Dictionary of Theories, Laws, and Concepts in Psychology

DICTIONARY OF THEORIES, LAWS, AND CONCEPTS IN PSYCHOLOGY

Jon E. Roeckelein

GREENWOOD PRESS
Westport, Connecticut • London

Library of Congress Cataloging-in-Publication Data

Roeckelein, Jon E.
    Dictionary of theories, laws, and concepts in psychology / Jon E.
Roeckelein.
        p.   cm.
    Includes bibliographical references (p.   ) and index.
    ISBN 0–313–30460–2 (alk. paper)
    1. Psychology—Dictionaries.   I. Title.
BF31.R625   1998
150'.3—dc21   97–43941

British Library Cataloguing in Publication Data is available.

Library of Congress Catalog Card Number: 97–43941
ISBN: 0–313–30460–2

First published in 1998

Greenwood Press, 88 Post Road West, Westport, CT 06881
An imprint of Greenwood Publishing Group, Inc.

Printed in the United States of America

The paper used in this book complies with the
Permanent Paper Standard issued by the National
Information Standards Organization (Z39.48–1984).

10 9 8 7 6 5 4 3 2 1

To Renée and Joshua, who appreciate semantic and theoretical distinctions and who show great faith, tolerance, understanding, and wisdom; and to Thom Verhave, who—using his unique pedagogy—taught us that discoveries and excitement are yet to be found lurking in the dusty musty area of the history of psychology.

CONTENTS

Preface   ix

Introduction   xi

Abbreviations   xvii

Dictionary of Theories, Laws, and Concepts in Psychology   1

Appendix A: Frequency of Usage of Concepts as Sampled in
            Psychology Textbooks, 1885–1996   495

Appendix B: References—Textbooks Surveyed for Collection of
            Laws and Theories in 112 Years of Psychology   521

Selected Bibliography   527

Subject Index   529

PREFACE

In discussing his imprinting experiments, Eckhard Hess once said that good psychologists try to make psychology a science.

The present work is my attempt to be a "good" psychologist. One of the purposes of writing this dictionary of psychological concepts is to provide a useful referent or baseline set of key concepts for examining the difficult topics of laws, theories, principles, effects, doctrines, and hypotheses in psychology. More specifically, it is hoped that this book of psychological concepts may serve as a valuable reference resource for answering questions in research concerning the semantic issues and problems surrounding the important terms of "law" and "theory" as they have appeared in the history of psychology. For example, How far has psychology come in the last 130 years concerning its development of lawful cause–effect relationship statements? Where does psychology go from here in its usage of the key descriptor concepts? How scientific is the science of psychology as judged by the quality and quantity of its laws, theories, and other descriptor terms and concepts? How does psychology measure up to the other sciences, especially the "natural" sciences of physics, chemistry, and biology, regarding the establishment of laws and theories? Since some concepts are more firmly established in psychology than others, which of the terms in psychology provide the most agreement among psychologists? Can we make psychology more scientific through examination of the terms and concepts that is uses? If so, what new measures and methods can we use *specifically* to accomplish this? Which are the "stronger" laws in psychology, and which are the "weaker" laws? What are the measurable mechanisms through which laws change in significance and status from weak to strong, or vice versa? How long does it take a theory to become a law? How valid, useful, or "good" are particular laws and theories in psychology?

This dictionary may provide a substantive basis and starting point for researching and answering these and many other such critical questions concerning the terminological issues in psychology.

I sincerely hope so.

INTRODUCTION

Psychology, like any other science, seeks to describe and explain its observations, data, and phenomena through the use of rigorous cause–effect statements. Some of these causal relationship statements lead to stronger and more certain predictions concerning outcomes than others. For example, the generalized term of scientific *law* contains the strongest and most rigorous descriptive account of how causal variables operate. Among the other, less rigorous, descriptors or concepts of how events are connected in science in general and psychology in particular are the generalized concepts of *theory, hypothesis, effect, doctrine,* and *principle*. The term "generalized concept" here refers to a cause–effect descriptor (e.g., "law"; "theory") that defines a particular set of events and an expected outcome (e.g., "*law* of effect"; "cognitive dissonance *theory*"; "serial position *effect*"). The following definitions of the various descriptor generalized concepts may serve as an initial guideline, or rule of thumb, for making distinctions among these generic terms.

The term *law* may be defined as "a verbal statement, supported by such ample evidence as not to be open to doubt unless much further evidence is obtained, of the way events of a certain class consistently and uniformly occur" (English & English, 1976, p. 288).

The term *theory* has been defined as "a coherent explanation (of an array of logically interrelated propositions about a set of phenomena) . . . which has undergone some validation and which may be applied to many data, but which does not have the status of a law" (Harriman, 1966, p. 201). Psychological theories are said to vary with respect to temporal duration of the target activity where theories confined to sequences of brief duration are termed "synchronic," and those concerned with extended durations are termed "diachronic" (Gergen, 1994). Another general distinction concerning theories is shown in Royce's (1994) two major facets of theoretical psychology: the construction of "substantive theory" and "metatheory." Substantive theory (e.g., "scientific theory'') focuses on explaining the observables and facts of a specifiable domain of investigation, whereas metatheory focuses on explaining the nature of theory using conceptual linguistic analyses to clarify the meanings and implications of theoretical terms. Marx and Goodson (1976) categorize scientific theories with respect to their mode of construction into three major types: "deductive" (characterized by the derivation of propositions, to be empirically tested, on the basis of logically related prior premises); "inductive" (emphasizes the accumulation or collection of disparate bits and pieces of data that are gradually articulated into theoretical propositions without any explicit guidance); and "functional" (an approach combining the best of deductive and inductive theory where small, frequently modified hypotheses are employed as investigation tools and focus their empirical attacks on specific behavioral problems). No theory, whatever its qualities, is ever final, even though all the predictive statements made from it have been verified perfectly. There always remains the possibility that any given theory will be replaced by another theory that is simpler, more general, or more consistent with other relevant theories (Marx & Hillix, 1979).

The term *hypothesis* has been defined as a statement that "attempts to explain a small or limited set of facts, whereas a theory attempts to encompass a broad range of facts and may even include several hypotheses" (Buss, 1973, p. 27).

The term *effect* refers to "an event that invariably follows a specific other phenomenon as in a causal relationship; a result" (Wolman, 1973).

The term *doctrine* has been defined as "a principle established through past decisions and interpretations; a principle of faith; dogma; tenet of belief supported by a teacher, a school, or a sect" (*Webster's*, 1986). The term *principle* may be defined as "a general inference that is derived from empirical studies but that cannot be stated unequivocally as a law" (Harriman, 1966, p. 148).

Since all these terms (i.e., *law, theory, hypothesis, effect, doctrine,* and *principle*) may be considered in the class of "generalized concepts"—or terms that convey differing amounts of certainty, predictability, and uniformity in psychology—the problem arises as to the choice of the "best" term to use from this class when describing any particular or specific causal phenomenon. As some studies have pointed out (e.g., Roeckelein, 1996c), there are many semantic issues and problems associated with distinguishing among these generalized terms in psychology. For instance, is the term *law*, in a scientific context, itself overly "pretentious"? Hill (1970, p. 14) believes that it is, because the term *law* seems to suggest that, given certain conditions, such and such will necessarily always occur. In reality, says Hill, most scientific *laws* are less precise than such cause–effect statements would imply, and, especially when referring to *psychological laws*, these statements need to be qualified by phrases such as "on the average" or "other things being equal."

One semantic problem that will have to be resolved eventually in this area of generalized terms and concepts is the question, How does a presumed cause–effect relationship come to be called a *law*? Furthermore, what are the measurable dynamics and criteria that go into the semantic transformation of phenomena from the status of tentative *theory* or *hypothesis* to that of rigorous *law*? As Marx (1976, p. 44) points out, "The development of laws is not an all-or-none process, and the gradual achievement of increasingly reliable relationships must be accepted as the normal manner in which fully accepted laws are obtained." Turner (1967, pp. 250–252) reminds us: "There are different aspects to laws. Some laws are derived from within a theory (laws as 'theorems of a formal theory'), and some laws do not fall within the corpus of theorems of a theory; the term *law* itself in science is ambiguous." Moreover, says Turner, it is the nature of a law to be true, but the "truth" or "falsity" of laws is in itself another set of interpretive issues requiring clarification both as to semantic-definitional assumptions and as to philosophical orientation. Perhaps, in the final analysis, as Hume (1739–1740) and Einstein (1959) suggested, it may be that nature's "laws" are more in the mind of the perceiver than in the external world.

Other semantic and "interpretive" questions concerning the generalized concepts in psychology are, Do specific *persons* sometimes "invent" laws, theories, and hypotheses? Are personalities ("great man theory") involved in "lawmaking" and "theorizing" in psychology? Is the major process surrounding the development of a generalized concept merely a social convention, or does it reflect "true" and impersonal descriptions and discoveries of natural events? Is there a pattern or direction in the development of the generalized concepts in psychology that is analogous, generally, to the pattern and direction in the development of history itself? For instance, Viney (1993, pp. 7–9) discusses various perspectives and hypotheses in the philosophy of history (e.g., cyclical hypothesis; linear-progressive hypothesis; chaos hypothesis). Do developmental ideas and schemas such as "cyclical" and "chaos" apply equally well to analyses of the development of the generalized concepts in psychology?

Unanimity and consensus of agreement by psychologists concerning such questions about the status of many generalized concepts and terms in psychology do not seem to be forthcoming in the immediate future. A simple set of statements regarding the "true" distinctions among the terms *law, theory, hypothesis, doctrine, effect*, and *principle* is probably largely illusory and indefensible at this stage of psychology's maturity. Therefore, in attempting to understand the various events and phenomena that employ the generalized concepts in psychology, a reasonable approach would be first to define the term or concept in question and then to cite the historical and current references that are pertinent in the development of that cause–effect relationship statement (cf: Roe & Frederick, 1981). It seems to be a well-established fact concerning the generalized concepts in psychology that certain concepts (theories, laws, etc.) are evolving in the field and are constantly subject to future change (e.g., is it *theories* of Gestalt perceptual organization or *laws* of Gestalt perceptual organization?).

The present book is an attempt to define and describe by source-referencing and cross-referencing the key or major (and some interesting minor) generalized concepts in psychology and to provide access to the literature on the concepts that *explicitly* employ the generalized descriptors of law, theory, hypothesis, effect, doctrine, and principle in the field. The method used here is to provide descriptive entries regarding the concepts and then to cite original sources and reviews in which the concepts are explained and, thereby, give the reader exposure to the genesis, foundation, and development of each concept as well as to its historical definition, analysis, and criticism. In addition, I have attempted to cite introductory psychology textbooks that were current when a given concept was first introduced, as well as later textbooks in order to indicate how some concepts have maintained their referencing status over decades of use in psychology. For example, the "law of effect" and "Weber's law" have remained high in frequency of usage by textbook authors since these concepts were first enunciated. On the other hand, the "law of dynamogenesis" and the "law of habit," for instance, have shown a decrease in usage over the years. The psychological concepts in this work have been selected from journal articles, books, reviews, monographs, and histories of psychology. These sources are primarily in the English language, but there are some references in the German, French, Italian, and Spanish languages. The sources include references published through the year 1996.

Appendix A located at the end of this book is a data bank of the frequency counts of concepts containing the key descriptors of *law* and *theory* across five time periods (1885–1919, 1920–1939, 1940–1959, 1960–1979, 1980–1996) covering 112 years of introductory psychology textbooks. Appendix B is a listing of the textbooks surveyed across 112 years of introductory psychology textbooks. The criterion for choosing the concepts shown in Appendix A was the same as the standard used for choosing concepts in this dictionary: the *explicit* attachment of a descriptor term (e.g., "law"; "theory") to concepts (e.g., "*law* of effect"; "recapitulation *theory*") as used by writers in the psychological literature. Appendix A may serve as a useful resource for investigators conducting empirical research in this area of key concepts and descriptors in psychology. For example, which of the key concepts cited in psychology textbooks are "borrowed" or "shared" and have their origination in *other* sciences such as physics, chemistry, biology, sociology, or anthropology? Another possible use for the data in Appendix A is to "track" the usage of specific laws and theories across 112 years of psychology textbooks in order to detect historical trends and changes in writers' usage of such terms (e.g., Roeckelein, 1996c).

Occasionally, a single concept may be known by several names (e.g., the "law of parsimony" is the same as "Occam's razor" and "Morgan's canon"), and, when this occurs, a cross-referencing method is used to connect the equivalent names. For example, entries for "Occam's razor" and "Morgan's canon" are included in the entry for the "law of parsimony." Also, in order to save page space concerning the single multinamed concepts, the set of references applying to such concepts are listed under whichever name is most commonly cited, regardless of conceptual, logical, or theoretical levels. Thus, for example, the specific concept name of "Hering's color theory" is subordinate here to the more general concept name of "tetrachromatic theory," but the former name becomes the main entry in this book because it is cited more frequently (perhaps because of its "eponymous" or surname nature; see Roeckelein, 1995, 1996a, b, 1997a, b). Terms may appear in the psychological literature with more than one descriptor term (e.g., "*law* of disuse"; "*theory* of disuse"), and, when this occurs, the entry is given multiple descriptors, with the first one signifying the more frequent usage (e.g., "Disuse, law/theory of," which indicates that in the literature "Disuse" appears as both a law and a theory with primary reference made to the concept as a law and only secondary reference made to it as a theory). Many of the concepts having a generalized descriptor have very definite origins and are explicitly named in the first entries in which they are discussed, while other concepts may be discussed without explicitly being named. In such cases of dubious origins of a concept, the first source to name the concept is cited as well as earlier "precursors" of the concept and later "interpretive reviews" of that concept.

There is some variation in entry length due to the following reasons: the entry refers to a broad or general area (e.g., learning; personality; perception) requiring greater length; or the entry refers to a specific, narrow, or technical phenomenon that invites only a brief description. There is limited page space, overall, available in the present volume to accommodate entries for all the concepts I collected. However, many concepts *not* appearing as regular entries are cited in Appendix A along with useful references in Appendix B.

In summary, the definitions of particular concepts (which *explicitly* employ one of the descriptor generalized terms) often change with the passage of time, especially in psychology, and may vary also from author to author (e.g., the concept "Yerkes–Dodson *law*" may be referred to by authors as the "inverted U curve *hypothesis* of motivation"). The approach taken in this book is to provide widely accepted definitions of the generalized concepts and also to provide historical references and current citations concerning the concepts in psychology as reflected by the authoritative accounts in the literature. Typically, the references and citations are listed chronologically, directly under the defining or descriptive entry for each concept, in order to show the historical development of the concept. Synonymous and related concept names are listed under each entry, as appropriate, with an = sign. For example, "Hering's color theory" = "tetrachromatic theory" = "opponent-process theory."

The following abbreviations are used in the references and citations in this book and refer to the journals and sources in which the concepts have been described, defined, and discussed.

Abbreviations

Ab. Konigl. Preuss. Ak. Wissen.	Abhandlung der Koniglische Preussisch Akademie der Wissenschaftlich
Acta Physio. Scan.	Acta Physiology Scandinavia
Acta Psy.	Acta Psychologica
Acta Psy. Tai.	Acta Psychologica Taiwanica (Taipei)
Acta Psychiat. Neur.	Acta Psychiatrica et Neurologica
Add. & Proc. Nat. Ed. Assoc.	Addresses and Proceedings of the National Education Association
Admin. Sci. Quar.	Administrative Science Quarterly
Adv. Exp. Soc. Psy.	Advances in Experimental Social Psychology
Adv. Stud. Beh.	Advances in the Study of Behavior
Advanc. Sci.	Advancement of Science
Amer. Anthro.	American Anthropologist
Amer. Ed. Res.	American Educational Research
Amer. Ed. Res. J.	American Educational Research Journal
Amer. Imago	American Imago
Amer. J. Clin. Hyp.	American Journal of Clinical Hypnosis
Amer. J. Hum. Genet.	American Journal of Human Genetics
Amer. J. Med. Sci.	American Journal of Medical Science
Amer. J. Ophthal.	American Journal of Ophthalmology
Amer. J. Orthopsychiat.	American Journal of Orthopsychiatry
Amer. J. Phys. Anthro.	American Journal of Physical Anthropology
Amer. J. Physics	American Journal of Physics
Amer. J. Physio.	American Journal of Physiology

Amer. J. Psy.	American Journal of Psychology
Amer. J. Psychiat.	American Journal of Psychiatry
Amer. J. Psychoan.	American Journal of Psychoanalysis
Amer. J. Psychother.	American Journal of Psychotherapy
Amer. J. Sci.	American Journal of Science
Amer. Pol. Quar.	American Politics Quarterly
Amer. Pol. Sci. Rev.	American Political Science Review
Amer. Psy.	American Psychologist
Amer. Psy. Soc.	American Psychological Society
Amer. Sci.	American Scientist
Amer. Soc. Rev.	American Sociological Review
Anim. Learn. Beh.	Animal Learning and Behavior
Ann. Amer. Acad. Pol. & Soc. Sci.	Annals of the American Academy of Political and Social Science
Ann. Clin. Res.	Annals of Clinical Research
Ann. Inter. Med.	Annals of Internal Medicine
Ann. Internat. Med.	Annals of International Medicine
Ann. Neur.	Annals of Neurology
Ann. N.Y. Acad. Sci.	Annals of the New York Academy of Sciences
Ann. Physik	Annals der Physik
Ann. Psy.	l'Annee Psychologie
Ann. Rev. Anthro.	Annual Review of Anthropology
Ann. Rev. Neurosci.	Annual Review of Neuroscience
Ann. Rev. Pharm. & Tox.	Annual Review of Pharmacology & Toxicology
Ann. Rev. Physio.	Annual Review of Physiology
Ann. Rev. Psy.	Annual Review of Psychology
APA	American Psychological Association
App. Cog. Psy.	Applied Cognitive Psychology
Ar. Anat. Physio.	Archiv fur Anatomie und Physiologie
Ar. Anat. Physio., Leipzig	Archiv der Anatomisch und Physiologie, Leipzig
Ar. Anat. Psy.	Archives of Anatomy and Psychology
Ar. Gen. Psychiat.	Archives of General Psychiatry
Ar. ges. Physio.	Archiv fur die gesamte Physiologie
Ar. ges. Psy.	Archiv fur die gesamte Psychologie
Ar. Mikr. Anat.	Archiv der Mikroskopische Anatomisch
Ar. Neur. Psychiat.	Archives of Neurological Psychiatry
Ar. Neuro.	Archives of Neurology

Ar. Neuro. Psychiat.	Archives of Neurological Psychiatry
Ar. Psy.	Archives of Psychology
Ar. Psy., N.Y.	Archives of Psychology, New York
Ar. Psychiat. Nervenkr.	Archiv der Psychiatrie und Nervenkrankheiten
Aud. Inst.	Audiovisual Instruction
Aust. Psy.	Australian Psychologist
Basic & App. Soc. Psy.	Basic and Applied Social Psychology
Beh. & Brain Sci.	Behavioral and Brain Sciences
Beh. Anal. Letters	Behavior Analysis Letters
Beh. Mono.	Behavior Monographs
Beh. Neuro.	Behavioral Neuroscience
Beh. Res. Meth., Inst., & Comp.	Behavior Research Methods, Instruments, & Computers
Beh. Res. Theory	Behavioral Research Theory
Beh. Sci. & Law	Behavioral Sciences and the Law
Beh. Sci.	Behavioral Science
Beh. Supp.	Behavior Supplements
Beh. Ther.	Behavior Therapy
Ber. Inter. Cong. Exp. Psy.	Berlin International Congress of Experimental Psychology
Ber. Sachs. Ges. Wiss. Leipzig Math-Phys.	Berichte Gesellschaft/Wissenschaft, Leipzig, Math./ Physiks.
Bio. Psy.	Biological Psychology
Brit. J. Crim.	British Journal of Criminology
Brit. J. Guid. Coun.	British Journal of Guidance and Counseling
Brit. J. Pol. Sci.	British Journal of Political Science
Brit. J. Psy.	British Journal of Psychology
Brit. J. Psy. Mono. Supp.	British Journal of Psychology Monograph Supplements
Brit. J. Psychiat.	British Journal of Psychiatry
Brit. Med. Bull.	British Medical Bulletin
Bull. Bur. Stan.	Bulletin of the Bureau of Standards
Bull. l'Aca. Roy. Sci. Brux.	Bulletins de l'Academie Royale des Sciences, de Bruxelles
Bull. l'Acad. R. S. Let. Beaux-Arts Bel.	Bulletin, Royal Academie/Sciences/Lettres/Beaux-Arts/Belgium
Bull. Math. Biophys.	Bulletin of Mathematical Biophysics
Bull. Menn. Clin.	Bulletin of the Menninger Clinic

Bull. Nat. Res. Coun.	Bulletin of the National Research Council
Bull. Psychonom. Soc.	Bulletin of the Psychonomic Society
Bull. Soc. d'Anat.	Bulletin Societe d'Anatomie
C.R. Soc. Bio. Mem.	Comptes Rendus Societe Biologique Memoir
C.R. Soc. Bio. Paris	Comptes Rendus Societe Biologique Paris
Can. J. Admin. Sci.	Canadian Journal of Administrative Science
Can. J. Psy.	Canadian Journal of Psychology
Can. Med. Assoc. J.	Canadian Medical Association Journal
Char. & Pers.	Character and Personality
Child Dev.	Child Development
Child Dev. Mono.	Child Development Monographs
Clin. Psy. Rev.	Clinical Psychology Review
Cog. Psy.	Cognitive Psychology
Cog. Ther. Res.	Cognitive Therapy and Research
Com. Ren. Soc. Bio.	Comptes Rendus de la Societe de Biologie
Comm. Mono.	Communications Monographs
Comp. Psy. Mono.	Comparative Psychology Monographs
Contemp. Psy.	Contemporary Psychology
Contr. Psy. Theor.	Contributions to Psychological Theory
Coun. Psy.	The Counseling Psychologist
Dev. Med. Child Neur.	Developmental Medicine and Child Neurology
Dev. Psy.	Developmental Psychology
Diss. Abs. Inter.	Dissertation Abstracts International
Ed. & Psy. Meas.	Educational and Psychological Measurement
Ed. Psy.	Educational Psychologist
EEG & Clin. Neurophysio.	Electroencephalography and Clinical Neurophysiology
Elem. School J.	Elementary School Journal
Ency. Psy.	Encyclopedia of Psychology
Ergebn. Physio.	Ergebnis Physiologie
Eug. Quart.	Eugenics Quarterly
Eur. J. Soc. Psy.	European Journal of Social Psychology
Excep. Child.	Exceptional Children
Exp. & Clin. Pharm.	Experimental & Clinical Pharmacology
Fed. Proc.	Federation Proceedings
Genet. Psy. Mono.	Genetic Psychology Monographs
Geron.	Gerontologist

Handbk. Exp. Psy.	Handbook of Experimental Psychology
Handbk. Gen. Exp. Psy.	Handbook of General Experimental Psychology
Handbk. Norm. Path. Physio.	Handbuch der Normalen und Pathological Physiologie
Har. Bus. Rev.	Harvard Business Review
Har. Ed. Rev.	Harvard Educational Review
Health Psy.	Health Psychology
Hum. Beh.	Human Behavior
Hum. Comm. Res.	Human Communications Research
Hum. Dev.	Human Development
Hum. Fact.	Human Factors
Hum. Rel.	Human Relations
Imp. Hum. Perf. Res. Quar.	Improving Human Performance: A Research Quarterly
Indiv. Psy. Bull.	Individual Psychology Bulletin
Inst. Child Welf. Mono.	Institute of Child Welfare Monographs
Instr. Sci.	Instructional Science
Int. Ency. Unif. Sci.	International Encyclopedia of Unified Science
Int. J. Beh. Dev.	International Journal of Behavioral Development
Int. J. Clin. Exp. Hyp.	International Journal of Clinical and Experimental Hypnosis
Int. J. Group Psychother.	International Journal of Group Psychotherapy
Int. J. Indiv. Psy.	International Journal of Individual Psychology
Int. J. Pol. Ed.	International Journal of Political Education
Int. J. Psy.	International Journal of Psychology
Int. J. Psychiat.	International Journal of Psychiatry
Int. J. Psychoanal.	International Journal of Psychoanalysis
Int. J. Soc. Psychiat.	International Journal of Social Psychiatry
J. Abn. Psy.	Journal of Abnormal Psychology
J. Abn. Soc. Psy.	Journal of Abnormal and Social Psychology
J. Acou. Soc. Amer.	Journal of the Acoustical Society of America
J. Alt. States Cons.	Journal of Altered States of Consciousness
J. Amer. Aca. Child Psychiat.	Journal of the American Academy of Child Psychiatry
J. Amer. Acad. Psychiat.	Journal of the American Academy of Psychiatry
J. Amer. Acad. Psychother.	Journal of the American Academy of Psychotherapists
J. Amer. Med. Assoc.	Journal of the American Medical Association

J. Amer. Psychoan. Assoc.	Journal of the American Psychoanalytic Association
J. Amer. Psychoan. Assoc. Mono.	Journal of the American Psychoanalytic Association Monographs
J. Amer. Soc. Psyc. Res.	Journal of the American Society for Psychical Research
J. Amer. Stat. Assoc.	Journal of the American Statistical Association
J. Anal. Psy.	Journal of Analytical Psychology
J. Anat. & Physio.	Journal of Anatomy and Physiology
J. Anat. Physio., Lon.	Journal of Anatomy and Physiology, London
J. App. Beh. Anal.	Journal of Applied Behavior Analysis
J. App. Physio.	Journal of Applied Physiology
J. App. Psy.	Journal of Applied Psychology
J. App. Soc. Psy.	Journal of Applied Social Psychology
J. Beh. Med.	Journal of Behavioral Medicine
J. Beh. Ther. Exp. Psychiat.	Journal of Behavior Therapy and Experimental Psychiatry
J. Black Stud.	Journal of Black Studies
J. Cell. Comp. Physio.	Journal of Cellular and Comparative Physiology
J. Clin. Endo. Met.	Journal of Clinical Endocrinology and Metabolism
J. Comp. Neurol. & Psy.	Journal of Comparative Neurology & Psychology
J. Comp. Neurol.	Journal of Comparative Neurology
J. Comp. Physio. Psy.	Journal of Comparative and Physiological Psychology
J. Comp. Psy.	Journal of Comparative Psychology
J. Cons. & Clin. Psy.	Journal of Consulting & Clinical Psychology
J. Cons. Psy.	Journal of Consulting Psychology
J. Consumer Res.	Journal of Consumer Research
J. Coun. Psy.	Journal of Counseling Psychology
J. Cross-Cult. Psy.	Journal of Cross-Cultural Psychology
J. de Phys.	Journal de Physiologie
J. Ed. Psy.	Journal of Educational Psychology
J. Ed. Psy. Mono. Supp.	Journal of Educational Psychology Monograph Supplements
J. Exp. Anal. Beh.	Journal of the Experimental Analysis of Behavior
J. Exp. Ed.	Journal of Experimental Education
J. Exp. Psy.	Journal of Experimental Psychology
J. Exp. Psy.: Anim. Beh. Proc.	Journal of Experimental Psychology: Animal Behavior Processes

J. Exp. Psy.: Gen.	Journal of Experimental Psychology: General
J. Exp. Psy.: Hum. Perc. & Perf.	Journal of Experimental Psychology: Human Perception/Performance
J. Exp. Psy.: Learn./Mem./Cog.	Journal of Experimental Psychology: Learning/Memory/Cognition
J. Frank. Inst.	Journal of the Franklin Institute
J. Gen. Physio.	Journal of General Physiology
J. Gen. Psy.	Journal of General Psychology
J. Genet. Psy.	Journal of Genetic Psychology
J. Heal. Soc. Beh.	Journal of Health and Social Behavior
J. Hist. Beh. Sci.	Journal of the History of the Behavioral Sciences
J. Hum. Psy.	Journal of Humanistic Psychology
J. Hum. Stress	Journal of Human Stress
J. Indiv. Psy.	Journal of Individual Psychology
J. Learn. Dis.	Journal of Learning Disabilities
J. Marr. & Fam.	Journal of Marriage and the Family
J. Math. Beh.	Journal of Mathematical Behavior
J. Math. Psy.	Journal of Mathematical Psychology
J. Mem. & Lang.	Journal of Memory and Language
J. Ment. Imag.	Journal of Mental Imagery
J. Ment. Sci.	Journal of Mental Science
J. Mind & Beh.	Journal of Mind and Behavior
J. Missouri Med. Assoc.	Journal of the Missouri Medical Association
J. Morph.	Journal of Morphology
J. Nerv. & Ment. Dis.	Journal of Nervous and Mental Disorders
J. Neurophysio.	Journal of Neurophysiology
J. N.Y. Acad. Soc. Sci.	Journal of the New York Academy of Social Sciences
J. Opt. Soc. Amer.	Journal of the Optical Society of America
J. Org. Beh.	Journal of Organizational Behavior
J. Parapsy.	Journal of Parapsychology
J. Pers.	Journal of Personality
J. Pers. Assess.	Journal of Personality Assessment
J. Pers. Soc. Beh.	Journal of Personality and Social Behavior
J. Pers. Soc. Psy.	Journal of Personality and Social Psychology
J. Pers. Soc. Psy. Mono.	Journal of Personality and Social Psychology Monographs
J. Pers. Soc. Psy. Mono. Supp.	Journal of Personality and Social Psychology Monographs Supplement

J. Phenom. Psy.	Journal of Phenomenological Psychology
J. Phil.	Journal of Philosophy
J. Phil., Psy., & Sci. Meth.	Journal of Philosophy, Psychology, and Scientific Method
J. Physio.	Journal of Physiology
J. Pol.	Journal of Politics
J. Pol. Mil. Soc.	Journal of Political and Military Sociology
J. Pop.	Journal of Population
J. Psychiat. Res.	Journal of Psychiatric Research
J. Psychosom. Res.	Journal of Psychosomatic Research
J. Rehab.	Journal of Rehabilitation
J. Res. Pers.	Journal of Research in Personality
J. Sex Res.	Journal of Sex Research
J. Soc. & Pers. Rel.	Journal of Social and Personal Relationships
J. Soc. Beh. & Pers.	Journal of Social Behavior and Personality
J. Soc. Clin. Psy.	Journal of Social and Clinical Psychology
J. Soc. Iss.	Journal of Social Issues
J. Struc. Learn.	Journal of Structural Learning
J. Stud. Alc.	Journal of Studies on Alcohol
J. Transper. Psy.	Journal of Transpersonal Psychology
J. Unif. Sci.	Journal of Unified Sciences
J. Verb. Learn. Verb. Beh.	Journal of Verbal Learning and Verbal Behavior
J. Voc. Beh.	Journal of Vocational Behavior
J. Wash. Acad. Sci.	Journal of the Washington Academy of Sciences
Klin. Monatb. Augenheilk.	Klinical Monatsblatter der Augenheilkunde
Learn. & Mot.	Learning and Motivation
Lunds Univ. Ars.	Lunds Universities Arsskrift
Marr. & Fam. Liv.	Marriage and Family Living
Mem. & Cog.	Memory and Cognition
Mem. Reg. Acc. Sci. Let. Art. Mod.	Memorie della Regia Accademia di Scienze, Lettre/ Arti in Modena
Mem. Soc. Bio.	Memories de la Societe de Biologie
Minn. Med.	Minnesota Medicine
Mono. Soc. Res. Child Dev.	Monographs of the Society for Research in Child Development
Mot. & Emo.	Motivation and Emotion
Multivar. Beh. Res.	Multivariate Behavior Research
Neb. Sym. Mot.	Nebraska Symposium on Motivation

New Eng. J. Med.	New England Journal of Medicine
Occup. Ment. Heal.	Occupational Mental Health
Org. & Admin. Sci.	Organization and Administrative Sciences
Org. Beh. & Hum. Dec. Proc.	Organizational Behavior & Human Decision Processes
Org. Beh. & Hum. Per.	Organizational Behavior and Human Performance
Pap. Amer. Congr. Gen. Semant.	Papers of the American Congress of General Semantics
Perc. & Mot. Skills	Perceptual and Motor Skills
Perc. & Psychophys.	Perception and Psychophysics
Pers. Indiv. Diff.	Personality and Individual Differences
Personnel Psy.	Personnel Psychology
Pers. Soc. Psy. Bull.	Personality and Social Psychology Bulletin
Pflug. Ar. ges. Physio.	Pflugers Archiv Gesamte Physiologie
Phil. Mag.	Philosophy Magazine
Phil. Sci.	Philosophy of Science
Phil. Ser.	Philosophical Series
Phil. Stud.	Philosophische Studien
Phil. Trans.	Philosophical Transactions
Phil. Trans. Roy. Soc. Lon.	Philosophical Transactions of the Royal Society of London
Phys. Soc. Yearbk.	Physical Society Yearbook
Physio. & Beh.	Physiology and Behavior
Physio. Rev.	Physiological Review
Physio. Zoo.	Physiological Zoology
Pogg. Ann. Phys. Chem.	Poggendorf Annales der Physiologie und Chemie
Pogg. Ann. Physik	Poggendorf Annales der Physik
Proc. Amer. Phil. Soc.	Proceedings of the American Philosophical Society
Proc. Nat. Acad. Sci.	Proceedings of the National Academy of Sciences
Proc. Phy. Soc. Lon.	Proceedings of the Physics Society of London
Proc. R.S. Lon.	Proceedings of the Royal Society of London
Proc. Soc. Psyc. Res.	Proceedings of the Society for Psychical Research
Proc. West. J. Comp. Conf.	Proceedings of the Western Joint Computer Conference
Prof. Psy.	Professional Psychology
Psy. Bull.	Psychological Bulletin
Psy. Bull. Mono. Supp.	Psychological Bulletin Monograph Supplement
Psy. Forsch.	Psychologische Forschung

Psy. Inq.	Psychological Inquiry
Psy. Iss.	Psychological Issues
Psy. Mono.	Psychological Monographs
Psy. Rec.	Psychological Record
Psy. Rep.	Psychological Reports
Psy. Rev.	Psychological Review
Psy. Rev. Mono. Supp.	Psychological Review Monograph Supplement
Psy. Sci.	Psychological Science
Psy. Stud.	Psychological Studies
Psy. Today	Psychology Today
Psychiat. Ann.	Psychiatric Annals
Psychiat. Quar.	Psychiatric Quarterly
Psychiat. Quar. Supp.	Psychiatric Quarterly Supplement
Psychoan. Psychother.	Psychoanalytic Psychotherapy
Psychoan. Rev.	Psychoanalytic Review
Psychoan. Study Child	Psychoanalytic Study of the Child
Psychoanal. Psy.	Psychoanalytic Psychology
Psychonom. Sci.	Psychonomic Science
Psychopharm. Bull.	Psychopharmacology Bulletin
Psychophy.	Psychophysiology
Psychosom. Med.	Psychosomatic Medicine
Psychother.: Theory Res. Prac.	Psychotherapy: Theory, Research, and Practice
Pub. Opin. Quar.	Public Opinion Quarterly
Quar. J. Exp. Psy.	Quarterly Journal of Experimental Psychology
Quar. Rev. Bio.	Quarterly Review of Biology
Rep. Res. Soc. Psy.	Representative Research in Social Psychology
Repl. Soc. Psy.	Replications in Social Psychology
Res. Mar.	Research in Marketing
Res. Publ. Assoc. Nerv. Ment. Dis.	Research Publication of the Association of Nervous/ Mental Disease
Rev. Anthro.	Review of Anthropology
Rev. Ed. Res.	Review of Educational Research
Rev. Fran. Endo.	Revue Francaise d'Endocrinologie
Rev. Pers. & Soc. Psy.	Review of Personality and Social Psychology
Rev. Res. Ed.	Review of Research in Education
Rev. Soc. Econ.	Review of Social Economy
S. Afr. J. Psy.	South African Journal of Psychology
S. Afr. Med. J.	South African Medical Journal

Schizo. Bull.	Schizophrenia Bulletin
Schweiz Z. Psy. An.	Schweiz Zeitschrift fur Psychologie Anwend
Sci. Amer.	Scientific American
Sci. Mon.	Scientific Monthly
Sitzber. Akad. Wiss. Berlin	Sitzungsberichte Akademie Wissenschaft der Berlin
Soc. Beh. & Pers.	Social Behavior and Personality
Soc. Bio.	Societe des Biologique
Soc. Bio. Mem. Paris	Societe Biologique Memoirs, Paris
Soc. For.	Social Forces
Soc. Prob.	Social Problems
Soc. Psy. Quar.	Social Psychology Quarterly
Soc. Res.	Social Research
Soc. Sci. Natl. Bull.	Societe Science National Bulletin
Society Adv. Soc. Psy. News.	Society for the Advancement of Social Psychology Newsletter
Stud. Ed. Psy., Nat. Cen. Univ.	Studies in Educational Psychology, National Center of Universities
Teach. Coll. Contr. Ed.	Teachers College Contributions to Education
Theory & Psy.	Theory and Psychology
Theory Res. Soc. Ed.	Theory and Research in Social Education
U. Iowa Stud. Child Welf.	University of Iowa Studies of Child Welfare
U. Ore. Pub. Stud. Psy.	University of Oregon Publications of Studies in Psychology
Univ. Cal. Pub. Psy.	University of California Publications in Psychology
Vis. Res.	Vision Research
Voc. Guid. Quar.	Vocational Guidance Quarterly
Youth Soc.	Youth and Society
Z. Bio.	Zeitschrift fur Biologisch
Z. Klin. Psy. Psychother.	Zeitschrift fur Klinische Psychologie und Psychotherapie
Z. Psy.	Zeitschrift fur Psychologie
Z. Psy. Physio. Sinn.	Zeitschrift fur Psychologie und Physiologie Sinnesorgange
Z. Sinn.	Zeitschrift fur Sinnesphysiologie
Z. Tierpsy.	Zeitschrift fur Tierpsychologie
Zb. Psychoan.	Zentlichblatt Psychoanalyse
Zbl. Physio.	Zeitblatter der Physiologie

Dictionary of Theories, Laws, and Concepts in Psychology

A

ABC THEORY. The American psychologist Albert Ellis (1913–) developed rational-emotive therapy (RET), which is a directive, confrontational psychotherapy designed to challenge and modify clients' irrational beliefs thought to cause their personal distress (Ellis, 1961, 1977, 1987). RET is based on Ellis' *ABC theory* (Wood & Wood, 1993). The *A* refers to the *activating* event, the *B* to the person's *belief* about the event, and the *C* to the emotional *consequence* that follows. Ellis claims that it is not the event that causes the emotional consequence, but rather the person's belief about the event; that is, *A* does not cause *C*, but *B* causes *C*. If the belief is irrational, then the emotional consequence can be extreme distress. Because reality does not conform to such irrational beliefs as "Everyone should love me" or "I must be perfect," patients who hold such beliefs are open to frustration and unhappiness. Irrational beliefs cause people to view an undesirable event as a catastrophe rather than merely as a disappointment, anxiety, or inconvenience; in addition, persons may go on to feel anxious about their anxiety and depressed about their depression (Ellis, 1987). RET and *ABC theory* help clients to see rationally and logically that their false beliefs and unrealistic expectations are the real causes of their problems. As clients begin to replace irrational beliefs with rational beliefs, their emotional reactions become more appropriate, less distressing, and more likely to lead to constructive behavior (Ellis, 1979). See also COGNITIVE THERAPY, THEORIES OF.

REFERENCES

Ellis, A. (1961). *A guide to rational living*. Englewood Cliffs, NJ: Prentice-Hall.

Ellis, A. (1977). The basic clinical theory of rational-emotive therapy. In A. Ellis & R. Grieger (Eds.), *Handbook of rational-emotive therapy*. New York: Springer.

Ellis, A. (1979). Rational emotive therapy. In R. J. Corsini (Ed.), *Current psychotherapies*. Itasca, IL: Peacock.

Ellis, A. (1987). The impossibility of achieving consistently good mental health. *Amer. Psy., 42*, 364–375.
Wood, E., & Wood, S. (1993). *The world of psychology*. Boston: Allyn & Bacon.

ABNEY'S EFFECT. See ABNEY'S LAW.

ABNEY'S LAW. The English chemist and physiologist William de Wiveleslie Abney (1844–1920) developed this principle concerning the additivity of heterochromatic luminances ("brightnesses"), which states that the luminance of a mixture of differently colored lights is equal to the sum of the luminances of the components. *Abney's law* has not generally been fully supported by later research, and, interestingly, questions about the law lie at the root of a theoretical debate in colorimetry (Judd, 1955). The deficiencies of *Abney's law* have been known for a long time (Graham, 1965), but the weaknesses have been evaded or tolerated by scientists only until recently (cf: Ives, 1912, 1915; Dresler, 1953). A phenomenon of perception called *Abney's effect* refers to visual conditions involving the sudden illumination of a large surface area (cf: *Lambert's law/ cosine law*, which states that the illumination on a surface varies directly as the cosine of the angle between the incident ray and the perpendicular to the surface; Warren, 1934). The perception of light in *Abney's effect* is that it seems to come on first in the center of the patch of area and then spread to the edges instead of appearing on the total area equally all at the same time. Subsequently, when the light is extinguished, the outer edges disappear first, first followed by the center area disappearing last (Reber, 1995). In addition to these phenomena, Abney is prominent for his contributions to the science of photography, including stellar photography, and for his discovery of how to make photographic plates that are sensitive to red and infrared light (Muir, 1994). See also COLOR MIXTURE LAWS/THEORY OF; GRASSMANN'S LAWS; NEWTON'S LAW/PRINCIPLE(S) OF COLOR MIXTURE.

REFERENCES

Abney, W., & Festing, E. (1886). Colour photometry. *Phil. Trans. Roy. Soc., Lon., 177,* 423–456.
Abney, W. (1897). The sensitiveness of the retina to light and colour. *Phil. Trans. Roy. Soc., Lon. 190A,* 155–193.
Ives, H. (1912). Studies in the photometry of lights of different colors. IV. The addition of luminosities of different color. *Phil. Mag., 24,* 845–853.
Abney, W. (1913). *Researches in colour vision*. London: Longmans, Green.
Ives, H. (1915). The transformation of color-mixture equations from one system to another. *J. Frank. Inst., 180,* 673–701.
Warren, H. (Ed.) (1934). *Dictionary of psychology*. Cambridge, MA: Houghton Mifflin.
LeGrand, Y., & Geblewicz, E. (1937). La dualite de la vision aux brilliances elevees. *Ann. Psy., 38,* 1–21.
Peiron, H. (1939). La dissociation de l'adaptation lumineuse et de l'adaptation chromatique. *Ann. Psy., 40,* 1–14.

Dresler, A. (1953). The non-additivity of heterochromatic brightnesses. *Transactions of the Illumination Engineering Society, London, 18*, 141–165.

Judd, D. (1955). Radical changes in photometry and colorimetry foreshadowed by CIE actions in Zurich. *J. Opt. Soc. Amer., 45*, 897–898.

Sperling, H. (1958). An experimental investigation of the relationship between colour mixture and luminous efficiency. In *Visual problems of colour.* Symposium, National Physical Laboratory, September 23–25, 1957. London: Her Majesty's Stationery Office.

Graham, C. (1965). Color mixture and color systems. In C. Graham (Ed.), *Vision and visual perception.* New York: Wiley.

Muir, H. (Ed.) (1994). *Larousse dictionary of scientists.* New York. Larousse.

Reber, A. (1995). *The Penguin dictionary of psychology.* New York: Penguin Books.

ABNORMALITY, THEORIES OF. See PSYCHOPATHOLOGY, THEORIES OF.

ABSTRACTION, LAWS/PRINCIPLES OF. See COGNITIVE STYLE MODELS.

ACCOMMODATION, LAW/PRINCIPLE OF. The concept of *accommodation* in psychology has a variety of meanings depending on the context in which it is used. In general terms, it refers to any movement or adjustment (physical or psychological) that is made to prepare the organism for some stimulus input. In the context of vision (Alpern, 1962), it refers to the automatic adjustment process wherein the shape of the lens of the eye changes to focus on objects situated at different distances from the observer. The suspensory ligaments hold the lens in a relatively flattened position when the normal eye is at rest and can focus clearly on objects that are about 20 feet away (distant vision). When objects are closer than 20 feet (near vision), the ciliary muscles contract, which causes relaxation of the suspensory ligaments and which, in turn, allows the flattened lens to thicken or bulge in shape, causing a sharper focus of light rays on the retina (Hochberg, 1965). The term *accommodation sensation* refers to a sensation that accompanies changes of visual adjustment that is attributable to changes in tension of the ciliary muscles that control the shape of the lens, and the term *accommodation time* refers to temporal duration from the moment a visual stimulus is presented in the line of vision until the lenses of the eyes have adjusted for clear vision of an object (Warren, 1934). Bartley (1951) reported that level of illumination has an effect on visual accommodation and that the most likely theory of the physiological mechanism for accommodation is that of a basic tonal background caused by vascular innervation of the sympathetic nervous system that affects the oculomotor nerve to make specific focusing adjustments. In the context of infant and childhood development, Jean Piaget (1954, 1970) used the term *accommodation* to refer to the child's modification of ideas or concepts of the world in response to new experiences in the environment or in response to experiences that are inconsistent with previously known ideas or concepts. Related terms in Piaget's theoretical viewpoint are *assimilation* (incorporating new or modified ideas and concepts into the child's existing cognitive structure) and *schema* (the development of an organized cognitive structure or pattern as a result of accommodation and assimilation). According to Piaget, schema (or "scheme" or "schemata") normally develop during the first two years of the child's life. When accommodation is used in the context of nerve activity, it describes the increased excitability of the nerve that occurs when a constant stimulus (such as an electric current) is applied to the nerve, and the subsequent slow decrease ("accommodation") in nerve excitability with continued stimulation. When the stimulus is terminated, a sudden drop in nerve excitability occurs. After such a sequence of events and following termination of the stimulating event, the nerve is less sensitive briefly to stimulation than it was before initiation of the original stimulus. *Accommodation* is used in a social psychological and sociological context to refer to a process of social adjustment that is designed to create or maintain group harmony (Reber, 1995). The notion of *accommodation* in the case of social behavior may take the form of bargaining, conciliation, conflict resolution, compromise, arbitration, negotiation, or truce-making among the concerned or antagonistic individuals, groups, or nations (Rubin & Brown, 1975; Druckman, 1977). In a historical context, in the area of attention, the term *accommodation* is archaic and referred to the person's adjustment or readjustment that was essential to the maximal clearness (Titchener, 1908, referred to "sensory clearness" or "attensity") of an impression when the normal mean *accommodation time* was measured to be about one and one-half second with a range between 0.2 and 3.0 seconds (Warren, 1934). See also BALANCE, PRINCIPLES/THEORY OF; FESTINGER'S COGNITIVE DISSONANCE THEORY; PIAGET'S THEORY OF DEVELOPMENTAL STAGES.

REFERENCES

Baldwin, J. (1894). *Handbook of psychology*. New York: Holt.
Titchener, E. (1908). *Lectures on the experimental psychology of feeling and attention*. New York: Macmillan.
Warren, H. (1919). *Human psychology*. Boston: Houghton Mifflin.
Warren, H. (Ed.) (1934). *Dictionary of psychology*. Cambridge, MA: Houghton Mifflin.
Bartley, S. (1951). The psychophysiology of vision. In S. S. Stevens (Ed.), *Handbook of experimental psychology*. New York: Wiley.
Piaget, J. (1954). *The construction of reality in the child*. New York: Basic Books.
Alpern, M. (1962). Accommodation. In H. Darson (Ed.), *The eye*. Vol. 3. New York: Academic Press.
Hochberg, J. (1965). *Perception*. Englewood Cliffs, NJ: Prentice-Hall.
Piaget, J. (1970). Piaget's theory. In P. Mussen (Ed.), *Carmichael's manual of child psychology*. New York: Wiley.
Rubin, J., & Brown, B. (1975). *The social psychology of bargaining and negotiation*. New York: Academic Press.

Druckman, D. (Ed.) (1977). *Negotiations: Social psychological perspectives*. Beverly Hills, CA: Sage.

Reber, A. (1995). *The Penguin dictionary of psychology*. New York: Penguin Books.

ACHIEVEMENT MOTIVATION, THEORY OF. = need achievement = achievement need. The American psychologist Henry A. Murray (1893–1988) first defined an individual's need for achievement (*achievement motivation*, or *nAch*) as a desire for significant accomplishments, for mastering skills, for overcoming obstacles in the way of one's success, or for rapidly attaining high standard(s) (Murray, 1938). Murray and other researchers, such as the American psychologists David C. McClelland (1917–   ) and John W. Atkinson (1923–   ), developed various ways to measure the concept of *achievement motivation*, prominent among which is the use of personality "projective" tests (such as the Thematic Apperception Test, or TAT, where the person's task is to invent stories about the content of ambiguous pictures or photos). McClelland (1961) extended the concept of *nAch* from the level of analysis of the individual to that of entire societies or cultures. The theoretical underpinnings of *achievement motivation*, including both "intrinsic" and "extrinsic" motives, have two essential components: an assumed energizing or motivating mechanism that directs a person toward goals and a set of internalized conditions or standards (whether created by oneself or by others) that represent personal fulfillment or achievement. A number of studies have criticized the *theory of nAch*. For example, Weinstein (1969) found low reliability and questionable validity assessments for the TAT measures; Maehr and Nicholls (1980) criticized the *nAch* researchers' narrow emphasis on personality as a crucial determinant of behavior and their inability to find adequate results concerning *nAch* in women (cf: Weiner, Johnson, & Mehrabian, 1968; Horner, 1972). On the other hand, Lindgren (1976) suggests that the unsatisfactory validity and reliability assessments of *nAch* measures may be due to the attempt to measure a spectrum of personality traits that is too broad, and proposed that forced-choice types of questions, rather than projective-types of tests, be used where individuals being tested would choose between "achievement-related" and "affiliation-related" personal styles. The *nAch* viewpoint was augmented in the 1970s when the field of *cognitive psychology* first appeared and placed emphasis upon a person's "cognitions" about the nature and purpose of achievement in a cultural context (Maehr & Nicholls, 1980). Then, by the 1980s, the unresolved question was raised as to whether *nAch* should be studied as a personality trait, as suggested by personality psychologists, or as a cognitive behavior, as suggested by cognitive psychologists. Perhaps future research on the concept of *nAch* may show greater reconciliation of the areas of personality psychology and cognitive psychology. See also MOTIVATION, THEORIES OF.

REFERENCES

Murray, H. (1938). *Explorations in personality*. New York: Oxford University Press.

Atkinson, J. (1958). *Motives in fantasy, action, and society.* New York: Van Nostrand.

McClelland, D. (1961). *The achieving society.* New York: Van Nostrand.

Atkinson, J. (1964). *An introduction to motivation.* New York: Van Nostrand.

McClelland, D. (1965). Need achievement and entrepreneurship: A longitudinal study. *J. Pers. Soc. Psy., 1,* 389–392.

Atkinson, J., & Feather, N. (Eds.) (1966). *A theory of achievement motivation.* New York: Wiley.

Heckhausen, H. (1967). *The anatomy of achievement motivation.* New York: Academic Press.

Heckhausen, H. (1968). Achievement motivation research: Current problems and some contributions toward a general theory of motivation. In W. Arnold (Ed.), *Nebraska Symposium on Motivation.* Lincoln: University of Nebraska Press.

Weiner, B., Johnson, P., & Mehrabian, A. (1968). Achievement motivation and the recall of incompleted and completed exam questions. *J. Ed. Psy., 59,* 181–185.

Weinstein, M. (1969). Achievement motivation and risk preference. *J. Pers. Soc. Psy., 13,* 153–172.

McClelland, D., & Winter, D. (1971). *Motivating economic achievement.* New York: Free Press.

Horner, M. (1972). Toward an understanding of achievement-related conflicts in women. *J. Soc. Iss., 28,* 147–172.

McClelland, D. (1973). Testing for competence rather than for "intelligence." *Amer. Psy., 28,* 1–14.

Atkinson, J., & Raynor, J. (Eds.) (1974). *Motivation and achievement.* Washington, DC: Winston.

Weiner, B. (Ed.) (1974). *Achievement motivation and attribution theory.* Morristown, NJ: General Learning Press.

Lindgren, H. (1976). Measuring need to achieve by Nach Naff scale—A forced-choice questionnaire. *Psy. Rep., 39,* 907–910.

McClelland, D., Atkinson, J., Clark, R., & Lowell, E. (1976). *The achievement motive.* New York: Irvington.

Heckhausen, H. (1977). Achievement motivation and its constructs: A cognitive model. *Mot. & Emo., 1,* 283–329.

McClelland, D. (1978). Managing motivation to expand human freedom. *Amer. Psy., 33,* 201–210.

Maehr, M., & Nicholls, J. (1980). Culture and achievement motivation: A second look. In N. Warren (Ed.), *Studies in cross-cultural psychology.* Vol. 3. New York: Academic Press.

Heckhausen, H. (1982). The development of achievement motivation. In W. Hartup (Ed.), *Review of child development research.* Vol. 6. Chicago: University of Chicago Press.

Cooper, W. (1983). An achievement motivation nomological network. *J. Pers. Soc. Psy., 44,* 841–861.

Dweck, C., & Elliott, E. (1983). Achievement motivation. In P. Mussen & E. Hetherington (Eds.), *Handbook of child psychology.* Vol. 4. New York: Wiley.

McClelland, D. (1983). Sources of adult motives in patterns of parent behavior in early childhood. *J. Pers. Soc. Psy., 44,* 564–574.

McClelland, D. (1985). *Human motivation.* Glenview, IL: Scott, Foresman.

ACHIEVEMENT MOTIVATION THEORY OF WORK. See WORK/
CAREER/OCCUPATION, THEORIES OF.

ACH'S LAWS/PRINCIPLES/THEORY. The German psychologist Narziss
Ach (1871–1946) was one member of the group of researchers (others included
O. Kulpe, H. Watt, K. Marbe, and K. Buhler) at the famous Wurzburg "new"
experimental school in Germany during the early 1900s. The Wurzburg group
studied thought processes via verbalized introspection and complex cognitive
events (as opposed to studying sensations, which was the primary emphasis at
the University of Leipzig under Wilhelm Wundt's leadership). Ach's work on
systematic experimental introspection, awareness, and *determining tendency* was
germinal to the exodus of experimental psychologists away from the exclusive
use of introspection as a research method. Ach's method of experimental introspection was systematic in that it clearly delineated the limits of a participant's
introspection (i.e., "looking into one's own experience and reporting on it") to
the "fore," the "mid," and the "after" periods for making introspective reports
during the conduct of an experiment. Ach also achieved relatively high levels
of precision in his studies by using devices such as the "Hipp chronoscope"
(an apparatus for measuring time intervals, first made by Mathias Hipp, a watch-
maker, in 1843; Warren, 1934; Ach, 1905) during his experiments. Ach's principles concerning *determining tendency* in experiments contain what are,
perhaps, the most important aspects of his work for present-day experimental
psychologists. Ach showed that there were *unconscious influences* operating on
the behavior of the participants in his experiments, including the instructions
that were given by the experimenter to the participant. The *determining tendencies* were thought to be known by some means other than the participant's
introspection. An example of *determining tendency* is provided by Boring, Langfeld, and Weld (1939, p. 389), who describe an experiment on hypnosis (cf:
Orne, 1979). After the subject (the word "participant" seems to be the favored
term to use today in experimental contexts) was hypnotized, the suggestion was
made that after waking, two cards with two digits on each would be shown. For
the first card, the person was to give the sum of the digits, and for the second
card, he was to give the difference between the two digits. Upon waking from
the hypnotic state, a card was shown on which the digits 6 and 2 were written;
the person immediately said "8." When the second card was shown, containing
the digits 4 and 2, the same individual said "2." The person had no memory
of the prior suggestion and could give no explanation of what he had said about
the cards, nor did it occur to the person that 8 was the sum of 2 and 6 or that
2 was the difference between 4 and 2. According to *Ach's principle*, the determining tendencies "fix" the course of thought by favoring certain "associations" that spring from the immediate or current situation and inhibit other
associations. In this way, the tendencies give directive order in a situation containing a number of competing possibilities and enable an answer to be given

to the question of why a particular possibility is materialized rather than any other one. Other experiments have indicated that determining tendencies function to give completion to already established patterns of thought (cf: Zeigarnik effect; mind/mental set) and may reinforce old associations that the individual may have partially established. According to *Ach's principle*, the directive or determining tendency makes the action of a person more than a rigid mechanical sequence of events such as is found in the movements of a machine. The term *determining tendencies* is somewhat archaic today and is replaced by validity- and control-sensitive terms in experimental psychology such as "preparatory set," "demand characteristics of the situation," "ecological validity of the experiment," and "experimenter effect" (Brunswik, 1947; Ray, 1996). Such contemporary terms seek to sensitize and motivate the experimenter to control various potentially confounding variables that may exist in the psychological experiment where there is a dynamic interplay between the participant, the experimenter, and the experimental setting or context. See also ASSOCIATION, LAWS/PRINCIPLES OF; MIND/MENTAL SET, LAW OF; PERCEPTION (I. GENERAL), THEORIES OF; ZEIGARNIK EFFECT/PHENOMENON.

REFERENCES

Ach, N. (1905). *Uber die Willenstatigkeit und das Denken. Eine experimentalle Untersuchung mit einem Anhange: Uber das Hippsche Chronoskop*. Gottingen, West Germany: Vandenhoeck & Ruprecht.

Warren, H. (Ed.) (1934). *Dictionary of psychology*. Cambridge, MA: Houghton Mifflin.

Boring, E. G., Langfeld, H., & Weld, H. (1935). *Psychology: A factual textbook*. New York: Wiley.

Stroud, J. (1938). *Introduction to general psychology*. New York: Prentice-Hall.

Boring, E. G., Langfeld, H., & Weld, H. (1939). *Introduction to psychology*. New York: Wiley.

Ach, N. (1944). *Lehrbuch der psychologie*. Vol. 3: *Praktische psychologie*. Bamberg: Buchner.

Brunswik, E. (1947). *Systematic and representative design of psychological experiments*. Berkeley: University of California Press.

Orne, M. (1979). On the simulating subject as a quasi-control group in hypnosis research: What, why, and how. In E. Fromm & R. Shor (Eds.), *Hypnosis: Developments in research and new perspectives*. New York: Aldine.

Ray, W. (1996). *Methods toward a science of behavior and experience*. Pacific Grove, CA: Brooks/Cole.

ACTIVATION/AROUSAL THEORY. The term *activation theory* was most prominently used by Donald B. Lindsley (1951) as a working theory for emotion. The concept *activate* means not only "to make active" but also "to render capable of reacting" (Woodworth & Schlosberg, 1965). At one end of a continuum of activation is a strong reaction to stimulation, and at the other end is the condition of quiescence, sleep, or death, with little or no reaction to stimulation. The *activation/arousal theory* developed from work in the area of physiology, specifically on the electrical activity of the brain where the cerebral cortex was seen to be aroused by discharge of a lower center of the brain in the hypothalamic region. The general form of the *activation theory* is a form of the older "energy-mobilization" concept of emotion (Cannon, 1915) where early studies showed how the body prepares for emergency action during states of rage and fear. The use of the term *activation* is generally restricted to the energizing influence of one internal system, such as the reticular activating system, on another one and is not an exact synonym for either "arousal" (a general term) or "stimulation" (activation produced by specific external sources). Historically, the concept of *activation* was central to the study and development of drives, motives, and emotions in psychology. It has been relatively easy to identify behavioral states as levels of arousal (cf: Berlyne's, 1960, 1971, "aesthetic arousal," which can be raised through properties of stimulus patterns such as novelty), but parallel physiological processes were more difficult to discover. The electroencephalograph (EEG) has been a somewhat successful indicator of arousal level where the lower frequency EEG is observed when behavioral arousal declines, but, given certain exceptions to this simple relationship, the EEG is only an approximate indicator of arousal. Also associated with the *arousal theory* is the sleep–wakefulness cycle of organisms where an individual goes to sleep when input falls below a certain level. This hypothesis (Bremer, 1935) is tenable when considering the general nocturnal sleeping habits of humans, but it has difficulty when explaining the behavior of certain animal species that sleep during the day and are most active at night. The sensory input interpretation of arousal was predominant until the studies by Moruzzi and Magoun (1949) at the University of Pisa in Italy and Lindsley, Bowden, and Magoun (1949) at the University of California at Los Angeles (UCLA) in the United States showed that severing all the sensory nerves in cats (without damaging the reticular formation) was accompanied by normal wakefulness–sleep patterns in the EEG. The view today (Levinthal, 1983) has changed somewhat from the simple picture of the reticular formation as the major activator for arousal patterns and includes the recognition that EEG arousal signs are not always consistent with changes in behavioral arousal. See also CANNON/CANNON–BARD THEORY; DRIVE, THEORIES OF; EMOTION, THEORIES/LAWS OF; LINDSLEY'S ACTIVATION THEORY; MOTIVATION, THEORIES OF; SPREADING-ACTIVATION MODEL OF MEMORY.

REFERENCES

Cannon, W. (1915). *Bodily changes in pain, hunger, fear, and rage*. New York: Appleton.

Bremer, F. (1935). Cerveau isole et physiologie du sommeil. *Com. Ren. Soc. Bio., (Paris), 118*, 1235–1241.

Darrow, C. (1946). The electroencephalogram and psychophysiological regulation of the brain. *Amer. J. Psychiat., 102*, 791–798.

Duffy, E., & Lacey, O. (1946). Adaptation in energy mobilization: Changes in general level of palmar skin conductance. *J. Exp. Psy., 36*, 437–452.

Lindsley, D., Bowden, J., & Magoun, H. (1949). Effect upon EEG of acute injury to the brain stem activating system. *EEG & Clin. Neurophysio., 1*, 475–486.

Moruzzi, G., & Magoun, H. (1949). Brain stem reticular formation and activation of the
    EEG. *EEG & Clin. Neurophysio., 1*, 455–473.
Lindsley, D., Schreiner, L., Knowles, W., & Magoun, H. (1950). Behavioral and EEG
    changes following chronic brain stem lesions in the cat. *EEG & Clin. Neurophy-
    sio., 2*, 483–498.
Duffy, E. (1951). The concept of energy mobilization. *Psy. Rev., 58*, 30–40.
Lindsley, D. (1951). Emotion. In S. S. Stevens (Ed.), *Handbk. Exp. Psy.*, pp. 473–516.
    New York: Wiley.
Duffy, E. (1957). The psychological significance of the concept of "arousal" or "acti-
    vation." *Psy. Rev., 64*, 265–275.
Malmo, R. (1959). Activation: A neuropsychological dimension. *Psy. Rev., 66*, 367–386.
Berlyne, D. (1960). *Conflict, arousal, and curiosity.* New York: McGraw-Hill.
Duffy, E. (1962). *Activation and behavior.* New York: Wiley.
Woodworth, R., & Schlosberg, H. (1965). *Experimental psychology.* New York: Holt,
    Rinehart, & Winston.
Berlyne, D. (1971). *Psychobiology and aesthetics.* New York: Appleton-Century-Crofts.
Levinthal, C. (1983). *Introduction to physiological psychology.* Englewood Cliffs, NJ:
    Prentice-Hall.

ACTIVATION MODEL OF MEMORY ORGANIZATION. See FORGET-
TING/MEMORY, THEORIES OF.

ACTIVATION-SYNTHESIS THEORY. See DREAM THEORY.

ADAPTATION, PRINCIPLES/LAWS OF. The term *adaptation* derives from
the Latin word *adaptare*, meaning "to fit," and has a variety of meanings in
science. In the discipline of biology, *adaptation* refers to structural or behavioral
changes of an organism, or part of an organism, that fit it more perfectly for
the environmental conditions in which it lives where the changes have evolutionary survival value. In the area of physiology, *adaptation* is the change or
adjustment of a sense organ to some incoming stimulation, and the term *sensory
adaptation* includes a decreased sensitivity to stimuli due to prolonged stimulation (also called *negative adaptation*; Warren, 1934). In psychology, in general, *adaptation* is the change in quality, clarity, or intensity of a sensory
experience that occurs with continuous and unchanged stimulation. In psychology, in particular, *adaptation* may be discussed in a multitude of contexts,
among which are visual adaptation, olfactory adaptation, pain adaptation, cutaneous adaptation, and gustatory adaptation (Woodworth & Schlosberg, 1965).
In *visual adaptation*, a set of processes takes place after change of exposure
from dark to light (or light to dark) whereby the eye is more capable of receiving
stimuli under the new conditions; included here are dark, light, and chromatic
adaptation. *Dark* ("scotopic") *adaptation* is the process of adjustment of the
eyes to low intensities of illumination that takes about four hours to complete,
even though effective dark adaptation takes only about 30 minutes (where the
retinal cones take only about 7 minutes to adapt, and the rods take the full four

hours to adapt). It is estimated that the totally dark-adapted eye is about 1 million times as sensitive as the normally illuminated eye (Reber, 1995). *Light* (''photopic'') *adaptation* is the process of adjustment of the eye to a high level of light intensity where the pupil of the eye is constricted, and the retinal cones are activated, making the eye relatively insensitive to light of lower intensities. *Dark adaptation* is the shift in retinal receptors from the photopic (cones) system to the scotopic (rods) system, while *light adaptation* is the shift from the scotopic to the photopic system. The term *brightness adaptation* refers to a decrease in the brilliance of a stimulus that is caused by an increase in the general illumination of the surrounding visual field. *Color* (''chromatic'' or ''spectral'') *adaptation* is alteration of hue or saturation or both, due to a previous exposure to light of some other wavelength (also called *color fatigue*; Warren, 1934); during color adaptation, an individual's absolute threshold of sensitivity to hue is raised. *Cross adaptation* (Reber, 1995) is adjustment to all stimuli of a group of stimuli after exposure to only one of the stimuli from that group. In *olfactory adaptation*, for instance, a person may become adapted to one odor that subsequently will produce in her or him a diminution in sensitivity to a large number and variety of other odors. *Social* (or ''cultural'') *adaptation* is the modification or adjustment of personal behavior that is necessary to maintain harmonious interaction with other individuals in the group (''social accommodation''), such as exhibiting conformity behavior to the customs (or taboos) of a particular social group. When used in a learning context, *adaptation* refers to a change in an organism's mode of behavior that results in more effective or more satisfactory adjustment to the prevailing situation, as well as the elimination of irrelevant behavior as learning progresses (Wolman, 1973). As used in the area of personality psychology, *adaptation* has been used to denote a process of upward adjustment and compensation for one's innate deficiencies (Adler, 1956), as a modification in drives, emotions, and attitudes in adjusting to the environment (Fromm, 1941), and as a critical concept in a theory of the ego (Hartmann, 1964). The term *adaptation time* is defined as the time that elapses from the onset of a continuous stimulus up to the point where any further stimulation causes no further change in the responsiveness of the sensory organ or system. As used in more informal terms, *adaptation time* is the time needed in adjustment for efficient performance of a task. Also, there is *genetic adaptation* (species-specific characteristics, such as long necks in giraffes, that are distillations of evolutionary processes over many generations that help the organism to survive in a changing environment), *phenotypic adaptation* (temporary adjustments of the individual, such as the return of one's ability to see clearly after a period in a darkened room following exposure to bright lights), and *perceptual adaptation* (the ability to adjust to an artificially displaced, or even inverted, visual field). The related concept of *habituation*, whose older definition was ''the process of becoming adapted to a given stimulus, situation, or general environment'' (Warren, 1934), has been redefined today in more modern terms as ''the gradual elimination of an unconditioned response, especially an orienting response, by the repeated presentation of the unconditional stimulus, and will not occur to highly noxious stimuli'' (Carlson, 1990). Thus, the principle/law of *adaptation* has been a valuable omnibus concept in the history of psychology and other disciplines, where it has helped to advance the scientific understanding of organisms' functional, physical, and social adjustments to an ever-changing environment. See also DARWIN'S EVOLUTION THEORY; HABIT/HABIT FORMATION, LAWS/PRINCIPLES OF; HABITUATION, PRINCIPLE/LAW OF; HELSON'S ADAPTATION-LEVEL THEORY; PURKINJE EFFECT/PHENOMENON/SHIFT; SELYE'S THEORY/MODEL OF STRESS.

REFERENCES

Stratton, G. (1897). Vision without inversion of the retinal image. *Psy. Rev., 4,* 341–360.

Seashore, C. (1923). *Introduction to psychology.* New York: Macmillan.

Titchener, E. (1928). *A textbook of psychology.* New York: Macmillan.

Warren, H. (Ed.) (1934). *Dictionary of psychology.* Cambridge, MA: Houghton Mifflin.

Hecht, S., & Shlaer, S. (1938). An adaptometer for measuring human dark adaptation. *J. Opt. Soc. Amer., 28,* 269–275.

Crozier, W. (1940). The theory of the visual threshold. II. On the kinetics of adaptation. *Proc. Nat. Acad. Sci., 26,* 334–339.

Fromm, E. (1941). *Escape from freedom.* New York: Avon Books.

Hecht, S., & Hsia, Y. (1945). Dark adaptation following light adaptation to red and white lights. *J. Opt. Soc. Amer., 35,* 261–267.

Cohen, J. (1946a). Color adaptation of the human eye. *Amer. J. Psy., 59,* 84–110.

Cohen, J. (1946b). Color adaptation to 1945. *Psy. Bull., 43,* 121–140.

Osgood, C. (1953). *Method and theory in experimental psychology.* New York: Oxford University Press.

Adler, A. (1956). *The individual psychology of Alfred Adler: A systematic presentation in selections from his writings.* New York: Harper & Row.

Hess, E. (1956). Space perception in the chick. *Sci. Amer., 195,* 71–80.

Hartmann, H. (1964). *Ego psychology and the problem of adaptation.* New York: International Universities Press.

Kohler, I. (1964). *The formation and transformation of the perceptual world.* New York: International Universities Press.

Woodworth, R., & Schlosberg, H. (1965). *Experimental psychology.* New York: Holt, Rinehart, & Winston.

Rock, I. (1966). *The nature of perceptual adaptation.* New York: Basic Books.

Wolman, B. (Ed.) (1973). *Dictionary of behavioral science.* New York: Van Nostrand Reinhold.

Carlson, N. (1990). *Psychology: The science of behavior.* Boston: Allyn & Bacon.

Reber, A. (1995). *The Penguin dictionary of psychology.* New York: Penguin Books.

ADAPTATION-LEVEL THEORY. See HELSON'S ADAPTATION-LEVEL THEORY.

ADAPTIVE NONRESPONDING THEORY. See SLEEP, THEORIES OF.

ADDITIVE COLOR MIXTURE, PRINCIPLE OF. See COLOR MIXTURE, LAWS/THEORY OF.

ADDITIVE LAW OF PROBABILITY. See PROBABILITY THEORY/ LAWS.

ADLER'S THEORY OF PERSONALITY. The Austrian psychoanalyst Alfred Adler (1870–1937) received his medical degree in 1895 from the University of Vienna with a specialty in ophthalmology but then changed to psychiatry after a period of practice in general medicine. Adler was one of the charter members of the Vienna Psychoanalytic Society, serving as its president in 1910, but resigned from the society in 1911 because of theoretical differences with Sigmund Freud (Colby, 1951; Ansbacher & Ansbacher, 1956, 1964). Adler went on to establish his own school, called the Society for Free Psychoanalytic Research (later called the Society of Individual Psychology; Adler, 1930), which attracted followers throughout the world and also inspired the establishment of an experimental school in Vienna that employed his theories of education (Adler, 1957). After moving to New York City in 1934, Adler continued to practice psychiatry and was a professor at the Long Island College of Medicine. His theoretical approach to personality (Adler, 1927) generally emphasized the concepts of goal striving, unity, and active participation of the individual and stressed the cognitive rather than the unconscious processes of personality (cf: Freud, 1940). Adler's *theory of personality* is an extremely "economical" one (Hall & Lindzey, 1978) where a few basic assumptions (cf: Shulman, 1994) sustain the whole theoretical structure: (1) fictional finalism—humans are motivated more by their subjective expectations of the future than by their objective experiences of the past; (2) striving for superiority (formerly called the "will to power" by Adler)—humans' final goal is to be aggressive, powerful, and superior where one strives for perfect completion and is driven "upwardly" toward "higher" goals; (3) inferiority feelings and compensation (Adler accepted being called the "father of the inferiority complex"; Ansbacher, 1994)—humans are motivated by the need to overcome any perceived or felt level of inferiority (cf: Adler, 1917) that arises from a sense of incompletion or imperfection in any area of their lives; (4) innate social interest (Adler, 1929a, 1939)—humans' striving for superiority becomes socialized where working for the common good permits individuals to compensate for their weaknesses; (5) style of life (Adler, 1929b, 1937)—the system principle, or self-created life plan, by which the unique individual personality achieves a higher level of functioning in life and where all the person's drives, feelings, memories, emotions, and cognitive processes are subordinate to that individual's lifestyle; (6) the creative self—this doctrine asserts that humans construct their own personalities out of the raw material of heredity and experience and that one's creative self gives meaning to life by creating the goals themselves, as well as the means to get to the goals in life; the creative self is the "active" principle of human life and is not unlike the older concept of the *soul* (Hall & Lindzey, 1978). Adler's *theory of therapy* emphasizes the goals of the therapist to be the establishment of a relationship of trust, to discover and understand the patient's "assumptive universe," to reveal these assumptions to the person in such a way that they become subject to self-correction and facilitate change, to convey a sense of worth and faith in the person's inner strength, and to offer the patient a model for good behavior and effective coping strategies (Dreikurs, 1967; Dinkmeyer, Pew, & Dinkmeyer, 1979; Shulman, 1994). Adler's *personality theory* exemplifies a humanistic orientation toward individual development that is contrary to Freud's more materialistic conception of the person and gives humans the characteristics of altruism, cooperation, humanitarianism, awareness, uniqueness, dignity, and creativity. Adler's work and concepts (while yet unrecognized by some psychologists) have been generally validated, have influenced most current personality theories (including psychoanalytic approaches), and have led to a continuation of the Adlerian tradition in this country (Dreikurs, 1950; Dreikurs, Corsini, Lowe, & Sonstegard, 1959; Ellis, 1971; Corsini, 1977). See also ALLPORT'S THEORY OF PERSONALITY; BIRTH ORDER THEORY; FREUD'S THEORY OF PERSONALITY; MASLOW'S THEORY OF PERSONALITY; ROGERS' THEORY OF PERSONALITY.

REFERENCES

Adler, A. (1910). Uber mannliche Einstellung bei Weiblichen Neurofiken. *Zb. Psychoan., 1,* 174–178.

Adler, A. (1912). *The neurotic constitution.* New York: Arno Press.

Adler, A. (1917). *Study of organ inferiority and its psychical compensation.* New York: Nervous and Mental Diseases.

Adler, A. (1927). *The practice and theory of individual psychology.* New York: Harcourt, Brace, & World.

Adler, A. (1929a). *Problems of neurosis.* London: Kegan Paul.

Adler, A. (1929b). *The science of living.* New York: Greenberg.

Adler, A. (1930). Individual psychology. In C. Murchison (Ed.), *Psychologies of 1930.* Worcester, MA: Clark University Press.

Adler, A. (1931). *What life should mean to you.* Boston: Little, Brown.

Adler, A. (1937). Position in family constellation influences life style. *Inter. J. Indiv. Psy., 3,* 211–227.

Adler, A. (1939). *Social interest: A challenge to mankind.* New York: Putnam.

Bottome, P. (1939). *Alfred Adler: A biography.* New York: Putnam.

Freud, S. (1940). *An outline of psychoanalysis.* New York: Norton.

James, W. (1947). Karen Horney and Erich Fromm in relation to Alfred Adler. *Indiv. Psy. Bull., 6,* 105–116.

Dreikurs, R. (1950). *Fundamentals of Adlerian psychology.* Chicago: Adler Institute.

Colby, K. (1951). On the disagreement between Freud and Adler. *Amer. Imago, 8,* 229–238.

Ansbacher, H., & Ansbacher, R. (Eds.) (1956). *The individual psychology of Alfred Adler.* New York: Basic Books.

Adler, A. (1957). *The education of children.* London: Allen & Unwin.

Dreikurs, R., Corsini, R., Lowe, R., & Sonstegard, M. (1959). *Adlerian family counseling*. Eugene: University of Oregon Press.

Way, L. (1962). *Adler's place in psychology*. New York: Collier Books.

Orgler, H. (1963). *Alfred Adler: The man and his work*. New York: Liveright.

Ansbacher, H., & Ansbacher, R. (Eds.) (1964). *Superiority and social interest by Alfred Adler*. Evanston, IL: Northwestern University Press.

Clark, K. (1967). Implications of Adlerian theory for an understanding of civil rights problems and action. *J. Indiv. Psy., 23*, 181–190.

Dreikurs, R. (1967). *Psychodynamics, psychotherapy, and counseling: Collected papers*. Chicago: Adler Institute.

Ellis, A. (1971). Reason and emotion in the individual psychology of Alfred Adler. *J. Indiv. Psy., 27*, 50–64.

Mosak, H. (Ed.) (1973). *Alfred Adler: His influence on psychology today*. Park Ridge, IL: Noyes Press.

Sperber, M. (1974). *Masks of loneliness: Alfred Adler in perspective*. New York: Macmillan.

Corsini, R. (1977). Individual education. *J. Indiv. Psy., 33*, 295–349.

Hall, C., & Lindzey, G. (1978). *Theories of personality*. New York: Wiley.

Dinkmeyer, D., Pew, W., & Dinkmeyer, D., Jr. (1979). *Adlerian counseling and psychotherapy*. Monterey, CA: Brooks/Cole.

Ansbacher, H. (1994). Alfred Adler. In R. J. Corsini (Ed.), *Ency. Psy*. New York: Wiley.

Shulman, B. (1994). Adlerian psychotherapy. In R. J. Corsini (Ed.), *Ency. Psy*. New York: Wiley.

AESTHETICS, PRINCIPLE OF. See ZEISING'S PRINCIPLE.

AFTERDISCHARGE, LAW OF. See SKINNER'S DESCRIPTIVE BEHAVIOR/OPERANT CONDITIONING THEORY.

AFTERIMAGE LAW. See EMMERT'S LAW.

AGGRESSION, THEORIES OF. The concept of *aggression* is a very general and complex phenomenon that refers to a wide variety of acts, has many causes, and is hard to predict and control. Commonly, the term is used for behaviors that may be motivated by frustration or fear, by a desire to cause fear in others, or by a desire to promote one's own interests and ideas. Patterns of usage of the concept of *aggression* usually indicate some theoretical orientation bias on the writer's part (Reber, 1995). For instance, ethologists consider aggression to be an evolutionarily/genetically determined instinctual pattern of behaviors involving specific environmental stimuli (e.g., territorial invasion); classical psychoanalysts (i.e., Freudians) consider aggression to be a conscious correlate of Thanatos (e.g., death wish behaviors; Weisman, 1975); learning theorists may regard aggression as a displaced response to any frustrating situation (e.g., *frustration-aggression hypothesis*, Miller, 1941, where one person may attack an innocent bystander out of inability to achieve some unrelated goal); and social-learning theorists may consider aggression to be a form of learned and reinforced behavior gained by imitating or observing some other individual who engages in aggressive acts (e.g., young boy imitates his father's aggression toward an ethnic-minority person). The concept of *aggression*, much like the concept of *personality*, seems to play a central role in many theoretical orientations where usage follows theory, and it is difficult to discover mutually agreed-upon definitions of the term. Goldstein (1994) has categorized the *theories of aggression* as to their theoretical contexts and as to their association with concepts such as instincts, drives, and learning/social-learning factors. There is a persistent popular belief that aggression is *instinctual*, where acts of aggression are merely the manifestation of an innate tendency to fight. According to this view (e.g., Ardrey, 1966; Lorenz, 1966; Morris, 1967), aggressive energy stemming from this uncontrollable instinct is generated spontaneously, continuously, and at a constant rate in the individual. Such aggressive energy builds up over time (e.g., Lorenz's *hydraulic model of aggression*), and the more that accumulates, the weaker the stimulus that is needed to set it off into overt aggressive acts. Also, if too much time elapses since the last aggressive act, it may occur spontaneously for no apparent reason. Thus, according to this orientation, aggressive energy inevitably accumulates, and inevitably it must be expressed. Perhaps this is the reason that competitive sports events (particularly ''bodily contact'' sports) have been so popular throughout history. Even though empirical studies do not verify the ''draining off'' or ''cathartic-expression'' rationale for aggression, *instinct theory* is attractive to many people as a basis for aggression because it is a comprehensive and easy blend of anecdote, analogical leaps, unsystematic journalism, self-serving rationalization, irresponsibility, and undefined concepts (Goldstein, 1994). According to the *drive theory* of aggression, aggressive acts stem from a heightened state of arousal or drive that is reduced through overt expression of aggressive behavior (Baron, 1977). Consistent with this approach is the classical *frustration-aggression hypothesis* (Dollard, Doob, Miller, Mowrer, & Sears, 1939), which states in its modified form (Miller, 1941) that frustration produces instigations to a number of different types of responses, one of which is an instigation to aggression. Variations of this hypothesis have been the *frustration-regression hypothesis* (Barker, Dembo, & Lewin, 1941) and the *frustration-fixation hypothesis* (Maier, 1949). Certain other aspects of the *drive theory* approach to understanding aggression emphasize the strength of the instigating events, the importance of the frustrated goal response to the individual, the number of frustrated response sequences, the degree of frustration, the amount of potential punishment for aggression, and the dynamics of displacement and catharsis in dealing with aggression. The research on the *frustration-aggression hypothesis* (Buss, 1961; Berkowitz, 1962; Feshbach, 1970; Zillman, 1979) and its related ideas was eventually tempered by the fact that it essentially involved a logical circularity of reasoning (Johnson, 1972; cf: *law of effect*), and the *drive theory* approach gave way somewhat to the *social learning theory* of aggression (e.g., Bandura, 1973), which emphasizes that the causes of aggressive behavior are not found exclusively in the organism but in environmental forces as well. *Social learning theory* focuses on the processes that are responsible for the individual's *acquisition* (physiological as well as psychological) of aggressive behaviors (e.g., Moyer, 1974, 1976; Thiesen, 1976), the *instigation* of overt aggressive acts at particular times (e.g., Toch, 1969; Feshbach, 1970), and the *maintenance* of aggressive behavior (e.g., Feldman, 1977). Research in this area has also been concerned with the *prediction* of aggression (e.g., Goldstein, 1974; McCord, 1979; Monahan, 1981) and the *control* of aggression (e.g., Bostow & Bailey, 1969; Hamberger & Lohr, 1980; Goldstein, Carr, Davidson, & Wehr, 1981). In general terms, research on aggression has indicated that aggressive criminal behavior correlates with the factors of past criminal behavior, sex, age, race, socioeconomic status, and alcohol or opiate abuse (Goldstein, 1994). However, such actuarial probabilities concerning criminal aggression most likely contain, at best, only modest value for the prediction of overt aggressive acts in any given individual at any given time. See also BANDURA'S THEORY; HYDRAULIC THEORY; PERSONALITY THEORIES.

REFERENCES

Dollard, J., Doob, L., Miller, N., Mowrer, O. H., & Sears, R. (1939). *Frustration and aggression.* New Haven, CT: Yale University Press.

Barker, R., Dembo, T., & Lewin, K. (1941). Frustration and regression. In R. Barker, J. Kounin, & H. Wright (Eds.), *Child behavior and development.* New York: McGraw-Hill.

Miller, N. (1941). The frustration-aggression hypothesis. *Psy. Rev., 48,* 337–342.

Maier, N. (1949). *Frustration: The study of behavior without a goal.* New York: McGraw-Hill.

Buss, A. (1961). *The psychology of aggression.* New York: Wiley.

Berkowitz, L. (1962). *Aggression: A social psychological analysis.* New York: McGraw-Hill.

Ardrey, R. (1966). *The territorial imperative.* New York: Atheneum.

Lorenz, K. (1966). *On aggression.* New York: Harcourt Brace Jovanovich.

Morris, D. (1967). *The naked ape.* New York: McGraw-Hill.

Bostow, D., & Bailey, J. (1969). Modification of severe disruptive and aggressive behavior using brief timeout and reinforcement procedures. *J. App. Beh. Anal., 2,* 31–37.

Toch, H. (1969). *Violent men.* Chicago: Aldine.

Feshbach, S. (1970). Aggression. In P. Mussen (Ed.), *Carmichael's manual of child psychology.* Vol. 2. New York: Wiley.

Johnson, R. (1972). *Aggression in man and animals.* Philadelphia: Saunders.

Bandura, A. (1973). *Aggression: A social learning analysis.* Englewood Cliffs, NJ: Prentice-Hall.

Goldstein, R. (1974). Brain research and violent behavior. *Ar. Neuro., 30,* 1–18.

Kornadt, H.-J. (1974). Toward a motivation theory of aggression and aggression inhibition. In J. deWit & W. Hartup (Eds.), *Determinants and origins of aggressive behavior.* The Hague: Mouton.

Moyer, K. (1974). *The psychobiology of aggression.* New York: Harper & Row.

Weisman, A. (1975). Thanatology. In A. Friedman, H. Kaplan, & B. Sadock (Eds.), *Comprehensive textbook of psychiatry*. Baltimore: Williams & Wilkins.

Moyer, K. (Ed.) (1976). *Physiology of aggression*. New York: Raven Press.

Rosenzweig, S. (1976). Aggressive behavior and the Rosenzweig Picture-Frustration (P-F) study. *J. Clin. Psy., 32*, 885–891.

Thiessen, D. (1976). *The evolution and chemistry of aggression*. Springfield, IL: Thomas.

Baron, R. (1977). *Human aggression*. New York: Plenum.

Feldman, M. (1977). *Criminal behavior: A psychological analysis*. New York: Wiley.

Frodi, A., Macaulay, J., & Thome, P. (1977). Are women always less aggressive than men? A review of the experimental literature. *Psy. Bull., 84*, 634–660.

Lefkowitz, M., Eron, L., Walder, L., & Heusmann, L. (1977). *Growing up to be violent*. New York: Pergamon Press.

McCord, J. (1979). Some child rearing antecedents to criminal behavior in adult men. *J. Pers. Soc. Psy., 37*, 1477–1486.

Zillman, D. (1979). *Hostility and aggression*. Hillsdale, NJ: Erlbaum.

Hamberger, K., & Lohr, J. (1980). Rational restructuring for anger control: A quasi-experimental case study. *Cog. Ther. Res., 4*, 99–102.

Maccoby, E., & Jacklin, C. (1980). Sex differences in aggression: A rejoinder and reprise. *Child. Dev., 51*, 964–980.

Goldstein, A., Carr, E., Davidson, W., & Wehr, P. (1981). *In response to aggression*. New York: Pergamon Press.

Monahan, J. (Ed.) (1981). *The clinical prediction of violent behavior*. Washington, DC: National Institute of Mental Health.

Goldstein, A., & Rosenbaum, A. (1982). *Aggress-less*. Englewood Cliffs, NJ: Prentice-Hall.

Kornadt, H.-J. (1982). *Aggressionsmotiv und Aggressionshemmung*. Bern: Huber.

Freedman, J. (1984). Effect of television violence on aggressiveness. *Psy. Bull., 96*, 227–246.

Freedman, J. (1986). Television violence and aggression: A rejoinder. *Psy. Bull., 100*, 372–378.

Josephson, W. (1987). Television violence and children's aggression: Testing the priming, social script, and disinhibition predictions. *J. Pers. Soc. Psy., 53*, 882–890.

Berkowitz, L. (1989). Frustration-aggression hypothesis: Examination and reformulation. *Psy. Bull., 106*, 59–73.

Widom, C. (1989). Does violence beget violence? A critical examination of the literature. *Psy. Bull., 106*, 3–28.

Berkowitz, L. (1990). On the formation and regulation of anger and aggression. *Amer. Psy., 45*, 494–503.

Goldstein, A. (1994). Aggression. In R. J. Corsini (Ed.), *Ency. Psy*. New York: Wiley.

Reber, A. (1995). *The Penguin dictionary of psychology*. New York: Penguin Books.

AGING, THEORIES OF. Studies of aging and behavior changes over the entire life span have led to the conclusion that cognitive and other functions increase and improve through the first 20 years or so of life, hold that level for the next 40–60 years, and then narrow and close down in a final deterioration phase (Ames, 1994). Research at the Gesell Institute of Child Development (Gesell, 1928; Gesell & Ilg, 1946; Gesell, Ilg, & Ames, 1956; Ames, Gillespie,

Haines, & Ilg, 1979) has suggested the principle that children should be pro-
moted in school on the basis of their *behavioral* age rather than their *chronological* age and, by extension, that this same basic principle should guide one's
expectations of an individual's functioning. Differences in individuals as a result
of age have been studied by *cross-sectional* (groups of persons of different ages
are observed at the same time), *longitudinal* (the same group of persons is
observed at different ages), and *sequential* methods (combination of cross-
sectional with longitudinal methods to study *cohort effects* or influences that
occur in the experiences of disparate age groups; Schaie, 1965; Baltes, 1968).
The relatively new field called *geriatric psychology* (the science of the behavior
and diseases of the aged; Silverman, 1994) has emerged in the last 50 years
where experimental studies of the aging process have been conducted (cf: the
broader science of aging called *gerontology*; Manaster, 1994). A number of
generalizations, some fairly obvious and predictable, concerning behavior
changes in later life have been described (Denny, 1994). For example, about
40% of one's cortical cells may be lost by age 80–90; fats increase, and water
content decreases over the life span; visual abilities start to decline in middle
age, where accommodation and acuity lessen due to elasticity loss in the eyes'
lens and where changes in the retina in older age increase sensitivity to glare
and affect color vision; auditory abilities begin to decline in middle age, where
perception of the higher frequencies may disappear and where hearing loss later
in life may lead to stress, depression, and emotional disturbances; long-term
memory deficits in the aged are usually retrieval problems, and short-term memory difficulties occur when the learning task requires divided attention, but span
of memory remains intact until extreme old age; Alzheimer's disease (named
after the German neurologist Alois Alzheimer, 1864–1915, who first described
it in 1907), involving progressive mental impairment that usually begins with a
deficit in recent memory and is caused by consistent cellular changes in the
aging brain, may be observed beginning in middle age (45–60 years of age);
and, in problem-solving situations, older people tend to ask uninformative questions, to be distracted by redundant and irrelevant information, and to treat both
negative and positive instances of a concept as positive, and apparent rigidity
in old persons may be due to their inability to profit from negative information.
Theories of aging are basically models of *balance* or "trade-off": in old age,
a person may lose energy reserve but gain an ability to control emotional reactions and, thereby, conserve energy. According to this view, two general kinds
of changes (i.e., *losses* or *gains*) can be expected with old age (Baltes, 1987).
Paul Baltes (1939–   ), a pioneer of *life-span developmental psychology*, stresses
that persons continue to maintain a capacity for change across the entire life
span. Baltes and his colleagues (Baltes & Schaie, 1973; Nesselroade & Baltes,
1979; Baltes & Willis, 1982) argue for the plasticity of intelligence in aging
persons and also advance the notion of interdisciplinary collaboration in order
to more fully understand the role of social change in psychological development.
Various perspectives on the causes of aging have been proposed (Baron, 1992),

and many fall under the major headings of *genetic programming theories* (which suggest that aging is the result of built-in, genetically determined biological clocks) and *wear-and-tear theories* (which suggest that aging results from gradual wearing out of organ systems or other parts of the body). Two principal theories concerning one's successful adjustment to the social and physical changes of aging are the *disengagement theory* and the *activity theory*. According to the *disengagement theory*, it is assumed to be normal and desirable for individuals to withdraw from society as they age since it relieves them of roles and responsibilities they become less able to fulfill (Cumming & Henry, 1961; Brown, 1974). The *disengagement theory* of social aging, however, has been discredited largely for a number of reasons. For instance, not all social contact is limited or eliminated in older people, and emotional detachment does not always necessarily occur in older people as *disengagement theory* falsely implies (Zimbardo & Weber, 1994). The *activity theory* of aging, a "use-it-or-lose-it" approach, assumes that activity is the essence of life for people of all ages and predicts that people who remain active physically, mentally, and socially will adjust better to aging (Havighurst, 1961; Barrow & Smith, 1979). Another theoretical approach, the *selective social interaction* viewpoint, suggests that as people age, they become more selective in choosing their social partners. This perspective suggests a practical way for older persons to regulate emotional experiences and conserve physical energy (Carstensen, 1991). The discrimination or prejudice against individuals on the basis of age is called *ageism* (Coon, 1992) and may be countered by dispelling some of the myths that have developed over time concerning the aged. For example, the myth that older workers perform less effectively on jobs requiring both speed and skill may be disputed (Salthouse, 1987; Schaie, 1988), and the myths that older persons become isolated and neglected by their families or that the majority of elderly persons show signs of senility, mental decay, or mental illness may be refuted. On the positive side, several prescriptions for well-being in old age emphasize that older persons should establish patterns for self-acceptance, positive relations with others, autonomy or personal freedom, mastery over the environment, a purpose in life, and continued personal growth (Ryff, 1989). See also DEVELOPMENTAL THEORY.

REFERENCES

Gesell, A. (1928). *Infancy and human growth.* New York: Macmillan.

Gesell, A., & Ilg, F. (1946). *The child from five to ten.* New York: Harper.

Gesell, A., Ilg, F., & Ames, L. (1956). *Youth: The years from ten to sixteen.* New York: Harper.

Cumming, E., & Henry, W. (1961). *Growing old: The process of disengagement.* New York: Basic Books.

Havighurst, R. (1961). Successful aging. *Geron., 1,* 8–13.

Schaie, K. (1965). A genetic model for the study of developmental problems. *Psy. Bull., 64,* 92–107.

Baltes, P. (1968). Longitudinal and cross-sectional sequences in the study of age and generation effects. *Hum. Dev., 11*, 145–171.

Goulet, L., & Baltes, P. (Eds.) (1970). *Life-span developmental psychology: Research and theory.* New York: Academic Press.

Baltes, P., & Labouvie, G. (1973). Adult development of intellectual performance: Description, explanation, and modification. In C. Eisdorfer & M. Lawton (Eds.), *The psychology of adult development and aging.* Washington, DC: American Psychological Association.

Baltes, P., & Schaie, K. (Eds.) (1973). *Life-span developmental psychology: Personality and socialization.* New York: Academic Press.

Ames, L. (1974). Calibration of aging. *J. Pers. Assess., 38*, 505–529.

Brown, A. (1974). Satisfying relationships for the elderly and their patterns of disengagement. *Geron., 14*, 258–262.

Walsh, D. (1975). Age differences in learning and memory. In D. Woodruff & J. Birren (Eds.), *Aging: Scientific perspectives and social issues.* New York: Van Nostrand Reinhold.

Binstock, R., & Shanas, E. (Eds.) (1976). *Handbook of aging and the social sciences.* New York: Van Nostrand Reinhold.

Sheehy, C. (1976). *Passages: Predictable crises of adult life.* New York: Dutton.

Craik, F. (1977). Age differences in human memory. In J. Birren & K. Schaie (Eds.), *Handbook of the psychology of aging.* New York: Van Nostrand Reinhold.

Frich, C., & Hayflick, L. (Eds.) (1977). *Handbook of the biology of aging.* New York: Van Nostrand Reinhold.

Ames, L., Gillespie, C., Haines, J., & Ilg, F. (1979). *The Gesell Institute's child from one to six.* New York: Harper & Row.

Barrow, G., & Smith, P. (1979). *Aging, ageism, and society.* St. Paul, MN: West.

Nesselroade, J., & Baltes, P. (Eds.) (1979). *Longitudinal research in the study of behavior and development.* New York: Academic Press.

Birren, J., & Sloane, R. (Eds.) (1980). *Handbook of mental health and aging.* Englewood Cliffs, NJ: Prentice-Hall.

Baltes, P., & Willis, S. (1982). Plasticity and enhancement of intellectual functioning in old age: Penn State's Adult Development and Enrichment Project (ADEPT). In F. Craik & S. Trehub (Eds.), *Aging and cognitive processes.* New York: Plenum.

Baltes, P. (1987). Theoretical propositions on life-span developmental psychology: On the dynamics between growth and decline. *Dev. Psy., 23*, 611–626.

Salthouse, T. (1987). Age, experience, and compensation. In C. Schooler & K. Schaie (Eds.), *Cognitive functioning and social structure over the life course.* NY: Ablex.

Schaie, K. (1988). Ageism in psychological research. *Amer. Psy., 43*, 179–183.

Ryff, C. (1989). Beyond Ponce de Leon and life satisfaction: New directions in quest of successful ageing. *Int. J. Beh. Dev., 12*, 35–55.

Palmore, E. (1990). *Ageism: Negative and positive.* New York: Springer.

Carstensen, L. (1991). Selectivity theory: Social activity in life-span context. In K. Schaie (Ed.), *Annual review of geriatrics and gerontology.* New York: Springer.

Baron, R. (1992). *Psychology.* Boston: Allyn & Bacon.

Coon, D. (1992). *Introduction to psychology.* St. Paul, MN: West.

Palmore, E. (Ed.) (1993). *Developments and research on aging: An international handbook.* Westport, CT: Greenwood Press.

Ames, L. (1994). Aging: Behavior changes. In R. J. Corsini (Ed.), *Ency. Psy.* New York: Wiley.

Denny, M. (1994). Age differences. In R. J. Corsini (Ed.), *Ency. Psy.* New York: Wiley.

Manaster, G. (1994). Gerontology. In R. J. Corsini (Ed.), *Ency. Psy.* New York: Wiley.

Silverman, H. (1994). Geriatric psychology. In R. J. Corsini (Ed.), *Ency. Psy.* New York: Wiley.

Zimbardo, P., & Weber, A. (1994). *Psychology.* New York: HarperCollins.

ALEXANDER'S LAW. See VISION/SIGHT, THEORIES OF.

ALGEBRAIC SUMMATION, LAW OF. See SKINNER'S DESCRIPTIVE BEHAVIOR/OPERANT CONDITIONING THEORY.

ALGORITHMIC-HEURISTIC THEORY. The term *algorithm* refers to a precise and unambiguous direction (''prescription'') for carrying out a defined sequence of relatively elementary operations in order to solve a certain class or type of problem (Landa, 1994). An example of an algorithm is the use of a flowchart (i.e., a technique that first poses a question and then, depending on the answer, directs the individual to go to another question, etc., until a final answer is achieved) for finding the greatest common denominator of two natural numbers. The execution of the cognitive operations according to the directions of an algorithm is called the *algorithmic process*, and, since each algorithm is applicable to a wide set of problems that belong to a certain class, it represents a general and guaranteed method for problem solving. The related term *heuristic*, however, denotes only a ''rule of thumb'' approach that may direct a problem-solving process but does not guarantee a solution to the problem. An example of a heuristic rule is, Try to solve a related problem if the proposed problem cannot immediately be solved. In this case, the set of directions is called a *heuristic prescription*. Heuristic prescriptions, as compared to algorithmic prescriptions, contain a certain amount of ambiguity and uncertainty. Classes of problems, according to this approach, may be viewed as ''algorithmically solvable,'' ''algorithmically unsolvable,'' or ''unknown as to algorithmical solvability.'' Thus, in the case of some problems, an appropriate algorithm may not exist (e.g., algorithms for proving most mathematical theorems), or an algorithm may be inefficient (e.g., an algorithm for finding the optimum move in a chess game) (Reber, 1995). The practical significance of using algorithms for problem-solving tasks is that it allows children and average adult learners to solve certain problems that, otherwise, might seem to be beyond their cognitive, intellectual, or sensorimotor capabilities. The *algorithmic-heuristic theory* (AHT), formulated by Lev Landa in 1952–1961 while in the USSR, is able to deal with a wide variety of learning, instructional, and performance problems, which include the development of general methods of thinking in students; the psychological and logical structure of different methods of thinking; classification of particular methods by different functional and logical characteristics; differences between algorithmic prescriptions and processes and their interactions; formation in students of the ability for self-programming, self-regulation, and self-control of their cognitive and practical activities; and methods of designing individualized adaptive instruction in algo-heuristics, including usage of computers. The area of research involving *instructional theory* prescribes the steps used to design effective instructional strategies, such as the identification of the educational goals (i.e., what the learner should be able to do after instruction) and the identification of prototypic cognitive processes/rules (i.e., what the learner must learn in order to perform successfully on tasks associated with the educational goals) (e.g., Gagne, 1965, 1994; Bruner's *theory of instruction*, 1966; Scandura, 1973, 1980; Reigeluth, 1981). Historically, the theory/doctrine of *formal discipline/training* (e.g., Lund, 1933; Munn, 1946) was an approach to education that advocated that some subjects/courses (e.g., Latin) ought to be studied, independently of any content that they might have, because they acquainted the student with basic principles (or "forms") that will ultimately prove of value in other ways and generally serve to "train the mind." The enthusiasm for this theory has waxed and waned several times over the years (Reber, 1995). Contemporary *instructional theory* provides a generalized basis for instructional prescriptions that, in principle, may be used with any particular subject matter that might be of interest—no matter how complex that subject matter (Scandura, 1994). See also COGNITIVE STYLE MODELS.

REFERENCES

Lund, F. (1933). *Psychology: An empirical study of behavior*. New York: Ronald Press.
Polya, G. (1945). *How to solve it: A new concept of mathematical method*. Princeton, NJ: Princeton University Press.
Munn, N. (1946). *Psychology*. New York: Houghton Mifflin.
Gagne, R. (1965). *The conditions of learning*. New York: Holt, Rinehart, & Winston.
Bruner, J. (1966). *Toward a theory of instruction*. Cambridge: Harvard University Press.
Scandura, J. (1973). *Structural learning. I. Theory and research*. London: Gordon & Breach.
Landa, L. (1974). *Algorithmization in learning and instruction*. Englewood Cliffs, NJ: Educational Technology Publications.
Merrill, P. (1977). Algorithmic organization in teaching and learning: Literature and research in the U.S.A. *Imp. Hum. Perf. Res. Quar., 6*, 93–112.
Landa, L. (1978). Some problems in algo-heuristic theory of thinking, learning, and instruction. In J. Scandura & C. Bainerd (Eds.), *Structural/process models of complex human behavior*. Alphen aan den Rijn: Sijthoff & Noordhoff.
Scandura, J. (1980). Theoretical foundations of instruction: A systems alternative to cognitive psychology. *J. Struc. Learn., 6*, 347–394.
Reigeluth, C. (Ed.) (1981). *Prescriptive theories of instruction*. New York: Academic Press.
Groner, R., Groner, M., & Bischof, W. (Eds.) (1983). *Methods of heuristics*. Hillsdale, NJ: Erlbaum.

Landa, L. (1983). *Instructional regulation and control: Cybernetics, algorithmization, and heuristics in education*. Englewood Cliffs, NJ: Educational Technology Publications.

Glaser, R. (1990). The reemergence of learning theory within instructional research. *Amer. Psy., 45*, 29–39.

Gagne, R. (1994). Learning outcomes. I. In R. J. Corsini (Ed.), *Ency. Psy.* New York: Wiley.

Landa, L. (1994). Algorithmic-heuristic theory. In R. J. Corsini (Ed.), *Ency. Psy.* New York: Wiley.

Marton, F. (1994). Learning outcomes. II. In R. J. Corsini (Ed.), *Ency. Psy.* New York: Wiley.

Scandura, J. (1994). Instructional theory. In R. J. Corsini (Ed.), *Ency. Psy.* New York: Wiley.

Reber, A. (1995). *The Penguin dictionary of psychology*. New York: Penguin Books.

McGuire, W. (1997). Creative hypothesis generating in psychology: Some useful heuristics. *Ann. Rev. Psy., 48*, 1–30.

ALIENATION THEORIES. See HORNEY'S THEORY OF PERSONALITY; PSYCHOPATHOLOGY, THEORIES OF.

ALL-OR-NONE LAW/PRINCIPLE. This principle, discovered by the American physiologist Henry Pickering Bowditch (1840–1917) while he was studying cardiac muscle (Warren, 1934), states that in any single nerve or muscle fiber the response to a stimulus above threshold level is maximal, independent of the intensity of the stimulus, and dependent only on the condition of the cell at the moment of stimulation. The *all-or-none* property of the nerve impulse is contained in the fact that its amplitude is always the same where the neural code is determined by frequency rather than size of the nerve response. Stronger stimuli result in more impulses being generated per second, but each stimulus has the same amplitude (Adrian, 1914, 1933). The process of nerve conduction has been likened to the burning of a fuse because both processes involve the progressive release of energy by local action (Woodworth & Schlosberg, 1965). However, it is true that not all fuses or all nerve fibers have the same amount of energy available; thick fuses and thick nerve fibers transmit a larger disturbance and transmit it faster. It is also true that the available energy in any nerve fiber varies from time to time with corresponding changes in the magnitude and speed of the impulse. The *all-or-none law*, however, is still valid because the nerve fiber either reacts with all of its available energy, or else (if the stimulus is too weak) it does not react at all. The top speed of the nerve impulse is estimated to be 100 meters per second and is attained only in the larger fibers of the body. Thin fibers conduct impulses at much slower rates, down to about 1 meter per second in some animal species. The major difference between the fuse and the nerve fiber in this analogy is that the nerve fiber restores itself after each impulse occurs, while the fuse does not. Only a small amount of the stored energy is momentarily available at the surface of the nerve fiber where the local activity takes place. The energy is promptly replaced as soon as this portion is consumed by the single nerve impulse. However, the replacement process takes a short amount of time, and a second impulse cannot follow immediately. At this stage in the process, the fiber is said to be in its *absolute refractory phase* (Osgood, 1953, refers to these events collectively as the *refractory law*). Then, within a millisecond or so, the fiber has recovered enough to allow a very strong stimulus to create a very weak impulse. Following this *relative refractory phase* of firing, there is a gradual buildup of available energy where the stimulus threshold is decreased, and the magnitude and speed of the impulse are increased. Osgood (1953) coins the term *essential identity law*, which is related to the physiological *all-or-none law* and refers to the fact that nerve impulses are all the same in kind. For example, impulses traveling in optic nerve fibers differ qualitatively in no way from impulses in cutaneous fibers, and activity in the visual areas of the cortex does not appear to differ qualitatively from activity in the somesthetic, or even in the motor, areas. The *all-or-none principle* from physiology has been expanded conceptually to the area of the psychology of learning where it refers to associations of learned materials that are either formed completely on a single trial or not formed at all (cf: *one-trial learning* of Guthrie, 1952; Skinner, 1953). The *all-or-none law/principle* has been consistently well referenced and represented in psychology textbooks from 1885 through 1996 (Roeckelein, 1996). See also CONTINUITY THEORY; GUTHRIE'S THEORY OF BEHAVIOR; SKINNER'S DESCRIPTIVE BEHAVIOR/OPERANT CONDITIONING THEORY.

REFERENCES

Adrian, E. (1914). The all-or-none principle in nerve. *J. Physio., 47*, 450–474.

Watson, J. B. (1919). *Psychology: From the standpoint of a behaviorist*. Philadelphia: Lippincott.

Dunlap, K. (1922). *The elements of scientific psychology*. St. Louis, MO: Mosby.

Adrian, W. (1933). The all-or-nothing reaction. *Ergebn. Physio., 35*, 744–755.

Warren, H. (Ed.) (1934). *Dictionary of psychology*. Cambridge, MA: Houghton Mifflin.

Boring, E. G., Langfeld, H., & Weld, H. (1935). *Psychology: A factual textbook*. New York: Wiley.

Munn, N. (1946). *Psychology*. New York: Houghton Mifflin.

Brink, F. (1951). Excitation and conduction in the neuron. In S. S. Stevens (Ed.), *Handbk. Exp. Psy.* New York: Wiley.

Guthrie, E. (1952). *The psychology of learning*. New York: Harper & Row.

Osgood, C. (1953). *Method and theory in experimental psychology*. New York: Oxford University Press.

Skinner, B. F. (1953). *Science and human behavior*. New York: Macmillan.

Woodworth, R., & Schlosberg, H. (1965). *Experimental psychology*. New York: Holt, Rinehart, & Winston.

Roeckelein, J. E. (1996). Citation of *laws* and *theories* in textbooks across 112 years of psychology. *Psy. Rep., 79*, 979–998.

ALLPORT'S CONFORMITY HYPOTHESIS. The American social psychologist Floyd Henry Allport (1890–1978) proposed that *conforming* behavior can be recognized by its distinctive distribution, which takes the shape of an inverted J curve (Allport, 1934). A few people overconform (are to the left of the curve's peak), the overwhelming majority are positioned exactly at the peak, which accounts for the spike of the J, and a minority deviate from the norm, which accounts for an elongated, but low-level, tail. Allport validated his *conformity hypothesis* mainly by observations in field situations involving activities such as reporting to work, using holy water in a Catholic church, and stopping at a stop sign. Allport's data refer primarily to situations where adherence to standards is enforced (''compliant behavior''). *Conformity* is seen as an intermediate stage between superficial compliance and permanent internalization and as a conflict between what a person basically is and what group membership induces from the individual (Corsini, 1994). See also ATTITUDE/ATTITUDE CHANGE, THEORIES OF; BYSTANDER INTERVENTION EFFECT; CONFLICT, THEORIES OF; GROUPTHINK PHENOMENON.

REFERENCES

Allport, F. (1924). *Social psychology*. Boston: Houghton Mifflin.

Allport, F. (1934). The J-curve hypothesis of conforming behavior. *J. Soc. Psy., 5*, 141–183.

Sherif, M. (1935). A study of some social factors in perception. *Ar. Psy., 27*, no. 187.

Festinger, L., Schachter, S., & Back, K. (1950). *Social pressures in informal groups: A study of human factors in housing*. New York: Harper.

Asch, S. (1951). Effects of group pressure upon the modification and distortion of judgment. In H. Guetzkow (Ed.), *Groups, leadership, and men*. Pittsburgh: Carnegie.

Asch, S. (1955). Opinions and social pressure. *Sci. Amer., 193*, 31–35.

Asch, S. (1956). Studies of independence and conformity. I. A minority of one against a unanimous majority. *Psy. Mono., 70*, no. 416.

Sherif, M., & Sherif, C. (1964). *Reference groups: Explorations into conformity and deviation of adolescents*. New York: Harper & Row.

Vaughan, G. (1964). The trans-situational aspect of conformity behavior. *J. Pers., 32*, 335–354.

Allen, V. (1965). Situational factors in conformity. In L. Berkowitz (Ed.), *Advances in experimental social psychology*. Vol. 2. New York: Academic Press.

Hollander, E., & Willis, R. (1967). Some current issues in the psychology of conformity and nonconformity. *Psy. Bull., 68*, 62–76.

Eagly, A. (1978). Sex differences in influenceability. *Psy. Bull., 85*, 86–116.

Cooper, H. (1979). Statistically combining independent studies: A meta-analysis of sex differences in conformity research. *J. Pers. Soc. Psy., 37*, 131–146.

Corsini, R. J. (1994). Conformity. In R. J. Corsini (Ed.), *Ency. Psy*. New York: Wiley.

Samuel, W. (1994). Conforming personality. In R. J. Corsini (Ed.), *Ency. Psy*. New York: Wiley.

ALLPORT'S FUNCTIONAL AUTONOMY PRINCIPLE. The American psychologist Gordon Willard Allport (1897–1967) studied, researched, and taught in the area of personality, which he regarded as the natural subject matter of psychology. In his exploration and development of personality theory, Allport conceived of personality as an organized whole (rather than merely a collection of habits) where one's *self* can make choices and influence the growth or outcome of its own personality (Allport, 1955). Allport formulated the concept of *functional autonomy of motives*, which emphasized the emergence of new motivational systems in a person's life (Allport, 1937). The *principle of functional autonomy* describes the case where well-established habits (such as a person's going to work for 12 hours a day for many years and earning a great deal of money) can become ends or motives in themselves (such as continuing to go to work for 12 hours a day, even though the person has become wealthy, could easily retire, and actually does not need to work at all). According to the *principle of functional autonomy of motives*, means to a goal become ends in themselves where the original activities have now become motives and function independently of the purposes or needs that they initially served. When it was first introduced, the concept of *functional autonomy* was both controversial and radical because it ran counter to the prevailing theories of motivation, which stressed mechanisms directly linked to basic physiological needs (Goranson, 1994). Allport's idea raised the possibility that simple and complex motives can function quite separately from any direct physiological drive or need. The concept of *functional autonomy* liberalized the area of motivation inasmuch as it allowed the individual to be an active (rather than a passive) entity whose behavior could be present-oriented, as well as future-oriented, and not merely past-oriented. Judging by its absence in most current introductory psychology textbooks, the *principle of functional autonomy of motives* seems to be less referenced generally today than it was years ago, even though the term seems, from casual observation, to have become part of psychologists' informal vocabulary. Thus, the notion of *functionally autonomous motives* (though controversial at one time; Hall & Lindzey, 1978) no longer seems particularly strange and has been accepted and absorbed into the mainstream of psychology. Indeed, recent theories of motivation have proposed and described "supra-" or "extra-physiologically based" needs in shaping individuals' personality such as motives for exploration, curiosity, mastery, manipulation, self-actualization, sensation-seeking, and competence (Goranson, 1994). See also ALLPORT'S THEORY OF PERSONALITY; MOTIVATION, THEORIES OF.

REFERENCES

Allport, G. (1937). The functional autonomy of motives. *Amer. J. Psy., 50*, 141–156.

Allport, G. (1940). The psychologist's frame of reference. *Psy. Bull., 37*, 1–28.

Allport, G. (1953). The trend in motivational theory. *Amer. J. Orthopsychiat., 23*, 107–119.

Allport, G. (1955). *Becoming: Basic considerations for a psychology of personality.* New Haven, CT: Yale University Press.

Mischel, W., Ebbesen, E., & Zeiss, A. (1973). Selective attention to the self: Situational and dispositional determinants. *J. Pers. Soc. Psy., 27*, 129–142.

Hall, C., & Lindzey, G. (1978). *Theories of personality.* New York: Wiley.

Mischel, W., & Peake, P. (1982). Beyond deja vu in the search for cross-situational consistency. *Psy. Rev., 89,* 730–755.

Goranson, R. (1994). Functional autonomy. In R. J. Corsini (Ed.), *Ency. Psy.* New York: Wiley.

ALLPORT'S THEORY OF ENESTRUENCE. = event-structure theory. This theory of perception, developed by Floyd Henry Allport (1890–1978), whom many consider to be the father of experimental social psychology, consists of a kinetic geometry (''kinematics'') of the self-closedness of ongoing-event series and associative probability concepts of the energies (i.e., events) involved in the self-closed structures and their interrelationships. As one can sense here, the programmatic nature of this rather intriguing theory is stated in somewhat abstract terms. This is because the model was intended to be applied to many different phenomena at various levels of analysis. Allport's theoretical model of *event-structure* attempted to cast the laws of nature under two headings: a formal principle of nature in terms *other* than ''quantitative'' and a principle of ''corporation'' of many perceptual and social phenomena. If the theory is true, said Allport (1955, p. 666), ''nature is not a machine, nor are organisms controlled by quantitative or mechanical laws. . . . [T]he theory is advanced merely as one way of looking at the problem of structure, one attempt to fathom the mystery of the form and unity of nature which have thus far been left largely untouched by science.'' Allport's *theory of enestruence* holds that social structure has no physical or anatomical basis but consists of cycles of events that ''hoop'' and return upon themselves to complete and sustain the cycle. To many psychologists, the *event-structure theory* suggested by Allport seems to be a rather ambitious prescription for the synthesis and consolidation of other theories of perception and social behavior into a unifying and cohesive system. Allport's 1967 article in the *American Psychologist* is recommended, especially, to the interested reader. See also PERCEPTION (I. GENERAL), THEORIES OF; PERCEPTION (II. COMPARATIVE APPRAISAL), THEORIES OF.

REFERENCES

Allport, F. (1940). An event-system of collective action. *J. Soc. Psy., 11,* 417–445.

Allport, F. (1954). The structuring of events: Outline of a general theory with applications to psychology. *Psy. Rev., 61,* 281–303.

Allport, F. (1955). *Theories of perception and the concept of structure.* New York: Wiley.

Tannenbaum, A., & Allport, F. (1956). Personality structure and group structure: An interpretive study of their relationship through an event-structure hypothesis. *J. Abn. Soc. Psy., 53,* 272–280.

Heider, F. (1959). On perception and event structure, and the psychological environment: Selected papers. *Psy. Iss., 1,* 1–123.

Allport, F. (1962). A structuronomic concept of behavior: Individual and collective. I. Structural theory and the master problem of social psychology. *J. Abn. Soc. Psy., 64,* 3–30.

Allport, F. (1967). A theory of enestruence (event-structure). *Amer. Psy., 22,* 1–14.

ALLPORT'S THEORY OF PERSONALITY. In taking an eclectic and humanistic approach to the study of personality, Gordon Willard Allport (1897–1967) drew on a wide variety of sources, from William McDougall's theory of motives (McDougall, 1923) to the experimental-social psychological analysis of behavior (Allport, 1960). While Allport also drew some of his ideas from the psychodynamic theories of personality (e.g., Freud, 1940), he was opposed strongly to the Freudian views of the unconscious, and he rejected any reductionist theory that attributed human behavior to innate instincts, childhood conditioning, or repressed complexes (Vernon, 1994). In examining the other sciences and scientific models, Allport (1947) opposed extensive borrowing from the natural sciences and believed that the methods and theoretical models that have been useful in the physical sciences may only mislead one when attempting to study complex human behavior. Allport thought of personality as an organized entity that is future-oriented and not merely a bundle of habits and fixations (Allport, 1955). He argued that one's *self* (or *proprium)* is able to make choices where it can influence the development of its own personality along with adjusting to the emergence of new motivational systems ("functional autonomy of motives"). Allport emphasized a multifaceted methodological approach toward personality study that combined the *idiographic* (study and analysis of single cases) and the *nomothetic* (discovery of general or universal laws that apply to all humans) viewpoints (Allport, 1962a). Even though Allport himself developed various tests of personality traits, values, and attitudes, he saw little merit in conducting factorial-type studies of personality (Allport, Vernon, & Lindzey, 1931/1951; Allport, 1937; cf: Cattell, 1946, 1952). Allport's *theory of personality* (Allport, 1937, 1961) is often called a *trait theory* where traits (i.e., enduring predispositions to respond in certain ways) occupy the position of a major motivational construct (cf: Murray's, 1938, *need*; Freud's, 1940, *instinct*; and McDougall's, 1923, *sentiment* theories). One of Allport's early studies (Allport & Odbert, 1936) found almost 18,000 words in the dictionary that could be used as *trait* names to describe personality. Using an *idiographic* approach of analysis (Allport, 1937) where an individual's unique personality traits were arranged into a hierarchy from "most important" at the top to "least important" at the bottom, Allport subsequently divided the hierarchy into three separate groups of traits: *cardinal* (the uncommon, but pervasive and all-encompassing characteristics that influence most areas of only a few people's lives, such as humanitarianism and honesty), *central* (specific behavioral tendencies that are highly characteristic of an individual, such as outgoing and ambitious), and *secondary* (the less-enduring and transitory characteristics such as liking to hike or cycle). Allport emphasized that no two people have exactly the same traits, and his *trait theory* of personality stressed the uniqueness of the individual. Although few psychologists have embraced Allport's personality theory in its total form, it has nevertheless been influential and useful, especially in its restoration and purification of the *ego* concept (Allport, 1943), and Allport himself was one of the few theorists who have provided an effective bridge between academic psychology and clinical-personality psychology (Hall & Lindzey, 1978). While Allport's main work was on the development of a comprehensive personality theory, his interests were wide-ranging, including studies on rumor, social attitudes, religion, graphology, eidetic imagery, radio voices, and prejudice (Allport & Vernon, 1933; Allport & Cantril, 1934; Allport & Postman, 1947; Allport, 1954, 1960, 1962b). Critics of Allport's theoretical orientation and work (cf: Allport, 1966) have included Bertocci (1940), Coutu (1949), Seward (1948), Skaggs (1945), and Sanford (1963). Perhaps the most remarkable aspect of Allport's work has been its ability to exert a broad influence and sense of novelty in psychology in spite of its pluralism and eclecticism (Hall & Lindzey, 1978). See also ALLPORT'S FUNCTIONAL AUTONOMY PRINCIPLE; IDIOGRAPHIC/NOMOTHETIC LAWS; MCDOUGALL'S HORMIC/INSTINCT THEORY/DOCTRINE.

REFERENCES

Allport, F., & Allport, G. (1921). Personality traits: Their classification and measurement. *J. Abn. Soc. Psy., 16*, 6–40.

McDougall, W. (1923). *Outline of psychology.* New York: Scribners.

Allport, G. (1929). The study of personality by the intuitive method. *J. Abn. Soc. Psy., 24*, 14–27.

Allport, G., Vernon, P., & Lindzey, G. (1931/1951). *A study of values.* Boston: Houghton Mifflin.

Allport, G., & Vernon, P. (1933). *Studies in expressive movement.* New York: Macmillan.

Allport, G., & Cantril, H. (1934). Judging personality from voice. *J. Soc. Psy., 5*, 37–55.

Allport, G., & Odbert, H. (1936). Trait names: A psycho-lexical study. *Psy. Mono., 47*, no. 211.

Allport, G. (1937). *Personality: A psychological interpretation.* New York: Holt, Rinehart, & Winston.

Murray, H. (1938). *Explorations in personality.* New York: Oxford University Press.

Allport, G. (1940). Motivation in personality: Reply to Mr. Bertocci. *Psy. Rev., 47*, 533–554.

Bertocci, P. (1940). A critique of G. W. Allport's theory of motivation. *Psy. Rev., 47*, 501–532.

Freud, S. (1940). *An outline of psychoanalysis.* New York: Norton.

Allport, G. (1943). The ego in contemporary psychology. *Psy. Rev., 50*, 451–478.

Skaggs, E. (1945). Personalistic psychology as science. *Psy. Rev., 52*, 234–238.

Allport, G. (1946). Effect: A secondary principle of learning. *Psy. Rev., 53*, 335–347.

Cattell, R. (1946). *Description and measurement of personality.* New York: World.

Allport, G. (1947). Scientific models and human morals. *Psy. Rev., 54*, 182–192.

Allport, G., & Postman, L. (1947). *The psychology of rumor.* New York: Holt.

Seward, J. (1948). The sign of a symbol: A reply to Professor Allport. *Psy. Rev., 55*, 277–296.

Coutu, W. (1949). *Emergent human nature.* New York: Knopf.

Cattell, R. (1952). *Factor analysis: An introduction and manual for psychologist and social scientist.* New York: Harper.

Allport, G. (1954). *The nature of prejudice.* Cambridge, MA: Addison-Wesley.

Allport, G. (1955). *Becoming: Basic considerations for a psychology of personality.* New Haven, CT: Yale University Press.

Allport, G. (1960). *Personality and social encounter.* Boston: Beacon Press.

Allport, G. (1961). *Pattern and growth in personality.* New York: Holt, Rinehart, & Winston.

Allport, G. (1962a). The general and the unique in psychological science. *J. Pers., 30,* 405–422.

Allport, G. (1962b). *The individual and his religion.* New York: Macmillan.

Sanford, N. (1963). Personality: Its place in psychology. In S. Koch (Ed.), *Psychology: A study of a science.* Vol. 5. New York: McGraw-Hill.

Allport, G. (1966). Traits revisited. *Amer. Psy., 21,* 1–10.

Hall, C., & Lindzey, G. (1978). *Theories of personality.* New York: Wiley.

Vernon, P. (1994). Gordon Willard Allport. In R. J. Corsini (Ed.), *Ency. Psy.* New York: Wiley.

ALRUTZ'S THEORY. The German researcher S. Alrutz made the suggestion at the turn of the century that the simultaneous arousal of both warm and cold receptors in the skin give the resultant sensation of heat. A clear demonstration of a hot sensation that results from the simultaneous stimulation of neighboring warmth and cold receptors is the so-called *synthetic heat* experiment (Burnett & Dallenbach, 1927, 1928), where no genuine heat is applied, but warm spots are subjected to moderate warmth and cold spots to cold. Under these conditions, the first sensation is usually cold, which is followed by heat, which disappears after a few seconds and then gives the sensation of cold again. This theory is related to the phenomenon of *paradoxical cold*, where the sensation of cold results from a warm stimulus (von Frey, 1895). The case for *paradoxical cold* and *synthetic heat* is not completely conclusive, and there is some evidence against the *Alrutz theory* (Jenkins, 1938). Related theories in this area of the stimulation of cutaneous senses are the *concentration theory of cutaneous cold* and the *spot theory of temperature senses* (Jenkins, 1940, 1941; Woodworth & Schlosberg, 1965). See also NAFE'S THEORY OF CUTANEOUS SENSITIVITY.

REFERENCES

von Frey, M. (1895). Beitrage zur Sinnesphysiologie des Haut. *Ber. Sachs. Ges. Wiss. Leipzig Math-Phys. 47,* 166–184.

Alrutz, S. (1897). Omfornimmelsen ''hett.'' *Uppsala Lakforen, 2,* 340–359.

von Frey, M. (1904). *Vorlesungen uber physiologie.* Berlin.

Alrutz, S. (1908). Untersuchungen uber die Temperatursinne. *Z. Psy., 47,* 161–202, 241–286.

Burnett, N., & Dallenbach, K. (1927). The experience of heat. *Amer. J. Psy., 38,* 418–431.

Burnett, N., & Dallenbach, K. (1928). Heat intensity. *Amer. J. Psy., 40,* 484–494.

Jenkins, W. (1938). Studies in thermal sensitivity. Further evidence against the Alrutz theory. *J. Exp. Psy., 23,* 411–422.

Jenkins, W. (1940). Studies in thermal sensitivity. Part–whole relations in seriatim warm-
    mapping. *J. Exp. Psy., 27,* 76–80.
Jenkins, W. (1941). Studies in thermal sensitivity. Further evidence on the effects of
    stimulus temperature. *J. Exp. Psy., 29,* 413–419.
Boring, E. G. (1942). *Sensation and perception in the history of experimental psychology.*
    New York: Appleton-Century-Crofts.
Woodworth, R., & Schlosberg, H. (1965). *Experimental psychology.* New York: Holt,
    Rinehart, & Winston.

AMSEL'S HYPOTHESIS/THEORY. The American psychologist Abram Amsel (1958, 1962, 1967) enunciated the *frustration hypothesis* concerning nonreward and extinction of instrumental behavior where the occurrence of
nonreward at a moment when the organism is expecting a reward causes the
elicitation of a primary "frustration reaction." The feedback stimulation from
this frustration reaction is aversive and has short-term, persisting motivational
effects upon subsequent instrumental behavior. Amsel states that fractional parts
of the frustration reaction become classically conditioned to stimuli preceding
its elicitation; cues from "anticipatory" frustration are connected to avoidance
responses where the connections are modifiable through training. Earlier treatments and interpretations of the nonreward situation had viewed it in a passive
role (e.g., Tolman, 1932, assumed that nonreward served simply to weaken an
organism's expectancy of reward; Hull, 1943, conceived of nonreward trials as
allowing the buildup of inhibitory factors without being offset by corresponding
increases in habit or incentive motivation). On the other hand, Amsel's *frustration hypothesis* considers the condition of nonreward as an actively punishing
and aversive event, rather than as a passive condition. The consequence of Amsel's position is that many of the effects of nonreward upon responding are
viewed today as analogous to the effects produced upon that same behavior by
the application of punishment (cf: Spence, 1960; Wagner, 1963, 1966; Daly,
1974). While Amsel's *frustration theory* is one of the dominant conceptions of
extinction, it does require critical analysis in light of a few failings. For example,
Levy and Seward (1969) suggest that no frustration effect occurs if the organism
is expecting different incentives in two goal locations; Bower (1960) observes
that Amsel's *extinction theory* applies only to instrumental, appetitive responses
and not to extinction in classical conditioning or instrumental escape conditioning situations; Capaldi (1967) and others have produced different resistance
levels to extinction by variations in the sequential pattern of reward and nonreward trials during acquisition of responses; and Robbins (1971) reviews some
studies that suggest that extinction is a multiple-determinant process while Amsel's *frustration hypothesis* is only one component of the total phenomenon
(Bower & Hilgard, 1981). See also CAPALDI'S THEORY; HULL'S LEARN-
ING THEORY; TOLMAN'S THEORY.

REFERENCES

Tolman, E. (1932). *Purposive behavior in animals and men.* New York: Appleton-
    Century-Crofts.

Hull, C. (1943). *Principles of behavior*. New York: Appleton-Century-Crofts.

Amsel, A. (1958). The role of frustrative nonreward in noncontinuous reward situations. *Psy. Bull., 55*, 102–119.

Bower, G. (1960). Partial and correlated reward in escape learning. *J. Exp. Psy., 59*, 126–130.

Spence, K. (1960). The roles of reinforcement and nonreinforcement in simple learning. In *Behavior theory and learning: Selected papers of K. W. Spence*. Englewood Cliffs, NJ: Prentice-Hall.

Amsel, A. (1962). Frustrative nonreward in partial reinforcement and discrimination learning. *Psy. Bull., 69*, 306–328.

Bower, G. (1962). The influence of graded reductions in reward and prior frustrating events upon the magnitude of the frustration effect. *J. Comp. Physio. Psy., 55*, 582–587.

Wagner, A. (1963). Conditioned frustration as a learned drive. *J. Exp. Psy., 66*, 142–148.

Ross, R. (1964). Positive and negative partial-reinforcement effects carried through continuous reinforcement, changed motivation, and changed response. *J. Exp. Psy., 68*, 492–502.

Amsel, A., & Ward, J. (1965). Frustration and persistence: Resistance to discrimination following prior experience with the discriminanda. *Psy. Mono., 79*, no. 597.

Wagner, A. (1966). Frustration and punishment. In R. Haber (Ed.), *Research on motivation*. New York: Holt, Rinehart, & Winston.

Amsel, A. (1967). Partial reinforcement effects on vigor and persistence. In K. Spence & J. Spence (Eds.), *The psychology of learning and motivation*. Vol. 1. New York: Academic Press.

Capaldi, E. (1967). A sequential hypothesis of instrumental learning. In K. Spence & J. Spence (Eds.), *The psychology of learning and motivation*. Vol. 1. New York: Academic Press.

Levy, N., & Seward, J. (1969). Frustration and homogeneity of rewards in the double runway. *J. Exp. Psy., 81*, 460–463.

Robbins, D. (1971). Partial reinforcement: A selective review of the alleyway literature since 1960. *Psy. Bull., 76*, 415–431.

Daly, H. (1974). Reinforcing properties of escape from frustration aroused in various learning situations. In G. Bower (Ed.), *The psychology of learning and motivation*. Vol. 8. New York: Academic Press.

Bower, G., & Hilgard, E. (1981). *Theories of learning*. Englewood Cliffs, NJ: Prentice-Hall.

Hergenhahn, B. (1982). *An introduction to theories of learning*. Englewood Cliffs, NJ: Prentice-Hall.

ANALOGUE THEORY OF MEMORY. See FORGETTING/MEMORY, THEORIES OF.

ANCESTRAL INHERITANCE, LAW OF. See GALTON'S LAWS.

ANGYAL'S PERSONALITY THEORY. The Hungarian American Andras Angyal (1902–1960) developed a theory of personality in which he described two basic types of motivational processes in humans: striving toward love ("homonomy") and striving toward mastery ("autonomy") (Angyal, 1941). Angyal conceived of personality as an interdependent system where tensions arise between the person and the environment and which is controlled by both homonomy and autonomy processes. In Angyal's formulation, the connection between the parts of the system are subordinate to the overall whole where, for example, neurosis is one system, and overall health is another system. Also, when the systems (through "system analysis") become disturbed or disrupted, the process of therapy is indicated and refers to the restoration of the health system to its normally dominant role. In its dynamics, Angyal's *personality theory* may be characterized as *organismic* or *holistic* (Angyal, 1965; cf: Bernard, 1866/1957; Wertheimer, 1923; Kantor, 1924, 1933; Smuts, 1926; Coghill, 1929; Goldstein, 1939; Murphy, 1947). In the genesis of his personality theory, Angyal emphasized the need for a new science that was not primarily psychological, physiological, or sociological in character but that viewed the person as a whole. Angyal, unlike Kurt Goldstein (1939), insisted that it is impossible to differentiate the organism from the environment (Angyal coined the term *biospheric* to indicate the holistic relationship between one individual and the environment) because they interpenetrate one another in such a complex fashion that any attempt to distinguish them would be artificial and tend to destroy the natural unity of the whole (Hall & Lindzey, 1978). Angyal's *personality theory* has not had a significant impact on academic psychology, perhaps because it was developed predominantly within a clinical, or nonacademic, context (Lichtenstein, 1994). See also GOLDSTEIN'S ORGANISMIC THEORY; MURPHY'S BIOSOCIAL THEORY.

REFERENCES

Bernard, C. (1866/1957). *An introduction to the study of experimental medicine*. New York: Dover.

Wertheimer, M. (1923). Untersuchungen zur Lehre von der Gestalt. *Psy. Forsch., 4,* 301–350.

Kantor, J. R. (1924). *Principles of psychology*. New York: Knopf.

Smuts, J. (1926). *Holism and evolution*. New York: Macmillan.

Coghill, G. (1929). *Anatomy and the problem of behavior*. London: Cambridge University Press.

Kantor, J. R. (1933). *A survey of the science of psychology*. Bloomington, IN: Principia Press.

Goldstein, K. (1939). *The organism: A holistic approach to biology derived from pathological data in man*. New York: American Book.

Angyal, A. (1941). *Foundations for a science of personality*. New York: Commonwealth Foundation.

Murphy, G. (1947). *Personality: A biosocial approach to origins and structure*. New York: Harper.

Angyal, A. (1948). The holistic approach in psychiatry. *Amer. J. Psychiat., 105,* 178–182.

Angyal, A. (1951). A theoretical model for personality studies. *J. Pers., 20,* 131–142.

Angyal, A. (1965). *Neurosis and treatment: A holistic theory*. New York: Wiley.

Hall, C., & Lindzey, G. (1978). *Theories of personality*. New York: Wiley.

Lichtenstein, P. (1994). Andras Angyal. In R. J. Corsini (Ed.), *Ency. Psy.* New York: Wiley.

ANIMAL MAGNETISM, THEORY OF. See HYPNOSIS/HYPNOTISM, THEORIES OF.

ANSBACHER EFFECT. See PERCEPTION (I. GENERAL), THEORIES OF.

ANXIETY, THEORIES OF. Anxiety is a subjective emotional state that is characterized by pervasive feelings such as dread and apprehension and is often accompanied by physical symptoms such as tremors, muscle tension, chest pain, palpitations, dizziness, headache, and gastrointestinal distress (Thorn-Gray, 1994). Anxiety may or may not be associated with fearful or stressful stimuli; it is an emotional attitude or sentiment concerning the future, characterized by an unpleasant alternation or mingling of dread and hope. Anxiety neurosis is a functional disorder of the nervous system for which no actual lesion is found and whose most prominent symptom is a marked degree of morbid and objectively unfounded dread (Warren, 1934). Anxiety is often distinguished from fear in that an anxiety state is often objectless, whereas fear assumes a specific feared object, person, or event; and anxiety disorder is a cover term for a variety of maladaptive syndromes that have severe anxiety as the dominant disturbance (Reber, 1995). *Theories of anxiety* may be classified generally as *psychoanalytic/ psychodynamic* theories or as *learning/behavioral* theories (Kutash, 1994). The concept of *anxiety neurosis* was first formulated in a psychoanalytic context in 1895 by Sigmund Freud, who thought it to be a result of the discharge of repressed *libido* (accumulated somatic sexual tension). Freud theorized that when libidinal excitation produced threatening sexual wishes, fantasies, or experiences, such mental constructions were repressed, and the blocked libidinal energy subsequently developed into anxiety or somatic symptoms. Freud later reformulated his notion of anxiety to relate it to the conflict between the *ego* (reality principle) and the *id* (pleasure principle). The emotion that was experienced during the traumatic state created by the tension between ego and id was called *anxiety* (Freud, 1923, 1936, 1964). Freud's development of his *anxiety theory* included a chronological sequence of early sources of anxiety that emphasized absence of mother, punishments leading to fear of losing parental love, castration fear during the oedipal stage, and disapproval by the *superego* (conscience). In such instances of anxiety, a child may come to fear her or his own instinctual wishes, and the means by which the ego opposes the id's wishes are revealed by the various defense systems that are sent into action by the anxiety. The defense systems/mechanisms include identification, denial, intellectualization, projection, and repression, among others. Other *psychoanalytic/ psychodynamic* theories of anxiety are those of Melanie Klein (1932, 1952), Rollo May (1950), Harry Stack Sullivan (1953), and I. Kutash (1980). Klein's theory focused on the child's fear of death as the basic cause of anxiety. May's theory emphasized the creation of anxiety as a result of one's value system being threatened; Sullivan's theory examined the unpleasant state of tension that was caused by disapproval involved in interpersonal relationships; and Kutash's *anxiety-stress theory* points to the disequilibrium (anxiety) that occurs when one is not experiencing optimal stress levels for one's constitution either in a healthy balance (equilibrium) or in an unhealthy balance (malequilibrium), and where anxiety can be adaptive (when a need to change is indicated by an optimal stress level) or maladaptive (when stress is either too high or too low). *Learning/ behavioral* theories of anxiety have been distinguished from the *psychoanalytic/ psychodynamic* theories concerning the type of stimuli (proximal versus distal) that are involved (Bootzin & Max, 1980), where proximal cues/stimuli (such as reinforcement in a stimulus–response sequence) are associated with *learning/ behavioral* theories, and the distal cues/stimuli (such as some intrapsychic conflict) are associated with the *psychoanalytic/psychodynamic* theories. The *learning/behavioral anxiety theories* have been developed based on the work of researchers such as Watson and Rayner (1920), Pavlov (1927), Wagner and Rescorla (1972), Mowrer (1960a, b), Herrnstein (1969), Bandura (1977), Berger (1962), and Rachman (1978). This approach is characterized by empirical conditioning studies (rather than personality and clinical studies) and attempts to understand, explain, and treat anxiety by invoking concepts such as *reinforcement* (the increase in the frequency of a response caused by pleasant/rewarding consequences), *punishment* (the decrease in the frequency of behaviors due to unpleasant consequences), *information processing, expectancy, efficacy expectations, fear reduction, discriminative* or *signaling value* of stimuli, *predictive value* of stimuli, *avoidance behavior, successive approximations* of desired behavior, *incompatible* behaviors, *cognitive processes, modeling* behaviors, *observational learning*, and *biofeedback* (Kutash, 1994). Various *antianxiety* drugs (such as the ''sedative-hypnotics'' named Valium and Librium) have been prescribed by physicians for individuals who experience the often overwhelming effects of anxiety (Thorn-Gray, 1994). See also FREUD'S THEORY OF PERSONALITY; LEARNING THEORIES/LAWS.

REFERENCES

Watson, J. B., & Rayner, R. (1920). Conditioned emotional reactions. *J. Exp. Psy., 3,* 1–14.
Freud, S. (1923). *The ego and the id.* New York: Norton.
Pavlov, I. (1927). *Conditioned reflexes.* New York: Dover.
Klein, M. (1932). *The psychoanalysis of children.* London: Hogarth Press.
Warren, H. (Ed.) (1934). *Dictionary of psychology.* Cambridge, MA: Houghton Mifflin.
Freud, S. (1936). *The problem of anxiety.* New York: Norton.
May, R. (1950). *The meaning of anxiety.* New York: Ronald Press.
Klein, M. (1952). On the theory of anxiety and guilt. In J. Riviere (Ed.), *Developments in psychoanalysis.* London: Hogarth Press.
Sullivan, H. S. (1953). *The interpersonal theory of psychiatry.* New York: Norton.

Mowrer, O. H. (1960a). *Learning theory and behavior.* New York: Wiley.

Mowrer, O. H. (1960b). *Learning theory and symbolic processes.* New York: Wiley.

Berger, S. (1962). Conditioning through vicarious instigation. *Psy. Rev., 69,* 450–466.

Freud, S. (1964). *The complete psychological works of Sigmund Freud.* Vols. 1–24. London: Hogarth Press.

Herrnstein, R. (1969). Method and theory in the study of avoidance. *Psy. Rev., 76,* 49–69.

Wagner, A., & Rescorla, R. (1972). Inhibition in Pavlovian conditioning: Applications of a theory. In R. Bokes & M. Halliday (Eds.), *Inhibition and learning.* New York: Academic Press.

Bandura, A. (1977). *Social learning theory.* Englewood Cliffs, NJ: Prentice-Hall.

Rachman, S. (1978). *Fear and courage.* San Francisco: Freeman.

Bootzin, R., & Max, D. (1980). Learning and behavioral theories. In I. Kutash & L. Schlesinger (Eds.), *Handbook on stress and anxiety.* San. Francisco: Jossey-Bass.

Kutash, I. (1980). Prevention and equilibrium-disequilibrium theory. In I. Kutash & L. Schlesinger (Eds.), *Handbook on stress and anxiety.* San Francisco: Jossey-Bass.

Kutash, I. (1994). Anxiety. In R. J. Corsini (Ed.), *Ency. Psy.* New York: Wiley.

Thorn-Gray, B. (1994). Antianxiety drugs. In R. J. Corsini (Ed.), *Ency. Psy.* New York: Wiley.

Reber, A. (1995). *The Penguin dictionary of psychology.* New York: Penguin Books.

APPARENT MOVEMENT, PRINCIPLES/THEORIES OF. The phenomenon of *apparent movement* refers to the subjective visual perception of movement in the absence of any real or objective physical motion. Common types of apparent movement include the *phi phenomenon*, the *autokinetic effect*, and the *aftereffects of seen movement*. Other kinds of apparent movement are *alpha-*, *beta-*, *delta-*, *epsilon-*, *gamma-*, *induced-*, and *stroboscopic* movement (Kenkel, 1913; Wolman, 1973). The *phi phenomenon*, or *stroboscopic* movement, may be observed when two adjacent stimulus lights are flashed in rapid succession. If the interstimulus period is too long, the lights appear to go on and off separately. If the interstimulus period is too short, the lights appear to flash at the same time. When the interstimulus period is about 30–200 milliseconds, however, one gets the sensation of a light moving from one location to another location (stroboscopic movement is the basis for the effect of motion seen on television and motion pictures). The *autokinetic effect* refers to movement that seems to occur when a stationary object is viewed against a dark or ill-defined background, and where the stationary object appears to move after looking at it for a few minutes. *Aftereffects of seen movement* may occur when an individual stares for a few minutes at some continuous motion of an object in one direction and then shifts the gaze to a different surface (such as looking at a waterfall for a few minutes and then looking away to a textured surface where the surface now appears to be going in the opposite, or upward, direction; James, 1890, p. 89). *Induced movement* refers to the illusion of movement where a visual frame of reference is actually moving in one direction (such as clouds moving across the moon), and a stationary object (such as the moon) subsequently seems to move in the opposite direction. *Alpha movement* occurs when there appears to be a change of size in parts of a figure that are exposed in succession. *Beta movement* refers the illusion of movement when differently sized, or positioned, objects are exposed in succession. *Delta movement* refers to the apparent movement of a light stimulus to a darker stimulus after successive exposure when the variables of stimulus size, distance, and interstimulus interval are controlled. *Epsilon movement* is the visual perception of movement when a white line viewed against a black background is changed so that subsequently one now views a black line against a white background. *Gamma movement* refers to the apparent contraction and expansion of a figure that is shown suddenly (or is withdrawn) or a figure that is exposed to sudden illumination changes. Various *theories of apparent movement* have been developed and described (e.g., Woodworth & Schlosberg, 1965) and include the *inference theory* (where we actually see only the initial and terminal positions and infer that the object must have moved; Wertheimer, 1912, 1925); the *eye-movement theory* (in which emphasis is placed on the fact that the eyes objectively move across from the initial stimulus position to the final position, and where eye movement itself contributes to the sensation of motion; cf: Guilford & Helson, 1929; Wendt, 1952); and the *brain-field theory* (which suggested that the retina, or the visual cortex, was actually stimulated in the region lying between the initial and the terminal positions of the stimuli; Exner, 1875; Kohler, 1938, 1940). Woodworth and Schlosberg (1965) observed that there is no generally acceptable *theory of apparent movement* except, perhaps, for the development of a novel theory that would regard perception as a type of response to the incoming sensory stimulation and that subsequently applies the principle of *stimulus generalization* to the ultimate explanation of movement. Thus, if the stimuli that are received are sufficiently similar to those that were received from real movement, then the perceptual response would likely be the same (cf: Koffka, 1931, 1935; Neff, 1936; Graham, 1951). Graham (1965) suggested that new analyses and investigations in the field of perceptual/apparent movement would lead to needed theoretical improvements. See also KORTE'S LAWS.

REFERENCES

Exner, S. (1875). Experimentelle Untersuchungen der einfachsten psychischen Processe. III. Abhandlung: Der personlichen Gleichung zweiter Theil. *Pflug. Ar. ges. Physio., 11*, 403–432.

Vierordt, K. (1876). Die Bewegungsempfindung. *Z. Bio., 12*, 226–240.

Aubert, H. (1886). Die Bewegungsempfindung. *Ar. ges. Physio., 39*, 347–370.

James, W. (1890). *Principles of psychology*. Vol. 2. New York: Holt.

Stern, L. (1894). Die Wahrnehmung von Bewegungen vermittelst des Auges. *Z. Psy., 7*, 321–385.

Marbe, K. (1898). Die Stroboskopischen Erscheinungen. *Phil. Stud., 14*, 376–401.

Durr, E. (1900). Uber die Stroboskopischen Erscheinungen. *Phil. Stud., 15*, 501–523.

Wertheimer, M. (1912). Experimentelle Studien uber das Sehen von Bewegung. *Z. Psy., 61*, 161–265.

Kenkel, F. (1913). Untersuchungen uber den Zusammenhang zwischen Erscheinungs grosse und Erscheinungsbewegung bei einigen sogenannten optischen Tauschungen. *Z. Psy.*, *67*, 358–449.

Wertheimer, M. (1925). *Drei Abhandlungen zur Gestalttheorie*. Erlangen: Philosophischen Akademie.

Higginson, G. (1926). The visual apprehension of movement under successive retinal excitations. *Amer. J. Psy.*, *37*, 63–115.

Guilford, J., & Helson, H. (1929). Eye-movements and the phi phenomenon. *Amer. J. Psy.*, *41*, 595–606.

Neuhaus, W. (1930). Experimentelle Untersuchung der Scheinbewegung. *Ar. ges. Psy.*, *75*, 315–458.

Koffka, K. (1931). Die Wahrnehmung von Bewegung. In A. Bethe (Ed.), *Handbk. Norm. Path. Physio.* Berlin: Springer.

Koffka, K. (1935). *Principles of Gestalt psychology*. New York: Harcourt, Brace.

Neff, W. (1936). A critical investigation of the visual apprehension of movement. *Amer. J. Psy.*, *48*, 1–42.

Kohler, W. (1938). *The place of value in a world of facts*. New York: Liveright.

Kohler, W. (1940). *Dynamics in psychology*. New York: Liveright.

Boring, E. G. (1942). *Sensation and perception in the history of experimental psychology*. New York: Appleton-Century-Crofts.

Graham, C. (1951). Visual perception. In S. S. Stevens (Ed.), *Handbk. Exp. Psy.* New York: Wiley.

Wendt, P. (1952). Development of an eye camera for use with motion pictures. *Psy. Mono.*, *66*, no. 339.

Bartley, S. (1958). *Principles of perception*. New York: Harper.

Graham, C. (1963). On some aspects of real and apparent visual movement. *J. Opt. Soc. Amer.*, *53*, 1019–1025.

Kolers, P. (1963). Some differences between real and apparent visual movement. *Vis. Res.*, *3*, 191–206.

Graham, C. (1965). Perception of movement. In C. Graham (Ed.), *Vision and visual perception*. New York: Wiley.

Woodworth, R., & Schlosberg, H. (1965). *Experimental psychology*. New York: Holt, Rinehart, & Winston.

Wolman, B. (Ed.) (1973). *Dictionary of behavioral science*. New York: Van Nostrand Reinhold.

APPERCEPTION, DOCTRINE OF. See HERBART'S DOCTRINE OF APPERCEPTION; WUNDT'S THEORIES.

APPRAISAL THEORIES OF EMOTION. See COGNITIVE THEORIES OF EMOTION.

ARISTOTLE'S DOCTRINES/THEORIES. The Greek philosopher Aristotle (384–322 B.C.) was a student of Plato's Academy in Athens, where he was schooled in the *theory of ideas*. Aristotle argued that man was a rational animal endowed with an innate capacity for attaining knowledge from sense perception (and ''memory/associations'') and that knowledge is the result of deduction of universals and principles from perceptual information and not the recovering of innate ideas, as Plato taught. Aristotle's *empirical* methodology parallels his psychological theory when he advocated the use of close observation and accurate classification of natural phenomena; he also formalized a system of deductive propositional logic. The term *Aristotelian* is used to indicate the principle of careful deduction of scientific or personal knowledge from systematic observations of natural events. Aristotle's work exerted an immense influence on medieval philosophy, especially through St. Thomas Aquinas, on Islamic philosophy, and on the whole Western intellectual and scientific tradition. In the Middle Ages, Aristotle was referred to simply as "the Philosopher," and the uncritical and religious acceptance of his doctrines was to hamper the progress of science until the scientific revolution of the sixteenth and seventeenth centuries. Aristotle's writings represented an enormous encyclopedic output over virtually every field of knowledge: logic, metaphysics, ethics, politics, rhetoric, poetry, biology, zoology, physics, and psychology (Muir, 1994; Reber, 1995). See also ASSOCIATION, LAWS/PRINCIPLES OF; HEDONISM, THEORY/ LAW OF; PLEASURE–PAIN, DOCTRINE/THEORY/LAW OF.

REFERENCES

Robertson, G. (1896). *Elements of psychology*. New York: Scribners.

Maher, M. (1900). *Psychology*. New York: Longmans, Green.

Hoffding, H. (1908). *Outlines of psychology*. London: Macmillan.

Aristotle. (1910). *Physiognomica*. Oxford: Oxford University Press.

Aristotle. (1941a). De anima (On the soul). In R. McKeon (Ed.), *The basic works of Aristotle*. New York: Random House.

Aristotle. (1941b). De memoria et reminiscentia (On memory and reminiscence). In R. McKeon (Ed.), *The basic works of Aristotle*. New York: Random House.

Aristotle. (1952). Physics. In R. Hutchins (Ed.), *Great books of the Western world*. Vol. 8. Chicago: Encyclopaedia Britannica.

Muir, H. (Ed.) (1994). *Larousse dictionary of scientists*. New York: Larousse.

Reber, A. (1995). *The Penguin dictionary of psychology*. New York: Penguin Books.

ARNOLD'S THEORY OF EMOTIONS. Magda B. *Arnold's theory of emotions* emphasizes the *cognitive* factors associated with emotional behavior that involves a continuous sequence of reaction and appraisal where a series of information-processing steps takes place (Arnold, 1954, 1960, 1970, 1984). In the first phase of processing, the individual typically *perceives* some event, object, or person and is prepared to evaluate it in a particular way: as "good," which leads to approach behavior, as "bad," which leads to avoidance behavior, or as "indifferent," which leads to ignoring the event. The next phase is *appraisal*, where the person decides whether what is happening will hurt, help, or have no effect on him or her. The third and fourth phases are *bodily change* and *emotion*, both of which typically occur at almost the same time. Phase five is *action*; some individuals in certain situations skip from the bodily changes in stage three and go directly to stage five. For example, if a strange dog comes running toward you with its teeth bared, you take rapid action and run away without thinking as epinephrine rushes into your system. When you reach safety, you become aware of your heart pounding, and, at that time, you experience the *emotion* of fear. *Arnold's theory* assumes that the entire appraisal sequence takes place in an instant. Arnold distinguishes among a few basic emotions that are simple reactions to the appraisal of basic situations: dislike, love (liking), aversion, despair, desire, anger, fear, hope, daring, sorrow, and joy. Her theory stresses that the intuitive, spontaneous appraisal in an emotional episode is supplemented by a deliberate value judgment, especially in adults, and it functions in the same way that one's sensory knowledge is complemented by cognitions. According to *Arnold's cognitive theory*, emotions can be socialized where social attitudes and customs influence one's intuitive appraisal of events, and where *affective memory* preserves one's previous encounters with intense emotion-arousing stimuli (Arnold, 1984). *Affective memory* may account for many of the "instinctive" feelings one experiences, such as immediate dislikes or likes for something or someone, reactions to fearful stimuli that later become phobias, prejudice connected with unresolved and unpleasant situations from the past, and even love at first sight. See also COGNITIVE THEORIES OF EMOTIONS; EMOTIONS, THEORIES/LAWS OF; LAZARUS' THEORY OF EMOTIONS; SCHACHTER–SINGER'S THEORY OF EMOTIONS.

REFERENCES

Arnold, M. (1954). Feelings and emotions as dynamic factors in personality integration. In M. Arnold & J. Gasson (Eds.), *The human person*. New York: Ronald Press.

Arnold, M. (1960). *Emotion and personality*. New York: Columbia University Press.

Lazarus, R. (1968). Emotions and adaptation. Conceptual and empirical relations. In W. Arnold (Ed.), *Nebraska Symposium of Motivation*. Vol. 16. Lincoln: University of Nebraska Press.

Arnold, M. (1970). *Feelings and emotions: The Loyola Symposium*. New York: Academic Press.

Arnold, M. (1984). *Memory and the brain*. Hillsdale, NJ: Erlbaum.

Strongman, K. (1987). *The psychology of emotion*. New York: Wiley.

Arnold, M. (1994). Cognitive theories of emotion. In R. J. Corsini (Ed.), *Ency. Psy.* New York: Wiley.

Baum, A. (1994). Emotions. In R. J. Corsini (Ed.), *Ency. Psy.* New York: Wiley.

AROUSAL THEORY. See ACTIVATION/AROUSAL THEORY.

AROUSAL-COGNITIVE THEORIES OF EMOTION. See COGNITIVE THEORIES OF EMOTIONS.

ASCH CONFORMITY EFFECT. The American social psychologist Solomon E. Asch (1907–1995) conducted a series of experiments where American college students were asked to make judgments about the length of vertical lines. Seven male students made these simple judgments out loud, one by one, in a group

setting, but the sixth student in the sequence was the only true subject/partici-
pant. The other students were Asch's accomplices (called *confederates*), and,
without the true subject's knowledge, on many trials they all deliberately made
the same incorrect guess. Asch's results were interesting: even in this simple
judgment task, only about one-fourth of the subjects completely resisted the
other students' answers and made no errors. Other subjects followed the unanimous, but incorrect, opinion on every trial, showing complete acquiescence to
the group's pressure. In later debriefing sessions, the subjects greatly underestimated their degree of *conformity* (Asch, 1955, 1956). Similar experiments with
French, Norwegian, Arabian, and British students supported Asch's findings
with American subjects. The *Asch effect*, then, refers to the powerful influence
of a unanimous group and its decision on the behavior of an individual that
results in *conformity* to that group. *Conformity*, for better or worse, is defined
as the tendency for people to adopt the behaviors, attitudes, and values of other
members of a reference group (Zimbardo & Weber, 1994). In subsequent studies, group size and group unanimity turned out to be key determinants of *conformity* (Asch, 1956). The factor of gender, however, does not seem to be a
distinguishing factor in *conformity* (Eagly & Johnson, 1990; Baron, 1992). Some
mixed results have appeared in recent years concerning Asch's paradigm and
make the *Asch effect* a topic of continued interest in current psychology (e.g.,
Amir, 1984; Friend, Rafferty, & Bramel, 1990; Larsen, 1990). See also BY-
STANDER INTERVENTION EFFECT; DECISION-MAKING THEORIES;
DEINDIVIDUATION THEORY; GROUPTHINK PHENOMENON.

REFERENCES

Asch, S. (1940). Studies in the principles of judgments and attitudes. II. Determination
        of judgments by group and by ego standards. *J. Soc. Psy., 12*, 433–465.
Asch, S. (1946). Forming impressions of personality. *J. Abn. Soc. Psy., 41*, 258–290.
Asch, S. (1951). Effects of group pressure upon the modification and distortion of judg-
        ment. In H. Guetzkow (Ed.), *Groups, leadership, and men*. Pittsburgh: Carnegie.
Asch, S. (1952). *Social psychology*. New York: Prentice-Hall.
Asch, S. (1955). Opinions and social pressure. *Sci. Amer., 193*, 31–35.
Deutsch, M., & Gerard, H. (1955). A study of normative and informational social influ-
        ences upon individual judgment. *J. Abn. Soc. Psy., 51*, 629–636.
Asch, S. (1956). Studies of independence and conformity. I. A minority of one against
        a unanimous majority. *Psy. Mono., 70*, no. 416.
Morris, W., & Miller, R. (1975). The effects of consensus-breaking and consensus-
        preempting partners on reduction of conformity. *J. Pers. Soc. Psy., 11*, 215–223.
Morris, W., Miller, R., & Spangenberg, S. (1977). The effects of dissenter position and
        task difficulty on conformity and response to conflict. *J. Pers., 45*, 251–266.
Amir, T. (1984). The Asch conformity effect: A study in Kuwait. *J. Soc. Beh. & Pers.,
        12*, 187–190.
Tanford, S., & Penrod, S. (1984). Social influence model: A forward integration of re-
        search on majority and minority influence processes. *Psy. Bull., 95*, 189–225.
Eagly, A., & Johnson, B. (1990). Gender and leadership style: A meta-analysis. *Psy.
        Bull., 108*, 233–256.

Friend, R., Rafferty, Y., & Bramel, D. (1990). A puzzling misinterpretation of the Asch "conformity" study. *Eur. J. Soc. Psy., 20,* 29–44.
Larsen, K. (1990). The Asch conformity experiment: Replication and transhistorical comparisons. *J. Soc. Beh. & Pers., 5,* 163–168.
Baron, R. (1992). *Psychology.* Boston: Allyn & Bacon.
Zimbardo, P., & Weber, A. (1994). *Psychology.* New York: HarperCollins.

ASHBY'S LAW OF REQUISITE VARIETY. See INFORMATION/ INFORMATION-PROCESSING THEORY.

ASSIMILATION, LAW OF. The "overload" term *assimilation* appears to be obsolete, as judged by its infrequent use by writers of psychology textbooks today (cf: Piaget, 1963), although it does find modern resuscitation in terms such as *generalization* and *analogy* (Reber, 1995). The *law of assimilation* states that when an individual is in a new situation, he or she will behave in a way that is similar to the way he or she did in similar circumstances in the past. Woodworth and Schlosberg (1965) consider the term *assimilation* to be under the rubric of *theory* rather than of *law.* Hovland (1951), however, refers to the *law* of assimilation. Piaget (1963) has employed the term *assimilation* as a working descriptive "functions" term in his study of the development of intellectual competence in children, where *assimilation* is a functional mechanism that preserves cognitive structure and promotes integration and similarity between the elements or content of the structure. The term *assimilation* itself was introduced by O. Lauenstein (1933), who was a student of the German-born American psychologist Wolfgang Kohler. In psychophysical experiments on hearing, where standard stimuli were studied against interpolated stimuli, Lauenstein obtained results on loudness that showed that experimental subjects "assimilated" or integrated standard stimulus "traces" toward an interpolated stimulus in such a way that assimilation occurred upward toward a loud interpolated stimulus but downward toward a soft one (Woodworth & Schlosberg, 1965). In human learning/retention contexts, the term *assimilation* has been characterized as a "law." The *law of assimilation,* according to Carr (1925), states that "each new stimulating condition tends to elicit the response which has been connected with similar stimulating conditions in the past." Terms related to *assimilation* in a learning/retention context (Hovland, 1951) are *associative interference* (when learning of a new association is made more difficult because of a prior association) and *associative facilitation* (when learning of a new association is made easier due to a prior association). More modern substitutes for these latter two terms in the current vocabulary of psychologists are *negative transfer of training* and *positive transfer of training,* respectively (cf: Reber, 1995). See also ASSOCIATION, LAWS/PRINCIPLES OF; GENERALIZATION, PRINCIPLE OF; PIAGET'S THEORY OF DEVELOPMENTAL STAGES; TRANSFER OF TRAINING, THORNDIKE'S THEORY OF.

REFERENCES

Carr, H. (1925). *Psychology: A study of mental activity*. New York: Longmans, Green.

Orata, P. (1928). *The theory of identical elements, being a critique of Thorndike's theory of identical elements and a re-interpretation of the problem of transfer of training.* Columbus: Ohio State University Press.

Yum, L. (1931). An experimental test of the law of assimilation. *J. Exp. Psy., 14,* 68–82.

Bruce, R. (1933). Conditions of transfer of training. *J. Exp. Psy., 16,* 343–361.

Lauenstein, O. (1933). Ansatz zu einer physiologischen Theorie des Vergleichs und der Zeitfehler. *Psy. Forsch., 17,* 130–177.

Woodworth, R. (1938). *Experimental psychology*. New York: Holt.

Hovland, C. (1951). Human learning and retention. In S. S. Stevens (Ed.), *Handbk. Exp. Psy.* New York: Wiley.

Piaget, J. (1963). *The origins of intelligence in children*. New York: Norton.

Woodworth, R., & Schlosberg, H. (1965). *Experimental psychology*. New York: Holt, Rinehart, & Winston.

Reber, A. (1995). *The Penguin dictionary of psychology*. New York: Penguin Books.

ASSOCIATION, LAWS/PRINCIPLES OF. = association, doctrine of = associationism. The term *association* referred originally to an association of ideas and was used by the early Greeks in their philosophies. For example, Empedocles (495–435 B.C.) believed that the process of thinking was the creation and destruction of percepts that took place in the churning of blood in the heart after being carried from the sense organs by the bloodstream; Plato (427–347 B.C.) enunciated a *theory of learning* based on association where recollection of similar ideas was emphasized; Aristotle (384–322 B.C.) observed that when a person thought of something, it would remind that person of something else, where one idea led to another idea in a manner that the two ideas had some kind of relation, connection, or association. Aristotle proposed in his essays on memory (McKeon, 1941) that three "relations" exist between elements that lead to associations: *contiguity, similarity,* and *contrast.* Thomas Hobbes (1588–1679) was the first to suggest that Aristotle's "relations" could serve as an associationistic model of human cognition (Reber, 1995). Later, John Locke (1632–1704) coined the phrase *association of ideas* (Locke, 1700) and regarded associations as interruptions to rational ways of thinking. Other eighteenth- and nineteenth-century philosophers transformed the notion of the association of ideas into the systematic viewpoint called *associationism.* Chief among these British empiricists or "associationistic" philosophers were George Berkeley (1685–1753), David Hume (1711–1776), David Hartley (1705–1757), James Mill (1773–1836), John Stuart Mill (1806–1873), Alexander Bain (1818–1903), and Thomas Brown (1778–1820). Hume reduced the mind to the association of ideas and maintained that the mind contains either perceptions or their copies ("ideas"), and ideas were glued together by two *laws of association*: *similarity* and *contiguity.* Hartley is usually recognized as the founder of *psychological associa-*

tionism, and he speculated on *physiological laws of association* between nerve vibrations to explain the *mental laws of association* (Leahey, 1994). The principle of *associative learning* was further refined by the Mills and Bain, who developed a type of psychological associationism that made the association of ideas the central process of acting and thinking. From this initial philosophical context, the *principle of association* moved toward an empirically researchable form as developed by Thomas Brown in his *secondary laws of association* (Warren, 1921; Woodworth & Schlosberg, 1965): *duration, liveliness, frequency*, and *recency*. These first four of Brown's secondary laws perhaps have the most vital significance for associationism (Murphy & Kovach, 1972). The other secondary laws include the concepts of "fewer alternative associates," "constitutional differences," "variations in the same individual," "diversities of state," and "habits of life" (Warren, 1921). Brown's terminological approach permitted casting the general laws of "suggestion" into a form that contained the concepts of the relative recency, frequency, and liveliness of particular experiences. Brown's emphasis on emotional and constitutional factors was also significant and contrasted with the associationists' usual neglect of individual differences (Murphy & Kovach, 1972). Marx and Hillix (1963, p. 109) show that of the three primary *principles/laws of association* (contiguity, similarity, and contrast) the *principle of contiguity* was the most popular among the early writers, including Aristotle, Hobbes, Locke, Berkeley, Hume, Hartley, J. Mill, J. S. Mill, Bain, and Spencer. At one time, the notion of *association* was characterized as "mental chemistry" (J. S. Mill), in which simple ideas could be linked to form more complex ideas. The decomposition of mental life into elements (simple ideas) and the compounding of these elements to form complex ideas subsequently formed the core of the new scientific psychology (Schultz, 1981). Historically noteworthy, also, in the advancement of *associationism* was the systematic research based on associationistic principles that was conducted by Herman Ebbinghaus (1850–1909), Ivan Pavlov (1849–1936), and Edward L. Thorndike (1874–1949). Ebbinghaus constructed lists of "nonsense syllables" as learning material and used himself over many years as subject ("n = 1") in his memory studies (Ebbinghaus, 1885). He found that the more times he repeated a list of syllables, the better his memory of it, thus supporting Brown's *law of frequency*. Ebbinghaus was also able to show that memory was influenced by such factors as the number of syllables on the list and the time between learning the list and having to recall the syllables (*law of recency*). Such factors are still studied today in memory research. Ivan Pavlov, the Russian physiologist, is credited (along with Vladimir Bekhterev, 1857–1927) for shifting the kind of association studied from philosophical ideas to laboratory-based stimulus–response connections. Pavlov's (and Bekhterev's) prior research on the conditioned reflex helped to objectify psychology as well as strengthen the concept of *association* (Pavlov, 1927; Bekhterev, 1913). E. L. Thorndike (1898) had developed the most complete account up to that time of psychological phenomena along associationistic lines (e.g., Thorndike's, 1931, *connectionism*), and his system was considered the most appropriate representative of *associationism* in psychology (Marx & Hillix, 1963). More recently, in the twentieth century and under the influence of the behavioristic viewpoint (e.g., Watson, 1919), the *laws of association* became the *laws of learning*, the *law of frequency* became the gradually rising learning curve, the *law of similarity* became the generalization gradient, and the *law of contiguity* became the temporal relationship between unconditioned and conditioned stimuli. Currently, the eighteenth-century association concepts have been revived somewhat with the advent and development of the field of *cognitive psychology*, which considers memory to be an associative network of ideas that are embedded in a complex information-processing system (e.g., Anderson & Bower, 1973). In its historical development, the *principle of association* was challenged by various psychologists, especially by the Gestalt psychologists who renounced it completely (Leahey, 1994). However, many *associative laws* were developed during the history of the doctrine of *associationism*, and these principles have been used often as hypotheses or as explanatory concepts in psychology (Pettijohn, 1986). Perhaps the most popular principle has been *temporal contiguity* (where things that occur close together in time tend to become associated with each other). The other surviving *associative laws* deriving mainly from Aristotle's "relations" and Brown's "secondary laws" are *vividness/clearness/intensity* (the more vivid, lively, or intense the experience, the stronger the associative bond); *frequency/repetition* (things that occur repeatedly together tend to become associated with each other; cf: *Marbe's law*, which is the generalization that in word association tasks the more *frequently* a response occurs, the more *rapidly* it tends to occur, and where latency is inversely related to frequency; Reber, 1995; Wolman, 1973); *recency* (associations that are formed recently are easiest to recall); *similarity/resemblance* (aspects of ideas, sensations, or movements that are similar tend to become associated with each other); and *contrast* (when two contrary or opposing sensations or other mental data are juxtaposed, the contrary characteristics are intensified, where given the idea of one, the idea of its opposite tends to be recalled) (Warren, 1934). William James (1890, vol. 1, p. 506) stated a *law of dissociation by varying concomitants* as follows: "What is associated now with one thing and now with another tends to become dissociated from either, and to grow into an object of abstract contemplation of the mind" (cf: Thorndike, 1907). The difficulty with the *associative laws*, even though they may be quite valid generally, is that all too often they have been expected to assume an explanatory role far beyond their capacities. For instance, the *principle of contiguity* has been valuable in the area of *learning theory*, but it cannot account for all mental experiences and events, many of which have emotional or motivational characteristics (Pettijohn, 1986). Also, in recent years, the concept of *associationism* may have lost some of its explanatory power in the fields of cognition, perception, psycholinguistics, and developmental psychology because of the feeling that most cognitive processes are too complex to submit to an analysis based simply on associative connections (Reber, 1995).

Nevertheless, the *doctrine of the association of ideas* and the concept of *association*, along with their various laws and principles, have shown themselves to be some of the most durable of psychological concepts, having maintained an unbroken record of influence for over 2,000 years from Plato to the present (cf: consistent citation of the *association* concept in introductory psychology textbooks for more than 112 years; Roeckelein, 1996). See also GUTHRIE'S THEORY OF BEHAVIOR; HULL'S LEARNING THEORY; THORNDIKE'S LAW OF EFFECT; TOLMAN'S THEORY; LEARNING THEORIES/LAWS.

REFERENCES

Locke, J. (1700). *Essay concerning human understanding.* London: Dent.

Spencer, H. (1855). *Principles of psychology.* London: Williams & Norgate.

Ebbinghaus, H. (1885). *Uber das Gedachtnis.* Leipzig: Duncker.

James, W. (1890). *Principles of psychology.* New York: Holt.

Calkins, M. (1896). Association. *Psy. Rev., 3,* 32–49.

Robertson, G. (1896). *Elements of psychology.* New York: Scribners.

Thorndike, E. L. (1898). *Animal intelligence.* New York: Macmillan.

Titchener, E. B. (1898). *An outline of psychology.* New York: Macmillan.

Calkins, M. (1905). *An introduction to psychology.* New York: Macmillan.

Thorndike, E. L. (1907). *The elements of psychology.* New York: Seiler.

Bekhterev, V. (1913). *Objektive Psychologie: oder Psychoreflexologie, die Lehre von den Assoziationsreflexen.* Leipzig: Teubner.

Watson, J. B. (1919). *Psychology from the standpoint of a behaviorist.* Philadelphia: Lippincott.

Warren, H. (1921). *A history of the association psychology.* New York: Scribners.

Pavlov, I. (1927). *Conditioned reflexes.* New York: Dover.

Thorndike, E. L. (1931). *Human learning.* New York: Appleton.

Robinson, E. (1932). *Association theory today.* New York: Appleton-Century-Crofts.

Warren, H. (Ed.) (1934). *Dictionary of psychology.* Cambridge, MA: Houghton Mifflin.

McKeon, R. (Ed.) (1941). *The basic works of Aristotle: De anima; De memoria et reminiscentia.* New York: Random House.

Marx, M., & Hillix, W. (1963). *Systems and theories in psychology.* New York: McGraw-Hill.

Woodworth, R., & Schlosberg, H. (1965). *Experimental psychology.* New York: Holt, Rinehart, & Winston.

Murphy, G., & Kovach, J. (1972). *Historical introduction to modern psychology.* New York: Harcourt Brace Jovanovich.

Anderson, J., & Bower, G. (1973). *Human associative memory.* Washington, DC: Winston.

Wolman, B. (Ed.) (1973). *Dictionary of behavioral science.* New York: Van Nostrand Reinhold.

Rapaport, D. (1974). *The history of the concept of association of ideas.* New York: International Universities Press.

Schultz, D. (1981). *A history of modern psychology.* New York: Academic Press.

Pettijohn, T. (Ed.) (1986). *The encyclopedic dictionary of psychology.* Guilford, CT: Dushkin.

Leahey, T. (1994). Associationism. In R. J. Corsini (Ed.), *Ency. Psy.* New York: Wiley.

Reber, A. (1995). *The Penguin dictionary of psychology*. New York: Penguin Books.
Roeckelein, J. (1996). Citation of *laws* and *theories* in textbooks across 112 years of psychology. *Psy. Rep., 79*, 979–998.

ASSOCIATIVE/CONTIGUITY THEORY. See GUTHRIE'S THEORY OF BEHAVIOR; REINFORCEMENT THEORY.

ASSOCIATIVE SHIFTING, LAW OF. One of E. L. Thorndike's (1874–1949) minor subsidiary laws to his *law of effect* that is similar to Ivan Pavlov's *principle of stimulus association* and also bears some resemblance to the conditioning *principle of generalization*. The *law of associative shifting* states that when two stimuli are present, and one elicits a response, the other takes on the ability to elicit the same response. This law became a central axiom to E. R. Guthrie's *contiguity learning theory*. Thorndike considered the general aspects of conditioning to be akin to associative shifting where the occurrence of a ''trial-and-error'' process may not be necessary. An example of *associative shifting* is the learning by a child to come to you when you call her or his name using different variations (e.g., differences in tone, pronunciation, intensity, inflection, etc.) of the name (and you subsequently hug her or him). According to Thorndike, the ancillary concepts of *belongingness* and *satisfaction* operate in *associative shifting*, but other scientists (e.g., Pavlov, 1927) regarded the time relations between the stimulus–response event to be solely adequate for establishing conditioned responses. See also BELONGINGNESS, LAW/PRINCIPLE OF; EFFECT, LAW OF; GENERALIZATION, PRINCIPLE OF; GUTHRIE'S THEORY OF BEHAVIOR; TRANSFER OF TRAINING, THORNDIKE'S THEORY OF.

REFERENCES

Pavlov, I. (1927). *Conditioned reflexes*. New York: Oxford University Press.
Thorndike, E. L. (1932). *The fundamentals of learning*. New York: Teachers College, Columbia University.
Guthrie, E. R. (1935). *The psychology of learning*. New York: Harper.
Keller, F., & Schoenfeld, W. (1950). *Principles of psychology*. New York: Appleton-Century-Crofts.
Spence, K. (1966). Theoretical interpretations of learning. In S. S. Stevens (Ed.), *Handbk. Exp. Psy.* New York: Wiley.
Murphy, G., & Kovach, J. (1972). *Historical introduction to modern psychology*. New York: Harcourt Brace Jovanovich.

ATTACHMENT, PRINCIPLE OF. See CUPBOARD THEORY; INFANT ATTACHMENT THEORIES.

ATTENTION, LAWS/PRINCIPLES/THEORIES OF. The term *attention* is defined differently depending on the contexts in which it is used. In a *functional* sense, for example, attention is defined generally as the process of focusing on

certain portions of an experience so that the parts become relatively more distinctive. In a *behavioral* context (cf: behaviorist school context, where attention
was rejected as a more traditional mentalistic concept; Woodworth & Schlosberg, 1965), attention is defined more precisely as an adjustment of the sensory
apparatus that facilitates optimal excitation by a specific stimulus (or a complex
of stimuli) and inhibits the action of all other details (Warren, 1934). Attention
may be conscious, in that some stimulus elements are actively selected out of
the total input, even though there is no explicit awareness of the factors that
cause the individual to perceive only some small part of the total stimulus complex (Reber, 1995). Historically, G. F. Stout (1860–1944) considered attention
to be "conation" (i.e., craving, desire, or will) insofar as it required for its
satisfaction fuller cognizance of its object (Stout, 1896, 1898/1899); and M.
Maher (1900) distinguished between sensation and attention where sensation
involves a *passive* faculty, and attention is the exercise of an *activity* or the
application of intellectual energy. For E. B. Titchener (1867–1927), the concept
of *attention* was given attributive status where it was nothing more nor less than
that which changes in experience and where attentional shifts are due to the
clarity or vividness ("attensity") of the sensory processes (Titchener, 1908,
1909). Many early psychology textbook authors (who seemed, generally, to use
the term *law* quite liberally and effusively in "nonpositivistic" ways) referred
to the *laws* or *theories* of attention. For example, Buell (1900) listed six *laws*
of attention: intensity of the stimulus, curiosity, size, adaptation, motive, and
change. Seashore (1923) listed 14 *laws* of attention: tension, novelty, intensity,
action change, periodicity, timing, rest, grouping, division of energy, purpose,
interest, effort, form, and skill. Ebbinghaus (1908) referred to the *laws* of *practice*, *memory*, and *attention*. Halleck (1895), Baldwin (1894), and Titchener
(1928) described *laws of attention*. Calkins (1916) described eight *theories* of
attention: activity theory, motor theory, negative theories, element theory, Bradley's theory, inhibition theory, Ribot's theory, and Wundt's theory. Baldwin
(1894), in addition to referring to the *general law of attention*, described *Horwicz's theory of attention* and the *spiritual theories of reflex attention*. Hoffding
(1908) described *Condillac's theory of attention*; and Woodworth (1921) referred to a *theory of attention*, as well as to the *laws of attention*. In the late
nineteenth and early twentieth centuries, the structuralist and functionalist
schools of psychology considered the topic of attention to be a core problem in
the field and emphasized different aspects of it. For instance, the structuralists
viewed attention as a state of consciousness that consisted of increased concentration and sensory clearness; they studied the conditions that maximized the
clearness of a sensation. On the other hand, the functionalists focused on the
selective and volitional nature of attention; they studied the motivational state
and active functioning of the individual (Urbina, 1994). Recent experimental
work on attention has focused on variables (or "problems" of attention; Woodworth & Schlosberg, 1965, Chap. 4) such as stimulus intensity, distraction, shifts
and fluctuations, stimulus duration, attention span, attentional value of stimuli

in different sensory modalities, locations, levels of novelty, temporal relations of stimuli as determiners of attention/selectivity of attention (e.g., Broadbent, 1957, 1958; Treisman, 1960, 1964; Deutsch & Deutsch, 1963; Nielsen & Sarason, 1981), and the neurophysiological basis of attention (e.g., Hernandez-Peon, 1961). Attention may be controlled automatically (e.g., a loud sound captures one's attention), by instructions (e.g., "pay attention to the red one over there"), or by the demands of a particular task (e.g., when driving a car, the driver looks out for other cars, pedestrians, and road signs). An individual's attentional mechanisms serve to enhance responsiveness to certain stimuli and to tune out irrelevant information (Carlson, 1990). An interesting aspect of attention, called the *cocktail-party phenomenon* (Cherry, 1953; Wood & Cowan, 1995), refers to the ability to attend selectively to a single person's speech across a room and in the midst of the competing speech of many other people (such as at a noisy cocktail party). Three possible *functions* of attention have been identified (Zimbardo & Weber, 1994): as a sensory filter (e.g., Broadbent, 1958), as response selection (e.g., Driver & Tipper, 1989), and as a gateway to consciousness (e.g., Carver & Scheier, 1981). Recent formalized *theories of attention* (Gray, 1994) include Broadbent's (1958) *filter theory/model* (where all sensory input is processed in parallel, initially in an automatic "preattentive compartment," and then some of it is selected to enter the "attentive compartment" for further processing; this theory can account for a person's ability to selectively hear or see things based on physical distinctions and for a person's failure to register the meanings of unattended stimuli); *late selection theories* (e.g., Shiffrin & Schneider, 1977; in this type of attention theory, the preattentive stage can process very familiar stimuli for meaning, and based on such processing, the selection can pass such stimuli onto the attentive stage, where they become conscious to the person; this theory can account for one's ability to hear one's own name in an unattended message or the ability to be influenced by the meaning of a stimulus that is not consciously perceived); and *early-selection theories* (e.g., Treisman's, 1969, *attentuation theory*; these theories suggest that a great quantity of information passes into the attentive stage and is analyzed for meaning at any of various levels of consciousness, but only some of the information is analyzed at a level of consciousness that permits the individual to describe it). Currently, research on the psychological, as well as the neurological, basis of attention continues unabated, and there are promising connections between the experimental work on attention and the eventual explanation and understanding of various psychopathological disorders such as hyperactivity, schizophrenia, and mental retardation (Urbina, 1994). See also CONDILLAC'S THEORY OF ATTENTION; VIGILANCE, THEORIES OF.

REFERENCES

Baldwin, J. (1894). *Handbook of psychology*. New York: Holt.
Halleck, R. (1895). *Psychology and psychic culture*. New York: American Book.

Stout, G. (1896). *Analytic psychology*. London: Sonnenschein.

Stout, G. (1898/1899). *A manual of psychology*. London: Clive.

Buell, C. (1900). *Essentials of psychology*. Boston: Ginn.

Maher, M. (1900). *Psychology: Empirical and rational*. London: Longmans, Green.

Ebbinghaus, H. (1908). *Psychology: An elementary textbook*. Boston: Heath.

Hoffding, H. (1908). *Outlines of psychology*. London: Macmillan.

Titchener, E. (1908). *Lectures on the experimental psychology of feeling and attention*. New York: Macmillan.

Titchener, E. (1909). *Lectures on the experimental psychology of the thought processes*. New York: Macmillan.

Calkins, M. (1916). *An introduction to psychology*. New York: Macmillan.

Woodworth, R. (1921). *Psychology: A study of mental life*. New York: Holt.

Seashore, C. (1923). *Introduction to psychology*. New York: Macmillan.

Titchener, E. (1928). *A textbook of psychology*. New York: Macmillan.

Warren, H. (Ed.) (1934). *Dictionary of psychology*. Cambridge, MA: Houghton Mifflin.

Cherry, E. (1953). Some experiments on the recognition of speech, with one and with two ears. *J. Acou. Soc. Amer., 25*, 975–979.

Broadbent, D. (1957). A mechanical model for human attention and immediate memory. *Psy. Rev., 64*, 205–215.

Broadbent, D. (1958). *Perception and communication*. New York: Pergamon Press.

Moray, N. (1959). Attention in dichotic listening: Affective cues and the influence of instructions. *Quar. J. Exp. Psy., 11*, 56–60.

Treisman, A. (1960). Contextual cues in selective listening. *Quar. J. Exp. Psy., 12*, 242–248.

Hernandez-Peon, R. (1961). Reticular mechanisms of sensory control. In W. Rosenblith (Ed.), *Sensory communication*. Cambridge: MIT Press.

Deutsch, J., & Deutsch, D. (1963). Attention: Some theoretical considerations. *Psy. Rev., 70*, 80–90.

Treisman, A. (1964). Selective attention in man. *Brit. Med. Bull., 20*, 12–16.

Woodworth, R., & Schlosberg, H. (1965). *Experimental psychology*. New York: Holt, Rinehart, & Winston.

Trabasso, T., & Bower, G. (1968). *Attention in learning: Theory and research*. New York: Wiley.

Treisman, A. (1969). Strategies and models of selective attention. *Psy. Rev., 76*, 282–299.

McKay, D. (1973). Aspects of the theory of comprehension, memory, and attention. *Quar. J. Exp. Psy., 25*, 22–40.

Mackintosh, N. (1975). A theory of attention: Variations in the associability of stimuli with reinforcement. *Psy. Rev., 82*, 276–298.

Neisser, U., & Becklen, R. (1975). Selective looking: Attending to visually significant events. *Cog. Psy., 7*, 480–494.

Rabbitt, P., & Dornic, S. (Eds.) (1975). *Attention and performance*. London: Academic Press.

Norman, D. (1977). *Memory and attention: An introduction to human information processing*. New York: Wiley.

Shiffrin, R., & Schneider, W. (1977). Controlled and automatic information processing. II. Perceptual learning, automatic attending, and a general theory. *Psy. Rev., 84*, 127–190.

Posner, M., Snyder, C., & Davidson, B. (1980). Attention and the detection of signals. *J. Exp. Psy.: Gen., 109*, 160–174.

Carver, C., & Scheier, M. (1981). *Attention and self-regulation: A control theory approach to human behavior.* New York: Springer.

Nielsen, L., & Sarason, I. (1981). Emotion, personality, and selective attention. *J. Pers. Soc. Psy., 41*, 945–960.

Posner, M. (1982). Cumulative development of attentional theory. *Amer. Psy., 37*, 168–179.

Becklen, R., & Cervone, D. (1983). Selective looking and the noticing of unexpected events. *Mem. & Cog., 11*, 601–608.

Kahneman, D., & Treisman, A. (1984). Changing views of attention and automaticity. In R. Parasuraman & D. Davies (Eds.), *Varieties of attention.* New York: Academic Press.

Driver, J., & Tipper, S. (1989). On the nonselectivity of ''selective'' seeing: Contrasts between interference and priming in selective attention. *J. Exp. Psy.: Hum. Perc. & Perf., 15*, 304–314.

Carlson, N. (1990). *Psychology: The science of behavior.* Boston: Allyn & Bacon.

Ayres, J. (1994). Selective attention. In R. J. Corsini (Ed.), *Ency. Psy.* New York: Wiley.

Gray, P. (1994). *Psychology.* New York: Worth.

Urbina, S. (1994). Attention. In R. J. Corsini (Ed.), *Ency. Psy.* New York: Wiley.

Zimbardo, P., & Weber, A. (1994). *Psychology.* New York: HarperCollins.

Reber, A. (1995). *The Penguin dictionary of psychology.* New York: Penguin Books.

Wood, N., & Cowan, N. (1995). The cocktail party phenomenon revisited: Attention and memory in the classic selective listening procedure of Cherry (1953). *J. Exp. Psy.: Gen., 124*, 243–262.

ATTITUDE/ATTITUDE CHANGE, THEORIES OF. The term *attitude* may be defined as a learned predisposition (''set'') to evaluate or react consistently in a particular manner, either positively or negatively, to certain persons, places, concepts, or things (Wolman, 1973). The concept of *attitude* was first introduced formally in the field of sociology by W. I. Thomas and F. Znaniecki in 1918 (cf: Thomas & Znaniecki, 1927) and has come to be a core concept in the field of social psychology. The *tricomponent model* of attitude states that attitudes contain three elements: affective/evaluative, cognitive/belief, and behavioral/action/conative. This model assumes both that there is a tendency within individuals to maintain consistency among the three components (Abelson, Aronson, McGuire, Newcomb, Rosenberg, & Tannenbaum, 1968; Breckler, 1984) and that, once formed, attitudes and the components become functional by preparing the person for ''unconflicted'' action. Of the three components, the most prominent is the affective/evaluative (feeling) dimension, where most attempts at changing attitudes by persuasion are aimed at changing the evaluative component (Ajzen, 1994). Psychologists in this field believe that a comprehensive *attitude theory* should be able to explain data in the five areas of the communication process that involve the *source* (i.e., who initiates the communication, and how credible is the person or institution?), the *message* (i.e., what is the nature of the communication, and does it involve fear tactics?), the *channel* (i.e., how is the communication transmitted: face-to-face, television, newspaper, etc.?), the *receiver* (i.e., who is the target audience, and what is the level of receiver intelligence, emotion, and motivation of the audience?), and the *destination* (i.e., what are the time frame, goal, and purpose for change of the communication?). Unfortunately, no single or unifying theory of attitudes is accepted by all scientists working in the field. There are over 30 distinct theoretical formulations described in textbooks on *attitude theory* (Ostrom, 1994). There are, however, common views among researchers concerning the notion that attitudes can be represented as an evaluative disposition on a continuum ranging from agreement to disagreement. Within these parameters, four separate classes of *attitude theory* can generally be identified: *evaluative disposition/undifferentiated* viewpoint (e.g., theories that employ principles of reinforcement and classical conditioning); *set of beliefs* (e.g., theories that suggest an averaging process across a person's cognitions or beliefs to get an overall evaluative disposition); *set of motivational forces* (e.g., theories that emphasize the more functional and enduring dispositions based on the person's values, needs, drives, and motives); and *attitude nonexistence* (e.g., theories that approach the concept of *attitude* as being a ''social fiction'' and advocate, instead, the examination of the processes of ''self-perception''). The ideal *attitude theory* should also contain accounts of both the antecedents and the consequences of attitude formation, but most theoretical efforts are limited and have concentrated only on the antecedent conditions (Ostrom, 1994). The following sample of four systematic *theories of attitude change* indicates the range of *attitude theories* acknowledged by most social psychologists today (Bridge, 1986): *cognitive-consistency theories, information-processing models/theories, functional theories*, and *perceptual theories*. The *cognitive-consistency theories* encompass the ''balance,'' ''congruity,'' ''dissonance,'' and ''probabilistic'' theories because they all assume that the person has an acquired/learned drive to maintain the optimal consistency among beliefs, and when inconsistency among beliefs (or between attitudes and overt behavior) occurs, the person will take action to avoid or reduce the resultant state of tension (e.g., Festinger, 1957; Cooper & Fazio, 1984). Various concepts of the ''dissonance'' theory approach include ''postdecisional dissonance'' (when a person must choose between two attractive alternatives, and after the choice is made, the individual rationalizes the decision by upgrading the features of the chosen alternative and downgrading the rejected alternative), ''selective exposure to information'' (persons may search out information that supports their beliefs and avoid information that challenges them in order to reduce dissonance), and ''forced compliance'' (the seemingly paradoxical notion of dissonance theory that the less a person is paid to engage in a distasteful task, the more the task will be enjoyed). The *information-processing models/theories* suggest that successful attitude change through persuasion involves the five sequential processes of attention (get the target audience's attention), comprehension (make arguments and expected behaviors of the audience clear), yielding (assess target audience's consent), retention (ensure that audience maintains its decision until action is required), and action (ensure that audience is motivated to act in accordance with the new attitude) (McGuire, 1985). According to this approach, if this sequence of processes is interrupted at any point, the expected attitude change will not occur. The *functional theories* (e.g., Katz, 1960; Herek, 1986, 1987; Snyder & DeBono, 1989) assume that individuals maintain a particular attitude because it has adaptive value and serves some personal basic need. The *functional theories* have examined the "author-itarian personality" (e.g., Christie & Jahoda, 1954; Rokeach, 1960, 1968) and have been favored by the psychoanalytically oriented theorists, who attempt to explain negative attitudes and prejudices in terms of past patterns of childhood socialization. The *perceptual theories* argue that attitudes change in conjunction with individuals' self-perceptions, their perceptions of the environment, and their own needs. This approach emphasizes the categories, frames of reference, and labels that individuals use to organize their social environment (e.g., Bem, 1972; Newman & Layton, 1984). A recent type of perceptual/social/cognitive theory called the *theory of planned behavior* (Ajzen, 1985, 1991) proposes that the conscious intention to behave in a particular way depends on the person's atti-tude toward the behavior (i.e., the desire to act in that way or not), subjective norm (i.e., the beliefs about what others would think about the action), and perceived behavioral control (i.e., sensing one's ability to carry out the action). Thus, according to this theory, people may perceive barriers to behaving ac-cording to their attitudes (Gray, 1994). Another current cognitive theoretical approach concerns the use of persuasion to change attitudes and is called the *elaboration likelihood model* (Petty & Cacioppo, 1986), which states that per-suasion can occur in either of two distinct ways, depending on how important or relevant the issues are to the individuals who are the target of persuasion: via a "central" route (where an "important" message is carefully processed, and degree of attitude change depends on the quality of the arguments advanced) and via a "perceptual" route (where an "unimportant" message is only casually processed, and degree of attitude change depends on the presence of persuasion cues such as the expertise or status of the persuader; cf: *heuristic theory of persuasion*; Sutherland, 1996). The formulation of *attitude theories* in psychol-ogy is an active area involving practical applications and consequences. However, various unresolved issues remain that are not yet well understood by attitude theorists. Among these are the lack of knowledge concerning the sudden and intense emotional arousal that attitudes may produce, the manner in which attitudes can lead individuals to make great personal sacrifices for their ideals and loved ones, and the dynamics underlying the dramatic attitude reversals that may occur in a person's life (such as love at first sight, religious conversion, etc.) (Ostrom, 1994). In psychology, the study of attitudes and the theories of attitude change reflect an overwhelming diversity of viewpoints and attitudes on the part of psychologists themselves about the relevant processes involved. As noted by Reber (1995, p. 65), psychology regularly gets itself into stormy def-initional waters, no more so than when a term like *attitude* is explored and where the domain of reference turns out to be much more complex than originally anticipated. See also ATTRIBUTION THEORY; CONFLICT, THEORIES OF; FESTINGER'S THEORY; PREJUDICE, THEORIES OF; REINFORCEMENT THEORY.

REFERENCES

Thomas, W., & Znaniecki, F. (1927). *The Polish peasant in Europe and America*. New York: Knopf.

LaPiere, R. (1934). Attitudes and actions. *Social Forces, 13*, 230–237.

Heider, F. (1946). Attitudes and cognitive organization. *J. Psy., 21*, 107–112.

Christie, R., & Jahoda, M. (Eds.) (1954). *Studies in the scope and method of the "authoritarian personality."* New York: Free Press.

Festinger, L. (1957). *A theory of cognitive dissonance*. Stanford, CA: Stanford University Press.

Katz, D. (1960). The functional approach to the study of attitudes. *Pub. Opin. Quar., 24*, 163–204.

Rokeach, M. (1960). *The open and closed mind*. New York: Basic Books.

Campbell, D. (1963). Social attitudes and other acquired behavioral dispositions. In S. Koch (Ed.), *Psychology: A study of a science*. Vol. 6. New York: McGraw-Hill.

Newcomb, T. (1963). Persistence and repression of changed attitudes: Long-range studies. *J. Soc. Iss., 19*, 3–14.

Fleming, D. (1967). Attitude: The history of a concept. *Perspectives in American History, 1*, 287–365.

Abelson, R., Aronson, E., McGuire, W., Newcomb, T., Rosenberg, M., & Tannenbaum, P. (Eds.) (1968). *Theories of cognitive consistency: A sourcebook*. Chicago: Rand-McNally.

Greenwald, A., Brock, T., & Ostrom, T. (Eds.) (1968). *Psychological foundations of attitudes*. New York: Academic Press.

Rokeach, M. (1968). *Beliefs, attitudes, and values*. San Francisco: Jossey-Bass.

Wicker, A. (1969). Attitudes versus actions: The relationship of verbal and overt behavioral responses to attitude objects. *J. Soc. Iss., 25*, 41–78.

Bem, D. (1972). Self-perception theory. In L. Berkowitz (Ed.), *Advances in experimental social psychology*. Vol. 6. New York: Academic Press.

Wolman, B. (Ed.) (1973). *Dictionary of behavioral science*. New York: Van Nostrand Reinhold.

Fishbein, M., & Ajzen, I. (1975). *Belief, attitude, intention, and behavior*. Reading, MA: Addison-Wesley.

Regan, D., & Fazio, R. (1977). On the consistency between attitudes and behavior: Look to the method of attitude formation. *J. Exp. Soc. Psy., 13*, 28–45.

Ajzen, I., & Fishbein, M. (1980). *Understanding attitudes and predicting social behavior*. Englewood Cliffs, NJ: Prentice-Hall.

Cialdini, R., Petty, R., & Cacioppo, J. (1981). Attitude and attitude change. *Ann. Rev. Psy., 32*, 357–404.

Breckler, S. (1984). Empirical validation of affect, behavior, and cognition as distinct components of attitude. *J. Pers. Soc. Psy., 47*, 1191–1205.

Cooper, J., & Croyle, R. (1984). Attitudes and attitude change. *Ann. Rev. Psy., 35*, 395–426.

Cooper, J., & Fazio, R. (1984). A new look at dissonance theory. In L. Berkowitz (Ed.), *Advances in experimental social psychology*. Vol. 17. New York: Academic Press.

Newman, J., & Layton, B. (1984). Overjustification: A self-perception perspective. *Pers. Soc. Psy. Bull., 10*, 419–425.

Ajzen, I. (1985). From intentions to actions: A theory of planned behavior. In J. Kuhl & J. Beckmann (Eds.), *Action control: From cognition to behavior*. Heidelberg: Springer.

McGuire, W. (1985). The nature of attitudes and attitude change. In G. Lindzey & E. Aronson (Eds.), *Handbook of social psychology*. Vol. 2. New York: Random House.

Bridge, R. (1986). Attitudes and attitude change. In T. Pettijohn (Ed.), *The encyclopedic dictionary of psychology*. Guilford, CT: Dushkin.

Frey, D. (1986). Recent research on selective exposure to information. *Adv. Exp. Soc. Psy., 19*, 41–80.

Herek, G. (1986). The instrumentality of attitudes: Toward a neofunctional theory. *J. Soc. Iss., 42*, 99–114.

Petty, R., & Cacioppo, J. (1986). The elaboration likelihood model of persuasion. In L. Berkowitz (Ed.), *Advances in experimental social psychology*. Vol. 19. New York: Academic Press.

Chaiken, S., & Strangor, C. (1987). Attitudes and attitude change. *Ann. Rev. Psy., 38*, 575–630.

Herek, G. (1987). Can functions be measured? A new perspective on the functional approach to attitudes. *Soc. Psy. Quar., 50*, 285–303.

Abelson, R. (1988). Conviction. *Amer. Psy., 43*, 267–275.

Fazio, R. (1989). Attitude accessibility. In M. Zanna (Ed.), *Advances in experimental social psychology*. New York: Academic Press.

Snyder, M., & DeBono, K. (1989). Understanding the functions of attitudes: Lessons from personality and social psychology. In A. Pratkanis, S. Breckler, & A. Greenwald (Eds.), *Attitude structure and function*. Hillsdale, NJ: Erlbaum.

Alessio, J. (1990). A synthesis and formalization of Heiderian balance and social exchange theory. *Social Forces, 68*, 1267–1286.

Tessor, A., & Shaffer, D. (1990). Attitude and attitude change. *Ann. Rev. Psy., 41*, 479–523.

Ajzen, I. (1991). The theory of planned behavior. *Org. Beh. & Hum. Dec. Proc., 50*, 179–211.

Cooper, J., & Scher, S. (1991). Actions and attitudes: The role of responsibility and aversive consequences in persuasion. In T. Brock & S. Shariff (Eds.), *The psychology of persuasion*. San Francisco: Freeman.

Johnson, B. (1991). Insights about attitudes: Meta-analytic perspectives. *Pers. Soc. Psy. Bull., 17*, 289–299.

Eagly, A., & Chaiken, S. (1993). *The psychology of attitudes*. Orlando, FL: Harcourt Brace Jovanovich.

Olson, J., & Zanna, M. (1993). Attitudes and attitude change. *Ann. Rev. Psy., 44*, 117–154.

Ajzen, I. (1994). Attitudes. In R. J. Corsini (Ed.), *Ency. Psy.* New York: Wiley.

Gray, P. (1994). *Psychology*. New York: Worth.

Ostrom, T. (1994). Attitude theory. In R. J. Corsini (Ed.), *Ency. Psy.* New York: Wiley.

Reber, A. (1995). *The Penguin dictionary of psychology*. New York: Penguin Books.

Sutherland, S. (1996). *The international dictionary of psychology*. New York: Crossroad.

ATTRIBUTION/ATTITUDE BOOMERANG EFFECT. See ATTRIBUTION THEORY.

ATTRIBUTION THEORY. The Austrian-American psychologist Fritz Heider (1896–1988) was preeminent in the formulation of *balance theory* in the study of attitudes (i.e., people are motivated to maintain balance, harmony, or "cognitive consonance" among their attitudes, perceptions, and beliefs; Heider, 1958; Newcomb, 1981; cf: state of imbalance, disharmony, or "cognitive dissonance"; Festinger, 1957) and of *attribution theory* in the study of social perception that originated in social psychology and is a general approach for describing the ways individuals use information to generate causal explanations for behavior and events (Heider, 1958). Heider argued that people continually make causal analyses about others' behavior where the behavior is attributed either to *dispositions* (internal factors or causes, such as one's personality) or to *situations* (external factors or causes, such as one's environment). For example, is the other person's overt hostility due to her or his aggressive personality (*dispositional attribution*) or due to abuse and stress in that person's environment (*situational attribution*)? Heider suggested that instead of developing theories of how people are supposed to act or think, psychologists should examine the personal theories (belief systems) that ordinary people themselves use as "intuitive psychologists" to assess the causes and effects of behavior (Ross, 1977). A prolific number of subtheories, hypotheses, effects, and principles relating to *attribution theory* have followed Heider's initial formulations (cf: *attribution/attitude boomerang effect*, which refers to a shift in attitude/attributions that not only goes against what was intended but actually is in the opposite direction; Reber, 1995). While it is possible that an individual may choose to make a *situational attribution* of another's behavior, most people tend to be biased toward making *dispositional attributions*. Thus, there seems to be a tendency to view persons as *origins* of events, and this leads many individuals to regard the needs, wishes, dispositions, skills, and motives of others as responsible for both natural and social phenomena (Heider, 1958; Misovich, 1986). This tendency of people to ignore the external circumstantial causes of behavior and to emphasize the internal personal-character causes is referred to as the *fundamental attribution error* (Ross, 1977; or the *overattribution effect*; Fernald, 1997). According to the *automaticity hypothesis* (Gilbert, 1989), such attributions to internal characteristics are automatic, while attributions to external causes are, by comparison, more controlled. Another hypothesis concerning attribution theory, the *cultural-norm hypothesis* (Jellison & Green, 1981; Lee, Hallahan, & Herzog, 1996), states that the fundamental attribution error (underestimating situational influences) is at least partly learned from one's larger culture. For example, individuals in a Western culture, which emphasizes the idea that people are in charge of their own destinies, will learn to attribute behavior more to internal character than to external environment. The *actor-observer discrepancy* is a concept in attribution theory that suggests that the fundamental attribution error is less likely to occur when people make attributions about their own behavior than when they make attributions about others' behaviors (Nisbett, Caputo, Legant, & Marecek, 1973). Various hypotheses have been offered to explain the *actor-observer discrepancy*: the *knowledge-across-situations hypothesis* states that people become more sensitized to the variations in their own behavior because they have seen themselves in many more situations than they have seen others (Sande, Goethals, & Radloff, 1988); the *visual-orientation hypothesis* stems from the basic characteristic of visual perception that our eyes point outward, and, when we watch someone else's behavior, our eyes are fixed on that person and, thereby, attribute internal causes to the person. On the other hand, when we ourselves engage in behaviors, we see the surrounding, external environment (not ourselves) and attribute external causes for our own behavior (Storms, 1973). The *correspondent inference theory* (Jones & Davis, 1965) is a systematic analysis of the processes described by Heider (1958) and describes the situational factors that influence the appearance of external and internal attributions. This theory states, among other things, that individuals observe actions and effects produced by actions where such action–effect connections become the basis for inferences about others' behaviors and intentions. When "knowledge" and "ability" intentions are attributed, an internal disposition is assumed to be the cause of the other person's behavior. In another case, the *just-world hypothesis* in attribution theory argues for the notion that people need to believe that the world is fair and that justice is served consistently, where bad people are punished, and good people are rewarded (Lerner, 1980). A theory related to the idea that people attribute and infer internal dispositions concerning others' behavior is the *self-perception theory* (Bem, 1967, 1972). This attribution theory proposes that individuals use the same information to make inferences about their own dispositional makeup as they use to make inferences about others'. Thus, according to this approach, we observe our own actions and subsequently attribute those actions to external or internal causes, and in the absence of a reasonable external cause for our own behavior, we attribute our behavior to an internal cause. In this way, for example, a person develops attitudes about issues and events by self-observation of the opinions she or he expresses. Another integrative theory of attribution processes has been formulated by Harold H. Kelley (1971, 1973). Kelley emphasized the idea that people often make causal attributions for events under conditions of uncertainty, and he developed a model of the logic that people might use to judge whether a specific behavior should be attributed to internal (personality-character) causes or to external (environmental) causes. According to Kelley's model, before making an attribution (either internal or external), one would ideally ask three questions about another's behavior: (1) Is it consistent? (2) Is it consensual/normative? (3) Is it distinctive? If the answer to (1) is no, the attribution will probably be external. If the answer to (1) is yes, either an external or internal attribution will be made, depending on the answers to (2) and (3). If the answer to both (1) and (2) is yes, the attribution will probably be external. If the answers to (1), (2), and (3) are yes, no, yes, respectively, the attribution will probably be internal. If the answers to (1), (2), and (3) are yes, no, no, respectively, the attribution will probably be a combination of both external and internal factors (cf: McArthur, 1972). According to Kelley (1971), a *covariation/correlation principle* is employed when people infer the causes of events, including the behavior of other people, by observing whether two events vary together or simply occur together (such as lightning and thunder). In this way, an effect is attributed to that condition that is present when the effect is present and that condition that is absent when the effect is absent. Kelley also refers to the concepts of *discounting principle* (cf: Cha's, 1971, *discounting effect*) and *augmentation principle* to describe the plausibility of internal versus external causes in the assessment of another's behavior. *Discounting* is the tendency to reject dispositional (internal) factors as causes of a behavior when the behavior is apparently one that most people would perform under the existing circumstances. *Augmenting* is the tendency for one to increase acceptance of an internal dispositional cause when a potential external cause is also present. Occasionally, the attributional process may be biased in a way where one's own personal goals, attitudes, and motives disrupt a rational and systematic analysis of the causes of behavior. One example of this type of attributional bias is called the *self-serving bias* (e.g., Arkin, Cooper, & Kolditz, 1980), which occurs when individuals tend to take credit for their successes but deny responsibility for their failures. Numerous studies have been conducted to extend and refine *attribution theory* (e.g., Fiske & Taylor, 1991), but they all attempt generally to examine the dynamics and conditions under which causal explanations about others' (and one's own) behaviors are made. In addition to social psychology, *attribution theory* has been used as an explanatory system or model in many other areas of psychology, including the study of marriage (Bradbury & Fincham, 1990), spousal abuse (Overholser & Moll, 1990), cultural influence (Lee, Hallahan, & Herzog, 1996), achievement motivation and emotions (Weiner, 1986), and clinical depression (Fletcher, Fitness, & Blampied, 1990). See also ACHIEVEMENT MOTIVATION, THEORY OF; ATTITUDE/ATTITUDE CHANGE, THEORIES OF; FESTINGER'S COGNITIVE DISSONANCE THEORY.

REFERENCES

Cartwright, D., & Harary, F. (1956). Structural balance: A generalization of Heider's theory. *Psy. Rev., 63*, 277–293.

Festinger, L. (1957). *A theory of cognitive dissonance*. Evanston, IL: Row, Peterson.

Heider, F. (1958). *The psychology of interpersonal relationships*. New York: Wiley.

Jones, E., & Davis, K. (1965). From acts to dispositions: The attribution process in person perception. In L. Berkowitz (Ed.), *Advances in experimental social psychology*. Vol. 2. New York: Academic Press.

Bem, D. (1967). Self-perception: An alternative interpretation of cognitive dissonance phenomena. *Psy. Rev., 74*, 183–200.

Cha, J. (1971). Clarity of the focal stimulus cue and the mediation of two opposing social perceptual effects. Unpublished doctoral dissertation. University of California at Los Angeles Library.

Kelley, H. (1971). *Attribution in social interaction*. Morristown, NJ: General Learning Press.

Bem, D. (1972). Self-perception theory. In L. Berkowitz (Ed.), *Advances in experimental social psychology*. Vol. 6. New York: Academic Press.

McArthur, L. (1972). The how and what of why: Some determinants and consequences of causal attribution. *J. Pers. Soc. Psy., 22*, 171–193.

Kelley, H. (1973). The process of causal attribution. *Amer. Psy., 28*, 107–128.

Nisbett, R., Caputo, C., Legant, P., & Marecek, J. (1973). Behavior as seen by the actor and as seen by the observer. *J. Pers. Soc. Psy., 27*, 154–164.

Storms, M. (1973). Videotape and the attribution process: Reversing actors' and observers' points of view. *J. Pers. Soc. Psy., 27*, 165–175.

Ross, L. (1977). The intuitive psychologist and his shortcomings: Distortions in the attribution process. In L. Berkowitz (Ed.), *Advances in experimental social psychology*. New York: Academic Press.

Arkin, R., Cooper, H., & Kolditz, T. (1980). A statistical review of the literature concerning the self-serving attribution bias in interpersonal influence situations. *J. Pers., 48*, 435–448.

Kruglanski, A. (1980). Lay epistemologic process and contents: Another look at attribution theory. *Psy. Rev., 87*, 70–87.

Lerner, M. (1980). *The belief in a just world: A fundamental delusion*. New York: Plenum.

Jellison, J., & Green, J. (1981). A self-presentation approach to the fundamental attribution error: The norm of internality. *J. Pers. Soc. Psy., 40*, 643–649.

Newcomb, T. (1981). Heiderian balance as a group phenomenon. *J. Pers. Soc. Psy., 40*, 862–867.

Misovich, S. (1986). Attribution theory. In T. Pettijohn (Ed.), *The encyclopedic dictionary of psychology*. Guilford, CT: Dushkin.

Weiner, B. (1986). *An attributional theory of motivation and emotion*. New York: Springer.

Sande, G., Goethals, G., & Radloff, C. (1988). Perceiving one's own traits and others': The multifaceted self. *J. Pers. Soc. Psy., 54*, 13–20.

Gilbert, D. (1989). Thinking lightly about others: Automatic components of the social inference process. In J. Uleman & J. Bargh (Eds.), *Unintended thought*. New York: Guilford.

Bradbury, T., & Fincham, F. (1990). Attributions in marriage: Review and critique. *Psy. Bull., 107*, 3–33.

Fletcher, G., Fitness, J., & Blampied, N. (1990). The link between attributions and happiness in close relationships: The roles of depression and explanatory style. *J. Soc. Clin. Psy., 9*, 243–255.

Overholser, J., & Moll, S. (1990). Who's to blame: Attributions regarding causality in spouse abuse. *Beh. Sci. & Law, 8*, 107–120.

Fiske, S., & Taylor, S. (1991). *Social cognition*. New York: McGraw-Hill.

Reber, A. (1995). *The Penguin dictionary of psychology*. New York: Penguin Books.

Lee, F., Hallahan, M., & Herzog, T. (1996). Explaining real life events: How culture and domain shape attributions. *Pers. Soc. Psy. Bull., 22*, 732–741.

Fernald, D. (1997). *Psychology*. Upper Saddle River, NJ: Prentice-Hall.

AUBERT–FLEISCHL PARADOX/PHENOMENON. See VISION/SIGHT, THEORIES OF.

AUBERT–FORSTER PHENOMENON/LAW. See VISION/SIGHT, THEORIES OF.

AUBERT PHENOMENON. See VISION/SIGHT, THEORIES OF.

AUDITION/HEARING, THEORIES OF. In general, the *audition theories* attempt to explain how physical sound vibrations are transformed into the neural impulses that are the basis of hearing (Bekesy & Rosenblith, 1948; Bekesy, 1957). Historically, there have been *five* (cf: Reber, 1995, who cites *two* major theories: *place theory* and *periodicity theory*) major audition theories (Wolman, 1973): *resonance/place theories*, *frequency theories*, *volley/periodicity theories*, *hydraulic theories*, and *sound-pattern theories*. The *resonance theory* of hearing, often called the *Helmholtz theory* (e.g., Helmholtz, 1863), asserts that pitch is determined by the place on the basilar membrane (i.e., a delicate membrane in the cochlea of the inner ear) that is stimulated, where the short fibers are sensitive to high-pitched sounds, the long fibers are sensitive to low-pitched sounds, and the fibers in the middle of the membrane are attuned to sounds of medium pitch. Loudness and tonal discriminability are assumed to be determined by the number of neurons activated by the incoming stimulus. The *resonance theory* is known also as the *harp theory*, the *place theory* (cf: Bekesy's *traveling-wave theory*, which states that sounds of different frequencies set up different wave patterns in the cochlear fluids; Ludel, 1978), and the *piano theory* (cf: Bekesy's, 1960, 1967, argument that this theory was incorrect because the basilar membrane fibers are not free to resonate like the strings of a piano with the sustaining pedal depressed; rather, the fibers are connected as if a sheet of light cloth were laid across the piano strings). The *frequency theory* of hearing (e.g., Rutherford, 1886) holds that the basilar membrane in the ear responds as a whole entity to aural stimuli and then transmits the stimuli to the brain for further analysis. Rutherford's *frequency theory*, often called the *telephone theory*, assumes that the basilar membrane responds much like a telephone diaphragm mechanism. The *volley/periodicity theory* of audition (e.g., Wever & Bray, 1930a, b, 1938; cf: Wever's, 1949, combined *resonance-volley theory*) maintains that nerve fibers of the basilar membrane respond in groups or "volleys," not in unison, which results in more transmission of aural impulses. Thus, *periodicity theory* emphasizes the synchronized firing of neurons and depends largely on the *volley principle*, which proposes that groups of basilar membrane fibers work as squads and fire in synchronized volleys; the *volley principle* is necessary to this theory because the auditory nerve follows signals only with frequencies up to 3,000–4,000 Hz (i.e., hertz, or cycles per second). The *Wever–Bray effect* refers to an aural potential that can be recorded using gross electrodes placed near the auditory nerve of an animal. It is made up of two separate potentials:

one is the whole nerve-action potential, and the other is the "cochlear micro-phonic." It is interesting to note that if the changes in the electrical potentials are amplified and fed through an ordinary telephone receiver, one can actually understand words spoken through it into the animal's ear (Reber, 1995). The *hydraulic theory* of hearing (Meyer, 1907, 1928) asserts that hearing is depen-dent on the amount of basilar membrane involved in the sensation of different tones. The *sound-pattern theory* (Ewald, 1899, 1903) states that the sense of hearing is dependent on the pattern of vibration on the basilar membrane; this theory assumes that different patterns of vibrations are imposed on the basilar membrane by stimuli of different complexities or pitches. The current view of audition seems to favor a form of amalgamation of the *place theory* and the *periodicity theory*: for stimuli below about 3,000 Hz, both *place* and *periodicity* combine, and for those frequencies above this level, the *place* on the basilar membrane is probably the critical factor. The variable of loudness seems to be mediated by the overall number of impulses arriving at the brain (cf: *Egan effect*—the loudness of speech in one ear is increased if noise is applied to the opposite ear; Zusne, 1987). Thus, in general, no one theory of audition/hearing seems adequate, perhaps because the sense of hearing is relatively complex (Reber, 1995). See also HYDRAULIC THEORY.

REFERENCES

Helmholtz, H. von (1863). *Die Lehre von den Tonempfindungen als physiologische Grun-dlage fur die Theorie der Musik*. Braunschweig: Wieweg.

Rutherford, E. (1886). A new theory of hearing. *J. Anat. Physio., Lon., 21*, 166–168.

Ewald, J. (1899). Zur Physiologie des Labyrinths. VI. Eine neue Hortheorie. *Ar. ges. Physio., 76*, 147–188.

Ewald, J. (1903). Zur Physiologie des Labyrinths. VII. Die Erzeugung von Schallbildern in der camer acustica. *Ar. ges. Physio., 93*, 485–500.

Meyer, M. (1907). An introduction to the mechanics of the inner ear. *University of Missouri Studies, Science Services, 2*, no. 1.

Meyer, M. (1928). The hydraulic principles governing the function of the cochlea. *J. Gen. Psy., 1*, 239–265.

Wever, E., & Bray, C. (1930a). Present possibilities for auditory theory. *Psy. Rev., 37*, 365–380.

Wever, E., & Bray, C. (1930b). The nature of acoustic response: The relation between sound frequency and frequency of impulses in the auditory nerve. *J. Exp. Psy., 13*, 373–387.

Stevens, S. S., & Davis, H. (1938). *Hearing: Its psychology and physiology*. New York: Wiley.

Wever, E., & Bray, C. (1938). Distortion in the ear as shown by the electrical responses of the cochlea. *J. Acou. Soc. Amer., 9*, 227–233.

Bekesy, G. von., & Rosenblith, W. (1948). The early history of hearing—Observations and theories. *J. Acou. Soc. Amer., 20*, 727–748.

Wever, E. (1949). *Theories of hearing*. New York: Wiley.

Davis, H. (1951). Psychophysiology of hearing and deafness. In S. S. Stevens (Ed.), *Handbk. Exp. Psy*. New York: Wiley.

Bekesy, G. von (1957). The ear. *Sci. Amer., 197*, 66–78.

Bekesy, G. von (1960). *Experiments in hearing.* New York: McGraw-Hill.

Bekesy, G. von (1967). *Sensory inhibition.* Princeton, NJ: Princeton University Press.

Gulick, W. (1971). *Hearing: Physiology and psychophysics.* New York: Oxford University Press.

Tobias, J. (Ed.) (1972). *Foundations of modern auditory theory.* New York: Academic Press.

Wolman, B. (Ed.) (1973). *Dictionary of behavioral science.* New York: Van Nostrand Reinhold.

Moore, B. (1977). *Introduction to the psychology of hearing.* Baltimore: University Park Press.

Carterette, E., & Friedman, M. (Eds.) (1978). *Handbook of perception.* Vol. 4: *Hearing.* New York: Academic Press.

Ludel, J. (1978). *Introduction to sensory processes.* San Francisco: Freeman.

Zusne, L. (1987). *Eponyms in psychology.* Westport, CT: Greenwood Press.

Reber, A. (1995). *The Penguin dictionary of psychology.* New York: Penguin Books.

AUFGABE, LAW OF THE. See MIND/MENTAL SET, LAW OF.

AUGMENTATION PRINCIPLE. See ATTRIBUTION THEORY.

AUTOKINETIC EFFECT. See APPARENT MOVEMENT, PRINCIPLES/ THEORIES OF.

AUTOMATICITY HYPOTHESIS. See ATTRIBUTION THEORY.

AUTOTELIC THEORY. See PLAY, THEORIES OF.

AVOIDANCE HYPOTHESIS. See PUNISHMENT, THEORIES OF.

B

BAER/VON BAER'S LAW. See RECAPITULATION, THEORY/LAW OF.

BALANCE, PRINCIPLES/THEORY OF. See ATTRIBUTION THEORY; FESTINGER'S COGNITIVE DISSONANCE THEORY.

BALDWIN EFFECT. The American developmental psychologist James Mark Baldwin (1861–1934) developed a refined Darwinian genetic psychology (Baldwin, 1894b, 1902). Baldwin's chief goal was to explain the adaptive correspondence of mental life and thoughts to material things, which he argued evolved through the formation and transformation of habits via the interacting processes of assimilation and imitation (Baldwin, 1906–1911). Baldwin held a functional view of mind as sensorimotor process and emphasized the importance of intentional action as the mechanism of selection in the development of mental faculties. In his approach, Baldwin combined Darwinian and Lamarckian ideas of evolution to formulate his own sophisticated hypothesis of organic selection, which accounted for the course and direction of growth. Baldwin's notion of organic selection came to be known as the *Baldwin effect* (Broughton, 1994). Baldwin also applied his model of intentional action to the moral, religious, and social aspects of human behavior where cycles of suggestion and imitation were mechanisms by which individuals developed socially, and where social progress was viewed as *social selection* along with the transmission and conservation of adaptive values. In some of his writings, Baldwin referred to numerous *laws* that occur in psychology. For example, Baldwin (1894a) described *laws* of nervous accommodation, habit, inheritance, evolution, motives, contradictory representation, reversion to type, mental dynamogenesis, attention, and voluntary interest. Also, in another case (Baldwin, 1906), he referred to *laws* of imagination, association, associative reproduction, correlation, preference in associations, identity in judgment, contiguity, contradiction, partial effect, sensation, passive imagination, sufficient reason, habit, and thought. Thus, Baldwin, like many other early psychologists who were schooled and grounded in *mental philosophy*, seemed to demonstrate a penchant for a rather generous, liberal, and nonrigorous use of the term *law* in describing various psychological phenomena. See also ATTENTION, LAWS/PRINCIPLES/THEORIES OF; DARWIN'S EVOLUTION THEORY; DYNAMOGENESIS, LAW OF.

REFERENCES

Baldwin, J. (1889–1891). *Handbook of psychology*. 2 vols. New York: A.M.S. Press.

Baldwin, J. (1894a). *Handbook of psychology*. New York: Holt.

Baldwin, J. (1894b). *Mental development in the child and in the race*. New York: Macmillan.

Baldwin, J. (1897a). *Social and ethical interpretations in mental development: A study in social psychology*. New York: Macmillan.

Baldwin, J. (Ed.) (1901–1905). *Dictionary of philosophy and psychology*. 4 vols. New York: Macmillan.

Baldwin, J. (1902). *Development and evolution*. New York: A.M.S. Press.

Baldwin, J. (1906). *Handbook of psychology (Senses and intellect)*. New York: Holt.

Baldwin, J. (1906–1911). *Thought and things*. 3 vols. London: Swan, Sonnenschein.

Broughton, J. (1994). James Mark Baldwin. In J. R. Corsini (Ed.), *Ency. Psy*. New York: Wiley.

BANDURA'S THEORY. The Canadian-American psychologist Albert Bandura (1925–   ) is a proponent of *social/cognitive learning theory*, which attempts to explain human behavior in terms of a reciprocal interaction between the three aspects of behavior, cognitions, and environmental events. While *social learning theory* had its origins in the behaviorally oriented writings of Ivan Pavlov, J. B.Watson, and B. F. Skinner (and in the work of J. Dollard and N. Miller, K. Lewin, E. Tolman, G. H. Mead, and H. S. Sullivan), Bandura is preeminent (along with Julian Rotter, Walter Mischel, and Arthur Staats) in the formulation and application of *social learning theory*. According to *Bandura's theory* (1969, 1986), humans learn to satisfy their needs, wishes, and desires by observing the outcomes of behaviors and events, where the observations lead to expectations about what will happen in the future and about one's ability to perform behaviors and to express emotions. Individuals compare their behaviors with those of others and make value judgments about their own and others' behaviors. In this way, according to *social/cognitive theory*, it is not simply the external conditions alone that determine behavior (as extreme behaviorists might claim), but it is also the decisions one makes based on one's cognitions ("knowledge") about the conditions. *Bandura's theory* includes several key concepts concerning the development of personal and social behaviors, among which are *reciprocal determination*—the idea that the person's behavior and the social learning environment continually influence each other in reciprocal ways; one learns behavior from interactions with other persons, and our behavior influences how other persons interact with us (Bandura, 1977b, 1978);

self-efficacy—the perception that one is capable of achieving one's goals (Bandura, 1977a, 1982); *self-regulation*—the process of cognitively punishing and reinforcing one's own behavior depending on whether or not it meets one's personal standards (Bandura, 1977b, 1989); *modeling/observational learning*—a procedure in which an individual observes another person perform some behavior, notes the consequences of that behavior, and then attempts to imitate that behavior (Bandura & Jeffrey, 1937; Bandura, Ross, & Ross, 1963; Bandura, 1968, 1971, 1986); *vicarious punishment*—the observation of the punishment of a model's behavior that results in the decrease of the probability of that same behavior in the observer; and *vicarious reinforcement*—the observation of the reinforcement of a model's behavior that results in the increase of the probability of that same behavior in the observer (Bandura, 1965, 1969, 1973). Bandura's essential research and theoretical formulations have focused on observational learning, the role of thought in establishing and maintaining behavior, the application of behavior principles and social learning to therapeutic contexts, and the ways in which children learn to be aggressive. See also AGGRESSION, THEORIES OF; BEHAVIOR THERAPY/COGNITIVE THERAPY, THEORIES OF; ROTTER'S SOCIAL LEARNING THEORY.

REFERENCES

Bandura, A., & Jeffrey, R. (1937). Role of symbolic coding and rehearsal processes in observational learning. *J. Abn. Soc. Psy., 26*, 122–130.

Bandura, A., & Walters, R. (1959). *Adolescent aggression*. New York: Ronald Press.

Bandura, A. (1961). Psychotherapy as a learning process. *Psy. Bull., 58*, 143–159.

Bandura, A., Ross, D., & Ross, S. (1963). Imitation of film-mediated aggressive models. *J. Abn. Soc. Psy., 66*, 3–11.

Bandura, A., & Walters, R. (1963). *Social learning and personality development*. New York: Holt, Rinehart, & Winston.

Bandura, A. (1965). Vicarious processes: A case of no-trial learning. In L. Berkowitz (Ed.), *Advances in experimental social psychology*. Vol. 2. New York: Academic Press.

Bandura, A. (1968). Modeling approaches to the modification of phobic disorders. In R. Porter (Ed.), *The role of learning in psychotherapy*. London: Churchill.

Bandura, A. (1969). *Principles of behavior modification*. New York: Holt, Rinehart, & Winston.

Bandura, A. (Ed.) (1971). *Psychological modeling: Conflicting theories*. Chicago: Aldine-Atherton.

Bandura, A. (1973). *Aggression: A social learning analysis*. Englewood Cliffs, NJ: Prentice-Hall.

Bandura, A. (1974). Behavior therapy and models of man. *Amer. Psy., 29*, 859–869.

Bandura, A. (1977a). Self-efficacy: Toward a unifying theory of behavioral change. *Psy. Rev., 84*, 191–215.

Bandura, A. (1977b). *Social learning theory*. Englewood Cliffs, NJ: Prentice-Hall.

Bandura, A. (1978). The self-system in reciprocal determinism. *Amer. Psy., 33*, 344–358.

Bandura, A. (1982). Self-efficacy mechanism in human agency. *Amer. Psy., 37*, 122–147.

Bandura, A. (1986). *Social foundations of thought and action: A social cognitive theory.* Englewood Cliffs, NJ: Prentice-Hall.

Bandura, A. (1989). Human agency in social cognitive theory. *Amer. Psy., 44,* 1175–1184.

BARNUM EFFECT. The *Barnum effect/phenomenon,* named after the American showman, charlatan, and entrepreneur Phineas T. Barnum (1810–1891), refers to the fact that a cleverly worded "personal" description based on general, stereotyped statements will be readily accepted as an accurate self-description by most people (Forer, 1949). The *Barnum effect* is behind the fakery of fortune-tellers, astrologers, and mind readers and has often contaminated legitimate study of personality assessment (Reber, 1995). The effect is consistent with Barnum's often-quoted aphorism "There's a sucker born every minute." Barnum, a circus showman, knew that the formula for success was to "have a little something for everybody" (Rathus, 1993). An early study of the *Barnum effect* (Forer, 1949) had a group of college students take a projective test on which they were given subsequent bogus feedback. In fact, each student was given the *same* interpretation. In general, the students each felt that these interpretations were accurate and fitted them well. Thus, the tendency to accept standard feedback of a vague, universalist nature is the *Barnum effect.* Other studies also report that when the same vague, positive, and flattering statements are given to individuals as a personalized horoscope, personality profile, or handwriting analysis, they believe them to be accurate descriptions of them personally (Snyder & Shenkel, 1975; French, Fowler, McCarthy, & Peers, 1991; cf: Layne, 1979; Johnson, Cain, Falke, Hayman, & Perillo, 1985). Some researchers report that people are more willing to believe flattering statements about themselves than statements that are scientifically accurate (e.g., Thiriart, 1991). Various suggestions have been offered by researchers to avoid falling prey to the *Barnum effect,* such as beware of all-purpose descriptions that could apply to anyone, beware of one's own selective perceptions, and resist undue flattery (Wade & Tavris, 1996). See also PERSONALITY THEORIES.

REFERENCES

Forer, B. (1949). The fallacy of personal validation: A classroom demonstration of gullibility. *J. Abn. Soc. Psy., 44,* 118–123.

Hill, W. (1970). *Psychology: Principles and problems.* Philadelphia: Lippincott.

Snyder, C., & Shenkel, R. (1975). The P. T. Barnum effect. *Psy. Today, 8,* 52–54.

Halperin, K., & Snyder, C. (1979). Effects of enhanced psychological test feedback on treatment outcome: Therapeutic implications of the Barnum effect. *J. Cons. & Clin. Psy., 47,* 140–146.

Layne, C. (1979). The Barnum effect: Rationality versus gullibility. *J. Cons. & Clin. Psy., 47,* 219–221.

Johnson, J., Cain, L., Falke, T., Hayman, J., & Perillo, E. (1985). The "Barnum effect" revisited: Cognitive and motivational factors in the acceptance of personality descriptions. *J. Pers. Soc. Psy., 49,* 1378–1391.

French, C., Fowler, M., McCarthy, K., & Peers, D. (1991). Belief in astrology: A test of the Barnum effect. *Skeptical Inquirer, 15*, 166–172.

Thiriart, P. (1991). Acceptance of personality test results. *Skeptical Inquirer, 15*, 161–165.

Rathus, S. (1993). *Psychology*. New York: Harcourt Brace Jovanovich.

Reber, A. (1995). *The Penguin dictionary of psychology*. New York: Penguin Books.

Wade, C., & Tavris, C. (1996). *Psychology*. New York: HarperCollins.

BARTLETT'S SCHEMATA THEORY. The British psychologist Frederic C. Bartlett (1886–1979) proposed an admittedly vague theory—the *schemata theory of memory*—as a way of invalidating and repudiating the classical *trace theory of memory* (i.e., the hypothesized modification of neural tissue resulting from any form of stimulation such as learning new material). Bartlett (1932) stressed the constructive, over the reproductive, aspects of recall and adapted his *schematic theory* (based on the assumption that *schemata* are cognitive, mental plans that are abstract guides for action, structures for interpreting and retrieving information, and organized frameworks for solving problems) from Henry Head's (1920) work on neurology, sensation, and the cerebral cortex. Unfortunately, *Bartlett's theory* seemed to be too speculative to gain wide acceptance in the psychological community (Zangwill, 1994), even though it led many people to think somewhat differently about the dynamics and nature of memory (Oldfield & Zangwill, 1943; Zangwill, 1972). See also MEMORY, THEORIES OF; TRACE THEORY.

REFERENCES

Head, H. (1920). *Studies in neurology II*. London: Oxford University Press.

Head, H. (1926). *Aphasia and kindred disorders of speech*. Cambridge, England: Cambridge University Press.

Bartlett, F. (1932). *Remembering: A study in experimental and social psychology*. Cambridge, England: Cambridge University Press.

Oldfield, R., & Zangwill, O. (1943). Head's concept of the schema and its application in contemporary British psychology: Part III. Bartlett's theory of memory. *Brit. J. Psy., 33*, 113–129.

Bartlett, F. (1948). Challenge to experimental psychology. In *Proceedings and Papers of the 12th International Congress of Psychology at Edinburgh*. Edinburgh: Oliver & Boyd.

Zangwill, O. (1972). "Remembering" revisited. *Quar. J. Exp. Psy., 24*, 124–138.

Zangwill, O. (1994). Frederic C. Bartlett. In R. J. Corsini (Ed.), *Ency. Psy.* New York: Wiley.

BATESON'S VIBRATORY THEORY. See MENDEL'S LAWS/PRINCIPLES.

BECK'S COGNITIVE THERAPY THEORY. See BEHAVIOR THERAPY/ COGNITIVE THERAPY, THEORIES OF.

BEHAVIOR THEORY OF PERCEPTION. See PERCEPTION (II. COM-PARATIVE APPRAISAL), THEORIES OF.

BEHAVIOR THERAPY/COGNITIVE THERAPY, THEORIES OF. The term *behavior therapy* originated in a hospital report by Lindsley, Skinner, and Solomon (1953) that described their use of operant conditioning principles with psychotic patients. Later, Lazarus (1958) used the term in referring to Wolpe's application of the technique of *reciprocal inhibition* to neurotic patients, and Eysenck (1959) used *behavior therapy* to refer to the application of *modern learning theory* to neurotic patients' behavior. The early usage of the term *behavior therapy* was linked consistently to *learning theory* (Krasner, 1994). It was also called *conditioning therapy*, which had as its goal the elimination of unadaptive behavior and the initiation and strengthening of adaptive habits (Wolpe, 1969). Krasner (1971) asserts that 15 factors within psychology coalesced during the 1950s and 1960s to create and form the *behavior therapy* theoretical approach: the concept of *behaviorism* in experimental psychology (e.g., Kantor, 1969); instrumental/operant conditioning research (Thorndike, 1931; Skinner, 1938); the treatment procedure of *reciprocal inhibition* (Wolpe, 1958); studies at Maudsley Hospital in London (Eysenck, 1964); the application of conditioning/learning concepts to human behavior problems in the United States from the 1920s through the 1950s; *learning theory* interpretations of psychoanalysis (e.g., Dollard & Miller, 1950); use of Pavlovian/classical conditioning to explain and change both normal and deviant behaviors; impact of concepts and research from social role learning and interactionism in social psychology and sociology (e.g., Mead, 1934; Parsons, 1949; Homans, 1961); research in developmental/child psychology emphasizing modeling and vicarious learning (e.g., Bandura, 1969, 1971); formulation of social influence variables and concepts such as demand characteristics, experimenter bias, placebo, and hypnosis; development of the *social learning model* as an alternative to the *disease model* of behavior (e.g., Ullman & Krasner, 1963); dissatisfaction with, and critiques of, traditional psychotherapy and the psychoanalytic model (e.g., Eysenck, 1952; cf: Gross, 1979); advancement of the idea of the clinical psychologist as "scientist-practitioner"; development in psychiatry of human/social interaction and environmental influences (e.g., Sullivan, 1953); and resurgence of utopian views of social-environmental planning (e.g., Skinner, 1948). The unifying theme in *behavior therapy* is its derivation from empirically based principles and procedures. Four general types of *behavior therapy* have been acknowledged by psychologists (Kanfer & Phillips, 1970): interactive, instigation, replication, and intervention therapies; and five different approaches in contemporary *behavior therapy* are recognized (Kazdin & Wilson, 1978): applied behavior analysis, neobehavioristic mediational S-R model, social learning theory, multimodal behavior therapy, and cognitive-behavior modification. A number of specific behavior and cognitive therapies based on these principles and theories have been developed since the 1960s, such as *rational-emotive therapy* (Ellis, 1973), *cognitive therapy* (Beck, 1974; Beck is called the "father of cognitive therapy"; Reber, 1995), *self-instructional/stress inoculation* (Meichenbaum, 1977), and *covert modeling therapy* (Cautela, 1971). It has been suggested that the various challenges facing *behavior/cognitive therapy theories* today concerning their procedures and effectiveness may best be met by the use of a "technical eclecticism" (Lazarus, 1981), where there is a willingness to employ appropriate techniques across the various theoretical points of view. However, the specific methods used in the various different *behavior therapy theories* all have the common attributes of scientific examination of behavior grounded in *learning theory*, including the control of appropriate variables, the appreciation of data-based concepts, and the high regard for operational definitions of terms and replicability of results. The development of *behavior therapy* was not monolithic in concept, theory, or practice, and its roots were wide and varied. Thus, *behavior therapy theory* may best be characterized, generally, as the application of the laws of modern *learning theory* to all types of disorder, including individual, situational, and environmental (Franks, 1994). See also ABC THEORY; BANDURA'S THEORY; SKINNER'S DESCRIPTIVE BEHAVIOR/OPERANT CONDITIONING THEORY; WOLPE'S THEORY/TECHNIQUE OF RECIPROCAL INHIBITION.

REFERENCES

Thorndike, E. (1931). *Human learning*. New York: Appleton.

Mead, G. (1934). *Mind, self, and society: From the standpoint of a social behaviorist*. Chicago: University of Chicago Press.

Skinner, B. F. (1938). *The behavior of organisms: An experimental analysis*. New York: Appleton-Century.

Skinner, B. F. (1948). *Walden two*. New York: Macmillan.

Parsons, T. (1949). *The structure of social action*. Glencoe, IL: Free Press.

Dollard, J., & Miller, N. (1950). *Personality and psychotherapy: An analysis in terms of learning, thinking, and culture*. New York: McGraw-Hill.

Eysenck, H. (1952). The effects of psychotherapy: An evaluation. *J. Cons. Psy., 16*, 319–324.

Lindsley, O., Skinner, B. F., & Solomon, H. (1953). *Studies in behavior therapy*. Waltham, MA: Metropolitan State Hospital.

Sullivan, H. S. (1953). *The interpersonal theory of psychiatry*. New York: Norton.

Lazarus, A. (1958). New methods in psychotherapy: A case study. *S. Afr. Med. J., 33*, 660–664.

Wolpe, J. (1958). *Psychotherapy by reciprocal inhibition*. Stanford, CA: Stanford University Press.

Eysenck, H. (1959). Learning theory and behaviour therapy. *J. Ment. Sci., 195*, 61–75.

Homans, G. (1961). *Social behavior: Its elementary forms*. New York: Harcourt Brace Jovanovich.

Ullman, L., & Krasner, L. (1963). *Case studies in behavior modification*. New York: Holt, Rinehart, & Winston.

Eysenck, H. (Ed.) (1964). *Experiments in behavior therapy: Readings in modern methods of mental disorders derived from learning theory*. Oxford: Pergamon Press.

Bandura, A. (1969). *Principles of behavior modification*. New York: Holt, Rinehart, & Winston.

Kantor, J. R. (1969). *The scientific evolution of psychology*. Chicago: Principia Press.

Wolpe, J. (1969). *The practice of behavior therapy*. New York: Pergamon Press.

Kanfer, F., & Phillips, J. (1970). *Learning foundations of behavior therapy*. New York: Wiley.

Bandura, A. (Ed.) (1971). *Psychological modeling: Conflicting theories*. Chicago: Aldine-Atherton.

Cautela, J. (1971). Covert conditioning. In A. Jacobs & L. Sachs (Eds.), *The psychology of private events: Perspectives on covert response systems*. New York: Academic Press.

Krasner, L. (1971). Behavior therapy. *Ann. Rev. Psy., 22*, 483–532.

Ellis, A. (1973). Rational-emotive therapy. In R. J. Corsini (Ed.), *Current psychotherapies*. Itasca, IL: Peacock.

Beck, A. (1974). *Cognitive therapy and the emotional disorders*. New York: International Universities Press.

Meichenbaum, D. (1977). *Cognitive-behavior modification: An integrative approach*. New York: Plenum.

Kazdin, A., & Wilson, G. (1978). *Evaluation of behavior therapy*. Cambridge, MA: Ballinger.

Ledwidge, B. (1978). Cognitive behavior modification: A step in the wrong direction. *Psy. Bull., 85*, 353–375.

Gross, M. (1979). *The psychological society*. New York: Simon & Schuster.

Kendall, P., & Hollon, S. (Eds.) (1979). *Cognitive behavioral interventions: Theory, research, and procedures*. New York: Academic Press.

Lazarus, A. (1981). *Multimodal theory*. New York: Guilford Press.

Franks, C. (1994). Behavior therapy: Problems and issues. In R. J. Corsini (Ed.), *Ency. Psy.* New York: Wiley.

Krasner, L. (1994). Behavior therapy. In R. J. Corsini (Ed.), *Ency. Psy.* New York: Wiley.

Reber, A. (1995). *The Penguin dictionary of psychology*. New York: Penguin Books.

BEHAVIORAL CONTRAST EFFECT/PHENOMENON. See GENERALIZATION, PRINCIPLE OF.

BEHAVIORIST THEORY. *Behaviorist theory* (''behaviorism'') was the most significant movement in experimental psychology from 1900 to about 1975. It was launched in 1913 by John B. Watson but had its origins in the work of Ivan Pavlov and E. L. Thorndike. *Behaviorist theory* remains influential today in spite of much criticism leveled against it after about 1960 (Leahey, 1980, 1994). In general, *behaviorist theory* developed as an alternative orientation toward studying and explaining an individual's conscious experience, and it originally rejected both the methods and tenets of *mentalism* (where the proper subject matter of psychology was purported to be the study of mind, favoring the method of *introspection*, or ''looking into one's own experience''). In John B. Watson's (1913, 1919, 1925, 1928) classical approach, *behaviorist theory* was formulated as a purely objective experimental branch of natural science whose goal was the prediction and control of behavior, whose boundaries recognized no dividing line between man and "lower" animal, and which rejected concepts such as *mind, consciousness,* and *introspection.* Various reformulations and versions of Watson's classical behaviorist approach, called *neobehaviorist theory* (or "neobehaviorism"), have appeared in the twentieth century under the labels of *formal behaviorism* (including *logical behaviorism* and *purposive/ cognitive behaviorism), informal behaviorism,* and *radical behaviorism* (Leahey, 1980, 1994). *Formal behaviorist theory,* under the influence of *logical positivism* (where propositions in science needed to be verified by empirical and observable means), attempted to explain behavior in terms of a theory that consisted of operational definitions of concepts, processes, and events both directly observed and unobserved. The logical behaviorism of Clark L. Hull (1943, 1952), formulated in terms of a *hypothetico-deductive learning theory,* was the most systematized theory of the formal behaviorists. Another variation of the formal behaviorist theories was E. C. Tolman's (1932) *purposive/cognitive behaviorist theory,* which rejected the highly mechanistic approach of Watson and Hull and espoused the notion that organisms are always acting to move toward or away from some goal where their purpose is to learn about their environments, not simply to respond to stimuli. *Tolman's theory* developed the "internal" concepts of *purpose, cognition, cognitive maps,* and *expectancies* as a way of explaining behavior. *Informal behaviorist theory,* or *liberalized stimulus-response theory,* formulated covert mediating events (called "fractional, unobservable responses") between the initial stimulus and the final response in a learned behavior. In this way, the covert behaviors of memory, thinking, language, and problem solving could be cast into *behavior theory* terms where the notion of the "central mediating response" was a core concept (e.g., Miller, 1959). *Radical behaviorist theory* is closest of all the neobehaviorist variations to Watson's classical theory. This approach proposed that whatever cannot be observed and measured does not exist; it also rejected the "fuzzy" and ill-defined concepts in psychology such as *mind, free will, personality, self,* and *feelings,* even though it allowed an organism's "private world" to be studied scientifically (Skinner, 1938, 1950, 1953, 1963, 1974; Kantor, 1958). The theoretical approach of the radical behaviorists is the only type of *behaviorist theory* that is exerting a serious influence on mainstream psychology today, while the other behaviorist variations have passed into history. It is possible that present-day cognitive psychology is a new form of *behaviorist theory* with historical roots in Tolman's purposive/cognitive psychology and Hull's logical behaviorism, and a new term (such as *behavioralism;* cf: Ions, 1977) may be needed to combine the *behaviorist* position with the *cognitivist* position, both of which commonly reject the notion of traditional mentalism (Leahey, 1994; cf: Miller, Galanter, & Pribram, 1960). See also HULL'S LEARNING THEORY; SKINNER'S BEHAVIOR THEORY/OPERANT CONDITIONING THEORY; TOLMAN'S THEORY.

REFERENCES

LaMettrie, J. (1748/1961). *Man as machine*. LaSalle, IL: Open Court.

Watson, J. B. (1913). Psychology as the behaviorist views it. *Psy. Rev., 20*, 158–177.

Watson, J. B. (1919). *Psychology from the standpoint of a behaviorist*. Philadelphia: Lippincott.

Watson, J. B. (1925). *Behaviorism*. New York: Norton.

Watson, J. B. (1928). *The ways of behaviorism*. New York: Norton.

Watson, J. B., & McDougall, W. (1929). *The battle of behaviorism*. New York: Norton.

Tolman, E. C. (1932). *Purposive behavior*. New York: Appleton-Century.

Skinner, B. F. (1938). *The behavior of organisms: An experimental analysis*. New York: Appleton-Century.

Hull, C. L. (1943). *Principles of behavior*. New York: Appleton-Century-Crofts.

Skinner, B. F. (1950). Are theories of learning necessary? *Psy. Rev., 57*, 193–216.

Hull, C. L. (1952). *A behavior system: An introduction to behavior theory concerning the individual organism*. New Haven, CT: Yale University Press.

Skinner, B. F. (1953). *Science and human behavior*. New York: Macmillan.

Kantor, J. R. (1958). *Interbehavioral psychology*. Bloomington, IN: Principia Press.

Miller, N. (1959). Liberalization of basic S-R concepts: Extensions to conflict behavior, motivation, and social learning. In S. Koch (Ed.), *Psychology: A study of a science*. Vol. 2. New York: McGraw-Hill.

Miller, G., Galanter, E., & Pribram, K. (1960). *Plans and the structure of behavior*. New York: Holt, Rinehart, & Winston.

Skinner, B. F. (1963). Behaviorism at fifty. *Science, 140*, 951–958.

Skinner, B. F. (1974). *About behaviorism*. New York: Knopf.

Ions, E. (1977). *Against behavioralism*. Oxford, England: Blackwell.

Leahey, T. (1980). *A history of psychology: Main currents in psychological thought*. Englewood Cliffs, NJ: Prentice-Hall.

Krasner, L. (1994). Behaviorism: History. In R. J. Corsini (Ed.), *Ency. Psy.* New York: Wiley.

Leahey, T. (1994). Behaviorism. In R. J. Corsini (Ed.), *Ency. Psy.* New York: Wiley.

BEKESY'S THEORY. See AUDITION/HEARING, THEORIES OF.

BELL-MAGENDIE LAW. This generalized principle initially described by the Scottish anatomist, surgeon, and neurophysiological pioneer Sir Charles Bell (1774–1842) in 1811 was subsequently restated independently (in 1818) by the French physiologist François Magendie (1783–1855). The *Bell–Magendie law* states that the ventral roots of the spinal nerves have motor functions, while the dorsal roots of the spinal nerves have sensory functions. Bell's work in physiology was considered in his own time as the most important since William Harvey's (1578–1657) discovery of the circulation of the blood in 1628. The differentiation of the sensory and motor nerve functions had been known by the early Greek physician Galen (c. 130–200), but this knowledge was lost by later physiologists who believed that the nerves functioned nondifferentially in transmitting both sensory and motor impulses. Bell's explorations of the sensorimotor functions of the spinal nerves triggered a bitter and prolonged priority dispute (i.e., who discovered the principle first?) with Magendie. Apparently, Magendie did not know of Bell's discovery, which was published privately in 1811 as a monograph of only 100 copies. Today, both scientists are given credit for the discovery known as the *Bell–Magendie law* (Boring, 1957; Lundin, 1994; Muir, 1994). The discovery of the distinction between sensory and motor nerves in the *Bell–Magendie law* provided the basis for Marshall Hall's (1790–1857) work in physiology on the reflex arc and reflex functions. Bell's experimental work led to the discovery of the long thoracic nerve in the body named *Bell's nerve*. In addition, the term *Bell's palsy* refers to Bell's demonstration that lesions of the seventh cranial nerve could create facial paralysis. Magendie's work, on the other hand, was concerned with wide-ranging and comprehensive studies in experimental physiology extending from the relationships between sensations and the nervous system to the relationships between intellect and the number of convolutions in the brains of animals on different levels of the phylogenetic scale. The *Bell–Magendie law* was elaborated by later workers in physiology into the principle that conduction from cell to cell within the central nervous system occurs only in the direction from receptor to effector (Warren, 1934). See also NEURON/NEURAL/NERVE THEORY.

REFERENCES

Bell, C. (1811). *Idea of a new anatomy of the brain*. London: Strahan & Preston.
Hall, M. (1833). On the reflex action of the medulla oblongata and medulla spinalis. *Phil. Trans. Roy. Soc. Lon., 123,* 635–665.
Warren, H. (Ed.) (1934). *Dictionary of psychology*. Cambridge, MA: Houghton Mifflin.
Boring, E. G. (1957). *A history of experimental psychology*. New York: Appleton-Century-Crofts.
Lundin, R. (1994). Sir Charles Bell. In R. J. Corsini (Ed.), *Ency. Psy.* New York: Wiley.
Muir, H. (Ed.) (1994). *Larousse dictionary of scientists*. New York: Larousse.

BELONGINGNESS, LAW/PRINCIPLE OF. This is one of E. L. Thorndike's (1932, 1935) accessory or secondary laws to his main *law of effect*, whereby the properties of one item, when closely related to the properties of another item, cause a bond to be formed easily between the two items. This principle implicitly acknowledges the contributions made by the *Gestalt theory* and Gestalt school in psychology (Koffka, 1935; Kohler, 1940), especially when considering the Gestaltists' *laws of perceptual organization*, whereby some kinds of stimuli seem to go together more naturally than others. For example, first and last names presented together may be perceptually grouped or learned better than a set of first names only or a set of last names only. The *principle of belongingness* has been reactivated in recent work on learning, where the basic principles of classical and operant conditioning are incomplete without some recognition of the relationship that exists between the items to be associated and the specific properties of the organism undergoing the learning experience (Reber, 1995). See also ASSOCIATIVE SHIFTING, LAW OF; EFFECT, LAW OF; GESTALT THEORY/LAWS; PERCEPTUAL ORGANIZATION, LAWS OF; REINFORCEMENT, THORNDIKE'S THEORY OF.

REFERENCES

Thorndike, E. L. (1932). *The fundamentals of learning.* New York: Teachers College, Columbia University.
Koffka, K. (1935). *The principles of Gestalt psychology.* New York: Harcourt Brace Jovanovich.
Thorndike, E. L. (1935). *The psychology of wants, interests, and attitudes.* New York: Appleton.
Cole, L. (1939). *General psychology.* New York: McGraw-Hill.
Kohler, W. (1940). *Dynamics in psychology.* New York: Liveright.
Reber, A. (1995). *The Penguin dictionary of psychology.* New York: Penguin Books.

BEM'S SELF-PERCEPTION THEORY. See ATTRIBUTION THEORY.

BENEKE'S DOCTRINE OF TRACES. See GESTALT THEORY/LAWS.

BERKELEY'S THEORY OF VISUAL SPACE PERCEPTION. In 1709, the Irish philosopher and theologian Bishop George Berkeley (1685–1753) argued for an *empiricist* (experience) position of vision and against a *nativist* (inborn) ability of individuals to judge distance (cf: Gibson & Walk, 1960; Walk, 1966). Berkeley's position on perceptual distance was that various cues (such as the size of objects encountered in one's experience) were learned previously and that individuals made the association between particular distances and the sensations that arose from their eye muscle movements and positions. Thus, *Berkeley's theory* posited that the perception of distance was an act of judgment that was grounded in experience, and he described the equivalents of what today are the *secondary* criteria or factors for appreciating visual space perception (such as aerial perspective, interposition, and relative size). Berkeley also listed three *primary* criteria for the appraisal of distance: (1) the physical space between the pupils, which is changed by turning one's eyes as an object approaches or recedes (today this is called the cue of *convergence*); (2) the "blurring" of objects when they are too close to the eye (this factor is probably not valid today as a distance cue); and (3) the "straining" of the eye (the cue that today may be called *accommodation*, involving the adjustment of the shape of the lens of the eye to compensate for the distance of the object of focus from the retina). Boring (1957) suggests that one must not be deceived about the extent of Berkeley's knowledge of visual space perception because he only vaguely understood the mechanism of the perception of distance. Berkeley was correct essentially in two of his three *primary* criteria, but he was a long way off from knowing about the physiology of convergence, corresponding points and the *horopter theory* (Graham, 1965), and *Helmholtz's theory* of the physiology of accommodation.

According to Boring (1957), Berkeley made the question of the perception of distance a matter of sensation or idea when he exemplified the introspectionist's *context theory* of the visual perception of distance, and, in so doing, Berkeley generally anticipated the ideas of modern associationism. Berkeley's "subjective idealism" (Boring, 1957) was influential in the historical development of the role of association in psychology as well as in advancing arguments for experiential factors in perception and against innate factors as the basis for vision (cf: *Hamilton's hypothesis of space*; Spencer, 1892). See also ASSOCIATION, LAWS/PRINCIPLES OF; EMMERT'S LAW; PERCEPTION (I. GENERAL), THEORIES OF; PERCEPTION (II. COMPARATIVE APPRAISAL), THEORIES OF; WITKINS' PERCEPTION THEORY.

REFERENCES

Berkeley, G. (1709/1948). Essay toward a new theory of vision. In A. Luce & T. Jessop (Eds.), *The works of George Berkeley, bishop of Cloyne.* Toronto: Nelson.

Berkeley, G. (1710/1950). *A treatise concerning the principles of human knowledge.* LaSalle, IL: Open Court.

Fraser, A. (Ed.) (1744/1901). *The works of George Berkeley.* Oxford: Clarendon Press.

James, W. (1890). *Principles of psychology.* Vol. 2. New York: Holt.

Spencer, H. (1892). *The principles of psychology.* New York: Appleton.

Ladd, G. (1898). *Outlines of descriptive psychology.* New York: Scribners.

Maher, M. (1900). *Psychology.* New York: Longmans, Green.

Smith, N. (1905). Malebranche's theory of the perception of distance and magnitude. *Brit. J. Psy., 1,* 191–204.

Boring, E. G. (1957). *A history of experimental psychology.* New York: Appleton-Century-Crofts.

Gibson, E., & Walk, R. (1960). The visual cliff. *Sci. Amer., 202,* 67–71.

Graham, C. (1965). Visual space perception. In C. Graham (Ed.), *Vision and visual perception.* New York: Wiley.

Hochberg, J. (1965). *Perception.* Englewood Cliffs, NJ: Prentice-Hall.

Walk, R. (1966). The development of depth perception in animals and infants. *Child Dev. Mono., 31,* no. 5.

BERNE'S SCRIPT THEORY. The Canadian-born American psychologist/psychiatrist Eric L. Berne (1910–1970) formulated his *script theory* concerning personality (ego) development and relationships between individuals (cf: Adler's, 1927, 1937, concept of *lifestyle*), which states that each person creates a *life script* early in life as a way of meeting one's needs, and it is usually carried out unknowingly. *Berne's theory* assumes that individuals develop one of four life positions: "I'm OK, you're OK," "I'm OK, you're not OK," "I'm not OK, you're OK," and "I'm not OK, you're not OK," and persons engage in games to play out their life script in order to obtain "stroking" (i.e., the attention and time of other people). The life position of "I'm not OK, you're OK" (or the "kick me" life script) indicates a maladaptive person who most likely suffers from depression. Treating maladaptive individuals involves explanation of the roles ("games") people play and how they treat other people in those roles, and where interpersonal transactions are analyzed (in *transactional analysis*; Berne, 1961) concerning *parent* (P), *adult* (A), and *child* (C) roles. According to this once-popular approach (Berne, 1964, 1966), when a person's PAC roles are positioned opposite another person's PAC roles, and the lines of communication or interaction between them are crossed, the transaction is considered to be unhealthy. On the other hand, when the lines of communication between two sets of aligned PAC roles are parallel, the interpersonal transaction is considered to be healthy. An example of an unhealthy transaction is a patient's "A" personality (or "ego state") saying to a nurse's "A" personality: "I think working in a hospital would be challenging," but having the nurse's "P" personality reply to the patient's "C" personality by saying, "You're sick because you can't cope with your problems" (a crossed interchange from "P" to "C," crossing the "A" to "A" communication line). *Berne's theory* and the "PAC" concepts contain obvious similarities to Sigmund Freud's (1920, 1933) *tripartite personality theory* concepts of *id*, *ego*, and *superego*, an accusation that Berne denied (Peyser, 1994). See also ADLER'S THEORY OF PERSONALITY; FREUD'S THEORY OF PERSONALITY.

REFERENCES

Freud, S. (1920). *A general introduction to psychoanalysis.* New York: Pocket Books.

Adler, A. (1927). *Practice and theory of individual psychology.* New York: Humanities Press.

Freud, S. (1933). *New introductory lectures on psychoanalysis.* In J. Strachey (Trans. & Ed.), *The standard edition of the complete psychological works of Sigmund Freud.* Vol. 20. London: Hogarth Press.

Adler, A. (1937). Position in family constellation influences life style. *Inter. J. Indiv. Psy., 3,* 211–227.

Berne, E. (1949). The nature of intuition. *Psychiat. Quar., 23,* 203–226.

Berne, E. (1961). *Transactional analysis in psychotherapy: A systematic individual and social psychiatry.* New York: Grove Press.

Berne, E. (1964). *Games people play: The psychology of human relationships.* New York: Grove Press.

Berne, E. (1966). *Principles of group treatment.* New York: Oxford University Press.

Berne, E. (1972). *What do you say after you say hello?* New York: Grove Press.

Peyser, C. (1994). Eric L. Berne. In R. J. Corsini (Ed.), *Ency. Psy.* New York: Wiley.

BEZOLD–BRUCKE EFFECT/PHENOMENON/HUE SHIFT. This phenomenon is credited to the German physicist Johann Bezold (1837–1907) and the German physiologist Ernst Brucke (1819–1892), who found that the hue of spectral colors of objects changes with the level of illumination. The effect applies to bluish reds and bluish greens, where the reds and greens are perceived as bluer with increased illumination, and to yellowish reds and yellowish greens, where the reds and greens are perceived as yellower with increased illumination. However, the *Bezold–Brucke effect* does not occur with the "purer" reds, greens, blues, and yellows. The phenomenon is usually obtained as an aspect of the negative afterimage produced by retinal adaptation. See also ADAPTA-TION, PRINCIPLES/LAWS OF; AFTER-IMAGE LAW; COLOR VISION, THEORIES/LAWS OF.

REFERENCES

Brucke, E. (1851). Untersuchungen uber subjective Farben. *Pogg. Ann. Phys. Chem., 84,* 418–452.
Brucke, E. (1884). *Vorlesungen uber Physiologie.* Vol. 2. Vienna: Braumueller.
Muller, G. E. (1930). Uber die Farben empfindungen. *Z. Psy., 17–18,* 46, 508.
Troland, L. (1930). *Principles of psychophysiology.* Vol. 2. New York: Van Nostrand.
Purdy, D. (1931). On the saturations and chromatic thresholds of the spectral colours. *Brit. J. Psy., 21,* 283.
Judd, D. (1951). Basic correlates of the visual system. In S. S. Stevens (Ed.), *Handbk. Exp. Psy.* New York: Wiley.
Graham, C. (1965). Color: Data and theories. In C. Graham (Ed.), *Vision and visual perception.* New York: Wiley.
Shaver, K., & Tarpy, R. (1993). *Psychology.* New York: Macmillan.

BICHAT, LAW OF. The French physician, pathologist, and anatomist Marie François Xavier Bichat (1771–1802) proposed the principle that there are two main body systems, which are in inverse relationship, called the *vegetative* and the *animal*, with the vegetative system providing for assimilation and augmentation of mass and the animal system providing for the transformation of energy (Wolman, 1989). Bichat's main contribution to medicine and physiology was his perception that the diverse organs of the body contain particular tissues or *membranes*, and he described 21 such membranes, including connective, muscle, and nerve tissues. Bichat maintained that in the case of disease in an organ, generally not the whole organ but only certain tissues are affected. Bichat did not use the microscope, which he distrusted, so his tissue analysis did not include any acknowledgment of their cellular structure. Bichat established the significance and centrality of the study of tissues ("histology"), and his lasting importance lay in simplifying anatomy and physiology by showing how the complex structures of organs could be ascertained in terms of their elementary tissues (Muir, 1994). Bichat's work, done with great intensity during the last years of his short life (he performed over 600 postmortems), had much influence in medical science, and he formed a bridge between the earlier *organ pathology* of Giovanni Battista Morgagni (1682–1771) and the later *cell pathology* of Rudolf Ludwig Carl Virchow (1821–1902) (Millar, Millar, Millar, & Millar, 1996). See also GENERAL SYSTEMS THEORY.

REFERENCES

Wolman, B. (Ed.) (1989). *Dictionary of behavioral science.* San Diego: Academic Press.
Muir, H. (Ed.) (1994). *Larousse dictionary of scientists.* New York: Larousse.

Millar, D., Millar, I., Millar, J., & Millar, M. (1996). *The Cambridge dictionary of scientists*. New York: Cambridge University Press.

BIEDERMAN'S RECOGNITION BY COMPONENTS THEORY. See PATTERN/OBJECT RECOGNITION THEORY.

BIG FIVE MODEL/THEORY OF PERSONALITY. See PERSONALITY THEORIES.

BIOCHEMICAL THEORIES OF PERSONALITY. See PSYCHOPATHOLOGY, THEORIES OF.

BIOCHEMICAL/NEUROLOGICAL THEORIES OF SCHIZOPHRENIA. See SCHIZOPHRENIA, THEORIES OF.

BIOFEEDBACK, PRINCIPLE OF. See CONTROL/SYSTEMS THEORY.

BIOGENETIC RECAPITULATION THEORY. See RECAPITULATION, THEORY/LAW OF.

BIOLOGICAL EVOLUTION, DOCTRINE OF. See DARWIN'S EVOLUTION THEORY.

BIRTH ORDER THEORY. While there has been a wealth of empirical research on *birth order* and its influence on personality (e.g., Sampson, 1965; Forer, 1977; Driscoll & Eckstein, 1982), most of the results are restricted to isolated phenomena and incomplete explanations because of an absence of an underlying and comprehensive *theory of birth order* (Driscoll & Eckstein, 1994). However, one of Alfred Adler's most significant contributions to psychology has been his formulation of the relationship between *birth order* and personality development. Adler (1927, 1937) hypothesized that the child's position in the family creates specific problems that are handled by families generally in the same way, and such *birth order* experiences may reveal a characteristic personality pattern for each ordinal birth position. According to Adler, as the family group develops, different demands arise, and need-fulfillment is assigned to each child in order of birth. The style of coping is never the same for any two children as the situation changes. Adler believed that the needs that influence a specific lifestyle correspond to the child's *perceived* birth order, where it isn't the child's number in order of successive births that influences her or his character, but the *situation* into which she or he is born and the way in which it is *interpreted*. Thus, according to Adler and others (Shulman & Mosak, 1977), "psychological positioning" is the most important factor, where an individual's own *subjective psychological birth order perception* is superordinate to mere *biological birth order*. Research has indicated that personality differences emerge in children, within a specific birth order group, relative to factors of absence or presence of a sibling, sex of the sibling, aspects of the parents' relationship, age, family size, exceptional status, available roles, and relationships with the extended family (Eckstein, 1982). In distinguishing between *idiographic* and *nomothetic laws* as related to Adler's *theory of birth order*, Dinkmeyer, Pew, and Dinkmeyer (1979) state that one may make general guesses about an individual's personality based upon ordinal position, where the guesses are based on *nomothetic laws* (such as youngest children tend to be. . . . , oldest children tend to be. . . . , etc.), but the actual, specific case may be different depending on how the individual perceives the situation and what that person does about it (which are called *idiographic laws*). Thus, *nomothetic laws* concerning the family constellation help in understanding the person's *idiographic laws* or "lifestyle." The major reviews of the literature concerning the influence of *birth order* on personality have shown the rubrics of "firstborn," "middle-born," "youngest," and "only children" to be the most common and frequently used divisions (e.g., Welch, 1977; cf: Shulman & Mosak, 1977). The assumption of *birth order theory* that birth order causes the different personality traits is false, and it would be erroneous to overgeneralize or typecast a person on that basis (Driscoll & Eckstein, 1994). Adler's approach, which emphasized the social determinants of personality and the predisposition of early influences to a faulty "lifestyle," seems to have merit for some psychologists where they believe that no two people develop in exactly the same way. Some persons strive for "superiority," some attempt to cope with "basic inferiority," and one's family constellation may intensify or modify the child's feelings in either case. The problems of *birth order theory* are numerous, and psychologists generally may be pessimistic (e.g., Schooler, 1972) or optimistic (e.g., Driscoll & Eckstein, 1994) concerning its long-range development and importance in explaining personality. See also ADLER'S THEORY OF PERSONALITY; IDIOGRAPHIC/NOMOTHETIC LAWS.

REFERENCES

Adler, A. (1927). *Practice and theory of individual psychology*. New York: Humanities Press.

Adler, A. (1937). Position in family constellation influences life style. *Inter. J. Indiv. Psy., 3*, 211–227.

Sampson, E. (1965). The study of ordinal position: Antecedents and conditions. In B. Maher (Ed.), *Progress in experimental personality research*. New York: Academic Press.

MacDonald, A. (1971). Birth order and personality. *J. Cons. & Clin. Psy., 36*, 171–176.

Schooler, C. (1972). Birth order effects: Not here not now! *Psy. Bull., 78*, 161–175.

Ko, Y. (1973). Birth order and psychological needs. *Acta Psy. Tai., 15*, 68–80.

Vockell, E., Felker, D., & Miley, C. (1973). Birth order literature 1967–1972. *J. Indiv. Psy., 29*, 39–53.

Rosenblatt, P., & Skoogberg, G. (1974). Birth order in cross-cultural perspective. *Dev. Psy., 10*, 48–54.

Forer, L. (1977). Bibliography of birth order literature in the 70's. *J. Indiv. Psy., 33,*
    122–141.
Shulman, B., & Mosak, H. (1977). Birth order and ordinal position: Two Adlerian views.
    J. Indiv. Psy., 33, 114–121.
Welch, B. (1977). A psychological study of only children. Unpublished Ph.D. disserta-
    tion. University of North Carolina Library.
Dinkmeyer, D., Pew, W., & Dinkmeyer, D. (1979). *Adlerian counseling and psycho-
    therapy.* Monterey, CA: Brooks/Cole.
Driscoll, R., & Eckstein, D. (1982). Empirical studies of the relationship between birth
    order and personality. In D. Eckstein (Ed.), *Life style: What it is and how to do
    it.* Dubuque, IA: Kendall/Hunt.
Eckstein, D. (1982). *Life style: What it is and how to do it.* Dubuque, IA: Kendall/Hunt.
Driscoll, R., & Eckstein, D. (1994). Birth order and personality. In R. J. Corsini (Ed.),
    Ency. Psy. New York: Wiley.

BLENDING, LAW OF. See SKINNER'S DESCRIPTIVE BEHAVIOR/
OPERANT CONDITIONING THEORY.

BLOCH'S LAW. See BUNSEN–ROSCOE LAW.

BLOCKING, PHENOMENON/EFFECT OF. The phenomenon of *blocking*
is an example in the psychology of learning and conditioning that the temporal
contiguity alone between events is not sufficient for an association to be formed
between them. Although the *blocking effect* was at one time claimed by *selective
attention theories* (Trabasso & Bower, 1968), Leon J. Kamin (1968, 1969) first
described the *blocking* experiment where two groups of subjects are used. One
group is presented with a compound stimulus (called "AX") that is paired with
an unconditioned stimulus (UCS), such as a noxious puff of air to the eye. A
second group, before receiving an identical treatment, is given pretraining during
which the "A" component of the compound stimulus is paired with the UCS
(air puff). Following the "AX–UCS" pairing, the portion "X" of the compound
stimulus is tested alone. It is found that "X" is more likely to elicit a conditioned response (CR), such as the eye blink, when the subject did *not* have prior
training with the "A" component alone. The stimulus portion "X" of the compound stimulus was paired with the UCS (and, therefore, with the unconditioned
response, UCR) the same number of times in both groups. Contiguity between
stimulus and response was established equally in both groups, and yet learning
was not equal. The *blocking phenomenon/effect* indicates that there must be
something more to conditioning and learning than mere stimulus–response contiguity. That is, if stimulus–response contiguity was a sufficient condition for
learning to occur, then "X" should have become an equally effective CS in
both groups, which it did not (Bower & Hilgard, 1981; Houston, 1981). Thus,
blocking occurs when conditioning to a stimulus is attenuated, or "blocked,"
because that stimulus signals an outcome that was previously predicted by another stimulus or cue. Kamin's (1968, 1969) interpretation of the *blocking effect*

was that conditioning depends on the predictability of reinforcement such that stimuli support learning only to the extent that the outcomes (that they signal) are "surprising." The first formal model to use Kamin's idea of "surprise" was developed by Rescorla and Wagner (1972). Their model differed from previous theories by assuming that the associative strength of a CS decreases over trials because the UCS becomes less effective when it is signaled by a stimulus with increasingly greater associative strength; thus, the UCS is reinforcing only to the extent that it is "surprising." Theories that have followed the *Rescorla–Wagner model* have been distinguished on the basis of whether they focus attention on the processing of the UCS or on the processing of the CS. The *information-processing theory* of Wagner (1978) focuses on the processing of the UCS; the *attentional theory* of Mackintosh (1975) and research by Pearce and Hall (1980) focus on the processing of the CS. However, none of the theories as yet developed can accommodate all the observations that are made from the *blocking* experiments, even though they have stimulated much research in the field of learning and conditioning (Rickert, 1994). See also ASSOCIATION, LAWS/PRINCIPLES OF; ATTENTION, LAWS/PRINCIPLES/THEORIES OF; INFORMATION/INFORMATION-PROCESSING THEORIES; LEARNING THEORIES/LAWS.

REFERENCES

Kamin, L. (1968). "Attention-like" processes in classical conditioning. In M. Jones (Ed.), *Miami symposium on the prediction of behavior.* Miami, FL: University of Miami Press.

Trabasso, T., & Bower, G. (1968). *Attention in learning: Theory and research.* New York: Wiley.

Kamin, L. (1969). Predictability, surprise, attention, and conditioning. In B. Campbell & R. Church (Eds.), *Punishment and aversive behavior.* New York: Appleton-Century-Crofts.

Rescorla, R., & Wagner, A. (1972). A theory of Pavlovian conditioning. Variations in the effectiveness of reinforcement and nonreinforcement. In A. Black & W. Prokasy (Eds.), *Classical conditioning. II. Current research and theory.* New York: Appleton-Century-Crofts.

Mackintosh, N. (1975). A theory of attention: Variations in the associability of stimuli with reinforcement. *Psy. Rev., 82,* 276–298.

Cheafle, M., & Rudy, J. (1978). Analysis of second-order odor-aversion conditioning in neonatal rats: Implications for Kamin's blocking effect. *J. Exp. Psy.: Anim. Beh. Proc., 4,* 237–249.

Wagner, A. (1978). Expectancies and the priming of STM. In S. Hulse, H. Fowler, & W. Honig (Eds.), *Cognitive processes in animal behavior.* Hillsdale, NJ: Erlbaum.

Kohler, E., & Ayres, J. (1979). The Kamin blocking effect with variable-duration CSs. *Anim. Learn. Beh., 7,* 347–350.

Pearce, J., & Hall, G. (1980). A model for Pavlovian learning: Variations in the effectiveness of conditioned but not of unconditioned stimuli. *Psy. Rev., 87,* 532–552.

Bower, G., & Hilgard, E. (1981). *Theories of learning.* Englewood Cliffs, NJ: Prentice-Hall.

Houston, J. (1981). *Fundamentals of learning and memory*. New York: Academic Press.
Rickert, E. (1994). Blocking. In R. J. Corsini (Ed.), *Ency. Psy.* New York: Wiley.

BOHR'S COMPLEMENTARITY PRINCIPLE. See VISION/SIGHT, THEORIES OF.

BOTTOM-UP PROCESSING THEORIES. *Bottom-up theories* is a general term referring to the direction of processing of information in any given aspect of *perceptual* or *cognitive theory*. For example, in *object perception theory*, the analysis of objects into parts is called *bottom-up processing* because processing starts with basic units, and one's perception is then built on the foundation laid by these units (Goldstein, 1996). Object perception is influenced not only by the nature of the units that make up objects but also by the observer's knowledge of the world (cf: *top-down processing*). In *cognitive theory*, similarly, *bottom-up processing* refers to the determination of a process primarily by the physical stimulus. The notion is that observers deal with the information in a given situation by beginning with the "raw" stimulus and then "work their way up" to the more abstract, cognitive operations (Reber, 1995). Thus, taking sensory data into the perceptual system first by the receptors and then sending it upward for extraction and analysis of relevant information is called *bottom-up processing* or *data-driven processing*. Sensations of visual features and perceptions of organized objects are largely the result of *bottom-up processes* (Zimbardo & Weber, 1994). See also INFORMATION/INFORMATION-PROCESSING THEORY; PATTERN/OBJECT RECOGNITION THEORY; PERCEPTION (I. GENERAL), THEORIES OF; PERCEPTION (II. COMPARATIVE APPRAISAL), THEORIES OF; TOP-DOWN PROCESSING/THEORIES.

REFERENCES

Zimbardo, P., & Weber, A. (1994). *Psychology*. New York: HarperCollins.
Reber, A. (1995). *The Penguin dictionary of psychology*. New York: Penguin Books.
Goldstein, E. (1996). *Sensation and perception*. Pacific Grove, CA: Brooks/Cole.

BOWDITCH'S LAW. See MULLER'S DOCTRINE OF SPECIFIC NERVE ENERGIES.

BRAIN-FIELD THEORY. See APPARENT MOVEMENT, PRINCIPLES OF.

BROADBENT'S FILTER MODEL. See ATTENTION, LAWS/THEORIES OF.

BRUCE EFFECT. This phenomenon describes the influence of social odor communication from one organism to another, where a female mouse that has mated with one male will display a blockage of pregnancy (called the *Bruce effect*) if she is exposed to a strange male, or the odor of a strange male, a few days later (Dewsbury, 1994). The *Bruce effect* was first observed in mice by Hilda Bruce, where the termination of a pregnancy was brought about by substances in the urine of a virile male mouse other than the one that impregnated the female. Having thus eliminated the offspring of the other male, the animal was now able to impregnate the female himself and thus increase the likelihood of passing his own genes on to future generations (Reber, 1995). Other related chemical signals that facilitate communication among members of a species are pheromones and allomones (chemical substances that signal within, and among, a species messages of sexual receptivity, alarm, or territoriality). Female rats emit a maternal pheromone that helps the offspring find them (Leon, 1974). Also, female rats that are housed near each other tend to have estrous cycles that become synchronized over time; a similar menstrual synchrony has been found between human females who live together (Graham & McGrew, 1980). See also COMMUNICATION THEORY; OLFACTION/SMELL, THEORIES OF.

REFERENCES

Wilson, E. (1963). Pheromones. *Sci. Amer., 208*, 100–115.

Leon, M. (1974). Maternal pheromone. *Phys. Beh., 13*, 441–453.

Sebeok, T. (Ed.) (1977). *How animals communicate*. Bloomington: Indiana University Press.

Smith, W. (1977). *The behavior of communicating*. Cambridge: Harvard University Press.

Brown, R. (1979). Mammalian social odors: A critical review. *Adv. Stud. Beh., 10*, 103–162.

Graham, C., & McGrew, W. (1980). Menstrual synchrony in female undergraduates living on a coeducational campus. *Psychoneuroendocrinology, 5*, 245–252.

Dewsbury, D. (1994). Animal communication. In R. J. Corsini (Ed.), *Ency. Psy*. New York: Wiley.

Reber, A. (1995). *The Penguin dictionary of psychology*. New York: Penguin Books.

BRUNER'S THEORY OF INSTRUCTION. See ALGORITHMIC-HEURISTIC THEORY.

BRUNSWIK'S PROBABILISTIC FUNCTIONALISM THEORY. See PERCEPTION (II. COMPARATIVE APPRAISAL), THEORIES OF.

BUNSEN-ROSCOE LAW. = Bloch's law = reciprocity law. This generalized principle developed by the German chemist and physicist Robert Wilhelm Bunsen (1811–1899) and the English chemist Sir Henry Enfield Roscoe (1833–1915) states that the absolute threshold for vision is a reciprocity relation and multiplicative function of the intensity and duration of the stimulus. For example, a flash of light of short duration, presented to the eye under adaptation, provides a given effect that can be achieved by the reciprocal manipulation of duration and luminance of the flash. This means that the given effect may be produced by an intense flash that acts for a short time or by a dim light that acts for a relatively long time. This relationship, when applied to many photochemical systems, is known as the *Bunsen–Roscoe law* (also called the *photographic law* when used in the context of the effect of light on photographic emulsion; Zusne, 1987). For instance, when chlorine and hydrogen are combined in the presence of light, the extent of the photochemical action varies inversely with the distance from the light source and is directly proportional to its intensity. However, when this relationship is applied to studies of human vision, it is sometimes known as *Bloch's law* (Graham, 1965; Bartlett, 1965). Considerable confirming evidence has accrued over the years that verifies the applicability of *Bloch's law* for threshold determination with durations of one millisecond or longer (e.g., Blondel & Rey, 1911; Karn, 1936), and, as long as the area of stimulation is small, and the duration is not excessive, a further critical factor in the law is the total energy involved in the stimulation for very short durations (Brindley, 1952). Another synonym for the *Bunsen–Roscoe law* is the *reciprocity law*, which states that response is determined by the product of the intensity and duration of the stimulus, independently of the magnitude of either one alone, and holds within rather narrow limits for various visual and other biological phenomena (cf: *Broca–Sulzer effect*, also called *Brucke effect* and *Brewster effect*—a flash of light appears brighter than a steady light of the same intensity; Zusne, 1987). See also RICCO'S/PIPER'S LAWS.

REFERENCES

Bloch, A. (1885). Experiences sur la vision. *Soc. Bio. Mem., Paris, 37*, 493–495.

Blondel, A., & Rey, J. (1911). Sur la perception des lumieres breves a la limite de leur portee. *J. de Phys., 1*, 530–550.

Hartline, H. (1934). Intensity and duration in the excitation of single photoreceptor units. *J. Cell. Comp. Physio., 5*, 229–247.

Warren, H. (Ed.) (1934). *Dictionary of psychology*. Cambridge, MA: Houghton Mifflin.

Karn, H. (1936). Area and the intensity-time relation in the fovea. *J. Gen. Psy., 14*, 360–369.

Brindley, G. (1952). The Bunsen-Roscoe law for the human eye at very short durations. *J. Physio., 118*, 135–139.

Bartlett, N. (1965). Thresholds as dependent on some energy relations and characteristics of the subject. In C. Graham (Ed.), *Vision and visual perception*. New York: Wiley.

Graham, C. (1965). Some fundamental data. In C. Graham (Ed.), *Vision and visual perception*. New York: Wiley.

Zusne, L. (1987). *Eponyms in psychology*. Westport, CT: Greenwood Press.

Muir, H. (Ed.) (1994). *Larousse dictionary of scientists*. New York: Larousse.

BYSTANDER INTERVENTION EFFECT. This phenomenon/model was described by Bibb Latane and John Darley (1968, 1970) and suggests that bystanders are engaged in a series of decisions, rather than a single decision, as whether to intervene or not in situations when help is needed by another person: (1) the bystander must notice that something is happening; (2) the bystander must interpret the happening as an emergency event; (3) the bystander must decide that she or he has a responsibility to become involved; (4) the bystander must decide on the form of assistance to give the "victim"; and (5) the bystander must make a decision as to how to implement the previous decision. Research findings from the laboratory and field settings indicate the importance that social factors play in the *bystander effect* where the actions of others in the situation (such as passivity versus activity on the part of other onlookers) may serve as cues to the bystander's involvement. The *bystander effect* concerning "altruism," "pro-social behavior," or "helping behavior" refers to the finding that the more people who are present when help is needed, the less likely any one of them is to provide assistance. Even when a bystander interprets the event to be an emergency, the presence of other people may help to "diffuse responsibility" for taking any action. Factors that relate to the bystander's personality and demographic characteristics have been found to provide a poorer prediction of bystander behavior than do the particular features of the "emergency" situation (Greenberg, 1994). See also ALLPORT'S CONFORMITY HYPOTHESIS; DECISION-MAKING THEORIES; DEINDIVIDUATION THEORY.

REFERENCES

Latane, B., & Darley, J. (1968). Group inhibition of bystander intervention in emergencies. *J. Pers. Soc. Psy., 10,* 215–221.

Latane, B., & Darley, J. (1970). *The unresponsive bystander: Why doesn't he help?* New York: Appleton-Century-Crofts.

Bar-Tal, D. (1976). *Prosocial behavior: Theory and research.* New York: Halsted.

Eisenberg-Berg, N. (1982). *Development of prosocial behavior.* New York: Academic Press.

Dovidio, J. (1984). Helping behavior and altruism: An empirical and conceptual overview. In L. Berkowitz (Ed.), *Advances in experimental social psychology.* Vol. 17. New York: Academic Press.

Bar-Tal, D. (1994). Helping behavior. In R. J. Corsini (Ed.), *Ency. Psy.* New York: Wiley.

Greenberg, M. (1994). Bystander involvement. In R. J. Corsini (Ed.), *Ency. Psy.* New York: Wiley.

Reber, A. (1995). *The Penguin dictionary of psychology.* New York: Penguin Books.

C

CANALIZATION HYPOTHESIS. See MURPHY'S BIOSOCIAL THEORY.

CANNON/CANNON-BARD THEORY. The American physiologist Walter B. Cannon (1871–1945) is given the major initial credit for this theory, and the American psychologist Philip Bard (1898–1977) is given partial recognition for his research support in its development and refinement (Cannon, 1915, 1928, 1932; Bard, 1934a, b, 1950). Another name for this theory is the *thalamic theory* of emotion (Cannon, 1931). The *Cannon–Bard theory* proposes that the integration of emotional expressiveness is controlled and directed by the thalamus, which sends relevant excitation patterns to the cortex at the same time that the hypothalamus controls the behavior, and emphasizes the simultaneous arousal of both the central and autonomic nervous systems. Cannon argued that the function of the autonomic nervous system arousal was to prepare the organism to deal with the immediate event—to fight or to flee, for example. An event that might cause harm generates arousal (an "emergency response"), which prepares the individual to cope with the event. Other alternative names for the *Cannon–Bard theory*, therefore, have been the *fight or flight theory* and the *emergency theory*. The *Cannon–Bard theory* was based on evolutionary survival value for the organism where increased heart rate, respiration, and so on permitted it to respond more quickly and strongly and, thereby, increased its chances of survival. The *Cannon–Bard theory* was a predominant opponent to the earlier *James–Lange theory* and argued that emotionality results from a removal of the inhibition that is normally exerted by the neocortex upon the thalamus. The neocortex, according to the Cannon–Bard approach, ordinarily suppresses the activity of the thalamus, but if emotion-eliciting stimuli reach the cortex, impulses are sent downward and act to release the inhibitory influences. Subsequently, the thalamus signals the neocortex to initiate the emotional experience while it also signals the rest of the body to begin the pattern of behavior associated with the specific emotion. The *Cannon–Bard theory* would predict that the removal of an animal's thalamus in a laboratory procedure called "decortication" would reduce its emotional hyperreactivity, but research showed this not to be the case. Thus, the research findings did not confirm a key feature of the theory. However, the *Cannon–Bard theory* has been important historically for two reasons: (1) it focused attention on possible central nervous system structures that may handle emotionality; and (2) it focused attention on the possible ways the neocortex may interact with structures in the lower brain regions. Today, the Cannon–Bard idea of cortical-subcortical interaction and involvement in emotionality is reflected in modern emotion theories. The difficulty with the *Cannon–Bard theory* was that it concentrated too heavily on the thalamus rather than the hypothalamus, and other physiological-behavioral research showed that the hypothalamus seems to dominate emotional behavior (Levinthal, 1983). See also EMOTION, THEORIES/LAWS OF; JAMES-LANGE/LANGE-JAMES THEORY OF EMOTIONS.

REFERENCES

Cannon, W. (1915). *Bodily changes in pain, hunger, fear, and rage: An account of recent researches into the function of emotional excitement.* New York: Appleton-Century-Crofts.

Cannon, W. (1928). The mechanism of emotional disturbance of bodily functions. *New Eng. J. Med., 198,* 877–884.

Cannon, W. (1931). Again the James-Lange and the thalamic theories of emotion. *Psy. Rev., 38,* 281–295.

Cannon, W. (1932). *The wisdom of the body.* New York: Norton.

Bard, P. (1934a). Emotion: I. The neuro-humoral basis of emotional reactions. In C. Murchison (Ed.), *Handbk. Gen. Exp. Psy.* Worcester, MA: Clark University Press.

Bard, P. (1934b). On emotional expression after decortication with some remarks on certain theoretical views. *Psy. Rev., 41,* 309–329, 424–449.

Cannon, W. (1936). Gray's objective theory of emotion. *Psy. Rev., 43,* 100–106.

Cannon, W., & Rosenblueth, A. (1937). *Autonomic neuro-effector systems.* New York: Macmillan.

Lashley, K. (1938). The thalamus and emotion. *Psy. Rev., 45,* 42–61.

Arnold, M. (1945). Physiological differentiation of emotional states. *Psy. Rev., 52,* 35–48.

Duffy, E. (1948). Leeper's "motivational theory of emotions." *Psy. Rev., 55,* 324–328.

Leeper, R. (1948). A motivational theory of emotion to replace "emotion as disorganized response." *Psy. Rev., 55,* 5–21.

Webb, W. (1948). A motivational theory of emotion. *Psy. Rev., 55,* 329–335.

Cannon, W., & Rosenblueth, A. (1949). *The supersensitivity of denervated structures: A law of denervation.* New York: Macmillan.

Young, P. T. (1949). Emotion as disorganized response—A reply to Professor Leeper. *Psy. Rev., 56,* 184–191.

Bard, P. (1950). Central nervous mechanisms for the expression of anger. In M. Reymert (Ed.), *The second international symposium on feelings and emotions.* New York: McGraw-Hill.

Levinthal, C. (1983). *Introduction to physiological psychology*. Englewood Cliffs, NJ: Prentice-Hall.

CAPALDI'S THEORY. With the development in the contemporary conception of *reinforcement* and the *law of effect* in the last 20 years (e.g., Premack, 1965; Timberlake & Allison, 1974; Timberlake, 1980), there have also been changes in the interpretation of the concepts of *extinction* and *nonreward* where a number of new hypotheses have been proposed. For example, E. J. Capaldi's (1966, 1967) *sequential patterning theory* of nonreward and the *partial reinforcement extinction effect* are refinements of two earlier hypotheses: the *discrimination/ generalization hypothesis*, which supposes that subjects will persist in responding as long as they cannot discriminate the extinction series from a run of nonreinforcements embedded within the training series, and the *stimulus aftereffects hypothesis*, which supposes that reward and nonreward events on one trial set up distinctive stimulus traces that persist over the intertrial interval and are part of the stimulus complex at the time the next response occurs (Sheffield, 1949). The *stimulus aftereffects hypothesis* assumes that during partial reinforcement training, persisting stimulus traces from nonreinforced trials become conditioned to the next response because of frequent reinforced trials following a nonreinforced trial, and lead to stimuli arising during extinction which maintains responding (Bower & Hilgard, 1981). *Capaldi's theory* deviates from the older *aftereffects hypothesis* concerning the time decay of information about the reinforcing event of the prior trial. The *aftereffects hypothesis* suggested that reward and nonreward events set up relatively short-term stimulus traces that decay after a few minutes, but this approach has no way to explain the *partial reinforcement effects* that have been obtained with widely spaced trials (such as one trial every 24 hours). *Capaldi's theory*, on the other hand, assumes that a trace of the prior reward or nonreward event persists indefinitely until it is modified or replaced by the next event to happen in the goal box of this situation. For Capaldi, the prior reward or nonreward stimuli are now available in something like a ''memory,'' which is reactivated when the animal is placed back in the stimulus or testing situation. This ''memory'' interpretation is somewhat more heuristic than the stimulus trace interpretation (Bower & Hilgard, 1981). Capaldi (1967) uses his hypothesis to explain a wide range of different scheduling phenomena such as the accelerated extinction and relearning that occur in multiple blocks of extinction and acquisition trials, the effects of patterned schedules and their discrimination, the effects of reward delay, the contrast effects in shifts of reward magnitude, the effects of different intertrial intervals, human probability learning, and application to *statistical learning theory* (Koteskey, 1972). There is current consensus among researchers that *Capaldi's sequential theory* is the best one available for predicting extinction resistance produced by most reinforcement schedules. However, a theoretical problem that remains to be solved is the combination of the *sequential hypothesis* with the concepts of frustrative reward and inhibition in order to produce a more general theory of extinction and nonreinforcement (Bower & Hilgard, 1981). See also AMSEL'S HYPOTHESIS/THEORY; PREMACK'S PRINCIPLE/LAW; TOLMAN'S THEORY.

REFERENCES

Sheffield, V. (1949). Extinction as a function of partial reinforcement and distribution of practice. *J. Exp., Psy., 39*, 511–526.

Meehl, P. (1950). On the circularity of the law of effect. *Psy. Bull., 47*, 52–75.

Sheffield, V. (1950). Resistance to extinction as a function of the distribution of extinction trials. *J. Exp. Psy., 40*, 305–313.

Premack, D. (1965). Reinforcement theory. In M. Jones (Ed.), *Nebraska symposium on motivation*. Lincoln: University of Nebraska Press.

Capaldi, E. J. (1966). Partial reinforcement: An hypothesis of sequential effects. *Psy. Rev., 73*, 459–477.

Capaldi, E. J. (1967). A sequential hypothesis of instrumental learning. In K. Spence & J. Spence (Eds.), *The psychology of learning and motivation: Advances in research and theory*. Vol. 1. New York: Academic Press.

Leonard, D. (1969). Amount and sequence of reward in partial and continuous reinforcement. *J. Comp. Physio. Psy., 67*, 204–211.

Capaldi, E. J., & Capaldi, E. D. (1970). Magnitude of partial reward, irregular reward schedules, and a 24–hour ITI: A test of several hypotheses. *J. Comp. Physio. Psy., 72*, 203–209.

Koteskey, R. (1972). A stimulus sampling model of the partial reinforcement effect. *Psy. Rev., 79*, 161–171.

Timberlake, W., & Allison, J. (1974). Response deprivation: An empirical approach to instrumental performance. *Psy. Rev., 81*, 146–164.

Timberlake, W. (1980). A molar equilibrium theory of learned performance. In G. Bower (Ed.), *The psychology of learning and motivation*. Vol. 14. New York: Academic Press.

Bower, G., & Hilgard, E. (1981). *Theories of learning*. Englewood Cliffs, NJ: Prentice-Hall.

CAREER THEORIES. See WORK/CAREER/OCCUPATION, THEORIES OF.

CATECHOLAMINE HYPOTHESIS/THEORY OF DEPRESSION. See DEPRESSION, THEORIES OF.

CATTELL'S THEORY OF PERSONALITY. The British-born American psychologist Raymond Bernard Cattell (1905–   ) developed a comprehensive theory of personality based on the statistical procedure of factor analysis introduced by Charles Spearman (1904, 1927) and expanded by L. L. Thurstone (1931, 1948) in the formulation of multiple factor analysis. The factor analytic approach typically begins with a large number of scores derived from tests, then applies a statistical technique to such *surface* scores to determine the underlying *basic* factors whose operation theoretically accounts for the variation in the large number of initial scores. Once the *basic* factors are identified, the theorist can then develop ways of measuring the factors in a more efficient manner. Thus, factor analysis is a procedure in which variables may be formulated to account for the diverse complexity of *surface* behaviors (e.g., Harman, 1967). Personality is defined by Cattell as "that which permits a prediction of what a person will do in a given situation" (Cattell, 1950, p. 2) and is considered to be a complex and differentiated structure of *traits* ("mental structures" inferred from observed behavior). Cattell distinguishes between the concepts of *surface traits*—clusters of overt variables that have common aspects, such as a syndrome of behaviors— and *source traits*—underlying variables that determine surface variables, such as physiological and temperamental factors; between *environmental-mold traits*—traits resulting from external environmental conditions—and *constitutional traits*—traits resulting from internal/hereditary conditions; and between *dynamic traits*—which set the person into action toward some goal—*ability traits*—effectiveness of the person in reaching a goal—and *temperament traits*— constitutional response aspects such as energy, speed, and emotional reactivity. Cattell identified 16 bipolar personality factors (i.e., source traits of the *core personality*) that are derived from testing protocols such as a person's life record and self-rating questionnaires: outgoing-reserved, more intelligent-less intelligent, stable-emotional, assertive-humble, happy-go-lucky–sober, conscientious-expedient, venturesome-shy, tender-minded–tough-minded, suspicious-trusting, imaginative-practical, shrewd-forthright, apprehensive-placid, conservative-experimenting, group-dependent–self-sufficient, uncontrolled-controlled, and relaxed-tense (Cattell, 1966; Cattell, Eber, & Tatsuoka, 1978; Cattell, 1990). Based on the premise that personality may be described in terms of ability, temperament, and other types of traits, Cattell developed a *specification equation* that implies a multidimensional representation of the individual within a given psychological situation to yield a predicted response. Such specification equations have practical applications in settings such as employment screening situations and in academic achievement contexts (Cattell, 1957). The important *dynamic traits* in *Cattell's theory* are "attitudes" (observable or measurable expression of one's dynamic structure); "ergs" (biologically based drives; cf: McDougall, 1908); and "sentiments" (environmental-mold, acquired attitude structures). A *dynamic lattice* is Cattell's (pictorial) representation of the inter-relationships among the *dynamic traits* and forms a pattern of "subsidiation" where, generally, attitudes are subsidiary to sentiments, sentiments are subsidiary to ergs, and ergs are the basic driving forces in the personality. One of the most important of Cattell's "sentiments" is the "master" sentiment of *self-sentiment*, which is similar to Freud's concepts of *ego* and *superego* and G. Allport's concept of *ego* and has the crucial role of integrating the different aspects of the personality (Cattell, 1966). Cattell has proposed that a useful way of assessing the degree of conflict that a person may have in a specific situation is to state the *specification equation* that expresses the involvement of the person's ergs and sentiments in a given course of action. Various other concepts in *Cat-

tell's theory (e.g., *states, roles, sets*) have been described (Cattell, 1963a) and have been investigated, also, by the factor analytic technique. Cattell developed an interesting method for assessing the relative weight of genetic and environmental factors in traits called *multiple abstract variance analyses (MAVA)* (Cattell, 1960) where initial results showed negative correlations between heredity and environmental factors. Cattell interpreted this result as evidence for a *law of coercion to the biosocial mean*, which refers to the tendency for environmental influences to oppose the systematic expression of genetic variation (e.g., when parents require that their two different children behave in the same way, even though one child is outgoing, and the other one is bashful). Cattell has extended his concepts of traits from his *personality theory* to descriptions of group behavior (called *syntality*; Cattell, 1948), including the behavior of nations (Cattell, 1949; Cattell & Gorsuch, 1965). Evaluations and reviews of Cattell's work have indicated a mixture of both admiration and uneasiness (cf: Sells, 1959; Becker, 1960; Gordon, 1966). *Cattell's personality theory* may not be popular in the sense that S. Freud's, C. Rogers', H. S. Sullivan's, G. Allport's, or H. Murray's theories have been popular, but it has attracted an active band of adherents, many of whom appreciate the widespread empirical grounding and economy of factor analytic formulations that his theory contains (Hall & Lindzey, 1978). See also PERSONALITY THEORIES.

REFERENCES

Spearman, C. (1904). "General intelligence" objectively determined and measured. *Amer. J. Psy., 15*, 201–293.

McDougall, W. (1908). *An introduction to social psychology.* Boston: Luce.

Spearman, C. (1927). *Abilities of man.* New York: Macmillan.

Thurstone, L. (1931). Multiple factor analysis. *Psy. Rev., 38*, 406–427.

Cattell, R., & Luborsky, L. (1947). Personality factors in response to humor. *J. Abn. Soc. Psy., 42*, 402–421.

Cattell, R. (1948). Concepts and methods in the measurement of group syntality. *Psy. Rev., 55*, 48–63.

Thurstone, L. (1948). Psychological implications of factor analysis. *Amer. Psy., 3*, 402–408.

Cattell, R. (1949). The dimensions of culture patterns by factorization of national character. *J. Abn. Soc. Psy., 44*, 443–469.

Cattell, R. (1950). *Personality: A systematic, theoretical, and factual study.* New York: McGraw-Hill.

Cattell, R., & Stice, G. (1954). Four formulae for selecting leaders on the basis of personality. *Hum. Rel., 7*, 493–507.

Cattell, R. (1957). *Personality and motivation: Structure and measurement.* New York: Harcourt Brace Jovanovich.

Sells, S. (1959). Structured measurement of personality and motivation: A review of contributions of Raymond B. Cattell. *J. Clin. Psy., 15*, 3–21.

Becker, W. (1960). The matching of behavior rating and questionnaire personality factors. *Psy. Bull., 57*, 201–212.

Cattell, R. (1960). The multiple abstract variance analysis equations and solutions: For nature-nurture research on continuous variables. *Psy. Rev., 67*, 353–372.

Cattell, R. (1963a). Personality, role, mood, and situation-perception: A unifying theory of modulators. *Psy. Rev., 70*, 1–18.

Cattell, R. (1963b). Theory of fluid and crystallized intelligence: A critical experiment. *J. Ed. Psy., 54*, 1–22.

Cattell, R. (1964). *Personality and social psychology*. San Diego: Knapp.

Cattell, R., & Gorsuch, R. (1965). The definition and measurement of national morale and morality. *J. Soc. Psy., 67*, 77–96.

Cattell, R. (1966). *The scientific analysis of personality*. Chicago: Aldine.

Cattell, R., & Tatro, D. (1966). The personality factors, objectively measured, which distinguish psychotics from normals. *Beh. Res. Ther., 4*, 39–51.

Gordon, J. (1966). Archetypical, Germanic, factorial, brilliant and contradictory. *Contemp. Psy., 11*, 236–238.

Harman, H. (1967). *Modern factor analysis*. Chicago: University of Chicago Press.

Cattell, R. (1971). *Abilities: Their structure, growth, and action*. Boston: Houghton Mifflin.

Cattell, R., Eber, H., & Tatsuoka, M. (1978). *Handbook for the Sixteen Personality Factor Questionnaire (16PF)*. Champaign, IL: Institute for Personality and Ability Testing.

Hall, C., & Lindzey, G. (1978). *Theories of personality*. New York: Wiley.

Cattell, R. (1979–1980). *Personality and learning theory*. New York: Springer.

Cattell, R. (1990). Advances in Cattellian personality theory. In L. Pervin (Ed.), *Handbook of personality: Theory and research*. New York: Guilford Press.

CELL ASSEMBLY THEORY. See PERCEPTION (II. COMPARATIVE APPRAISAL), THEORIES OF.

CHAINING, LAW OF. See SKINNER'S DESCRIPTIVE BEHAVIOR THEORY.

CHANCE, LAWS OF. See PROBABILITY THEORY/LAWS.

CHARPENTIER'S LAW. See VISION/SIGHT, THEORIES OF.

CHEMICAL PROFILE THEORY. See HUNGER, THEORIES OF.

CHOICE, THEORY OF. See DEMBER-EARL THEORY OF CHOICE/ PREFERENCE.

CHOMSKY'S PSYCHOLINGUISTIC THEORY. The American psychologist, linguist, and philosopher Noam Avram Chomsky (1928–) formulated a *theory of psycholinguistics* that views language as genetically determined where it develops in ways similar to other bodily organs (Chomsky, 1957, 1964, 1965, 1966, 1968, 1972, 1980). According to Chomsky's prominent theory, the human brain is preprogrammed by a cognitive mechanism called the *language acqui-sition device (LAD)*, which allows individuals to generate grammatically correct sentences in a universal or culture-free manner. Chomsky believes that humans have an innate capacity for understanding and emitting language behaviors. Only humans have language acquisition capabilities (a "species-specific" feature), and all human languages share a common logical structure (a "species-uniform" feature). Chomsky's conceptualization of a *transformational generative gram-mar (TGG)* is an important advancement over the older viewpoint of language acquisition known as *phase-structure grammars* (i.e., a formal system for ana-lyzing the structure of a sentence by assigning labels, such as noun, noun phrase, verb, etc. to parts of the sentence). Transformational grammar is grounded in the hypothesization of several necessary components (Reber, 1995): *semantics*— the rules for "meaning"; *deep structure*—the representation of underlying "meaning"; *transformational deviation*—the rules for mapping deep structures on a *surface structure* (i.e., consistency of the sequence of elements, such as phonemes, syllables, words, phrases, and sentences that constitute a written or spoken message); and *phonological*—the rules for providing the appropriate sound patterns, or phonetic sounds, of the language. Thus, based on his intro-duction of the important distinction between *deep* and *surface* structure (Chom-sky, 1957, 1965) into psycholinguistics, Chomsky's *TGG* is a system that integrates both the deep (logical) and the surface (phonetic) structure of lan-guage. *Chomsky's theory of language acquisition* has been challenged most no-tably by proponents of behaviorism (e.g., Skinner, 1957) and the behavioristic viewpoint concerning verbal learning (cf: Bower & Hilgard, 1981). According to the behavioristic approach, children learn to talk through the processes of classical and operant conditioning. This approach helps to explain why one child may be more skilled in the use of language than another child. Chomsky's cognitivist approach, on the other hand, helps to explain why children all over the world follow similar or invariant sequences of language development (cf: Chomsky, 1959). While both the behaviorist and the cognitivist viewpoints can account for some of the data of language acquisition, a third perspective em-phasizes the "interaction" between infant and caregiver, between one person and another, and between the person and the environment as the heart of lan-guage learning (Bruner, 1977; Berger, 1994; cf: *neurolinguistic theory*, Lamen-della, 1979; Haynie, 1994; and *semiotic theory*, Percy, 1961; Quagliano, 1994). Chomsky's notions concerning transformational grammar, although they revo-lutionized the field of linguistics, have not provided all the answers to the many problems of language acquisition. Psychologists, while maintaining many of Chomsky's ideas, have moved on to new concerns (Houston, 1981). See also SKINNER'S DESCRIPTIVE BEHAVIOR/OPERANT CONDITIONING THE-ORY; WHORF–SAPIR HYPOTHESIS/THEORY.

REFERENCES

Chomsky, N. (1957). *Syntactic structures*. The Hague: Mouton.

Skinner, B. F. (1957). *Verbal behavior*. New York: Appleton-Century-Crofts.

Chomsky, N. (1959). A review of Skinner's "Verbal Behavior," *Language, 35*, 26–58.

Percy, W. (1961). The symbolic structure of interpersonal processes. *Psychiatry, 24*, 39–52.

Vygotsky, L. (1962). *Thought and language*. Cambridge: M.I.T. Press.

Chomsky, N. (1964). *Current issues in linguistic theory*. The Hague: Mouton.

Chomsky, N. (1965). *Aspects of the theory of syntax*. Cambridge: M.I.T. Press.

Chomsky, N. (1966). *Topics in the theory of generative grammar*. The Hague: Mouton.

Smith, F., & Miller, G. (Eds.) (1966). *The genesis of language: A psycholinguistic approach*. Cambridge: M.I.T. Press.

Chomsky, N. (1968). *Language and the mind*. New York: Harcourt, Brace, & World.

McNeill, D. (1970). *The acquisition of language: The study of developmental psycholinguistics*. New York: Harper & Row.

Chomsky, N. (1972). *Studies on semantics in generative grammar*. The Hague: Mouton.

Dale, P. (1972). *Language development: Structure and function*. New York: Holt.

Bruner, J. (1977). Early social interaction and language acquisition. In H. Schaffer (Ed.), *Studies in mother–infant interaction*. London: Academic Press.

DeVilliers, J., & DeVilliers, P. (1978). *Language acquisition*. Cambridge: Harvard University Press.

Lamendella, J. (1979). Neurolinguistics. *Ann. Rev. Anthro., 8*, 373–391.

Chomsky, N. (1980). *Rules and representations*. New York: Columbia University Press.

Bower, G., & Hilgard, E. (1981). *Theories of learning*. Englewood Cliffs, NJ: Prentice-Hall.

Houston, J. (1981). *Fundamentals of learning and memory*. New York: Academic Press.

Berger, K. (1994). Language development. In R. J. Corsini (Ed.), *Ency. Psy.* New York: Wiley.

Haynie, N. (1994). Neurolinguistics. In R. J. Corsini (Ed.), *Ency. Psy.* New York: Wiley.

Quagliano, A. (1994). Signs and symbols. In R. J. Corsini (Ed.), *Ency. Psy.* New York: Wiley.

Siguan, M. (1994). Psycholinguistics. In R. J. Corsini (Ed.), *Ency. Psy.* New York: Wiley.

Reber, A. (1995). *The Penguin dictionary of psychology*. New York: Penguin Books.

CLASSICAL CONDITIONING, LAWS OF. See PAVLOVIAN CONDITIONING PRINCIPLES/LAWS/THEORIES.

CLASSICAL STRENGTH THEORY. See DECISION-MAKING THEORIES.

CLASSICAL THEORY OF SENSORY DISCRIMINATION. See NEURAL QUANTUM THEORY.

CLEVER HANS EFFECT/PHENOMENON. Hans was the name of a "talented" horse, among the world-famous Elberfeld horses of Germany, that was trained by Wilhelm von Osten of Berlin (Block, 1904; Pfungst, 1911; Warren,

1934; Rosenthal, 1965). Hans' talent was his ability to perform some rather remarkable mental tasks such as addition, subtraction, division, multiplication, obtaining square roots, and spelling various words. After many people were thoroughly mystified by Hans' abilities, the German psychologist Oskar Pfungst tested Hans and ultimately discovered that the horse was actually performing and solving his mathematical and mental problems by responding to subtle and totally unintentional, very tiny visual cues that were provided by von Osten (such as the questioner's bending forward slightly after presenting the horse with a problem and bending backward and upward slightly when the correct tap of the hoof was reached). That is, the horse's method was to "count up" to the answer of a problem by stamping his hoof the required number of times. Hans "knew" when to stop stamping by taking his cues from the humans around him who unconsciously responded with changes in breathing patterns and bodily positions. Thus, Hans was simply responding to visual cues that were, to him, the "start" and "stop" signals for hoof tapping. The term *Clever Hans effect/ phenomenon* has come to stand for communication that is transmitted through slight, unintentional, nonverbal cues. Prior to Pfungst's (1911) work, such cues had not been reported in the scientific/research literature, yet today they are recognized as unconscious signals in posture, gesture, and vocal tone emitted by individuals even as they speak their language (Ambady & Rosenthal, 1992, 1993; Scheflen, 1964). The *Clever Hans effect* may be an important concern in psychological experiments where the experimenter's expectations, hopes, habits, and personal characteristics can influence, unwittingly, the outcome of a research investigation (Rosenthal, 1976). Such conditions of unintentional cuing are also called *experimenter effects*, *experimenter bias*, *Rosenthal effect*, or *Der Kluge Hans* (Reber, 1995). See also EXPERIMENTER EFFECTS.

REFERENCES

Block, P. (1904). Der Kluge Hans. *Berliner Tageblatt*, August 15, p. 1.

Pfungst, O. (1911). *The horse of Mr. von Osten*. C. Rahn (Trans.). New York: Holt.

Warren, H. (Ed.) (1934). *Dictionary of psychology* Cambridge, MA: Houghton Mifflin.

Scheflen, A. (1964). The significance of posture in communication systems. *Psychiatry, 27*, 316–331.

Rosenthal, R. (Ed.) (1965). *Clever Hans: The horse of Mr. von Osten*. New York: Holt, Rinehart, & Winston.

Rosenthal, R. (1976). *Experimenter effects in behavioral research*. New York: Appleton-Century-Crofts.

Ambady, N., & Rosenthal, R. (1992). Thin slices of expressive behavior as predictors of interpersonal consequences: A meta-analysis. *Psy. Bull., 111*, 256–274.

Ambady, N., & Rosenthal, R. (1993). Half a minute: Predicting teacher evaluations from thin slices of nonverbal behavior and physical attractiveness. *J. Pers. Soc. Psy., 64*, 431–441.

Reber, A. (1995). *The Penguin dictionary of psychology*. New York: Penguin Books.

CLOSURE, PRINCIPLE OF. See GESTALT THEORY/LAWS.

COCKTAIL-PARTY PHENOMENON. See ATTENTION, LAWS/PRIN-CIPLES/THEORIES OF.

CODING THEORIES. In general, a *code* is a system of symbols or signals representing information. Examples of codes are semaphore signals, magnetic fields on a recording tape, spoken English, written German, and the electrical zeroes and ones in a computer's memory chip. As long as one knows the rules of a code, a message can be converted from one medium to another without losing any information. Although the precise rules that sensory systems use to transmit information to the brain are not known, it is known that they take two forms (Carlson, 1990): *anatomical coding* (activity of particular neurons) and *temporal coding* (time or rate of neuron firing). The term *coding* is used in many content areas of psychology when examining and describing various aspects of stimuli and responses. In sensation, the sensory organs collect environmental physical energies as input and prepare the stimuli for the next process, called *transduction* of the stimulus energy into neural impulse form, after which coding occurs at higher neural centers. In this way, stimulus information is translated or coded into the different aspects of sensation that are experiences. Some of the coded information concerns the factors of stimulus intensity (e.g., a loud versus a quiet sound) and stimulus quality (e.g., a high pitch versus a low pitch sound). Coding occurs in the processing of certain kinds of visual information, but individuals also have a verbal "channel" for processing information contained in words and ideas. Paivio (1982, 1991) refers to the process of coding information by both visual and verbal means as a *dual-coding system* or *theory*. Coding is used also in the area of cognitive psychology to describe the mechanisms of memory where concepts such as "encoding," "recoding," "decoding," "chunks," "subjective units," "functional stimuli," and "coding responses" are described, and where coding processes and responses need not be conscious or reportable (e.g., Melton & Martin, 1972). In one case, the *encoding specificity hypothesis/principle* refers to the generalization that the initial encoding (i.e., the process of choosing the information to be retained and transforming that information into a form that can be saved) of learned material will reflect the influence of the context in which the learning took place (Tulving & Thomson, 1973; Bower & Hilgard, 1981; Reber, 1995). In terms of terminological analysis and experimental methodology, the phenomenon of *coding* is a construct that is defined by *converging operations* (Garner, Hake, & Eriksen, 1956) where it is viewed as a system for representing thoughts of any type, including schemata, propositions, concepts, percepts, ideas, images, segments, features, and "knowing" responses. Thus, there are many attributes to stimuli, and not all of them are involved in every memory, action, or thought, but cortical regions provide the neural *coding* processes necessary to register one's experiences (Anderson, 1994). See also NEURON/NEURAL/NERVE THEORY; INFORMATION/INFORMATION-PROCESSING THEORY; MEMORY, THEORIES OF.

REFERENCES

Garner, W., Hake, H., & Eriksen, C. (1956). Operationism and the concept of perception. *Psy. Rev., 63,* 149–159.

Sternberg, S. (1966). High speed scanning in human memory. *Science, 153,* 652–654.

Wickens, D. (1970). Encoding categories of words: An empirical approach to meaning. *Psy. Rev., 77,* 1–15.

Melton, A., & Martin, E. (Eds.) (1972). *Coding processes in human memory.* Washington, DC: Winston.

Tulving, E., & Thomson, D. (1973). Encoding specificity and retrieval processes in episodic memory. *Psy. Rev., 80,* 352–373.

Uttal, W. (1973). *The psychology of sensory coding.* New York: Harper & Row.

Anderson, J., & Bower, G. (1974). A propositional theory of recognition memory. *Mem. & Cog., 2,* 406–412.

DeValois, R., & DeValois, K. (1975). Neural coding of color. In E. Carterette & M. Friedman (Eds.), *Handbook of perception.* Vol. 5. New York: Academic Press.

Anderson, N. (1981). *Foundations of information integration theory.* New York: Academic Press.

Bower, G., & Hilgard, E. (1981). *Theories of learning.* Englewood Cliffs, NJ: Prentice-Hall.

Paivio, A. (1982). The empirical case for dual coding. In J. Yuille (Ed.), *Imagery, cognition, and memory.* Hillsdale, NJ: Erlbaum.

Carlson, N. (1990). *Psychology: The science of behavior.* Boston: Allyn & Bacon.

Paivio, A. (1991). Dual coding theory: Retrospect and current status. *Can. J. Psy., 45,* 255–287.

Anderson, N. (1994). Coding. In R. J. Corsini (Ed.), *Ency. Psy.* New York: Wiley.

Reber, A. (1995). *The Penguin dictionary of psychology.* New York: Penguin Books.

Goldstein, E. (1996). *Sensation and perception.* Pacific Grove, CA: Brooks/Cole.

COGNITIVE ALGEBRA THEORY. See IMPRESSION FORMATION, THEORIES OF.

COGNITIVE APPRAISAL THEORY. See COGNITIVE THEORIES OF EMOTION.

COGNITIVE STYLE MODELS. Kagan, Moss, and Sigel (1963) define the construct of *cognitive learning style* as the relatively stable individual preferences for perceptual and conceptual organization and categorization of the external environment (cf: the early *laws/principles of abstraction*; Moore, 1910; Titchener, 1915; Freeman, 1939). The term *cognitive style* has been introduced and reintroduced into the psychological literature over a period of time extending back to the German psychologists at the turn of the century (Haynie, 1994). Because *cognitive style* deals with qualitative, rather than quantitative, differences and dimensions and is concerned with behavior and preference, it is value-free and resists moral judgments. A number of *cognitive style models* (or *learning styles*) on a dimensional/continuum basis have been formulated and include the following factors (Roeckelein, 1980; Haynie, 1994): field independence versus field dependence; scanning versus focusing; broad versus narrow categorizing; leveling versus sharpening; constricted versus flexible control; tolerance versus intolerance for incongruity; impulsive versus reflective responding; analytic versus nonanalytic conceptualizing styles; risk-taking versus cautious; perceptive versus receptive; systematic versus intuitive; and cognitive complexity versus simplicity. In general, a person's *cognitive style* may be determined by the way she or he assesses her or his surroundings, seeks out meanings, and becomes informed. In particular, a battery of tests concerning preferences for different ways of learning may be given to individuals, and results can be interpreted to produce a ''map'' of the many ways each person seeks meaning, such as preferences for theoretical symbolic input, qualitative code input, modalities of inference, and cultural determinants. Thus, a *cognitive map* describes each person's *cognitive style* by relating score results on about two dozen elements where the resultant map indicates a preferred or optimal learning environment. *Cognitive style mapping* is a diagnostic testing program useful for educational planning and may be used to identify and maximize an individual's strengths in a learning setting (Hill, 1973). *Cognitive style* is represented in observable behaviors where inconsistencies may occur in the choice of particular behaviors to be examined. Various researchers have developed measuring instruments to elicit specific behaviors for analyzing a person's *cognitive style*, but it has been found that some measures of *cognitive style* do not correlate highly with other measures (Coop & Sigel, 1971). The philosophy behind *cognitive style models* and *cognitive style mapping* is that individuals learn in diverse and unique ways, and no single educational method can serve everyone in an equal or optimal fashion (Ferguson, 1980). See also KELLY'S PERSONAL CONSTRUCT THEORY; PIAGET'S THEORY OF DEVELOPMENTAL STAGES.

REFERENCES

Moore, T. (1910). The process of abstraction. *Univ. Calif. Pub. Psy., 1*, 73–197.

Titchener, E. (1915). *A beginner's psychology.* New York: Macmillan.

Freeman, E. (1939). *Principles of general psychology.* New York: Holt.

Bieri, J. (1955). Cognitive complexity-simplicity and predictive behaviors. *J. Abn. Soc. Psy., 51*, 263–268.

Kagan, J., Moss, H., & Sigel, I. (1963). The psychological significance of styles of conceptualization. In J. Wright & J. Kagan (Eds.), *Basic cognitive processes in children. Monograph of the Society for Research in Child Development.* No. 28, 73–112.

Bruner, J. (1964). The course of cognitive thought. *Amer. Psy., 19*, 1–15.

Crockett, W. (1965). Cognitive complexity and impression formation. In B. Maher (Ed.), *Progress in experimental personality research.* Vol. 2. New York: Academic Press.

Miller, A. (1969). Amount of information and stimulus valence as determinants of cognitive complexity. *J. Pers., 37*, 141–157.

Coop, R., & Sigel, I. (1971). Cognitive style: Implications for learning and instruction. *Psychology in the Schools, 8*, 152–161.

Hill, J. (1973). *The educational sciences*. Bloomfield Hills, MI: Oakland Community College Press.

Kreitler, H., & Kreitler, S. (1976). *Cognitive orientation and behavior*. New York: Springer.

Ferguson, M. (1980). *The Aquarian conspiracy: Personal and social transformations in the 1980s*. Los Angeles: Tarcher.

Roeckelein, J. (1980). *Psychology: Theory and practice*. Dubuque, IA: Kendall/Hunt.

Entwistle, N. (1981). *Styles of learning and teaching*. New York: Wiley.

Haynie, N. (1994). Cognitive learning styles. In R. J. Corsini (Ed.), *Ency. Psy.* New York: Wiley.

COGNITIVE THEORIES OF EMOTIONS. *Cognitive theory of emotion* is a general term for a relatively recent class of theories of emotion that view the cognitive interpretation and appraisal of emotional stimuli from both inside and outside the body to be the major event in emotions. *Cognitive theories* have a long history, going back to the early Greek philosophers (Arnold, 1994). Aristotle (384–322 B.C.) suggested that humans and animals can make sensory evaluations of things as being good or bad for them where the evaluation involves the arousal of emotions (Aristotle, 1941); Thomas Aquinas (1225–1274) agreed with Aristotle in his explanation of the arousal of emotions. Rene Descartes (1596–1650) believed that all emotions are aroused directly through excitation of "animal spirits" or by arousal of innate reflex actions in combination with physiological changes that are necessary for the organism's survival (Descartes, 1650); Charles Darwin (1809–1882) essentially shared Descartes' notion of emotions (Darwin, 1872). Later, William James (1842–1910) and Carl Lange (1834–1900) reversed the classical, intuitive, or commonsense view that emotion produces bodily changes by arguing that bodily changes occur after the perception of the arousing event where one's sensation of the bodily changes is the emotion (James, 1890). Sigmund Freud (1856–1939) conceived of emotions as an "affect change" of the twin drives of love and aggression, and fear as the reliving of the birth trauma (Freud, 1933). Alfred Adler (1870–1937), rejecting Freud's concept of libido as the source of all motivation, accounted for human motivation and emotion in terms of a desire for power (Adler, 1927). Carl Jung (1875–1961) proposed that feelings are a kind of psychological function different from intellectual judgment that is somewhat similar in nature to the ideas of Aristotle and Aquinas (Jung, 1921). Jung's insistence on feeling as a rational judgment function makes him the first modern *cognitive theorist* of feeling; however, Jung did not connect the "feeling function" with emotion, which he viewed as an irrational phenomenon arising from the unconscious (Arnold, 1994). With the appearance of the school of behaviorism (Watson, 1919), where internal concepts such as feeling and emotion were considered to be too mentalistic, the topic of emotion was either subordinated to motivation or almost completely lost in the stimulus–response paradigm of the behaviorists. Between the 1920s and the 1950s, the topic of emotion seems to have been abandoned in psychology, even as a chapter heading. By the 1950s and 1960s, however, theorists (e.g., Kelly, 1955; Polanyi, 1964) began to return to the intuitive idea that a situation must be interpreted in some way before it can instigate an emotion. Arnold (1954) introduced the concept of *appraisal* into academic psychology where emotion was defined as a felt action tendency toward things that are intuitively appraised as good for oneself or away from things that are appraised as bad, and where a pattern of physiological changes is organized around particular types of approach or withdrawal. Arnold (1960) suggested that emotions depend not only on intuitive appraisals of things as "good or bad for me" but also on the appraisal of potential actions as suitable or unsuitable. It is interesting to note how some of the early writers in psychology anticipated the modern notion of *cognitive theory* in emotions. For instance, Pillsbury (1918, p. 272) states that "all emotions have an instinctive basis; movements in emotional expression are the outcome of instinct. So true is this, that the emotion is defined as the *conscious* side of instinct" (italics added). In a later edition of the same book, Pillsbury (1926, p. 305) ascribes this idea of emotion as the *conscious* side of instinct to both John Dewey and William McDougall. As used today, the *cognitive theory of emotions* is regarded often as a single theory (e.g., Leventhal & Tomarken, 1986; Frijda, 1988; Lazarus, 1991), even though a number of different investigators over many years have contributed various aspects and refinements to the theory. For example, Arnold (1960), Ellis (1962), and Schachter and Singer (1962) have been prominent in the development of the *cognitive theory of emotions* and collectively propose, in general, that there are two steps in the process of cognitive interpretation of an emotional episode: (1) the interpretation and appraisal of stimuli from the external environment and (2) the interpretation and appraisal of stimuli from the internal autonomic arousal system. See also ABC THEORY; ACTIVATION/AROUSAL THEORY; ADLER'S THEORY OF PERSONALITY; ARNOLD'S THEORY OF EMOTIONS; EMOTIONS, THEORIES/LAWS OF; FREUD'S THEORY OF PERSONALITY; JAMES–LANGE/LANGE–JAMES THEORY OF EMOTIONS; JUNG'S THEORY OF PERSONALITY; KELLY'S PERSONAL CONSTRUCT THEORY; LAZARUS' THEORY OF EMOTIONS; SCHACHTER-SINGER'S THEORY OF EMOTIONS; ZAJONC'S AROUSAL AND CONFLUENCE THEORIES.

REFERENCES

Descartes, R. (1650). *Les passions de l'ame*. Paris: Loyson.

Darwin, C. (1872). *The expression of the emotions in man and animals*. Chicago: University of Chicago Press.

James, W. (1890). *Principles of psychology*. New York: Holt.

Pillsbury, W. (1918). *The essentials of psychology*. New York: Macmillan.

Watson, J. (1919). *Psychology from the standpoint of a behaviorist*. Philadelphia: Lippincott.

Jung, C. (1921). *Psychological types*. Princeton, NJ: Princeton University Press.

Pillsbury, W. (1926). *The essentials of psychology*. New York: Macmillan.

Adler, A. (1927). *Practice and theory of individual psychology*. New York: Humanities Press.

Freud, S. (1933). New introductory lectures on psychoanalysis. In *The standard edition of the complete psychological works of Sigmund Freud*. Vol. 22. London: Hogarth Press.

Aristotle. (1941). De anima (On the soul). In R. McKeon (Ed.), *The basic works of Aristotle*. New York: Random House.

Thomas Aquinas. (1951). *Commentary of St. Thomas Aquinas*. New Haven, CT: Yale University Press.

Arnold, M. (1954). Feelings and emotions as dynamic factors in personality integration. In M. Arnold & J. Gasson (Eds.), *The human person*. New York: Ronald Press.

Kelly, G. (1955). *The psychology of personal constructs*. New York: Norton.

Arnold, M. (1960). *Emotion and personality*. New York: Columbia University Press.

Ellis, A. (1962). *Reason and emotion in psychotherapy*. New York: Lyle Stuart.

Schachter, S., & Singer, J. (1962). Cognitive, social, and physiological determinants of emotional state. *Psy. Rev., 69*, 379–399.

Polanyi, M. (1964). *Personal knowledge*. New York: Harper & Row.

Lazarus, R. (1984). On the primacy of cognition. *Amer. Psy., 39*, 117–123.

Leventhal, H., & Tomarken, A. (1986). Emotion: Today's problem. *Ann. Rev. Psy, 37*, 565–610.

Frijda, N. (1988). The laws of emotion. *Amer. Psy., 43*, 349–357.

Lazarus, R. (1991). *Emotion and adaptation*. New York: Oxford University Press.

Arnold, M. (1994). Cognitive theories of emotion. In R. J. Corsini (Ed.), *Ency. Psy*. New York: Wiley.

COGNITIVE THERAPY, THEORIES OF. See BEHAVIOR THERAPY/ COGNITIVE THERAPY, THEORIES OF.

COLOR MIXING, PRINCIPLES OF. See COLOR MIXTURE, LAWS/THEORY OF.

COLOR MIXTURE, LAWS/THEORY OF. = additive color mixture, principles of. = subtractive color mixture, principles of. = color mixing, principles of. The colors of objects in the environment are determined by pigments that are chemicals on the objects' surface that absorb some wavelengths of light and, consequently, prevent those wavelengths of light from being reflected. Also, different pigments permit different wavelengths to be reflected. For example, a pigment that absorbs short and medium wavelengths of light appears to be "red" because only long ("red") wavelengths are reflected; a pigment that permits only short wavelengths to be reflected appears to be "blue"; and a pigment that permits only medium wavelengths to be reflected appears to be "yellow" or "green." When all wavelengths are reflected equally by a pigment, one gets the experience of "white," "gray," or "black," depending on whether the relative amount of light reflected is high ("white"), medium ("gray"), or low ("black"). The term *additive color mixing* refers to the mixture of colored *lights*, while the term *subtractive color mixing* refers to the mixture of *pigments* (such as paints). *Subtractive color mixing* occurs when pigments create the perception of color by "subtracting" (i.e., absorbing) some of the light waves that would otherwise be reflected to the eye. For instance, if a blue pigment (which absorbs long wavelengths of light) is mixed with a yellow pigment (which absorbs short wavelengths of light), only the medium-length waves will be reflected, and the resultant mixture will be perceived as "green." Amateur painters, working with pigments, experience *subtractive color mixing* when they mix all of the paints on the palette together, with the result of a muddy "brown" or "black" color. In this case, the painter "subtracts out" *all* of the wavelengths by mixing all of the pigments together. *Additive color mixing*, on the other hand, describes the results of mixing colored lights together. For example, shining a blue light together with red and green-yellow lights on the same spot on a white screen reflects the mixed lights back and gives the perception of a "white" light. Two general *laws of additive color mixing*, known to scientists as early as the eighteenth century (e.g., Newton, 1704), are called the *three-primaries law* and the *law of complementarity*. The *three-primaries law* states that three different wavelengths of light (the "primaries") can be used to match any color that the eye can see, if they are mixed in the proper proportions. The "primaries" can be any three wavelengths as long as each one is taken from the three types of wavelengths: one from the long-wave end ("red") of the spectrum, one from the medium-wave ("green," "green-yellow") end, and one from the short-wave ("blue," "violet") end of the visible spectrum. The *law of complementarity* states that pairs ("complements") of wavelengths of light can be reflected so that, when they are added together, they give the visual sensation of a "white" light. An important subfield in the area of color vision and color mixture is called *colorimetry*, which is the science that aims at specifying and reproducing colors as a result of measurement. Colorimeters may be of three types: (1) color filter samples for empirical comparison; (2) monochromatic colorimeters that match colors with a mixture of monochromatic and white lights; and (3) trichromatic colorimeters in which a match is effected by a mixture of three colors (Illingworth, 1991). See also ABNEY'S LAW; COLOR VISION, THEORIES/LAWS OF; GRASSMANN'S LAWS; NEWTON'S LAW/PRINCIPLES OF COLOR MIXTURE; VISION/SIGHT, THEORIES/LAWS OF.

REFERENCES

Newton, I. (1704). *Opticks*. London: Smith.

Grassmann, H. (1853). Zur Theorie der Farbenmischung. *Pogg. Ann. Physik., 89*, 69.

Judd, C. (1907). *Psychology: General introduction*. New York: Scribners.

Kulpe, O. (1909). *Outlines of psychology*. New York: Macmillan.

Titchener, E. (1928). *A textbook of psychology*. New York: Macmillan.

OSA Committee on Colorimetry. (1943). The concept of color. *J. Opt. Soc. Amer., 33*, 544.

OSA Committee on Colorimetry. (1944). The psychophysics of color. *J. Opt. Soc. Amer.,* *34*, 246, 254–255.

Judd, D. (1951). Basic correlates of the visual stimulus. In S. S. Stevens (Ed.), *Handbk. Exp. Psy.* New York: Wiley.

Mueller, C. (1965). *Sensory psychology.* Englewood Cliffs, NJ: Prentice-Hall.

Woodworth, R., & Schlosberg, H. (1965). *Experimental psychology.* New York: Holt, Rinehart, & Winston.

Carlson, N. (1990). *Psychology: The science of behavior.* Boston: Allyn & Bacon.

Illingworth, V. (Ed.) (1991). *The Penguin dictionary of physics.* New York: Penguin Books.

COLOR VISION, THEORIES/LAWS OF. The concept of *color* is a psychological (subjective) experience or sensation that is associated with the presence of a physical light source and depends on three aspects of the actual physical energy: intensity (''brightness''), wavelength (''hue''), and purity (''saturation''). Most humans see the shorter visible wavelengths (''hues'') of the electromagnetic radiation spectrum as ''bluish'' (about 480 nanometers, or *nm*); the medium wavelengths as ''greenish'' (about 510 *nm*) and ''yellowish'' (about 580 *nm*); and the longer wavelengths as ''reddish'' (about 700 *nm*). The term *chromatic* refers to stimuli that have all three of these aspects (and have *color*), while the term *achromatic* refers to stimuli that have only the ''brightness'' aspect (and are ''white-gray-black''). Typically, the better *theories of color vision* can account for several phenomena: (1) the *primary colors* (''unique hues'') of ''blue,'' ''green,'' ''yellow,'' and ''red''; (2) the *complementary colors* (i.e., any of the colors that are opposite to each other on the color wheel and when additively mixed produce an achromatic gray) and their influence in afterimages and contrast effects; (3) the *laws of color mixture*; and (4) the different symptoms of various types of *color blindness* (e.g., protanopes, deuteranopes, tritanopes; cf: *Horner's law*, which is the genetic principle that the most common form of color blindness, red-green, is transmitted from male to male through unaffected females; Reber, 1995; cf: *Konig's theory*, 1897; Calkins, 1905). Wheeler (1929) described a number of minor *theories of color vision*, such as those by Venable, Schanz, and Forbes. Another early writer (Reid, 1938) listed the *laws* (cf: *theories*) of *color vision* as adapting, color mixture, contrast, and induction. *Kirschmann's law of contrast* (1891) is the principle that the contrast is proportional to the logarithm of the saturation of the contrast-inducing color (Graham & Brown, 1965). Judd (1951) summarized a few of the better-known visual theories, citing their fundamental colors and their chief limitations: *Young–Helmholtz three components theory* (red, green, violet)—fails to explain dichromatic vision and color perceptions of protanopes (red-color deficiency) and deuteranopes (green-color deficiency); *dominator-modulator theory* (''late-Konig'' theory; red, green, violet)—fails to explain color perceptions of protanopes and deuteranopes; *Ladd–Franklin three components theory* (''early Konig'' theory; red, green, blue)—implies that the blue function has a negative luminosity for normals and deuteranopes and a positive luminosity for protanopes; *Hering opponent colors theory* (red-green, yellow-blue, white-black)—fails to give an account of protanopia and tritanopia (blue-light deficiency); *von Kries-Schrodinger zone theory* (red, green blue; and green-red, blue-yellow, white-black)—implies that the blue function has a negative luminosity for normals and deuteranopes and a positive luminosity for protanopes, and fails to account for tritanopia; *Adams zone theory* (red, green, violet; red, green, blue; red-green, blue-yellow, white-black)—explanations of protanopia and tritanopia are based on other "extra" or "subsidiary" assumptions; *Muller zone theory* (red, green, violet; red-green, yellow-blue, white-black)—implausible explanation of protanopic luminosity. It is a well-accepted fact that the cones and rods of the retina are the immediate organs of vision and that they contain substances, or mixtures of substances, that absorb radiant energy falling on these receptors. In turn, the receptors respond by initiating nerve impulses that go to the fibers of the optic nerve. It is also well established that the response of the rods is due to a photochemical substance called *rhodopsin* (Hecht & Williams, 1922), but the substances giving the cones their precise spectral characteristics are still being researched, as well as the combinations of cone responses that produce impulses in the optic nerve. Recent theories of the underlying mechanisms mediating color vision feature a merger of two accounts that were initially considered to be in conflict (Fobes, 1994). One approach, the *trichromatic theory* of Thomas Young and Hermann von Helmholtz, stressed the relative activity of cones that are maximally sensitive to red, blue, or green. The other approach, the *opponent-process theory* of Ewald Hering, Leo Hurvich, and Dorothea Jameson, considered red-green as well as blue-yellow to be antagonistic processes. These two accounts have been reconciled now so that the *trichromatic theory* describes activity at the "lower" receptor level, and the *opponent-process theory* describes integration events at the "higher" level of neural organization. A current *theory of color vision*, the *retinex theory*, formulated by the American sensory psychologist Edwin Herbert Land (1909–   ), maintains the existence of three separate visual systems ("retinexes") where one is responsive primarily to long-wavelength light, one to moderate-wavelength light, and the third to short-wavelength light. Each system is represented as an analog to a black-and-white picture taken through a particular filter with each one producing maximum activity in response to red, green, and blue light for the long-, moderate-, and short-wavelength retinexes respectively (Land, 1959; Graham & Brown, 1965; Reber, 1995). See also COLOR MIXTURE, LAWS/THEORY OF; HECHT'S COLOR VISION THEORY; HERING–HURVICH-JAMESON COLOR VISION THEORY; LADD-FRANKLIN/FRANKLIN COLOR VISION THEORY; YOUNG–HELMHOLTZ COLOR VISION THEORY.

REFERENCES

Kirschmann, A. (1891). Uber die quantitativen Verhaltnisse des simultanen Helligkeits-
    und Farben-Contrastes. *Phil. Stud., 6,* 417–491.

Konig, A. (1897). Uber Blaublindheit. *Sitzungsberichte Akademie der Wissenschaffen, Berlin*.

Calkins, M. (1905). *An introduction to psychology*. New York: Macmillan.

Hecht, S., & Williams, R. (1922). The visibility of monochromatic radiation and the absorption spectrum of visual purple. *J. Gen. Physio., 5*, 1.

Wheeler, R. (1929). *The science of psychology: An introductory study*. New York: Crowell.

Reid, A. (1938). *Elements of psychology*. New York: Prentice-Hall.

Judd, D. (1951). Basic correlates of the visual system. In S. S. Stevens (Ed.), *Handbk. Exp. Psy*. New York: Wiley.

Dartnall, H. (1957). *The visual pigments*. New York: Wiley.

Land, E. (1959). Color vision and the natural image. *Proc. Nat. Acad. Sci., 45*, 115–129; 636–644.

Rushton, W. (1962). *Visual pigments in man*. London: Liverpool University Press.

MacNichol, E. (1964). Retinal mechanisms of color vision. *Vis. Res., 4*, 119–133.

Graham, C. (1965). Color: Data and theories. In C. Graham (Ed.), *Vision and visual perception*. New York: Wiley.

Graham, C., & Brown, J. (1965). Color contrast and color appearances: Brightness constancy and color constancy. In C. Graham (Ed.), *Vision and visual perception*. New York: Wiley.

Wyszecki, G., & Stiles, W. (1967). *Color science: Concepts and methods, quantitative data and formulas*. New York: Wiley.

Michael, C. (1969). Retinal processing of visual images. *Sci. Amer., 220*, 104–114.

Symposium on New Developments in the Study of Color Vision (1969). *Proc. Nat. Acad. Sci., 45*, 89–115.

Boynton, R. (1971). Color vision. In J. Kling & L. Riggs (Eds.), *Woodworth and Schlosberg's experimental psychology*. New York: Holt, Rinehart, & Winston.

Geldard, F. (1972). *The human senses*. New York: Wiley.

Nathans, J., Thomas, P., Diantandia, R., Eddy, T., Shows, D., & Hogness, D. (1986). Molecular genetics of inherited variations in human color vision. *Science, 232*, 203–210.

Fobes, J. (1994). Color vision. In R. J. Corsini (Ed.), *Ency. Psy*. New York: Wiley.

Reber, A. (1995). *The Penguin dictionary of psychology*. New York: Penguin Books.

COMMUNICATION THEORY. In broad terms, *communication* refers to the transmission of something from one location to another where the "thing" that is transmitted may be a message, a signal, a meaning, and so on, and where both the transmitter and the receiver must share a common code so that the meaning of information contained in the message may be interpreted without error (Reber, 1995). *Communication theory* is the process whereby one system influences another system by regulation of the transmitted signals (Wolman, 1973). In psychology, *communication theory* has proven useful in developing models of interpersonal interaction, memory processes, language, and physiological functions. The general *communication process* consists of five steps (Shannon & Weaver, 1949): (1) the source; (2) the transmitter; (3) the channel; (4) the source of potential noise; and (5) the receiver (cf: the social psychological analysis of persuasion involving the basic elements of source, message, and audience; Hovland, Janis, & Kelley, 1953). The channel may alter a certain amount and type of data where the translation of data into a form acceptable to the channel (coding) and the reverse process for use by the receiver (decoding) are critical problems in the analysis and design of communication systems. The concept of *noise* is defined as the origin of errors in transmission where the signal received by the receiver is a function of the original signal plus noise (cf: the concept of *noise* in *signal detection theory*; Green & Swets, 1966). The *communication model* proposed by Shannon and Weaver (1949) invites mathematical analysis and quantitative measurements of the concepts of information, channel capacity, error reduction, redundancy, and efficiency of coding systems. This approach allows analyses to be made of communication processes in different areas of investigation from molecular genetics to literary criticism (Back, 1994). Communication in the social sciences may be divided into interpersonal versus mass communication categories. In interpersonal communication, the receiver can respond immediately and create a network of several communication chains, while in mass communication each transmission link is largely separated. The theoretical approaches in the study of interpersonal communication are dependent on particular methods of research, experiments, observation, or field study. Two models/theories that emphasize the type of message in the communication process are those of Bales (1950) and Chapple (1949). Bales (1950) developed 12 formal categories for describing the communication/interaction process occurring among members in small groups. By combining some of the 12 categories in certain ways, Bales was able to define and elaborate various subsets of communication/interaction "climates," as well as to identify problems of communication, evaluation, control, decision making, tension reduction, and reintegration. Chapple's (1949) model is more abstract than Bales' system and measures only the amount of talking, overlap, and lengths of contradiction. Both Bales' and Chapple's approaches avoid any mention of communication *content* per se. In other theoretical approaches, however, such as the experimental approach to measuring communication, the actual communication processes are inferred from measurement of the conditions and the effect of the process (e.g., Bavelas, 1951; Leavitt, 1951). Some experimental approaches may control informal social communication processes by instruction and inputs by the experimenter with outcomes measured via questionnaires or joint actions by the group members (e.g., Festinger, 1950; Festinger, Schachter, & Back, 1950; cf: "actual" communication sequences, Grimshaw, 1981). Theories and studies of interpersonal communication have focused also on the practical aspects of communication, such as intimacy and communication (e.g., Gottman & Krokoff, 1989; Long & Andrews, 1990), and on effective communication (e.g., Goldstein & Gilliam, 1990; Hartgrove-Freile, 1990). It has been recognized that the method of field observation and analysis of interpersonal communication is a relatively weak approach—without a good theory to guide data collection—due to the paucity of results relative to the large technical apparatus necessary to collect data (Back, 1994). On the other hand, the theoretical work of some investigators has succeeded in bridging the gap between the interpersonal and the mass communication approaches (e.g., Katz & Lazarsfeld's, 1955, *two-step theory of communications*; Lerner's, 1958, *societal progress theory*; McLuan's, 1962, *communication theory*; Klapp's, 1978, *sociological theory of communication*). Thus, *communication theory* includes a number of disciplines where each focuses on a number of different factors. Lin (1973) outlines three approaches to the study of both verbal and nonverbal communication: the *dimensional* approach (delineates specific components of communication, including a source, a message, a channel, and a receiver where there is typically a two-way exchange of communication); the *process* approach (focuses on the internal and external dynamics of the sender and receiver of a message); and the *functional* approach (studies the functions and purposes of communication, including syntactics [structural elements], semantics [meanings], and pragmatics [practical consequences of communication]). Fisher (1978) described four major "perspectives" on the study of communication: *mechanistic* (physical elements of communication, including the transmission and reception of messages along a linear model); *psychological* (a behavioristic conceptualization of communication, including concepts such as stimulus field, sensory inputs, emitted responses, reinforcement, and processing of cognitive-behavioral events); *interactional* (a humanistic orientation where communication focuses on the development of one's potential via social interaction, including concepts such as self, social roles, cultural symbols, self-understanding, and self-disclosure); and *pragmatic* (focuses on outcomes and consequences of communication, especially as developed in the field of psychotherapy). Apparently, no matter what particular theoretical perspective, approach, or direction one takes, most investigators of communication subscribe to the principle that an individual cannot *not* communicate. Even without verbal signals, people would emit an infinite variety and number of nonverbal behaviors that essentially communicate meaning (Baron, 1994).   See also ATTITUDE/ATTITUDE CHANGE, THEORIES OF; CODING THEORIES; INFORMATION/INFORMATION–PROCESSING THEORY; SIGNAL DETECTION THEORY.

REFERENCES

Chapple, E. (1949). The interaction chronograph: Its evolution and present applications. *Personnel, 25*, 295–307.

Shannon, C., & Weaver, W. (1949). *The mathematical theory of communication*. Urbana: University of Illinois Press.

Bales, R. (1950). *Interaction process analysis: A method for the study of small groups*. Reading, MA: Addison-Wesley.

Festinger, L. (1950). Informal social communication. *Psy. Rev., 57*, 271–282.

Festinger, L., Schachter, S., & Back, K. (1950). *Social pressures in informal groups: A study of human factors in housing*. New York: Harper.

Bavelas, A. (1951). Communication patterns in task-oriented groups. In D. Lerner & H. Laswell (Eds.), *The policy sciences*. Stanford, CA: Stanford University Press.

Leavitt, H. (1951). Some effects of certain communication patterns on group perform-ance. *J. Abn. Soc. Psy., 46*, 38–50.

Hovland, C., Janis, I., & Kelley, H. (1953). *Communication and persuasion: Psycholog-ical studies of opinion changes*. New Haven, CT: Yale University Press.

Katz, E., & Lazarsfeld, P. (1955). *Personal influence: The part played by people in the flow of mass communications*. Glencoe, IL: Free Press.

Lerner, D. (1958). *The passing of traditional society*. Glencoe, IL: Free Press.

McLuan, M. (1962). *The Gutenberg galaxy*. Toronto: University of Toronto Press.

Green, D., & Swets, J. (1966). *Signal detection theory and psychophysics*. New York: Wiley.

Borden, G. (1971). *An introduction to human communication theory*. Dubuque, IA: Brown.

Lin, N. (1973). *The study of human communication*. New York: Bobbs-Merrill.

Miller, G. (Ed.) (1973). *Communication, language, and meaning: Psychological per-spectives*. New York: Basic Books.

Wolman, B. (Ed.) (1973). *Dictionary of behavioral science*. New York: Van Nostrand Reinhold.

Fisher, B. (1978). *Perspectives on human communication*. New York: Macmillan.

Klapp, O. (1978). *Opening and closing*. Cambridge, England: Cambridge University Press.

Grimshaw, A. (1981). Talk and social control. In M. Rosenberg & R. Turner (Eds.), *Social psychology*. New York: Basic Books.

Gottman, J., & Krokoff, L. (1989). Marital interaction and satisfaction: A longitudinal view. *J. Cons. Clin. Psy., 57*, 47–52.

Goldstein, I., & Gilliam, P. (1990). Training system issues in the year 2000. *Amer. Psy., 45*, 134–143.

Hartgrove-Freile, J. (1990). *Organizations, communication, and culture*. St. Paul, MN: West.

Long, E., & Andrews, D. (1990). Perspective taking as a predictor of marital adjustment. *J. Pers. Soc. Psy., 59*, 126–131.

Back, K. (1994). Communication processes. In R. J. Corsini (Ed.), *Ency. Psy.* New York: Wiley.

Baron, A. (1994). Communication theory. In R. J. Corsini (Ed.), *Ency. Psy.* New York: Wiley.

Reber, A. (1995). *The Penguin dictionary of psychology*. New York: Penguin Books.

COMPARATIVE JUDGMENT, LAW OF. See THURSTONE'S LAW OF COMPARATIVE JUDGMENT.

COMPATIBILITY, LAW OF. See SKINNER'S DESCRIPTIVE BEHAV-IOR/OPERANT CONDITIONING THEORY.

COMPENSATORY THEORY OF DREAMING. See DREAM THEORY.

COMPETENCE THEORY. See PLAY, THEORIES OF.

COMPLEMENTARY NEEDS, THEORY OF. See LOVE, THEORIES OF.

COMPLEMENTARY ODORS, LAW OF. See OLFACTION/SMELL, THEORIES OF.

COMPONENTIAL RECOVERY, PRINCIPLE OF. See PATTERN/OBJECT RECOGNITION THEORY.

COMTE'S LAW. The French philosopher and sociologist Auguste Comte (1798–1857) initially belonged to the French philosophical movement of *materialism* (which viewed humans as machines) but subsequently founded another movement called *positivism*. According to Comte's *positivistic* approach, the only knowledge that is valid is observable and objective knowledge. Introspection, which focused on the inner analysis of conscious experience, was rejected completely. Concerning the evolution of thought, Comte believed that individuals passed through three stages, called *Comte's law of three stages* (Carlson, 1993): the theological, the metaphysical, and the positivistic, with the last being the basis for scientific thought. Comte considered the psychology of his time (which emphasized the subjective analysis of one's consciousness via the introspective method) to be the last phase of theology. Comte argued that science itself was a matter of description, prediction, and control, and the good scientist should avoid giving explanations to phenomena, particularly if there are unobservable entities involved. Postulation of unseen causes was regarded as a dangerous relapse into religion or metaphysical superstition (Leahey, 1994b). Since the time of Comte, *positivists* have organized the sciences hierarchically from the oldest and most basic (i.e., physics) up to the science of social planners (i.e., sociology). Each science is held to be reducible to the next lower level, with the overall effect that all sciences are, in principle, branches of physics (cf: Roeckelein, 1997). Comte's approach had a strong influence on the social theories of his time. He stressed that humans must rely on direct experience in a dynamic society where the aim of society (''sociology'') should be to remove the study of social factors from the influence of the theological and metaphysical stages of thought. Comte believed that phenomena in the social sciences may be examined and evaluated with the same criteria as used in discovering scientific laws in the natural sciences. Comte's notions have had a strong impact on modern behaviorism, and some psychologists consider Comte to have been the first behaviorist (Lundin, 1994). Today, there is another type of *positivism*, inspired by Comte's original notion, called *logical positivism* (e.g., Carnap & Morris, 1948), which holds that the basic data of experience are the operations of scientific observation, and which led historically to the important prescriptions in science called *operationism* and *operational definitions* (Bridgman, 1927; Boring, 1957; cf: Bridgman, 1959; Leahey, 1980). See also BEHAVIORIST THEORY.

REFERENCES

Comte, A. (1853). *The positive philosophy*. London: Bell.
Martineau, H. (1853). *Comte's positive philosophy*. London: Chapman.

Bridgman, P. (1927). *The logic of modern physics*. New York: Macmillan.

Carnap, R., & Morris, C. (Eds.) (1948). *International encyclopedia of unified science*. Chicago: University of Chicago Press.

Boring, E. G. (1957). *A history of experimental psychology*. New York: Appleton-Century-Crofts.

Bridgman, P. (1959). *The way things are*. Cambridge: Harvard University Press.

Suppe, F. (1974). *The structure of scientific theories*. Urbana: University of Illinois Press.

Leahey, T. (1980). The myth of operationism. *J. Mind & Beh., 1*, 127–143.

Carlson, N. (1993). *Psychology: The science of behavior*. Boston: Allyn & Bacon.

Leahey, T. (1994a). Operationalism. In R. J. Corsini (Ed.), *Ency. Psy.* New York: Wiley.

Leahey, T. (1994b). Positivism. In R. J. Corsini (Ed.), *Ency. Psy.* New York: Wiley.

Lundin, R. (1994). Auguste Comte. In R. J. Corsini (Ed.), *Ency. Psy.* New York: Wiley.

Roeckelein, J. (1997). Psychology among the sciences: Comparisons of numbers of theories and laws cited in textbooks. *Psy. Rep., 80*, 131–141.

CONCEPT LEARNING/CONCEPT FORMATION, THEORIES OF. A *concept* may be defined as a symbol or group of symbols that stands for a class of objects or events that possess common properties. Thus, *tree* is a concept because it is a symbol that stands for a larger group of objects, all of which possess common characteristics (e.g., a trunk, branches, leaves, etc.). Most words, with the exception of proper nouns that refer to only a single object, are concepts. Concepts may be nonverbal as well as verbal; for instance, infants can have a concept of *mother* long before they have achieved language skills. The power of using concepts is that they help individuals to think efficiently because they free one from having to create a unique label for each new instance of an object or event. The term *concept formation* refers to the problem-solving process one goes through to acquire concepts. Learning psychologists are interested particularly in understanding how individuals, both human and nonhuman, learn to identify objects or events as examples of specific concepts (Houston, 1981). The terms *concept formation* and *concept learning* are often used synonymously to refer to the process of abstraction of a quality, property, or set of features that can be taken to represent a concept; however, there is considerable latitude in actual usage. The literature in *cognitive psychology* abounds with synonymous terms that have been introduced to refer to these processes: concept acquisition, concept development, concept discovery, concept identification, concept use, concept attainment, concept construction, and concept induction. There seems to be little agreement about terminology in this area of *concept learning/concept formation*, and the most useful counsel is careful reading and critical reflection (Reber, 1995). Several theories have attempted to account for the processes operating in *concept learning/concept formation*. The *behaviorist*, or *stimulus–response*, *theory* of concept learning was supported by Clark Hull (1920). Although many of the subjects in Hull's experiments on concept learning were able to learn the tasks, none of them were able to explain "how" they were classifying symbols and objects into different categories. Hull was impressed by subjects' inabilities to describe their performance and emphasized the importance of analyzing individuals' behavior and not their introspective accounts of behavior. Thus, the behaviorist viewpoint was advanced by Hull's work. Introspection was deemed unscientific, and speculations about what goes on "inside one's head" during concept learning were avoided. Other theories are based on more *cognitive* notions, however, such as the assumption that people try to "solve" concepts by making up hypotheses or tentative guesses and then testing these hypotheses (Bourne, Dominowski, & Loftus, 1979; Matlin, 1994). Bruner, Goodnow, and Austin (1956) proposed that people use strategies in order to learn concepts, where strategy was defined as an orderly method for making decisions that allows people to solve the concept accurately and quickly without taxing their reasoning skills or memories. Levine (1975) formulated a *concept learning theory* that suggested subjects begin a concept formation task with a subset of hypotheses, one of which is the "working" hypothesis; if their feedback on the tasks is consistent with the working hypothesis, subjects retained that hypothesis, and if the feedback was inconsistent, they shifted their emphasis to a different working hypothesis that was selected from the original subset. Another theoretical approach is offered by Bower and Trabasso (1964) and Trabasso and Bower (1968), who argue that concept learning occurs in an *all-or-none* fashion, and is contrasted with the *incremental* position, which argues that learning takes place gradually over a series of trials. According to the findings of Bower and Trabasso, it appears that concept learning may at least sometimes occur in a fashion resembling an all-or-none process, but a final answer with respect to the adequacy of the all-or-none conception must wait for further experimentation (Houston, 1981). Other approaches in explaining concept learning involve the use of terms and procedures such as *decision trees* (e.g., Hunt, Marin, & Stone, 1966), *prototype acquisition* (e.g., Posner, 1973; Rosch & Lloyd, 1978), *animals' concept formation* (e.g., Hulse, Fowler, & Honig, 1978), *rule learning and complexity* (e.g., Anglin, 1977; Fodor, 1975), *information-processing theories* (e.g., Hunt, 1962), *quantitative/mathematical theories* (e.g., Bourne & Restle, 1959), *abstracting ability* (e.g., Osgood, 1953), and *mediational theories* and *cue-selection models* (e.g., Kling & Riggs, 1971). See also INFORMATION/INFORMATION-PROCESSING THEORY; LEARNING THEORIES/LAWS.

REFERENCES

Hull, C. (1920). Quantitative aspects of the evolution of concepts. *Psy. Mono., 28,* no. 123.

Hovland, C. (1952). A "communication analysis" of concept learning. *Psy. Rev., 59,* 461–472.

Osgood, C. (1953). *Method and theory in experimental psychology.* New York: Oxford University Press.

Bruner, J., Goodnow, J., & Austin, G. (1956). *A study of thinking.* New York: Wiley.

Bourne, L., & Restle, F. (1959). Mathematical theory of concept identification. *Psy. Rev., 66,* 278–296.

Hunt, E. (1962). *Concept learning: An information-processing problem.* New York: Wiley.

Bower, G., & Trabasso, T. (1964). Concept identification. In R. Atkinson (Ed.), *Studies in mathematical psychology.* Stanford, CA: Stanford University Press.

Hunt, E., Marin, J., & Stone, P. (1966). *Experiments in induction.* New York: Academic Press.

Klausmeier, H., & Harris, C. (Eds.) (1966). *Analyses of concept learning.* New York: Academic Press.

Trabasso, T., & Bower, G. (1968). *Attention in learning.* New York: Wiley.

Piaget, J. (1970). Piaget's theory. In P. Mussen (Ed.), *Carmichael's manual of child psychology.* New York: Wiley.

Kling, J., & Riggs, L. (Eds.) (1971). *Woodworth and Schlosberg's experimental psychology.* New York: Holt, Rinehart, & Winston.

Posner, M. (1973). *Cognition: An introduction.* Glenview, IL: Scott, Foresman.

Fodor, J. (1975). *The language of thought.* New York: Crowell.

Levine, M. (1975). *A cognitive theory of learning.* Hillsdale, NJ: Erlbaum.

Anglin, J. (1977). *Word, object, and conceptual development.* New York: Norton.

Hulse, S., Fowler, H., & Honig, W. (1978). *Cognitive processes in animal behavior.* Hillsdale, NJ: Erlbaum.

Rosch, E., & Lloyd, B. (Eds.) (1978). *Cognition and categorization.* Hillsdale, NJ: Erlbaum.

Bourne, L., Dominowski, R., & Loftus, E. (1979). *Cognitive processes.* Englewood Cliffs, NJ: Prentice-Hall.

Klausmeier, H. (1980). *Learning and teaching process concepts: A strategy for testing applications of theory.* New York: Academic Press.

Houston, J. (1981). *Fundamentals of learning and memory.* New York: Academic Press.

Klausmeier, H. (1994). Conceptual learning and development. In R. J. Corsini (Ed.), *Ency. Psy.* New York: Wiley.

Matlin, M. (1994). Concept learning. In R. J. Corsini (Ed.), *Ency. Psy.* New York: Wiley.

Reber, A. (1995). *The Penguin dictionary of psychology.* New York: Penguin Books.

CONDILLAC'S THEORY OF ATTENTION. The French philosopher Etienne Bonnot de Condillac (1715–1780) successfully transported John Locke's method and theory of empiricism from England to France. The *theory* of empiricism states that all knowledge comes from experience, while the *method* of empiricism advocates the collection and evaluation of data where experimentation is emphasized, and induction via observation is advocated over deduction from theoretical constructs (Reber, 1995). Condillac reacted against Descartes' *theory of innate ideas,* Malebranche's *faculties,* and Leibnitz's *theory of the monad* (Boring, 1957). In 1754, Condillac presented his famous analogy or parable of the *sentient statue* to emphasize that the whole of mental life can be derived in experience from sensation alone. One is asked to imagine a statue that is endowed with only a single sense, such as the simple sense of smell. The statue smells a rose (where the statue *is* a rose for the time being because there is nothing else to its existence than this odor) and is, thereby, said to be *attending* to the odor. Thus, one may see how *attention* comes into mental life: the first odor goes, and another odor comes; then the first returns, and the statue knows that what was can come again; that is "memory." When what was recurs with what is, the statue may be said to be comparing: one odor is pleasant, another odor is unpleasant. Also, in the inherent values of the odors, the statue learns of desire and aversion. In like fashion, judgment, discernment, imagination, and other sorts of abstract notions were represented by Condillac as possible of development in experience with only a single sense as the medium. Later, the addition of other senses would still further enhance the statue's capacities. Thus, the essential point of Condillac's *statue analogy* is that all mental life, including *attention*, can be derived from sensory experience, and if a statue were endowed with only a single sense, it could develop all the mental processes currently possessed by humans (Wolman, 1973). Condillac argued that the sum total of all human mental processes would develop without any need to presuppose the *laws of association*, and variations in the quality of sensations would necessarily produce all the qualities that were needed for human comprehension (Lundin, 1994). Condillac's brand of sensational empiricism eventually failed because it was too simple: it was difficult to reduce the mind to sensory experience alone. The nineteenth-century French writers felt that Condillac's approach was too cold; twentieth-century psychologists could not ignore the "whole" person and tended to stress the notion that analysis without synthesis is open to failure in theorizing (Boring, 1957). However, on the positive side, Condillac fostered the *empirical* attitude, which had a strong impact on the movement of French materialism, and, like John Locke, he adopted a philosophical approach and strategy that provided the basis for development of the natural sciences (Lundin, 1994). See also ASSOCIATION, LAWS/PRINCIPLES OF; ATTENTION, LAWS/PRINCIPLES/THEORIES OF.

REFERENCES

Condillac, E. (1746/1974). *Essay on the origin of human knowledge*. New York: AMS.
Condillac, E. (1754/1930). *Treatise on sensations*. Los Angeles: University of Southern California Press.
Hoffding, H. (1908). *Outlines of psychology*. London: Macmillan.
Boring, E. G. (1957). *A history of experimental psychology*. New York: Appleton-Century-Crofts.
Wolman, B. (Ed.) (1973). *Dictionary of behavioral science*. New York: Van Nostrand Reinhold.
Lundin, R. (1994). Etienne Bonnot de Condillac. In R. J. Corsini (Ed.), *Ency. Psy.* New York: Wiley.
Reber, A. (1995). *The Penguin dictionary of psychology*. New York: Penguin Books.

CONDITIONING OF TYPE R, LAW OF. See SKINNER'S DESCRIPTIVE BEHAVIOR/OPERANT CONDITIONING THEORY.

CONDITIONING OF TYPE S, LAW OF. See SKINNER'S DESCRIPTIVE BEHAVIOR/OPERANT CONDITIONING THEORY.

CONFLICT, THEORIES OF. The term *conflict* is an extremely broad concept used to refer to any situation where there are mutually antagonistic events, motives, behaviors, impulses, or purposes (Reber, 1995). In the area of learning and motivation psychology, Miller (1944), Miller and Murray (1952), and Miller (1959) developed a precise formulation of *conflict theory* based on some preliminary ideas of Lewin (1935). According to Lewin (1931) and Miller (1944), there are four major types of conflicts involving "approach" and "avoidance" behavioral tendencies: *approach-approach*—situation in which the person must choose between two positive goals of the same value; *avoidance-avoidance*—the person must choose between two negative outcomes of approximately equal value; *approach-avoidance*—circumstances where achieving a positive goal will produce a negative outcome as well; and *double/multiple approach-avoidance*—the person is required to choose between two or more alternatives, each of which contains both positive and negative consequences. The concept of *ambivalence* (i.e., mixed positive and negative feelings concerning objects, people, or events) is a central characteristic of *approach-avoidance* conflicts and is usually translated into "partial approach" (Miller, 1944). Within Miller's (1944) conflict paradigm, Epstein & Fenz (1965) and Epstein (1982) have demonstrated the stressfulness of conflicts in their studies of parachute jumpers. The sympathetic autonomic arousal reaction of the jumpers rose dramatically to a peak at the moment of the jump, then returned to normal levels immediately after they landed. In the area of *social conflict* (e.g., Pruitt, 1986), the study of conflict is an interdisciplinary enterprise, involving sociologists, political scientists, game theorists, and social psychologists. Some psychologists have viewed *conflict* as a manifestation of individual aggression that is usually attributed to frustrations experienced by the person; others see *conflict* as arising from images that persons or groups have of one another (e.g., in the mutual perception of threat). During the late 1940s and early 1950s, conflict theorists began to study empirically the social phenomena of *cooperation* and *competition* (Alcock, 1994). The terms *cooperation* and *competition* refer to collaborative effort and rivalry, respectively, concerning mutually desired goals or the means of achieving individual or mutual goals. In a "pure" cooperation situation (e.g., Deutsch, 1950), the goal of one individual can be reached only if the other members also attain their goals. In the case of "pure" competition, a person's goals can be attained only if the others do not attain theirs. However, the extremes of pure cooperation and pure competition are rarely encountered in realistic contexts, and most situations are a blend of both types. One theoretical approach (Neumann & Morgenstern, 1947) used *mathematical games and models* to describe the behavior of "rational" individuals in situations of interdependence. Other approaches study laboratory interactions of *bargaining* situations (e.g., Siegel & Fouraker, 1960), *prisoner's dilemma games* (e.g., Rapoport & Chammah, 1965; cf: Pruitt & Kimmel, 1977), *locomotion games* (e.g., Deutsch & Krauss, 1960), and realistic *field scenarios* (e.g., Sherif, Harvey, White, Hood, & Sherif, 1961). In general, psychological research shows that cooperative activity most likely emerges when the interacting parties both share a common goal and a common means of attaining that goal, and competition most likely occurs when either the individual goals of the parties involved or the means of obtaining them are incompatible (Raven & Rubin, 1976). Interest has also been shown by *conflict theorists* in the social sciences for practical methods of *conflict resolution*, such as bargaining and mediation (e.g., Pruitt, 1972; Smith, 1994; Leviton & Greenstone, 1994). Theories of conflict between groups, called *image theories*, have been proposed where diabolical images of the enemy and virile/moral images of the self have been employed (e.g., Pruitt, 1986). Study of direct intergroup conflict concerning the variable of competition has led to the formulation of the *realistic conflict theory* of prejudice, which states that prejudice arises from competition between social groups over scarce commodities or opportunities (Baron, 1992). The *realistic conflict theory* further suggests that as such competition persists, the members of the groups involved come to view each other in increasingly negative ways, much as indicated in the *image theories* (e.g., White, 1977; cf: Hovland & Sears, 1940; Hepworth & West, 1988). The concept of *conflict* has been invoked, also, in the history of psychology by Johann Friedrich Herbart (1776–1841). Based on the popular assumption that elementary bits of ideas or experiences may combine harmoniously into wholes, Herbart taught that ideas may come into relation with each other through *conflict* or struggle as well. Thus, according to Herbart, ideas that are incapable of combining compete with one another, and this competition occurs in order to gain a place in consciousness. Recent writers, including the psychoanalysts, emphasize that objects of thought do not conflict with each other because they are in logical opposition, as Herbart proposed, but because they lead to divergent lines of conduct; ideas are in conflict if they lead individuals to do opposite things (Murphy & Kovach, 1972). The concept of *conflict* has been invoked, also, in the area of perception. For example, Ames (1955) and Ittelson (1952) discussed *conflict of cues* related to demonstrations of the influence of visual context upon monocular and binocular perception. Ames produced surprising, sometimes startling, effects in his "Ames room demonstrations"—such as seeing someone changed into a giant or a dwarf, and red spots on playing cards change to black—because of sheer congruity and the perceiver's need for internal unity. In the Ames room situation, affective and familiarity factors may destroy the intended illusion. For example, the *Honi effect/phenomenon* refers to the failure of the well-known perceptual distortion effects of the Ames room to occur when a very familiar person such as a parent or spouse is placed in the room (Reber, 1995; cf: Dion & Dion, 1976). The term *conflict*, when used in the area of psychoanalysis, refers to a painful emotional state that results from a tension between opposed and contradictory wishes and is due to the fact that an unconscious (repressed) wish is forcibly prevented from entering the conscious system. The term *major conflict* refers to the more dominant emotional state in a current conflict between opposed and contradictory wishes (Warren, 1934). *Actual con-*

flict is a presently occurring conflict where, in the psychoanalytic context, such conflicts are assumed to derive from "root conflicts" (i.e., the underlying conflict that is assumed to be primarily responsible for an observed psychological disorder; cf: *nuclear conflict*, which tends to be used in a broader fashion). *Nuclear conflict* is a fundamental conflict occurring during infancy or early childhood that is assumed to be a root cause of a number of psychoneurotic disorders that may emerge only later in life. For Freud, the *Oedipus complex* fulfilled this hypothesized role; for Horney, it was a child's *feeling of helplessness*; and for Adler, it was *feelings of inferiority*. The term *basic conflict* was Horney's term for the fundamental conflicts that emerge when "neurotic needs" are discoordinate (Wolman, 1973; Reber, 1995). In Horney's (1937, 1945) theory of personality, the term *central conflict* is the psychic conflict between one's "real self" and one's "idealized self." The term *conflict-free ego sphere* is Heinz Hartmann's (1958) concept in his *ego theory* for the part of the ego called "primary autonomy," which includes the individual's perception, motility, and memory. In the area of measurement and statistics, the concept called *conflict index (C)* is a statistic that gives an exact value for the total amount of energy that an organism (or other dynamic system) has bound up in its internal conflict (Wolman, 1973). Thus, *conflict theories* and the concept of *conflict* have been used, among other things, to refer to individual or group preferences for incompatible actions in a given learning or motivation situation, to particular aspects of different psychoanalytic theories, to philosophical analyses concerning ideas, to perceptual demonstrations, to a statistical index, and to practical contexts concerning resolution, resolution therapy, cooperation/competition, and negotiations/mediation of conflicts. See also AGGRESSION, THEORIES OF; DECISION-MAKING THEORIES; EQUITY THEORY; FESTINGER'S COGNITIVE DISSONANCE THEORY; FREUD'S THEORY OF PERSONALITY; HORNEY'S THEORY OF PERSONALITY; PREJUDICE, THEORIES OF.

REFERENCES

Lewin, K. (1931). Environmental forces in child behavior and development. In C. Murchison (Ed.), *Handbook of child psychology*. Worcester, MA: Clark University Press.

Warren, H. (Ed.) (1934). *Dictionary of psychology*. Cambridge, MA: Houghton Mifflin.

Lewin, K. (1935). *A dynamic theory of personality*. New York: McGraw-Hill.

Horney, K. (1937). *Neurotic personality of our times*. New York: Norton.

Hovland, C., & Sears, R. (1940). Minor studies in aggression: VI. Correlation of lynchings with economic indices. *J. Psy., 9*, 301–310.

Miller, N. (1944). Experimental studies in conflict. In J. McV. Hunt (Ed.), *Personality and the behavior disorders*. New York: Ronald Press.

Horney, K. (1945). *Our inner conflicts*. New York: Norton.

Neumann, J. von., & Morgenstern, O. (1947). *Theory of games and economic behavior*. Princeton, NJ: Princeton University Press.

Deutsch, M. (1950). A theory of cooperation and competition. *Hum. Rel.*, *2*, 129–152.

Miller, N. (1951). Comment on theoretical models illustrated by the development of a theory of conflict. *J. Pers.*, *20*, 82–100.

Ittelson, W. (1952). *The Ames demonstrations in perception*. Princeton, NJ: Princeton University Press.

Miller, N., & Murray, E. (1952). Displacement and conflict: Learnable drive as a basis for the steeper gradient of avoidance than of approach. *J. Exp. Psy.*, *43*, 227–231.

Ames, A. (1955). *An interpretive manual for the demonstrations in the Psychological Research Center, Princeton University*. Princeton, NJ: Princeton University Press.

Hartmann, H. (1958). *Ego psychology and the problem of adaptation*. New York: International Universities Press.

Miller, N. (1959). Liberalization of basic S-R concepts: Extensions to conflict behavior, motivation, and social learning. In S. Koch (Ed.), *Psychology: A study of a science*. Vol. 2. New York: McGraw-Hill.

Deutsch, M., & Krauss, R. (1960). The effect of threat upon interpersonal bargaining. *J. Abn. Soc. Psy.*, *61*, 181–189.

Siegel, S., & Fouraker, L. (1960). *Bargaining and group decision-making: Experiments in bilateral monopoly*. New York: McGraw-Hill.

Sherif, M., Harvey, O., White, B., Hood, W., & Sherif, C. (1961). *Intergroup conflict and cooperation: The Robber's Cave experiment*. Norman: University of Oklahoma Press.

Epstein, S., & Fenz, W. (1965). Steepness of approach and avoidance gradients in humans as a function of experience: Theory and experiment. *J. Exp. Psy.*, *70*, 1–12.

Rapoport, A., & Chammah, A. (1965). *Prisoner's dilemma: A study in conflict and cooperation*. Ann Arbor: Universtiy of Michigan Press.

Raven, B., & Kruglanski, A. (1970). Conflict and power. In P. Swingle (Ed.), *The structure of conflict*. New York: Academic Press.

Miller, N. (1971). *Selected papers on conflict, displacement, learned drives, and theory*. Chicago: Aldine.

Murphy, G., & Kovach, J. (1972). *Historical introduction to modern psychology*. New York: Harcourt Brace Jovanovich.

Pruitt, D. (1972). Methods for resolving conflicts of interest: A theoretical analysis. *J. Soc. Iss.*, *28*, 133–154.

Wolman, B. (Ed.) (1973). *Dictionary of behavioral science*. New York: Van Nostrand Reinhold.

Dion, K. L., & Dion, K. K. (1976). The Honi phenomenon revisited: Factors underlying the resistance to perceptual distortion of one's partner. *J. Pers. Soc. Psy.*, *33*, 170–177.

Raven, B., & Rubin, J. (1976). *Social psychology*. New York: Wiley.

Pruitt, D., & Kimmel, M. (1977). Twenty years of experimental gaming: Critique, synthesis, and suggestions for the future. *Ann. Rev. Psy.*, *28*, 363–392.

White, R. (1977). Misperception in the Arab–Israeli conflict. *J. Soc. Iss.*, *33*, 190–221.

Epstein, S. (1982). Conflict and stress. In L. Goldberger & S. Breznitz (Eds.), *Handbook of stress*. New York: Free Press.

Pruitt, D. (1986). Social conflict. In T. Pettijohn (Ed.), *The encyclopedic dictionary of psychology*. Guilford, CT: Dushkin.

Hepworth, J., & West, S. (1988). Lynchings and the economy: A time-series reanalysis of Hovland and Sears (1940). *J. Pers. Soc. Psy., 55*, 238–247.

Baron, R. (1992). *Psychology*. Boston: Allyn & Bacon.

Alcock, J. (1994). Cooperation/competition. In R. J. Corsini (Ed.), *Ency. Psy.* New York: Wiley.

Leviton, S., & Greenstone, J. (1994). Conflict mediation. In R. J. Corsini (Ed.), *Ency. Psy.* New York: Wiley.

Smith, W. (1994). Conflict resolution. In R. J. Corsini (Ed.), *Ency. Psy.* New York: Wiley.

Reber, A. (1995). *The Penguin dictionary of psychology*. New York: Penguin Books.

CONFLUENCE THEORY. See ZAJONC'S AROUSAL THEORY.

CONNECTION, LAWS OF. See REINFORCEMENT, THORNDIKE'S THEORY OF.

CONSERVATION OF ENERGY, LAW/PRINCIPLE OF. See GESTALT THEORY/LAWS.

CONSOLIDATION HYPOTHESIS/THEORY. See FORGETTING/MEMORY, THEORIES OF.

CONSTITUTIONAL THEORIES OF PERSONALITY. See SHELDON'S TYPE THEORY; KRETSCHMER'S THEORY OF PERSONALITY.

CONSTRUCTIVIST THEORY OF PERCEPTION. This approach toward explaining perceptual phenomena and processes focuses on how the mind *constructs* perceptions. *Constructivist theory* takes a number of different forms, including research on the connection between perception and neural processing and research on how perception is determined by mental processing. The idea of approaching perception by asking what the mind does during the perceptual process is an old notion whose roots go back to the nineteenth century, when Hermann von Helmholtz proposed the *likelihood principle*: one perceives the object that is "most likely" to occur in "that particular situation" (Goldstein, 1996). A modern descendant of Helmholtz's *likelihood principle* is Gregory's (1973) notion that perception is governed by a mechanism he calls *hypothesis testing*, which refers to a function of sensory stimulation as providing data for hypotheses concerning the state of the external world. *Hypothesis testing* does not always occur at a conscious level, and perceivers are usually not aware of the complex mental processes that occur during a perceptual act. The idea that mental operations occur during the perceptual process is illustrated by an early study by Kulpe (1904): displays of various colors were presented to subjects who were asked to pay attention to a particular aspect of the display (such as the positions of certain letters), but when the subjects were asked subsequently to describe another aspect of the display (such as the color of a particular letter), they were not able to do it. This indicates that even though all of the information from the stimulus display reached the observer's eye, a selection process took place somewhere between the reception of this information and the person's perception so that only part of the information was actually perceived and re-membered. Thus, perception seems to depend on more than simply the properties of the stimulus, and the observer makes a contribution to the perceptual process. Another way that the *cognitive/constructivist* aspect of processing has been ap-proached is by considering the *eye movements* that people make when observing an object (e.g., Hochberg, 1971). According to the *eye movement theory*, as an observer looks at a scene, information is taken in by a series of "fixations" (i.e., pauses of the eye that occur one to three times per second as the person examines part of the stimulus) and "eye movements" that propel the eye from one fixation to the next. Such eye movements are necessary in order to see all of the details of the scene, because a single fixation would reveal only the details near the fixation point. According to Hochberg (1971), *eye movements* have another purpose: the information they take in about different parts of the scene is used to create a "mental map" of the scene by a process of "integration" or "piecing together." Thus, Helmholtz's *likelihood principle*, Gregory's idea of *hypothesis testing*, and Hochberg's *eye movement theory* all treat perception as involving an active, constructing observer who processes stimulus informa-tion. The *constructivist* approach also assumes that perception of a whole object is constructed from information taken in from smaller parts. The essence of all *constructivist theories* is that perceptual experience is viewed as more than a direct response to stimulation (cf: *direct perception theory*); it is, instead, viewed as an elaboration or "construction" based on hypothesized cognitive and affec-tive operations (Reber, 1995). See also ATTENTION, LAWS/PRINCIPLES/ THEORIES OF; DIRECT PERCEPTION THEORY; PERCEPTION (I. GEN-ERAL), THEORIES OF; PERCEPTION (II. COMPARATIVE APPRAISAL), THEORIES OF; UNCONSCIOUS INFERENCE, DOCTRINE OF.

REFERENCES

Kulpe, O. (1904). Versuche uber Abstraktion. *Ber. Inter. Cong. Exp. Psy.*, 56–68.
Hochberg, J. (1971). Perception. In J. Kling & L. Riggs (Eds.), *Woodworth and Schlos-berg's experimental psychology*. New York: Holt, Rinehart, & Winston.
Gregory, R. (1973). *Eye and brain*. New York: McGraw-Hill.
Reber, A. (1995). *The Penguin dictionary of psychology*. New York: Penguin Books.
Goldstein, E. (1996). *Sensation and perception*. Pacific Grove, CA: Brooks/Cole.

CONTACT HYPOTHESIS OF PREJUDICE. See PREJUDICE, THEORIES OF.

CONTEXT, LAW OF. See INTERFERENCE THEORIES OF FORGETTING.

CONTIGUITY, LAW OF. See ASSOCIATION, LAWS/PRINCIPLES OF.

CONTINGENCY THEORIES OF WORK MOTIVATION. See WORK/ CAREER/OCCUPATION, THEORIES OF.

CONTINGENCY THEORY OF LEADERSHIP. See LEADERSHIP, THE-ORIES OF.

CONTINUITY, LAW/PRINCIPLE OF. See GESTALT THEORY/LAWS.

CONTINUITY THEORY. See SPENCE'S THEORY; DEVELOPMENTAL THEORY.

CONTRAST, LAW OF. See ASSOCIATION, LAWS/PRINCIPLES OF.

CONTROL/SYSTEMS THEORY. The terms *control theory* and *control the-ory psychology* (e.g., Powers, 1973a, b, 1979) are recent names for describing the development of a body of theory based on a *feedback-system* paradigm or model. Other current synonymous names for this approach include *cybernetic psychology*, *general feedback theory* of human behavior, and *systems theory psychology* (Robertson, 1994; Royce, 1994). In the area of learning/condition-ing, the *biofeedback principles* and procedures (i.e., the process of providing an organism with information about its biological functions such as alpha waves, heart rate, blood pressure, blood flow in the extremities) have demonstrated *control/systems* approaches in both laboratory and practical settings (e.g., Miller, 1969, 1978, 1983; Schwartz, 1973, 1978). The notion of self-regulating systems of the body is not new (cf: Bernard, 1865; Cannon, 1932; Buckley, 1967). However, the idea of applying the same principles to the study of the mind is relatively more recent (e.g., Ashby, 1952; Sluckin, 1954; Annett, 1969; Emery, 1969). Various unresolved issues confounded initial attempts to develop a com-prehensive and precise feedback model, for instance, the concept of *homeostasis* (internal stability and balance) versus the concept of *adaptation* (external shap-ing and modifiability). That is, how could behavior be controlled so as to ac-commodate both internal and external systems? (cf: Mowrer, 1954; Slack, 1955; Deutsch, 1968). Another problem was the development of mechanisms to account for integration of different feedback systems in the organism (cf: Pow-ers, Clark, & McFarland, 1960). Powers (1973a, b) described an *integration theory* and model involving a negative feedback control loop that consisted of five elements: a *feedback* function involving a transducer/signal sensitive to identifiable environmental variables; a *comparator* function involving the feed-back/reference/error signal; a *compatibility* function between the reference and feedback signals; an error signal *discrepancy* function between the feedback and reference signals; and an *output* function that exerts its effect upon the environ-ment so as to make a match between the feedback and reference signals and reduce the error signal to zero. A profound consequence of Powers' (1973a) theory for psychology is the implication that living organisms do not control their environments by controlling their outputs. They control their *inputs*; that is, they control their "perceptions" (cf: Rogers, 1959). Thus, according to this theoretical orientation, control over the environment results as a by-product of controlling one's perceptions (Powers, 1973a). *Control theory* research breaks with more traditional approaches to research methodology in psychology. Most current research is based on a *causal model* where influence is expected to flow in one direction, but *cybernetic theory* (e.g.,Wiener, 1948) shows that the concept of *cause* becomes ambiguous when variables under the control of negative feedback systems are examined. Among other positive features, *control theory* provides a natural theoretical basis for *humanistic psychology*; that is, behavior originates not in stimuli from the environment but within the organism itself (Robertson, 1994). See also ORGANIZATIONAL/INDUSTRIAL/SYSTEMS THEORY; REACTANCE THEORY.

REFERENCES

Bernard, C. (1865). *An introduction to the study of experimental medicine*. New York: Dover.

Cannon, W. (1932). *The wisdom of the body*. New York: Norton.

Craik, K. (1943). *The nature of explanation*. Cambridge, England: Cambridge University Press.

Wiener, N. (1948). *Cybernetics: Control and communication in the animal and the machine*. Cambridge: MIT Press.

Ashby, R. (1952). *Design for a brain*. New York: Wiley.

Mowrer, O. H. (1954). Ego psychology, cybernetics, and learning theory. In D. Adams (Ed.), *Learning theory and clinical research*. New York: Wiley.

Sluckin, W. (1954). *Minds and machines*. London: Pelican Books.

Slack, C. (1955). Feedback theory and the reflex arc concept. *Psy. Rev., 62*, 263–267.

Rogers, C. (1959). A theory of therapy, personality, and interpersonal relationships as developed in the client-centered framework. In S. Koch (Ed.), *Psychology: A study of a science*. Vol. 3. New York: McGraw-Hill.

Maltz, M. (1960). *Psycho-cybernetics: A new way to get more living out of life*. Englewood Cliffs, NJ: Prentice-Hall.

Miller, G., Galanter, E., & Pribram, K. (1960). *Plans and the structure of behavior*. New York: Holt, Rinehart, & Winston.

Powers, W., Clark, R., & McFarland, R. (1960). A general feedback theory of human behavior. Part 1. *Percep. Mot. Skills Mono., 11*, no. 7.

Smith, K., & Smith, M. (1966). *Cybernetic principles of learning and educational design*. New York: Holt, Rinehart, & Winston.

Buckley, W. (1967). *Sociology and modern systems theory*. Englewood Cliffs, NJ: Prentice-Hall.

Bertalanffy, L. von (1968). *General systems theory*. New York: Braziller.

Deutsch, K. (1968). Toward a cybernetic model of man and society. In W. Buckley (Ed.), *Modern systems theory for the behavioral scientist*. Chicago: Aldine.

Annett, J. (1969). *Feedback and human behavior*. Baltimore: Penguin Books.

Emery, F. (1969). *System thinking*. Hammondsworth, England: Penguin Books.

Klir, G. (1969). *An approach to general systems theory*. New York: Van Nostrand Reinhold.

Miller, N. (1969). Learning of visceral and glandular responses. *Science, 163*, 434–445.

Powers, W. (1973a). *Behavior: The control of perception*. Chicago: Aldine.

Powers, W. (1973b). Feedback beyond behaviorism. *Science, 179*, 351–356.

Schwartz, G. (1973). Biofeedback as therapy: Some theoretical and practical issues. *Amer. Psy., 28*, 666–673.

Miller, N. (1978). Biofeedback and visceral learning. *Ann. Rev. Psy., 29*, 373–404.

Schwartz, G. (1978). Disregulation and systems theory: A biobehavioral framework for biofeedback and behavioral medicine. In N. Birbaumer & H. Kimmel (Eds.), *Biofeedback and self-regulation*. Hillsdale, NJ: Erlbaum.

Powers, W. (1979). A cybernetic model for research in human development. In M. Ozer (Ed.), *A cybernetic approach to assessment of children: Toward a more humane use of human beings*. Boulder, CO: Westview Press.

Carver, C., & Scheier, M. (1982). Control theory: A useful conceptual framework for personality, social, clinical, and health psychology. *Psy. Bull., 92*, 111–135.

Miller, N. (1983). Behavioral medicine: Symbiosis between laboratory and clinic. *Ann. Rev. Psy., 34*, 1–31.

Deci, E. (1994). Control systems. In R. J. Corsini (Ed.), *Ency. Psy.* New York: Wiley.

Robertson, R. (1994). Control theory. In R. J. Corsini (Ed.). *Ency. Psy.* New York: Wiley.

Royce, J. (1994). Systems theory. In R. J. Corsini (Ed.), *Ency. Psy.* New York: Wiley.

COOLIDGE EFFECT. See LOVE, THEORIES OF.

COOPERATION/COMPETITION, THEORIES OF. See CONFLICT, THEORIES OF.

CORE-CONTEXT THEORY. See PERCEPTION (II. COMPARATIVE APPRAISAL), THEORIES OF.

CORRESPONDENT INFERENCE THEORY. See ATTRIBUTION THEORY.

COVARIATION/CORRELATION PRINCIPLE. See ATTRIBUTION THEORY.

CREATIVE SYNTHESIS, PRINCIPLE OF. See WUNDT'S THEORIES.

CRESPI EFFECT. The American psychologist Leo P. Crespi (1916–) is credited with the finding that in learning experiments on lower animals there is a disproportionate increase in a response with an increase in incentive. For example, if an animal is pressing a lever for one gram of food reinforcement and is then shifted suddenly to five grams of reinforcement, it will characteristically respond at a higher rate than a comparable animal that has been receiving five gram reinforcements all along (Reber, 1995). This sudden shift in "attractiveness" of a reward is called the *Crespi effect* or the *contrast effect* (Crespi, 1942, 1944). Another example of the *Crespi effect* is seen in rats learning to run a maze: if a large amount of food provides the incentive, the rats run to the goal faster than if the amount of food is small. Thus, with practice, the rats in these two conditions (large reward versus small reward) show a significant difference in running speeds. Subsequently, once the levels of running are established in each condition, switching the amounts of food for the two groups has an immediate effect on maze-running performance. Rats that had received a large reward and now receive a small reward run more slowly. On the other hand, rats that had received a small reward and now receive a large reward run faster. In addition, the rats' performance with the changed reward often "overshoots" the mark expected from their earlier behavior. The rats switched from a large reward to a small reward run more slowly than predicted, while those rats switched from a small to a large reward run faster than expected (Kimble, 1994). Increased performance as a result of going from a small to a large reward was termed *positive contrast* or an *elation effect*, whereas the poorer performance associated with going from a large to a small amount of reward was termed *negative contrast* or a *depression effect* (Hall, 1966, 1976). The replicability of Crespi's findings has been controversial. While many studies support the *Crespi effect* and Crespi's (1942) earlier findings (e.g., Zeaman, 1949; DiLollo, 1964), a number of other investigators have been unable to obtain such effects (e.g., Homzie & Ross, 1962; Rosen, 1966). Spence (1956) failed to find *positive contrast effects* and suggested that the *positive contrast effect* obtained by Crespi was a function of the original high-reward group subjects' not having reached their asymptote and that the shift group responded at the higher level because of the additional training trials. Spence (1956) did report, however, finding *negative contrast effects* (cf: Bower, 1961). Thus, although the *negative contrast effect* seems to stand as a viable concept in the field (Peters & McHose, 1974), there have been questions about the validity of the *positive contrast effect* (e.g., Dunham, 1968; Dunham & Kilps, 1969). Optimal explanations for the *contrast effects* may depend, ultimately, on whether only *negative contrast effects* are thought to be obtainable, or whether both *positive* and *negative contrast effects* can be considered bona fide phenomena. If it is assumed that both types are obtainable, a theory such as Helson's (1964) *adaptation-level theory* as applied to conditioning and reinforcement may be a feasible option (Hall, 1976). See also HELSON'S ADAPTATION-LEVEL THEORY; LEARNING THEORIES/ LAWS.

REFERENCES

Crespi, L. (1942). Quantitative variation of incentive and performance in the white rat. *Amer. J. Psy., 55*, 467–517.
Crespi, L. (1944). Amount of reinforcement and level of performance. *Psy. Rev., 51*, 341–357.

Zeaman, D. (1949). Response latency as a function of the amount of reinforcement. *J. Exp. Psy., 39*, 466–483.

Spence, K. (1956). *Behavior theory and conditioning.* New Haven, CT: Yale University Press.

Bower, G. (1961). A contrast effect in differential conditioning. *J. Exp. Psy., 62*, 196–199.

Homzie, M., & Ross, L. (1962). Runway performance following a reduction in the concentration of a liquid reward. *J. Comp. Physio. Psy., 55*, 1029–1033.

DiLollo, V. (1964). Runway performance in relation to runway goal-box similarity and changes in incentive amount. *J. Comp. Physio. Psy., 58*, 327–329.

Helson, H. (1964). *Adaptation-level theory: An experimental and systematic approach to behavior.* New York: Harper & Row.

Hall, J. (1966). *The psychology of learning.* Philadelphia: Lippincott.

Rosen, A. (1966). Incentive-shift performance as a function of magnitude and number of sucrose rewards. *J. Comp. Physio. Psy., 62*, 487–490.

Dunham, P. (1968). Contrasted conditions of reinforcement: A selective critique. *Psy. Bull., 69*, 295–315.

Dunham, P., & Kilps, B. (1969). Shifts in magnitude of reinforcement: Confounded factors or contrast effects? *J. Exp. Psy., 79*, 373–374.

Peters, D., & McHose, J. (1974). Effects of varied preshift reward magnitude on successive negative contrast effects in rats. *J. Comp. Physio. Psy., 86*, 85–95.

Hall, J. (1976). *Classical conditioning and instrumental learning: A contemporary approach.* Philadelphia: Lippincott.

Kimble, G. (1994). Crespi effect. In R. J. Corsini (Ed.), *Ency. Psy.* New York: Wiley.

Reber, A. (1995). *The Penguin dictionary of psychology.* New York: Penguin Books.

CULTURAL BIAS HYPOTHESIS. See INTELLIGENCE, THEORIES/ LAWS OF.

CULTURAL-NORM HYPOTHESIS. See ATTRIBUTION THEORY.

CULTURE-EPOCH THEORY. See RECAPITULATION, THEORY/LAW OF.

CUMULATIVE DEFICITS PHENOMENON/THEORY. The American psychologist Morton Deutsch (1920–   ) and the Nigerian psychologist Christopher Bakare (1935–   ) have both suggested the *cumulative deficits phenomenon/theory*, and Bakare has formulated a *theory of the cumulative cognitive deficit syndrome.* The *theory of cumulative deficits* refers to the condition where, with persistent influence from a disadvantaged environment, there is over time an increasingly larger negative effect on the behavior in question. Bakare has studied the phenomenon in African children and has developed a number of cognitive-stimulation materials for correcting such deficits once they are diagnosed (cf: Hutt's, 1980, *theory of microdiagnosis,* which proposes that in all exceptional cases an examiner or clinician should develop relevant hypotheses concerning test scores that would help to explain any suspected deviance from the "true score" of individuals). In addition to his study of the phenomenon, Deutsch has done research on interracial housing, cooperation and competition, interpersonal conflict, and distributive justice. See also INTELLIGENCE, THEORIES/LAWS OF.

REFERENCES

Deutsch, M., & Brown, B. (1964). Social influences in negro–white intelligence differences. *J. Soc. Iss., 20,* 24–35.

Deutsch, M., & Krauss, R. (1965). *Theories of social psychology.* New York: Basic Books.

Bakare, C. (1972). Social class differences in the performance of Nigerian children on the Draw-a-Man test. In L. Cronbach & P. Drenth (Eds.), *Mental tests and cultural adaptation.* The Hague: Mouton.

Wolman, B. (Ed.) (1973). *Dictionary of behavioral science.* New York: Van Nostrand Reinhold.

Deutsch, M., & Hornstein, H. (Eds.) (1975). *Applying social psychology.* Hillsdale, NJ: Erlbaum.

Hutt, M. (1980). Microdiagnosis and misuse of scores and standards. *Psy. Rep., 50,* 239–255.

CUPBOARD THEORY. The *cupboard theory* is one of the earliest explanations for the phenomenon of *infant attachment* (Carlson, 1990). The theory refers to the mother's providing food when her infant is hungry, warmth when the child is cold, and dryness when the infant is wet and uncomfortable. That is, the mother functions virtually as a *cupboard* of supplies for her infant. Through her association with the infant and giving such needed supplies, the mother herself becomes a positive stimulus (*conditioned reinforcer*), and, as a result of the association process, the infant clings to her and demonstrates other signs of attachment. A number of experiments conducted on the phenomenon of *infant attachment* in the monkey (Harlow & Zimmerman, 1959; Harlow & Suomi, 1970; Harlow, 1974), however, showed unequivocally that the *cupboard theory* cannot account exclusively for attachment behavior in infants. Rather, the clinging behavior (in the case of the monkeys, clinging to a soft, cuddly form) in infants appears to be an innate response. Harry Harlow (1905–1981) and his associates isolated baby monkeys from their mothers immediately after birth and raised them alone in a cage containing two inanimate "surrogate" (substitute) mothers, one that was made of bare wire mesh but providing milk nourishment and the other padded and covered with terry cloth but providing no nourishment. If the *cupboard theory* were valid, the infants should have learned to cling to the surrogate mother that provided them with milk (the wire surrogate). However, the infants did not cling to the wire mother; they preferred to cling to the cuddly, cloth, warmer surrogate mother and went to the wire mother only to drink milk. Harlow's results suggest that close physical contact with a cuddly object is a biological need for infant monkeys (as well as for human infants), and infants cling and attach to their mothers not simply because the infant receives food from the mother but also because the physical contact with the mother is innately reinforcing (cf: Hong & Townes, 1976; Passman & Halonen, 1979; Cohen & Clark, 1984; Mahalski, Silva, & Spears, 1985). See also IN-FANT ATTACHMENT THEORIES.

REFERENCES

Harlow, H., & Zimmerman, R. (1959). Affectional responses in the infant monkey. *Science, 130*, 421–432.

Harlow, H., & Suomi, S. (1970). Nature of love—simplified. *Amer. Psy., 25*, 161–168.

Harlow, H. (1974). *Learning to love*. New York: Aronson.

Hong, K., & Townes, B. (1976). Infants' attachment to inanimate objects. *J. Amer. Acad. Child Psychiat., 15*, 49–61.

Ainsworth, M., Blehar, M., Waters, E., & Wall, S. (1978). *Patterns of attachment*. Hillsdale, NJ: Erlbaum.

Passman, R., & Halonen, J. (1979). A developmental survey of young children's attachment to inanimate objects. *J. Genet. Psy., 134*, 165–178.

Cohen, K., & Clark, J. (1984). Transitional object attachments in early childhood and personality characteristics in later life. *J. Pers. Soc. Psy., 46*, 106–111.

Mahalski, P., Silva, P., & Spears, G. (1985). Children's attachment to soft objects at bedtime, child rearing, and child development. *J. Amer. Acad. Child Psychiat., 24*, 442–446.

Carlson, N. (1990). *Psychology: The science of behavior*. Boston: Allyn & Bacon.

CYBERNETIC THEORY. See CONTROL/SYSTEMS THEORY.

CYBERNETIC THEORY OF PERCEPTION. See PERCEPTION (II. COMPARATIVE APPRAISAL), THEORIES OF.

D

DARWIN'S EVOLUTION THEORY/EVOLUTION, THEORY/LAWS OF.
= Darwinism. = biological evolution, doctrine of. The English naturalists Charles Robert Darwin (1809–1882) and Alfred Russel Wallace (1823–1913) independently formulated the basic tenets of the *theory of evolution*, which was first publicly presented in 1858 at a meeting of the Linnaean Society (named in honor of the Swedish botanist and taxonomist Carolus Linnaeus, 1707–1778). Darwin (1859) firmly established the *theory of organic evolution* known as *Darwinism*, and his name is better known than Wallace's today in connection with the origination of *evolutionary theory*. However, both men were exceptionally modest concerning ''ownership'' of the theory, and they first published summaries of their ideas simultaneously in 1858 (Harris & Levey, 1975). At first, Wallace held that human evolution could be explained by his and Darwin's theory, but he later departed from Darwin on this point, believing instead that a guiding spiritual force was necessary to account for the human soul. Wallace also considered ''sexual selection'' to be less important in evolution than did Darwin, holding that (unlike Darwin) it had no role in the evolution of human intellect (Thain & Hickman, 1995). The *theory of evolution* states that all naturally occurring populations are gradually and constantly changing as a result of natural selection that operates on individual organisms and varies according to their biological fitness. According to the theory, the process of evolution led to an enormous diversity in animal and plant forms where one of these lines evolved into hominids and, eventually, into humans. The implication of this *biological theory* for the discipline of psychology was that the human mind and behavior were as subject to natural law as was animal behavior. Darwin viewed mental processes in humans and animals as products of evolution and a proper subject for scientific investigation. Darwin recognized that the evolutionary process was characterized by constant divergence and diversification where it could be likened to an enormously elaborate branching tree with living species rep-

resented by the tip of the branches, while the remainder of the tree denotes extinct species; as many as 98% of all species that ever existed are now extinct (King, 1994). One ramification of the branching tree analogy is that it is meaningless to place different species in an ordinal sequence from lower to higher (e.g., Hodos & Campbell, 1969). For instance, birds evolved from a line of reptiles different from those that evolved into mammals, and carnivores evolved along a different branch of the mammals than did primates. Therefore, birds, cats, monkeys, and humans do not form a continuum of evolution; they are *distinct* types of animals. Evolution has not been an orderly process that produced organisms of consistently increasing subtlety and complexity that culminated in the appearance of humans; rather, the line of organisms leading to humans is only one branch among numerous other branches, and the human species perhaps does not deserve the universal evolutionary importance often given to it (King, 1994). Evolution is assumed, generally, to account for the variety of species on the earth today where over millions of years changes have taken place that are due to variation in the genes of a population and to survival and transmission of certain variations by natural selection. The *law of natural selection* is defined as the elimination of those individual organisms that are least well adapted to the environment, with the survival and greater proportionate increase of those that are better adapted. The operative factor, according to *evolutionary theory*, is *competition* (or struggle) for existence where the result is *survival of the fittest*. The phrase "survival of the fittest" was devised by the English philosopher/psychologist/sociologist Herbert Spencer (1820–1903) to describe the results of biological competition and is equivalent to the phrase "survival of the best adapted organisms" (Warren, 1934). Darwin (1859) postulated that natural selection interacts with genetic variation so that the fittest members of the population contribute most significantly to the gene pool of subsequent generations. Rate of evolutionary change is determined by rate of advantageous mutations and intensity of selection pressures (Denny, 1994). The process of evolution produces new species (called *speciation*) when two or more populations of a species become separated and isolated from each other in different environments; such populations evolve differently and thus become different species. The process of *adaptation* occurs when the environment remains fairly constant, and the entire species becomes better suited to the environment through natural selection, and, thus, behaviors as well as anatomical structures evolve through the mechanism of natural selection (Darwin, 1859). Evolutionary change does not need to be slow, gradual, and continuous, and there are not necessarily any "missing links" in the fossil record of the evolution of humans (Stanley, 1981). Although evolution is a theory, it is a well-established one; it is not a hypothesis but a theory that is the end product of an empirical science that rests on masses of accumulated data (Denny, 1994). The terms *evolution*, *evolutionary theory*, and *theory of evolution* are used by most people as though they were synonyms and all indicating the Darwinian position. However, this pattern of usage tends to be misleading. *Evolution* is not theory but a fact; the *gradualist* position of origin of species by natural selection advanced by Darwin (*Darwinism*) is one attempt to explain that fact. Defenders of *creationism* often mistake disputes over the best characterization of the evolutionary process as indications that biologists themselves regard evolution as merely a "theoretical" concept (Reber, 1995). The influence of *evolutionary doctrine* in psychology has been both powerful and productive: it encouraged the study of individual differences, helped establish the fields of *comparative psychology* and *behavior genetics*, provided the useful concepts of *adaptation, purpose,* and *function* in twentieth-century psychology, and advanced the scientific study of *developmental psychology*. It is interesting to note that the *theory of evolution* is the only theory that is referenced and described in John Dewey's (1898) introductory psychology textbook. A comprehensive *theory of evolution* called the *modern synthesis*, or *neo-Darwinism*, was forged in the early 1940s and emphasized the integration of the concepts of *natural selection, gradualism,* and *population genetics* as the fundamental units of evolutionary change (Campbell, 1993). The relatively new area of *animal sociobiology*, which is the application of principles from evolutionary and population biology to animals' social behavior, has invoked the *modern synthetic theory of evolution* (Wynne-Edwards, 1962; Dewsbury, 1994). This approach has stimulated scientists from various disciplines to reexamine the evolution of social behavior and to reconsider how the principle of *natural selection* works in this context (e.g., Wilson, 1975). See also LAMARCK'S THEORY; MENDEL'S LAWS/PRINCIPLES; PARSIMONY, LAW/PRINCIPLE OF; WEISMANN'S THEORY.

REFERENCES

Darwin, C. (1859). *On the origin of species by means of natural selection*. London: Murray.

Darwin, C. (1868). *The variation of plants and animals under domestication*. London: Murray.

Darwin, C. (1871). *The descent of man and selection in relation to sex*. London: Murray.

Spencer, H. (1892). *The principles of psychology*. New York: Appleton.

Dewey, J. (1898). *Psychology*. New York: Harper & Bros.

Ebbinghaus, H. (1908). *Psychology: An elementary textbook*. Boston: Heath.

Titchener, E. (1928). *A textbook of psychology*. New York: Macmillan.

Warren, H. (Ed.) (1934). *Dictionary of psychology*. Cambridge, MA: Houghton Mifflin.

Wynne-Edwards, V. (1962). *Animal dispersion in relation to social behavior*. Edinburgh: Oliver & Boyd.

Hodos, W., & Campbell, C. (1969). *Scala Naturae*: Why there is no theory in comparative psychology. *Psy. Rev., 4*, 337–350.

Gruber, H. (1974). *Darwin on man: A psychological study of scientific creativity*. New York: Dutton.

Harris, W., & Levey, J. (Eds.) (1975). *The new Columbia encyclopedia*. New York: Columbia University Press.

Wilson, E. (1975). *Sociobiology: The new synthesis*. Cambridge: Harvard University Press.

Denny, M. (1980). *Comparative psychology: An evolutionary analysis of animal behavior*. New York: Wiley.

Stanley, S. (1981). *The new evolutionary timetable*. New York: Basic Books.

Desmond, A., & Moore, J. (1992). *Darwin*. New York: Warner.

Campbell, N. (1993). *Biology*. Redwood City, CA: Benjamin/Cummings.

Denny, M. (1994). Evolution. In R. J. Corsini (Ed.), *Ency. Psy.* New York: Wiley.

Dewsbury, D. (1994). Animal sociobiology. In R. J. Corsini (Ed.), *Ency. Psy.* New York: Wiley.

King, J. (1994). Comparative psychology. In R. J. Corsini (Ed.), *Ency. Psy.* New York: Wiley.

Reber, A. (1995). *The Penguin dictionary of psychology*. New York: Penguin Books.

Thain, M., & Hickman, M. (1995). *The Penguin dictionary of biology*. New York: Penguin Books.

DARWIN'S THEORY OF EMOTIONS. The English naturalist Charles Darwin (1809–1882) speculated that in prehistoric times before communication that used words was common, one's ability to communicate with facial expressions increased an individual's chances of survival. Facial expressions could convey the various important messages of threat, submission, happiness, anger, and so on. (Darwin, 1872/1965). *Darwin's theory* held that the basic emotions demonstrated by facial expressions were a universal language among all humans no matter what their cultural setting. Today, however, it is an accepted belief that although cultures share a universal facial language, they differ in how and how much they express emotion (Matsumoto, Kudoh, Scherer, & Wallbott, 1988; Markus & Kitayama, 1991; cf: Ekman, 1993). For example, Americans grimace when viewing a film of someone's hand being cut, while Japanese viewers tend to hide their emotions, especially in the presence of others (Triandis, 1994). See also EKMAN-FRIESEN THEORY OF EMOTIONS; EMOTIONS, THEORIES/ LAWS OF; FACIAL-FEEDBACK HYPOTHESIS; IZARD'S THEORY OF EMOTIONS.

REFERENCES

Darwin, C. (1872/1965). *The expression of the emotions in man and animals*. London: Appleton/Chicago: University of Chicago Press.

Matsumoto, D., Kudoh, T., Scherer, K., & Wallbott, H. (1988). Antecedents of, and reactions to, emotions in the United States and Japan. *J. Cross-Cult. Psy., 19*, 267–286.

Markus, H., & Kitayama, S. (1991). Culture and the self: Implications for cognition, emotion, and motivation. *Psy. Rev., 98*, 224–253.

Ekman, P. (1993). Facial expressions and emotion. *Amer. Psy., 48*, 384–392.

Triandis, H. (1994). *Culture and social behavior*. New York: McGraw-Hill.

DECAY THEORY OF MEMORY. See FORGETTING/MEMORY, THEORIES OF.

DECISION-MAKING THEORIES. Decision-making research, generally regarded as a subarea within the field of cognitive psychology, investigates the question of how organisms make choices between alternatives where the major focus is on human decision making. *Decision theories* and *choice behavior theories* (e.g., Luce, 1959) seek to explain decision making and vary from the highly *formal* mathematical approaches (e.g., Greeno, 1973) based on *game theory* (i.e., the decision-making process that takes account of the actions and options for action of another individual whose own decisions are in conflict with yours; variations on the basic theory have been directed at studies of interpersonal interactions, economics, labor–management negotiations, and international diplomacy; e.g., Rubin & Brown, 1975); *probability theory* (i.e., the discipline within mathematics that deals with probability and forms the basis for all the statistical techniques of psychology where, given a relatively small number of observations in an experimental setting, one needs to make decisions about the likelihood of such observations in the long run; e.g., Hays, 1994); *classical strength theory* (Restle & Greeno, 1970; Neimark & Estes, 1967); and *utility theory* (i.e., utility is taken as the value to an individual of arriving at a particular decision, playing a game according to a particular strategy, or making a particular choice—such as reflected in *subjective expected utility* situations where the utility of any choice between alternatives is given by the sum of the person's *subjective probability estimates* of each alternative times the *utility value* of each one; e.g., Luce & Suppes, 1965; Tversky, 1967), to the more *informal*, intuitive theories that deal with beliefs, attitudes, and other subjective factors (Reber, 1995). The *rational decision-making* viewpoint assumes that people calculate the costs and benefits of various actions and pick the best alternative in a fairly logical, reasoned way. They choose the alternative that gives them the greatest benefit at the least cost. Typical of this approach is the *expectancy-value theory* (Edwards, 1954), which argues that decisions are made on the basis of the product of two factors: the value of the various possible outcomes of the decision and the probability or likelihood that each outcome will actually result from the decision. Theories of decision making in the area of political psychology include *conflict theory* (e.g., Janis & Mann, 1977), which emphasizes the emotion-laden decisional conflicts, the various patterns of coping behavior common in such conflicts, the antecedents of coping patterns, and the various consequences for decisional rationality. Group decision making may sometimes lead to the phenomenon called *groupthink* (Janis, 1982), which is an impairment in decision making and sound judgment that can occur in highly cohesive groups with a strong, dynamic leader, and where group members isolate themselves from outside information, try to please the group leader, and agree on a decision even if it is irrational. Another group decision-making phenomenon is called the *risky-shift/choice-shift effect*, which reflects a more general process of "group polarization" (Isenberg, 1986) and is defined as situations where people are sometimes willing to support riskier decisions after taking part in a group discussion than they were before the discussion. *Risky-shift* can lead either to riskier or to more cautious decisions, depending on the initial views of group members (Wallach, Kogan, & Bem, 1962; Kogan & Wallach, 1967). In personal decision-making situations, the process frequently arouses *postdecision dissonance* (Brehm, 1956) or *cognitive dissonance* (Festinger, 1957), which is the theoretical approach that assumes people have a drive toward consistency in their attitudes, beliefs, and decisions. According to this viewpoint, whenever one must decide between two or more alternatives, the final choice is, to some extent, inconsistent with some of the decision maker's beliefs. After the decision is made, all the *good* aspects of the *unchosen* alternative and all the *bad* aspects of the *chosen* alternative are dissonant with the decision. Dissonance can be reduced by improving one's evaluation of the chosen alternative, because everything positive about it is consonant with the decision; dissonance can also be reduced by lowering the evaluation of the unchosen alternative, as the less attractive it is, the less dissonance is aroused by rejecting it. Therefore, after people make decisions, there is a tendency for them to increase their liking for what they chose and to decrease their liking for what they did not choose. See also CONFLICT, THEORIES OF; FESTINGER'S COGNITIVE DISSONANCE THEORY; ORGANIZATIONAL/INDUSTRIAL/SYSTEMS THEORY; PROBABILITY THEORY/LAWS; THURSTONE'S LAW OF COMPARATIVE JUDGMENT.

REFERENCES

Cartwright, D., & Festinger, L. (1943). A quantitative theory of decision. *Psy. Rev., 50*, 595–621.

Edwards, W. (1954). The theory of decision-making. *Psy. Bull., 51*, 380–417.

Brehm, J. (1956). Post-decision changes in desirability of alternatives. *J. Abn. Soc. Psy., 52*, 384–389.

Festinger, L. (1957). *A theory of cognitive dissonance*. Evanston, IL: Row, Peterson.

Luce, R. (1959). *Individual choice behavior: A theoretical analysis*. New York: Wiley.

Wallach, M., Kogan, N., & Bem, D. (1962). Group influence on individual risk taking. *J. Abn. Soc. Psy., 65*, 75–86.

Luce, R., & Suppes, P. (1965). Preference, utility, and subjective probability. In R. Luce, R. Bush, & E. Galanter (Eds.), *Handbook of mathematical psychology*. Vol. 3. New York: Wiley.

Kogan, N., & Wallach, M. (1967). Risk taking as a function of the situation, the person, and the group. In G. Mandler (Ed.), *New directions in psychology*. Vol. 3. New York: Holt, Rinehart, & Winston.

Neimark, E., & Estes, W. (1967). *Stimulus sampling theory*. San Francisco: Holden-Day.

Tversky, A. (1967). Utility theory and additivity analysis of risky choices. *J. Exp. Psy., 75*, 27–36.

Restle, R., & Greeno, J. (1970). *Introduction to mathematical psychology*. Reading, MA: Addison-Wesley.

Greeno, J. (1973). A survey of mathematical models in experimental psychology. In B. Wolman (Ed.), *Handbook of general psychology*. Englewood Cliffs, NJ: Prentice-Hall.

Rubin, J., & Brown, B. (1975). *The social psychology of bargaining and negotiation.* New York: Academic Press.

Janis, I., & Mann, L. (1977). *Decision making.* New York: Free Press.

Janis, I. (1982). *Groupthink: Psychological studies of policy decisions and fiascoes.* Boston: Houghton Mifflin.

Isenberg, D. (1986). Group polarization: A critical review and meta-analysis. *J. Pers. Soc. Psy., 50,* 1141–1151.

Hays, W. (1994). *Statistics.* New York: Harcourt, Brace.

Reber, A. (1995). *The Penguin dictionary of psychology* New York: Penguin Books.

DEGENERACY THEORY OF GENIUS. See LOMBROSIAN THEORY.

DEGRADATION, LAW OF. See WEBER'S LAW.

DEINDIVIDUATION THEORY. The term *deindividuation* refers to the loss of one's sense of individuality during which the person behaves with little or no reference to personal internal values or standards of conduct. Deindividuated states are characterized as pleasurable wherein the person feels free to act on impulse and without regard to consequences. However, they can also be extremely dangerous in that they can result in violent and antisocial behavior (Pettijohn, 1986). In the late 1800s, the French sociologist Gustave LeBon (1896) postulated the concept of a *group mind* and asserted that people in a crowd may lose their sense of personal responsibility and behave as if governed by a primitive, irrational, hedonistic mind that seems to belong more to the group as a whole than to any one individual. Thus, the state of *deindividuation* seems to be brought on by a combination of "reduced accountability" that comes from being a relatively anonymous member of a crowd and "shifting attention" away from the self and toward the highly arousing external stimulation associated with the mob's actions (Diener, 1977). Various theoretical approaches have been developed concerning the phenomenon of *deindividuation.* Festinger, Pepitone, and Newcomb (1952) suggested that the person's focus on the group (which is associated with their attraction to the group) lessens the attention given to individuals. Thus, the members of the group are deindividuated by their submergence and moral subordination to the group. Therefore, according to Festinger et al. (1952), *deindividuation* lowers the person's inhibitions toward exercising counternormative actions. In another viewpoint, Ziller (1964) argues that persons learn to associate individuation with rewarding conditions and deindividuation with potentially punishing conditions. Thus, whenever the person expects punishment, there will be a tendency to diffuse responsibility by submerging oneself into a group, whereas when one learns to expect rewards for jobs well done, he or she wants to appear uniquely responsible for such behaviors. Zimbardo's (1970) *deindividuation theory* postulates that the expression of normally inhibited behavior may include creative and loving behavior as well as negative or counternormative behaviors. Zimbardo proposed that a number of factors may lead to deindividuation in addition to focus on the group and avoidance of negative evaluation of moral responsibility: anonymity, group size, level of emotional arousal, altered time perspectives, novelty/ambiguity of the situation, and degree of involvement in group functioning. Such factors lead to a *loss of identity* or self-consciousness, which, in turn, causes the person to become unresponsive to external stimuli and to lose cognitive control over motivations and emotions. Consequently, the deindividuated person becomes less compliant to positive or negative sanctions from influences outside the group. Diener's (1980) theoretical approach emphasizes the association of deindividuation with *self-awareness*: deindividuated persons do not attend to their own behavior and lack awareness of themselves as entities distinct from the group. With such little awareness of self, the individual is more likely to respond to immediate stimuli, motives, and emotions. According to Diener, the term *deindividuation* is a construct referring to a set of circumstances or relationships among emotional states, cognitive processes, situations, and behavioral reactions. In such circumstances, various antinormative behaviors such as drug abuse, riots, lynchings, mob violence, and even reactions involving loss of inhibition in marathon, encounter, and other noncognitive therapy groups are associated with a state of deindividuation (Tedeschi, 1994). See also ALLPORT'S CONFORMITY HYPOTHESIS; ASCH CONFORMITY EFFECT; BYSTANDER INTERVENTION EFFECT.

REFERENCES

LeBon, G. (1896). *The crowd.* London: Ernest Benn.

Festinger, L., Pepitone, A., & Newcomb, T. (1952). Some consequences of deindividuation in a group. *J. Abn. Soc. Psy., 47,* 382–389.

Ziller, R. (1964). Individuation and socialization. *Hum. Rel., 17,* 341–360.

Singer, J., Brush, C., & Lublin, S. (1965). Some aspects of deindividuation and conformity. *J. Exp. Soc. Psy., 1,* 356–378.

Zimbardo, P. (1970). The human choice: Individuation, reason, and order versus deindividuation, impulse, and chaos. In W. Arnold & D. Levine (Eds.), *Nebraska Symposium on Motivation.* Lincoln: University of Nebraska Press.

Diener, E. (1977). Deindividuation: Causes and consequences. *J. Soc. Beh. & Pers., 5,* 143–155.

Diener, E. (1980). Deindividuation: The absence of self-awareness and self-regulation in group members. In P. Paulus (Ed.), *The psychology of group influence.* Hillsdale, NJ: Erlbaum.

Pettijohn, T. (Ed.) (1986). *The encyclopedic dictionary of psychology.* Guilford, CT: Dushkin.

Spivey, C., & Prentice-Dunn, S. (1990). Assessing the directionality of deindividuated behavior: Effects of deindividuation, modeling, and private self-consciousness on aggressiveness and prosocial responses. *Basic & App. Soc. Psy., 11,* 387–403.

Tedeschi, J. (1994). Deindividuation. In R. J. Corsini (Ed.), *Ency. Psy.* NY: Wiley.

DE JONG'S LAW. See TOTAL TIME HYPOTHESIS/LAW.

DEMBER–EARL THEORY OF CHOICE/PREFERENCE. W. Dember and R. Earl formulated this *theory of choice/preference*, which concerns the influence of stimulus complexity on organisms' behaviors (Dember, 1956; Dember & Earl, 1957; Dember, Earl, & Paradise, 1957). The theory holds that every stimulus object has a certain *complexity* value that is also its *information* value (cf: Glanzer, 1958; Berlyne, 1960). One assumption behind the *theory of choice/ preference* is that every individual (both human and nonhuman) has its own "ideal level" of complexity, that is, the level of stimulation for which it has a preference. Individuals seek out objects containing their ideal level of complexity, will choose them from among other objects, will work for them, and will learn what needs to be done in order to obtain them. In addition, individuals will explore objects of a somewhat higher complexity level called "pacer stimuli." As organisms master the new level of complexity of the pacer stimuli, their own ideal level rises, and they are now ready to deal with new pacers and, again, raise their own ideal level. Thus, according to the *Dember–Earl theory of choice*, the need for stimulus variability in an individual's experience provides a basis and reinforcement for increasingly complicated kinds of learning. The results of several experiments (e.g., Munsinger & Kessen, 1964; Dorfman & McKenna, 1966; Kammann, 1966; Vitz, 1966; Thomas, 1969) confirm the predicted relation between complexity and preference in accordance with the *theory of choice/preference* and attest to its generality over a wide range of stimulus materials and types of subjects (Dember & Warm, 1979). See also PERCEPTION (I. GENERAL), THEORIES OF.

REFERENCES

Krechevsky, I. (1937). Brain mechanisms and variability. II. Variability where no learning is involved. *J. Comp. Psy., 23*, 139–163 (also, 121–138, 351–364).

Dember, W. (1956). Response by the rat to environmental change. *J. Comp. Physio. Psy., 49*, 93–95.

Dember, W., & Earl, R. (1957). Analysis of exploratory, manipulatory, and curiosity behaviors. *Psy. Rev., 64*, 91–96.

Dember, W., Earl, R., & Paradise, N. (1957). Response by rats to differential stimulus complexity. *J. Comp. Physio. Psy., 50*, 514–518.

Glanzer, M. (1958). Curiosity, exploratory drive, and stimulus satiation. *Psy. Bull., 55*, 302–315.

Berlyne, D. (1960). *Conflict, arousal, and curiosity.* New York: McGraw-Hill.

Munsinger, H., & Kessen, W. (1964). Uncertainty, structure, and preference. *Psy. Mono., 78*, no. 9.

Dorfman, D., & McKenna, H. (1966). Pattern preference as a function of pattern uncertainty. *Can. J. Psy., 62*, 171–183.

Kammann, R. (1966). Verbal complexity and preferences in poetry. *J. Verb. Learn. Verb. Beh., 5*, 536–540.

Vitz, P. (1966). Preference for different amounts of visual complexity. *Beh. Sci., 11*, 105–114.

Thomas, H. (1969). Unidirectional changes in preference for increasing visual complexity in the cat. *J. Comp. Physio. Psy., 68*, 296–302.

Coombs, C., & Avrunin, G. (1977). Single-peaked functions and the theory of preference. *Psy. Rev., 84,* 216–230.

Dember, W., & Warm, J. (1979). *Psychology of perception.* New York: Holt, Rinehart, & Winston.

DEMORALIZATION HYPOTHESIS. See DODO HYPOTHESIS.

DENERVATION, LAW OF. This principle, formulated by W. B. Cannon and A. Rosenblueth (1949), states that *denervation* (i.e., the removal of the nerve supply to an organ or other tissue, where removal is either actual or "functional") results in a progressive sensitization of sites higher in the nervous system. The *law of denervation* has been cited in the contexts of sensory deprivation (SD) and perceptual deprivation (PD) experiments (Zubek, 1969) where the latter employ research formats and methods that lead to a "functional" form of denervation. A potential explanation for SD and PD is that they may sensitize the individual's sensory system and act to lower thresholds for subsequently presented stimuli (as well as resulting in the attribution of activity within higher sites) to an external stimulus affecting the unstimulated receptor. Also, the *phantom-limb* phenomenon occasionally observed in amputees may be accounted for by neurophysiological theories that invoke the *law of denervation.* See also HABITUATION, PRINCIPLE/LAW OF.

REFERENCES

Cannon, W., & Rosenblueth, A. (1949). *The supersensitivity of denervated structures.* New York: Macmillan.

Doane, B., Mahatoo, W., Heron, W., Scott, T. (1959). Changes in perceptual functions after isolation. *Can. J. Psy., 13,* 210–219.

Zubek, J. (Ed.) (1969). *Sensory deprivation: Fifteen years of research.* New York: Appleton-Century-Crofts.

DEPRESSION, THEORIES OF. In general, *depression* is a mood state characterized by a sense of inadequacy, feelings of despondency, sadness, pessimism, and decrease in activity or reactivity. Depressive disorders involve a spectrum of psychological dysfunctions that vary in frequency, duration, and severity. At one end of the continuum is the experience of normal depression (a transient period, usually lasting no longer than two weeks), consisting of fatigue and sadness and precipitated by identifiable stressors. At the other end of the spectrum is the longer-lasting period of depressed mood approaching clinical depressive disorders, which is accompanied by sleep difficulties, eating problems, and growing thoughts of despair and hopelessness. In *psychotic depression*, the individual suffers deep despair and sadness and may lose contact with reality and develop delusions, hallucinations, and severe motor and psychological retardation. In this sense, depression may be a symptom of some other psychological disorder, a part or syndrome of related symptoms that appears as secondary to another disorder, or a specific disorder itself. A major difficulty in studying depression is that the term is often used indiscriminately for an entire spectrum of experiences where it has come to describe a mood, a symptom, and a syndrome (Marsella, 1994; Reber, 1995). The terminology of depression includes *dualistic* systems where the concepts of "reactive versus autonomous," "neurotic versus psychotic," "primary versus secondary," "exogenous versus endogenous," "unipolar versus bipolar," and "justified versus somatic" depression have been used (cf: Winokur, 1979). *Pluralistic* systems of depression classification describe many types of disorders. For example, Grinker, Miller, Sabshin, Nunn, and Nunnally (1961) proposed four patterns of depression based on a factor analysis of moods, behaviors, and treatment responses: empty-, angry-, anxious-, and hypochondriacal-depression. Other pluralistic classification systems of depression are provided in the American Psychiatric Association's *Diagnostic and Statistical Manual* (1994), which lists more than a dozen different kinds of depressive disorders, including various depressive personality types, as well as schizoaffective and psychotic depressive disorders. Concerning the diagnosis of depression, the American psychiatrist Aaron Temkin Beck (1921–   ) designed the Beck Depression Inventory (BDI), which is based on observations of attitudes and symptoms characteristic of depressed patients. The BDI contains 21 categories of symptoms and attitudes, such as sense of failure, dissatisfaction, guilt, sense of punishment, self-accusations, and sleep disturbance. The various *theories of depression* may be grouped generally into *biological* or *psychological* types (Marsella, 1994). The *biological theories* include the *genetic theories*, in which it is assumed that genetic factors interact with environmental factors and where heredity influences emotional lability, cellular functioning, basic arousal levels, stimulus threshold levels, and other physiological substrates of behavior (cf: Depue, 1979; Nurnberger & Gershon, 1982); and the *biochemical theories*, which are further subdivided into *biogenic amine* (neurotransmitters) *theories*, which include *catecholamine, indoleamine*, and *permissive amine hypotheses* (e.g., Schildkraut, 1965, 1978; Wilson, Prange, & Lynn, 1974; Goodwin & Potter, 1979), the *electrolyte metabolism theories*, which focus on sodium and potassium in the brain (e.g., Shaw & Coppen, 1966), and the *pituitaryadrenal axis theories*, which argue that the primary problem in depression disorders rests in the hypothalamic-pituitary-adrenal axis (e.g., Sachar, 1982). The *psychobehavioral theories* (e.g., Friedman & Katz, 1974) may be subdivided into the *reconposre theory*, where the term *reconposre* stands for "response contingent positive reinforcement" and which argues that depression develops when individuals receive inadequate amounts of positive reinforcement in their lives (e.g., Lewinsohn, 1974); the *learned helplessness theory*, which proposes that when humans or animals are trapped in situations in which they cannot avoid threat or harm, and where uncontrollable aversive events produce an expectancy that one cannot control stressors, they develop a sense of helplessness, resignation, or hopelessness and act "depressed" (e.g., Seligman, 1975); the *cognitive the-*

ory, which emphasizes the role of one's faulty thought processes, including factors such as logic errors, selective abstraction, arbitrary inferences, overgeneralizations, excessive magnification, and dichotomous/distorted thinking (e.g., Beck, 1967a, b, 1973); and the *psychoanalytic theory*, which argues that depression results from the loss of an ambivalently loved person or loss of a "love object," which leads to a self-directed hostility and constitutes the depressive experience; this approach suggests that the self-punishment that accompanies depression may actually be an unconscious effort to regain maternal love and support, or that in cases of traumatic experiences in childhood there is resultant faulty ego and libido development with fixation at an earlier state of insecurity and helplessness (e.g., Abraham, 1927, 1966). The most current theories and perspectives of depression focus on the interaction of biological, psychological, and sociological levels of functioning (e.g., Akiskal, 1979). Such new approaches integrate the older theories and offer the promise of new insights into depression, its manifestations, diagnosis, and treatment (Marsella, 1994). See also LEARNED HELPLESSNESS EFFECT/THEORY; PSYCHOPATHOLOGY, THEORIES OF.

REFERENCES

Abraham, K. (1927). *Selected papers on psychoanalysis*. London: Hogarth.
Grinker, R., Miller, J., Sabshin, M., Nunn, R., & Nunnally, J. (1961). *The phenomena of depressions*. New York: Hoeber.
Schildkraut, J. (1965). The catecholamine hypothesis of affective disorders: A review of supporting evidence. *Amer. J. Psychiat., 122*, 509–522.
Abraham, K. (1966). *On character and libido development: Six essays by Karl Abraham*. New York: Norton.
Shaw, D., & Coppen, A. (1966). Potassium and water distribution in depression. *Brit. J. Psychiat., 112*, 269–279.
Beck, A. (1967a). *Depression: Causes and treatment*. Philadelphia: University of Pennsylvania Press.
Beck, A. (1967b). *Depression: Clinical, experimental, and theoretical aspects*. New York: Hoeber.
Beck, A. (1973). *The diagnosis and management of depression*. Philadelphia: University of Pennsylvania Press.
Friedman, R., & Katz, M. (Eds.) (1974). *The psychology of depression*. Washington, DC: Winston.
Lewinsohn, P. (1974). A behavioral approach to depression. In R. Friedman & M. Katz (Eds.), *The psychology of depression*. Washington, DC: Winston.
Wilson, I., Prange, A., & Lynn, C. (1974). L-tryptophan mania: Contribution to a permissive amine hypothesis of affective disorder. *Ar. Gen. Psychiat., 30*, 56–62.
Seligman, M. (1975). *Helplessness: On depression, development, and death*. San Francisco: Freeman.
Schildkraut, J. (1978). Current status of the catecholamine hypothesis of affective disorders. In M. Lipton, A. DiMascio, & K. Killam (Eds.), *Psychopharmacology: A generation of progress*. New York: Raven Press.
Akiskal, H. (1979). A biobehavioral approach to depression. In R. Depue (Ed.), *The psychobiology of the depressive disorders*. New York: Academic Press.

Depue, R. (Ed.) (1979). *The psychobiology of depressive disorders*. New York: Academic Press.

Goodwin, F., & Potter, W. (1979). Catecholamines. In E. Usdin, I. Kopen, & J. Barchas (Eds.), *Catecholamines: Basic and clinical frontiers*. New York: Pergamon Press.

Winokur, G. (1979). Unipolar depression: Is it divisible into autonomous subtypes? *Ar. Gen. Psychiat., 36*, 47–52.

Nurnberger, J., & Gershon, E. (1982). Genetics. In E. Paykel (Ed.), *Handbook of affective disorders*. New York: Guilford Press.

Sachar, E. (1982). Endocrine abnormalities in depression. In E. Paykel (Ed.), *Handbook of affective disorders*. New York: Guilford Press.

American Psychiatric Association. (1994). *Diagnostic and statistical manual of mental disorders*. Washington, DC: American Psychiatric Association.

Gorman, B. (1994). Manic-depressive personality. In R. J. Corsini (Ed.), *Ency. Psy.* New York: Wiley.

Marsella, A. (1994). Depression. In R. J. Corsini (Ed.), *Ency. Psy.* New York: Wiley.

Reber, A. (1995). *The Penguin dictionary of psychology*. New York: Penguin Books.

DETERMINISM, DOCTRINE/THEORY OF. The doctrine of *determinism* assumes that every event has causes, and it is the theory or working principle according to which all phenomena are considered as necessary consequents of antecedent conditions (Warren, 1934). The concept of *determinism* is central to science because it maintains that if one knew all the factors involved in a forthcoming event, it could be predicted exactly. *Determinism* implies a chain of events, each following the other, to produce a necessary conclusion where everything and every event in the world (and universe) is the result of natural laws that can be ascertained by use of the scientific methods. A distinction is made often between *hard determinism* (or "nomological" laws) and *soft determinism* (e.g., Reber, 1995). For instance, concerning *hard determinism*, in *classical* mechanics in physics it was assumed that if one knew the position and momentum of every particle of matter at one instant in time, then one could know its position and momentum at any other point in future time. This position, however, was "softened" somewhat with the development of *quantum* mechanics, where the levels of cause and effect are probabilistic in nature and which, thereby, shifted the idea of perfect ("hard") prediction to probabilistic ("soft") prediction. In psychology, the question of *determinism* generally revolves around the *humanist's* and *existentialist's* advocacy of "free will." However, if one wishes to study behavior and the mind in scientific terms, it must be assumed that there are *deterministic*, cause–effect relationships to take into serious consideration. Scientific psychology assumes a degree of *determinism* in behavior where three categories of *determinants* are usually studied as they interact to influence behavior: *biological* factors (include heredity, bodily constitution, and physiological health and disease), *psychological* factors (include emotions, drives, attitudes, learning experiences, and conscious and unconscious conflicts), and *social/cultural* factors (include economic status, customs and mores, social status, and social conflicts) (Pettijohn, 1986). *Deterministic* relationships, or laws, are discovered in various ways. For example, Aristotle (Hutchins, 1952) first observed a phenomenon and then followed up by thinking about the event, classifying it, and putting it into a category so that predictions could be made. Many methods of basic scientific inquiry are available, including observation, interpretation, conclusions, and hypotheses-testing, but they all depend on the fundamental notion of *deterministic* causality. The doctrine of dialectical materialism developed by the German social theorist and philosopher Karl Marx (1818–1883) in the field of political science is in the *deterministic* tradition (Marx & Engels, 1848; Marx, 1867–1879). Recent events in the field of physics, however, have modulated the scientific regnancy of *determinism*. In particular, it appears to be highly uncertain or impossible to determine at the same time the momentum of an electron particle as well as its position. The German theoretical physicist Werner Karl Heisenberg (1901–1976) formulated this conclusion in 1927, which has come to be known today as *Heisenberg's principle of uncertainty* or the *Heisenberg indeterminacy principle* (Heisenberg, 1958) and demonstrated that Newtonian physics does not apply at the level of analysis of atoms. In translating this principle to psychology, if one views one human as the equivalent of an atom, it is true that *determinacy* holds for the human species (which leads to *deterministic nomothetic laws*), but it is also true that *indeterminacy* holds for the human individual, whose "free will" behavior is only partially explainable in terms of antecedent events, and, in which case, it makes it impossible to predict the individual's behavior with complete accuracy. The *theory of indeterminism* means that one can act in relative independence of given stimuli and that the individual has freedom of choice or "free will" (Warren, 1934). The laws of most societies and the dogma of many religions are based on the ideas of individual responsibility and free will where the consequences of punishment, whether on earth or in heaven, are justified regarding a person's moral judgments and behavior. Psychologists seem to take a number of positions on the question of *determinism* versus *indeterminism*, where rigid *behaviorists* tend to be *strict determinists*, and *humanistic/existentialists* tend to be *indeterminists*, even though most psychologists straddle the fence by asserting the necessity of *determinism* as part of scientific methodology, on one hand, and, on the other hand, operating pragmatically day in and day out in terms of *indeterminism* (Sutton, 1994). See also IDIOGRAPHIC/NOMOTHETIC LAWS.

REFERENCES

Marx, K., & Engels, F. (1848). *Communist manifesto*. New York: Washington Square Press.
Marx, K. (1867–1879). *Capital: A critique of political economy*. Chicago: Kerr.
Warren, H. (Ed.) (1934). *Dictionary of psychology*. Cambridge, MA: Houghton Mifflin.
Hutchins, R. (Ed.) (1952). Aristotle's *Physics. Great books of the Western world*. Vol. 8. Chicago: Encyclopedia Britannica.
Heisenberg, W. (1958). *The physicist's conception of nature*. New York: Harcourt, Brace, & World.

Pettijohn, T. (1986). *The encyclopedic dictionary of psychology.* Guilford, CT: Dushkin.
Sutton, W. (1994). Determinism/indeterminism. In R. J. Corsini (Ed.), *Ency. Psy.* New
        York: Wiley.
Reber, A. (1995). *The Penguin dictionary of psychology.* New York: Penguin Books.

DEVELOPMENTAL THEORY. Development is the sequence of changes that
occur over the full life span of an organism. The area of *developmental psychology* initially (via G. Stanley Hall in the early 1900s, who proposed a *biogenetic theory* of development) referred to the study of the full life span from
birth to death, but today the tendency is also to use the term in more specific
ways (e.g., developmental aphasia, developmental articulation disorder, developmental psycholinguistics, etc.). The "thing" that develops in *developmental
theory* may be almost anything: molecular systems, bones and organs, emotions,
ideas and cognitive processes, moral systems, personality, relationships, groups,
societies, and cultures (Reber, 1995). The period of *early childhood* has received
a great deal of theoretical attention in developmental psychology. Childhood is
a culturally defined period in human development between infancy and adulthood where, only in the past 400 years or so (from J. A. Comenius, 1592–1670),
childhood has been a part of Western culture with the recognition of this special
class of individuals and special growth phases, stages, and sequences of each
person (Wertlieb, 1994). In general, *continuity theories of development* maintain
that psychological development is a gradual, continuous process. On the other
hand, *stage theories of development* maintain that psychological development is
discontinuous, with plateaus (periods of relative stability) separated by periods
of rapid change (Gray, 1994). *Psychoanalytic theories of development* hypoth-
esize that early childhood is the critical period in development where major
personality orientations emerge and continue into childhood, adolescence, and
adulthood. An individual's sense of *self*, and as a female or male, is formed in
important ways during early childhood (cf: various *theories of ego development;*
e.g., H. S. Sullivan; L. Kohlberg; S. Ferenczi; D. Ausubel; W. Perry) (Loevinger,
1994). Two of the most prominent *psychoanalytic theories of development* are
Sigmund Freud's (1920, 1940) *theory of psychosexual development,* which describes the oral, anal, phallic/oedipal, and genital stages of development, and
Erik Erikson's (1950, 1968) *theory of psychosocial development,* which describes the "crises" of early childhood (such as trust versus mistrust, autonomy
versus shame/doubt, industry versus inferiority). The *cognitive developmental
theories* (e.g., Piaget, 1929, 1970; Bruner, 1968) also emphasize early childhood
as a period of critical construction of the child's knowledge and sense of reality.
For example, according to Piaget, the child passes through cognitive stages of
sensorimotor, preoperational, concrete operational, and formal operational
modes of thinking that are based on a complex series of interactions of the child
with the environment. Many of the *learning theorists* (e.g., Thorndike, 1931;
Guthrie, 1935; Hull, 1943) have tended to consider developmental behavior as
based on environmental, rather than organismic, factors and (like Freud) view

the individual as a passive receptacle rather than active in its own development (cf: the *humanist's* "active" approach). The emergence of *social learning theory* (e.g., Rotter, 1954; Bandura, 1977) may be viewed, in some respects for *developmental theory*, as a combination of *psychoanalytic* and *learning theory* concepts (McKinney, 1994). See also AGING, THEORIES OF; ERIKSON'S THEORY OF PERSONALITY; FREUD'S THEORY OF PERSONALITY; LEARNING THEORIES/LAWS; PIAGET'S THEORY OF DEVELOPMENTAL STAGES.

REFERENCES

Freud, S. (1920). *A general introduction to psychoanalysis.* New York: Pocket Books.

Piaget, J. (1929). *The child's conception of the world.* New York: Littlefield, Adams.

Thorndike, E. (1931). *Human learning.* New York: Appleton-Century-Crofts.

Guthrie, E. (1935). *The psychology of learning.* New York: Harper & Row.

Freud, S. (1940). *An outline of psychoanalysis.* New York: Norton.

Hull, C. (1943). *Principles of behavior.* New York: Appleton-Century-Crofts.

Erikson, E. (1950). *Childhood and society.* New York: Norton.

Rotter, J. (1954). *Social learning and clinical psychology.* New York: Johnson.

Rogers, C. (1961). *On becoming a person.* Boston: Houghton Mifflin.

Maslow, A. (1962). *Toward a psychology of being.* Princeton, NJ: Van Nostrand.

Bruner, J. (1968). *Processes of cognitive growth: Infancy.* Worcester, MA: Clark University Press.

Erikson, E. (1968). *Identity: Youth and crisis.* New York: Norton.

Piaget, J. (1970). Piaget's theory. In P. Mussen (Ed.), *Carmichael's manual of child psychology.* New York: Wiley.

Bandura, A. (1977). *Social learning theory.* Englewood Cliffs, NJ: Prentice-Hall.

Gray, P. (1994). *Psychology.* New York: Worth.

Loevinger, J. (1994). Ego development. In R. J. Corsini (Ed.), *Ency. Psy.* New York: Wiley.

McKinney, J. (1994). Child psychology. In R. J. Corsini (Ed.), *Ency. Psy.* New York: Wiley.

Wertlieb, D. (1994). Early childhood development. In R. J. Corsini (Ed.), *Ency. Psy.* New York: Wiley.

Reber, A. (1995). *The Penguin dictionary of psychology.* New York: Penguin Books.

DIAGNOSIS OF PSYCHOPATHOLOGY. See PSYCHOPATHOLOGY, THEORIES OF.

DIATHESIS-STRESS THEORY OF ABNORMALITY. See PSYCHOPATHOLOGY, THEORIES OF; SCHIZOPHRENIA, THEORIES OF.

DIFFERENTIAL FORGETTING, THEORY OF. See INTERFERENCE THEORIES OF FORGETTING.

DIFFERENTIATION HYPOTHESIS. See INTERFERENCE THEORIES OF FORGETTING.

DIMINISHING RETURNS, LAW OF. See JOST'S LAWS.

DIRECTIVE-STATE THEORY. See PERCEPTION (II. COMPARATIVE APPRAISAL), THEORIES OF.

DIRECT PERCEPTION THEORY. See PERCEPTION (I. GENERAL), THEORIES OF.

DISCOUNTING PRINCIPLE. See ATTRIBUTION THEORY.

DISCREPANCY-EVALUATION THEORY. See SCHACHTER–SINGER'S THEORY OF EMOTIONS.

DISCRIMINATION LEARNING THEORY. See SPENCE'S THEORY.

DISEQUILIBRIUM PRINCIPLE. See REINFORCEMENT THEORY.

DISPOSITIONAL (TYPE/TRAIT) THEORIES OF PERSONALITY. See PERSONALITY THEORIES.

DISSOCIATION, LAW OF. See ASSOCIATION, LAWS/PRINCIPLES OF.

DISSONANCE THEORY. See FESTINGER'S COGNITIVE DISSONANCE THEORY.

DISUSE, LAW/THEORY OF. A generalization of conditioning by E. L. Thorndike, derived from his *law of exercise*, which states that a learned stimulus–response bond or association will decrease and become weakened through disuse or through lack of practice. The *law of disuse* had been invoked in early discussions in psychology of how forgetting occurs. That is, following the analogy that a muscle is weakened through disuse (and strengthened through exercise or use), lack of practice of learned materials may weaken the ability to recall those materials. The *law of disuse* was stated, also, in the following way early in this century (Gates, 1926, p. 284): "When a modifiable connection between a stimulus and a response is not exercised during a length of time, the strength of the connection is decreased." Recently, however, Plotnik (1993, p. 258) points out that the *law of disuse* is not widely held today because it is not supported by adequate data, and there are many common instances of its failure to predict the expected outcome (e.g., you may actually remember your Spanish vocabulary and the names of high school classmates after 30–40 years, even if these materials have not been used during that time). See also EFFECT, LAW OF; EXERCISE, LAW OF; FORGETTING, THEORIES OF; USE, LAW OF.

REFERENCES

Gates, A. (1926). *Elementary psychology*. New York: Macmillan.
Bregman, E., & Thorndike, E., & Woodyard, E. (1943). The retention of the ability to draw lines of a given length blindfolded. *J. Exp. Psy., 33*, 78–80.
Hilgard, E., & Bower, G. (1966). *Theories of learning*. New York: Appleton-Century-Crofts.
Kimble, G., & Schlesinger, K. (1985). *Topics in the history of psychology*. Hillsdale, NJ: Erlbaum.
Plotnik, R. (1993). *Introduction to psychology*. Pacific Grove, CA: Brooks/Cole.

DITCHBURN–RIGGS EFFECT. See VISION/SIGHT, THEORIES OF.

DODO HYPOTHESIS. This proposition states that all mental health therapies are roughly equal and was first proposed by Lester B. Luborsky, Barton Singer, and Lise Luborsky in 1975 (cf: the *demoralization hypothesis*, which states that because all forms of psychotherapy are helpful, their shared features must counteract a type of distress and disability common to most seekers of psychotherapy; Frank, 1994). The *Dodo hypothesis* alludes to the Dodo in Lewis Carroll's *Alice's Adventures in Wonderland*, who tells racers in a foot race that "*everyone has won, and all must have prizes!*" Luborsky and his colleagues conducted reviews of studies of the efficacy of various psychotherapies and concluded that the *Dodo hypothesis* is essentially correct: all of the contenders in the psychotherapy race were successful. There is a huge amount of evidence that psychotherapy works, they say, but no evidence across a broad range of samples that any one mode of psychotherapy, or talk therapies, is superior to the others. In addition, Luborsky and his group found support for an *allegiance effect*, which is the tendency of researchers to find evidence that favors the particular type of therapy that they themselves practice. However, another interpretation of the *Dodo hypothesis* has been offered by E. Fuller Torrey (1992), who states that everyone has *lost*, and *none* must have prizes. Torrey has criticized psychoanalysis and all other talk therapies as pseudoscience (cf: Gross, 1979) and disputes the underlying assumption of all talk therapies that the human psyche is shaped by childhood experiences and can be reshaped through psychotherapy. Torrey believes that drugs, gene therapy, and other biological remedies will make talking cures obsolete, and, for now, psychotherapy should be excluded from health care coverage. According to Horgan (1996), bashing Freud and the talk therapies is not a novel pastime: the eminent Austrian-born English philosopher Karl Popper (1902–1994) recalled more than 60 years ago that "psychoanalysis was the treatment of the id by the odd." Thus, the debate concerning the efficacy of psychotherapy in general and Freudian psychoanalysis in particular continues. See also FREUD'S THEORY OF PERSONALITY.

REFERENCES

Holt, R., & Luborsky, L. (1958). *Personality patterns of psychiatrists: A study of methods for selecting residents*. New York: Basic Books.

Strupp, H., & Luborsky, L. (Eds.) (1962). *Research in psychotherapy*. Vol. 2. Washington, DC: American Psychological Association.

Luborsky, L., Auerbach, A., Chandler, M., Cohen, J., & Bachrach, H. (1971). Factors influencing the outcome of psychotherapy. *Psy. Bull., 75*, 145–185.

Torrey, E. (1972a). *The mind game: Witchdoctors and psychiatrists*. New York: Bantam Books.

Torrey, E. (1972b). What Western psychotherapists can learn from witchdoctors. *Amer. J. Orthopsychiat., 42*, 69–76.

Strupp, H. (1973). *Psychotherapy: Clinical, research, and theoretical issues*. New York: Aronson.

Luborsky, L., Singer, B., & Luborsky, L. (1975). Comparative studies of psychotherapies. *Ar. Gen. Psychiat., 32*, 995–1008.

Orlinsky, D., & Howard, K. (1978). The relation of process to outcome in psychotherapy. In S. Garfield & A. Bergin (Eds.), *Handbook of psychotherapy and behavior change: An empirical analysis*. New York: Wiley.

Gross, M. (1979). *The psychological society*. New York: Simon & Schuster.

Fisher, S., & Greenberg, R. (1989). *The limits of biological treatments for psychological distress*. New York: Erlbaum.

Torrey, E. (1992). *Freudian fraud*. New York: HarperCollins.

Dawes, R. (1994). *House of cards: Psychology and psychotherapy built on myth*. New York: Free Press.

Frank, J. (1994). Effective components of psychotherapy. In R. J. Corsini (Ed.), *Ency. Psy.* New York: Wiley.

Mendel, W. (1994). Treatment outcome. In R. J. Corsini (Ed.), *Ency. Psy.* New York: Wiley.

Raskin, N. (1994). Psychotherapy research. In R. J. Corsini (Ed.), *Ency. Psy.* New York: Wiley.

Fisher, S., & Greenberg, R. (1996). *Freud scientifically reappraised*. New York: Wiley.

Horgan, J. (1996). Why Freud isn't dead. *Sci. Amer., 275*, 106–111.

DONDERS' LAW; DONDERS' REACTION TIME TECHNIQUES. The Dutch physiologist and ophthalmologist Franciscus Cornelis Donders (1818–1889) formulated this principle of visual fixation in 1846, according to which every position of the lines of regard in relation to the head corresponds to a definite, invariable angle of torsion of the eyes, regardless of the path by which that position has been reached (Warren, 1934). Another version of *Donders' law* is given by Wolman (1973): the principle that the position of the eyes in looking at an object is independent of the movement of the eyes to that position; regardless of previous fixation points, every point on the line corresponds to a definite, invariable angle of the eyes. Aided in part by Hermann von Helmholtz's invention of the ophthalmoscope in 1850, Donders established himself as a specialist in diseases of the eye, setting up a polyclinic for eye diseases at Utrecht University. Donders improved the efficiency of spectacles through the introduction of prismatic and cylindrical lenses and wrote extensively on eye physiology (Muir, 1994). Donders is most remembered for his studies on *reaction time* (i.e., the minimum time between the presentation of a stimulus and the subject's response to it) and the *subtraction method*, which refers to any of several methods for measuring the time it takes for particular psychological processes to occur (Donders, 1868). Donders studied three kinds of *reaction time* (RT) tasks: (1) *simple RT*—the minimum lag between a single simple stimulus, such as a tone or light, and the subject's making of a single simple response, such as pressing a button; (2) *discrimination RT*—there are two distinctive stimuli and the subject is asked to respond to only one of them and refrain from making a response to the other; and (3) *choice RT*—an extension of simple RT where the subject is confronted with two or more stimuli and two or more corresponding responses. By subtracting the time it took subjects to carry out task (2) from the time it took to carry out task (3), Donders obtained an estimate of how long it took to make a choice; and by subtracting task (1) time from task (2) time, he obtained an estimate of the individual's discrimination time (Woodworth & Schlosberg, 1965; Reber, 1995). In view of the originality and ingenuity of this first attempt to measure the speed of higher mental processes, it is astonishing to see the small amount of data upon which Donders based his judgments (30 trials or less with some of his subjects). The validity of the *method of subtraction* has never been fully accepted by most investigators. However, Donders' work is important for several reasons: he showed that some of the variability of results was not due to simple differences in speed of conduction but to central processes, he laid down the foundation for the analysis of the time relations of mental processes, and he found that the RT for the different senses showed characteristic differences (Murphy & Kovach, 1972). See also HICK'S LAW.

REFERENCES

Donders, F. (1868). Die Schnelligkeit psychischer Processe. *Ar. Anat. Physio., 6*, 657–681.

Warren, H. (Ed.) (1934). *Dictionary of psychology*. Cambridge, MA: Houghton Mifflin.

Teichner, W. (1954). Recent studies of simple reaction time. *Psy. Bull., 51*, 128–149.

Woodworth, R., & Schlosberg, H. (1965). *Experimental psychology*. New York: Holt, Rinehart, & Winston.

Brozek, J. (1970). Wayward history: F. C. Donders (1818–1889) and the timing of mental operations. *Psy. Rep., 26*, 563–569.

Murphy, G., & Kovach, J. (1972). *Historical introduction to modern psychology*. New York: Harcourt Brace Jovanovich.

Teichner, W., & Krebs, M. (1972). Laws of the simple visual reaction time. *Psy. Rev., 79*, 344–358.

Wolman, B. (Ed.) (1973). *Dictionary of behavioral science*. New York: Van Nostrand Reinhold.

Muir, H. (Ed.) (1994). *Larousse dictionary of scientists*. New York: Larousse.

Reber, A. (1995). *The Penguin dictionary of psychology*. New York: Penguin Books.

DOPAMINE THEORY OF SCHIZOPHRENIA. See SCHIZOPHRENIA, THEORIES OF.

DOPPLER EFFECT/PRINCIPLE/SHIFT. The Austrian physicist Christian Johann Doppler (1803–1853) enunciated this principle in 1842, which explains the variation of frequency observed (lower or higher than that which is actually emitted) when a vibrating source of waves and the observer, respectively, recede from, or approach, one another. In other terms, the *Doppler effect* refers to the change in apparent frequency of a source due to relative motion of source and observer. An interesting experimental validation of the *Doppler effect* was conducted at Utrecht in the Netherlands in 1845: a locomotive pulling an open car containing several individuals playing trumpets passed by a group of musicians (who had perfect pitch) standing at a fixed location. The result was as expected: the apparent frequency of waves from the source (the trumpeters) when *moving toward* the observers (the musicians) was *increased*, and the apparent sound waves from the source (the trumpeters) when *moving away from* the observers (the musicians) was *decreased*. The *Doppler shift* (also called *redshift* in the context of astronomy and wavelengths in the visible spectrum) refers to the magnitude of the change in frequency or wavelength of waves that results from the *Doppler effect*. C. J. Doppler's name is honored, also, in the concepts of ''Doppler broadening'' (thermal motion of molecules, atoms, or nuclei), ''Doppler width'' (distribution of velocities), and ''Doppler radar'' (Illingworth, 1991). The *Doppler effect* has been used to measure the speed of the sun's rotation and Saturn's rings, to serve as the basis for police radar speed traps for vehicles, to act in ''Doppler satellites'' (used by aircraft and ships to locate their position), and to measure physiological events in echocardiography (''Doppler reflection'') such as heart defects. In astronomy, the *Doppler effect* provides a basis for collecting valuable evidence for cosmological conceptions of the universe (e.g., an ''expanding'' universe) by studying the changes in spectral wavelengths as celestial bodies approach or recede from a fixed observation point on the earth (Hawking, 1988). Doppler himself recognized that the frequency effect he described applied to light as well as sound, and the French physicist Armand Fizeau (1819–1896) pointed out in 1848 that the spectral hues of stars should be shifted toward the red end of the spectrum according to the speed at which they are receding from us (i.e., the *Doppler shift*). Other astronomers have used the *redshift effect* to infer the speed of recession of other galaxies from the earth.

REFERENCES

Kimble, G., & Garmezy, N. (1956). *Principles of general psychology*. New York: Ronald Press.

Shepard, D. (1977). *Psychology: The science of human behavior*. Chicago: Science Research Associates.

Hawking, S. (1988). *A brief history of time*. New York: Bantam Books.

Illingworth, V. (Ed.) (1991). *The Penguin dictionary of physics*. New York: Penguin Books.

Roediger, H., Capaldi, E., Paris, S., & Polivy, J. (1991). *Psychology*. New York: HarperCollins.

Muir, H. (Ed.) (1994). *Larousse dictionary of scientists*. New York: Larousse.

DOUBLE-ASPECT THEORY. See MIND–BODY THEORIES.

DOUBLE-BIND HYPOTHESIS/THEORY. See SCHIZOPHRENIA, THEO-RIES OF.

DOUBLE-DEPLETION HYPOTHESIS. See THIRST, THEORIES OF.

DREAM THEORY. A dream may be defined as "a more or less coherent imagery sequence which ordinarily occurs during sleep" (Warren, 1934) or as "imagery during sleep" (Reber, 1995). Before mid-nineteenth- and twentieth-century scientific investigations took place, a *popular dream theory* was that they were divine messages with prophetic intent where the messages were coded, and the decoding task was performed by persons with a "gift" for dream interpretation (such as tribal leaders, chiefs, or witch doctors in uncivilized/primitive societies or by psychoanalysts in modern/civilized societies). Hall (1994) divides the history of the scientific study and theories of dreams and dreaming into three periods: 1861–1900, 1900–1953, and 1953–present. A French scientist, Alfred Maury (1861), described the effects of external stimuli on his dreams (e.g., his dreaming of a guillotine sequence was interrupted by the headboard of his bed falling on his neck). Henri Bergson (1901) believed that explanations of dreaming and dreams transcended a mere accounting of correlations between external and internal stimuli and anticipated the later interest in the influence of the unconscious on dreams. In 1900, Sigmund Freud initiated a period dominated by the clinical investigations of dreams where the functions of dreams were to help uncover the origins of patients' symptoms and to understand one's unconscious ("wish fulfillment") mental processes. According to Freud (1900), a dream has different components: the *manifest content*—the dream as it is consciously recalled—and the *latent content*—the "true" meaning of the dream, which is unconscious. In Freud's approach, the dream as recalled represents a compromise between the fulfillment of a repressed wish and the desire to remain asleep; dreams were considered as guardians of sleep and protected the sleeper from being disturbed by unconscious conflicts and annoying external stimuli. The Swiss psychiatrist Carl Jung distinguished "little dreams" (which are a continuation during sleep of one's waking preoccupations) from "big dreams" (which carry messages from the deepest layer of the unconscious, called the *collective unconscious*, and are the same in every individual in every culture; Jung, 1936). The contents of the *collective unconscious* are defined as mental structures ("archetypes") inherited from previous generations. Jung developed the *method of amplification*, or guided questioning, to identify the expression of an archetype in a "big dream." The symbols one uses in dreaming are not disguises, according to Jung, but are attempts of the archetypes to express themselves. Jung believed that symbols reveal, rather than conceal, meaning—in contrast to Freud's viewpoint. On the other hand, both Jung and Freud agreed that dreams are *compensatory* (cf: Boss, 1958, who argued that dreams are neither symbolic nor compensatory; they should merely be taken at "face value"). For Jung, dreams compensate for undeveloped archetypes, and for Freud dreams compensate for unfulfilled wishes (Hall, 1994). Other theoretical approaches to the functions of dreams are provided by Wolman (1973), who notes the wide variety and range of viewpoints: A. Adler suggested that dreams serve a problem-solving function offering cryptic solutions to difficulties the dreamer faces (cf: Warren, 1934, who ascribes to Adler the idea that the dream is always interpreted as a reflection of the dreamer's attitudes toward the future, especially his or her drive toward superiority); H. S. Sullivan believed that dreams satisfy in symbolic ways the needs that could not be discharged in wakeful states and thus reduce tension; W. Dement and C. Fisher suggested that dreams are safety valves reducing the danger of emotional disturbance where deprivation could produce psychosis; R. Hernandez-Peon considered dreams to be related to disinhibition of cortical and limbic neurons associated with the motivational and muscular systems where the neurons associated with memory functions determine the manifest dream content, and the limbic neurons determine the latent dream content; and M. Jouvet and J. Jouvet identified the causal-positive area in the thromboencephalic part of the brain as the locus and center of dreaming. An objective, laboratory-based analysis of dreaming was provided by Aserinsky and Kleitman (1953), who correlated the rapid, conjugate eye movements (REMs) that sleepers made periodically throughout the night with the experience of dreaming. They discovered that subjects recalled few dreams during non-REM (NREM) sleep and a great many dreams during REM periods of sleep. Other physiological characteristics of REM periods that were found were high frequency/low amplitude brain waves during REM (but low frequency/higher amplitude during NREM), irregularities of breathing, blood pressure, and heart rate, and penile erections. The early *scanning hypothesis* of Aserinsky and Kleitman (which stated that the dreamer's eye movements were correlated with the specific events the dreamer was "watching" in a dream) was not corroborated by later experiments. Later studies discovered, also, that dreams are recalled on awakening from *every* sleep stage, not just from REM awakenings (cf: Dement & Kleitman, 1957; Foulkes, 1978). Thus, it appears that all sleep is dreaming sleep, yielding to the current conclusion that, as yet, there are not dependable physiological indicators or correlates of dreaming (Hall, 1994). Another theoretical approach toward the study of dreams is the *content analysis* procedure of Hall (1953), where different categories were devised for describing various elements in dream reports, such as human characters (distinguished by age, sex, family members, friends, strangers), animals, interactions among characters, objects, and emotions. Generalizations from such content analyses are that women and men differ in their dreams: men dream more about male characters, strangers, physical aggression, sexuality, physical activities, tools/weapons, and outdoor settings than do women, while women dream more about female characters, known characters, verbal activities, clothes, and indoor settings than do men. Hall's approach indicated that what an adult dreams about from one year to the next changes very little, and that there is considerable congruence (*continuity principle*) between what one dreams about and one's preoccupations in waking life (Hall, 1994). The various theoretical approaches to dreaming have been challenged recently by a controversial, biologically based approach called the *activation-synthesis theory*, which states that all dreams begin with random electrical discharges from deep within the brain. The signals emerge from the brain stem and go on to stimulate higher areas of the cortex. According to the *activation-synthesis theory*, the brain deals with this strange event by attempting to make sense out of all the input it receives and attempts to give order to chaos and to "synthesize" the separate bursts of electrical stimulation into a coherent story by "creating" a dream (Hobson & McCarley, 1977). Proponents of the *activation-synthesis theory* argue that REM sleep furnishes the brain with an internal source of activation (when external stimulation is minimized) to promote the growth and development of the brain. The content of a dream results from such random stimulation, not unconscious wishes (cf: Freud, 1900). In this view, the meaning of a dream comes as a "brainstorm afterthought" where meaningless activations, once synthesized, give a feeling of familiarity and meaningfulness (Hobson, 1988). The *activation-synthesis theory* helps explain some of the "mysteries" of sleep where the essence of dreams may actually be a brain chemical (i.e., acetylcholine) that is turned on by one set of neurons in the brain stem during REM, and those neurons are "on" only when the others, which trigger the release of serotonin and norepinephrine, are "off." These two brain chemicals are necessary to store memories; people forget about 95 percent of their dreams because they are stored only temporarily in short-term memory, and they cannot be transferred to more permanent memory because serotonin and norepinephrine are shut off during the dream. Hobson (1988) and others believe this approach has opened the door to the molecular biology of sleep and closed it on the *psychoanalytic theory of dreams*. In another current theory, Antrobus' (1991) *neurocognitive theory*, dreams are regarded as variations of normal perceptual, cognitive, and motor activities. Under a high level of cortical arousal, produced by stimulation of the cortex by the reticular formation, together with a blocking of sensory input and motor output, various modules in the cortex interact with one another to produce the images and themes present in dreams, together with emotional responses to the dream content. It appears that humans are so competent at making sense out of chaos in waking life, they even do it in their sleep (cf: the *Potzl phenomenon*—after single tachistoscopic exposures of scenes, of about 1/100th second, the person's dreams the next night reflect with the greatest clarity those portions of the scene that the person fails to report immediately after exposure or does not remember seeing; Zusne, 1987). By understanding the mechanisms of dreaming, knowledge of the waking aspects of imagery and conscious thought processes is enhanced (Antrobus, 1991). See also SLEEP, THEORIES OF.

REFERENCES

Maury, A. (1861). *Le Sommeil et les reves*. Paris: Didier.

Freud, S. (1900). The interpretation of dreams. In *The standard edition of the complete psychological works of Sigmund Freud*. Vols. 4, 5. London: Hogarth Press.

Bergson, H. (1901). *Dreams*. New York: Huebsch.

Warren, H. (Ed.) (1934). *Dictionary of psychology*. Cambridge, MA: Houghton Mifflin.

Jung, C. (1936). The concept of the collective unconscious. In *Collected works*. Vol. 9. Princeton, NJ: Princeton University Press.

Aserinsky, E., & Kleitman, N. (1953). Regularly occurring periods of eye motility and concomitant phenomena during sleep. *Science, 118*, 273–274.

Hall, C. (1953). *The meaning of dreams*. New York: McGraw-Hill.

Dement, W., & Kleitman, N. (1957). Cyclical variations in EEG during sleep and their relation to eye movements, bodily motility, and dreaming. *EEG & Clin. Neurophysio., 9*, 673–690.

Boss, M. (1958). *The analysis of dreams*. New York: Philosophical Library.

Wolman, B. (Ed.) (1973). *Dictionary of behavioral science*. New York: Van Nostrand Reinhold.

Hobson, J., & McCarley, R. (1977). The brain as a dream state generator: An activation-synthesis hypothesis of the dream process. *Amer. J. Psychiat., 134*, 1335–1348.

Foulkes, D. (1978). *A grammar of dreams*. New York: Basic Books.

Zusne, L. (1987). *Eponyms in psychology*. Westport, CT: Greenwood Press.

Hobson, J. (1988). *The dreaming brain*. New York: Basic Books.

Antrobus, J. (1991). Dreaming: Cognitive processes during cortical activation and high afferent thresholds. *Psy. Rev., 98*, 96–121.

Hall, C. (1994). Dreams. In R. J. Corsini (Ed.), *Ency. Psy*. New York: Wiley.

Reber, A. (1995). *The Penguin dictionary of psychology*. New York: Penguin Books.

DRIVE, THEORIES OF. See MOTIVATION, THEORIES OF.

DRIVE-REDUCTION THEORY. See HULL'S LEARNING THEORY; MOTIVATION, THEORIES OF; MOWRER'S THEORY.

DRY-MOUTH THEORY. See THIRST, THEORIES OF.

DUAL CODING HYPOTHESIS/MODEL. See IMAGERY/MENTAL IMAGERY, THEORIES OF.

DUAL-PROCESSES THEORY. See PREJUDICE, THEORIES OF.

DUPLICITY/DUPLEXITY THEORY. See VON KRIES' COLOR VISION THEORY.

DYNAMIC LAWS OF REFLEX STRENGTH. See SKINNER'S DESCRIPTIVE BEHAVIOR/OPERANT CONDITIONING THEORY.

DYNAMIC THEORY. See MOTIVATION, THEORIES OF; PERCEPTION (II. COMPARATIVE APPRAISAL), THEORIES OF.

DYNAMOGENESIS, LAW OF. See PERCEPTION (II. COMPARATIVE APPRAISAL), THEORIES OF.

E

EARLY SELECTION THEORIES. See ATTENTION, LAWS/PRINCIPLES/ THEORIES OF.

EBBINGHAUS' DOCTRINE OF REMOTE ASSOCIATIONS. See SERIAL-POSITION EFFECT.

ECONOMY, PRINCIPLE OF. See PARSIMONY, LAW/PRINCIPLE OF.

EFFECT, LAW OF. = empirical law of effect = Thorndike's law of effect. This is one of the major principles of E. L. *Thorndike's* (1874–1949) *learning theory*, which states that "satisfaction" strengthens a stimulus–response connection or bond, and "annoyance" weakens or gradually eliminates a stimulus–response bond. The *law of effect* has also been called the *empirical law of effect* and the *law of selection*. In its original (1911) form, the *law of effect* stated that of several responses made to the same situation, those that are accompanied or closely followed by satisfaction to the organism will, other things being equal, be more firmly connected with the situation, and those that are accompanied or closely followed by discomfort to the organism will, other things being equal, have their connections with that situation weakened. The greater the satisfaction (or discomfort), the greater the strengthening (or weakening) of the bond. Other forms of the *law of effect* are called *strong law of effect*, *weak law of effect*, and *negative law of effect*. The *weak law of effect* states that a response is more likely to recur if it is followed by a reinforcer, a "satisfier," or a "satisfying state of affairs." The *strong law of effect*, which is an extension of the *empirical* or *weak law of effect*, states that the *necessary* condition for a response to be learned is the explicit occurrence of a reinforcer(s) or a "satisfying state of affairs" after the response is exhibited (this is not a necessary requirement in other learning theories, such as Guthrie's, 1935, *contiguity theory*). The *negative law of effect*, as a reciprocal of the *weak law of effect*, states that responses that are followed by an "annoying state of affairs" are less likely to be repeated. The *negative law of effect* was dropped by Thorndike in his later writings when he became convinced that punishment ("annoying state of affairs") did not simply "stamp out" behavior in the same way that reinforcers ("satisfiers") "stamp in" behavior. Historically, much confusion concerning the *law of effect* has resulted from failure to differentiate the law on three bases: (1) as an empirical statement; (2) as a general theory of reinforcement; and (3) as special hypotheses concerning the nature of reinforcers and their action characteristics. Consistent criticism against the *law of effect* has focused on the tautology or circularity inherent in the law (Woodworth & Schlosberg, 1965). That is, it is difficult to explain an instance of learning in terms of its "effects" because the effects happen after the behavior or learning has already occurred, or the only way one can tell whether or not a given result is satisfying is by observing to see whether or not the organism repeats the behavior that produced the supposed reward. The circular reasoning is that a "satisfying state of affairs" is one that increases responding, and any event that increases responding is a "satisfying state of affairs." Thus, for example, an individual likes a stimulus (e.g., applause) because he or she repeats a behavior (e.g., acting on stage), and the individual repeats a behavior (e.g., acting on stage) because he or she likes the stimulus (e.g., applause) (cf: Meehl, 1950). See also GUTHRIE'S THEORY; HERRNSTEIN'S MATCHING LAW; READINESS, LAW OF; REINFORCEMENT, THORNDIKE'S THEORY OF.

REFERENCES

Thorndike, E. L. (1905). *The elements of psychology*. New York: Seiler.

Thorndike, E. L. (1911). *Animal intelligence, experimental studies*. New York: Macmillan.

Thorndike, E. L. (1913). *Educational psychology*. Vol. 2. *The psychology of learning*. New York: Teachers College, Columbia University.

Thorndike, E. L. (1927). The law of effect. *Amer. J. Psy., 39,* 212–222.

Thorndike, E. L. (1931). *Human learning*. New York: Appleton-Century-Crofts.

Thorndike, E. L. (1932). *The fundamentals of learning*. New York: Teachers College, Columbia University.

Tolman, E., Hall, C., & Bretnall, E. (1932). A disproof of the law of effect and a substitution of the laws of emphasis, motivation, and disruption. *J. Exp. Psy., 15,* 601–614.

Guthrie, E. R. (1935). *The psychology of learning*. New York: Harper.

Tolman, E. (1938). The law of effect: A roundtable discussion. II. *Psy. Rev., 45,* 200–203.

Razran, G. (1939). The law of effect or the law of qualitative conditioning. *Psy. Rev., 46,* 445–463.

Tilton, J. (1945). Gradients of effect. *J. Genet. Psy., 66,* 3–19.

Allport, G. (1946). Effect: A secondary principle of learning. *Psy. Rev., 53,* 335–347.

Mowrer, O. H. (1946). The law of effect and ego psychology. *Psy. Rev., 53,* 321–334.

Rice, P. (1946). The ego and the law of effect. *Psy. Rev., 53,* 307–320.

Postman, L. (1947). The history and present status of the law of effect. *Psy. Bull., 44,* 489–563.

Meehl, P. (1950). On the circularity of the law of effect. *Psy. Bull., 47*, 52–75.

Marx, M. (1956). Spread of effect: A critical review. *Genet. Psy. Mono., 53*, 119–186.

Boring, E. G. (1957). *A history of experimental psychology*. New York: Appleton-Century-Crofts.

Kimble, G. (1961). *Hilgard and Marquis' conditioning and learning*. New York: Appleton-Century-Crofts.

Postman, L. (1961). Spread of effect as a function of time and intraserial similarity. *Amer. J. Psy., 74*, 493–505.

Woodworth, R., & Schlosberg, H. (1965). *Experimental psychology*. New York: Appleton-Century-Crofts.

Herrnstein, R. (1970). On the law of effect. *J. Exp. Anal. Beh., 13*, 243–266.

Brown, R., & Herrnstein, R. (1975). *Psychology*. Boston: Little, Brown.

Bower, G., & Hilgard, E. (1981). *Theories of learning*. Englewood Cliffs, NJ: Prentice-Hall.

Bugelski, B. R. (1994). Thorndike's laws of learning. In R. J. Corsini (Ed.), *Ency. Psy.* New York: Wiley.

EGO-STATE THEORY. See HYPNOSIS/HYPNOTISM, THEORIES OF.

EINSTELLUNG EFFECT. See MIND/MENTAL SET, LAW OF.

EKMAN–FRIESEN THEORY OF EMOTIONS. This current theory by Paul Ekman (1934–   ) and his associates combines a *somatic theory of emotions* (the somatic nervous system controls many bodily muscles, including facial muscles) with an *evolutionary theory of emotions* (based on the *Darwinian theory* that some ways of expressing emotions are inborn). The *Ekman–Friesen theory* (Ekman & Friesen, 1971, 1975; Ekman, 1982, 1993) argues that there are distinct facial expressions that accompany a number of emotions, including fear, joy, surprise, anger, excitement, scorn, and sadness. When an environmental event occurs, the person's facial muscles react with an emotional expression. The information of how the face is responding is transmitted to the brain, which then labels a specific emotional state. In this way, autonomic arousal may occur either before or after the labeling of an emotion. When it occurs before the labeling process, it may be incorporated into the label and influence the interpretation of the intensity of the emotion. This theory has been proposed to account for emotional behavior across cultures, and Ekman and Friesen (1971) found many similarities in the way people from different cultures express specific emotions. However, while such cross-cultural studies demonstrate some degree of universality in emotional expression, research continues to help decide if emotional expression is inborn, as the *Darwinian evolutionary theory* suggests. See also DARWIN'S EVOLUTION THEORY; EMOTIONS, THEORIES/LAWS OF; FACIAL FEEDBACK HYPOTHESIS; IZARD'S THEORY OF EMOTIONS; JAMES–LANGE/LANGE–JAMES THEORY OF EMOTIONS; PLUTCHIK'S MODEL OF EMOTIONS.

REFERENCES

Feleky, A. (1914). The expression of the emotions. *Psy. Rev., 21*, 33–41.

Feleky, A. (1916). The influence of emotions on respiration. *J. Exp. Psy., 1*, 218–241.

Langfeld, H. (1918). The judgment of emotion by facial expression. *J. Abn. Soc. Psy., 13*, 172–184.

Feleky, A. (1922). *Feelings and emotions*. New York: Pioneer Press.

Landis, C. (1924). Studies of emotional reactons. II. General behavior and facial expression. *J. Comp. Psy., 4*, 447–509.

Frois-Wittmann, J. (1930). The judgment of facial expressions. *J. Exp. Psy., 13*, 113–151.

Munn, N. (1940). The effect of knowledge of the situation upon judgment of emotions from facial expressions. *J. Abn. Soc. Psy., 35*, 324–338.

Andrew, R. (1965). The origins of facial expressions. *Sci. Amer., 4*, 88–94.

Ekman, P., & Friesen, W. (1971). Constants across culture in the face and emotions. *J. Pers. Soc. Psy., 17*, 124–129.

Ekman, P., Friesen, W., & Ellsworth, P. (1972). *Emotion in the human face: Guidelines for research and an integration of findings*. Elmsford, NY: Pergamon.

Ekman, P., & Friesen, W. (1975). *Unmasking the face*. Englewood Cliffs, NJ: Prentice-Hall.

Ekman, P. (Ed.) (1982). *Emotion in the human face*. New York: Cambridge University Press.

Ekman, P., Levenson, R., & Friesen, W. (1983). Autonomic nervous system activity distinguishes among emotions. *Science, 221*, 1208–1210.

Ekman, P., Friesen, W., & Simons, R. (1985). Is the startle reaction an emotion? *J. Pers. Soc. Beh., 49*, 1416–1426.

Ekman, P., Davidson, R., & Friesen, W. (1990). The Duchenne smile: Emotional expression and brain physiology. II. *J. Pers. Soc. Psy., 58*, 342–353.

Ekman, P., & O'Sullivan, M. (1991). Who can catch a liar? *Amer. Psy., 46*, 913–920.

Ekman, P. (1993). Facial expressions and emotion. *Amer. Psy., 48*, 384–392.

Ekman, P., & Davidson, R. (1993). Voluntary smiling changes regional brain activity. *Psy. Sci., 14*, 342–345.

Davidoff, L. (1994). Facial expressions. In R. J. Corsini (Ed.), *Ency. Psy*. New York: Wiley.

Ekman, P. (1994). Strong evidence for universals in facial expressions: A reply to Russell's mistaken critique. *Psy. Bull., 115*, 268–287.

Lindauer, M. (1994). Physiognomic perception. In R. J. Corsini (Ed.), *Ency. Psy*. New York: Wiley.

ELECTRODERMAL ACTIVITY/PHENOMENA. The term *electrodermal activity* (EDA) is used by psychophysiologists to refer to the electrical activity of the skin on the palms of the hand or on the fingers (Stern, 1994). The first individuals to use this measure thought that it indicated the secrets of mental life (Newmann & Blauton, 1970). However, today, EDA is considered merely as a state of the organism's interaction with the environment. The terms used to describe EDA have changed over the years. The term *psychogalvanic reflex* (PGR) was used during the early 1900s, and later the term *galvanic skin re-*

sponse (GSR) was popular (named in honor of the Italian physiologist Luigi Galvani, 1737–1798, who discovered animal electricity; Muir, 1994). The difficulty found later with the term GSR was that it came to describe several different aspects of electrodermal activity (e.g., basal level, response amplitude), and most psychophysiologists today seem to prefer the term EDA. The electrical activity of the skin can be measured in two ways: the Fere method and the Tarchanoff method. The French neurologist Charles Fere (?–1907) used an "exosomatic" method, often referred to as the *Fere phenomenon*, where a small current was passed through the skin from an external source, following which the resistances to the passage of current were measured (Fere, 1888). The Russian physiologist Ivan Romanovich Tarchanoff (1846–1908) used an "endosomatic" method, often referred to as the *Tarchanoff phenomenon*, where the electrical activity was measured at the surface of the skin with no externally imposed current (Tarchanoff, 1890). The Fere method has been modified today into the measurement of *skin conductance* (SC), which is the reciprocal of skin "resistance." Tarchanoff's method is still used today to measure *skin potential* (SP). The "galvanometer" is an instrument that measures electric current and provides a measure of the electrical response of the skin. Thus, Fere's measure records changes in the resistance of the skin to the passage of a weak electric current, and Tarchanoff's measure records weak current actually produced by the body. Because the Fere measure increases with increasing perspiration, it has often been assumed to be an indication of emotional tension or anxiety (as employed in the so-called lie detection or polygraph procedure). This assumption has proven difficult to substantiate, however, and it is probably best to consider it as merely a measure of physiological arousal (Reber, 1995). See also EMOTIONS, THEORIES/LAWS OF.

REFERENCES

Fere, C. (1888). Note sur les modifications de la resistance electrique sous l'influence des excitations sensorielles et des emotions. *C. R. Soc. Bio. Mem., 40*, 217–219.

Tarchanoff, J. (1890). Ueber die galvanischen Erscheinungen in der Haut des menschen bei Reizungen der Sinnesorgane und bei verschiedennen Formen der psychischen Thatigkeit. *Pflug. Ar. ges. Physio., 46*, 46–55.

Woodworth, R., & Schlosberg, H. (1965). *Experimental psychology*. New York: Holt, Rinehart, & Winston.

Newmann, E., & Blauton, R. (1970). The early history of electrodermal research. *Psychophysiology, 6*, 453–475.

Stern, R., Ray, W., & Davis, C. (1980). *Psychophysiological recording*. New York: Oxford University Press.

Muir, H. (Ed.) (1994). *Larousse dictionary of scientists*. New York: Larousse.

Stern, R. (1994). Electrodermal activity. In R. J. Corsini (Ed.), *Ency. Psy.* New York: Wiley.

Reber, A. (1995). *The Penguin dictionary of psychology*. New York: Penguin Books.

ELECTROLYTE METABOLISM THEORY OF DEPRESSION. See DEPRESSION, THEORIES OF.

ELICITED OBSERVING RATE HYPOTHESIS. This hypothesis (Jerison, 1970) describes the complex relation between observing activity, decision processes, and vigilance in sustained attention tasks. The hypothesis also attempts to formulate the topic of vigilance within the framework of *signal detection theory*. The *elicited observing rate hypothesis* makes the assumption that during a vigilance activity (e.g., a sailor's monitoring a sonar screen to detect enemy submarines) the observer constantly makes sequential decisions as to emit or not to emit an observing response toward a display that is being monitored. In general terms, observing responses are termed *unitary attentive acts* and may involve "internal" message selection by the central nervous system. The hypothesis says that signal detection failures (e.g., an enemy sub was present, and the sailor didn't see or hear it) occur when the individual does not emit the observing responses and also proposes that the effort involved in observing has a quantifiable energy "cost" where decisions to observe or not to observe are based upon their *utility* (i.e., the "cost" of observing relative to the "reward" of correct signal detection). Poor vigilance, according to the hypothesis, results from the decrement in quality and quantity of elicited observing behavior over a period of time and where factors such as fatigue and low motivation account for the high "costs" of the observing activity. Definitive tests of the hypothesis are difficult because of the imprecise specification of the nature of the "internal" observing mechanism (Dember & Warm, 1979). See also SIGNAL DETECTION, THEORY OF; UTILITY THEORY; VIGILANCE, THEORIES OF.

REFERENCES

Baker, C. (1960). Observing behavior in a vigilance task. *Science, 132,* 674–675.

Jerison, H., & Pickett, R. (1963). Vigilance: A review and reevaluation. *Hum. Fact., 5,* 211–238.

Jerison, H., & Pickett, R. (1964). Vigilance: The importance of the elicited observing rate. *Science, 143,* 970–971.

Jerison, H. (1967). Activation and long-term performance. *Acta Psy., 27,* 373–389.

Jerison, H. (1970). Vigilance, discrimination, and attention. In D. Mostofsky (Ed.), *Attention: Contemporary theory and analysis.* New York: Appleton-Century-Crofts.

Jerison, H. (1977). Vigilance, biology, psychology, theory, and practice. In R. Mackie (Ed.), *Vigilance: Theory, operational performance, and physiological correlates.* New York: Plenum.

Dember, W., & Warm, J. (1979). *Psychology of perception.* New York: Holt, Rinehart, & Winston.

EMBOITEMENT, THEORY OF. This biologically based theory has been stated by the English philosopher Herbert Spencer (1820–1903) as follows: "[I]n the germ of every living creature the future adult exists . . . and within this exist the immeasurably more minute forms of adults which will eventually descend from it, and so on *ad infinitum*" (Spencer, 1892, p. 655). The term *emboitement*, according to Webster's unabridged dictionary (Merriam-Webster, 1986), is defined as "encasement; to put into a box; encase; fit together." While it does have a certain intuitive appeal (much like the *theory of recapitulation*), as a theory in psychology the concept of *emboitement* appears to be archaic and is only infrequently referenced by authors of psychology textbooks. For example, in a study that sampled 136 textbooks published from 1885 to 1996 (Roeckelein, 1996), only one writer (Spencer, 1892) referenced the *theory of emboitement*. See also RECAPITULATION, THEORY/LAW OF.

REFERENCES

Spencer, H. (1892). *The principles of psychology*. New York: Appleton.
Merriam-Webster. (1986). *Webster's third new international dictionary of the English language*. Unabridged. Springfield, MA: Author.
Roeckelein, J. E. (1996). Citation of *laws* and *theories* in textbooks across 112 years of psychology. *Psy. Rep., 79*, 979–998.

EMERGENCY THEORY. See CANNON/CANNON–BARD THEORY.

EMMERT'S LAW. = size-distance invariance hypothesis. This generalized principle is named in honor of the Swiss ophthalmologist Emil Emmert (1844–1911) and refers to the tendency of a projected image (usually an *afterimage*) to increase in size in proportion to the distance to which it is projected onto a background surface. Boring, Langfeld, and Weld (1939) refer to *Emmert's law* as an *afterimage law*; earlier, Ebbecke (1929) proposed a *theory of positive and negative afterimages*. Another *afterimage* phenomenon is the *McCollough effect/ color-contingent aftereffect*, which is a persistent afterimage produced by saturating the eye with red and green patterns of different angularity: in a typical experiment, a pattern of bright red and black horizontal lines is alternated with a pattern of bright green and black vertical lines every five seconds for several minutes. Following these exposures a pattern of black and white lines at various angles is presented, and, when the afterimage appears, the horizontal white lines are seen as tinged with green and the vertical with red. If the head is tilted 90 degrees, the colors change, taking on the appropriate coloration. The *Mc-Collough effect* may last up to four or five days (McCollough, 1965; Reber, 1995; cf: Brown, 1965). *Emmert's law* is based on the use of size as a cue in estimating distance and involves the geometry of visual size and depth (Schlosberg, 1950) that suggests the following equation (this equation has been called *Euclid's law*; Woodworth & Schlosberg, 1965): $a = A/D$, where a is the retinal image of an object, A is the actual size of the object, and D is the distance from the object to the retina. This equation says, at face value, that the farther away an object is, the smaller it should look (''retinal size''). However, there is an apparent exception to *Euclid's law*. In 1881, Emmert reported that an *afterimage* actually looks bigger if it is projected on a more distant surface; that is, the judged size of the image is proportional to the distance (*Emmert's law*). Thus, *Emmert's law* is essentially a special case of *Euclid's law*. The relationship of the variable of size to the variable of distance was studied, also, by Helmholtz (1856–1866), who argued that observers learn through experience that an object's physical size remains the same (invariant), although its retinal image size varies with distance. Thus, one's perceptual system records the size of the retinal image and then changes or corrects this information in light of available cues about distance to arrive at judgments of object size. Helmholtz suggested also that in perceiving object size, people implicitly solve the equation: object size = retinal size × distance (cf: *Euclid's law*). More recently, this view of size constancy constitutes the *size-distance invariance hypothesis* (Kilpatrick & Ittelson, 1953; Epstein, Park, & Casey, 1961), which implies that accurate perception of an object's distance leads to accurate perception of its size. Thus, the link between the *size-distance invariance hypothesis* and *Emmert's law* is the use in the latter of an *afterimage* of an object that is projected onto a background surface. The basic principles concerning the relationship between perceived size and perceived distance remain the same in either case (cf: Weintraub & Gardner, 1970). The *size-distance invariance hypothesis* has been generally useful in the psychology of perception. For instance, it is the most widely cited account of the phenomenon of *size constancy*, but it has also generated controversy, and there are limits to its applicability (cf: Vogel & Teghtsoonian, 1972). *Emmert's law* and the *size-distance invariance hypothesis* have been invoked as a possible explanation for one of the classical illusions, the *moon illusion* (i.e., the experience where the perceived size of a full moon observed on the horizon seems much larger than the same moon when viewed overhead at its zenith a few hours later; also called the *celestial illusion* because the effect may also occur with respect to the sun), which has been a puzzle since antiquity and has been discussed repeatedly in ancient and medieval literature (Ross & Ross, 1976). However, Dember and Warm (1979) point out that there may be no single answer or explanation, such as *Emmert's law*, to the ancient puzzle and curiosity of the *moon illusion* (cf: Boring, 1943, 1962; Wallach, 1962). See also PERCEPTION (I. GENERAL), THEORIES OF; PERCEPTION (II. COMPARATIVE APPRAISAL) THEORIES OF; VISION/SIGHT, THEORIES OF.

REFERENCES

Emmert, E. (1881). Grossenverhaltnisse der Nachbilder. *Klin. Monatb. Augenheilk.*, 443–450.

Helmholtz, H. von (1856–1866). *Handbuch der physiologischen Optik*. Trans. by J. Southall. Rochester, NY: Optical Society of America.

Ebbecke, U. (1929). *Ar. ges. Physio.*, *221*, 160–212.

Boring, E. G., Langfeld, H., & Weld, H. (1939). *Introduction to psychology*. New York: Wiley.

Boring, E. G. (1940). Size-constancy and Emmert's law. *Amer. J. Psy.*, *53*, 293–295.

Holway, A., & Boring, E. G. (1941). Determinants of apparent visual size with distance variant. *Amer. J. Psy.*, *54*, 21–37.

Boring, E. G. (1943). The moon illusion. *Amer. J. Physics*, *11*, 55–60.

Edwards, W. (1950). Emmert's law and Euclid's optics. *Amer. J. Psy., 63*, 607–612.

Schlosberg, H. (1950). A note on depth perception, size constancy, and related topics. *Psy. Rev., 57*, 314–317.

Young, F. (1950). Boring's interpretation of Emmert's law. *Amer. J. Psy., 63*, 277–280.

Boring, E. G., & Edwards, W. (1951). What is Emmert's law? *Amer. J. Psy., 64*, 416–422.

Young, F. (1951). Concerning Emmert's law. *Amer. J. Psy., 64*, 124–128.

Kilpatrick, F., & Ittelson, W. (1953). The size-distance invariance hypothesis. *Psy. Rev., 60*, 223–231.

Rock, I., & Ebenholtz, S. (1959). The relational determination of perceived size. *Psy. Rev., 66*, 387–401.

Epstein, W., Park, J., & Casey, A. (1961). The current status of the size-distance hypothesis. *Psy. Bull., 58*, 491–514.

Boring, E. G. (1962). On the moon illusion. *Science, 137*, 902–906.

Kaufman, L., & Rock, I. (1962). The moon illusion. *Sci. Amer., 207*, 120–130.

Wallach, H. (1962). On the moon illusion. *Science, 137*, 900–902.

Epstein, W. (1963). Attitudes of judgment and the size-distance invariance hypothesis. *J. Exp. Psy., 66*, 78–83.

Gruber, H., King, W., & Link, S. (1963). Moon illusion: An event in imaginary space. *Science, 139*, 750–751.

Brown, J. (1965). Afterimages. In C. Graham (Ed.), *Vision and visual perception*. New York: Wiley.

McCollough, C. (1965). Color adaptation of edge-detectors in the human visual system. *Science, 149*, 1115–1116.

Woodworth, R., & Schlosberg, H. (1965). *Experimental psychology*. New York: Holt, Rinehart, & Winston.

Gogel, W. (1968). The measurement of perceived size and distance. In W. Neff (Ed.), *Contributions to sensory physiology*. New York: Academic Press.

Weintraub, D., & Gardner, G. (1970). Emmert's laws: Size constancy vs. optical geometry. *Amer. J. Psy., 83*, 40–51.

Vogel, J., & Teghtsoonian, M. (1972). The effects of perspective alterations on apparent size and distance scales. *Perc. & Psychophys., 11*, 294–298.

Favreau, O., & Corballis, M. (1976). Negative aftereffects in visual perception. *Sci. Amer., 235*, 42–48.

Ross, H., & Ross, G. (1976). Did Ptolemy understand the moon illusion? *Perception, 5*, 377–385.

Dember, W., & Warm, J. (1979). *Psychology of perception*. New York: Holt, Rinehart, & Winston.

Reber, A. (1995). *The Penguin dictionary of psychology*. New York: Penguin Books.

EMOTIONAL CONTAGION/PRIMITIVE EMOTIONAL CONTAGION, THEORY OF. See FACIAL FEEDBACK HYPOTHESIS.

EMOTIONS, THEORIES/LAWS OF. The term *emotion* derives from the Latin *emovere*, meaning to excite, to move, to agitate, or to stir up. Historically, the term *emotion* has defied exact definition, even though it is widely used as if implicit agreement existed, and most textbook authors employ it as the title of a chapter, allowing the material presented to be a substitute for a precise definition (Reber, 1995). Despite the long history of the concept of *emotion*, which goes back to the early Greek philosophers, as well as Descartes' (1650) analysis of emotions into *six passions of the soul* (i.e., wonder, love, hate, desire, joy, sadness), there had been little discussion of emotion as theory (Lindsley, 1951). Modern interest in *theories of emotion* began with the writings of William James (1884, 1890), and there currently exist a number of specific theoretical orientations toward emotion (see cross-referenced terms). Current usage of the term *emotion* falls into two categories: (1) the identification of a number of subjectively experienced states (e.g., fear, anger, love, surprise, disgust) and (2) the reference to a field of scientific research that examines the physiological, behavioral, cognitive, and environmental factors underlying the subjective aspects of emotion. The definitions of terms in the second category amount to *minitheories of emotion*, where there seems to be consensus on at least four generally important factors for study (Reber, 1995): (1) instigating stimuli— exogenous (external stimuli such as environmental events) and endogenous (internal stimuli such as images or thoughts); (2) physiological correlates—general biological systems (such as central and autonomic nervous system events) and specific action patterns (such as hypothalamic-thalamic interactions; e.g., *Papez's theory* and *MacLean's theory* of emotion; Papez, 1937; MacLean, 1958); (3) cognitive appraisal—individualistic or personal significance of potential and actual emotional events (such as exhibiting fear reactions to caged lions at a zoo); and (4) motivational aspects—the organismic arousal associated with emotions is consistently associated with the activation involved in motivation (such as becoming angry for some reason and then displacing aggression onto an innocent bystander). In general, emotional states have other characteristics that distinguish them from allied concepts in the history of psychology. For example, emotions are *acute* (i.e., they are momentary conditions of high intensity), which sets them apart from *sentiments* (i.e., general complex dispositions toward action), *feelings* (i.e., general sensing or experiencing of events in the world such as happiness or well-being), and *organized behaviors* (i.e., nonerratic, nonchaotic, well-integrated, and controlled behavioral responses to the environment). Also, in general, emotions tend not to be cyclical or regular (aside from psychopathological conditions such as the *affective disorders*, which show inappropriate, chronic expression of an emotional state) but seem in "normally" functioning individuals to be dependent on specific situations and are tied to one's particular personal perception and meaning. The difficulty in studying emotions is due to a number of causes and problems, prominent among which is the pervasive tendency by investigators to separate emotion from cognition or rational thought processes. The physiological and psychological processes involved in emotion are most likely interrelated, and, according to some writers (e.g., Baum, 1994), separation by theorists of emotion from these other aspects of experience may not be productive; rather, integration of the psychological and physiological realms in the study of emotions is a desideratum. It is interesting to note that recently, in only 30 years from 1954 to 1984, it is estimated that there have been at least 20 new *theories of emotions* advanced by psychologists (Scarr & VanderZanden, 1984). Coon (1997, p. 433) provides a synthesis (*contemporary model of emotions*) of the main factors of several of the most popular theories of emotions in psychology. In this model, the following feedback sequence occurs in an emotional episode: an emotional stimulus triggers a cognitive appraisal of the situation, which then gives rise to arousal, behavior, facial/postural expressions, and emotional feelings. Arousal, behavior, and expressions then add to emotional feelings. Emotional feelings influence appraisal, which further affects arousal, behavior, expressions, and feelings. Sound circular? Some few writers have argued that the study of emotions achieved the status of lawful phenomena where the *laws of emotion* may now be cited. For example, Frijda (1988) describes the following set of *laws of emotion*: the law of situational meaning; the law of concern; the law of reality; the laws of change, habituation, and comparative feeling; the law of hedonic asymmetry; the law of conservatism of emotional momentum; the law of closure; and the laws of care for consequence, of lightest load, and of greatest gain. Time will tell, perhaps, which of these *laws of emotion*, if any, will be generally acknowledged and honored by psychologists. See also ACTIVATION/ AROUSAL THEORY; ARNOLD'S THEORY OF EMOTIONS; BEHAVIORISTIC THEORY; CANNON/CANNON–BARD THEORY; COGNITIVE-APPRAISAL THEORY; DARWIN'S THEORY OF EMOTIONS; EKMAN–FRIESEN THEORY OF EMOTIONS; FACIAL-FEEDBACK HYPOTHESIS; IZARD'S THEORY OF EMOTIONS; JAMES–LANGE/LANGE-JAMES THEORY OF EMOTIONS; MOTIVATION, THEORIES OF; PLUTCHIK'S MODEL OF EMOTIONS; SCHACHTER–SINGER'S THEORY OF EMOTIONS; SOLOMON'S OPPONENT-PROCESS THEORY OF EMOTIONS.

REFERENCES

Descartes, R. (1650). *Les passions de l'ame*. Paris: Loyson.

Bain, A. (1859). *The emotions and the will*. London: Longmans.

James, W. (1884). What is an emotion? *Mind, 9*, 188–205.

James, W. (1890). *Principles of psychology*. New York: Holt.

Cannon, W. (1915). *Bodily changes in pain, hunger, fear, and rage*. New York: Appleton.

Cannon, W. (1932). *The wisdom of the body*. New York: Norton.

Duffy, E. (1934). Emotion: An example of the need for reorientation in psychology. *Psy. Rev., 41*, 184–198.

Papez, J. (1937). A proposed mechanism of emotion. *Ar. Neuro. Psychiat., 38*, 725–743.

Duffy, E. (1941). An explanation of "emotional" phenomena without the use of the concept "emotion." *J. Gen. Psy., 25*, 283–293.

Lindsley, D. (1951). Emotion. In S. S. Stevens (Ed.), *Handbk. Exp. Psy.* New York: Wiley.

Funkenstein, D. (1955). The physiology of fear and anger. *Sci. Amer., 192*, 74–80.

MacLean, P. (1958). Contrasting functions of limbic and neocortical systems of the brain and their relevance of psychophysiological aspects of medicine. *Amer. J. Med.,* *25,* 611–626.

Davitz, J. (1969). *The language of emotion.* New York: Academic Press.

Levi, L. (Ed.) (1975). *Emotions: Their parameters and measurement.* New York: Raven Press.

Averill, J. (1980). A constructionist view of emotion. In R. Plutchik & H. Kellerman (Eds.), *Emotion: Theory, research, and experience.* New York: Academic Press.

Scarr, S., & VanderZanden, J. (1984). *Understanding psychology.* New York: Random House.

Frijda, N. (1986). *The emotions.* London: Cambridge University Press.

Strongman, K. (1987). *The psychology of emotion.* New York: Wiley.

Frijda, N. (1988). The laws of emotion. *Amer. Psy., 43,* 349–358.

Baum, A. (1994). Emotions. In R. J. Corsini (Ed.), *Ency. Psy.* New York: Wiley.

Reber, A. (1995). *The Penguin dictionary of psychology.* New York: Penguin Books.

Coon, D. (1997). *Essentials of psychology.* Pacific Grove, CA: Brooks/Cole.

EMPIRICAL LAW OF EFFECT. See EFFECT, LAW OF.

ENCODING SPECIFICITY HYPOTHESIS/PRINCIPLE. See CODING THEORIES.

ENERGY CONSERVATION THEORY. See SLEEP, THEORIES OF.

ENERGY METABOLISM THEORY. See HUNGER, THEORIES OF.

ENESTRUENCE/EVENT-STRUCTURE, THEORY OF. See ALLPORT'S THEORY OF ENESTRUENCE.

ENTROPY PRINCIPLE. See JUNG'S THEORY OF PERSONALITY.

EPIPHENOMENALISM, THEORY OF. See MIND–BODY THEORIES.

EQUIPOTENTIALITY THEORY. See LASHLEY'S THEORY.

EQUITY THEORY. The essential structure of *equity theory* is that it consists of four interdependent, or interlocking, propositions (Hatfield, 1994): (1) people attempt to maximize *outcomes* (where an outcome equals reward minus punishment); (2) people in groups may maximize collective reward by devising systems for equitable apportionment of resources and will reward group members who treat others in an equitable fashion while punishing group members who treat each other inequitably; (3) people who find themselves participating in inequitable relationships will become distressed at a level that is directly proportionate to the level of inequitability; and (4) people will attempt to eliminate distress and restore equity when they find themselves in an inequitable situation. *Equity theory* has been applied to areas of human interaction such as intimate and exploitative interpersonal relationships, philanthropic and altruistic relationships, and business relationships. *Equity theory* research has indicated that people who discover that they are in an inequitable relationship attempt to reduce their resultant distress by restoring either "actual" or "psychological" equity to their relationship. Actual equity may be restored by altering one's own or one's partner's relative gains in certain ways. For instance, if a worker discovers that he is getting paid less than was contracted for, he can establish equity in a number of different ways: he can lower his own personal effort or input into the job, he can raise his outcomes by stealing from the company, he can raise the employer's inputs by making deliberate job-related mistakes, or he can lower the employer's outcomes by deliberately damaging company equipment. An employee can also insist that equity be restored to the employee–employer relationship by demanding various types of restitution. Other research on *equity theory* has indicated that the "overbenefited" often voluntarily compensate the "underbenefited" (e.g., Carlsmith & Gross, 1969). Psychological equity may be used also to restore equity in an unbalanced relationship: the individual can distort reality and convince herself that the unjust relationship really is perfectly fair. For instance, if a worker feels that she is being underpaid, but there is nothing she can do about it, she may restore psychological equity by lowering her own self-esteem (such as feeling that she is really unambitious), by raising her outcomes through compensatory thoughts (such as convincing herself that this four-day-a-week job gives her more time to engage in other more valuable activities), by raising her employer's inputs (such as praising the company for its community contributions), or by lowering her employer's outcomes (such as feeling that the bosses will get sick from overwork on the job). Thus, the chief argument made by proponents of *equity theory* is that such diverse topics as cooperation, aggression, power, altruism, and other social psychological phenomena can be accounted for by an analysis of *outcomes, inputs, equity,* and *inequity* in various interpersonal relationship situations. See also CONFLICT, THEORIES OF; EXCHANGE/SOCIAL EXCHANGE THEORY; FESTINGER'S COGNITIVE DISSONANCE THEORY.

REFERENCES

Adams, J. (1963). Toward an understanding of inequity. *J. Abn. Soc. Psy., 67*, 422–436.
Brock, T., & Buss, A. (1964). Effects of justification for aggression in communication with the victim on post-aggression dissonance. *J. Abn. Soc. Psy., 68*, 403–412.
Adams, J. (1965). Inequity in social exchange. In L. Berkowitz (Ed.), *Advances in experimental social psychology*. Vol. 2. New York: Academic Press.
Walster (Hatfield), E., & Prestholdt, P. (1966). The effect of misjudging another: Overcompensation or dissonance reduction? *J. Exp. Soc. Psy., 2*, 85–97.
Carlsmith, J., & Gross, A. (1969). Some effects of guilt on compliance. *J. Pers. Soc. Psy., 11*, 232–239.
Walster (Hatfield), E., Berscheid, E., & Walster, G. (1973). New directions in equity research. *J. Pers. Soc. Psy., 25*, 151–176.

Walster (Hatfield), E., Walster, G., & Berscheid, E. (1978). *Equity: Theory and research.* Boston: Allyn & Bacon.

Hatfield, E., Utne, M., & Traupmann, H. (1979). Equity theory and intimate relationships. In R. Burgess & T. Huston (Eds.), *Social exchange in developing relationships.* New York: Academic Press.

Hatfield, E. (1994). Equity. In R. J. Corsini (Ed.), *Ency. Psy.* New York: Wiley.

EQUITY THEORY OF WORK. See WORK/CAREER/OCCUPATION, THEORIES OF.

EQUIVALENCE PRINCIPLE. See JUNG'S THEORY OF PERSONALITY.

ERIKSON'S THEORY OF PERSONALITY. The German-born American psychoanalyst Erik Homburger Erikson (1902–1994) attempted to revive the structure of psychoanalysis after the death of Sigmund Freud in 1939. Erikson considered himself a Freudian psychoanalyst in spite of some opinions that he fell outside the Freudian tradition (e.g., Roazen, 1976; cf: Coles, 1970). Erikson's major contributions to contemporary *psychoanalytic theory* included a *psychosocial theory of development* and psychohistorical analyses of famous persons (Hall & Lindzey, 1978). According to Erikson's theoretical approach, the term *psychosocial* refers to the stages of an individual's life from birth to death and focuses on the social/environmental influences that interact with the physical and psychological growth of the individual. Erikson's *psychosocial theory*, which describes "stages" of development, supplements Freud's *psychosexual stage development theory*, Piaget's *cognitive stage development theory*, and Sullivan's *interpersonal stage development theory*. The notion of "stage" in developmental theories refers to the more or less clearly defined ages at which new forms of behavior appear in response to new maturational and social variables. Erikson coined the term *identity crisis* and posited that development proceeds in eight consecutive stages, where the first four stages occur during infancy and childhood, the fifth stage occurs during adolescence, and the final three stages occur during adulthood up to old age. Each stage contributes to an individual's whole personality in an "epigenetic" sense (i.e., overall development unfolds via interaction with the environment), but different people may have different timetables for entering and progressing through each stage. Erikson (1950/1963) believed that each stage was characterized by a specific conflict that seeks resolution. The eight stages are *basic trust versus basic mistrust*—infancy period, when very young children develop attitudes of trust or mistrust concerning people; *autonomy versus shame/doubt*—early childhood, when the child grows older and, in its attempt to gain control over muscles and bones, develops attitudes of autonomy, independence, and success, or shame, doubt, and failure; *initiative versus guilt*—occurs during preschool age, when the child is about four years old and is seeking behavior roles to imitate; if she learns the socially acceptable behaviors, then initiative is required, but if there is failure, a sense of lasting guilt develops; *industry versus inferiority*—when the child begins school, he attempts to master the world in certain social ways, and success is characterized by industry or competence, while failure is associated with the development of inferiority feelings; *identity versus identity confusion/diffusion*—when the young adult approaches adolescence and puberty, she must decide "who she is" and "where she's going"; at this stage decisions concerning sexual identity, occupation, and adult life plans are made; *intimacy versus isolation*—during young adulthood, when the person has "found himself" and knows where he's going, then intimacy with another person is possible; however, if adolescence has passed without proper role identity and resolution, isolation from others may be the result; *generativity versus stagnation*—while in middle or full adulthood, the person must choose to continue her mental growth, health, creativity, and productivity or else risk the chance of stagnation and loss of growth; *integrity versus despair*—this last stage is a crisis of old age or maturity that challenges a person to choose between maintaining feelings of worth and integrity that have been built up or to yield to opposing feelings of despair and resignation where one senses that life has been a futile waste of energy. Also, according to Erikson's *psychosocial theory*, each person's personality may be viewed as the result of an encounter between the *person's needs* and the *society's needs* at or during a particular historical time frame ("epoch") wherein each individual develops a unique *psychohistory*. Erikson (1974, p. 13) defines *psychohistory* as "the study of individual and collective life with the combined methods of psychoanalysis and history." His interest in psychoanalyzing famous historical personages included Martin Luther (Erikson, 1958; cf: Domhoff, 1970), William James (Erikson, 1968), and Thomas Jefferson (Erikson, 1974). Evaluations by psychologists of Erikson's theoretical approach often indicate a positive attitude toward the face validity of his formulations, which are a rich source of hypotheses that can be tested, eventually, and also indicate a preference for Erikson's *psychosocial stage theory* over Freud's *psychosexual stage theory*. Some psychologists feel that Erikson has done for personality development what Piaget has done for cognitive/intellectual development. On the other hand, however, Erikson has been criticized for "watering down" Freudian theory, for creating an overly optimistic view of the concept of *ego* and of human beings (just as Freud has been criticized for his overly pessimistic view of people), and for the poor quality of the empirical foundations (i.e., personal, subjective observation method) of his theory (Hall & Lindzey, 1978). *Erikson's theory*, taken as a heuristic scheme, has had a marked impact on contemporary developmental psychology, especially the psychology of adolescence, and investigations of adolescent identity formation have started to move in the direction of testing specific predictions based on his theory (Berzonsky, 1994). See also FREUD'S THEORY OF PERSONALITY; PERSONALITY THEORIES; PIAGET'S THEORY OF DEVELOPMENTAL STAGES; SULLIVAN'S THEORY OF PERSONALITY.

REFERENCES

Erikson, E. (1950/1963). *Childhood and society.* New York: Norton.
Erikson, E. (1954). The dream specimen of psychoanalysis. *J. Amer. Psychoan. Assoc.,* 2, 5–56.
Erikson, E. (1958). *Young man Luther.* New York: Norton.
Erikson, E. (1968). *Identity: Youth and crisis.* New York: Norton.
Coles, R. (1970). *Erik H. Erikson: The growth of his work.* Boston: Little, Brown.
Domhoff, G. (1970). Two Luthers: The orthodox and heretical in psychoanalytic thinking. *Psychoan. Rev., 57,* 5–17.
Erikson, E. (1974). *Dimensions of a new identity.* New York: Norton.
Erikson, E. (1975). *Life history and the historical moment.* New York: Norton.
Roazen, P. (1976). *Erik H. Erikson: The power and limits of his vision.* New York: Free Press.
Hall, C., & Lindzey, G. (1978). *Theories of personality.* New York: Wiley.
Berzonsky, M. (1994). Eriksonian developmental stages. In R. J. Corsini (Ed.), *Ency. Psy.* New York: Wiley.
Motet, D. (1994). Identity crisis. In R. J. Corsini (Ed.), *Ency. Psy.* New York: Wiley.

ERRORS, THEORY OF. See PROBABILITY THEORY/LAWS.

ESTES' STIMULUS SAMPLING THEORY. The American psychologist William Kaye Estes (1919–   ) formulated a *mathematical learning theory* that seeks to predict the exact numerical details of experimental results. The term *mathematical learning theory* denotes a type of approach to theory construction rather than a single, specific set of postulates that could technically be called a theory (cf: Hull, 1943, 1951, 1952). Estes developed a form of *mathematical learning theory* in the 1950s called *stimulus sampling theory* (*SST*). *SST* started as a form of stimulus–response associationism (cf: Guthrie, 1935/1952) that assumed that organisms learn by attaching new adaptive behaviors to stimulus situations where they formerly had inappropriate behaviors. Estes accepted Thorndike's *empirical law of effect* (i.e., reinforcers strengthen and guide behavior), although he did not subscribe to the "satisfaction" or "drive-reduction" properties of rewards. In *SST*, learning and performance are treated explicitly as a *probabilistic* or *stochastic* (i.e., a sequence of events that can be analyzed in terms of probability) process. The main dependent variable of *statistical learning theory* is the probability of various responses of a subject at any point in time (within a given learning theory), and a *statistical learning model* consists of assumptions about how the subject's probability of a correct response changes from trial to trial as a result of the outcomes experienced on each trial. In *SST*, the stimulus situation is represented as a population of independent variable components and the total environment ("stimulus elements"). At any given moment, only a sample of elements from the total population is effective or active, where the less variable the experimental conditions, the less variable are the successive trial samples of stimulus elements. The assumption of *SST* concerning responses is that their probabilities are determined by the proportions of stimulus elements in the sample connected to the various responses. The early experimental work in *SST* employed the probability-learning paradigm where the subject's task was to predict on each trial which one of two events was going to occur; after the predictive response was made, the actual event was shown. Events in these *probability learning* experiments occur in a random sequence with no information available to help in predicting perfectly which event will occur (cf: Suppes & Donio, 1967). The phenomena of forgetting and spontaneous recovery were interpreted by Estes (1955a, b) in terms of random changes in factors in the stimulating environment from one experimental session to the next (e.g., factors such as temperature, humidity, subjects' receptor sensitivity and attitudes). Estes' *fluctuation theory* of stimulus change accounts for the shapes of forgetting and recovery curves; it has also been applied to the phenomena of retroactive and proactive inhibition (Estes, 1959b) and verbal short-term memory (Estes, 1971; Bower, 1972). *SST* considers *stimulus generalization* in a manner similar to Thorndike's *identical elements theory*: a response associated with a stimulus population will generalize to a test stimulus to the extent that the second population shares common stimulus elements with the first population. Concerning *discrimination learning*, *SST* adopts the concept of *selective attention* and its associative relevant cues to help explain behavioral outcomes (e.g., Restle, 1955; Lovejoy, 1968; cf: Trabasso & Bower, 1968). Estes (1959a) indicated that different learning models follow from *SST* when a small number of stimulus elements is assumed. Such "small-element models" fit the experimental data as well as do the original large-element models. Recent developments in *Estes' theory* have changed in a direction closer to cognitive psychology and away from his original Guthrian stimulus–response approach. For example, Estes deals with the issue of subjects' decision making in preferential choice situations through his *scanning model*, which provides a viable approach to a *process theory of decision making* (Estes, 1976). Estes (1972) has also recently developed a *hierarchical associations theory of memory* that compares favorably with the "duplex" ideas of British associationism and with the "higher-order memory nodes" in Anderson and Bower's (1973) *theory of memory*. Although *SST* has relatively few adherents as a "total" theory today, the basic ideas of *SST* have been assimilated into a common stock of useful theoretical constructs. To date, Estes' *SST* is probably the most significant and rational attempt at a global *quantitative learning theory* in psychology (Bower & Hilgard, 1981). See also GENERALIZATION, PRINCIPLE OF; GUTHRIE'S THEORY OF BEHAVIOR; HULL'S LEARNING THEORY; IDENTICAL ELEMENTS THEORY; PROBABILITY THEORY/ LAWS; THORNDIKE'S LAW OF EFFECT.

REFERENCES

Guthrie, E. (1935/1952). *The psychology of learning*. New York: Harper & Row.

Estes, W., & Skinner, B. F. (1941). Some quantitative properties of anxiety. *J. Exp. Psy., 29*, 390–400.

Hull, C. (1943). *Principles of behavior*. New York: Appleton-Century-Crofts.

Hull, C. (1951). *Essentials of behavior*. New Haven, CT: Yale University Press.

Hull, C. (1952). *A behavior system: An introduction to behavior theory concerning the individual organism*. New Haven, CT: Yale University Press.

Estes, W., & Straughan, J. (1954). Analysis of a verbal conditioning situation in terms of statistical learning theory. *J. Exp. Psy., 47*, 225–234.

Estes, W. (1955a). Statistical theory of distributional phenomena in learning. *Psy. Rev., 62*, 369–377.

Estes, W. (1955b). Statistical theory of spontaneous recovery and regression. *Psy. Rev., 62*, 145–154.

Restle, F. (1955). A theory of discrimination learning. *Psy. Rev., 62*, 11–19.

Estes, W. (1959a). Component and pattern models with Markovian interpretations. In R. Bush & W. Estes (Eds.), *Studies in mathematical learning theory*. Stanford, CA: Stanford University Press.

Estes, W. (1959b). The statistical approach to learning theory. In S. Koch (Ed.), *Psychology: A study of a science*. Vol. 2. New York: McGraw-Hill.

Luce, R., Bush, R., & Galanter, E. (Eds.) (1963/1965). *Handbook of mathematical psychology*. New York: Wiley.

Suppes, P., & Donio, J. (1967). Foundations of stimulus-sampling theory for continuous-time processes. *J. Math. Psy., 4*, 202–225.

Lovejoy, E. (1968). *Attention in discrimination learning*. San Francisco: Holden-Day.

Trabasso, T., & Bower, G. (1968). *Attention in learning: Theory and research*. New York: Wiley.

Estes, W. (1971). Learning and memory. In E. Beckenbach & C. Tompkins (Eds.), *Concepts of communication*. New York: Wiley.

Bower, G. (1972). Stimulus-sampling theory of encoding variability. In E. Martin & A. Melton (Eds.), *Coding theory and memory*. Washington, DC: Hemisphere.

Estes, W. (1972). An associative basis for coding and organization in memory. In A. Melton & E. Martin (Eds.), *Coding processes in human memory*. Washington, DC: Winston.

Anderson, J., & Bower, G. (1973). *Human associative memory*. Washington, DC: Winston.

Estes, W. (Ed.) (1975–1978). *Handbook of learning and cognitive processes*. Hillsdale, NJ: Erlbaum.

Estes, W. (1976). The cognitive side of probability learning. *Psy. Rev., 83*, 37–64.

Bower, G., & Hilgard, E. (1981). *Theories of learning*. Englewood Cliffs, NJ: Prentice-Hall.

Robbins, D. (1994). Mathematical learning theory. In R. J. Corsini (Ed.), *Ency. Psy.* New York: Wiley.

EVOLUTION, LAWS OF. See DARWIN'S EVOLUTION THEORY.

EVOLUTIONARY/CIRCADIAN THEORY. See SLEEP, THEORIES OF.

EWALD'S SOUND-PATTERN THEORY. See AUDITION/HEARING, THEORIES OF.

EXCHANGE/SOCIAL EXCHANGE THEORY. The terms *exchange* and *social exchange* refer to a model of social structure that is based on the principle that most social behavior is predicated in the individual's expectation that one's actions with respect to others will result in some type of commensurate return (Reber, 1995). *Exchange theory* is a body of theoretical work in sociology and social psychology that emphasizes the importance of the *reward-cost* interdependence of group members in shaping their social interaction patterns as well as their psychological responses to one another. *Exchange theories* assume that the basis of social life is found in the *rewards* and *costs* that people mediate for one another (Smith, 1994). The most comprehensive *social exchange theories* are those of John Thibaut and Harold Kelley (1959, 1978), George Homans (1961), and Peter Blau (1964). *Social exchange theories* involve an analogy between economic relationships and other kinds of social relationships where an exchange is assumed to occur when each of the parties involved controls goods valued by the others, and each values at least some of the goods that others control more than at least some of the goods that she or he controls (goods may be any commodity, condition, person, or act that has value for the individual). *Social exchange theories* differ in their conceptual language and in the explicit reference to economic or behavioral psychology concepts. *Homans'* (1961) *theory* borrowed concepts and language from B. F. Skinner's (1938) behavioral psychology (e.g., concepts such as *frequency, value, reward, satiation,* and *extinction*). *Homans' theory* focused on concepts of equilibration in exchange and attempted to explain social interaction in small groups. He also used the concepts of *expectancy* and *distributive justice* in which the parties to an exchange should receive rewards proportional to their costs and investments. *Blau's* (1964) *theory*, while similar to Homans', makes more explicit use of economic concepts such as *indifference curves, power,* and *normative obligation.* Much of *Blau's theory* is concerned with the roots of emergent social structure in social exchange patterns in small groups. *Thibaut and Kelley's* (1959) *theory* used the language of group problem solving (with two-person, dyadic groups) in which many of the assumptions are common to the reinforcement concepts of behavioral psychology. Thibaut and Kelley made extensive use of *reward-cost matrices* derived from *game theory,* which led to the development of various indices of individuals' interdependence, such as definition of parties' power over each other and their conflicts of interest (''correspondence'' versus ''noncorrespondence'' of outcomes). Thibaut and Kelley (1978) later used the concept of *reflexive control,* which refers to the extent that an individual can unilaterally affect his or her own outcomes in a relationship through chosen behaviors. Through analyzing the particular combination of power in a given encounter, Thibaut and Kelley were able to predict the likely course of social interaction. They also analyzed persons' attractions to relationships based on how the outcomes received in a relationship compare to the individual's "comparison level" (i.e., a standard for evaluating the goodness of outcomes from a relationship based on a central tendency of the distribution of all outcomes from previous salient relationships; cf: Smith, 1993). Although Thibaut and Kelley's analyses were primarily concerned with dyadic relationships, their same principles were applied to larger groups in studying topics such as coalition formation, status, and role differentiation in groups. Some theoretical approaches to social exchange argue that the concrete nature of the outcome sought will affect the nature of the exchange. For example, Foa and Foa (1974) advanced a classification of rewards based on their "concreteness" versus "abstractness" and on their situational specificity where some outcomes are not exchangeable (e.g., love will be exchanged for love, but not for money; cf: Gergen, Greenberg, & Willis, 1980). According to Altman and Taylor's (1973) *social penetration theory*, which addresses the nature and quality of social exchange and close relationships, relationships progress from superficial exchanges to more intimate ones as people begin to give more of themselves to one another. Their exchanges become both broader (including more areas of their lives) and deeper (involving more intimate and personally meaningful areas). The social penetration process may involve a greater sharing of possessions or physical intimacy, but the most important commodity of all may be the sharing of innermost thoughts and feelings with another in the act of "self-disclosure" (e.g., Hendrick, 1989; Miller, 1990). Aronson (1984), in his *gain-loss theory*, has also applied the principles of *social exchange theory* to the factors that promote interpersonal attraction. For example, long-distance relationships may have the potential to be as rewarding as proximal relationships. However, the former have higher costs associated with them in terms of time, effort, and financial expenditure, and, thus, people usually opt for relationships with individuals who live close by. See also EQUITY THEORY; INTERPERSONAL ATTRACTION THEORIES; LOVE, THEORIES OF.

REFERENCES

Skinner, B. F. (1938). *The behavior of organisms: An experimental analysis*. New York: Appleton-Century.

Thibaut, J., & Kelley, H. (1959). *The social psychology of groups*. New York: Wiley.

Homans, G. (1961). *Social behavior: Its elementary forms*. New York: Harcourt, Brace, & World.

Blau, P. (1964). *Exchange and power in social life*. New York: Wiley.

Foa, U. (1971). Interpersonal and economic resources. *Science, 171*, 345–351.

Altman, I., & Taylor, D. (1973). *Social penetration: The development of interpersonal relationships*. New York: Holt, Rinehart, & Winston.

Simpson, R. (1973). *Theories of social exchange*. Morristown, NJ: General Learning Press.

Foa, U., & Foa, E. (1974). *Societal structures of the mind*. Springfield, IL: Thomas.

Heath, A. (1976). *Rational choice and social exchange: A critique of exchange theory*. Cambridge, England: Cambridge University Press.

Thibaut, J., & Kelley, H. (1978). *Interpersonal relations: A theory of interdependence.* New York: Wiley.

Gergen, K., Greenberg, M., & Willis, R. (Eds.) (1980). *Social exchange: Advances in theory and research.* New York: Plenum.

Aronson, E. (1984). *The social animal.* San Francisco: Freeman.

Hendrick, C. (Ed.) (1989). *Close relationships.* Newbury Park, CA: Sage.

Miller, L. (1990). Intimacy and liking: Mutual influence and the role of unique relationships. *J. Pers. Soc. Psy., 59,* 50–60.

Smith, R. (1993). *Psychology.* St. Paul, MN: West.

Smith, W. (1994). Exchange theory. In R. J. Corsini (Ed.), *Ency. Psy.* New York: Wiley.

Reber, A. (1995). *The Penguin dictionary of psychology.* New York: Penguin Books.

EXERCISE, LAW OF. In his *law of exercise,* E. L. Thorndike (1898) recognized and renamed an older generalization in psychology and education concerning learning called the *law of frequency.* The *law of exercise* states that, other things being equal, the repeated occurrence of any act makes that behavior easier to perform and is less vulnerable or subject to error; that is, ''practice makes perfect.'' Thorndike regarded his *law of exercise* and his *law of effect* to be of equal importance until 1931, when the *law of exercise* was given a subordinate position in his system. Thus, Thorndike was led by his own research to renounce his former position and to argue against exercise as a factor working independently of effect. The phrase ''other things being equal'' in the definition of the *law of exercise* has been the topic of debate among learning theorists for decades. Another criticism of the *law of exercise* was that it did not take into account the factor of ''incentive'' (i.e., reinforcement value). See also DISUSE, LAW/THEORY OF; EFFECT, LAW OF; FREQUENCY, LAW OF; USE, LAW OF.

REFERENCES

Thorndike, E. (1898). Animal intelligence: An experimental study of the associative processes in animals. *Psy. Rev. Mono. Supp., 2,* no. 8.

Thorndike, E. (1898/1911). *Animal intelligence.* New York: Macmillan.

Woodworth, R. (1921). *Psychology: A study of mental life.* New York: Holt.

Finch, G., & Culler, E. (1934). Higher order conditioning with constant motivation. *Amer. J. Psy., 46,* 596–602.

Culler, E. (1938). Recent advances in some concepts of conditioning. *Psy. Rev., 45* 134–153.

Woodworth, R., & Schlosberg, H. (1965). *Experimental psychology.* New York: Holt, Rinehart, & Winston.

Hilgard, E. (1987). *Psychology in America: A historical survey.* New York: Harcourt Brace Jovanovich.

EXISTENTIAL/PHENOMENOLOGICAL THEORIES OF ABNORMALITY. See PSYCHOPATHOLOGY, THEORIES OF.

EXPECTANCY EFFECT. See EXPERIMENTER EFFECTS.

EXPECTANCY THEORY OF WORK. See WORK/CAREER/OCCUPA-TION, THEORIES OF.

EXPECTANCY-VALUE THEORY. See DECISION-MAKING THEORIES.

EXPERIMENTER EFFECTS. When a researcher conducts an experiment, she or he hypothesizes that one or several variables will have a particular outcome. The experiment is planned to test the hypotheses under investigation and to eliminate as many alternative or "rival" explanations as possible. A major set of rival explanations in this process is called *experimenter effect* (also known as *observer effect* or *Rosenthal effect*; Zusne, 1987), which refers to a number of possible effects upon participants in an experiment that can be traced to the biases or behaviors of the experimenter (Rosenthal, 1976; Ray, 1996). One such effect is called the *experimenter-expectancy effect* or *expectancy effect*, which refers to an experimenter artifact that results when the hypothesis held by the experimenter leads unintentionally to behavior toward the participants that, in turn, increases the likelihood that the hypothesis will be confirmed; this is also called *self-fulfilling prophesy* (Rosnow & Rosenthal, 1996; cf: Barber & Silver, 1968). The phenomenon called *experimenter bias* (where experimenters may unwittingly influence behavior in the direction of their expectations) is illustrated by the case of "Clever Hans" (Pfungst, 1911/1965), which points out that researchers often give cues to subjects unintentionally through facial expressions and tones of voice. With this in mind, researchers are constantly attempting to eliminate experimenter–participant interactions that may lead to biased data. Another type of *experimenter effect* focuses on the factor of attention, especially on how attention paid to participants by the experimenter may bias the research results. The classic illustration here is the study by Roethlisberger and Dickson (1939), who are credited with discovering the *Hawthorne effect*. This effect (named after the locale of the research—the Hawthorne plant of the Western Electric Company—where they studied ways to increase worker productivity) refers to the positive influence of attention on participants' performance. In the Hawthorne study, the effects of attention were so powerful that performance improved even when the objective working conditions worsened (cf: Parsons, 1974). Thus, the *Hawthorne effect* has come today to refer generally to the fact that one's performance in an experiment is affected by knowledge that one is in an experiment (Bracht & Glass, 1968; Benson, 1994; cf: Rice, 1982). A phenomenon similar to the *Hawthorne effect* is called the *novelty/disruption effect*, which refers to a treatment effect that may result when an experimental treatment condition involves something new or unusual. For instance, inserting a red-colored nonsense syllable in the most difficult position in a serial list of black-on-white nonsense syllables facilitates the learning of that novel stimulus (VanBuskirk, 1932). When the novelty or disruption diminishes, the treatment effect may disappear (Christensen, 1994). Experimenters may also provide the conditions for the *pretesting effect*, which refers to the influence that administering a pretest may have on the experimental treatment effect: it may sensitize the participant in such a way to behave differently than participants who did not receive the pretest (Lana, 1959; Rosnow & Suls, 1970; Rosenthal & Rosnow, 1975). Another category of effects that may occur in psychological experiments is called *subject effects*, which refer to any response by subjects/participants in a study that does not represent the way they would normally behave if not under study (cf: *Hawthorne effect*). Two powerful subject effects are the *placebo effect* (i.e., in a treatment study, any observed improvement in response to a sham treatment that is probably due to the subject's expectations for treatment effectiveness) and the *demand characteristics of the situation* (i.e., cues inadvertently given to individuals in a study concerning how they are expected to behave, including not only characteristics of the setting and procedures but also information and even rumors about the researcher and the nature of the research). Researchers conducting psychological experiments should, ideally, include *controls* for these and other possible *experimenter and subject effects* to prevent confounding and the reduction of a study's validity (Graziano & Raulin, 1997). See also CLEVER HANS EFFECT/PHENOMENON; HALO EFFECT; PYGMALION EFFECT.

REFERENCES

Pfungst, O. (1911/1965). *Clever Hans (the horse of Mr. von Osten): A contribution to experimental animal and human psychology.* New York: Holt, Rinehart, & Winston.
VanBuskirk, W. (1932). An experimental study of vividness in learning and retention. *J. Exp. Psy., 15,* 563–573.
Roethlisberger, F., & Dickson, W. (1939). *Management and the worker.* Cambridge: Harvard University Press.
Lana, R. (1959). Pretest-treatment interaction effects in longitudinal studies. *Psy. Bull., 56,* 293–300.
Rosenthal, R., & Lawson, R. (1964). A longitudinal study of the effects of experimenter bias on the operant learning of rats. *J. Psychiat. Res., 2,* 61–72.
Barber, T. X., & Silver, M. (1968). Fact, fiction, and the experimenter bias effect. *Psy. Bull. Mono. Supp., 70,* 1–29.
Bracht, G., & Glass, G. (1968). The external validity of experiments. *Amer. Ed. Res. J., 5,* 437–474.
Rosnow, R., & Suls, J. (1970). Reactive effects of pretesting in attitude research. *J. Pers. Soc. Psy., 15,* 338–343.
Parsons, H. (1974). What happened at Hawthorne? *Science, 183,* 922–932.
Rosenthal, R., & Rosnow, R. (1975). *The volunteer subject.* New York: Wiley.
Barber, T. X. (1976). *Pitfalls in human research: Ten pivotal points.* New York: Pergamon.
Rosenthal, R. (1976). *Experimenter effects in behavioral research.* New York: Irvington.
Rosenthal, R., & Rubin, D. (1978). Interpersonal expectancy effects: The first 345 studies. *Beh. & Brain Sci., 1,* 377–386.
Rice, B. (1982). The Hawthorne defect: Persistence of a flawed theory. *Psy. Today, 16,* 70–74.

Zusne, L. (1987). *Eponyms in psychology*. Westport, CT: Greenwood Press.

Benson, P. (1994). Hawthorne effect. In R. J. Corsini (Ed.), *Ency. Psy*. New York: Wiley.

Christensen, L. (1994). *Experimental methodology*. Boston: Allyn & Bacon.

Rosnow, R., & Rosenthal, R. (1996). *Beginning behavioral research*. Englewood Cliffs, NJ: Prentice-Hall.

Ray, W. (1996). *Methods toward a science of behavior and experience*. Pacific Grove, CA: Brooks/Cole.

Graziano, A., & Raulin, M. (1997). *Research methods: A process of inquiry*. New York: Longman.

EXTENSIONS-OF-WAKING-LIFE THEORY. See SLEEP, THEORIES OF.

EXTINCTION OF CHAINED REFLEXES, LAW OF. See SKINNER'S DE-SCRIPTIVE BEHAVIOR/OPERANT CONDITIONING THEORY.

EXTINCTION OF TYPE R, LAW OF. See SKINNER'S DESCRIPTIVE BEHAVIOR/OPERANT CONDITIONING THEORY.

EXTINCTION OF TYPE S, LAW OF. See SKINNER'S DESCRIPTIVE BE-HAVIOR/OPERANT CONDITIONING THEORY.

EYE MOVEMENT THEORY. See APPARENT MOVEMENT, PRINCI-PLES/THEORIES OF; CONSTRUCTIVIST THEORY OF PERCEPTION.

EYSENCK'S THEORY OF PERSONALITY. The German-born English psy-chologist Hans Jurgen Eysenck (1916–   ) views personality as organized in a hierarchy where *types* are located at the most general level, *traits* at the next level (similar to R. B. Cattell's, 1965, *source traits*), *habitual responses* at the next level, and *specific responses* at the bottom of the hierarchy. Eysenck ana-lyzes personality at the *type* level along the three dimensions of "extraversion-introversion," "neuroticism-stability," and "normality-psychoticism" by using ratings, situational tests, questionnaires, and physiological measures. For ex-ample, an individual who scores high on the "psychoticism" dimension tends to be hostile, egocentric, and antisocial and is generally considered to be "pe-culiar" by other people (Huffman, Vernoy, & Vernoy, 1995). Eysenck devel-oped an innovative aspect of factor analysis called *criterion analysis*, in which a given factor is adjusted in such a way as to give maximal separation in the analysis to a specific criterion group (e.g., the factor of "neuroticism" may be aligned to differentiate it maximally between a group of nonneurotic persons versus a group of neurotic individuals; Eysenck, 1952). Thus, the use of the technique of factor analysis within an articulated theoretical framework is char-acteristic of Eysenck's approach to personality study (Eysenck & Eysenck, 1968a). There is a duality to *Eysenck's personality theory*: (1) *theory of per-sonality structure*, consisting of the extraversion-introversion, neuroticism, and psychoticism dimensions, where the first two dimensions have been studied most and may be assessed via the Eysenck Personality Inventory (EPI) and (2) *theory of cause*, which proposes that behaviors are caused by characteristic brain functions or other neurophysiological functions. Eysenck's model for the causation of high degrees of neuroticism, for example, holds that the hypothalamus is likely to discharge excessive stimulation into the cerebral cortex and into the autonomic nervous system in such cases, and his model of extraversion-introversion holds that when the balance of inhibition versus excitation of the cortex is disrupted, the behavior of turning outward or turning inward occurs (Cartwright, 1979). *Eysenck's personality theory* and his view of humans are governed by the idea that people are biosocial organisms whose actions are determined equally by biological (genetic, physiological, endocrine) factors and social (historical, economic, interactional) factors. His insistence on seeing individuals as a product of evolution is regarded by Eysenck as essential for a proper understanding of people (Corsini, 1994). See also CATTELL'S PERSONALITY THEORY; PERSONALITY THEORIES.

REFERENCES

Guilford, J., & Guilford, R. (1934). An analysis of the factors in a typical test of introversion-extraversion. *J. Abn. Soc. Psy., 28*, 377–399.

Eysenck, H. (1947a). *Dimensions of personality*. London: Routledge & Kegan Paul.

Eysenck, H. (1947b). Types of personality. *J. Ment. Sci., 90*, 851–861.

Eysenck, H., & Prell, D. (1951). The inheritance of neuroticism: An experimental study. *J. Ment. Sci., 97*, 441–465.

Eysenck, H. (1952). *The scientific study of personality*. London: Routledge & Kegan Paul.

Eysenck, H. (1953). *The structure of human personality*. New York: Wiley.

Eysenck, H. (1955). A dynamic theory of anxiety and hysteria. *J. Ment. Sci., 101*, 28–51.

Eysenck, H. (1956). The inheritance of extraversion-introversion. *Acta Psy., 12*, 95–110.

Cattell, R. B. (1965). *The scientific analysis of personality*. Baltimore: Penguin Books.

Eysenck, H., & Rachman, S. (1965). *The causes and cures of neuroses*. San Diego: Knapp.

Eysenck, H., & Eysenck, S. (1968a). A factorial study of psychoticism as a dimension of personality. *Multivar. Beh. Res.* Clinical Psychology, Special Issue, 15–31.

Eysenck, H., & Eysenck, S. (1968b). *Manual for the Eysenck Personality Inventory*. San Diego: Educational and Industrial Testing Service.

Eysenck, H. (1969). *Personality structure and measurement*. San Diego: Knapp.

Eysenck, H. (1977). Personality and factor analysis: A reply to Guilford. *Psy. Bull., 84*, 405–411.

Guilford, J. (1977). Will the real factor of extraversion-introversion please stand up? A reply to Eysenck. *Psy. Bull., 84*, 412–416.

Cartwright, D. (1979). *Theories and models of personality*. Dubuque, IA: Brown.

Eysenck, H. (1979). The conditioning model of neurosis. *Beh. Brain Sci., 2*, 155–199.

Eysenck, H. (1990). Biological dimensions of personality. In L. Pervin (Ed.), *Handbook of personality: Theory and research*. New York: Guilford Press.

Eysenck, H. (1992). Four ways five factors are not basic. *Pers. Indiv. Diff., 13*, 667–673.

Eysenck, H. (1993). Creativity and personality: Suggestions for a theory. *Psy. Inq., 4*, 147–178.

Corsini, R. J. (Ed.) (1994). Hans J. Eysenck. In *Ency. Psy.* New York: Wiley.

Huffman, K., Vernoy, M., & Vernoy, J. (1995). *Essentials of psychology in action.* New York: Wiley.

F

FACIAL FEEDBACK HYPOTHESIS. This hypothesis refers to the notion that emotional activity causes genetically programmed changes to occur in facial expression where the face subsequently provides cues (''feedback'') to the brain that help a person to determine what emotion is being felt. In other terms, the *facial feedback hypothesis* states that having facial expressions and becoming aware of them are what lead to an emotional experience. Indeed, according to the *facial feedback hypothesis* (Tomkins, 1962; Izard, 1990; Ekman, 1993), when people deliberately form various facial expressions, emotion-like changes occur in their bodily activity. Thus, ''making faces'' can actually cause emotion (Ekman, 1993). The idea that sensory feedback from one's own facial expression can influence one's emotional feeling suggests a possible mechanism through which emotional ''contagion'' can occur: people may automatically mimic the facial expressions of others, and then perhaps feedback from one's own body alters the emotions to coincide with the expressions that are being mimicked. Recently, Hatfield, Cacioppo, and Rapson (1993) proposed this *theory of primitive emotional contagion* in which the mimicry of expressions does not involve higher cognitive processes. A considerable amount of research shows that people do automatically mimic the emotional expressions of others (e.g., Meltzoff & Moore, 1977; Davis, 1985; Reissland, 1988; Provine, 1992). The ability to synchronize emotions quickly with other people may have been an advantage in our evolution and may still be today, by helping to promote our acceptance of those around us. Perhaps overt facial expressions of emotion, coupled with an automatic tendency to mimic those expressions, came about in evolution partly to facilitate social acceptance (Gray, 1994). See also EKMAN–FRIESEN THEORY OF EMOTIONS; EMOTIONS, THEORIES OF; IZARD'S THEORY OF EMOTIONS.

REFERENCES

Tomkins, S. (1962). *Affect, imagery, consciousness, the positive effects*. Vol. 1. New York: Springer.

Gelhorn, E. (1964). Motion and emotion: The role of proprioception in the physiology and pathology of the emotions. *Psy. Rev., 71*, 457–472.

Meltzoff, A., & Moore, M. (1977). Imitation of facial and manual gestures by human neonates. *Science, 198*, 75–78.

Davis, M. (1985). Perceptual and affective reverberation components. In A. Goldstein & G. Michaels (Eds.), *Empathy: Development, training, and consequences*. Hillsdale, NJ: Erlbaum.

Reissland, N. (1988). Neonatal imitation in the first hour of life: Observations in rural Nepal. *Dev. Psy., 24*, 464–469.

Adelmann, P., & Zajonc, R. (1989). Facial efference and the experience of emotion. *Ann. Rev. Psy., 40*, 249–280.

Izard, C. (1990). Facial expressions and the regulation of emotions. *J. Pers. Soc. Psy., 58*, 487–498.

Provine, R. (1992). Contagious laughter: Laughter is a sufficient stimulus for laughs and smiles. *Bull, Psychonom. Soc., 30, 1*–4.

Ekman, P. (1993). Facial expression and emotion. *Amer. Psy., 48*, 384–392.

Hatfield, E., Cacioppo, J., & Rapson, R. (1993). *Emotional contagion*. Madison, WI: Brown.

Gray, P. (1994). *Psychology*. New York: Worth.

FACILITATION, LAW OF. See SKINNER'S DESCRIPTIVE BEHAVIOR/ OPERANT CONDITIONING THEORY.

FACULTY THEORY. See TRANSFER OF TRAINING, THORNDIKE'S THEORY OF.

FEATURE ANALYSIS THEORY. See PATTERN/OBJECT RECOGNITION THEORY.

FEATURE THEORY OF MEMORY. See FORGETTING/MEMORY, THEORIES OF.

FECHNER–HELMHOLTZ LAW. See FECHNER'S LAW.

FECHNER'S LAW. The German physiologist, physicist, mathematician, and philosopher Gustav Theodor Fechner (1801–1887) is best remembered in psychology for his development of psychophysics, that is, the study of the relationships between the mental world (''mind'') and the material world (''body''). From his work in psychophysics, Fechner formulated a lawful connection between mind (mental sensation) and body (material stimulus). This quantitative relationship, called *Fechner's law*, is stated in the equation $S = k \log I$, where S is the mental sensation, I is the material stimulus, log is the logarithmic value of a given I, and k is a constant referring to a particular sensory modality (e.g., vision, audition, touch). According to *Fechner's law*, as the stimulus intensity increases in geometrical series, the mental sensation increases in arithmetical series (Schultz, 1981; cf: *Fechner–Helmholtz law*—a visual stimulus reduces the excitability of the visual system so that the effect of an equal subsequent stimulus is diminished by approximately the same amount as would have been the case had the stimulus intensity itself been diminished proportionately; Zusne, 1987; and the *parallel law*—Fechner's assertion that when two stimuli of different intensity are presented for a period of time, although through adaptation the apparent magnitude of each will lessen, the ratio of their apparent magnitudes will remain the same; Sutherland, 1996). Fechner advanced the field of psychophysics by systematizing three methods: the methods of *average error*—where a mean represents the best approximation of a large number of measures; *constant stimuli*—determines the amount of difference in stimulation needed to indicate a sensory difference; and *limits*—determines the thresholds of sensory stimulations (also called *just noticeable differences* or *JND*). While Ernst Weber's (1795–1878) investigations using the *JND* method had preceded Fechner's work, Fechner's contribution is based in his mathematical statement of the relationship between the mental and the physical domains. Apparently, Weber himself had not recognized the general significance of his *JND law*; he had formulated no specific law. Fechner realized later that his own principle was essentially what Weber's earlier results showed, and Fechner gave the empirical relationship mathematical form and called it *Weber's law*. In recent times, there has been a tendency to correct Fechner's generosity and to give the name *Fechner's law* to what Fechner called *Weber's law*, reserving the latter term for Weber's simple statement that the *JND* in a stimulus bears a constant ratio to the stimulus (k = delta I/I). The immediate result of Fechner's idea was the formulation of the program of what he later called *psychophysics* (Boring, 1957). Inasmuch as *Fechner's law* was derived from *Weber's law*, the combination *Weber–Fechner law* was used occasionally by writers (e.g., Titchener, 1928) to encompass both generalizations. There is also some confusion in the older literature over whose law is called by which name (Reber, 1995). *Fechner's law* can be indicted on several grounds based on the data accumulated in the century since its formulation: Fechner's summated *JND* technique may introduce serious error into the form of the psychophysical relation between stimulus magnitude and subjective magnitude; Fechner's choice of the absolute threshold as an arbitrary starting point for scale of psychological magnitude may not have been a good one because the nature of the absolute threshold is in itself open to question; and Fechner's assumption that all *JND* are subjectively equal to each other (and therefore that each *JND* contributes an equal increment to perceived magnitude) is contradicted by empirical evidence (Stevens, 1957). The German physiologist, philosopher, and psychologist Wilhelm Wundt (1832–1920) is credited by most historians as the "founder" of modern experimental psychology in 1879, but some writers consider Fechner's publication in 1860 of his

"Elements of Psychophysics" to be a significant and noteworthy event in the development and advancement of psychology as a science (cf: Boring, 1942, 1957; Murphy & Kovach, 1972; Schultz, 1981). See also STEVENS' POWER LAW; WEBER'S LAW.

REFERENCES

Weber, E. (1842–1853). Der Tastsinn und das Gemeingefuhl. In R. Wagner (Ed.), *Handworterbuch der Physiologie*. 4 vols. Braunschweig: Vieweg.

Fechner, G. (1851). *Zend-Avesta*. Leipzig: Voss.

Fechner, G. (1860). *Elemente der Psychophysik*. Leipzig: Breitkopf, Hartel.

Fechner, G. (1877). *In Sachen der Psychophysik*. Leipzig: Breitkopf, Hartel.

Fechner, G. (1882). *Revision der Hauptpunkte der Psychophysik*. Leipzig: Breitkopf, Hartel.

Titchener, E. (1928). *A textbook of psychology*. New York: Macmillan.

Guilford, J. (1932). A generalized psychophysical law. *Psy. Rev., 39*, 73–85.

Boring, E. G. (1942). *Sensation and perception in the history of experimental psychology*. New York: Appleton-Century.

Boring, E. G. (1957). *A history of experimental psychology*. New York: Appleton-Century-Crofts.

Stevens, S. S. (1957). On the psychophysical law. *Psy. Rev., 64*, 153–181.

Murphy, G., & Kovach, J. (1972). *Historical introduction to modern psychology*. New York: Harcourt Brace Jovanovich.

Schultz, D. (1981). *A history of modern psychology*. New York: Academic Press.

Zusne, L. (1987). *Eponyms in psychology*. Westport, CT: Greenwood Press.

Corso, J. (1994). Psychophysical laws. In R. J. Corsini (Ed.), *Ency. Psy.* New York: Wiley.

Robinson, G. (1994). Psychophysics. In R. J. Corsini (Ed.), *Ency. Psy.* New York: Wiley.

Reber, A. (1995). *The Penguin dictionary of psychology*. New York: Penguin Books.

Sutherland, S. (1996). *The international dictionary of psychology*. New York: Crossroad.

FERE PHENOMENON. See ELECTRODERMAL ACTIVITY/PHENOMENA.

FERRY–PORTER LAW. = Porter's law. Named in honor of the American physicist Edwin Sidney Ferry (1868–1956) and the English scientist Thomas Cunningham Porter (late 1800s–early 1900s), this law states that *critical flicker frequency* (*cff*) increases by equal amounts for equal increases in the logarithm of the brightness or intensity of the stimulus. This generalization is independent of the wavelength composition/color of the stimulus. *Cff* is the frequency of intermittence of a visual stimulus just necessary to eliminate the sensation of "flicker," where the flicker phenomenon is defined as a rapid periodic change perceived in a visual impression due to a corresponding rapid periodic change in the intensity or some other character of the stimulus. Flicker disappears when the frequency of the stimulus change exceeds the *cff* rate, which is about 25 to 30 hertz (1 hertz, or Hz, = one cycle per second; this unit of measurement is named in honor of the German physicist Heinrich Rudolph Hertz, 1857–1894).

The *cff* rate is somewhat higher at higher intensity levels and lower for lower intensities, and the rate is lowered with decrease in the intensity difference between parts of the sequence/period. The *Ferry–Porter law* holds only over a very limited range of conditions, and this is particularly evident when considering the variations in the character of temporal modulation of the extant stimulus. The law does not hold at all for very low modulation amplitudes (Brown, 1965). See also TALBOT-PLATEAU LAW; VISION/SIGHT, THEORIES OF.

REFERENCES

Ferry, E. (1892). Persistence of vision. *Amer. J. Sci., 44*, 192–207.

Porter, T. (1902). Contributions to the study of flicker. II. *Proc. Roy. Soc. Lon., 70A*, 313–329.

Porter, T. (1912). Contributions to the study of flicker. III. *Proc. Roy. Soc. Lon., 86A*, 495–513.

Hecht, S. (1934). Vision: II. The nature of the photoreceptor process. In C. Murchison (Ed.), *A handbook of general experimental psychology*. Worcester, MA: Clark University Press.

de Lange, H. (1954). Relationship between critical flicker frequency and a set of low-frequency characteristics of the eye. *J. Opt. Soc. Amer., 44*, 380–389.

Brown, C., & Forsyth, D. (1959). Fusion contour for intermittent photic stimuli of alternating duration. *Science, 129*, 390–391.

Levinson, J., & Harmon, L. (1961). Studies with artificial neurons. III. Mechanisms of flicker-fusion. *Kybernetik, 1*, 107–117.

Brown, J. (1965). Flicker and intermittent stimulation. In C. Graham (Ed.), *Vision and visual perception*. New York: Wiley.

FESTINGER'S COGNITIVE DISSONANCE THEORY. The American psychologist Leon Festinger (1919–1989) developed the *theory of cognitive dissonance*, which is based on the tenet that an individual is motivated to maintain consistency/consonance among pairs of cognitive beliefs, ideas, perceptions, or attitudes about oneself, behavior, or the environment (Festinger, 1957, 1964; cf: Heider, 1946). According to the theory, when inconsistency occurs between cognitions, the person is assumed to be psychologically uncomfortable, and internal pressure is exerted both to reduce the dissonance and to avoid information and events that would increase the dissonance. Festinger's position is similar to Kelly's (1955) approach, which assumes that cognitions are the basic elements relevant to achieving consistency (Maddi, 1972). Festinger's theory concerns *psychological* inconsistency, not formal *logical* inconsistency. For example, the behavior-cognition pair "I smoke" and "Smoking is unhealthy" will produce dissonance only with the assumption that the smoker does not want to be unhealthy or to contract cancer. As Aronson (1980) points out, this ambiguity concerning type of inconsistency both increases the scope of *dissonance theory* and also makes it difficult to predict when dissonance will occur. Festinger's *theory of cognitive dissonance* is also an elaboration of Lewin's (1935) *field theory*, in which the situation existing prior to one's making a decision about events differs from the situation after a decision has been made (Hall & Lindzey, 1978). Festinger's experimental research on cognitive dissonance demonstrated that people are more likely to change their beliefs to conform to their public statements if they are underrewarded than if they are given large rewards, a finding that is at odds with traditional *reinforcement theory* (Festinger, 1964). Whereas *reinforcement theory* would suggest that one dislikes things associated with pain, *cognitive dissonance theory* suggests that persons come to like those things for which they suffer (Pervin, 1996). Festinger identified four types of dissonance (Campbell, 1994): postdecision dissonance (cf: double approach-avoidance situation of *conflict theory*; Miller, 1944), forced compliance disso-nance, maximized dissonance/consequent attitude change, and social support system dissonance. Occasionally, people behave in ways that run counter to their attitude and then, subsequently, are faced with their dissonant cognitions (such as saying, "I believe *this*, but I did *that*"). They can't undo their deed, but they can relieve their dissonance by changing, even reversing, their attitude to justify an action. This phenomenon is called the *insufficient-justification effect* and is defined as a change in attitude that occurs because, without the change, the individual cannot justify the already completed action. Hundreds of field studies and experiments have demonstrated the power of the *theory of cognitive dis-sonance* to change behavior and attitudes (Wicklund & Brehm, 1976). Festinger (1954) was also among the first to point out that group membership fills needs for social comparison. Festinger's *theory of social comparison* holds that in an ambiguous situation (i.e., when one is not certain about what to do or how to feel) the individual will affiliate with people with whom one can compare feel-ings and behaviors (cf: *Fiske & Maddi's*, 1961, *personality theory*, which is based on a consistency model concerning the match and mismatch between one's customary and actual levels of *activation/tension* rather than of *cogni-tions*). By the 1970s, the *theory of cognitive dissonance* was recognized as one of the most important and influential developments in social psychology up to that time (Aronson, 1992). Detractors of *cognitive dissonance theory* (e.g., Bem, 1967) have argued that dissonance phenomena could more parsimoniously be accounted for by assuming that actors infer their beliefs from observations of their own behavior. The strength of *cognitive dissonance theory* has also been its weakness: the postulation of cognitive mechanisms has had a positive impact, but the intricate experimental procedures used have led to alternative interpre-tations of results (Campbell, 1994). Recently, there has been a decline of interest in *cognitive dissonance theory*. Perhaps part of the reason for this has to do with its focus on the motivational concept of *tension-reduction*. By the mid- and late 1970s, psychologists' attraction to the theory began to wane as interest in the entire topic of motivation faded, and the journals were overwhelmed by studies concerning the purely cognitive approaches (absent motivational con-structs such as *drive-reduction* and *tension-reduction*) and it was fashionable to pretend that motivation did not exist. Perhaps *dissonance theory* will now make a comeback (Aronson, 1992). See also ATTRIBUTION THEORY; BEM'S

SELF-PERCEPTION THEORY; CONFLICT, THEORIES OF; DECISION-MAKING THEORIES; KELLY'S PERSONAL CONSTRUCT THEORY; LEWIN'S FIELD THEORY.

REFERENCES

Lewin, K. (1935). *A dynamic theory of personality*. New York: McGraw-Hill.

Miller, N. (1944). Experimental studies of conflict. In J. McV. Hunt (Ed.), *Personality and the behavior disorders*. Vol. 1. New York: Ronald Press.

Heider, F. (1946). Attitudes and cognitive organization. *J. Psy., 21*, 107–112.

Festinger, L. (1954). A theory of social comparison processes. *Hum. Rel., 7*, 117–140.

Kelly, G. (1955). *The psychology of personal constructs*. New York: Norton.

Festinger, L. (1957). *A theory of cognitive dissonance*. Stanford, CA: Stanford University Press.

Fiske, D., & Maddi, S. (Eds.) (1961). *Functions of varied experience*. Homewood, IL: Dorsey Press.

Chapanis, N., & Chapanis, A. (1964). Cognitive dissonance: Five years later. *Psy. Bull., 61*, 1–22.

Festinger, L. (1964). *Conflict, decision, and dissonance*. Stanford, CA: Stanford University Press.

Bem, D. (1967). Self-perception: An alternative interpretation of cognitive dissonance phenomena. *Psy. Rev., 74*, 183–200.

Maddi, S. (1972). *Personality theories: A comparative analysis*. Homewood, IL: Dorsey Press.

Wicklund, R., & Brehm, J. (1976). *Perspectives on cognitive dissonance*. Hillsdale, NJ: Erlbaum.

Hall, C., & Lindzey, G. (1978). *Theories of personality*. New York: Wiley.

Aronson, E. (1980). Persuasion via self-justification: Large commitments for small rewards. In L. Festinger (Ed.), *Retrospections on social psychology*. New York: Oxford University Press.

Aronson, E. (1992). The return of the repressed: Dissonance theory makes a comeback. *Psy. Inq., 3*, 303–311.

Campbell, J. (1994). Cognitive dissonance. In R. J. Corsini (Ed.), *Ency. Psy.* New York: Wiley.

Pervin, L. (1996). *The science of personality*. New York: Wiley.

FIELD DEPENDENCE/INDEPENDENCE. See WITKIN'S PERCEPTION THEORY.

FIELD THEORY. See LEWIN'S FIELD THEORY.

FIGHT OR FLIGHT THEORY. See CANNON/CANNON-BARD THEORY.

FILIAL REGRESSION, LAW OF. See GALTON'S LAWS.

FILTER THEORY/MODEL. See ATTENTION, LAWS/PRINCIPLES/THEORIES OF.

FISKE AND MADDI'S PERSONALITY THEORY. See FESTINGER'S COGNITIVE DISSONANCE THEORY.

FITTS' LAW. See INFORMATION/INFORMATION-PROCESSING THEORY.

FIXATION, LAW OF. See TOTAL TIME HYPOTHESIS/LAW.

FORBES–GREGG HYPOTHESIS. See NEURON/NEURAL/NERVE THEORY.

FORGETTING, LAW OF. See FORGETTING/MEMORY, THEORIES OF.

FORGETTING/MEMORY, THEORIES OF. Four major *theories of forgetting/memory* have been described consistently in the psychological literature: *decay/trace theory, interference theory, reconstruction theory,* and *theory of motivated forgetting* (cf: the *law of forgetting*—the principle that forgetting increases linearly with the logarithm of the time since learning occurred; Sutherland, 1996). According to the *decay/trace theory,* which is a classical, intuitive, and commonsense approach to forgetting, memories that are not used gradually fade, deteriorate, and die over time (cf: the *obliteration theory,* which postulates a sudden, rather than a gradual, destruction of a memory trace; Fernald, 1997). The *decay theory* had been discarded by psychologists as being incorrect until recent years. The acceptance by most psychologists today of some version of the *three-stage theory of memory* (i.e., the stages of "sensory register," "short-term memory," and "long-term memory"; e.g., Atkinson & Shiffrin, 1968) has revived the *decay theory* somewhat. Apparently, the simple passage of time may be a cause of forgetting both in the sensory register and in short-term memory, but it does not appear that time-passage decay is a cause of forgetting in long-term memory. Memory "traces" seem to be permanent once they have been *consolidated* into long-term memory (see *consolidation hypothesis/theory;* Lamberth, McCullers, & Mellgren, 1976), and forgetting in long-term memory is probably due to other factors such as irretrievability of stored materials rather than simply to their disuse over time. The *interference theory* of forgetting refers to the blocking or disruption of memories due to the relative similarity of materials and acts on the storage or retrieval of information. When interference is built up by *prior* learning, it is called *proactive interference/inhibition,* and when interference is created by *later* learning, it is called *retroactive interference/inhibition.* Interference may cause forgetting in long-term memory by retrieval failure (see *retrieval failure theory;* Huffman, Vernoy, & Vernoy, 1997), but it may also cause forgetting in short-term memory in a different way, either by overloading the capacity of short-term memory or by weakening or completely "knocking an item out of storage" (e.g., Klatzky, 1980). A great deal of experimental evidence supports the *interference theory* of forgetting in both long-term and short-term memory for isolated facts and materials. However, other factors—such as "meaning"—may be operating in the forgetting of information (e.g., Tulving, 1972, 1985). One interesting phenomenon related to interference is called the *tip-of-the-tongue phenomenon* (*TOT*), which is a type of effortful retrieval that occurs when people are confident they know something but just can't quite retrieve it from long-term memory (e.g., Brown, 1991). *TOT* seems to become more frequent during stressful situations, as people get older, and with words that are seldom used. The *reconstruction theory* of forgetting was first stated by Sir Frederic Bartlett in 1932 and states that forgetting is due to changes in the structure of a memory that make it inaccurate when retrieved, and where some memory traces become so distorted over time that they are unrecognizable. According to this approach, memories change with time in such a way as to become less complex, more congruent, and more consistent with what the person already believes or knows. *Reconstruction theory* seems to be intuitively appealing, but, until recently, it seems to have had little impact on memory research, perhaps because of the vague terminology in Bartlett's (1932) original statements. More recent versions of *reconstruction theory* (e.g., Bransford & Franks, 1971) tend to employ the distinction made by Tulving (1972) between *episodic* and *semantic* memory where the "meaning" of events in *semantic* memory is stored better than the *episodic* details. In this approach, meaning takes precedence over details, where details may be created (reconstructed and distorted) in order to be consistent with the remembered meaning of events. The way *reconstruction theory* explains forgetting and memory is similar to the way in which the brain "constructs" full and complete perceptions out of a minimum or inadequate amount of sensory information (cf: the "filling-in" of the blind spot in visual perception). People sometimes construct their memories from minimal information. The *theory of motivated forgetting* was enunciated originally by Sigmund Freud (1915/1959) and states that forgetting is based on the threatening, anxiety-arousing, or upsetting nature of the forgotten information. In Freudian terms, the concept of *repression* refers to forgetting that occurs when the conscious mind deals with unpleasant information by pushing it into unconsciousness. Support for the *motivated forgetting theory* largely comes from clinical case studies (e.g., Bonanno, 1990) rather than from laboratory studies. However, case study evidence is not a good source of support for the theory because there is absence of precise experimental control, the effect of a stressful event may be to disrupt the biological process of consolidating the memory trace in long-term memory (rather than to cause repression of the memory), and it does not explain events in ordinary life but just in unusually stressful situations. Currently, psychologists are examining distinctions between visual versus verbal information types of memory. According to the *propositional theory* (also called the *feature theory* in the context of analyzing the mental representation of a "concept"; cf: Greenberg & Kuczaj, 1982), memories for visual scenes are similar to memories for verbal information where both types of memories are assumed to be stored as sets of *propositions* that are elementary units of meaningful information (e.g., Anderson, 1983). However, according to the *analogue theory* (also called the *prototype theory* in the context of analyzing mental representations of "concepts"; Rosch, 1975), visual memories are fundamentally different from verbal memories where it is assumed that visual information is stored in a way that preserves the spatial gradients of the original scene; that is, visual memory is produced in a way that is functionally equivalent or *analogous* to a picture (cf: Kosslyn, 1980). Another line of theorizing in memory research continues the *associationistic* tradition begun by Aristotle (384–322 B.C.) and his principles of association by *contiguity* and *similarity* (cf: Verhave, 1993). Today, cognitive psychologists depict the mind's storehouse of knowledge as a vast network of mental concepts (or "schemas") linked by associationistic ties. One such network model of memory organization is the *spreading-activation model of memory organization* (Collins & Loftus, 1975; Anderson, 1983), which hypothesizes that the degree to which one word speeds up the ability to recognize or recall another reflects the strength of the mental association between the two words or concepts. See also ASSOCIATION, LAWS/PRINCIPLES OF; IMAGERY/MENTAL IMAGERY, THEORIES OF; INFORMATION/INFORMATION-PROCESSING THEORIES; INTERFERENCE THEORIES OF FORGETTING; SERIAL POSITION EFFECT.

REFERENCES

Ebbinghaus, H. (1885/1964). *Memory: A contribution to experimental psychology.* New York: Dover.

Burnham, W. (1888). Memory, historically and experimentally considered. *Amer. J. Psy., 2,* 39–90.

Kennedy, F. (1898). On the experimental investigation of memory. *Psy. Rev., 5,* 477–554.

Bentley, I. (1899). The memory image and its qualitative fidelity. *Amer. J. Psy., 1,* 1–48.

Freud, S. (1915/1959). Repression. In E. Jones (Ed.), *Collected papers.* Vol. 4. New York: Basic Books.

Bartlett, F. (1932). *Remembering: A study in experimental and social psychology.* New York: Cambridge University Press.

Atkinson, R., & Shiffrin, R. (1968). Human memory: A proposed system and its control processes. In K. Spence & J. Spence (Eds.), *The psychology of learning and motivation.* Vol. 2. New York: Academic Press.

Bransford, J., & Franks, J. (1971). The abstraction of linguistic ideas. *Cog. Psy., 2,* 331–350.

Tulving, E. (1972). Episodic and semantic memory. In E. Tulving & W. Donaldson (Eds.), *Organization and memory.* New York: Academic Press.

Anderson, J., & Bower, G. (1974). A propositional theory of recognition memory. *Mem. & Cog., 2,* 406–412.

Collins, A., & Loftus, E. (1975). A spreading-activation theory of semantic processing. *Psy. Rev., 82,* 407–428.

Rosch, E. (1975). Cognitive representations of semantic categories. *J. Exp. Psy.: Gen., 104*, 192–223.

Lamberth, J., McCullers, J., & Mellgren, R. (1976). *Foundations of psychology*. New York: Harper & Row.

Klatzky, R. (1980). *Human memory: Structures and processes*. San Francisco: Freeman.

Kosslyn, S. (1980). *Image and mind*. Cambridge: Harvard University Press.

Greenberg, J., & Kuczaj, S. (1982). Towards a theory of substantive word-meaning acquisition. In S. Kuczaj (Ed.), *Language development*. Vol. 1. Hillsdale, NJ: Erlbaum.

Anderson, J. (1983). A spreading activation theory of memory. *J. Verb. Learn. Verb. Beh., 27*, 261–295.

Tulving, E. (1985). How many memory systems are there? *Amer. Psy., 40*, 385–398.

Baddeley, A. (1990). *Human memory: Theory and practice*. Boston: Allyn & Bacon.

Bonanno, G. (1990). Repression, accessibility, and the translation of private experience. *Psychoanal. Psy., 7*, 453–473.

Brown, A. (1991). A review of the tip-of-the-tongue experience. *Psy. Bull., 109*, 204–223.

Verhave, T. (1993). Network theories of memory: Before Wundt and Herbart. *Psy. Rec., 43*, 547–552.

Sutherland, S. (1996). *The international dictionary of psychology*. New York: Crossroad.

Fernald, D. (1997). *Psychology*. Upper Saddle River, NJ: Prentice-Hall.

Huffman, K., Vernoy, M., & Vernoy, J. (1997). *Psychology in action*. New York: Wiley.

FORMAL DISCIPLINE/TRAINING, THEORY/DOCTRINE OF. See ALGORITHMIC-HEURISTIC THEORY.

FOURIER'S LAW/SERIES/ANALYSIS. The French mathematician Jean Baptiste Joseph Fourier (1768–1830) formulated the mathematically demonstrable generalization (*Fourier's law*) that any complex periodic pattern (such as sound waves) may be described as a particular sum of a number of "sine waves" (i.e., a wave form characterized by regular oscillations with a set period and amplitude such that the displacement amplitude at each point is proportional to the sine of the phase angle of the displacement; a pure tone is propagated as a sine wave). The sine waves so used are called a *Fourier series*, and the description itself is called a *Fourier analysis*. Thus, a *Fourier analysis* is a mathematical procedure whereby any intensity pattern can be broken down into a number of sine-wave components, and such an analysis may be applied to visual stimulation as well as to auditory phenomena (Kaufman, 1979). That is, any visual stimulus can be broken down into sine waves with different spatial frequencies, amplitudes, contrasts, and phases. The notion behind *Fourier analyses* in vision is that the visual system carries out an analysis by breaking a scene down into a number of sine-wave components. This information is contained in the firing of spatial frequency detectors (neurons that fire best to specific frequencies). The visual system then uses the information from these neurons to carry out the reverse process, called *Fourier synthesis*, in which the information is combined to create the visual scene (Campbell & Robson, 1968; Goldstein,

1996). See also AUDITION/HEARING, THEORIES OF; OHM'S ACOUSTIC/ AUDITORY LAW; VISION/SIGHT, THEORIES OF.

REFERENCES

Wheeler, R. (1929). *The science of psychology: An introductory study*. New York: Crowell.
Campbell, F., & Robson, J. (1968). Application of Fourier analysis to the visibility of gratings. *J. Physio., 197*, 551–566.
Kaufman, L. (1979). *Perception: The world transformed*. New York: Oxford University Press.
Goldstein, E. (1996). *Sensation and perception*. Pacific Grove, CA: Brooks/Cole.

FREQUENCY, LAW OF. A correlate of the *law of use*, the *law of frequency* attempted to explain generally that exercise up to a certain physiological limit is cumulative in effect, and if one response strengthens the connection somewhat, then two responses have a greater effect than one, and so on. The *law of frequency*, also known as the *law of repetition*, states that, other things being equal, the more frequently a connection has been exercised, the stronger the connection and the more resistant it is to extinction. The concept of *frequency* as an important factor in experimental psychology and learning has been traced back to the British school of association psychologists and Thomas Brown (1820). Brown maintained that there were three *primary laws of association* (Aristotle's *laws of similarity, contrast*, and *nearness in time and space*). In addition, he formulated several *secondary laws: duration, liveliness/vividness*, and *frequency*. Thus, *frequency* as a general principle operating in philosophical and psychological descriptions of individual differences and behavior goes back more than 170 years. See also EXERCISE, LAW OF; READINESS, LAW OF; USE, LAW OF.

REFERENCES

Brown, T. (1820). *Lectures on the philosophy of the human mind*. Edinburgh: Tait.
Warren, H. (1919). *Human psychology*. Boston: Houghton Mifflin.
Carr, H. (1925). *Psychology: A study of mental activity*. New York: Longmans, Green.
Perrin, F. (1932). *Psychology: Its methods and principles*. New York: Holt.
Woodworth, R., & Schlosberg, H. (1965). *Experimental psychology*. New York: Holt, Rinehart, & Winston.
Chaplin, J., & Krawiec, T. (1968). *Systems and theories of psychology*. New York: Holt, Rinehart, & Winston.

FREQUENCY/REPETITION, PRINCIPLE OF. See ASSOCIATION, LAWS/PRINCIPLES OF; FREQUENCY, LAW OF; SKINNER'S DESCRIPTIVE BEHAVIOR/OPERANT CONDITIONING THEORY.

FREQUENCY/TELEPHONE THEORY. See AUDITION/HEARING, THEORIES OF.

FREQUENCY THEORIES OF HEARING. See AUDITION/HEARING, THEORIES OF.

FREUD'S DOCTRINE OF CATHARSIS. See FREUD'S THEORY OF PERSONALITY.

FREUD'S INSTINCT THEORY. Sigmund Freud (1856–1939) argued that all animals, human and nonhuman, are born with powerful *aggression instincts* (Freud, 1907/1959, 1934). Such instincts create a drive to engage in acts of aggression that must be satisfied. Through the operation of a type of ''pressure-building'' mechanism, the instincts create an uncomfortable tension within the individual that must be released, often in the form of overt acts of aggression. According to Freud's *instinct theory*, the way to curb violence and other anti-social aggressive acts is to find nonviolent ways to release the aggressive energy, such as engaging in competitive activities, reading about violent crimes, or watching aggressive sporting events. Freud's viewpoint that the behavior of aggression is inborn/instinctual has been reinforced by a number of other re-searchers, often ethologists and biologists, who suggest that violence is an element of *evolutionary theory* and is necessary for the survival of the fittest. Perhaps the most debatable aspect of Freud's theory is his belief that instinctual aggressive energy needs to be released in some fashion. Freud referred to the process of releasing instinctual energy as *catharsis* (from the Greek word *katharsis*, meaning ''purgation or cleansing, especially of guilt''; Hansen, 1994) and suggested that societies should develop methods whereby the nonviolent catharsis of aggressive energy may occur. Some psychologists agree generally with Freud that aggression is an inborn aspect of human behavior but do not agree, in particular, that it stems from an overwhelming instinctual urge to aggress. The counterview is that aggression is a natural reaction to the blocking (''frustration'') of important motives and goals. Thus, the *frustration-aggression theory* (e.g., Dollard, Doob, Miller, Mowrer, & Sears, 1939; Berkowitz, 1989) suggests that not only people but entire nations as well whose intended motives and goals are frustrated will react with aggression and anger. Other psychologists argue that Freud's notions of the ways in which catharsis may be exhibited actually have the opposite effect of increasing aggression, rather than dissipating it (e.g., Bandura, 1973; Geen & Quanty, 1977). Such *social learning theory* approaches suggest that individuals are aggressive only if they have learned that it is to their benefit to be aggressive. Thus, the *social learning theorists* disagree with Freud concerning the concept of *catharsis*. Where *Freudian theory* em-phasizes that cathartic outlets need to be found for aggressive energy in order to keep it from appearing as actual aggression, *social learning theory* argues that cathartic outlets such as yelling when angry, hitting or punching a bag, or watching violent sporting events will not decrease violence but will actually increase it by teaching violence to the person. See also AGGRESSION, THE-ORIES OF; BANDURA'S THEORY; FREUD'S THEORY OF PERSONAL-ITY.

REFERENCES

Freud, S. (1907/1959). *The collected papers of Sigmund Freud*. New York: Basic Books.

Freud, S. (1934). Instincts and their vicissitudes. In *Collected papers*. Vol. 4. London: Hogarth Press.

Dollard, J., Doob, L., Miller, N., Mowrer, O. H., & Sears, R. (1939). *Frustration and aggression*. New Haven, CT: Yale University Press.

Bandura, A. (1973). *Aggression: A social learning analysis*. Englewood Cliffs, NJ: Prentice-Hall.

Geen, R., & Quanty, M. (1977). The catharsis of aggression: An evaluation of a hypothesis. In L. Berkowitz (Ed.), *Advances in experimental social psychology*. Vol. 10. New York: Academic Press.

Liebert, R., Neale, J., & Davidson, E. (1983). *The early window: The effects of television on children and youth*. New York: Pergamon Press.

Berkowitz, L. (1989). Frustration-aggression hypothesis: Examination and reformulation. *Psy. Bull., 106*, 59–73.

Wood, W., Wong, F., & Chachere, J. (1991). Effects of media violence on viewer's aggression in unconstrained social interaction. *Psy. Bull., 109*, 371–383.

Hansen, F. (1994). Catharsis. In R. J. Corsini (Ed.), *Ency. Psy.* New York: Wiley.

FREUD'S THEORY OF PERSONALITY. The Austrian neurologist/psycho-analyst Sigmund Freud (1856–1939) had early associations with the Austrian physician Josef Breuer and the French physician Jean Charcot, who gave him an appreciation of the value of the "talking cure," "catharsis," and "hypnosis" for treating hysterical neuroses and also of the sexual etiology of neuroses. These experiences served as the basis for the development of the *Freudian theory* and method called *psychoanalysis*, formally initiated in 1895 (Breuer & Freud, 1895). For over 40 years, Freud examined the structure and function of one of his most important concepts, the *unconscious*, through the methods of free as-sociation and dream analysis and developed the first comprehensive *theory of personality* (Hall & Lindzey, 1978). The psychoanalytic movement was pro-moted in 1902 by Freud, who invited Alfred Adler, Otto Rank, and Carl Jung to join him in regular discussions concerning problems of neurosis and the applied techniques of the new method. This group became known as the Vienna Psychological Society and later, the Vienna Psychoanalytical Association. The group was disrupted, however, over theoretical differences after about 10 years, with Adler's leaving the group in 1911 and Jung's leaving in 1914. The three major systems in Freud's *structure* of personality are called the *id*—instinctual, biological, animal-like sexual and aggressive urges of self-gratification under the aegis of the *pleasure principle* (Freud, 1920, 1934); the *ego*—the objective aspect of personality and reason, operating under the *reality principle* (Freud, 1923); and the *superego*—the idealistic, moral, and social aspect of the con-science that strives for perfection (Freud, 1926; cf: Turiell, 1967). According to Freud, an individual's behavior is almost always the product of an interaction among the three systems of the *id, ego,* and *superego,* where they work together as a team under the administrative leadership of the *ego*. A state of anxiety results, theoretically, whenever the *ego* becomes too overwhelmed with the triple impact of the *id's* powerful psychic energies, the *ego's* tension-reduction need to manipulate reality, and the *superego's* relentless quest for perfection. Freud's *dynamics* of personality involve the concepts of *instincts*—inborn and constant psychological representations of inner somatic sources of excitation that are the sole motives for human behavior (includes *life instincts* operating via sexual energy or *libido*, and *death instincts/wishes* with corresponding self-destructive aggressiveness); *distribution of psychic energy*—diversion of psychic energy from the *id* into the *ego* via operation of the *identification* mechanism, which matches subjective mental representations with objective physical reality, and use of the coping strategies (cf: *defense mechanisms*; A. Freud, 1937); and *anxiety*—a state of tension that may be one of three types: *reality* anxiety or fear of external world dangers, *neurotic* anxiety or fear of punishment, and *moral* anxiety or fear of the conscience involving violations of moral codes (Freud, 1926). Freud's *development* of personality involves the concepts of *identification*—the modeling of one's behavior after that of another person, usually a parental figure; *displacement*—the development of a new "cathexis" or libidinal energy fixation when "anticathexis" or blocking actions and events occur (*sublimation* may result when the displacement produces a higher cultural achievement); *ego defense mechanisms*—the unconscious, reality-distorting measures taken by the *ego* to reduce psychic pressure and relieve anxiety that include *repression* (information below conscious awareness), *projection* or displacing unacceptable urges onto someone else, *reaction formation* or replacing an anxiety-producing impulse with an opposite impulse, and *fixation/regression* or arrested personality growth at a particular stage such as an earlier, more comfortable stage of development; and *psychosexual stages of development*—the psychodynamically differentiated stages during the individual's first few years of life that are decisive in the permanent formation of one's personality that include the *oral* stage, where primary pleasure is gained by activity in the oral cavity, the *anal* stage, where successful toilet training must take place, the *phallic* stage, where the *Oedipus* and *castration complexes* must be resolved for proper sexual development to occur, the *latent* stage, where physical/chemical changes take place in the body acting as a transition from childhood to adulthood, and the *genital* stage, where truly socialized and adult relationships with others are developed. *Freud's theory* and method of treating personality problems identified resistances and repressions ("motivated forgetting") that an individual used to get protection from pain. In this approach, the "talking techniques" of dream analysis, free association of ideas, and working through *transference* (where the patient shifts his emotional attitudes from parental figures onto the therapist) were employed to cure patients' neurotic behaviors (cf: the case of Anna O.—a woman treated for hysteria by Joseph Breuer, who rightly or wrongly attributed her recovery to the new "talking cure"; she thus became the first—and possibly the last—success of psychoanalysis; Sutherland, 1996). Freud's approach, theories, and methods have been criticized for several reasons (Canning, 1966; Haynie, 1994): the unsystematic and uncontrolled manner of data collection and interpretation; an overemphasis on biological factors, especially sex, as the major force in personality development; and an excessive deterministic/mechanistic view of the influence of past behavior on a person's present functioning. On the other hand, while many of the methods and mechanisms of psychoanalysis have not been absorbed completely into the mainstream of general psychological thought, various Freudian conceptualizations (such as unconscious motivation, emphasis on important childhood experiences, defense mechanisms, and the case study method) have gained wide acceptance in the contemporary psychological community (Schultz, 1981). References to Freud's work (via use of the eponyms *Freud's theory, Freudian,* and *Freudianism*) have steadily increased in citation frequency in psychology textbooks, and Freud's name continues to be one of the most popular referents in psychology over the last 75 years (Roeckelein, 1995, 1996a, b). See also DODO HYPOTHESIS; FREUD'S INSTINCT THEORY; PERSONALITY THEORIES.

REFERENCES

Freud, S., & Breuer, J. (1892). On the psychical mechanism of hysterical phenomena. In *Collected papers.* Vol. 1. London: Hogarth Press.

Breuer, J., & Freud, S. (1895). *Studies on hysteria.* New York: Basic Books.

Freud, S. (1920). Beyond the pleasure principle. In *Standard edition.* Vol. 18. London: Hogarth Press.

Freud, S. (1923). *The ego and the id.* New York: Norton.

Freud, S. (1926). Inhibitions, symptoms, and anxiety. In *Standard edition.* Vol. 20. London: Hogarth Press.

Freud, S. (1934). Instincts and their vicissitudes. In *Collected papers.* Vol. 4. London: Hogarth Press.

Freud, A. (1937). *The ego and mechanisms of defense.* New York: International Universities Press.

Jones, E. (1953–1957). *The life and work of Sigmund Freud.* 3 vols. New York: Basic Books.

Strachey, J. (Ed.) (1953–1964). *The standard edition of the complete psychological works of Sigmund Freud.* 24 vols. London: Hogarth Press.

Amarcher, P. (1965). Freud's neurological education and its influence on psychoanalytic theory. *Psy. Iss., 4,* 1–93.

Canning, J. (1966). A logical analysis of criticisms directed at Freudian psychoanalytic theory. Unpublished doctoral dissertation. University of Maryland Library.

Turiell, E. (1967). A historical analysis of the Freudian concept of the superego. *Psychoan. Rev., 54,* 118–140.

Hall, C., & Lindzey, G. (1978). *Theories of personality.* New York: Wiley.

Schultz, D. (1981). *Theories of personality.* Monterey, CA: Brooks/Cole.

Haynie, N. (1994). Sigmund Freud. In R. J. Corsini (Ed.), *Ency. Psy.* New York: Wiley.

Roeckelein, J. (1995). Naming in psychology: Analyses of citation counts and eponyms. *Psy. Rep., 77,* 163–174.

Roeckelein, J. (1996a). Citation of *laws* and *theories* in textbooks across 112 years of psychology. *Psy. Rep., 79,* 979–998.

Roeckelein, J. (1996b). Contributions to the history of psychology: CIV. Eminence in psychology as measured by name counts and eponyms. *Psy. Rep., 78,* 243–253.

Sutherland, S. (1996). *The international dictionary of psychology.* New York: Crossroad.

FROMM'S THEORY OF PERSONALITY. In the development of his "dialectic humanistic" *personality theory*, the German-born American psychoanalyst Erich Fromm (1900–1980) departed from the standard *Freudian theory* in stressing the effect of social forces on personality and was greatly influenced by the German social philosopher Karl Marx (e.g., Fromm, 1961, 1962). The fundamental notion that underlies Fromm's writings is that individuals feel lonely and isolated because they have become separated from other people and from nature. Inherent in this theme is a basic dilemma of humans that consists of a person's being both a part of nature and separate from it, where a person is both an animal and a social human being. In his *personality theory*, Fromm (1941) suggests that as humans have gained more freedom throughout the centuries, they have also felt more alone, and freedom then becomes an aversive condition from which people try to escape. There were two solutions to such a dilemma: to submit to authority and conform to society or to join with others in a spirit of love and social productivity. Fromm chose "productive love" as an important theme in his theory. Fromm (1947) proposed five *needs* that arise from the condition of being human and through which humans attempt to resolve the contradictions of existence: *relatedness* (also called *frame of devotion*; Fromm, 1968), *transcendence*, *rootedness*, *identity*, and *frame of orientation*. Fromm discussed the concept of *character* from two points of view: individual and social. From an individualistic viewpoint, *character* was thought to be dynamic and structured in infancy, and it involved the functions of facilitation of personal action, selection of world-confirming judgments and ideas, adaptation to one's own culture, and orientations toward death and life. From a societal viewpoint, *character* was seen as ways in which persons relate to the world and to each other and included five *social character types*: receptive, exploitative, hoarding, marketing, and productive. Of these five types, Fromm regarded only the *productive* type to be a healthy condition of character development. Fromm emphasized the role that socioeconomic factors play in one's life, believing that through a kind of "dialectic" process—that is, the process through which an idea or event (thesis) generates its opposite (antithesis), leading to a reconciliation of opposites (synthesis)—one's socioeconomic class influences social character, which, in turn, influences the adaptation of free individuals to the prevailing social conditions. Thus, in other terms, social character internalizes the external needs and orients individuals toward tasks required by the particular socioeconomic system (Nunez, 1994). Fromm's formulations in his *personality theory*—where an individual's relationship to society is a key theme—may be summed up in the following assumptions: humans fundamentally have an inborn nature; society is created by humans in order to fulfill this essential nature; no society that has yet been devised meets the basic needs of human existence; and it is possible to create such a society. Fromm's name for such an ideal society was "humanistic communitarian socialism" (Fromm, 1968; cf: Schaar, 1961). Fromm's *personality theory* consistently focused on the thesis that character/ personality affects, and is affected by, social structure and social change. His major contribution to *personality theory* is the idea that through the productive type of character, people may realize their own potentialities and, in so doing, may subordinate themselves to the well-being and welfare of all humans. See also ADLER'S THEORY OF PERSONALITY; FREUD'S THEORY OF PERSONALITY; HORNEY'S THEORY OF PERSONALITY; MASLOW'S THEORY OF PERSONALITY; PERSONALITY THEORIES; ROGERS' THEORY OF PERSONALITY.

REFERENCES

Fromm, E. (1939). Selfishness and self-love. *Psychiatry, 2,* 507–523.

Fromm, E. (1941). *Escape from freedom.* New York: Avon Books.

Fromm, E. (1947). *Man for himself: An inquiry into the psychology of ethics.* New York: Holt, Rinehart, & Winston.

Fromm, E. (1950) *The sane society.* New York: Holt, Rinehart, & Winston.

Fromm, E. (1956). *The art of loving.* New York: Harper & Row.

Fromm, E. (1961). *Marx's concept of man.* New York: Ungar.

Schaar, J. (1961). *Escape from authority: The perspectives of Erich Fromm.* New York: Basic Books.

Fromm, E. (1962). *Beyond the chains of illusion: My encounter with Marx and Freud.* New York: Simon & Schuster.

Fromm, E. (1968). *The revolution of hope.* New York: Harper & Row.

Fromm, E. (1970). *The crisis of psychoanalysis.* New York: Holt, Rinehart, & Winston.

Hall, C., & Lindzey, G. (1978). *Theories of personality.* New York: Wiley.

Fromm, E. (1980). *Greatness and limitations in Freud's thought.* New York: Harper & Row.

Nunez, R. (1994). Fromm's theory. In R. J. Corsini (Ed.), *Ency. Psy.* New York: Wiley.

FRUSTRATION-AGGRESSION HYPOTHESIS/THEORY. See AGGRESSION, THEORIES OF; FREUD'S INSTINCT THEORY.

FUCHS PHENOMENON. See PERCEPTION (I. GENERAL), THEORIES OF.

FULLERTON–CATTELL LAW. This generalized formulation, called the *square root law* in the area of psychophysics, is credited to the American psychologists George Stuart Fullerton (1859–1925) and James McKeen Cattell (1860–1944) and states that the error of observation and *least noticeable difference*, or *just noticeable difference* (*JND*), are proportional to the square root of the value of the stimulus rather than to the stimulus value itself. Thus, in a psychophysical experiment, the error of a subject's observation is seen to increase with the square root of the intensity of the stimulus that is being administered. The *Fullerton–Cattell law* (1892) was proposed as a substitute for Ernst Weber's (1795–1878) earlier law of 1834 on the basis that one's observation errors may more validly be viewed as psychological processes (involving "confidence" in judgments and "guessing" responses) than as the results of the classical "introspective" methodology (i.e., looking into one's own experience and reporting on it) to determine actual *JND*. Woodworth (1914) proposed that a compromise between the two laws was theoretically sound where much psychophysical data do fall between the values predicted by the two laws. However, some writers suggest that the *Fullerton–Cattell law* may not be a more universal or accurate law of psychophysical judgment than is the *Weber law* (see Woodworth & Schlosberg, 1965, p. 224). See also FECHNER'S LAW; WEBER-FECHNER LAW; WEBER'S LAW; PSYCHOPHYSICAL LAWS/THEORY.

REFERENCES

Fullerton, G., & Cattell, J. McK. (1892). On the perception of small differences, with special reference to the extent, force, and time of movement. *Philo. Series*, no. 2, Philadelphia: University of Pennsylvania Press.

Woodworth, R. (1914). Professor Cattell's psychophysical contributions. *Ar. Psy., N.Y.*, no. 30.

Guilford, J. (1932). A generalized psychophysical law. *Psy. Rev., 39*, 73–85.

Woodworth, R., & Schlosberg, H. (1965). *Experimental psychology*. New York: Holt, Rinehart, & Winston.

Murphy, G., & Kovach, J. (1972). *Historical introduction to modern psychology*. New York: Harcourt Brace Jovanovich.

FUNDAMENTAL ATTRIBUTION ERROR. See ATTRIBUTION THEORY.

FUZZY SET THEORY. See MIND/MENTAL SET, LAW OF.

G

GAIN-LOSS THEORY. See INTERPERSONAL ATTRACTION THEORIES.

GALEN'S DOCTRINE OF THE FOUR TEMPERAMENTS. The ancient Greek physician/philosopher Claudius Galen (c. A.D. 130–200) formulated the *doctrine of the four temperaments* of personality based on the earlier *doctrine of bodily humors* as outlined by the Greek philosopher Empedocles (c. 495–435 B.C.) and the Greek physician Hippocrates (c. 460–377 B.C.). Empedocles posited that the universe was made up of the four basic elements of earth, fire, air, and water where combinations of these four elements, in one way or another, could explain all known substances. Each of the four elements had corresponding "qualities": *earth*—cold/dry; *fire*—warm/dry; *air*—warm/moist; and *water*—cold/moist. When the qualities were taken with respect to the human body, they assumed the form of four substances or *humors*: blood, yellow bile, black bile, and phlegm. Hippocrates considered these *humors* to be the basic constituents of the body where—depending on their deficiency, excess, or balance—they could cause both disease and health. In this sense, Hippocrates' naturalistic approach and explanations of cause–effect relationships anticipated modern medicine and psychology, rather than appealing to the presence of "evil spirits" as the cause of diseases. Later, Galen systematized the relationship of the Empedoclean/Hippocratic notions of elements/humors into a general *personality theory of temperaments* where an excess of blood characterized the *sanguine* (warmhearted, cheerful) person, a preponderance of black bile related to the *melancholic* (sad, fearful) personality, an excess of yellow bile led to the *choleric* (fiery, highly reactive) person, and an excess of phlegm typified the *phlegmatic* (slow) individual. Galen's *doctrine of the four humors* and their corresponding *temperaments* was viable until about A.D. 1400, when the Renaissance and the rebirth of medicine took place, and the doctrine faded. While Galen's doctrine is now chiefly of historical interest only, certain vestiges of terminology remain in our language, such as the expressions "bad humor," "good humor," and "humorless." Galen's doctrine also served as the intellectual basis for certain contemporary *theories of personality* that formulated and advanced the concept of *types*, such as Sheldon's (Sheldon, Stevens, & Tucker, 1940; Sheldon & Stevens, 1942) triad of personality types: *visceratonic*—outgoing, cheerful, happy; *somatotonic*—athletic, energetic, vigorous; and *cerebrotonic*—inward, bookish, shy (Lundin, 1994). In another case, Alfred Adler (1870–1937) related his hypothesized four *styles of life* to *Galen's four temperaments* (Peyser, 1994). The work of Hippocrates and Galen may have inspired some modern investigators to look for biochemical sources of variations in human personality and behavior, and the *four temperament types* themselves, detached from the humoral doctrine, have continued to interest prominent psychologists such as Wundt, Pavlov, and Eysenck (Coan, 1994). See also EMOTIONS, THEORIES/LAWS OF; EYSENCK'S THEORY OF PERSONALITY; KRETSCHMER'S THEORY OF PERSONALITY; PERSONALITY THEORIES; SHELDON'S TYPE THEORY.

REFERENCES

Spranger, E. (1920). *Types of men*. Halle, East Germany: Niemeyer.

Kretschmer, E. (1922). *Physique and character: An investigation of the nature of constitution and of the theory of temperament*. London: Paul, Trench, Trubner.

Viola, G. (1933). *La costituzione individuale*. Bologna, Italy: Cappeli.

Sheldon, W., Stevens, S. S., & Tucker, W. (1940). *The varieties of human physique*. New York: Harper.

Sheldon, W., & Stevens, S. S. (1942). *Varieties of human temperament: A psychology of constitutional differences*. New York: Harper.

Hutchins, R. (Ed.) (1952). *Writings of Hippocrates*. In *Great books of the Western world*. Vol. 10. Chicago: Encyclopaedia Britannica.

Galen, C. (1956). *On anatomical procedures*. London: Oxford University Press.

Coan, R. (1994). Personality types. In R. J. Corsini (Ed.), *Ency. Psy.* New York: Wiley.

Lundin, R. (1994). Humoral theory. In R. J. Corsini (Ed.), *Ency. Psy.* New York: Wiley.

Peyser, C. (1994). Galen. In R. J. Corsini (Ed.), *Ency. Psy.* New York: Wiley.

GALTON'S LAWS. The English natural scientist/psychologist Sir Francis Galton (1822–1911) has been called the "father of differential psychology" and was one of the foremost progenitors of psychometrics (Galton, 1883). Galton's contributions to *differential psychology* (i.e., the branch of psychology that studies the differences and variations in certain fundamental characters as manifested in different races, in different social groups, or in individuals of the same group) reflected his conviction that all human characteristics, both physical and mental, could ultimately be described in quantitative terms (Jensen, 1994a). Galton's long-term concern and study of heredity (Galton, 1889/1973) led him to anticipate the *polygenic theory of inheritance* of continuous characteristics that was later developed by the English geneticist/statistician Sir Ronald Fisher (1890–1962). Galton (1883) also anticipated the formalized *motor theory of thought*

(Watson, 1914) through his finding that many scientists seemed to have no visual imagery at all (Galton himself apparently had clear visual imagery). In attempting to explain how his "men of science" could have ideas without visual images, Galton said that the missing faculty was replaced by other modes of conception, chiefly that of the "incipient motor sense," not only of the eyeballs but of the muscles generally (Osgood, 1953). Galton was the first scientist to clearly formulate the *nature–nurture* question, that is, the relative contributions of heredity and environment to individual and group differences in human abilities, traits, and talents. He was also the first to note the methodological importance of monozygotic and dizygotic twins for estimating the relative effects of genetic and environmental factors in human variation. Galton (1869/1962) investigated the inheritance of general ability by studying nearly 1,000 men who had achieved eminence and recorded the frequency of eminent men among all their relatives (cf: Roeckelein, 1996). He found that as the degree of genetic kinship decreased, the percentage of eminent relatives also decreased in a markedly stepwise fashion—as predicted from Galton's *model of genetic inheritance*, which also explained in hereditary terms physical traits such as fingerprints and stature. From these data, Galton argued that mental ability is inherited in the same way as are many physical traits. For example, Galton's *law of filial regression to mediocrity* is demonstrated in the trait of stature: the offspring of a deviant parent are, on average, less deviant from the mean of the population than is the parent regarding the trait in question (Jensen, 1994a, b). Thus, the offspring of two very tall or two very short parents would be more nearly of average height than the parents themselves. A corollary to this law is Galton's *law of reversion*, which refers to the reappearance of a recessive genetic trait that had not been present in the phenotypes for one or more generations. Galton explained the phenomenon of *regression* in terms of his *law of ancestral inheritance*, by which the genetic contribution of each parent to an offspring is 1/4, of each grandparent is 1/16, of each great-grandparent is 1/64, and so on. Presumably, each further-removed ancestral generation comes closer to being a random sample of the general population. Therefore, the offspring's total genetic inheritance for the trait studied, being the sum of this infinite series of decreasing fractions, comes closer to the population mean than does that of the parents. This explanation for regression, however, has been totally rejected by modern geneticists (Jensen, 1994b). The concept of *regression* developed by Galton served as the basis for the statistical correlation methods formulated by the English statistician Karl Pearson (1857–1936). Galton first studied statistically the relationship between the heights of fathers and their sons; Galton hired Pearson as a statistician to work with him and his father on a series of investigations involving the contributions of heredity to the development of human attributes (Merenda, 1994; Well, 1994). In addition to regression and correlation, Galton's contributions to statistics and psychometrics include formulations and developments of the bivariate scatter diagram, multiple correlation, standardized or scale-free scores, percentile ranks, the use of median and geometric mean as measures of central tendency, and rating scales (Jensen, 1994a). The possible causes of *regression* among parents and offspring (or any other kinships) may be classified into three categories: errors of measurement, genetic factors, and environmental factors. There is nothing in the phenomenon of *regression* per se that proves either genetic or environmental causes or some combination of these. However, the complex methods of quantitative genetics that partition the total population variance in a trait into its genetic and environmental components may give an estimate of how much observed regression is attributable to genetic factors, to the environment, and to measurement error (Jensen, 1994b). See also INTELLIGENCE, THEORIES/LAWS OF.

REFERENCES

Galton, F. (1869/1962). *Hereditary genius: An inquiry into its laws and consequences.* London: Collins.

Galton, F. (1872). Statistical inquiries into the efficacy of prayer. *The Fortnightly Review, 12,* 125–135.

Galton, F. (1874). *English men of science: Their nature and nurture.* London: Macmillan.

Galton, F. (1879–1880). Psychometric experiments. *Brain, 2,* 149–162.

Galton, F. (1883). *Inquiries into human faculty and its development.* London: Macmillan.

Galton, F. (1888). Co-relations and their measurements, chiefly from anthropometric data. *Proc. R. S. Lon., 45,* 135–140.

Galton, F. (1889/1973). *Natural inheritance.* New York: AMS Press.

Watson, J. (1914). *Behavior: An introduction to comparative psychology.* New York: Holt.

Osgood, C. (1953). *Method and theory in experimental psychology.* New York: Oxford University Press.

Jensen, A. (1994a). Francis Galton. In R. J. Corsini (Ed.), *Ency. Psy.* New York: Wiley.

Jensen, A. (1994b). Law of filial regression. In R. J. Corsini (Ed.), *Ency. Psy.* New York: Wiley.

Merenda, P. (1994). Correlation methods. In R. J. Corsini (Ed.), *Ency. Psy.* New York: Wiley.

Well, A. (1994). Correlation and regression. In R. J. Corsini (Ed.), *Ency. Psy.* New York: Wiley.

Roeckelein, J. (1996). Contributions to the history of psychology: CIV. Eminence in psychology as measured by name counts and eponyms. *Psy. Rep., 78,* 243–253.

GAMBLER'S FALLACY. See PROBABILITY, THEORY/LAWS.

GAME THEORY. See DECISION-MAKING THEORIES.

GARCIA EFFECT. The American psychologist John Garcia (1917–   ) conducted extensive work in the area of learning, specifically on classically conditioned taste aversion. The *Garcia effect*, also called *bait-shyness, toxicosis,* and *learned taste aversion* (Reber, 1995), refers to an acquired syndrome in which an organism learns to avoid a particular food because of a conditioned aversion response to its smell or taste. A *toxicosis* reaction can be formed in a single trial during which consumption of a novel food is followed by nausea and sickness—even when the toxic reaction itself is not experienced for some hours after eating. Specifically, in one study (Garcia & Koelling, 1966), rats quickly acquired an aversion to a sweet-tasting liquid when it was followed by an injection that made them ill, but they did *not* readily acquire an aversion to the sweet taste when it was followed by an electric shock. In contrast, rats learned to avoid a light/noise stimulus combination when it was paired with shock but *not* when it was followed by a nausea-inducing injection. These findings indicate that classical conditioning cannot be established equally well for all stimuli. The key to conditioning in these types of studies is that the original association must be with an internal, digestively linked stimulus (either the smell or taste of the food substance), and the aversive outcome must be associated with alimentary function such as nausea. The *Garcia effect* is a particularly interesting phenomenon because it can be formed over such a long interval of time, whereas in all other forms of classical conditioning the optimal interval between stimuli is approximately only a half a second (Braverman & Bronstein, 1985; Reber, 1995). See also GUSTATION/TASTE, THEORIES OF; OLFAC-TION/SMELL, THEORIES OF; PAVLOVIAN CONDITIONING PRINCI-PLES/LAWS.

REFERENCES

Garcia, J., & Koelling, R. (1966). Relation of cue to consequence in avoidance learning. *Psychonom. Sci., 4,* 123.

Kalat, J., & Rozin, P. (1973). "Learned safety" as a mechanism in long-delay taste aversion learning in rats. *J. Comp. Physio. Psy., 83,* 198–207.

Garcia, J., Hankins, W., & Rusiniak, K. (1974). Behavioral regulation of the milieu internal in man and rat. *Science, 185,* 824–831.

Garcia, J., Rusiniak, K., & Brett, L. (1977). Conditioning food-illness aversions in wild animals: Caveat canonici. In H. Davis & H. Hurwitz (Eds.), *Operant-Pavlovian interactions*. Hillsdale, NJ: Erlbaum.

Revusky, S. (1977). Learning as a general process with an emphasis on data from feeding experiments. In N. Milgram, L. Krames, & T. Alloway (Eds.), *Food aversion learning*. New York: Plenum.

Braverman, N., & Bronstein, P. (1985). Experimental assessments and clinical applications of conditioned food aversions. *Ann. N.Y. Acad. Sci., 43,* 1–41.

Reber, A. (1995). *The Penguin dictionary of psychology*. New York: Penguin Books.

GARDNER'S MULTIPLE INTELLIGENCES THEORY. See INTELLI-GENCE, THEORIES/LAWS OF.

GAS CHROMATOGRAPHIC MODEL. See OLFACTION/SMELL, THE-ORIES OF.

GATE-CONTROL THEORY. Psychologist Ronald Melzack and biologist Patrick Wall (1965, 1982) formulated the *gate-control theory of pain*, which states that the spinal cord contains a type of neurological "gate" that either blocks or allows pain signals to pass on to higher centers in the brain. The spinal cord contains small nerve fibers ("C-fibers") that conduct most pain signals and larger fibers ("A-delta fibers") that transmit most other sensory information. When some bodily tissue is injured, suggest Melzack and Wall, the small fibers activate and open the "neural gate," and the person feels "pain." Large fiber activity, on the other hand, serves to close the pain gate and turns pain off. Thus, according to the *gate-control theory*, one way to treat chronic pain is to stimulate (via small electrical currents or by acupuncture) the "gate-closing" activity in the large neural fibers. This is called the "counterirritant" method for reducing pain (Baron, 1992). For example, ice applied to an arm bruise not only controls swelling but also triggers "cold messages" that close the gate on the pain signals. Patients suffering from arthritis may carry a small, portable electrical stimulation unit next to a chronically painful area, and when the unit stimulates nerves in that area, the individual feels a vibrating sensation rather than pain. The effectiveness of acupuncture may be adequately explained by *gate-control theory* where inserting needles into the large neural fibers transmits sensory signals that compete with pain signals of the small neural fibers and, thus, close the "pain gate." The *gate-control theory of pain* has been revised recently to account for the importance of several brain mechanisms in the perception of pain (Melzack & Wall, 1982; cf: Nathan, 1976), such as one's current emotional state interacting with the onset of a painful stimulus, which may alter the pain intensity one feels. Thus, the brain itself may affect pain perception by sending messages that either close the spinal gate (as when one relaxes) or keep it open (as when one is anxious). Opiate-like chemicals, called endorphins and enkephalins, that are produced in the body naturally may interact with the spinal gate also to lessen the sensations of pain (Millan, 1986). Certain areas of the spinal cord are rich in opiate receptors and endorphin-loaded neurons, and these substances may close the spinal gate by inhibiting the release of excitatory substances for neurons transmitting signals about pain (Neale, Barker, Uhl, & Snyder, 1978). It has been suggested that social and cognitive-behavioral factors can strongly affect pain, even though pain is a basic sensory experience, and the specific mechanisms accounting for such factors are still being researched (Weisenberg, 1984). See also COGNITIVE THERAPY, THEORIES OF.

REFERENCES

Melzack, R., & Scott, T. (1957). The effects of early experience on the response to pain. *J. Comp. Physio. Psy., 50*, 155–161.

Melzack, R., & Wall, P. (1965). Pain mechanism: A new theory. *Science, 150*, 971–979.

Melzack, R. (1976). Pain: Past, present, and future. In M. Weisenberg & B. Tursky (Eds.), *Pain: New perspectives in therapy and research.* New York: Plenum.

Nathan, P. (1976). The gate control theory of pain. *Brain, 99*, 123–158.

Neale, J., Barker, J., Uhl, G., & Snyder, S. (1978). Enkephalin-containing neurons visualized in spinal cord cultures. *Science, 201*, 467–469.

Melzack, R., & Wall, P. (1982). *The challenge of pain*. New York: Basic Books.

Melzack, R. (1983). *Pain measurement and assessment*. New York: Raven Press.

Melzack, R. (1984). The myth of painless childbirth. *Pain, 19,* 321–337.

Weisenberg, M. (1984). Cognitive aspects of pain. In P. Wall & R. Melzack (Eds.), *Textbook of pain*. Edinburgh: Churchill Livingstone.

Millan, M. (1986). Multiple opioid systems and pain. *Pain, 27,* 303–347.

Melzack, R. (1990). The tragedy of needless pain. *Sci. Amer., 262,* 27–33.

Baron, R. (1992). *Psychology*. Boston: Allyn & Bacon.

Melzack, R. (1992). Phantom limbs. *Sci. Amer., 266,* 120–126.

GELB PHENOMENON. See PERCEPTION (I. GENERAL), THEORIES OF.

GENERALIZATION, PRINCIPLES OF. The *principle of response generalization* states that an increase (or decrease) in the strength of one response through a reinforcement (or extinction) procedure is accompanied by a similar, but smaller, increase (or decrease) in the strength of other responses that have properties in common with the first response (Keller & Schoenfeld, 1950). The *principle of stimulus generalization* is the tendency for stimuli similar to the original stimulus in a learning situation to produce the response originally acquired (cf: the *unit hypothesis*—the amount of *generalization* along a continuum decreases with the number of test stimuli that lie between the training stimulus and a given test stimulus and increases with the number that lie beyond it; Sutherland, 1996). Although there has been a tendency to regard *stimulus generalization* as a "fundamental" process, it has been noted that when it occurs, it can be viewed simply as the failure of the organism to have established a "discrimination" (i.e., the ability to perceive and respond differentially to differences between two or more stimuli) between the original stimulus and the new one(s) (Reber, 1995). *Stimulus generalization* was first demonstrated by Pavlov (1927) in laboratory experiments with dogs: after the dog experienced a succession of pairings between a stimulus such as a tone (e.g., 200 Hz) and food reinforcement, a stimulus similar in character (e.g., 400 Hz) and yet discriminably different from the original tone would be presented without reinforcement. This procedure resulted in the establishment of the *excitatory gradient of generalization*, which showed that the intensity of the animal's response to the test stimulus was directly proportional to its similarity to the training stimulus. Pavlov placed great importance on *stimulus generalization* and saw it as biologically adaptive (Pavlov, 1927, p. 113); animals generalized their responses to stimuli other than the original one to compensate for the instability of the environment. The early emphasis on the adaptive value of *stimulus generalization* led later theorists to treat it as a fundamental and irreducible aspect of learning (e.g., Spence, 1936; Hull, 1943). The later theorists derived other, more complex psychological phenomena from the concept of *generalization*. The *theories of generalization* began with Pavlov's (1927) *physiological theory*, in which he argued that *generalization* from the training (original) stimulus to the testing (similar) stimuli was due to a *spreading wave of excitation* across the cortex. *Pavlov's theory* may be dismissed, however, with the observation that there was no physiological evidence for cortical waves then or now (Adams, 1980). Later, Hull (1943) wrote about *generalization* in terms of the *spread of habit strength* in a way similar to Pavlov's *spread of cortical excitation*. The common aspect to both *Pavlov's theory* and *Hull's theory* concerning *generalization* is that it was seen as an innate propensity of the brain whereby it was hypothesized to occur naturally via cortical waves or habit structures once a training stimulus came to elicit a response reliably. The theoretical development of *generalization* lay dormant for a number of years until the appearance of the *Lashley–Wade hypothesis*, which suggested that the view of innate *generalization* was incorrect. Rather, *generalization* occurs because of failure to discriminate the training stimulus from the test stimulus. According to Lashley and Wade (1946), the dimensions of a stimulus series are determined by comparison of two or more stimuli and do not exist for the organism until established by differential training. Thus, the *Lashley–Wade hypothesis* asserts that there is no *generalization* (or *generalization gradient*) without discrimination learning, and the organism learns about the dimensions of stimuli by training to discriminate differences between them. There is both a strong and a weak interpretation of the *Lashley–Wade hypothesis* (Adams, 1980). The strong interpretation is that all *generalization* is a function of discrimination experience with *no* contribution from innate sources. The weak interpretation is that there *may* be influences from innate sources, but, nevertheless, training in discriminating the values of a stimulus dimension will affect *generalization*. Conclusions from research concerning the strong interpretation have been negative, while studies focusing on the weak interpretation have shown positive evidence (e.g., Jenkins & Harrison, 1960; Newman & Baron, 1965). In addition to discrimination training, other variables such as schedules of reinforcement and amount of training are important for amount of *generalization*. *Generalization* can be excitatory, in which the spread of responding is with respect to the training stimulus that has been reinforced, or it can be inhibitory, in which there is a spread of nonresponding with respect to the stimulus that has not been reinforced. Recently, a *cognitively* oriented explanation of *stimulus generalization* (Riley & Lamb, 1979) has appeared to rival the earlier interpretations. In this approach, *stimulus generalization* is regarded as a special case of stimulus classification: the organism categorizes discriminably different events as equivalent and responds to them in terms of their class membership rather than to their peculiarities. In another area of research, the *behavioral contrast effect/phenomenon*—where a behavioral change occurs as a consequence of a transition from one condition of reinforcement to another—has attracted the interest of psychologists (e.g., Amsel, 1971; Capaldi, 1974) because it appears to be an exception to the *laws of extinction* and *stimulus generalization*. The issue as to whether *behavioral contrast* can be incorporated into existing laws of conditioning, or whether new laws must be formulated to account for the phenomenon is still unresolved (Rickert, 1994a).

While psychologists are closer now than they once were to a comprehensive explanation of *generalization*, they are still lacking a fundamental theory (Adams, 1980). See also ASSOCIATIVE SHIFTING, LAW OF; INTERFERENCE, THEORIES OF.

REFERENCES

Pavlov, I. (1927). *Conditioned reflexes*. New York: Oxford University Press.
Spence, K. (1936). The nature of discrimination learning in animals. *Psy. Rev., 43*, 427–449.
Hull, C. (1943). *Principles of behavior*. New York: Appleton-Century-Crofts.
Lashley, K., & Wade, M. (1946). The Pavlovian theory of generalization. *Psy. Rev., 53*, 72–87.
Keller, F., & Schoenfeld, W. (1950). *Principles of psychology*. New York: Appleton-Century-Crofts.
Guttman, N., & Kalish, H. (1956). Discriminability and stimulus generalization. *J. Exp. Psy., 51*, 79–88.
Jenkins, H., & Harrison, R. (1960). Effect of discrimination training on auditory generalization. *J. Exp. Psy., 59*, 246–253.
Newman, F., & Baron, M. (1965). Stimulus generalization along the dimension of angularity. *J. Comp. Physio. Psy., 60*, 59–63.
Amsel, A. (1971). Positive induction, behavioral contrast, and generalization of inhibition in discrimination learning. In H. Kendler & J. Spence (Eds.), *Essays in neobehaviorism: A memorial volume to Kenneth W. Spence*. New York: Appleton-Century-Crofts.
Capaldi, E. (1974). Partial reward either following or preceding consistent reward: A case of reinforcement level. *J. Exp. Psy., 102*, 954–962.
Riley, D., & Lamb, M. (1979). Stimulus generalization. In A. Pick (Ed.), *Perception and its development: A tribute to E.J. Gibson*. Hillsdale, NJ: Erlbaum.
Adams, J. (1980). *Learning and memory*. Homewood, IL: Dorsey Press.
Rickert, E. (1994a). Behavioral contrast. In R. J. Corsini (Ed.), *Ency. Psy*. New York: Wiley.
Rickert, E. (1994b). Stimulus generalization. In R. J. Corsini (Ed.), *Ency. Psy*. New York: Wiley.
Reber, A. (1995). *The Penguin dictionary of psychology*. New York: Penguin Books.
Sutherland, S. (1996). *The international dictionary of psychology*. New York: Crossroad.

GENERALIZATION-DIFFERENTIATION THEORY. See INTERFERENCE THEORIES OF FORGETTING.

GENERAL SYSTEMS THEORY. The Austrian-born biologist Ludwig von Bertalanffy (1901–1972) is generally considered to be the father of *general systems theory*, which he viewed comprehensively as "a science of science" (Gregory, 1994; Royce, 1994). Other precursors of *general systems theory* include the development of Gestalt psychology (e.g., Wertheimer, 1923) and development of the holistic approach (e.g., Smuts, 1926). The goal of *general systems theory* is to find models that are applicable across many diverse disciplines such as agriculture, metallurgy, music, business, psychology, sociology, and others. (Bertalanffy, 1968; cf: periodic attempts to establish a *unity of science* orientation across disciplines; Neurath, Carnap, & Morris, 1938). One of the most popular of such general models is the *open* versus *closed system model* where each system may be seen in terms of "openness/closedness" and in terms of how self-sufficient or independent it is regarding outside influences. Diverse examples of such systems are an eddy in a stream (open system), the solar system (closed system), an ant's behavior (closed system), a well-adjusted person (open system), learning theory in psychology (a limited, or open-closed, system), and personality psychology (a unisystem centering on the concepts of self-consistency, integrity, and balance; cf: Lecky, 1945). Other system models in psychology include the concepts of *homeostasis*—the maintenance of constancy in internal functioning, *self-concept*—constancy/consistency of personality (cf: Stagner, 1951), and *stress*—changes in personality structure as a result of psychological stress that are similar to changes in physiological structure as a result of biological stress (cf: Selye, 1956). Other concepts in *general systems theory* include *entropy*, *negative entropy*, *feedback*, *adaptation*, and *equifinality* (Bertalanffy, 1968). Distinctions are made between the terms *systems*, *general systems*, and *systems analysis* where *systems* applies to a model within a discipline (such as a communication system, a governmental system, an administrative system, etc.), *general systems* refers to common models that are incorporated into two or more fields, and *systems analysis* refers to the analysis of the structure of specific systems (Gregory, 1994). *General systems theory* tends to de-emphasize the tenets of elementarism and reductionism, which ignore the significance of "wholes" or "systems" (cf: Lewin's, 1936, *field theory*, which recognizes the importance of holistic, organismic, and field-emergent influences when analyzing human behavior). Any failures in the wide acceptance and application of *general systems theory* may be connected to some of the theory's shortcomings: it doesn't have a formulation of the system that is acceptable for a majority of the investigators, it hasn't revealed an organizing factor where the transfer into the system of the chaos of a great number of components into an organized multitude has occurred, and the system is portrayed as a homogeneous entity without any "operational architectonics" that would permit the evaluation of the system (Wolman, 1973). See also CONTROL/SYSTEMS THEORY; LEARNING THEORIES/LAWS; LEWIN'S FIELD THEORY; ORGANIZATIONAL/INDUSTRIAL/SYSTEMS THEORY; SELYE'S THEORY/MODEL OF STRESS.

REFERENCES

Wertheimer, M. (1923). Untersuchungen zur Lehre von der Gestalt. *Psy. Forsch., 4*, 301–350.

Smuts, J. (1926). *Holism and evolution.* New York: Viking Press.

Lewin, K. (1936). *Principles of topological and vectoral psychology.* New York: McGraw-Hill.

Neurath, O., Carnap, R., & Morris, C. (Eds.) (1938). *International encyclopedia of unified science*. Chicago: University of Chicago Press.

Lecky, P. (1945). *Self-consistency: A theory of personality*. Garden City, NY: Doubleday/ Anchor.

Bertalanffy, L. von (1950a). An outline of general systems theory. *Brit. J. Phil. Sci., 1*, 134–165.

Bertalanffy, L. von (1950b). The theory of open systems in physics and biology. *Science, 111*, 23–29.

Krech, D. (1950). Dynamic systems as open neurological systems. *Psy. Rev., 57*, 345–361.

Stagner, R. (1951). Homeostasis as a unifying concept in personality theory. *Psy. Rev., 58*, 5–17.

Bertalanffy, L. von (1955). General systems theory. *Main currents in modern thought, 11*, 75–83.

Selye, H. (1956). *Stress of life*. New York: McGraw-Hill.

Bertalanffy, L. von (1968). *General systems theory*. New York: Braziller.

Wolman, B. (Ed.) (1973). *Dictionary of behavioral science*. New York: Van Nostrand Reinhold.

Gregory, W. (1994). General systems. In R. J. Corsini (Ed.), *Ency. Psy.* New York: Wiley.

Royce, J. (1994). Ludwig von Bertalanffy. In R. J. Corsini (Ed.), *Ency. Psy.* New York: Wiley.

GENETIC CONTINUITY, PRINCIPLE OF. See WEISMANN'S THEORY.

GENETICS, LAWS OF. See MENDEL'S LAWS/PRINCIPLES.

GERM-PLASM/CONTINUITY THEORY. See WEISMANN'S THEORY.

GESTALT THEORY/LAWS. = perceptual organization, laws of. The German word *Gestalt* may be translated as "form" or "configuration." *Gestalt theory* is an example of a "rationalist" (i.e., progressing from abstract ideas to interpretations and demonstrations of the phenomena under study) theory in psychology that was developed initially by Wolfgang Kohler (1887–1967), Kurt Koffka (1886–1941), and Max Wertheimer (1880–1943). Wertheimer (1912, 1923a/1958, 1923b) is considered to be the official founder of Gestalt psychology (Bower & Hilgard, 1981). Gestalters—those who advocate the Gestaltist approach—were concerned originally with the predominant nature of perception, thinking, problem-solving processes (including "insight"; Kohler, 1925), and the structure of psychological experience, without primary reference to learning phenomena (cf: Koffka, 1935). Gestalters suggested, however, that what was learned in a learning/memory context was a product of the *laws of perceptual organization*. They argued that traces of perceptual events are stored in memory, and, since *organizational laws* determine the structuring of perception, those laws also determine the structure of what information is laid down in memory. The *laws of perceptual organization*, or "grouping" (Wertheimer, 1923b), indicate the priority of perception in *Gestalt theory* and show how a perceiver groups together certain stimuli and, thereby, how one structures and interprets a visual field. A few of these subsidiary laws are figure–ground, proximity, similarity, common direction/good continuation, continuity, simplicity, and common fate. The *principle of figure–ground relationships* (see Rubin, 1915/1958; cf: the *Liebmann effect*—as the luminosity of a colored figure increases, the contrast between the figure and the ground on which it lies begins to diminish, and, if the figure is complex, it becomes simpler; when the figure–ground luminosities are equal, the figure cannot be distinguished from the ground; Osgood, 1953; Zusne, 1987; cf: *law of surroundedness*—where one figure surrounds another, the surrounding figure is likely to be seen as *background* and the enclosed figure as *figure*; Sutherland, 1996) refers to the contrast between the *figure*—the area of a visual stimulus that is the focus of attention and appears closest to the perceiver, such as letters printed on paper—and the *background*—the area of the visual stimulus that recedes beyond the figure and constitutes the background upon which a figure is superimposed, such as the white paper upon which letters or symbols are printed. Sometimes, what is figure and what is ground in a given visual stimulus are ambiguous, where the perceiver may organize it in one way at a given time and then, a few seconds later, switch to seeing it another way (cf: the *Schafer–Murphy effect*—the alleged phenomenon that when subjects are rewarded for seeing an ambiguous figure in one way, they are more likely to see it in that way in the future; Sutherland, 1996). The relevance of the *principle of figure–ground* for *learning theory* is the notion that people learn primarily about the figure they focus in attention, rather than the background, and what becomes an important figure can be influenced by various factors (such as instructions given to human subjects). In the context of learning/ memory, it is emphasized that it is "perceptually interpreted" objects, not the raw stimuli themselves, that are learned. The *law of proximity* refers to the tendency for the perceiver to group together elements of a visual or auditory field based on their nearness/proximity to one another. The factor of *proximity* (cf: Thorndike's *principle of belongingness*) is used in the communication processes of reading, writing, or talking, as well as with relatively discrete, isolated, neutral, or meaningless stimuli. The *law of similarity* states that items similar in respect to some feature (such as color, shape, texture) will tend to be grouped together by the perceiver. This principle is consistently utilized when a person speaks or reads. For example, in the *cocktail party effect* it is possible to pick out and listen to a particular speaker against a noisy background because of the consistent voice quality of the speaker from one moment to another. The *law of common direction/good continuation/continuity* (cf: Judd, 1907) refers to the perceiver's tendency to group together a set of points if some appear to continue or complete a "lawful" series or complete a simple curve. The *law of simplicity* states that, other things being equal, the perceiver will see the visual field as organized into simple, regular figures (called "good gestalts" of symmetry, regularity, and smoothness). For example, figures containing "gaps" yield perceptions of closed, complete figures where the perceiver fills in the gap with the redundant, predictable extrapolation of the simplest description of the figure (this is also referred to as *closure*, in which closed areas or complete figures perceptually give more stability than unclosed areas or incomplete figures). The *law of common fate* states that elements that move in the same direction will be perceived as belonging together and forming a figure. For example, an animal in the forest is hidden if its surface is covered with the same elements found in the background because its boundary is unclear: there is no basis for grouping the elements or spots on the animal as long as the animal is stationary and it remains well hidden. However, once it moves, the elements on its surface will move together, and the animal's form will quickly be perceived. A practical application of the *laws of perceptual organization*, one that is especially relevant to the *law of common fate*, is illustrated in the art of "camouflage" (Wertheimer, 1923a/1958), where a significant figure is buried or hidden by supplementing its lines, shape, color, and contours so that attention is defocused from the original shape. An additional and more general law called the *law of pragnanz* (meaning "compact and significant"; "good figure"; Wertheimer, 1938) was formulated also to describe the common features of the subsidiary laws of grouping. The *law of pragnanz*, similar to the *law of simplicity*, states that people have a tendency to see things in the simplest form possible. Consistent with the *law of pragnanz* is the Gestalt principle called the *law of least action*, which states that an organism will tend to follow the course of action that requires the least effort or expended energy under prevailing conditions. In a personality context, course of action and energy expended can be influenced by the individual's personality characteristics so that an objectively easy course of action may be difficult for a person because of the amount of emotional investment required. The *law of least action* is also called the *principle of least-energy expenditure* and *least-effort principle* (Wolman, 1989). The German physicist/mathematician Hermann von Helmholtz (1821–1894) formulated the mathematical foundation for the *law of conservation of energy* (e.g., Hoffding, 1908; cf: Hamilton's *principle of least action/law of resistance/law of least constraint/law of least energy/law of greatest economy*; Thorndike, 1907). Up until the appearance of Gestalt psychology and *Gestalt theory* in America in the late 1920s and the early 1930s, the traditional method of scientific analysis was to describe the parts of a complex phenomenon and arrive at the whole by adding up the discrete descriptions. Developments in the fields of biology, physics, psychology, and sociology, however, began to suggest that such an approach did not account adequately for "field processes" (i.e., entities composed of interacting forces; cf: Kohler, 1920/1938). The contribution of *Gestalt theory* to psychology was in its emphasis on the value of accounting for field forces in scientific methodology in general. In particular, the *Gestalt theorists* emphasized that the whole perception one obtains in a perceptual field "emerges" from the relationships among the parts of the form, where the parts may lose their former properties and take on new properties determined by the form of the whole pattern. In short, "the whole of perceptual experience is *more* than the sum of the parts." An example of "emergent" properties of *physical* parts is the liquid nature of water when the gaseous elements of hydrogen and oxygen are combined. An example of "emergent" properties in *psychological* parts is the apparent motion (called the *phi phenomenon*) created in a perceiver when rapidly flipping a series of overlapping still photographs. The Gestaltist emphasis on the "wholism" of perceptual experience has been accepted largely in modern *perceptual theories*, where it often has been called *top-down* (or *context-determined*) *processing* of stimulus information (Bower & Hilgard, 1981). In a learning/memory context, the Gestalt conception of *memory* is comparable to Aristotle's earlier theory that perception is "stamped in" as a corresponding *memory trace* (cf: Beneke's, 1832, *doctrine of traces*). Gestalters argue that the neural processes active during perception can endure in a mitigated form as a *trace*, and, thus, information is stored in substantially the same form by the same neural processes as in the original perception (cf: *phenomenon/hypothesis of isomorphism*—the notion that there is a structural similarity between excitatory fields in the cortex and conscious experience; Kohler, 1929; Allport, 1955). The old *laws of association* (such as contiguity, similarity, and contrast), enunciated by the early philosophers, are analogous to the *Gestalt laws of perceptual organization* (such as proximity, similarity, and good continuation). In recent years, studies in perception have attempted to quantify the *laws of perceptual organization* as the Gestalters originally described them. The typical approach is to create a number of perceptual stimulus arrays, present them to individuals, and then ask the people to rank them numerically along certain stimulus dimensions (such as good continuation or similarity). Much of this work has provided experimental confirmation of many of the views of *Gestalt theory* (e.g., Restle, 1982). However, researchers are not able to explain *how* these *perceptual organization laws* work. Current investigations in the field of artificial intelligence are seeking to model and design human perceptual systems, including the *laws of perceptual organization* (e.g., Bruce & Green, 1985) but, to date, this work has met with only limited success. See also ASSOCIATION, LAWS/ PRINCIPLES OF; BELONGINGNESS, LAW/PRINCIPLE OF; COCKTAIL PARTY EFFECT; CODING THEORIES; INFORMATION/INFORMATION-PROCESSING THEORY; LEWIN'S FIELD THEORY; PERCEPTION, THEORIES OF; VON RESTORFF EFFECT.

REFERENCES

Beneke, F. (1832). *Lehrbuch der Psychologie als Naturwissenschaft.* Berlin: Mittler.

Judd, C. (1907). *Psychology: General introduction.* New York: Scribners.

Thorndike, E. (1907). *The elements of psychology.* New York: Seiler.

Hoffding, H. (1908). *Outline of psychology.* London: Macmillan.

Wertheimer, M. (1912). Experimental studies of the perception of movement. *Z. Psy., 61,* 161–265.

Rubin, E. (1915/1958). *Synsoplevede Figurer.* In D. Beardslee & M. Wertheimer (Eds.), *Readings in perception.* Princeton, NJ: Van Nostrand Reinhold.

Kohler, W. (1920/1938). Die physische gestalten in Ruhe und in Stationaren Zustand. In W. Ellis (Ed.), *A source book of Gestalt psychology*. New York: Harcourt, Brace, & World.

Rubin, E. (1921). *Visuelle wahrgenommene Figuren*. Copenhagen: Gyldendalske.

Wertheimer, M. (1923a/1958). Principles of perceptual organization. In D. Beardslee & M. Wertheimer (Eds.), *Readings in perception*. Princeton, NJ: Van Nostrand Reinhold.

Wertheimer, M. (1923b). Untersuchung zur Lehre von der Gestalt. II. *Psy. Forsch., 4*, 301–350.

Kohler, W. (1925). *The mentality of apes*. New York: Harcourt, Brace, & World.

Kohler, W. (1929). *Gestalt psychology*. New York: Liveright.

Koffka, K. (1935). *The principles of Gestalt psychology*. New York: Harcourt, Brace, & World.

Wertheimer, M. (1938). Laws of organization in perceptual forms. In W. Ellis (Ed.), *A sourcebook of Gestalt psychology*. London: Paul, Trench, Trubner.

Arnheim, R. (1949). The Gestalt theory of expression. *Psy. Rev., 56*, 156–171.

Osgood, C. (1953). *Method and theory in experimental psychology*. New York: Oxford University Press.

Allport, F. (1955). *Theories of perception and the concept of structure*. New York: Wiley.

Heider, R. (1970). Gestalt theory: Early history and reminiscences. *J. Hist. Beh. Sci., 6*, 131–139.

Bower, G., & Hilgard, E. (1981). *Theories of learning*. Englewood Cliffs, NJ: Prentice-Hall.

Restle, F. (1982). Coding theory as an integration of Gestalt psychology and information processing theory. In J. Beck (Ed.), *Organization and representation in perception*. Hillsdale, NJ: Erlbaum.

Wertheimer, M. (1982). Gestalt theory, holistic psychologies, and Max Wertheimer. *Z. Psy., 190*, 125–140.

Bruce, V., & Green, P. (1985). *Visual perception: Physiology, psychology, and ecology*. Hillsdale, NJ: Erlbaum.

Zusne, L. (1987). *Eponyms in psychology*. Westport, CT: Greenwood Press.

Wolman, B. (Ed.) (1989). *Dictionary of behavioral science*. San Diego: Academic Press.

Sutherland, S. (1996). *The international dictionary of psychology*. New York: Crossroad.

GIBSON EFFECT. See PERCEPTION (I. GENERAL), THEORIES OF.

GIBSON'S DIRECT PERCEPTION THEORY. See PERCEPTION (I. GENERAL), THEORIES OF.

GLUCOSTATIC THEORY. See HUNGER, THEORIES OF.

GOAL-SETTING THEORY. See ORGANIZATIONAL/INDUSTRIAL/SYSTEMS THEORY.

GOLDSTEIN'S ORGANISMIC THEORY. The German-American neuropsychiatrist Kurt Goldstein (1878–1965) was the leading exponent of *organismic* *theory*, even though there had been previous advocates (including writers and philosophers such as Aristotle, Goethe, Spinoza, and William James) of the *organismic* approach (i.e., treating the organism as a unified, organized whole rather than "atomizing" the individual into elementary particles of feelings, images, and sensations). The *holistic/organismic* viewpoint has appeared in studies in the fields of psychobiology (see Rennie, 1943), psychosomatics (Dunbar, 1954), developmental biology (Coghill, 1929), neurology (Jackson, 1931), physiology (Bernard, 1866/1957), philosophy (Smuts, 1926), and psychology (Dewey, 1896; Kantor, 1924; Murphy, 1947; Rogers, 1961). Organismic psychology may be regarded as the extension of Gestalt principles to the organism as a whole (Hall & Lindzey, 1978). The central features of *organismic theory*, as regards a theory of personality, are the following: an emphasis on the unity, consistency, coherence, and integration of the personality—where organization is normal, and disorganization is pathological; a belief that the organized system of the organism may be analyzed by differentiating the whole into its constituent membership parts—where the whole organism functions according to laws that cannot be found in study of the isolated parts separately; an assumption that the person is motivated by sovereign drive ("self-actualization/realization") rather than by a plurality of drives—where a singleness of purpose gives direction to the person's life; a tendency to stress the inherent potentialities of the organism for growth—where the influence of the external environment on normal development is minimized; and a belief in the advantages of studying comprehensively one individual rather than studying one isolated psychological function in many persons. The primary organization of organismic functioning, according to *Goldstein's* (1939) *theory*, is that of *figure* (any foreground process or conscious action that emerges and stands out as a contour against a background surface) and *ground* (the continuous, often unconscious, background or surrounding environment). Goldstein distinguished between different kinds of structural behavior: *performances*—consciously experienced, voluntary activities; *attitudes*—inner experiences such as moods and feelings; *processes*—indirect experiencing of bodily functions; *concrete behavior*—automatically responding to a stimulus; and *abstract behavior*—the organism acting upon a stimulus after cognitively considering it. Goldstein (1939) described the dynamics of the organism by developing the concepts of *equalization*—an "average" state of tension in the organism that acts as the "center" of the individual; the *principle of equalization*—explains the orderliness, coherence, and consistency of behavior; *self-actualization/self-realization*—the predominant motive that an organism possesses whereby all other drives, such as power, sex, hunger, and curiosity, are merely subordinate entities; self-actualization is the fulfillment and replenishment of one's needs; and *coming to terms* with the environment—the interaction between the organism and the environment where the person attempts to master the challenges of the environment, such as overcoming the physical and psychological threats and pressures that jeopardize one's drive toward self-actualization. If the discrepancy between the organism's goals and the realities of the environment becomes too great, the person either breaks down or makes compromises whereby some lower level of functioning is accepted for self-actualization. Many of Goldstein's theoretical notions were applied in his treatment and study of the behavior patterns/symptoms of brain-damaged persons (Goldstein, 1942). He and his colleagues also developed a number of psychological tests for diagnosing the degree of impairment in an individual's ability to abstract things about the environment, to plan ahead, and to think in symbolic terms (e.g., Goldstein & Scheerer, 1953). A critical analysis of Goldstein's concepts of abstract and concrete behavior was made by Pikas (1966). One charge that has been made against *Goldstein's theory* is that it is not sufficiently "holistic" (cf: Hunt, 1940, and the *organismic paradox*—the organismic theorist denies the validity of partitive concepts yet is forced to use them) where it treats the organism as a segregated unit that is set apart from the rest of the world (Hall & Lindzey, 1978). Other critiques of *Goldstein's theory* are provided by Katsoff (1942), who claimed that Goldstein did not distinguish adequately between what is inherent in the organism versus what is culturally determined, and Skinner (1940), who suggested that Goldstein's main concept of *self-actualization* is too metaphysical in character and not open to experimental testing. See also ANGYAL'S PERSONALITY THEORY; MURPHY'S BIO-SOCIAL THEORY; PERSONALITY THEORIES; REFLEX ARC THEORY/CONCEPT; ROGERS' THEORY OF PERSONALITY.

REFERENCES

Bernard, C. (1866/1957). *An introduction to the study of experimental medicine*. New York: Dover.

Dewey, J. (1896). The reflex arc concept in psychology. *Psy. Rev., 3*, 357–370.

Gelb, A., & Goldstein, K. (1920). *Psychologische Analysen hirnpathologischer Faelle*. Leipzig: Barth.

Kantor, J. R. (1924). *Principles of psychology*. New York: Knopf.

Smuts, J. (1926). *Holism and evolution*. New York: Macmillan.

Coghill, G. (1929). *Anatomy and the problem of behavior*. London: Cambridge University Press.

Jackson, J. H. (1931). *Selected writings of John Hughlings Jackson*. London: Hodder & Stoughton.

Goldstein, K. (1939). *The organism*. New York: American Book.

Hunt, W. (1940). Review of K. Goldstein's *The organism. Psy. Bull., 37*, 637–639.

Skinner, B. F. (1940). Review of K. Goldstein's *The organism. J. Abn. Soc. Psy., 35*, 462–465.

Goldstein, K. (1942). *After-effects of brain injuries in war*. New York: Grune & Stratton.

Katsoff, L. (1942). Review of K. Goldstein's *Human nature in the light of psychotherapy. J. Gen. Psy., 26*, 187–194.

Rennie, T. (1943). Adolf Meyer and psychobiology: The man, his methodology, and its relation to therapy. *Pap. Amer. Congr. Gen Semant., 2*, 156–165.

Murphy, G. (1947). *Personality: A biosocial approach to origins and structure*. New York: Harper & Row.

Goldstein, K., & Scheerer, M. (1953). Tests of abstract and concrete thinking. In A.

Weider (Ed.), *Contributions toward medical psychology*. New York: Ronald Press.

Dunbar, H. F. (1954). *Emotions and bodily change*. New York: Columbia University Press.

Rogers, C. (1961). *On becoming a person*. Boston: Houghton Mifflin.

Pikas, A. (1966). *Abstraction and concept formation*. Cambridge: Harvard University Press.

Hall, C., & Lindzey, G. (1978). *Theories of personality*. New York: Wiley.

GOOD CONTINUATION, PRINCIPLE OF. See GESTALT THEORY/ LAWS.

GRACEFUL DEGRADATION, PRINCIPLE OF. See INFORMATION/ INFORMATION-PROCESSING THEORY.

GRANIT–HARPER LAW. See GRANIT'S COLOR VISION THEORY.

GRANIT'S COLOR VISION THEORY. The viewpoint exemplified by Granit's (1943, 1945a, b, 1955) research in color vision has been characterized as *theory-neutral* and not so much of a theory as an approach that has established some limiting conditions for any good *theory of color vision* (Graham, 1965). Some aspects of Granit's research might be interpretable in a context of *trichromatic theory* (e.g., *Young–Helmholtz theory*), while other aspects may be taken within a context of *opponent-colors theory* (e.g., *Hering–Hurvich-Jameson theory*). Granit recorded the electrical reactions via microelectrodes in single and grouped optic nerve fibers and ganglion cells in the retinas of different animals when stimulated by lights of different wavelengths. Granit presented "scotopic dominator curves" (giving rod sensitivity), "photopic dominator curves" (giving cone sensitivity), and "modulator curves" based on wavelength stimulation of the retinas of various animals, including snakes (which have cone receptors only), frogs, cats, pigeons, fish, and tortoises. Granit (1947) asserts that the photopic dominator curve may be attributed to the combined activity of several modulator curves and where, at a more complex level, photopic visibility and hue discrimination may be explained by various modulator combinations. Also, according to Granit, it is likely that the photopic and scotopic dominators (which demonstrate the *Purkinje effect* between them) are responsible for the average spectral distributions of photopic and scotopic luminances. Thus, the photopic dominator can be considered as corresponding to the *Hering–Hurvich–Jameson* achromatic black-white process, and the modulators considered as cue-providers for wavelength discriminations. Granit (1947) describes various mechanisms of color blindness as well as the relationships of the scotopic-dominator, photopic-dominator, and modulator theory to the data of color vision, and indicates how modulators may combine to yield the human photopic luminosity curve (cf: the *Granit–Harper law*, formulated in 1930, which is the generalization that critical fusion frequency and the logarithm of the areas of the stimulus are linearly related over a luminance range of 1,000 to 1 and circular stimulus areas ranging from 0.98 to 5.0 degrees in diameter for retinal locations up to 10 degrees away from the fovea; Zusne, 1987). Bartley (1951) discusses hypotheses that are related to Granit's work, called the *polychromatic hypothesis* of Granit and Hartridge and the *cluster hypothesis* of Hartridge. See also COLOR VISION, THEORIES/LAWS OF; HERING–HURVICH–JAMESON COLOR VISION THEORY; PURKINJE EFFECT/PHENOMENON/ SHIFT; YOUNG–HELMHOLTZ COLOR VISION THEORY.

REFERENCES

Granit, R. (1933). The components of the retinal action potentials in mammals and their relation to the discharge in the optic nerve. *J. Physio., 77,* 207–239.
Granit, R. (1943). A physiological theory of colour perception. *Nature, 151,* 11–14.
Granit, R. (1945a). The color receptors of the mammalian retina. *J. Neurophysio., 8,* 195–210.
Granit, R. (1945b). The electrophysiological analysis of the fundamental problem of colour reception. *Proc. Phy. Soc. Lon., 57,* 447–463.
Granit, R. (1947). *Sensory mechanisms of the retina.* New York: Oxford University Press.
Hartridge, H. (1948). Recent advances in color vision. *Science, 108,* 395–404.
Hartridge, H. (1950). *Recent advances in the physiology of vision.* London: Churchill.
Bartley, S. (1951). The psychophysiology of vision. In S. S. Stevens (Ed.), *Handbk. Exp. Psy.* New York: Wiley.
Granit, R. (1955). *Receptors and sensory perception.* New Haven, CT: Yale University Press.
Granit, R. (1962). The visual pathway. In H. Davson (Ed.), *The eye.* New York: Academic Press.
Graham, C. (1965). Color: Data and theories. In C. Graham (Ed.), *Vision and visual perception.* New York: Wiley.
Zusne, L. (1987). *Eponyms in psychology.* Westport, CT: Greenwood Press.

GRASSMANN'S LAWS. This is a set of principles concerning the normal visual system that was summarized by the German scientist H. G. Grassmann (1853, 1854) and was foreshadowed by Isaac Newton's (1642–1727) *laws of color mixture.* The basic assumption of *Grassmann's laws* is that if a light composed of known amounts of three primary color components is equivalent in color to another light, the three known amounts may be used as a color specification for this light. Such amounts are called *tristimulus* values of the color. *Grassmann's laws* (Judd, 1951) state that (1) when equivalent lights are added to equivalent lights, the sums are also equivalent; (2) when equivalent lights are subtracted from equivalent lights, the differences are also equivalent; and (3) lights equivalent to the same light are equivalent to each other. Thus, *Grassmann's laws* indicate relationships among three primary colors that follow algebra-like rules under conditions where a person matches colors by adjusting the amounts of each of the three primary colors needed to match perceptually ("subjective equivalence") a test color. The term *color equation* describes the conditions and results of such a color-matching task. The principles expressed in *Grassmann's laws* have been established by numerous experiments conducted over a wide range of retinal illuminance (e.g., Hering, 1885) for all kinds of vision, both normal and abnormal. However, the principles tend to weaken for very high retinal illuminance (Wright, 1936) and for illuminance conditions of 10 minutes or more where retinal rod vision is initiated (Konig, 1887; Ladd-Franklin, 1929). Between these two extremes, *Grassmann's laws* hold independent of the particular adaptive state of the viewer's eye. See also COLOR MIXTURE, LAWS/THEORY OF; COLOR VISION, THEORIES OF; NEWTON'S LAWS/PRINCIPLES OF COLOR MIXTURE.

REFERENCES

Grassmann, H. (1853). Zur Theorie der Farbenmischung. *Pogg. Ann. Physik, 89*, 69.

Grassmann, H. (1854). On the theory of compound colours. *Phil. Mag., 7*, 254–264.

Hering, E. (1885). *Uber individuelle Verschiedenheiten des Farbensinnes*. Prague: Lotos.

Konig, A. (1887). Uber Newtons Gesetz der Farbenmischung und darauf bezugliche Versuch des Hrn. Eugen Brodhun. *Sitzber. Akad. Wiss. Berlin*, Mar. 31, p. 311.

Ladd-Franklin, C. (1929). *Colour and colour theories*. New York: Harcourt, Brace.

Wright, W. (1936). The breakdown of a colour match with high intensities of adaptation. *J. Physio., 87*, 23.

Judd, D. (1951). Basic correlates of the visual system. In S. S. Stevens (Ed.), *Handbk. Exp. Psy.* New York: Wiley.

GREAT MAN/GREAT PERSON THEORY. See LEADERSHIP, THEORIES OF; NATURALISTIC THEORY OF HISTORY.

GREAT MAN/GREAT WOMAN THEORY OF LEADERSHIP. See LEADERSHIP, THEORIES OF.

GREENSPOON EFFECT. The American psychologist Joel Greenspoon (1921–   ) conducted studies that indicate that verbal *awareness* of the learning situation or of the new responses is not a necessity for behavior to be altered. In the experimental condition showing the *Greenspoon effect*, participants were asked to say all the words they could think of in 50 minutes. The experimenter sat behind the individuals and uttered "mmm-hmm" (an assenting murmur) every time a plural noun was spoken. With other participants, the experimenter murmured "huh-uh" (dissenting) when plural nouns were spoken. Most of the individuals were unable to see any connection between the behavior of the experimenter and the words they were saying. Nevertheless, "mmm-hmm" increased the number of plural nouns that were said, and "huh-uh" decreased the number of plural nouns (Greenspoon, 1955, 1963; cf: Spielberger & DeNike, 1962, 1963). The *Greenspoon effect* has been taken by some, particularly behaviorists (e.g., Skinner, 1957; Verhave, 1966), as evidence that language can be brought under operant control and, by extension, as evidence that language learning takes place through a process of social reinforcement (Reber, 1995). The verbal conditioning paradigm seems to provide a valuable tool and method for bridging the gap between the clinical psychologist and the general-experimental psychologist. However, more basic research in verbal conditioning needs to be conducted (see Greenspoon, 1962; Holz & Azrin, 1966). See also CHOMSKY'S PSYCHOLINGUISTIC THEORY; SKINNER'S DESCRIPTIVE BEHAVIOR/OPERANT CONDITIONING THEORY.

REFERENCES

Greenspoon, J. (1955). The reinforcing effect of two spoken sounds on the frequency of two responses. *Amer. J. Psy., 68*, 409–416.

Mandler, G., & Kaplan, W. (1956). Subjective evaluation and reinforcing effect of a verbal stimulus. *Science, 124*, 582–583.

Skinner, B. F. (1957). *Verbal behavior*. New York: Appleton-Century-Crofts.

Krasner, L. (1958). Studies of the conditioning of verbal behavior. *Psy. Bull., 15*, 148–171.

Salzinger, K. (1959). Experimental manipulation of verbal behavior: A review. *J. Genet. Psy., 61*, 65–95.

Greenspoon, J. (1962). Verbal conditioning and clinical psychology. In A. J. Bachrach (Ed.), *Experimental foundations of clinical psychology*. New York: Basic Books.

Spielberger, C., & DeNike, L. (1962). Operant conditioning of plural nouns: A failure to replicate the Greenspoon effect. *Psy. Rep., 11*, 355–366.

Greenspoon, J. (1963). Reply to Spielberger and DeNike: Operant conditioning of plural nouns: A failure to replicate the Greenspoon effect. *Psy. Rep., 12*, 29–30.

Spielberger, C., & DeNike, L. (1963). Implicit epistemological bias and the problem of awareness in verbal conditioning: A reply to Greenspoon. *Psy. Rep., 12*, 103–106.

Holz, W., & Azrin, N. (1966). Conditioning human verbal behavior. In W. Honig (Ed.), *Operant behavior: Areas of research and application*. New York: Appleton-Century-Crofts.

Verhave, T. (1966). *The experimental analysis of behavior: Selected readings*. New York: Appleton-Century-Crofts.

Reber, A. (1995). *The Penguin dictionary of psychology*. New York: Penguin Books.

GROOS' THEORY OF PLAY. See PLAY, THEORIES OF.

GROUPTHINK PHENOMENON. See DECISION-MAKING THEORIES.

GUILFORD'S STRUCTURE-OF-INTELLECT MODEL/THEORY. See INTELLIGENCE, THEORIES/LAWS OF.

GUSTATION/TASTE, THEORIES OF. In terms of *evolutionary theory*, when life moved from sea to land, the undifferentiated chemical receptor systems of *taste* and *smell* became differentiated and began to serve different functions where the *taste* system served as a ''close-up'' sense that provided the last check on the acceptability of food, and *smell* served as a useful "distance" sense, although it also retained an important function in dealing with food (Coren & Ward, 1989; Rozin, 1982). The physical stimuli for the taste system are substances that can be dissolved in water, and, as is common for physical stimuli, the amount of a chemical substance present is related to the intensity of the experienced taste (cf: Baradi & Bourne's, 1951, *enzyme theory of taste*). However, which properties result in the various different taste qualities is still unknown in detail, even though there are several guesses, such as the size of the substances' individual molecules, how the molecule breaks apart when dissolved in water, or how molecules interact with cell membranes. Complete agreement on the basic dimensions of taste is still lacking (Erickson, 1985; cf: Boring, Langfeld, & Weld's, 1939, references to various *laws of taste* such as "fusion," "compensation," "adaptation," "successive contrast," and "sensitivity"), but there does seem to be general agreement on at least four primary *taste qualities* (cf: Henning's, 1916, *taste theory/taste pyramid*): sweet, salty, sour, and bitter (Bartoshuk, 1974, suggests a fifth quality: that of water). When considering the question of how taste quality is neurally encoded, it was originally thought that there would be different receptors for different taste qualities. However, most receptor cells seem to respond to all four of the basic kinds of taste stimuli but at different rates (e.g., Arvidson & Friberg, 1980). One *theory of taste*, called the *across-fiber pattern theory* (Pfaffmann, 1955; Erickson, 1985), holds that if the condition of various neural units having different stimulus-specific response rates is met, then the code for taste quality could be an *across-fiber pattern* of neural activity. According to this theory, unique taste fibers respond in a different pattern to each taste quality, even though all of the fibers respond to all taste inputs to some extent. Another *theory of taste quality encoding*, called the *labeled-line theory* (Pfaffmann, 1974), suggests that each taste fiber encodes the intensity of a single basic taste quality. This theory states that to the extent that a stimulus activates the "sweet" fibers, for example, it tastes sweet, and to the extent it activates the "bitter" fibers, it tastes bitter. The theory also suggests that "simple" stimuli could have a complex taste if they activate several types of fiber. The *labeled-line theory* is compatible with the *across-fiber pattern theory* except that in the former the code for taste quality is a profile across a few fiber types rather than a pattern across many thousands of unique fibers (cf: Scott, 1987). Different gustatory fibers seem to be "tuned" to certain taste stimuli, much as auditory nerve fibers are tuned to certain sound frequencies. Such fibers respond most intensely to their "best" substances and less intensely to others. In the future, it may be possible to classify such *taste fibers* into a few classes, corresponding to the basic *taste qualities* (cf: Pfaffmann, Frank, & Norgren, 1979). While it is unknown at present whether *labeled-lines* exist along the entire taste pathway, cortical neurons most responsive to the four basic tastes seem to be localized in different parts of the taste cortex (Yamamoto, Yayama, & Kawamura, 1981). Also, it is likely that some recoding of the taste information takes place in the cortex, where specific cortical cells give an "on" or "off" response to different taste stimuli, much like the feature-specific cells in the visual cortex (e.g., Funakoshi, Kasahara, Yamamoto, & Kawamura, 1972). See also GARCIA EFFECT; OLFACTION/SMELL, THEORIES OF.

REFERENCES

Henning, H. (1916). Die Qualitatenreihe des Geschmaks. Z. Psy., 74, 203–219.

Boring, E. G., Langfeld, H., & Weld, H. (1939). Introduction to psychology. New York: Wiley.

Beebe-Center, J., & Waddell, D. (1948). A general psychological scale of taste. J. Psy., 26, 517–524.

Lewis, D. (1948). Psychological scales of taste. J. Psy., 26, 437–446.

Baradi, A., & Bourne, G. (1951). Localization of gustatory and olfactory enzymes in the rabbit, and the problems of taste and smell. Nature, 168, 977–979.

Pfaffmann, C. (1951). Taste and smell. In S. S. Stevens (Ed.), Handbk. Exp. Psy. New York: Wiley.

Pfaffmann, C. (1955). Gustatory nerve impulses in rat, cat, and rabbit. J. Neurophysio., 18, 429–440.

Pfaffmann, C. (1965). De gustibus. Amer. Psy., 20, 21–33.

von Bekesy, G. (1966). Taste theories and the chemical stimulation of single papillae. J. App. Physio., 21, 1–9.

Schiffman, S., & Erikson, R. (1971). A theoretical review: A psychophysical model for gustatory quality. Physio. & Beh., 1, 617–633.

Funakoshi, M., Kasahara, Y., Yamamoto, T., & Kawamura, Y. (1972). Taste coding and central perception. In D. Schneider (Ed.), Olfaction and taste IV. Stuttgart: Wissenshaftliche Verlagsgesellschaft MBH.

Bartoshuk, L. (1974). NaCl thresholds in man: Thresholds for water taste or NaCl taste? J. Comp. Physio. Psy., 87, 310–325.

Pfaffmann, C. (1974). Specificity of the sweet receptors of the squirrel monkey. Chemical Senses and Flavor, 1, 61–67.

Pfaffmann, C., Frank, M., & Norgren, R. (1979). Neural mechanisms and behavioral aspects of taste. Ann. Rev. Psy., 30, 283–325.

Arvidson, K., & Friberg, U. (1980). Human taste response and taste bud number in fungiform papillae. Science, 209, 807–808.

Yamamoto, T., Yayama, N., & Kawamura, Y. (1981). Central processing of taste perception. In Y. Katsuki, R. Norgren, & M. Sato (Eds.), Brain mechanisms of sensation. New York: Wiley.

Rozin, P. (1982). "Taste-smell confusions" and the duality of the olfactory sense. Perc. & Psychophys., 31, 397–401.

Erickson, R. (1985). Definitions: A matter of taste. In D. Pfaff (Ed.), Taste, olfaction, and the central nervous system. New York: Rockefeller University Press.

Scott, T. (1987). Coding in the gustatory system. In T. Finger & W. Silver (Eds.), Neurobiology of taste and smell. New York: Wiley.

Coren, S., & Ward, L. (1989). Sensation and perception. New York: Harcourt Brace Jovanovich.

GUTHRIE'S THEORY OF BEHAVIOR. The American behaviorist/psychologist Edwin Ray Guthrie (1886–1959) formulated an objective stimulus–response association psychology system ("contiguous conditioning"). Guthrie's one primary law of association or learning was devised around the contiguity (nearness) of cue and response; that is, "a combination of stimuli which was accompanied by a movement will on its recurrence tend to be followed by that movement" (Guthrie, 1935, p. 26). In Guthrie's approach, E. L. Thorndike's concept of *associative shifting* (i.e., the shifting of a response to one stimulus onto another stimulus paired with it) was a central feature of his *behavior theory* (Guthrie did not accept, however, the more prominent *law of effect* as stated by Thorndike; cf: Guthrie, 1940). Guthrie's major emphasis on the single *principle of associative/contiguity learning* also separated him theoretically from Pavlov and the principles/procedures of classical conditioning. Pavlov criticized Guthrie for his solitary focus on the contiguity concept without concern for the many complexities of conditioning (Pavlov, 1932; cf: Guthrie, 1934). Guthrie (1935) explained the phenomena of *extinction* and *forgetting* (weakening of behaviors) through the process of associative competition or interference where the learning of a different and incompatible response to the initial stimulus situation occurred. He suggested three methods that contribute to the weakening of behaviors: the toleration method, the exhaustion (flooding) method, and the method of counterconditioning; cf: the modern technique of *systematic desensitization* (Wolpe, 1958), which is based on Guthrie's earlier methods. In *Guthrie's theory*, motives acted to provide "maintaining stimuli" to keep the organism active until a goal is reached, and conduct is organized into sequences in which the individual makes plans and carries them out. Guthrie followed the lead of Sherrington (1906) and Woodworth (1918) in considering sequences of behavior as composed of preparatory responses followed by consummatory responses where these "anticipatory responses" were conditioned to maintaining stimuli. Reward, according to Guthrie, is a secondary principle and is effective because it removes the organism from the stimulating situation in which the "correct" response has been made. Reward does not strengthen the correct response but prevents its weakening because no new response can become attached to the cues that led to the correct response. The effects of punishment for learning are determined by what it causes the organism to do and suggests the principle that the best predictor of learning is the response that *last* occurred in the situation (cf: *postremity principle*—Guthrie's notion that the organism always does what it *last* did in a given stimulus situation; Sutherland, 1996). When learning transfers to new situations, it is because of the common elements within the old and new, and when forgetting occurs, it is due to the learning of new responses that replace the old responses. Criticisms of *Guthrie's learning theory* include an uneasiness by some psychologists concerning Guthrie's assured answers to all the problems of learning, where "either the theory is miraculously inspired or it is not stated very precisely, and hence is not very sensitive to experimental data" (Bower & Hilgard, 1981, p. 93). In addition, critics have suggested that the simplicity of *Guthrie's theory* may be illusory, and that "many reviews of Guthrie in the literature have probably mistaken incompleteness for simplicity" (see O'Connor, 1946; Sheffield, 1949; Mueller & Schoenfeld, 1954). Guthrie was at heart an associationist with a strong behavioristic bias (e.g., in attempting to get rid of subjective terms, he referred to "inner speech" and "movement-produced stimuli" instead of "thinking"). According to Bower and Hilgard (1981), while the associationist tradition will doubtless continue on, Guthrie's particular version of it seems to have lost its appeal to succeeding generations. See also ASSOCIATIVE SHIFTING, LAW OF; LEARNING THEORIES/LAWS; THORNDIKE'S LAW OF EFFECT.

REFERENCES

Sherrington, C. (1906). *The integrative action of the nervous system.* New Haven, CT: Yale University Press.

Woodworth, R. (1918). *Dynamic psychology.* New York: Columbia University Press.

Guthrie, E. (1930). Conditioning as a principle of learning. *Psy. Rev., 37,* 412–428.

Pavlov, I. (1932). The reply of a physiologist to a psychologist. *Psy. Rev., 39,* 91–127.

Guthrie, E. (1934). Pavlov's theory of conditioning. *Psy. Rev., 41,* 199–206.

Guthrie, E. (1935). *The psychology of learning.* New York: Harper & Row.

Guthrie, E. (1940). Association and the law of effect. *Psy. Rev., 47,* 127–148.

Seward, J. (1942). An experimental study of Guthrie's theory of reinforcement. *J. Exp. Psy., 30,* 247–256.

O'Connor, V. (1946). Recency or effect? A critical analysis of Guthrie's theory of learning. *Harv. Ed. Rev., 16,* 194–206.

Sheffield, F. (1949). Hilgard's critique of Guthrie. *Psy. Rev., 56,* 284–291.

Mueller, C., & Schoenfeld, W. (1954). Edwin R. Guthrie. In W. Estes, S. Koch, K. MacCorquodale, P. Meehl, C. Mueller, W. Schoenfeld, and W. Verplanck. *Modern learning theory.* New York: Appleton-Century-Crofts.

Wolpe, J. (1958). *Psychotherapy by reciprocal inhibition.* Stanford, CA: Stanford University Press.

Bower, G., & Hilgard, E. (1981). *Theories of learning.* Englewood Cliffs, NJ: Prentice-Hall.

Sutherland, S. (1996). *The international dictionary of psychology.* New York: Crossroad.

H

HABIT/HABIT FORMATION, LAWS/PRINCIPLES OF. The *principle of habit* may be defined as any instrumentally learned response that occurs with regularity and occurs in response to specific environmental events. In some cases, the *habit* is connected to a number of frequently occurring stimuli while, in other cases, *habits* may be connected to stimuli that infrequently occur (Pettijohn, 1986). The concept of *habit/habit formation* has a long history in psychology (Aristotle considered *habit* to be of basic importance in the development of one's morality; Warren, 1934), where it originally referred only to motor or physical patterns of behavior (e.g., James, 1890; Baldwin, 1894), and has appeared most recently in the *learning theories* of Hull (1943, 1952) and Spence (1956, 1960) as a central term in their approaches where *habit* ("response tendency") interacts with *drive* to produce behavior and where learning was considered to be the organization and accumulation of response habits. However, currently, the concept of *habit* has been given less attention because most psychologists today acknowledge that it is better defined in terms of operational definitions, processes of acquisition, and generalization as well as other factors that directly influence *habits*, especially the role of various environmental cues in *habit formation*. When *habit* is defined within the context of personality psychology, it refers to a pattern of activity that has, through repetition, become fixed, automatic, and easily carried out. In this case, *habit* is close in meaning to the concept of *trait* (i.e., any enduring characteristic of an individual that may serve in the role of a theoretical entity as an explanation for the observed regularities/consistencies in behavior; Reber, 1995). When *habit* is defined within the area of ethology (i.e., the study of animal behavior), it usually refers to a pattern of action that is characteristic of a particular species of animal and where an innate or species-specific behavior pattern is implied (as opposed to a "learned" behavior). The term *habit formation* has presented some semantic problems, historically, where it has often been used as a synonym for *learning*, but today most psychologists would avoid such an equivalency and insist, instead, that all learning is not merely the formation of habits. Also, the term *formation* is ambiguous because it may apply to the actual acquisition of a new habit or the novel use of a previously acquired habit (Reber, 1995). Thus, the *principle of habit* has served historically as a generally useful (e.g., leading to fruitful experimental hypotheses and theories) and ubiquitous (i.e., covers a wide range of disciplines) concept throughout the development of the social and behavioral sciences, perhaps coming close to the overall influence and utility of other omnibus terms such as *adaptation, assimilation, association, accommodation, activation,* and *contiguity.* See also ADAPTATION, PRINCIPLES/ LAWS OF; HULL'S LEARNING THEORY; LEARNING THEORIES/LAWS; SPENCE'S THEORY.

REFERENCES

James, W. (1890). *Principles of psychology.* New York: Holt.
Baldwin, J. (1894). *Handbook of psychology.* New York: Holt.
Warren, H. (Ed.) (1934). *Dictionary of psychology.* Cambridge, MA: Houghton Mifflin.
Hull, C. (1943). *Principles of behavior.* New York: Appleton-Century-Crofts.
Hull, C. (1952). *A behavior system: An introduction to behavior theory concerning the individual organism.* New Haven, CT: Yale University Press.
Spence, K. (1956). *Behavior theory and conditioning.* New Haven, CT: Yale University Press.
Spence, K. (1960). *Behavior theory and learning.* Englewood Cliffs, NJ: Prentice-Hall.
Pettijohn T. (Ed.) (1986). *The encyclopedic dictionary of psychology.* Guilford, CT: Dushkin.
Reber, A. (1995). *The Penguin dictionary of psychology.* New York: Penguin Books.

HABITUATION, PRINCIPLE/LAW OF. The *principle of habituation* refers to the elimination of a response as a result of a continuous exposure to the stimulus that originally elicited the response. Another term for *habituation* is *negative adaptation* (Humphrey, 1930). The concept of *habituation* has been used to refer both to an empirical result and to a hypothetical construct, depending on the context, character, and depth of its study (Riopelle, 1994). Factors such as injury, fatigue, adaptation, and drugs are not usually included under *habituation,* even though these variables may produce a decline in responsiveness. An example of *habituation* is the *orienting reflex response,* which is an attentional response of an organism that functions to put it into a physical position or orientation whereby it is exposed optimally to the source of stimulation, such as a strange noise that alarms an animal, which then stops whatever it was doing, becomes motionless, and scans its surroundings in search of the sound source. After a few seconds, if there is no danger, the animal resumes its initial activity. If similar noises are made subsequently, and again no danger is present, the animal makes progressively weaker and shorter alerting responses whereupon *habituation* is said to have occurred to those types of noises. Distinctions have been made among the terms *specific habituation, general habit-*

uation, and *acclimatization/acclimation* (Riopelle, 1994). *Specific habituation* is the localization or restriction of a habitual response to a particular area or part of the body. *General habituation* is the change in the mental psychological *set* that results in a generalized reduction in response to a repeated stimulus. The term *acclimatization* refers to the compensation that results over a period of time (days or weeks) in response to a complex of changes, and *acclimation* is the same type of adjustment but, in this case, only to a simple, or single, environmental condition. The following characteristics have been associated with *habituation* (Hilgard & Bower, 1966; Riopelle, 1994): (1) spontaneous recovery of an originally strong response will occur after a long enough absence of stimulation; (2) habituation is faster when the evoking stimulus is given more frequently and regularly; (3) habituation is slower when the eliciting stimulus is stronger, and near-threshold stimuli may not habituate; (4) habituation is prolonged and spontaneous recovery is delayed when additional stimulation is given beyond the level that completely abolishes the original habituated response; (5) habituation may generalize its effects to other, similar stimuli; (6) "dishabituation" or restoration of an original response may occur when a stimulus is presented that is stronger (or, sometimes, weaker) than is customarily given; (7) habituation will not occur if the eliciting stimulus is converted through conditioning into a signal of biological importance (such as pairing a click with a painful shock or with food). Various models have been proposed to explain the nature of the neural mechanisms involved in *short-term habituation*. For example, the *synaptic depression model* states that sensory input energizes the small interneurons located in the periphery of the brain stem reticular formation (BSRF), and, assuming that *synaptic depression* occurs in this region, these neurons then activate the neurons in the BSRF core, which then lead to cortical arousal (in higher-order mammals). Another model of habituation, called the *match-mismatch model* (Sokolov, 1963), states that a stimulus elicits a neural representation ("engram") of itself in higher-order mammals that is relatively permanent and where the neural consequences of subsequent stimuli are compared with the representation of the original alerting stimulus. In this case, if there is a match between the subsequent stimuli and the original stimulus, then no BSRF arousal occurs, and the result is *habituation*. The term *sensitization* is distinguished from *habituation* where *sensitization* refers to an *initial* increase in the habituated response after a stimulus has been repeatedly presented, and where the alerting response has first increased and then decreased (Thompson & Spencer, 1966). The concept of *sensitization* has led to a good deal of empirical and theoretical controversy regarding the equivalence of responses in different species, in the parts of the nervous system involved, and in the time frames for the *sensitization* and *habituation* processes (Riopelle, 1994). The *principle of habituation* within the context of neurophysiological research is being actively and vigorously pursued (Hilgard & Bower, 1966). See also ADAPTATION, PRINCIPLES/LAWS OF; ATTENTION, LAWS/PRINCIPLES/THEORIES OF; DENERVATION, LAW OF; HABIT/HABIT FORMATION,

LAWS/PRINCIPLES OF; MIND/MENTAL SET, LAW OF; VIGILANCE, THEORIES OF.

REFERENCES

Dodge, R. (1923). Habituation to rotation. *J. Exp. Psy., 6*, 1–35.
Humphrey, G. (1930). Extinction and negative adaptation. *Psy. Rev., 37*, 361–363.
Sharpless, S., & Jasper, H. (1956). Habituation of the arousal reaction. *Brain, 79*, 655–680.
Sokolov, E. (1963). Higher neuron functions: The orienting reflex. *Ann. Rev. Physio., 25*, 545–580.
Hilgard, E., & Bower, G. (1966). *Theories of learning.* New York: Appleton-Century-Crofts.
Thompson, R., & Spencer, W. (1966). Habituation: A model phenomenon for the study of neuronal substrates of behavior. *Psy. Rev., 173*, 16–43.
Mackworth, J. (1968). Vigilance, arousal, and habituation. *Psy. Rev., 75*, 308–322.
Groves, P., & Thompson, R. (1970). Habituation: A dual process theory. *Psy. Rev., 77*, 419–450.
Riopelle, A. (1994). Habituation. In R. J. Corsini (Ed.), *Ency. Psy.* New York: Wiley.

HALO EFFECT. This phenomenon refers to the tendency to evaluate an individual high on many other traits because of a belief that the individual is high on one particular trait; that is, the rated trait seems to "spill over" onto other traits. The *halo effect* most often emerges as a bias on personal rating scales (Warren, 1934; Reber, 1995) but may also appear in the classroom (e.g., Nash, 1976). The effect was first supported empirically by Thorndike (1920). The *halo effect* is detrimental to rating systems because it masks the presence of individual variability across different rating scales. Many suggestions have been offered to cope with the effect. For example, rating all people on one trait before going on to the next, varying the anchors of the scale, pooling raters with equal knowledge, and giving intensive training to the raters (this technique seems to be the most effective). Related closely to the *halo effect* is the concept of the *devil effect* (or *reverse halo effect*), where a rater evaluates an individual low on many traits because of a belief that the person is low on one trait that is assumed to be critical. The *halo effect* and the *devil effect* usually increase to the degree that the rated characteristic is vague or difficult to measure (Berger, 1994). See also EXPERIMENTER EFFECTS; PYGMALION EFFECT.

REFERENCES

Thorndike, E. (1920). A constant error on psychological ratings. *J. App. Psy., 4*, 25–29.
Warren, H. (Ed.) (1934). *Dictionary of psychology.* Cambridge, MA: Houghton Mifflin.
Nash, R. (1976). *Teacher expectations and pupil learning.* London: Routledge & Kegan Paul.
Berger, L. (1994). Halo effect. In R. J. Corsini (Ed.), *Ency. Psy.* New York: Wiley.
Reber, A. (1995). *The Penguin dictionary of psychology.* New York: Penguin Books.

HAMILTON'S HYPOTHESIS OF SPACE. See BERKELEY'S THEORY OF VISUAL SPACE PERCEPTION.

HAMILTON'S PRINCIPLE OF LEAST ACTION/LAW OF LEAST RESISTANCE. See GESTALT THEORY/LAWS.

HARVEY'S PRINCIPLE. See VISION/SIGHT, THEORIES OF.

HAWTHORNE EFFECT. See EXPERIMENTER EFFECTS.

HEBB'S THEORY OF PERCEPTUAL LEARNING. See PERCEPTION (II. COMPARATIVE APPRAISAL), THEORIES OF.

HECHT'S COLOR VISION THEORY. Selig Hecht (1892–1947) carried out research in the areas of physical chemistry, physiology, and biophysics and studied, among other topics, the basic functioning of the eye, the sensitivity curve to different wavelengths under low-illumination viewing with the rods, and a hypothetico-deductive approach to the chemical breakdown and recombination in the rods and cones. Hecht's *color vision theory* (1930, 1931, 1932, 1937) is a mathematical account of the component physiological processes that intervene between visual data and a mathematical space and elaborates on the *line-element theory* of Helmholtz and Stiles. The theory assumes that there are three kinds of cones present in the retina and that in the fovea they exist in approximately equal numbers. The sensations that result from the action of the three types of cones are qualitatively specific and are described as blue, green, and red. Given a specific cone that contains a photosensitive substance whose spectral absorption is greater in the blue or in the green or in the red, and when the photosensitive substance is altered by light and initiates a nerve impulse, the nerve will register, respectively, as blue, green, or red in the brain. The type of *color vision theory* proposed by Hecht exhibited many desirable features; for example, it formulated mechanisms that offered many researchers a flexible basis for further exploration of visual processes. Certain aspects of color vision, however, could not be accounted for by *Hecht's theory*, such as the data generated by some studies of color blindness, as well as some of the data in the *two-color threshold* area of vision research (Graham, 1965). See also COLOR VISION, THEORIES/LAWS OF; HELMHOLTZ'S COLOR VISION THEORY; STILES' COLOR VISION THEORY.

REFERENCES

Hecht, S., & Williams, R. (1923). The visibility of monochromatic radiation and the absorption spectrum of visual purple. *J. Gen. Physio., 5*, 1–33.
Laurens, H., & Hamilton, W. (1923). The sensibility of the eye to differences in wavelength. *Amer. J. Physio., 65*, 547–568.

Hecht, S. (1928). On the binocular fusion of colors and its relation to theories of color vision. *Proc. Nat. Acad. Sci., 14,* 237–241.

Hecht, S. (1930). The development of Thomas Young's theory of color vision. *J. Opt. Soc. Amer., 20,* 231–270.

Hecht, S. (1931). The interrelations of various aspects of color vision. *J. Opt. Soc. Amer., 21,* 615–639.

Hecht, S. (1932). A quantitative formulation of colour vision. In *Report of a Joint Discussion on Vision, June 3, 1932, at the Imperial College of Science by the Physical and Optical Societies.* London: Physical Society.

Hecht, S. (1935). A theory of visual intensity discrimination. *J. Gen. Physio., 18,* 767–789.

Hecht, S. (1937). Rods, cones, and the chemical basis of vision. *Physio. Rev., 17,* 239–290.

Hecht, S., Shlaer, S., & Pirenne, M. (1942). Energy, quanta, and vision. *J. Gen. Physio., 25,* 819–840.

Hecht, S. (1944). Energy and vision. *Amer. Sci., 32,* 159–177.

Graham, C. (1965). Color: Data and theories. In C. Graham (Ed.), *Vision and visual perception.* New York: Wiley.

HEDONISM, THEORY/LAW OF. The ethical/philosophical *theory of hedonism* (the notion that pleasure is the ultimate goal) goes back to the Greek writings of Aristippus (435–360 B.C.) and Epicurus (341–270 B.C.). Aristippus developed the first coherent exposition of *hedonism*, which held pleasure to be the highest good, and virtue to be identical with the ability to enjoy. Epicurus defined philosophy as the art of making life happy and strictly subordinated metaphysics to ethics, naming pleasure as the highest and only good. Thus, ancient *hedonistic theory* was expressed in two ways: the cruder form proposed by Aristippus, who believed that pleasure was achieved by the complete gratification of all one's sensual desires, and the more refined form of Epicurus, who accepted the primacy of pleasure but equated it with the absence of pain and taught that it could best be attained through the rational control of one's desires. As a more modern *psychological theory, hedonism* is the assumption that individuals act so as to attain pleasant, and avoid unpleasant, feelings. *Motivational hedonic theory* states that people have tendencies to approach pleasure and to avoid pain. The English philosopher Jeremy Bentham (1748–1832) was one of the main proponents of the *motivation theory of hedonism,* which held that human activity arose out of a desire to avoid pain and to seek pleasure. Bentham (1789, 1798) defined principles of utility, happiness, good, and pleasure and proposed that the object of legislation should be the general happiness of the majority of people. The influence of Bentham's philosophy of *hedonism* and utility was widespread: it affected the writings of John Stuart Mill (1806–1873) and Herbert Spencer (1820–1903); Christian theologians emphasized the pleasures of heaven and the pain of hell; Sigmund Freud (1856–1939) described the *pleasure principle* as activity of the unconscious *id*; Edward Thorndike (1874–1949) formulated his *law of effect,* in which the hedonic principle operates—actions that lead to satisfying consequences are "stamped in"; and Clark Hull (1884–1952) and B. F. Skinner (1904–1990) developed the principle of *reinforcement*, in which hedonic expression is also found (Lundin, 1994). Warren (1919) elevated the status of *hedonic doctrine* somewhat by his reference to *hedonic law*. Other writers in psychology refer to *pleasure-pain theories, pleasure principle, law of pleasure-pain*, and *doctrine of pleasure-pain*. Ladd (1898) referred to a *law of pleasure*, which was one component of the Aristotelian compound concept of the *law of pleasure-pain*; Baldwin (1894) referred to this concept only as Aristotle's *theory of pleasure-pain*. Both Seashore (1923) and Stroud (1938) refer to *theories of pleasure-pain*. Maher (1900) gives a historical perspective and progression of *theories of pleasure-pain*, but he also describes the *laws of pleasure-pain*. According to Maher, other laws that are subsidiary to the *pleasure laws* are the *law of change* (concerns the relativity of pleasures), the *law of accommodation* (pleasures may become habituated), and the *law of repetition* (diminished pleasures may be revitalized). Maher (1900) represents an interesting "turn-of-the-century" amalgam of the disciplines of philosophy and psychology concerning the *doctrine of hedonism*. See also EFFECT, LAW OF; FREUD'S THEORY OF PERSONALITY; REINFORCEMENT THEORY.

REFERENCES

Bentham, J. (1789). *Principles of morals and legislation*. Oxford, England: Clarendon Press.

Bentham, J. (1798). *Theory of legislation*. Oxford, England: Clarendon Press.

Baldwin, J. (1894). *Handbook of psychology*. New York: Holt.

Ladd, G. (1898). *Outlines of descriptive psychology*. New York: Scribners.

Maher, M. (1900). *Psychology: Empirical and rational*. New York: Longmans, Green.

Warren, H. (1919). *Human psychology*. Boston: Houghton Mifflin.

Seashore, C. (1923). *Introduction to psychology*. New York: Macmillan.

Stroud, J. (1938). *Introduction to general psychology*. New York: Prentice-Hall.

Lundin, R. (1994). Jeremy Bentham. In R. J. Corsini (Ed.), *Ency. Psy.* New York: Wiley.

HEIDER'S BALANCE THEORY. See ATTRIBUTION THEORY.

HEISENBERG'S PRINCIPLE OF UNCERTAINTY/INDETERMINACY. See DETERMINISM, DOCTRINE/THEORY OF.

HELMHOLTZ'S COLOR VISION THEORY. See YOUNG–HELMHOLTZ COLOR VISION THEORY.

HELMHOLTZ'S LIKELIHOOD PRINCIPLE. See CONSTRUCTIVIST THEORY OF PERCEPTION.

HELMHOLTZ'S THEORY OF HEARING. See AUDITION/HEARING, THEORIES OF.

HELPLESSNESS/HOPELESSNESS THEORY OF DEPRESSION. See DE-PRESSION, THEORIES OF.

HELSON'S ADAPTATION-LEVEL THEORY. = adaptation-level affect/phenomenon. The American psychologist Harry Helson (1898–) developed this *psychological/perceptual theory* (Helson, 1947, 1964), which postulates a momentary state and subjective evaluation of the individual in which stimuli are judged to be indifferent or neutral on any given attribute. Stimuli above this *point of subjective equality* have specific features, and those below this point have complementary qualities. As an example, when one goes through the transition in a set of stimuli from pleasant stimuli (e.g., substances having a sweet taste) to unpleasant stimuli (e.g., substances having a sour taste), there is a stimulus (or group of stimuli) that is neutral (neither pleasant nor unpleasant). This transitional zone, called the *adaptation-level* (*AL*), represents the stimuli to which the individual is adapted concerning the particular magnitude, quality, or attributes of those stimuli. Another common example of the operation of *AL* is where cool water may be made to feel warm if the person first adapts to rather cold water (Reber, 1995). The *AL* may be defined operationally as the stimulus value that elicits a neutral response when a person judges a set of stimuli in terms of numerical (quantitative or qualitative) rating scales. *Helson's theory of AL* attempted to evaluate the variables that affect the neutral zone of stimuli in terms of their *background, focal,* and *residual* levels. Because the *AL* was rarely observed to be at the arithmetic mean (center point) of a stimulus series, the phenomenon of *AL* has been called *decentering*. It has been an accepted feature of *AL* that it is a weighted geometric mean consisting of *background, focal,* and *residual* stimuli. *Background* stimuli are "contextual" or "ground" (in the sense of a Gestalt "figure versus ground" relationship), *focal* stimuli are "attentional" or "figural" (in the sense of Gestalt *figure* versus *ground* relationships), and *residual* stimuli are "extra-situational" stimuli computed from differences between *background* and *focal* stimuli. Thus, *AL theory* maintains that the neutral or adapted background stimuli provide a basis, frame of reference, or standard against which new stimuli are perceived. See also ADAPTATION, LAWS/PRINCIPLES; CRESPI EFFECT; PERCEPTION (II. COMPARATIVE APPRAISAL), THEORIES OF; WEBER–FECHNER LAW.

REFERENCES

Shaad, D., & Helson, H. (1931). Group presentation in the method of constant stimuli as a time-saving device. *Amer. J. Psy., 43,* 422–433.

Helson, H., & Fehrer, E. (1932). The role of form in perception. *Amer. J. Psy., 44,* 79–102.

Helson, H. (1934). How do we see in the blind spot? *J. Exp. Psy., 17,* 763–772.

Helson, H. (1947). Adaptation-level as frame of reference for prediction of psychophysical data. *Amer. J. Psy., 60,* 1–29.

Helson, H. (1948). Adaptation-level as a basis for a quantitative theory of frames of reference. *Psy. Rev., 55*, 297–313.

Michels, W., & Helson, H. (1949). A reformulation of the Fechner law in terms of adaptation-level applied to rating-scale data. *Amer. J. Psy., 62*, 355–368.

Allport, F. (1955). *Theories of perception and the concept of structure.* New York: Wiley.

Helson, H. (1964). *Adaptation level theory: An experimental and systematic approach to behavior.* New York: Harper & Row.

Corso, J. (1971). Adaptation-level theory and psychophysical scaling. In M. Appley (Ed.), *Adaptation-level theory: A symposium.* New York: Academic Press.

Reber, A. (1995). *The Penguin dictionary of psychology.* New York: Penguin Books.

HENNING'S THEORY OF SMELL. See OLFACTION/SMELL, THEORIES OF.

HENNING'S THEORY OF TASTE. See GUSTATION/TASTE, THEORIES OF.

HERBART'S DOCTRINE OF APPERCEPTION. The German philosopher, psychologist, and mathematician Johann Friedrich Herbart (1776–1841) viewed psychology as a science that is based on experience, metaphysics, and mathematics. However, Herbart did not consider psychology to be experimental, because he could not conceive of ways to experiment on the mind. Herbart was in agreement with the German philosopher Immanuel Kant (1724–1804) concerning the nature of a unitary mind or soul (Kant, 1781/1929, 1798/1974), but he also proposed that the mind could be an entity composed of smaller units. That is, Herbart thought of the mind as an *apperceptive mass* made up of psychic states. Unconscious ideas existed in a kind of static state that had "forces" or intensities. When the "forces" became strong enough, they could overcome the "counterforces" already present in the *apperceptive mass*, cross the threshold, and enter into consciousness. The interaction of psychic states, in and out of consciousness, constituted Herbart's *psychic dynamics* (Herbart, 1816, 1824). In its original sense, the concept of *apperception* dates back to the German philosopher/mathematician Gottfried Wilhelm von Leibnitz (1646–1716), who referred to it as a final/clear phase of perception in which there is recognition, identification, or comprehension of what has been perceived (e.g., Leibnitz, 1714/1898). According to Leibnitz's *monad theory* (a "monad" was his term for the essential unit or individuality of all substances), the world consists of an infinite number of independently acting *monads*, which were points of "force" rather than substance, and where all *monads* had various degrees of clarity and consciousness ranging from the relatively unclear and unconscious to the most conscious and perceptible. Leibnitz called the lower degrees of consciousness (unconscious) the "little perceptions," which, when actualized, became *apperceptions.* Leibnitz was probably the first to develop a *theory of degrees of consciousness,* and it became the cornerstone of Sigmund Freud's conception of the *tripartite personality* (i.e., *id*, *ego*, and *superego*) and mental apparatus of opposing forces (i.e., *cathexis* and *anticathexis*), as well as Alfred Adler's and Carl Jung's approaches to degrees of consciousness and unconsciousness in their personality theories (Lundin, 1994b). For Herbart, however, *apperception* was considered to be the fundamental process of acquiring knowledge wherein the perceived qualities of a new object, event, or idea were assimilated with already existing knowledge. In some form or another, the basic notion of *apperception* that learning and understanding depend on recognizing relationships between new ideas and existing knowledge is axiomatic of nearly all *educational theory* and practice (Murphy & Kovach, 1972; Reber, 1995). The mathematics involved in Herbart's *psychic dynamics* focused on what could and could not enter consciousness where calculations concerned the amount of one force that was going to oppose another force. It was possible also for two forces or ideas to combine and suppress the ideas that were weaker (cf: Kantor, 1969). Herbart's contribution to psychology was the notion that it could be quantified, and, even though he denied that psychology could be experimental, his advocacy of quantification was crucial to the modern development of experimental psychology (Lundin, 1994a). See also ADLER'S THEORY OF PERSONALITY; FREUD'S THEORY OF PERSONALITY; JUNG'S THEORY OF PERSONALITY; PERSONALITY THEORIES; WUNDT'S THEORIES/DOCTRINES.

REFERENCES

Leibnitz, G. (1714/1898). *Monadology*. Oxford, England: Oxford University Press.

Kant, I. (1781/1929). *Critique of pure reason*. New York: St. Martin's Press.

Kant, I. (1798/1974). *Anthroponomy*. The Hague: Nijhoff.

Herbart, J. (1816). *A textbook of psychology: An attempt to found the science of psychology on experience, metaphysics, and mathematics*. New York: Appleton.

Herbart, J. (1824). *Psychologie als Wissenschaft*. 2 vols. Konigsberg: Unzer.

Kantor, J. R. (1969). *The scientific evolution of psychology*. Chicago: Principia Press.

Murphy, G., & Kovach, J. (1972). *Historical introduction to modern psychology*. New York: Harcourt Brace Jovanovich.

Lundin, R. (1994a). Gottfried Wilhelm Leibnitz. In R. J. Corsini (Ed.), *Ency. Psy.* New York: Wiley.

Lundin, R. (1994b). Johann Friedrich Herbart. In R. J. Corsini (Ed.), *Ency. Psy.* New York: Wiley.

Reber, A. (1995). *The Penguin dictionary of psychology*. New York: Penguin Books.

HERING–HURVICH–JAMESON COLOR VISION THEORY. = Hering's color theory = Hurvich–Jameson color vision theory = opponent-process color vision theory = tetrachromatic theory. The German physiologist Karl Ewald Hering (1834–1918) based his original *color vision theory* (1878, 1920) on the fact that individuals uniformly select four colors when asked to designate unique colors: primary blue (about 480 nanometers, or nm where 1 nm = one-billionth of one meter), primary green (about 510 nm), primary yellow (about 580 nm), and primary red (about 700 nm). *Hering's theory*, therefore, assumed that yellow was a fourth primary color in addition to the three primary colors of red, green, and blue. This was one of the factors that distinguished his theory from other *trireceptor* (red, blue, green) theories such as the *Young–Helmholtz theory*. Another distinguishing feature of *Hering's theory* was an *opponent-process* aspect where each of three sets of receptor systems in the retina responded to either of two complementary colors: blue–yellow, red–green, and black–white (each system was assumed to function as an antagonistic pair), and where other colors are formed by the combined stimulation of more than one type of color receptor. The term *opponent-processes* referred to the opposing reactions that occurred among the different substances in the retina where a "catabolism" or "breakdown" reaction corresponded to excitation of the red, yellow, and white substances, and an "anabolism" or "buildup" reaction corresponded to excitation of the opposite color substances of green, blue, and black. The intermediate hues (e.g., the color violet) depend on the interaction between the anabolic processes and the catabolic components (e.g., for violet, the combination of catabolic red with anabolic blue). *Hering's theory* was able to explain the red–green type of color blindness (called *deuteranopia* for green light vision deficiency and *protanopia* for red light vision deficiency) by assuming some dysfunction in the red or green visual receptors, while the blue or yellow receptors remain unaffected. This accounted for the fact that red–green color-blind persons can still discriminate the colors blue and yellow. The theory also explained the phenomena of *color contrast* and *negative afterimages*—where opposite reactions to an initial stimulation are observed. The term *tetrachromatism* is used to refer to color vision that is characterized by the ability to distinguish/discriminate among all four of the Hering primaries (red, green, yellow, and blue). The American psychologists Leo M. Hurvich and Dorothea Jameson (1955, 1957) expanded *Hering's opponent-process* (or opponent-colors) *theory* by giving it a more quantitative basis. They assumed, as did Hering, that there are four basic hues, along with their corresponding receptor-processes, paired in three sets of receptors: yellow–blue, red–green, and black–white. The Hurvich–Jameson modification of *Hering's theory* accounted for the facts of color mixture, for most color vision defects, and for the appearances of "dissimilarity," "similarity," and "purity" among the hues of the color circle (Hochberg, 1965). The effect of light, according to the *Hering–Hurvich–Jameson theory*, depends not only on its physical properties but also on the condition of the visual mechanism. According to this viewpoint, a phenomenon such as the *Bezold–Brucke effect* (where a change in hue is a function of brightness) can be ascribed to mechanisms and conditions of visual adaptation and compensation. The phenomenon of *simultaneous color contrast* can also be viewed as a condition where antagonistic processes are set up in areas adjacent to a stimulated zone, and the addition of complementary lights results in addition of brilliance, but also a subtraction process occurs where opponent colors react to each other and yield the color white (cf: Boring, 1942). Today, the *Hering–Hurvich–Jameson theory* is regarded as a better approximation to the true explanation and state of color vision than is the *Young–Helmholtz theory*. However, it is cautioned that any good color vision theory must eventually deal with the fact that the retina organizes and processes visual stimuli differently from the cortical and subcortical visual centers (Reber, 1995). See also BEZOLD–BRUCKE EFFECT; COLOR VISION, THEORIES/LAWS OF; YOUNG–HELMHOLTZ COLOR VISION THEORY.

REFERENCES

Hering, E. (1878). *Zur Lehre vom Lichtsinn*. Vienna: Gerolds.

Hering, E. (1890). Beitrage zur Lehre vom Simultankontrast. *Z. Psy.*, *1*, 18–28.

Hering, E. (1920). *Grundzuge der Lehre vom Lichtsinn*. Berlin: Springer.

Boring, E. G. (1942). *Sensation and perception in the history of experimental psychology*. New York: Appleton-Century-Crofts.

Hurvich, L., & Jameson, D. (1949). Helmholtz and the three-color theory: An historical note. *Amer. J. Psy.*, *62*, 111–114.

Hurvich, L., & Jameson, D. (1951). The binocular fusion of yellow in relation to color theories. *Science, 114*, 199–202.

Hurvich, L., & Jameson, D. (1955). Some quantitative aspects of an opponent-colors theory. II. Brightness, saturation, and hue in normal and dichromatic vision. *J. Opt. Soc. Amer.*, *45*, 602–616.

Jameson, D., & Hurvich, L. (1955). Some quantitative aspects of an opponent-colors theory. I. Chromatic responses and spectral saturation. *J. Opt. Soc. Amer., 45*, 546–552.

Hurvich, L., & Jameson, D. (1957). An opponent-process theory of color vision. *Psy. Rev., 64*, 384–404.

Hochberg, J. (1965). *Perception*. Englewood Cliffs, NJ: Prentice-Hall.

Hurvich, L., & Jameson, D. (1974). Opponent-processes as a model of neural organization. *Amer. Psy., 29*, 88–102.

Jameson, D., & Hurvich, L. (1989). Essay concerning color constancy. *Ann. Rev. Psy., 40*, 1–22.

Reber, A. (1995). *The Penguin dictionary of psychology*. New York: Penguin Books.

HERING'S COLOR THEORY. See HERING–HURVICH–JAMESON COLOR VISION THEORY.

HERING'S LAW OF EQUAL INNERVATION. See VISION/SIGHT, THEORIES OF.

HERRNSTEIN'S MATCHING LAW. The *matching law* was formulated by Richard Herrnstein (1961), who observed and recorded the behavior of pigeons pecking two keys for food reinforcement delivered on concurrent variable-interval (i.e., an average, nonfixed amount of elapsed time) schedules. The pigeons yielded response curves that conformed closely to a predicted line of perfect matching where response ratios are matched to ratios of obtained reinforcements (cf: Shimp, 1966; Herrnstein & Heyman, 1979; Lea & Tarpy, 1982). The *matching law* is defined as the matching of response ratios to reinforcement ratios where the match is most robust when dealing with concurrent variable interval/variable interval and concurrent variable interval/variable ratio reinforcement schedules of operant behavior (Herrnstein, 1970; cf: Rachlin, 1971). Experiments using pigeons, rats, and people as subjects show that the *matching law* applies when they choose between alternative sources of food, brain stimulation, and information, respectively. The three species, doing different things for different consequences, all crowd the theoretical "matching line." The acknowledged qualifications on the *matching law* involve three empirical issues (Brown & Herrnstein, 1975): the equivalence of responses, the equivalence of rewards, and the interactions among drives. Much is unsettled about matching as a general principle, but various quantitative conclusions can be drawn regarding the law. For example, experiments have consistently shown that a response rises in rate either when its reward increases or when the reward for other concurrent responses decreases. Inversely, a response declines either when its reward decreases or when other available responses gain reward (Herrnstein, 1970). Because pleasures and pains are always felt relative to a context ("total rewards that are available"), the traditional *law of effect* may more properly be called the *law of relative effect*. In this way, the *law of relative effect* is considered to be a *principle of hedonic relativity* (Herrnstein, 1971) where individuals that are subject to its workings allocate their behavior according to the relative gain connected with each. Therefore, an animal or person may work at a maximal rate for a pittance, if the alternatives are poor enough. In contrast, when the alternatives improve, even generous rewards may fail to produce much of any sort of activity. The *relativity* of the *law of effect* explains why context is so important for how people behave (Brown & Herrnstein, 1975). Herrnstein defined the *law of relative effect* as the rate of a given response that is proportional to its rate of reinforcement relative to the reinforcement for all other responses. However, while the *relative law of effect* predicts well for simple variable interval reinforcement schedules, it has failed to serve as a basis for a more general principle of reinforcement (Staddon & Ettinger, 1989). See also EFFECT, LAW OF.

REFERENCES

Herrnstein, R. (1961). Relative and absolute strength of response as a function of frequency of reinforcement. *J. Exp. Anal. Beh., 4*, 267–272.

Shimp, C. (1966). Probabilistically reinforced choice behavior in pigeons. *J. Exp. Anal. Beh., 9*, 443–455.

Herrnstein, R. (1970). On the law of effect. *J. Exp. Anal. Beh., 13*, 243–266.

Herrnstein, R. (1971). Quantitative hedonism. *J. Psychiat. Res., 8*, 399–412.

Rachlin, H. (1971). On the tautology of the matching law. *J. Exp. Anal. Beh., 15*, 249–251.

Herrnstein, R. (1974). Formal properties of the matching law. *J. Exp. Anal. Beh., 21*, 159–164.

Brown, R., & Herrnstein, R. (1975). *Psychology*. Boston: Little, Brown.

Herrnstein, R., & Heyman, G. (1979). Is matching compatible with reinforcement maximization on concurrent variable interval, variable ratio? *J. Exp. Anal. Beh., 31,* 209–223.

Lea, S., & Tarpy, R. (1982). Different demand curves from rats working under ratio and interval schedules. *Beh. Anal. Letters, 2,* 113–121.

Staddon, J., & Ettinger, R. (1989). *Learning: An introduction to the principles of adaptive behavior.* New York: Harcourt Brace Jovanovich.

HESS EFFECT. See PERCEPTION (I. GENERAL), THEORIES OF.

HEURISTIC THEORY OF PERSUASION. See ATTITUDE/ATTITUDE CHANGE, THEORIES OF.

HEYMAN'S LAW. See SKINNER'S DESCRIPTIVE BEHAVIOR/OPERANT CONDITIONING THEORY.

HICK'S LAW. W. E. Hick (1952) formulated this principle, which states that the rate of processing a signal is a linear increasing function of stimulus information (e.g., reaction time increases as a linear function of *stimulus uncertainty*), or that the rate of gain of information is a constant (Dember & Warm, 1979). The time between the occurrence of a stimulus and the initiation of a response is called reaction time (RT). The study of RT represents one of the oldest problems in psychology, dating from 1850, when Hermann von Helmholtz developed the RT experiment. Hirsch (1861–1865) measured the *physiological time* of the eye, ear, and sense of touch; Donders (1868) invented the *disjunctive RT experiment*; Exner (1873) introduced the term *reaction time*; Wilhelm Wundt's students began studies of single and complex RTs in 1879 (see Woodworth & Schlosberg, 1965); and Cattell (1886a, b) and his students worked extensively on RT investigations. One of the first experimental studies of the effects of *stimulus uncertainty* on choice RT was made by Merkel (1885), who found a predictable regularity in the nature of RT (cf: *Merkel's law,* which is the generalization that to equal differences between stimuli at above-threshold strength, there correspond equal differences in sensation; Zusne, 1987; however, this is an incorrect assumption/generalization; Sutherland, 1996). It was not until many years later and the advent of *information theory* that the general applicability of Merkel's (1885) finding became apparent. Hick (1952) realized that the uncertainty produced by variations in the number of stimulus alternatives could be viewed in *information theory* terms by expressing the number of alternatives in *bits* (i.e., "binary digit" where a *bit* is the amount of information needed to reduce the alternatives in a choice situation by one half). Hick found that RT increased as a linear function of the log (base 2) of the number of stimulus alternatives, and thus, in *information theory* terms, RT was proportional to stimulus uncertainty. Hick's discovery was not in itself new but was a confirmation of Merkel's earlier finding, using a different scale for describing the number of stimulus alternatives. Hick's approach made it possible to map a number of ways to manipulate stimulus uncertainty onto a common scale. While there is some disagreement (e.g., Kornblum, 1968), the general trend of the data seems to indicate that choice RT is proportional to stimulus information (cf: *symbolic distance effect*—when a subject has to gauge from memory the relative position of two items on a dimension, such as length, the smaller the difference between the two items on the dimension, the longer is the subject's RT; Sutherland, 1996). Within limits, it does not seem to matter if uncertainty is manipulated through variations in the number of stimulus alternatives or through variations in stimuli probabilities or their sequential dependencies (e.g., Garner, 1962; Smith, 1968; Alluisi, 1970; Teichner & Krebs, 1974). Reber (1995) defines a variation of *Hick's law*, called the *Hick–Hyman law*, as the generalization that RT increases as a function of the amount of information transmitted in making a response (cf: Hyman, 1953). According to Dember and Warm (1979), *Hick's law* apparently has generality because it applies to vigilance tasks as well as to the choice RT tasks for which it was originally formulated. See also DONDERS' LAW; INFORMATION/INFORMATION-PROCESSING THEORY; VIGILANCE, THEORIES OF.

REFERENCES

Hirsch, A. (1861–1865). Experiences chronoscopiques sur la vitesse des differentes sensations et de la transmission nerveuse. *Soc. Sci. Natl. Bull., 6*, 100–114.

Donders, F. (1868). Die Schnelligkeit psychischer Processe. *Ar. Anat. Physio.*, 657–681.

Exner, S. (1873). Experimentelle Untersuchung der einfachsten psychischen Processe. *Pflug. Ar. ges. Physio., 7*, 601–660.

Merkel, J. (1885). Die zeitlichen Verhaltnisse der Willensthatigkeit. *Phil. Stud., 2*, 73–127.

Cattell, J. McK. (1886a). Psychometrische Untersuchungen. *Phil. Stud., 3*, 305–335; 452–492.

Cattell, J. McK. (1886b). The time taken up by the cerebral operations. *Mind, 11*, 220–242, 377–392, 524–538.

Hick, W. (1948). The discontinuous functioning of the human operator in pursuit tasks. *Quar. J. Exp. Psy., 1*, 36–51.

Hick, W. (1952). On the rate of gain of information. *Quar. J. Exp. Psy., 4*, 11–26.

Hyman, R. (1953). Stimulus information as a determinant of reaction time. *J. Exp. Psy., 45*, 188–196.

Garner, W. (1962). *Uncertainty and structure as psychological concepts.* New York: Wiley.

Woodworth, R., & Schlosberg, H. (1965). *Experimental psychology.* New York: Holt, Rinehart, & Winston.

Kornblum, S. (1968). Serial-choice reaction time: Inadequacies of the information hypothesis. *Science, 159*, 432–434.

Smith, E. (1968). Choice reaction time: An analysis of the major theoretical positions. *Psy. Bull., 69*, 77–110.

Alluisi, E. (1970). Information and uncertainty: The metrics of communications. In K. DeGreene (Ed.), *Systems psychology.* New York: McGraw-Hill.

Teichner, W., & Krebs, M. (1974). Laws of visual choice reaction time. *Psy. Rev., 81*, 75–98.

Dember, W., & Warm, J. (1979). *Psychology of perception.* New York: Holt, Rinehart, & Winston.

Zusne, L. (1987). *Eponyms in psychology.* Westport, CT: Greenwood Press.

Reber, A. (1995). *The Penguin dictionary of psychology.* New York: Penguin Books.

Sutherland, S. (1996). *The international dictionary of psychology.* New York: Crossroad.

HIERARCHY OF NEEDS THEORY OF WORK MOTIVATION. See WORK/CAREER/OCCUPATION, THEORIES OF.

HIERARCHY THEORY OF MOTIVATION. See MASLOW'S THEORY OF PERSONALITY.

HILGARD'S HIDDEN OBSERVER HYPOTHESIS. See HYPNOSIS/HYP-NOTISM, THEORIES OF.

HISTORIC THEORIES OF ABNORMALITY. See PSYCHOPATHOL-OGY, THEORIES OF.

HOFFDING STEP/PHENOMENON. See PATTERN/OBJECT RECOGNI-TION THEORY.

HOMEOSTASIS, PRINCIPLE OF. See HUNGER, THEORIES OF.

HONI EFFECT/PHENOMENON. See CONFLICT, THEORIES OF.

HORMONAL THEORY OF HUNGER. See HUNGER, THEORIES OF.

HORNER'S LAW. See COLOR VISION, THEORIES/LAWS OF.

HORNEY'S THEORY OF PERSONALITY. The German-born American Karen D. Horney (1885–1952) was trained originally in the method of *Freudian psychoanalysis*, but she broke away eventually from the standard Freudian orthodoxy over the issue of female sexuality (cf: Freud, 1905/1931, 1925, 1933). Where Freud emphasized the concepts of penis envy, jealousy of the male, *libido theory*, and feelings of genital inferiority as determinants in the psychology of women, Horney argued that lack of confidence and overemphasis on the love relationship were at the heart of feminine psychology (Horney, 1967). Horney retained many of the basic Freudian concepts and methods, such as free association, transference, repression, and resistance, but she—like other analysts (e.g., Adler, Fromm, and Sullivan)—stressed the importance of environmental and social factors in developing the personality. She also kept the Freudian doctrine of unconscious motivation and psychic determinism. Horney redefined the meaning of the Freudian oedipal complex (it was anxiety that grew out of the parent–child relationship, not a sexual-aggressive conflict) and aggression (it was security-protection, not an inborn trait). Horney also criticized the Freudian notions of the *id, ego, superego*, anxiety, masochism, and repetition compulsion (Horney, 1939). The primary concepts in *Horney's personality theory* are *basic anxiety* and *idealized image*, which are pervasive learned characteristics of the child that result from feeling isolated and helpless in a hostile environment. A powerful drive for parental security and safety arises in the child out of the feeling of *basic anxiety*; the *idealized image* is a fictitious, self-deceiving creation of the individual that expresses discontent with one's "real" self (Ewen, 1994). Horney presented a list of ten *neurotic* (e.g., irrational) *needs* that are acquired as a consequence of trying to find solutions to disturbed human relationship problems. These are *neurotic needs* for approval and affection, a partner who will take over one's life, restriction of one's life within narrow borders, power, exploitation of others, prestige, personal admiration, personal achievement, self-sufficiency/independence, and perfection/unassailability (Hall & Lindzey, 1978). According to Horney, the *neurotic needs* are "insatiable" (the more one gets, the more one wants) and are sources from which inner conflicts develop. Horney classified the *neurotic needs* under the three orientations/headings of "moving toward people," "moving away from people," and "moving against people." It is these orientations where inner conflict develops (Horney, 1945). While the "normal" individual is able to resolve the inner conflicts posed by these orientations concerning others by integrating all three orientations, the "neurotic" person develops and utilizes artificial or irrational solutions. Such inner conflicts, however, are avoidable and resolvable if the child is reared in a home that has warmth, trust, love, respect, and tolerance of mistakes. Thus, Horney did not feel that conflict was innate, but that it stemmed from relationships with parents and other social conditions (Horney, 1937). *Horney's theory of personality* deals essentially with the dynamics and causes of neurosis. She incorporated into her theory a unique synthesis of some of the formulations and concepts both of Sigmund Freud and Alfred Adler. See also ADLER'S THEORY OF PERSONALITY; FREUD'S THEORY OF PERSONALITY; JUNG'S THEORY OF PERSONALITY; PERSONALITY THEORIES.

REFERENCES

Freud, S. (1905/1931). Three essays on the theory of sexuality/Female sexuality. In *The standard edition of the complete psychological works of Sigmund Freud*. Vols. 7, 21. London: Hogarth Press.

Freud, S. (1925). Some psychical consequences of the anatomical distinction between the sexes. In *The standard edition of the complete psychological works of Sigmund Freud*. Vol. 19. London: Hogarth Press.

Freud, S. (1933). The psychology of women. In *New introductory lectures on psychoanalysis*. New York: Norton.

Horney, K. (1937). *The neurotic personality of our times*. New York: Norton.

Horney, K. (1939). *New ways in psychoanalysis*. New York: Norton.

Horney, K. (1942). *Self-analysis*. New York: Norton.

Horney, K. (1945). *Our inner conflicts: A constructive theory of neurosis*. New York: Norton.

Horney, K. (1950). *Neurosis and human growth: The struggle toward self-realization*. New York: Norton.

Horney, K. (1967). *Feminine psychology*. New York: Norton.

Martin, A. (1975). Karen Horney's theory in today's world. *Amer. J. Psychoan., 35,* 297–302.

Hall, C., & Lindzey, G. (1978). *Theories of personality*. New York: Wiley.

Ewen, R. (1994). Horney's theory. In R. J. Corsini (Ed.), *Ency. Psy.* New York: Wiley.

HOROPTER THEORY. See BERKELEY'S THEORY OF VISUAL SPACE PERCEPTION.

HULL'S LEARNING THEORY. The American psychologist Clark Leonard Hull (1884–1952) formulated a hypothetico-deductive (cf: Pratt, 1994), behavioristic, reductive, mechanistic, and Darwinian/adaptive learning theory that used *habit* as its core concept, along with a number of intermediary theoretical constructs called *intervening variables*. In Hull's system, it was assumed that a given psychological state usually involves multiple causes and multiple effects, and this necessitated the postulation of various *intervening variables* that mediate between observable cause and observable effect events within the organism. For example, Hull described the *intervening variable* of "thirst" as mediating the input variable of "hours of water deprivation" and the output variable of "amount of water drunk." In his theory, Hull postulated about eight *intervening variables* (such as habit or thirst) and described their causal input variables. Several *intervening variables* were combined to determine the organism's final behavior observed in problem-solving and conditioning tasks. Among Hull's other theoretical concepts and constructions are habit strength, drive level, positive associative response strength, negative/inhibitory response strength, conditioned inhibition, reaction potential, net response strength, incentive motivation, drive stimuli, fatigue, general drive pool, evoking-stimulus goodness, anticipatory goal responses, gradient of reinforcement, habit-family hierarchy, and fractional anticipatory goal reaction (Hull, 1943, 1952; cf: Hilgard & Bower, 1966). In his ambitious behavior theory and program of experimentation, Hull developed sequences of calculational stages, equations, and mathematical derivations that described both acquisition and extinction of conditioned responses that, in the abstract, were similar to Pavlov's notions of behavior as being determined by the subtraction of internal inhibition from excitation and, also, to Guthrie's ideas of the conditioned response's competition against interfering movements evoked by the conditioned stimulus. Hull went beyond Thorndike's *law of effect* and hypothesized that all primary/biological reinforcers serve to reduce their corresponding drive/need; he concluded that any reduction of a drive would act as a reinforcing event (Bower & Hilgard, 1981). Criticisms against *Hull's theory* were that it did not have a tractable mathematical system, it had too many parameters to be measured and too weak a measurement theory to get leverage on the quantitative details of his experimental data, and its mathematical derivations were suspect in detail where ad hoc rules were often invented to handle special problems arising in each derivation (e.g., Cotton, 1955; Amsel, 1965; Bower & Hilgard, 1981). On the positive side, Hull's quantitative system and program—which arguably was the most influential of the learning theories between 1930 and 1955 (Spence, 1952)—set the stage for later development in the area of *mathematical learning theory*. Hull also influenced profoundly a number of his students (the "neo-Hullians") and other prominent researchers and writers in learning psychology, such as N. E. Miller, O. H. Mowrer, K. Spence, A. Amsel, and F. Logan. See also AMSEL'S HYPOTHESIS/THEORY; LEARNING THEORIES; LOGAN'S MICROMOLAR THEORY; MOWRER'S THEORY; SPENCE'S THEORY.

REFERENCES

Hull, C. (1932). The goal-gradient hypothesis and maze learning. *Psy. Rev., 39*, 25–43.
Hull, C. (1934). The concept of the habit-family hierarchy and maze learning. *Psy. Rev., 41*, 33–54.
Hull, C. (1935). The conflicting psychologies of learning—a way out. *Psy. Rev., 42*, 491–516.
Hull, C. (1937). Mind, mechanism, and adaptive behavior. *Psy. Rev., 44*, 1–32.
Hull, C. (1938). The goal-gradient hypothesis applied to some "field-force" problems in the behavior of young children. *Psy. Rev., 45*, 271–299.
Hull, C. (1943). *Principles of behavior*. New York: Appleton-Century-Crofts.
Koch, S. (1944). Review of Hull's *Principles of behavior*. *Psy. Bull., 41*, 269–286.
Skinner, B. F. (1944). Review of Hull's *Principles of behavior*. *Amer. J. Psy., 57*, 276–281.
Hull, C. (1951). *Essentials of behavior*. New Haven, CT: Yale University Press.
Hull, C. (1952). *A behavior system: An introduction to behavior theory concerning the individual organism*. New Haven, CT: Yale University Press.
Spence, K. (1952). Clark Leonard Hull: 1884–1952. *Amer. J. Psy., 65*, 639–646.
Seward, J. (1954). Hull's system of behavior: An evaluation. *Psy. Rev., 61*, 145–159.
Cotton, J. (1955). On making predictions from Hull's theory. *Psy. Rev., 62*, 303–314.
Logan, F. (1959). The Hull–Spence approach. In S. Koch (Ed.), *Psychology: A study of a science*. Vol. 2. New York: McGraw-Hill.
Ammons, R. (1962). Psychology of the scientist: II. Clark L. Hull and his "Idea Books." *Perc. Mot. Skills, 15*, 800–802.
Hull, C. (1962). Psychology of the scientist: IV. Passages from the "Idea Books" of Clark L. Hull. *Perc. Mot. Skills, 15*, 807–882.
Amsel, A. (1965). On inductive versus deductive approaches and neo-Hullian behaviorism. In B.Wolman (Ed.), *Scientific psychology*. New York: Basic Books.
Hilgard, E., & Bower, G. (1966). *Theories of learning*. New York: Appleton-Century-Crofts.
Bower, G., & Hilgard, E. (1981). *Theories of learning*. Englewood Cliffs, NJ: Prentice-Hall.

Pratt, A. (1994). Hypothetical-deductive reasoning. In R. J. Corsini (Ed.), *Ency. Psy.* New York: Wiley.

HUMORAL/HUMORS THEORY. See GALEN'S DOCTRINE OF THE FOUR TEMPERAMENTS.

HUMPHREY'S LAW. See STROOP EFFECT/INTERFERENCE EFFECT/ STROOP TEST.

HUNGER, THEORIES OF. An operational definition of the term *hunger* is the internal state that results from food deprivation and whose severity is measured by the duration of the deprivation. In terms of physiology, the state of hunger results from particular imbalances in nutrients in the body whose severity is determined by the degree of imbalance (Reber, 1995). The American physiologist Walter B. Cannon (1871–1945) introduced the useful *principle of homeostasis* (i.e., the body's natural tendency to maintain equilibrium among its various states, such as temperature and glucose level) to help understand the motivational aspects of organisms. Early *theories of hunger* focused on the *peripheral factors* in eating such as the way in which eating behavior was regulated where the obvious locus was the stomach and the digestive tract. It had been known for a long time that an empty stomach displayed vigorous contractions in addition to the peristaltic movements that occur normally during the digestion/ processing of food. One of the first formal theories of hunger, called the *stomach-contraction theory*, or the *hunger-pang theory* (Cannon & Washburne, 1912; Cannon, 1934) asserted that the stomach's contractions were signals to the central nervous system concerning hunger where the behavioral regulation of food intake resulted from such *peripheral* information from the stomach. However, Cannon's commonsense *stomach-contraction theory* has been discredited by evidence from animal studies where the sensory pathways leading from the stomach muscles to the brain and motor pathways leading from the brain to the stomach muscles have been severed surgically. Stomach contractions do occur, under normal circumstances, when one experiences hunger and may become important conditioned stimuli for eating, but they do not appear to be essential. It seems that hunger and satiety originate in brain mechanisms that collect information about the body's energy supply. Along these lines, the most widely accepted theory of hunger, the *lateral hypothalamus/feeding center theory*, or the *hypothalamic theory* (Stellar, 1954), holds that hunger is proportional to the neural activity in the lateral hypothalamus (LH) region of the brain, an area that is implicated also in the regulation of thirst. Satiety, according to this theory, is caused by the activation of the immediately adjacent medial/ventromedial hypothalamus (VMH). In simple terms, the LH area is seen as a ''turn-on'' eating center, and the VMH area is viewed as a ''turn-off'' eating center (cf: Teitelbaum & Epstein, 1962). Many puzzling questions have been asked about the *hypothalamic theory* of hunger and energy regulation. Damage to the

LH abolishes eating in experimental animals; however, it is not clear that the effect is necessarily attributed to destruction of a hunger center rather than to an interruption of some of the major pathways through the area. The *hypothalamic theory* is widely accepted today because no viable alternatives have been offered (Grossman, 1994). Concerning the question of how the hypothalamus is apprised of the state of constantly changing nutrients, the *glucostatic theory* (Mayer, 1955; cf: Kennedy's, 1953, hypothesized *lipostat mechanism*) suggests that the extent of glucose utilization in body cells is monitored by special "glucoreceptors" in the VMH (an earlier hypothesis, that simply the level of glucose in the bloodstream was important, had to be discarded because evidence from diabetic individuals showed them actually to eat more, rather than less as the *blood-glucose theory* would have predicted; Levinthal, 1983). Another theory of hunger, the *thermostatic theory* (Brobeck, 1948; cf: Stevenson, 1969) proposes that animals eat to maintain their body temperature and stop eating to prevent hyperthermia. However, while environmental temperature does affect food and water regulation, there is no evidence that internal temperature changes are responsible for such regulation (Friedman & Stricker, 1976). A *hormonal theory of hunger* (Davis, Gallagher, Ladove, & Turausky, 1969) holds that there is a hormonal inhibition of eating that is mediated through the blood supply. The *chemical profile theory* (Myers, 1975) suggests that a whole range of substances, making up a chemical "profile" reflecting the metabolic condition of the body, affect brain mechanisms controlling feeding and hunger. Another theory, the *energy metabolism theory* (Friedman & Stricker, 1976), maintains that the stimulus for hunger should be sought among changes that occur in the supply of metabolic fuels rather than in the utilization of specific nutrients or in levels of fuel reserves. The *peripheral theories of hunger* point to a variety of oropharyngeal and postingestional, gastric and humoral, factors in hunger. Each of these undoubtedly plays some role in the regulation of food intake; none of these, however, can be considered as critical or as the sole determinant of hunger (Schwartz, 1978). One theory that integrates the diverse findings on hunger, eating, and weight, called the *set-point theory* (Keesey, 1980), suggests that a homeostatic mechanism that regulates food intake, fat reserves, and metabolism operates to keep an organism at its predetermined weight. According to *set-point theory*, which was first suggested by research with rats, no single area in the brain keeps track of weight. Rather, an interaction of metabolism, fat cells, and hormones keeps people at the weight for which their bodies are designed. A common, persistent psychological theory holds that being overweight is a sign of emotional disturbance, but research has failed to support this popular belief. However, tension and irritability can result from constant dieting (being hungry much of the time), and unhappiness can result from being heavy in a society that discriminates against people who weigh more than the cultural ideal. Culture and ethnic background also contribute to understanding hunger and eating behavior; for example, how often one eats, what foods one eats, and with whom one eats are important social influences in the dynamics of hunger (Wade & Tavris, 1993). See also THIRST, THEORIES OF.

REFERENCES

Cannon, W., & Washburne, A. (1912). An explanation of hunger. *Amer. J. Physio., 29,* 444–454.

Cannon, W. (1934). Hunger and thirst. In C. Murchison (Ed.), *Handbook of general experimental psychology.* Worcester, MA: Clark University Press.

Brobeck, J. (1948). Food intake as a mechanism of temperature regulation in rats. *Federation Proceedings, American Physiological Society, 7,* 13.

Kennedy, G. (1953). The role of depot fat in the hypothalamic control of food intake in the rat. *Proc. R. S. Lon., 140,* 578–592.

Stellar, E. (1954). The physiology of motivation. *Psy. Rev., 61,* 5–22.

Mayer, J. (1955). Regulation of energy intake and the body weight: The glucostatic theory and the lipostatic theory. *Ann. N.Y. Aca. Sci., 63,* 15–42.

Teitelbaum, P., & Epstein, A. (1962). The lateral hypothalamic syndrome: Recovery of feeding and drinking after lateral hypothalamic lesions. *Psy. Rev., 69,* 74–90.

Davis, J., Gallagher, R., Ladove, R., & Turausky, A. (1969). Inhibition of food intake by a humoral factor. *J. Comp. Physio. Psy., 67,* 407–414.

Stevenson, J. (1969). Mechanisms in the control of food and water intake. *Ann. N.Y. Aca. Sci., 157,* 1069–1083.

Schachter, S. (1971). Some extraordinary facts about obese humans and rats. *Amer. Psy., 26,* 129–144.

Grossman, S. (1975). Role of the hypothalamus in the regulation of food and water intake. *Psy. Rev., 82,* 200–224.

Myers, R. (1975). Brain mechanisms in the control of feeding: A new neurochemical profile theory. *Pharmacology, Biochemistry, and Behavior, 3,* 75–83.

Friedman, M., & Stricker, E. (1976). The physiological psychology of hunger: A physiological perspective. *Psy. Rev., 83,* 409–431.

Schwartz, M. (1978). *Physiological psychology.* Englewood Cliffs, NJ: Prentice-Hall.

Keesey, R. (1980). A set-point analysis of the regulation of body weight. In A. Stunkard (Ed.), *Obesity.* Philadelphia: Saunders.

Levinthal, C. (1983). *Introduction to physiological psychology.* Englewood Cliffs, NJ: Prentice-Hall.

Wade, C., & Tavris, C. (1993). *Psychology.* New York: HarperCollins.

Grossman, S. (1994). Physiological needs. In R. J. Corsini (Ed.), *Ency. Psy.* New York: Wiley.

Reber, A. (1995). *The Penguin dictionary of psychology.* New York: Penguin Books.

HUNGER-PANG THEORY. See HUNGER, THEORIES OF.

HUNTER–McCRARY LAW. See SERIAL-POSITION EFFECT.

HURVICH–JAMESON COLOR VISION THEORY. See HERING–HURVICH–JAMESON COLOR VISION THEORY.

HUTT'S MICRODIAGNOSIS THEORY. See CUMULATIVE DEFICITS PHENOMENON/THEORY.

HUYGEN'S WAVE THEORY OF LIGHT. See VISION/SIGHT, THEORIES OF.

HYBRID THEORY. See LOGAN'S MICROMOLAR THEORY.

HYDRAULIC THEORY. This general notion—which underlies several theories that model the phenomena under study using a "hydraulic" or "pressure" principle—refers to the assumption that things behave like fluids under pressure and are ready to break through any weak spots in a boundary, barrier, or border should the pressure exceed some critical level (Reber, 1995). Examples of such *hydraulic theories* are Max Meyer's (1907, 1928) *theory of hearing*, Sigmund Freud's (1953–1964) *personality theory*, and the *ethological theory* of Konrad Lorenz and Nikolaas Tinbergen (Lorenz & Tinbergen, 1938). In one case, *Lorenz's hydraulic model of aggression*, it was hypothesized that stored instinctual energy needed to be discharged, and, once discharged, a refractory period is required for buildup because the full store of emotional energy is flushed— comparable to flushing a toilet. Lorenz claimed that aggressive behavior can detonate spontaneously, even in the absence of a stimulus, because of an "innate releasing mechanism" (Lorenz, 1966). See also AGGRESSION, THEORIES OF; AUDITION/HEARING, THEORIES OF; FREUD'S THEORY OF PERSONALITY.

REFERENCES

Meyer, M. (1907). An introduction to the mechanics of the inner ear. *University of Missouri Studies, Science Services, 2*, no. 1.

Meyer, M. (1928). The hydraulic principles governing the function of the cochlea. *J. Gen. Psy., 1*, 239–265.

Lorenz, K., & Tinbergen, N. (1938). Taxis und Instinkthandlung in der Eirollbewegung der Graugans. *Z. Tierpsy., 2*, 1–29.

Freud, S. (1953–1964). *The standard edition of the complete psychological works of Sigmund Freud.* J. Strachey (Ed.), 24 vols. London: Hogarth Press.

Lorenz, K. (1966). *On aggression.* New York: Harcourt Brace Jovanovich.

Reber, A. (1995). *The Penguin dictionary of psychology.* New York: Penguin Books.

HYPNOSIS/HYPNOTISM, THEORIES OF. The British surgeon James Braid (1795–1860) is credited by some writers (e.g., Lundin, 1994) to be the discoverer of *hypnosis* (Braid actually first introduced the term *hypnosis* in 1852), and others (e.g., Bloch, 1980; Evans, 1994) state that Franz Anton Mesmer (1734–1815) is commonly recognized as the founding father of modern *hypnosis* (which Mesmer called *animal magnetism*). It was Braid's idea that *hypnosis* was really nothing more than suggestion, and his significance for psychology was that he took the phenomenon out of the area of mystical explanation and placed it on a physical basis (Lundin, 1994). Mesmer applied the *principles of magnetism* developed in physics to the problems of mental health; his method was to have patients grasp metal rods that protruded from a tub of water filled with iron filings, join hands with other patients, and wait for Mesmer to "lay hands on" them as they became "hypnotized." However, a number of experiments conducted in Paris in 1784 headed by Benjamin Franklin led to the demise of Mesmer's *animal magnetism theory* (Evans, 1994). The phenomenon of *hypnosis* was also known and practiced by the British surgeon James Esdaile (1808–1859) in India, where he performed over 1,000 operations using hypnosis as his only anesthesia (Esdaile, 1847), by the English physician John Elliotson (1791–1868), who employed hypnosis in the treatment of a wide variety of medical disorders (Elliotson, 1843), by A. Liebeault (1866), H. Bernheim (1886/1964), and J. M. Charcot (1890) in France, who experimented and published papers on the use of hypnosis in therapy, and by Sigmund Freud and Josef Breuer (1892) in Vienna, who used hypnosis to help patients emotionally relive their early childhood traumas (a process called *abreaction*). Bernheim (1886/1964), like Braid, viewed hypnosis as a manifestation of suggestibility, and this persistent idea became the subject matter of a major research program on hypnosis conducted by the American learning theorist Clark Hull (1933). Other notable practitioners of hypnosis and hypnotherapy were G. Simmel in Germany and J. Hadfield in England, who treated war neuroses during World War I, J. Watkins (1949), who treated battle casualties during World War II, and M. Erickson, who made refinements in the use of hypnosis and expanded its use for a number of personality and behavioral disorders, including dentistry (Erickson & Rossi, 1981). Many modern counterparts to all the early developments in *hypnosis theory* still exist today and contribute to both the skepticism and enthusiasm of the phenomenon. Reber (1995) notes that few terms in the psychological lexicon are so thoroughly wrapped in confusion and mysticism as is the term *hypnosis*. The logical positivist and the cautious scientist find that it is difficult to give a satisfactory definition of *hypnosis*, and many of the arguments over the nature of the *theory of hypnosis* depend on which aspects one emphasizes: the hypnotist–patient/subject relationship, the type of suggestions given regarding cognitive, perceptual, and affective distortion, or the ability of some individuals to "relinquish control" temporarily (Evans, 1994). Given these qualifications, a number of standardized scales have been developed and used to measure hypnotic states (e.g., the Stanford Hypnotic Susceptibility Scales; the Harvard Group Scale of Hypnotic Susceptibility). Also, dreams may be initiated when under hypnosis (Hilgard, 1979), and persons may report dreams in detail that were forgotten apparently in the conscious, waking state. Research by Hilgard (1977) on "hypnotic analgesia"—which deals with the conscious perception of pain— led to the formulation of the *neodissociation theory of hypnosis*, which involves the concepts of *divided consciousness* and *hidden observer* whereby multiple control systems of thought and action may operate independently of each other.

A *hidden observer* is a hypothesized, concealed consciousness that is inferred to experience events differently from the hypnotized consciousness, although they operate in a parallel fashion. Hilgard's (1977) notion of a *hidden observer* impacts directly on certain central issues in cognitive psychology, such as the problem of serial versus parallel processing of information (Blum, 1994). The phenomenon of a *hidden observer* appears to be similar to the concept of *ego-state/ego-state theory* (Watkins, 1994a). The typical hypnotizable individual does not seem to be weak-willed, gullible, hysterical, passive, or submissive to the dominant personage of the hypnotist. Rather, he or she (there seem to be no sex differences on this issue) is an individual who has the capacity to become totally absorbed in some particular fantasy or ongoing experience and has a considerable ability to empathize with other people, both real and fictitious. Cognitive flexibility is the hallmark of the hypnotizable person (Evans, 1994). Due to its methodological sophistication, contemporary hypnosis research is significant in its contributions to general psychological theory (e.g., Hilgard, 1965, 1977, 1979; Barber, 1969; Sheehan & Perry, 1976; Orne, 1979). Watkins (1994b) cites many diverse clinical contexts in which *hypnotherapy* has been used successfully as a treatment, among which are the control of pain in general, relief of anxiety, postsurgical depression, impotence, and frigidity. When used in a research context, there are potential limitations to the validity of hypnosis-related data, such as possible deception/faking on the part of the subject concerning the execution of hypnotic instructions, possible *demand characteristics of the situation* where subjects are unconsciously predisposed to perform in ways they believe the experimenter expects, possible lack of *external validity* (i.e., generalizability of results to the population at large) through the use of specially selected subjects (e.g., using only high-scoring persons on standard tests of hypnotic susceptibility), and the extensive use of *small sample sizes* in studies involving hypnosis (Blum, 1994). See also EXPERIMENTER EFFECTS; FREUD'S THEORY OF PERSONALITY.

REFERENCES

Mesmer, F. (1799). *Memoir*. New York: Eden Press.

Braid, J. (1843). *Neurhypnology, or the rationale of nervous sleep considered in relation with animal magnetism*. London: Redway.

Elliotson, J. (1843). *Numerous cases of surgical operations without pain in the mesmeric state*. Philadelphia: Lea & Blanchard.

Esdaile, J. (1847). *Hypnosis in medicine and surgery*. New York: Julian Press.

Liebeault, A. (1866). *Du sommeil et das etats analogues, consideres surtout au point de vue de l'action du moral sur le physique*. Paris: Masson.

Bernheim, H. (1886/1964). *Hypnosis and suggestibility in psychotherapy: A treatise on the nature and use of hypnosis*. New Hyde Part, NY: University Books.

Charcot, J. (1890). *Complete works*. Vol. 9. *Metalotherapie et hypnotisme*. Paris: Fourneville & Brissand.

Freud, S., & Breuer, J. (1892). On the psychical mechanism of hysterical phenomena. In *Collected papers*. Vol. 1. London: Hogarth Press.

Hull, C. (1933). *Hypnosis and suggestibility* New York: Appleton-Century.

Watkins, J. (1949). *Hypnotherapy of war neuroses.* New York: Ronald Press.

Hilgard, E. (1965). *Hypnotic susceptibility.* New York: Harcourt, Brace, & World.

Barber, T. X. (1969). *Hypnosis: A scientific approach.* New York: Van Nostrand Reinhold.

Sheehan, P., & Perry, C. (1976). *Methodologies of hypnosis: A critical appraisal of contemporary paradigms of hypnosis.* New York: Wiley.

Hilgard, E. (1977). *Divided consciousness: Multiple controls in human thought and action.* New York: Wiley.

Hilgard, E. (1979). Imaginative and sensory-affective involvements in everyday life and in hypnosis. In E. Fromm & R. Shor (Eds.), *Hypnosis: Developments in research and new perspectives.* New York: Aldine.

Orne, M. (1979). On the simulating subject as a quasi-control group in hypnosis research: What, why, and how. In E. Fromm & R. Shor (Eds.), *Hypnosis: Developments in research and new perspectives.* New York: Aldine.

Bloch, G. (1980). *Mesmerism: A translation of the original medical and scientific writings of F. A. Mesmer, M.D.* Los Altos, CA: Kaufmann.

Erickson, M., & Rossi, E. (1981). *Experiencing hypnosis.* New York: Irvington.

Blum, G. (1994). Hypnosis as a research tool. In R. J. Corsini (Ed.), *Ency. Psy.* New York: Wiley.

Evans, F. (1994). Hypnosis. In R. J. Corsini (Ed.), *Ency. Psy.* New York: Wiley.

Lundin, R. (1994). James Braid. In R. J. Corsini (Ed.), *Ency. Psy.* New York: Wiley.

Watkins, J. (1994a). Ego-state theory and therapy. In R. J. Corsini (Ed.), *Ency. Psy.* New York: Wiley.

Watkins, J. (1994b). Hypnotherapy. In R. J. Corsini (Ed.), *Ency. Psy.* New York: Wiley.

Reber, A. (1995). *The Penguin dictionary of psychology.* New York: Penguin Books.

HYPNOTHERAPY, THEORIES OF. See HYPNOSIS/HYPNOTISM, THEORIES OF.

HYPOTHALAMIC THEORY. See HUNGER, THEORIES OF.

HYPOTHESIS-TESTING THEORY. See NULL HYPOTHESIS; CONSTRUCTIVIST THEORY OF PERCEPTION.

HYPOTHESIS THEORY. See PERCEPTION (II. COMPARATIVE APPRAISAL), THEORIES OF.

I

IDENTICAL ELEMENTS THEORY. See TRANSFER OF TRAINING, THORNDIKE'S THEORY OF.

IDENTITY HYPOTHESIS/THEORY. See MIND–BODY THEORIES.

IDIOGRAPHIC/NOMOTHETIC LAWS. The term *idiographic* (from the Greek word meaning "separate" or "distinct"; sometimes spelled *ideographic*; Denzin, 1994) relates to the unique/individualistic approach in science and is usually contrasted with the term *nomothetic* (from the Greek word meaning "general," "universal," or "abstract"; Reber, 1995), which refers to general scientific laws of nature. In simple terms, *idiographic* refers to the specific case, and *nomothetic* refers to the general perspective. In the psychological literature, the synonymous terms *idiographic laws, idiographic theory, ideographic approach, ideographic psychology,* and *idiographic science* are used, as well as the equivalent terms *nomothetic laws, nomothetic theory, nomothetic approach, nomothetic psychology,* and *nomothetic science.* In terms of research strategy, psychologists may choose to take an *idiographic* or a *nomothetic* approach concerning the descriptions, explanations, and interpretations of their subject matter. The *idiographic-nomothetic* distinction is due originally to Windelband (1921). The German philosopher Wilhelm Windelband (1848–1915) distinguished studying phenomena from a *nomothetic* versus an *idiographic* standpoint where the former concentrates on general laws or theories such as demonstrated by the empirical natural sciences, and the latter approach stresses the uniqueness and particularities of the individual case. This distinction has been used recently (Meissner, 1971) to describe Freud's method of psychoanalysis as a scientific hybrid tied into the two combined poles of *nomothetic,* which uses rules, laws, mathematics, physics, and energy, and *idiographic,* which represents ideas by various unique symbols and metaphors for understanding psychological phenomena. An examination of the history of the terms *idiographic* and *nomothetic* shows a conflict between these two models of science where the origins of the debate are traceable to the eighteenth and nineteenth centuries in academic disciplines including anthropology, sociology, psychology, history, religion, and geography (Gadamer, 1976). Today, there seems to be a renewal of interest in the *idiographic-nomothetic* debate where the basic assumptions concerning the philosophy of science, the goals and purposes of the sciences, and the nature of scientific inquiry are questioned. In the discipline of psychology, the question is asked whether psychology should be a cause–effect (lawful) science that seeks general relational statements (laws) of behavior (cf: Nagel, 1961), or whether it should be a personalistic/interpretive science capable of describing single cases (cf: Sahakian, 1977). In the area of personality psychology, Gordon Allport (1897–1967) acknowledged that there was a fundamental difference between the intuitive and scientific views concerning the explanation of human behavior (Allport, 1929) where the terms *idiographic* and *nomothetic* were invoked to emphasize and describe such a dichotomy. Allport attempted to combine and reconcile the two viewpoints where *nomothetic* characteristics could be measured by objective personality tests given to many people, and the *idiographic* approach could employ the individual case study method such as analyzing a person's diary or imaginative writings. The search for uniformity in patterns of human behavior is at the bottom of both the *idiographic* and *nomothetic* approaches, and such uniformities may be discovered and formulated ultimately in a diversity of ways (e.g., correlational, mathematical, structural, descriptive, analytical), and the unyielding adherence to only one theoretical approach or method may be unwise (Denzin, 1994). See also PERSONALISTIC/NATURALISTIC THEORIES OF HISTORY; PERSONALITY THEORIES.

REFERENCES

Dilthey, W. (1894). Ideas concerning a descriptive and analytic psychology. In R. Zaner & K. Heiges (Eds.), *Descriptive psychology and historical understanding*. The Hague: Nijhoff.

Windelband, W. (1921). *An introduction to philosophy*. London: Unwin.

Allport, G. (1929). The study of personality by the intuitive method. *J. Abn. Soc. Psy.*, *24*, 14–27.

Nagel, E. (1961). *The structure of science: Problems in the logic of scientific explanation*. New York: Harcourt, Brace, & World.

Meissner, W. (1971). Freud's methodology. *J. Amer. Psychoan. Assoc.*, *19*, 265–309.

Gadamer, H. (1976). *Philosophical hermeneutics*. Los Angeles: University of California Press.

Sahakian, W. (1977). Personalism. In R. J. Corsini (Ed.), *Current personality theories*. Itasca, IL: Peacock.

Denzin, N. (1994). Ideographic/nomothetic psychology. In R. J. Corsini (Ed.), *Ency. Psy.* New York: Wiley.

Reber, A. (1995). *The Penguin dictionary of psychology*. New York: Penguin Books.

IMAGERY/MENTAL IMAGERY, THEORIES OF. In the context of cognitive experiences, the term *image* refers to a mental representation of an earlier sensory stimulus or experience and represents a less vivid copy of that event. When *image* is used to mean a ''picture in one's head,'' it is assumed that this representation is not a literal one but merely acts ''as if'' one had a mental picture that was an analog of a real-world scene. Also, the *image* in this sense is assumed to be a ''construction'' or a ''synthesis'' of an earlier event and not merely a copy of some previously experienced sensory (visual, auditory, tactile, gustatory, or olfactory) stimulus (Reber, 1995). Four different classes of *mental images* have been described (Richardson, 1983): *afterimages*—a perceptual experience that occurs after the original source of stimulation has been removed; *eidetic images*—prolonged mental imagery that is vivid and persistent, commonly called ''photographic memory''; *memory/thought images*—images that are fragmented, pallid, indefinitely localized, and of brief duration; and *imagination images*—images that are influenced by motivational states and generally involve concentrated quasi-hypnotic attention along with inhibition of associations; this class includes hypnagogic, perceptual isolation, hallucinogenic drug, and sleep deprivation images. Around the turn of the century, mental images were mentioned frequently in controversies over cognitive experiences, such as whether *images* were critical to thinking and problem-solving processes (McMahon, 1973; Sheikh, 1994). After the waning of interest in *imagery* due to the early influence of behaviorism in psychology in the 1920s, it has become one of the most significant issues in current cognitive psychology (e.g., Holt, 1964; Paivio, 1969, 1971; Yuille & Marschark, 1983). In his *coding model*, Paivio (1971, 1982) suggests that there are two main modes of coding experience: *verbal processes*—which involve a functional symbolic system and are assumed to be auditory/motor; and *imaginal processes*—which constitute the representational mode for nonverbal thinking. Paivio's *dual coding hypothesis* states that higher imagery conditions are so effective in learning/memory because they increase the probability that both imaginal and verbal processes play a mediational role in item retrieval (cf: Bower, 1972). Both verbal-sequential and imagery-spatial-parallel processing are needed for optimal human functioning. However, because of its concrete/contextual nature, the *imagery* system appears more akin to perception (cf: the *Perky effect*—the subjective impression of imagery with the objective presence of a physical stimulus; when a person is asked to form a mental image of an object, and a very faint image of the object is then presented on a screen, the projected image may be taken to be the mental image; Zusne, 1987). It has been demonstrated that an image and a percept cannot be distinguished from each other on the basis of their intrinsic qualities (Sheikh, 1994). A number of other *theories/models of mental imagery* have been proposed (Pinker & Kosslyn, 1983): Neisser's *percept analogy*; Moran's *propositional model*; Kosslyn, Schwartz, and Pinker's *array theory*; Trehub's *neural networks model*; Finke's *levels of equivalence model*; Shepard's *psychophysical complementarity theory*; Pylyshyn's *tacit knowledge account theory*; and Hinton's *structural descriptions theory*. All these *theories/models of imagery* may be placed into one of two groups: the *iconophiles*—those who give mental imagery representations a special nature—and the *iconophobes*—those who hold that images have no special status concerning intrinsic spatial or pictorial characteristics. Shepard (1978) states that the current theoretical differences concerning *mental imagery* focus generally on two related issues: the degree of direct and functional relationships between imagery and thinking and the nature and extent of the physical/isomorphic processes that underlie mental images in the brain (cf: Pylyshyn, 1973). Throughout the history of psychology the concept of the *mental image* and *mental imagery* has been scrutinized and criticized. Today, however, there seems to be convincing evidence both for the importance of *mental images* in psychology in general and for their practical application in clinical and diagnostic settings, in particular (Sheikh, 1994). See also FORGETTING/MEMORY, THEORIES OF.

REFERENCES

Holt, R. (1964). Imagery: The return of the ostracized. *Amer. Psy., 19*, 254–264.

Paivio, A. (1969). Mental imagery in associative learning and memory. *Psy. Rev., 76*, 241–263.

Bugelski, B. R. (1970). Words and things and images. *Amer. Psy., 25*, 1002–1012.

Paivio, A. (1971). *Imagery and verbal processes.* New York: Holt, Rinehart, & Winston.

Bower, G. (1972). Mental imagery and associative learning. In L. Gregg (Ed.), *Cognition in learning and memory.* New York: Wiley.

Sheehan, F. (1972). *The function and nature of imagery.* New York: Academic Press.

McMahon, C. (1973). Images as motives and motivators: A historical perspective. *Amer. J. Psy., 86*, 465–490.

Pylyshyn, Z. (1973). What the mind's eye tells the mind's brain: A critique of mental imagery. *Psy. Bull., 80*, 1–24.

Sheikh, A., & Panagiotou, N. (1975). Use of mental imagery in psychotherapy: A critical review. *Perc. & Mot. Skills, 41*, 555–585.

Shepard, R. (1978). The mental image. *Amer. Psy., 33*, 125–137.

Paivio, A. (1982). The empirical case for dual coding. In J. Yuille (Ed.), *Imagery, cognitions, and memory.* Hillsdale, NJ: Erlbaum.

Pinker, S., & Kosslyn, S. (1983). Theories of mental imagery. In A. Sheikh (Ed.), *Imagery: Current theory, research, and application.* New York: Wiley.

Richardson, A. (1983). Imagery: Definition and types. In A. Sheikh (Ed.), *Imagery: Current theory, research, and application.* New York: Wiley.

Yuille, J., & Marschark, M. (1983). Imagery effects on memory: Theoretical interpretations. In A. Sheikh (Ed.), *Imagery: Current theory, research, and application.* New York: Wiley.

Zusne, L. (1987). *Eponyms in psychology.* Westport, CT: Greenwood Press.

Sheikh, A. (1994). Mental imagery. In R. J. Corsini (Ed.), *Ency. Psy.* New York: Wiley.

Reber, A. (1995). *The Penguin dictionary of psychology.* New York: Penguin Books.

IMMATERIALISM, THEORY OF. See MIND–BODY THEORIES.

IMPRESSION FORMATION, THEORIES OF. The original research on impression formation (i.e., how one individual perceives another person) is credited to Solomon Asch (1907–1995), who addressed two major issues in his work (Asch, 1946): the meaning people give to their observations of others and how to measure exactly a perceiver's impressions of another person. Asch used three methods to measure impressions: he asked the perceiver to write out in a brief paragraph impressions about another person (these were then evaluated in terms of the presence of consistent themes); the perceiver was asked to make up a list of words or phrases (i.e., a "free association" style) that came to mind when thinking about the other person; and the perceiver was given a list of prechosen adjectives and asked to place a check mark by the adjectives that applied to the other person. Recent research on impression formation has employed a fourth approach—the use of a rating scale defined by end labels such as "very favorable" and "very unfavorable" (Ostrom, 1994). Asch's main theoretical concern was the importance of understanding how people cope with the diverse information they receive about another individual. This concern is sometimes called the *information integration problem* (Anderson, 1981). Two major theoretical approaches toward impression formation and the information integration problem are the *Gestalt approach* and the *cognitive algebra approach*. The *Gestalt theory* maintains that people adopt a configural strategy where they appraise the entire information array and subsequently form a theoretical interpretation that integrates all the separate pieces of data into a coherent whole. This approach often involves the reinterpretation of some data and the discounting of other information (Ostrom, 1994). The *cognitive algebra theory* holds that each item of information contributes independently to one's overall impression. This approach (unlike the Gestalt view) assumes that the information items are not actively interrelated into a single thematic or meaningful configuration, but, rather, each item is evaluated separately and may be combined with any preexisting evaluations to yield a current evaluative impression of the person (Anderson, 1965). This viewpoint is called the *cognitive algebra approach* because information items are combined through algebra rules such as multiplying, adding, or averaging. Although the *Gestalt theory* and the *cognitive algebra theory* are different in their conceptual assumptions, they seem to be equally capable of accounting for the empirical findings in research on impression formation, including a variety of characteristics regarding the information items such as *primary-recency effects*—when perceivers' attention is paid either to the first, or last, part of a list of items; *meaning shift effects*—the rating of one item in a set in a particular way depending on the nature of other items in the set; and *set size effects*—the influence of the relative number of positive items to the number of negative items in a set (Ostrom, 1977, 1994). Another area linked theoretically to impression formation is the study of *interpersonal perception*. Person perception is a complex topic involving inferences and attributions made by an observer about others. Theoretical approaches in this area include those by Heider (1958), Kelley (1973), and Jones and Davis (1965). According to Heider (1958) and *attribution theory*, causes for behavior are attributed to either the environment or the person. When an action can be attributed to environmental causes, the actor is not held responsible for the positive or negative effects of her or his behavior, but when the actor is perceived as the originator, she or he is held accountable for the effect. Kelley (1973) proposed a *discounting principle* to account for causes of behavior where it was hypothesized that observers have a tendency to accept the first sufficient cause as the reason for behavior, but the impact of any particular cause in producing an effect is "discounted" if other plausible causes are present. Kelley also suggested an *augmentation principle* where the more "costs" the actor risks in order to act as she does, the more likely the observer is to attribute the behavior to "person causes." Kelley's rule of thumb is that the more the actor's behavior deviates from what the perceiver believes most people would do, the more likely the action is associated with an actor-specific feature or factor. The focus of attention on the actor to the exclusion of the environment is called the *fundamental attribution error* and leads observers to make stronger personal attributions than do actors. Jones and Davis (1965) argue that once an observer makes an attribution to personal causes, a *correspondent inference* will be made from the observed behavior and the motive that is inferred as underlying that behavior. According to this approach, the observer notes effects that occur in the environment and traces these back to the behavior of an actor; if the behavior is attributed to environmental factors, the information processing stops. However, if a personal attribution is made, the observer assumes the actor intended the effects observed. Most of the literature on interpersonal perception assumes that a stimulus person is basically inert, while the observer draws inferences from the behavior exhibited. However, the actor may have something to gain or lose by the impressions generated by behavior and may be motivated to effect them in some way such as engaging in a number of possible "impression management strategies" to negotiate an identity in the eyes of the observer. The study of *interpersonal perception* has not yet incorporated the dynamic interactions proposed by *impression management theory*, and the attribution process appears to be relatively static with an overreliance on rational models of information processing (Tedeschi, 1994). See also ATTITUDE/ATTITUDE CHANGE, THEORIES OF; ATTRIBUTION THEORY; BALANCE, PRINCIPLES/THEORY OF; PERCEPTION (I. GENERAL), THEORIES OF; PERSONALITY THEORIES.

REFERENCES

Asch, S. (1946). Forming impressions of personality. *J. Abn. Soc. Psy., 41*, 258–290.

Heider, F. (1958). *The psychology of interpersonal relations*. New York: Wiley.

Anderson, N. (1965). Averaging versus adding as a stimulus-combination rule in impression formation. *J. Exp. Psy., 70*, 394–400.

Jones, E., & Davis, K. (1965). From acts to dispositions: The attribution process in person perception. In L. Berkowitz (Ed.), *Advances in experimental social psychology*. Vol. 2. New York: Academic Press.

Kelley, H. (1973). The process of causal attribution. *Amer. Psy., 28*, 107–128.

Ostrom, T. (1977). Between theory and within theory conflict in explaining context effects in impression formation. *J. Exp. Soc. Psy., 13*, 492–503.

Schneider, D., Hastorf, A., & Ellsworth, P. (1979). *Person perception.* Reading, MA: Addison-Wesley.

Anderson, N. (1981). *Foundations of information integration theory.* New York: Academic Press.

Klein, J. (1991). Negativity effects in impression formation. *Pers. Soc. Psy. Bull., 17*, 412–418.

Mellers, B., Richards, V., & Birnhaum, M. (1992). Distributional theories of impression formation. *Org. Beh. & Hum. Dec. Proc., 51*, 313–343.

Ostrom, T. (1994). Impression formation. In R. J. Corsini (Ed.), *Ency. Psy.* New York: Wiley.

Tedeschi, J. (1994). Interpersonal perception. In R. J. Corsini (Ed.), *Ency. Psy.,* New York: Wiley.

INCENTIVE THEORY. See MOTIVATION, THEORIES OF; REINFORCEMENT THEORY.

INDEPENDENCE HYPOTHESIS. See INTERFERENCE THEORIES.

INDEPENDENT ASSORTMENT, LAW OF. See MENDEL'S LAWS/PRINCIPLES.

INDETERMINISM, DOCTRINE/THEORY OF. See DETERMINISM, DOCTRINE/THEORY OF.

INDIFFERENCE PRINCIPLE. See REINFORCEMENT THEORY.

INDIVIDUALITY THEORY. See INTELLIGENCE, THEORIES/LAWS OF.

INDUCTION, LAW OF. See SKINNER'S DESCRIPTIVE BEHAVIOR/OPERANT CONDITIONING THEORY.

INFANT ATTACHMENT THEORIES. The English psychiatrist John Bowlby (1907–1990) introduced the term *attachment* into psychology and psychiatry (Bowlby, 1958, 1969–1980), even though Sigmund Freud laid the foundation for attachment concepts by suggesting the *cathexis* (i.e., an "investment" or "holding") of libidinal energy onto a love object in order to establish an emotional connection for behavioral stability and organization. Bowlby argued that attachment is an expression of the biology of a species that is exhibited by species-specific behaviors (such as following, sucking, crying, smiling, and clinging) that occur at different ages and are focused on the infant's mother. Theories of infant attachment have appeared as subtheories and supporting concepts in *ethological theory*, *psychoanalytic theory*, and *learning theory* (Zaslow,

1994). In the area of *ethology* (the study of animal behavior), lasting attachments are created in the *imprinting* process whereby a newborn organism "attaches" itself to the first moving object (e.g., by exhibiting following behavior) it sees shortly after birth during a *critical period*. Thus, *ethological theory* (e.g., Lorenz & Tinbergen, 1938) assumes that genetically programmed behaviors interact with the environment during a *critical stage* of growth to develop bonding in the young organism with other individuals/organisms. In humans, attachments are generally more complex, require a longer time span for development, and are dependent upon bonding "networks" of behavior (such as "body-contact" bond and "eye-face-contact" bond; cf: Zaslow, 1982). According to *psycho-analytic theory* (e.g., Freud, 1933), attachment occurs during the nurturing-affectionate caretaking activities (such as feeding) where the infant's instinctual biological urge for oral gratification is met via sucking responses and contact with the mother's breast, which is then transferred into psychological attachment to the mother as a love object. In the area of *learning theory*, the behavior of feeding is the major drive-reducing reinforcement mechanism for learned at-tachment to the mother. In addition to oral satisfaction through feeding, the behaviors of touch, holding, and physical contact (e.g., Harlow, 1958) are con-sidered necessary for the development of comfort and attachment in the young child. Bowlby's (1969–1980) work on mother–child separation showed that the infant reacts to "loss" of the mother in three distinct stages: protests of anger/crying to get the mother back; a period of despair, withdrawal, depression, and decreased activity if the mother does not return as a result of the initial protests; and a *detachment* phase where the infant is relatively unresponsive to people and intensely hates the mother figure (see Bowlby, 1960). Bowlby (1979) asserts that *attachment theory*, vis-à-vis its relationship to psychopathology in the in-dividual, is a scientifically valid approach that combines concepts from the fields of psychoanalysis, cognitive theory, control theory, and ethology. See also CUP-BOARD THEORY; FREUD'S THEORY OF PERSONALITY.

REFERENCES

Freud, S. (1933). New introductory lectures on psycho-analysis. In *The standard edition of the complete psychological works of Sigmund Freud*. Vol. 22. London: Hogarth Press.

Lorenz, K., & Tinbergen, N. (1938). Taxis und Instinkthandlung in der Eirollbewegung der Graugans. *Z. Tierpsy., 2*, 1–29.

Spitz, R. (1945). Hospitalism: An inquiry into the genesis of psychiatric conditions in early childhood. *Psychoan. Study Child, 1*, 53–74.

Bowlby, J. (1958). The nature of the child's tie to his mother. *Inter. J. Psychoan., 39*, 350–373.

Harlow, H. (1958). The nature of love. *Amer. Psy., 13*, 673–685.

Bowlby, J. (1960). Separation anxiety. *Inter. J. Psychoan., 41*, 89–113.

Bowlby, J. (1969–1980). *Attachment and loss*. 3 vols. London: Hogarth Press.

Harlow, H. (1971). *Learning to love*. New York: Ballantine Books.

Ainsworth, M. (1973). The development of infant–mother attachment. In B. Caldwell & H. Ricciuti (Eds.), *Review of child development research.* Vol. 3. Chicago: University of Chicago Press.

Bowlby, J. (1979). *The making and breaking of affectional bonds.* London: Tavistock.

Zaslow, R. (1982). Der Medusa-Komplex. Die Psychopathologie der Menschlichen Aggression im Rahmen der Attachment-Theorie, Widergespiegelt im Medusa-Mythos, dem Autismus und der Schizophrenie. *Z. Klin. Psy. Psychother., 30,* 66–84.

Zaslow, R. (1994). Bonding and attachment. In R. J. Corsini (Ed.), *Ency. Psy.* New York: Wiley.

INFECTION THEORY/EFFECT. The viewpoint of *infection theory* is that theories in psychology generally cluster around some fundamental concept disseminated by researchers who are in personal touch with one another, but especially with the individual who originally proposed or developed the hypothesis (Sahakian, 1980). The *infection effect* is most noticeable in centers and institutes of learning and research (particularly in prestigious graduate schools) when a teacher shares ideas with high-ability students and with other professional colleagues. Promising students—who are "infected"—research their teachers' ideas, advance and perpetuate those ideas throughout their own careers, and strengthen them with published experimental research (cf: *social impact theory*—the larger the number of people influencing someone in the same direction, the more important they are, and the more immediate their influence, then the greater their influence will be; Sutherland, 1996). Once these students become influential in their field, their mentors' hypotheses and theories are cited in the psychological literature and, consequently, become known and supported in the discipline. A *snowball effect* occurs in this process where particular hypotheses and theories are published in one textbook, and then other authors pick them up and include them in their books, thus giving those hypotheses and theories greater circulation. According to *infection theory*, theoretical orientations such as Kurt Lewin's and B. F. Skinner's achieved wide audiences because many graduate students under their influence engaged in psychological research and prolific writing. One undesirable consequence of the *infection effect* is the inbreeding of ideas. Instead of a free and open exchange of ideas, hypotheses, and theories, authors with more personal contacts tend to have their orientations magnified or augmented. The *infection effect* tends to make psychology (and other disciplines) less diverse and varied. For example, the area of *personality theory* tends to contain a limited set of ideas due to the restricted interests of influential psychologists where the full spectrum of personality—involving study of traits such as humor, love, faith, and aesthetic sensitivity—is left virtually unexplored (Sahakian, 1994). See also DODO HYPOTHESIS.

REFERENCES

Sahakian, W. (1980). The infection theory in social psychology. *Society for the Advancement in Social Psychology Newsletter, 6,* 3–4.

Sahakian, W. (1982a). *History and systems of social psychology.* New York: McGraw-Hill Hemisphere.

Sahakian, W. (1982b). *Introduction to psychology of learning.* Itasca, IL: Peacock.

Sahakian, W. (1994). Infection theory. In R. J. Corsini (Ed.), *Ency. Psy.* New York: Wiley.

Sutherland, S. (1996). *The international dictionary of psychology.* New York: Crossroad.

INFERENCE THEORY. See APPARENT MOVEMENT, PRINCIPLES/THEORIES OF; UNCONSCIOUS INFERENCE, DOCTRINE OF.

INFORMATION/INFORMATION-PROCESSING THEORY. In general, *information-processing (IP) theory* is concerned with the way organisms attend to, select, and internalize information and how the information is subsequently used to make decisions and direct their behavior. *IP theories* have generated research in various areas of psychology, including memory, perception, attention, language, problem solving, and thinking (Estes, 1975–1978; Lachman, Lachman, & Butterfield, 1979). *Information theory* was introduced into psychology by Miller and Frick (1949). The term *IP theory* refers to some common presuppositions and research methods involving specialized scientific language and concepts in which the primary empirical domain is intelligent behavior and mental processes. At the broadest level, *IP* research and theory are aimed at studying the properties of adaptive mechanisms concerning the apprehension, storage, retrieval, and use of information that may be initiated in either internal states or external environments (see the *information-processing/levels of processing* model of memory; Craik & Lockhart, 1972; the *principle of graceful degradation*—Marr's principle that in any information-processing system, the effects of an error should be restricted and should not produce completely false results; the human mind appears to obey this principle, because few of the errors it makes are catastrophic; and the *principle of least commitment*—Marr's generalization that a task will be more efficiently executed if no decisions are taken that may subsequently have to be reversed, i.e., at each point in processing, a decision should be taken only when there is enough evidence to warrant it; Sutherland, 1996). *Theories of IP* that mainly originated in psychology derive from the behavioristic studies of Spence (1956), the verbal learning experiments of McGeoch (1942), the experimental analyses of attention and perception by Broadbent (1958), and studies of human engineering and performance (e.g., Howell & Goldstein, 1971; see *Fitt's law*—an equation that describes the movement between two similar targets, each of which must be touched in turn, where movement time decreases with the size of the target and increases with the amplitude of the movement; Sutherland, 1996). Other *IP theories* that originated outside psychology include Minsky's (1967) mathematical logic/computer science, Chomsky's (1965) transformational linguistics, and Shannon's (1948) communication engineering/information theory. Thus, *IP theory* has been influenced generally by movements and viewpoints in the areas of behaviorism, engineering/information theory, linguistics, and computer science. In particular, in a learning context, *IP theory* has progressed through *robotology* (e.g., Ashby, 1952; Hoffman, 1962; see Ashby's, 1952, *law of requisite variety*, which is a mathematical statement about *IP* that describes the procedure for choosing correct alternatives and rejecting incorrect ones), to computer models dealing with experimental synthesis of complex human behaviors and using specialized computer languages (e.g., Newell & Simon, 1963; cf: Miller, Galanter, & Pribram, 1960) and "artificial intelligence" (e.g., Newell & Simon, 1972; Hunt, 1975). Since the 1950s and 1960s and the major beginnings of modern information-processing models, there has been a proliferation of models, theories, simulations, and programs dealing with pattern recognition, perceptual learning, problem solving, language, and learning/memory. The development of computer technology has provided a valuable tool for understanding the complexities of human thought and information processing (Bower & Hilgard, 1981). See also ALGORITHMIC-HEURISTIC THEORY; ATTITUDE/ATTITUDE CHANGE, THEORIES OF; COMMUNICATION THEORY; CONTROL/SYSTEMS THEORY; DECISION-MAKING THEORIES; HICK'S LAW; LEARNING THEORIES/LAWS; PATTERN/OBJECT RECOGNITION THEORY.

REFERENCES

McGeoch, J. (1942). *The psychology of human learning: An introduction.* New York: Van Rees Press.

Shannon, C. (1948). A mathematical theory of communication. *Bell System Technical Journal, 27,* 379–423, 623–656.

Weiner, N. (1948). *Cybernetics.* New York: Wiley.

Miller, G., & Frick, F. (1949). Statistical behavioristics and sequences of responses. *Psy. Rev., 56,* 311–324.

Shannon, C., & Weaver, W. (1949). *The mathematical theory of communication.* Urbana: University of Illinois Press.

Ashby, W. (1952). *Design for a brain.* New York: Wiley.

Miller, G. (1953). What is information measurement? *Amer. Psy., 8,* 3–11.

Miller, G. (1956). The magical number seven, plus or minus two: Some limits on our capacity for processing information. *Psy. Rev., 63,* 81–97.

Spence, K. (1956). *Behavior theory and conditioning.* New Haven, CT: Yale University Press.

Broadbent, D. (1958). *Perception and communication.* London: Pergamon Press.

Attneave, F. (1959). *Applications of information theory to psychology.* New York: Holt, Rinehart, & Winston.

Miller, G., Galanter, E., & Pribram, K. (1960). *Plans and the structure of behavior.* New York: Holt, Rinehart, & Winston.

Hoffman, H. (1962). The analogue lab: A new kind of teaching device. *Amer. Psy., 17,* 684–694.

Newell, A., & Simon, H. (1963). Computers in psychology. In R. Luce, R. Bush, & E. Galanter (Eds.), *Handbook of mathematical psychology.* Vol. 1. New York: Wiley.

Chomsky, N. (1965). *Aspects of the theory of syntax.* Cambridge: MIT Press.

Minsky, M. (1967). *Computation: Finite and infinite machines.* Englewood Cliffs, NJ: Prentice-Hall.

Howell, W., & Goldstein, I. (Eds.). (1971). *Engineering psychology: Current perspectives in research.* New York: Appleton-Century-Crofts.

Craik, F., & Lockhart, R. (1972). Levels of processing: A framework for memory research. *J. Verb. Learn. Verb. Beh., 11,* 671–684.

Newell, A., & Simon, H. (1972). *Human problem solving.* Englewood Cliffs, NJ: Prentice-Hall.

Garner, W. (1974). *The processing of information and structure.* Englewood Cliffs, NJ: Prentice-Hall.

Hunt, E. (1975). *Artificial intelligence.* New York: Academic Press.

Estes, W. (Ed.) (1975–1978). *Handbook of learning and cognitive processes.* Hillsdale, NJ: Erlbaum.

Norman, D. (1977). *Memory and attention: An introduction to human information processing.* New York: Wiley.

Lachman, R., Lachman, J., & Butterfield, E. (1979). *Cognitive psychology and information processing: An introduction.* Hillsdale, NJ: Erlbaum.

Bower, G., & Hilgard, E. (1981). *Theories of learning.* Englewood Cliffs, NJ: Prentice-Hall.

Marr, D. (1982). *Vision.* San Francisco: Freeman.

Kantowitz, B. (1994). Information processing. In R. J. Corsini (Ed.), *Ency. Psy.* New York: Wiley.

Lachman, R. (1994). Information-processing theory. In R. J. Corsini (Ed.), *Ency. Psy.* New York: Wiley.

Marx, M. (1994). Information processing (unconscious). In R. J. Corsini (Ed.), *Ency. Psy.* New York: Wiley.

Sutherland, S. (1996). *The international dictionary of psychology.* New York: Crossroad.

INFORMATION-PROCESSING/LEVELS OF PROCESSING MODELS. See INFORMATION/INFORMATION-PROCESSING THEORY; PIAGET'S THEORY.

INFRARED THEORY. See OLFACTION/SMELL, THEORIES OF.

INHERITANCE, LAWS OF. See MENDEL'S LAWS/PRINCIPLES.

INHIBITION, LAWS OF. The term *inhibition* has different meanings depending on the context in which it is used (Warren, 1934; Reber, 1995). In general, *inhibition* is the restraining, repressing, preventing, decreasing, or prohibiting of any process or the process that brings about such restraining. In the context of physiology, *inhibition* is the partial or complete arrest of an already active function, especially of a muscular contraction; it is also that condition of a tissue or organ in which a function cannot be excited by the usual stimulus. In the area of psychoanalysis, *inhibition* refers to a mental condition that, through an opposing force, tends to check or prevent certain modes of expression, especially such as would expose to others the individual's thoughts or character (synonymous terms are *repression* and *suppression*; cf: Reber, 1995). In the context of learning/memory, *inhibition* (or "interference"; cf: Reber, 1995) is the reduction in, or prevention of, a response due to the operation of some other process, such as *retroactive inhibition* or *proactive inhibition* (see *interference theories of forgetting*). The term *central inhibition* is used whenever the assumed inhibitory action is taking place within the central nervous system; cf: *reciprocal inhibition* (Wolpe, 1958), where inhibition is shown by antagonistic muscles when the neural message to one muscle to contract is accompanied by a relaxation of the other, resulting from an inhibition of its motor nerve cells; and *reflex inhibition*, which is the prevention of one reflex by a mutually incompatible one. The terms *external inhibition* and *internal inhibition* refer, respectively, to the inhibition of a conditioned response produced when a novel or irrelevant stimulus is presented along with the conditioned stimulus and to the inhibition that depends on a conditioning process such as extinction (cf: Pavlov, 1927; also, see Pavlov's term *inhibition of inhibition*, or *disinhibition*, which refers to the removal of an inhibition by an extraneous stimulus). The term *latent inhibition* refers to inhibition that is established by nonreinforced exposure to a stimulus; for example, an animal learns not to attend to that stimulus so that when it is presented in a reinforcing situation, learning is inhibited; also called the *stimulus preexposure effect* (Reber, 1995). The terms *reactive inhibition* and *inhibitory potential* were used by Hull (1943, 1952) to refer, respectively, to the hypothesized inhibitory tendency that builds up as a result of effortful responding and to the hypothesized state that results from the performance of a response that reflects the organism's tendency to inhibit the making of the response. Among his *static laws of the reflex*, Skinner (1938) described the *law of inhibition*, where the strength of a reflex may be decreased through presentation of a second stimulus that has no other relation to the effector involved. Warren (1934) and Zusne (1987) define the *Wedensky inhibition principle/effect*, where a critical frequency for stimulating a nerve in a nerve-muscle preparation can be found, and at which rate the muscle responds with a very rapid series of twitches (e.g., 200 per sec.), whereas if the rate of stimulation is increased somewhat, the muscle responds with a single contraction followed by complete relaxation; this phenomenon is related to the *theory of neuromuscular inhibition* via its interference or "overcrowding" of nerve pulsations. Warren (1934) refers to *Heymans' law of inhibition*, formulated in 1901, which concerns visual stimulation where the threshold value of a given stimulus is increased proportionately to the intensity of the inhibitory stimulus, when an inhibitory stimulus is offered. Zusne (1987) and Reber (1995) describe the *Ranschburg inhibition effect* as the generalization that under tachistoscopic viewing conditions more individual stimuli can be recognized if all are different than if some are identical; that is, the effect refers to the inhibition among identical materials (see Ranschburg, 1901). See also FREUD'S THEORY OF PERSONALITY; INTERFERENCE THEORIES OF FORGETTING; PAVLOVIAN CONDITIONING PRINCIPLES/LAWS/THE-

ORIES; SKINNER'S DESCRIPTIVE BEHAVIOR/OPERANT CONDITION-ING THEORY.

REFERENCES

Heymans, G. (1896). Quantitative Untersuchungen uber das "optische Paradoxon." *Z. Psy., 9,* 221–255.

Ranschburg, P. (1901). Apparat und Methode zur Untersuchung des optischen Gedacht-nisses fur medizinische und padogogisch-psychologische Zwecke. *Monatsschrift Psychiatrie Neurologisch, 10,* 321–333.

Pavlov, I. (1927). *Conditioned reflexes.* New York: Dover.

Warren, H. (Ed.) (1934). *Dictionary of psychology.* Cambridge, MA: Houghton Mifflin.

Skinner, B. F. (1938). *The behavior of organisms: An experimental analysis.* New York: Appleton-Century-Crofts.

Hull, C. (1943). *Principles of behavior.* New York: Appleton-Century-Crofts.

Hull, C. (1952). *A behavior system.* New Haven, CT: Yale University Press.

Wolpe, J. (1958). *Psychotherapy by reciprocal inhibition.* Stanford, CA: Stanford University Press.

Zusne, L. (1987). *Eponyms in psychology.* Westport, CT: Greenwood Press.

Reber, A. (1995). *The Penguin dictionary of psychology.* New York: Penguin Books.

INSTINCT THEORY. See McDOUGALL'S HORMIC/INSTINCT THEORY/DOCTRINE.

INSTRUCTIONAL THEORY. See ALGORITHMIC-HEURISTIC THEORY.

INSTRUMENTAL CONDITIONING, PRINCIPLE OF. See REINFORCE-MENT THEORY; REINFORCEMENT, THORNDIKE'S THEORY OF; SKIN-NER'S DESCRIPTIVE BEHAVIOR/OPERANT CONDITIONING THEORY.

INSUFFICIENT-JUSTIFICATION EFFECT. See FESTINGER'S COGNI-TIVE DISSONANCE THEORY.

INTELLIGENCE, THEORIES/LAWS OF. The concept of *intelligence* is broad in nature and refers to a person's complex mental abilities, which include, among others, the variables of amount of knowledge available at a given time; speed with which new knowledge is acquired; the ability to adapt to new situations; and the ability to deal with new and old concepts, abstract symbols, and cognitive relationships. The process of developing mental "schemas" to classify events in the environment is called *abstract intelligence/reasoning* (Terman, 1916; cf: *concretistic reasoning*) and *formal operations* (Piaget, 1963) and may be measured/evaluated in various ways. Many of the *theories of intelligence* are tied to particular tests, methods, and measures of this complex concept, and these constitute what might be called *measured intelligence*. Some researchers in this area also refer to the "adaptive ability" (e.g., grades in school, performance and success at work) of the individual as an indication of *general intelligence*. The modern concept of *measured intelligence* in psychology began with the French psychologist Alfred Binet (1857–1911), who was called upon in 1904 by the Paris minister of public instruction to develop a test that would identify subnormal children in the Paris schools for the purpose of placing and educating them in special schools. In 1905, Binet presented a scale for the measurement of intelligence, along with the French psychologist Theodore Simon (1873–1961). The scale consisted of tasks that were arranged in increasing difficulty according to the age at which an "average" child (i.e., criterion of 60–90% students passing tasks) could master them. Using this method, Binet and Simon could identify a "mentally retarded" child, who performed below the average child for his or her particular age group. A total *mental age (MA)* score was calculated for each student and compared with his or her *chronological age (CA)* (Binet & Simon, 1915). Binet's work on intelligence was developed further after 1911 by the German psychologist Lewis William Stern (1871–1938), who formulated the concept of *intelligence quotient*, or *IQ*, where overall *IQ score* equals *MA* divided by *CA* $\times$ 100 (Stern, 1912; cf: *Heinis' constant/law of mental growth*; Zusne, 1987). Thus, in the case of Binet, Simon, and Stern, *intelligence* was considered to be one general or common factor of global functioning based on the individual's test score on their standardized test. The Binet–Simon Test was translated from French into English and brought to the United States by the American psychologist Henry Goddard (1866–1957) in 1908. In 1916, the American psychologist/psychometrician Lewis Terman (1877–1956) at Stanford University adapted the Binet–Simon Test to create the Stanford–Binet Test, which provided a single score of intelligence. In 1904, the English psychologist/psychometrician Charles Spearman (1863–1945) proposed a slightly different theoretical viewpoint (called the *two-factor theory*) concerning intelligence, where he showed the presence of one *general factor (g)* in classroom tests of intellectual ability and achievement (cf: Raven's, 1960, *progressive matrices theory*), as well as a number of *specific factors (s)*. The question of whether intelligence is basically a single ability (*g*) or a group of specific abilities (*s*) has been debated by psychologists for more than three generations and still remains unresolved (Matarazzo & Denver, 1994). The Romanian-American psychologist David Wechsler (1896–1981) developed a set of individually administered intelligence tests (e.g., Wechsler, 1974) that measured several factors such as comprehension, vocabulary, similarities, block design, and object assembly on scales that provide an overall intelligence score as well as subscale scores on verbal and performance abilities. The American psychologist/psychometrician Louis Leon Thurstone (1887–1955) devised a ratio scale for the measurement of intelligence in 1928 after he pointed out the psychometric inadequacies of the Binet-Simon-Stern concept of *MA* as a scale for mental ability and of the *IQ* concept when used as the ratio of *MA* to *CA* (Thurstone, 1926). That is, the concept of *MA* is ambiguous and can mean two different things: the average age of children obtaining a given score or the average test score of children of a given age. Thurstone's theoretical approach emphasizes the use of percentile ranks or standard scores instead of *MA* and *IQ*. This viewpoint is the basis for all modern intelligence tests, and such intelligence scores today are actually standard scores with a population mean of 100 and standard deviation of 15 or 16. Thurstone's approach is based also on the statistical method of *factor analysis* (Thurstone, 1947), wherein he extracted a number of factors he called *primary mental abilities* (Thurstone, 1938). Thurstone developed "factor-pure" tests for the seven factors of reasoning, verbal comprehension, word fluency, number, spatial visualization, perceptual speed, and associative memory. Currently, however, it is thought that each "factor-pure" test measures not only one of Thurstone's primary abilities but also Spearman's *g* factor to some degree (Jensen, 1994b). The American psychologist Joy Paul Guilford (1897–1987) made numerous factor analytic studies of intellectual abilities and developed an ambitious and creative model called the *structure-of-intellect model/theory*, which suggests the existence of as many as 150 separate and distinct functions or abilities (Guilford, 1956, 1967). In at least 120 of these "intelligences," Guilford conceives of a stack of building blocks six blocks high, four blocks wide, and five blocks deep, and where each block is a separate "intelligence." This theoretical approach suggests there are five "operations" (evaluation, convergent production, divergent production, memory, cognition), four "contents" (figural, symbolic, semantic, behavioral), and six "products" (units, classes, relations, systems, transformations, implications). According to Guilford, an individual uses various operations, contents, and products whenever she or he is engaged in intellectual activities (cf: *Sternberg & Lubart's theory of creativity*, 1991). Thus, to oversimplify the range of *classical theories of intelligence*, one may go from the Binet–Simon–Stern–Terman concept of one general/global factor, to the Spearman–Wechsler concept of one general plus several specific factors, to Piaget's emphasis on cognitive development, to Thurstone's seven (or eight) factors/abilities, and finally to Guilford's theoretical approach, which invokes 150 distinct abilities or "intelligences." The more *modern/contemporary theories of intelligence* focus on concepts such as *multiple intelligences* (Gardner, 1983), *triarchic* (componential, experiential, contextual) *intelligence* (Sternberg, 1985, 1988) and *mental self-government* (Sternberg, 1986). A general class of theories that attempts to account for individual differences ranging from reaction time, through intelligence, to study of personal values is called *individuality theory* (Royce, 1994). Questions concerning *intelligence* that remain to be answered by further theoretical and empirical developments before the "laws" of intelligence may be stated are, Is intelligence truly one general ability or several specific abilities? Is intelligence a matter of rapid information processing? Is intelligence genetically, environmentally, or culturally defined (cf: Jensen, 1994a)? One popular explanation for the observed social class and racial differences on intelligence tests is called the *cultural bias hypothesis*, which states that the typical experiences involving the acquisition of skills and knowledge are different for different subpopulations, and the content of test items is selected much more from the experiences of certain groups such as "whites," "Anglo-Saxons," "Protestants," and "middle class," than from the experiences of other groups such as "blacks," "poor," and "lower class" (McMillan, 1994). See also PIAGET'S THEORY OF DEVELOPMENTAL STAGES.

REFERENCES

Spearman, C. (1904). "General intelligence," objectively determined and measured. *Amer. J. Psy., 15,* 201–292.

Stern, W. (1912). *The psychological methods of testing intelligence.* Baltimore: Warwick & York.

Binet, A., & Simon, T. (1915). *A method of measuring the development of intelligence of young children.* Chicago: Medical Books.

Terman, L. (1916). *The measurement of intelligence.* Boston: Houghton Mifflin.

Thurstone, L. (1926). The mental age concept. *Psy. Rev., 33,* 268–278.

Thurstone, L. (1928). The absolute zero in intelligence measurement. *Psy. Rev., 35,* 175–197.

Thurstone, L. (1938). *Primary mental abilities.* Psychometric Monographs, no. 1. Chicago: University of Chicago Press.

Thurstone, L. (1947). *Multiple-factor analysis: A development and expansion of the vectors of the mind.* Chicago: University of Chicago Press.

Guilford, J. P. (1956). The structure of intellect. *Psy. Bull., 53,* 267–293.

Raven, J. (1960). *Guide to the standard progressive matrices.* London: Lewis.

Piaget, J. (1963). *The origins of intelligence in children.* New York: Norton.

Guilford, J. P. (1967). *The nature of human intelligence.* New York: McGraw-Hill.

Wechsler, D. (1974). *Wechsler Intelligence Scale for Children, revised.* New York: Psychological Corporation.

Gardner, H. (1983). *Frames of mind: The theory of multiple intelligences.* New York: Basic Books.

Sternberg, R. (1985). *Beyond IQ: A triarchic theory of human intelligence.* New York: Cambridge University Press.

Sternberg, R. (1986). Intelligence is mental self-government. In R. Sternberg & D. Detterman (Eds.), *What is intelligence? Contemporary viewpoints on its nature and definition.* Norwood, NJ: Ablex.

Zusne, L. (1987). *Eponyms in psychology.* Westport, CT: Greenwood Press.

Sternberg, R. (1988). *The triarchic mind: A new theory of human intelligence.* New York: Viking.

Sternberg, R., & Lubart, T. (1991). An investment theory of creativity and its development. *Hum. Dev., 34,* 1–31.

Jensen, A. (1994a). Cultural bias in tests. In R. J. Corsini (Ed.), *Ency. Psy.* New York: Wiley.

Jensen, A. (1994b). Louis Leon Thurstone. In R. J. Corsini (Ed.), *Ency. Psy.* New York: Wiley.

Matarazzo, J., & Denver, D. (1994). Intelligence measures. In R. J. Corsini (Ed.), *Ency. Psy.* New York: Wiley.

McMillan, J. (1994). Culture fair tests. In R. J. Corsini (Ed.), *Ency. Psy.* New York: Wiley.

Royce, J. (1994). Individuality theory. In R. J. Corsini (Ed.), *Ency. Psy.* New York: Wiley.

INTENSITY/VIVIDNESS, LAW OF. See ASSOCIATION, LAWS/PRINCI-PLES OF.

INTENTIONALISM, PSYCHOLOGICAL THEORY OF. See MIND–BODY THEORIES.

INTERACTION/INTERACTIONISM, THEORY/DOCTRINE OF. See MIND–BODY THEORIES.

INTERACTION OF REFLEXES, LAW OF. See SKINNER'S DESCRIPTIVE BEHAVIOR/OPERANT CONDITIONING THEORY.

INTERFERENCE THEORIES OF FORGETTING. *Interference theory* states that forgetting occurs because similar memories interfere with the storage or retrieval of information. Interference is an *active* theory of forgetting; without interfering events there is no forgetting (Adams, 1980). An early functionalist's view of the conditions that affect transfer of the forgetting of verbal materials is provided by McGeoch (1932), who accepted two major *laws of forgetting and transfer*: the *law of context*, which states that the degree of retention of material, as measured by performance, is a function of the *similarity* between the original learning situation and the retention situation, and the *law of proactive and retroactive inhibition*, which states that the retention of material is a function of *activities* occurring prior to, and subsequent to, the original learning (cf: *perseveration theory* of Muller & Pilzecker, 1900). The evolution of hypotheses regarding the similarity effects in retroaction and transfer is traced by Bower and Hilgard (1981): the early experiments, demonstrating retroactive interference and the possible role of similarity as a factor (e.g., McGeoch, 1932); Robinson's (1927) somewhat crude dimensional hypothesis, which led to a series of experiments that revealed multiple sources and kinds of intertask similarities requiring a generalization more complex than the *Skaggs–Robinson hypothesis* (Skaggs, 1925; Robinson, 1927); Osgood's (1949) synthesis (via his *transfer and retroaction surface*), incorporating the results on transfer and retroactive interference; and Martin's (1965) proposed "component transfer surfaces" to compensate for Osgood's (1949) simplistic synthesis. This type of succession of hypothesized generalizations, according to Bower and Hilgard (1981), with an interplay between data, analytical criticism, and theory, demonstrates a maturing functional analysis, as well as indicates some potential frustrations of a functionalistic approach. The most serviceable *theory of forgetting* that has emerged from laboratory experiments is the *interference theory* that is connected to the functionalists' analysis of negative transfer and interference. The *interference theory* is an "association" theory; that is, its basic primitive concept is an associative bond, or functional connection, between two or more elements where elements may be ideas, words, situational stimuli, or responses. Changes in *interference theory* have occurred over the years. For example, Postman's (1961, 1971) formulations may be compared with McGeoch's (1932) earlier statements where new concepts have been added, unsupported conjecture dropped, and new experimental methods devised to measure more exactly the relevant dependent variables (cf: Thune & Underwood, 1943; Slamecka & Ceraso, 1960). One major shift in *interference theory* over the years consisted of the powerful role assigned to *proactive* sources of interference in forgetting (see Underwood, 1957; Underwood & Postman, 1960). The history of research on verbal interference shows several subtheories of interference. In the 1930s, a viable theory of interference was the *independence hypothesis*, which held that interfering responses compete at recall, and the strongest one in the competition is the one that actually occurs. In a retroactive interference paradigm where the learning of material A and B is followed by the recall of A, the decrement in recall of A was explained by the dominance of B. The successor to the *independence hypothesis* was the *unlearning hypothesis*, which held that the decrement in A at recall was because the learning of B had brought about the extinction of A in part. Later, there was the *differentiation hypothesis/ theory of differential forgetting* (McGeoch, 1942), which asserted that interference reduced the discriminability, or differentiation, of the material where the learning of B reduced the discriminability of A and decreased its availability at recall (Adams, 1980; cf: *generalization-differentiation theory*; Gibson, 1940; Tighe & Tighe, 1968). The early studies of interference used "meaningless" materials such as "nonsense syllables" or randomly unrelated words as information to be learned. However, recent research provides evidence that similar interference processes operate in the learning and forgetting of meaningful text materials (e.g., single sentences and interrelated sets of sentences or paragraphs) as well (see Anderson & Bower, 1973). See also FORGETTING/MEMORY, THEORIES OF; INHIBITION, LAWS OF; SKAGGS–ROBINSON HYPOTHESIS; TRANSFER OF TRAINING, THORNDIKE'S THEORY OF.

REFERENCES

Muller, G., & Pilzecker, A. (1900). Experimentelle Beitrage zur Lehre vom Gedachtnis. *Z. Psy.* Ergbd. I.

Skaggs, E. (1925). Further studies in retroactive inhibition. *Psy. Mono., 34*, no. 161.

Robinson, E. (1927). The "similarity" factor in retroaction. *Amer. J. Psy., 39*, 297–312.

McGeoch, J. (1932). Forgetting and the law of disuse. *Psy. Rev., 39*, 352–370.

Gibson, E. (1940). A systematic application of the concepts of generalization and differentiation to verbal learning. *Psy. Rev., 47*, 196–229.

McGeoch, J. (1942). *The psychology of human learning*. New York: Longmans, Green.

Thune, L., & Underwood, B. (1943). Retroactive inhibition as a function of degree of interpolated learning. *J. Exp. Psy., 32*, 185–200.

Osgood, C. (1949). The similarity paradox in human learning: A resolution. *Psy. Rev.,* *56,* 132–143.

Underwood, B. (1957). Interference and forgetting. *Psy. Rev., 64,* 49–60.

Slamecka, N., & Ceraso, J. (1960). Retroactive and proactive inhibition of verbal learning. *Psy. Bull., 57,* 449–475.

Underwood, B., & Postman, L. (1960). Extra-experimental sources of interference in forgetting. *Psy. Rev., 67,* 73–95.

Postman, L. (1961). The present status of interference theory. In C. Cofer (Ed.), *Verbal learning and verbal behavior.* New York: McGraw-Hill.

Martin, E. (1965). Transfer of verbal paired associates. *Psy. Rev., 72,* 327–343.

Tighe, T., & Tighe, L. (1968). Differentiation theory and concept-shift behavior. *Psy. Bull., 70,* 756–761.

Postman, L. (1971). Transfer, interference, and forgetting. In J. Kling & L. Riggs (Eds.), *Woodworth and Schlosberg's experimental psychology.* New York: Holt, Rinehart, & Winston.

Anderson, J., & Bower, G. (1973). *Human associative memory.* Washington, DC: Winston.

Adams, J. (1980). *Learning and memory: An introduction.* Homewood, IL: Dorsey Press.

Bower, G., & Hilgard, E. (1981). *Theories of learning.* Englewood Cliffs, NJ: Prentice-Hall.

Bower, G., Thompson-Schill, S., & Tulving, E. (1994). Reducing retroactive interference: An interference analysis. *J. Exp. Psy.: Learn., Mem., & Cog., 20,* 51–66.

INTERPERSONAL ATTRACTION THEORIES. *Interpersonal attraction* refers to a favorable attitude toward, or feeling of liking for, another person (Ajzen, 1994). People are attracted to others for a variety of reasons, and there are many different kinds of attraction. One generalization concerning interpersonal attraction is the *reward theory,* which states that we like people whose behavior provides us with maximum reward at minimum cost (Thibaut & Kelley, 1959; Aronson, 1972). Aronson's *gain–loss theory* suggests that increases in positive, rewarding behavior from another person will have more impact on an individual than constant, invariant reward from that person. Thus, if one takes "being liked" as a reward, a person whose liking for us increases over time will be liked better than one who has always liked us (Aronson & Linder, 1965). Four other theories/principles that describe interpersonal attraction are *similarity, beauty/physical appearance, proximity,* and *social exchange.* The *similarity-attraction theory* suggests that we like other people whose attitudes, values, and beliefs appear to be similar to our own (e.g., Heider, 1958; Secord & Backman, 1964; Byrne, 1971). The principle of *beauty/physical appearance* refers to the rather obvious prediction that we tend to prefer physically attractive to physically unattractive individuals (e.g., Berscheid & Walster, 1969, 1974). Within a given culture, there is considerable agreement in judgments of a person's physical attractiveness, but little is known about the particular attributes that define "beauty." However, there is strong evidence to show a gender distinction where physical appearance has a greater influence on the attraction of males to females than vice versa (Ajzen, 1994). The *principle of proximity* states that we are more likely to be attracted to people who live and work close to us rather than to those who live/work farther away. Proximity is perhaps the most important determinant of who people choose as friends, lovers, and spouses; often, people end up marrying mates who live only a few blocks away. In general, the closer in distance people are to others, the more opportunities they have of becoming familiar with them: knowledge often leads to attraction and love (Hatfield, 1994). The *theory of social exchange* (e.g., Thibaut & Kelley, 1959) states that a relationship between two persons will be formed and maintained if, for each person, the rewards from the interaction are greater than the costs. A variation on the *social-exchange theory*, called *equity theory*, shifts the emphasis from the individual to mutual costs and benefits where a group of people can maximize their outcome in any interaction situation by working out an arrangement for equitably dividing the benefits and costs among group members (Baum, Fisher, & Singer, 1985). There is some evidence that attraction and liking are influenced by such nonverbal behaviors as smiling, eye contact, physical touch, and body posture (Ajzen, 1994). See also COOPERATION/COMPETITION, THEORIES OF; EQUITY THEORY; EXCHANGE/SOCIAL EXCHANGE THEORY; LOVE, THEORIES OF; SULLIVAN'S THEORY OF PERSONALITY.

REFERENCES

Heider, F. (1958). *The psychology of interpersonal relations.* New York: Wiley.
Thibaut, J., & Kelley, H. (1959). *The social psychology of groups.* New York: Wiley.
Secord, P., & Backman, C. (1964). Interpersonal congruency, perceived similarity, and friendship. *Sociometry, 27,* 115–127.
Aronson, E., & Linder, D. (1965). Gain and loss of esteem as determinants of interpersonal attractiveness. *J. Exp. Soc. Psy., 1,* 156–171.
Berscheid, E., & Walster, E. (1969). *Interpersonal attraction.* Reading, MA: Addison-Wesley.
Byrne, D. (1971). *The attraction paradigm.* New York: Academic Press.
Aronson, E. (1972). *The social animal.* San Francisco: Freeman.
Berscheid, E., & Walster, E. (1974). Physical attractiveness. In L. Berkowitz (Ed.), *Advances in experimental social psychology.* Vol. 7. New York: Academic Press.
Huston, T., & Levinger, G. (1978). Interpersonal attraction and relationships. *Ann. Rev. Psy., 29,* 115–156.
Baum, A., Fisher, J., & Singer, J. (1985). *Social psychology.* New York: Random House.
Ajzen, I. (1994). Interpersonal attraction. In R. J. Corsini (Ed.), *Ency. Psy.* New York: Wiley.
Hatfield, E. (1994). Love. In R. J. Corsini (Ed.), *Ency. Psy.* New York: Wiley.

INTERPERSONAL PERCEPTION. See IMPRESSION FORMATION, THEORIES OF.

INVERTED-U HYPOTHESIS. Also known as the *Yerkes–Dodson law*, this hypothesis refers to the results observed in a situation where performance on a task (e.g., taking a test) is seen as a function of one's arousal level (e.g., degree of motivation or anxiety), and where behavior is best at moderate levels but drops off with either decreases or increases in the individual's arousal level. When graphed, the distribution of potential results under such circumstances appears to be a curve in the shape of an upside down (inverted) letter U. Because the phenomenon described by the inverted-U relationship here between performance and arousal level may be categorized as either a *law* or a *hypothesis*, a semantic and labeling problem arises and becomes a decision for the reader/ researcher to make concerning the scientific validity and/or utility of the *hypothesis* (or *law*). See also AROUSAL THEORY; REINFORCEMENT THEORY; YERKES–DODSON LAW.

REFERENCES

Naatanen, R. (1973). The inverted-U relationship between activation and performance: A critical review. In S. Kornblum (Ed.), *Attention and performance*. IV. New York: Academic Press.

Anderson, K. (1990). Arousal and the inverted-U hypothesis: A critique of Neiss's "reconceptualizing arousal." *Psy. Bull., 107*, 96–100.

Neiss, R. (1990). Ending arousal's reign of error: A reply to Anderson. *Psy. Bull., 107*, 101–105.

Raglin, J., & Turner, P. (1993). Anxiety and performance in track and field athletes: A comparison of the inverted-U hypothesis with zone of optimal function theory. *Pers. Indiv. Diff., 14*, 163–171.

ISAKOWER PHENOMENON. See SLEEP, THEORIES OF.

ISOMORPHISM, PHENOMENON OF. See GESTALT THEORY/LAWS.

IZARD'S THEORY OF EMOTIONS. Carroll E. Izard's approach to emotions is strongly influenced by the *evolutionary theory* of Charles Darwin (1872), who argued that certain basic patterns of emotional expression are part of one's biological inheritance. Such patterns of emotion evolved because of their high survival value in giving humans mutual and beneficial systems of communication. For example, humans—including nonhuman animals such as dogs and baboons—grimace and bare their teeth when they become threatened and thus convey their dispositions and level of arousal to others of the species. *Izard's theory* is called a *differential emotions theory* because it emphasizes 10 distinct and discriminable emotions: joy, excitement, anguish, rage, startle, revulsion, scorn, humiliation, remorse, and terror. To this list of distinctive emotions— including various other physiological and cognitive components of emotion— Izard adds the variable of facial expression for displaying emotional expressiveness and suggests that each of the specific emotions has its own separate facial pattern. For example, when one experiences rage, a specific pattern of muscle firings that is physiologically connected to anger ''informs'' the person's brain that it is rage she or he is feeling and not some other emotion such as shame or fear. Thus, according to *Izard's theory*, facial patterning and facial muscle tension initiates, sustains, and increases one's experience of emotion, and the facial-muscular movement that occurs with each emotion is part of a biological and evolutionary program that is ''wired'' into the individual. Evolutionary emotion theories, such as Izard's (1971, 1977, 1994) and Plutchik's (1984), hold that emotion evolved before thought and that emotions originate in subcortical brain structures (such as the limbic system and the hypothalamus), which evolved before the cortical areas that are associated with more complex thought. The principal goal of the *neo-evolutionary theories of emotion* has been to come up with a list of the basic/primary emotions. Of course, not all theorists come up with the same list of emotional terms and concepts, but there is considerable overlap (Mandler, 1984). See also DARWIN'S THEORY OF EMOTIONS; EKMAN–FRIESEN THEORY OF EMOTIONS; EMOTIONS, THEORIES/LAWS OF; FACIAL-FEEDBACK HYPOTHESIS; PLUTCHIK'S MODEL OF EMOTIONS.

REFERENCES

Darwin, C. (1872). *The expression of emotions in man and animals*. London: Appleton.

Izard, C. (1971). *The faces of emotion*. New York: Appleton-Century-Crofts.

Izard, C. (1977). *Human emotions*. New York: Plenum.

Mandler, G. (1984). *Mind and body*. New York: Norton.

Plutchik, R. (1984). Emotions: A general psychoevolutionary theory. In K. Scherer & P. Ekman (Eds.), *Approaches to emotion*. Hillsdale, NJ: Erlbaum.

Izard, C. (1990). The substrata and function of emotional feeling: William James and current theory. *Pers. Soc. Psy. Bull., 16*, 625–635.

Mesquita, B., & Frijda, N. (1992). Cultural variations in emotions: A review. *Psy. Bull., 112*, 179–204.

Izard, C. (1994). Innate and universal facial expressions: Evidence from developmental and cross-cultural research. *Psy. Bull., 115*, 288–299.

J

JACKSON'S LAW. See NEURON/NEURAL/NERVE THEORY.

JAMES–LANGE/LANGE–JAMES THEORY OF EMOTIONS. This theory is credited to both the American philosopher/psychologist William James (1842–1910) and the Danish physiologist Carl Lange (1843–1900), who independently proposed the theory. The term *James–Lange theory* is seen more frequently in the psychological literature, but the *Lange–James theory* has been used as well (e.g., McDougall, 1924). The theory is sometimes called the *counterintuitive theory* of emotions because it states that overt, external action (e.g., laughter) precedes the internal/emotional response (e.g., happiness). The older, classical, popular, *commonsense*, or *intuitive theory* of emotions states the sequence of events in the opposite order: the internal event (e.g., happiness) precedes the external action (e.g., laughter). The *commonsense theory* says we laugh because we're happy, while the *James–Lange theory* says we're happy because we laugh. The empirical works by James (1884) and Lange (1885, 1922) were among the first to propose a theory that identified a physiological mechanism and neural basis for emotionality. However, the ancient Greeks set up four nonempirically based categories of physiological states (involving a predominant ingredient in one's bodily fluids) for emotionality: the *sanguine, melancholic, choleric*, and *phlegmatic* temperaments. The key idea behind the *James–Lange theory* was that an emotion was not a direct reaction to an environmental happening, but rather it was a reaction to how the body was responding to the environmental event. James (1890, p. 450) stated that "we feel sorry because we cry, angry because we strike, afraid because we tremble, and not that we cry, strike, or tremble because we are sorry, angry, or fearful, as the case may be." *James' theory* (1890) held that the bodily changes directly follow the perception of the exciting fact, that one's feeling of the same changes as they occur *is* the emotion, and that every one of the bodily changes is *felt* acutely or obscurely the moment it occurs. *Lange's theory* (1885) held that a stimulus object or situation immediately leads to vasomotor changes wherever blood vessels are found. According to Lange, the secondary changes that occur in the bodily tissues give rise to the sensations that constitute the emotion. Overall, the *James–Lange theory* did more than simply focus attention on bodily (somatic and autonomic) responses that occurred during stress; it proposed that these bodily responses formed the essential basis for an emotional experience. The strongest objections to the *James–Lange theory* were raised by Cannon (1927), who cited five principal criticisms: total separation of the viscera from the central nervous system does not alter emotional behavior; the same visceral changes occur in diverse emotional states and in nonemotional states; the viscera are relatively insensitive structures; the visceral changes are too slow to be a direct source of emotional feeling; and artificial induction of the visceral changes typical of strong emotions does not produce them. In the light of such criticisms, some writers (e.g., Lindsley, 1951) suggest that the *James–Lange theory* by its very nature and formulation is not a theory per se but rather an untestable hypothesis. It is clear today that greater attention is given to the influence of the central nervous system on emotions and one's cognition and interpretation of events, rather than merely to examine visceral processes in order to achieve the most comprehensive view of emotionality. See also CANNON/CANNON–BARD THEORY; EMOTIONS, THEORIES/LAWS OF.

REFERENCES

James, W. (1884). What is an emotion? *Mind, 9,* 188–205.

Lange, C. (1885). *Om Sindsbevagelser.* Copenhagen.

James, W. (1890). *Principles of psychology.* New York: Holt.

Lange, C. (1922). The emotions. In K. Dunlap (Ed.), *Psychology classics.* Vol. 1. Baltimore: Williams & Wilkins.

Maranon, G. (1924). Contribution a l'etude de l'action emotive de l'adrenaline. *Rev. Fran. Endo., 2,* 301–325.

McDougall, W. (1924). *Outline of psychology.* New York: Scribners.

Cannon, W. (1927). The James–Lange theory of emotions: A critical examination and an alternative theory. *Amer. J. Psy., 39,* 106–124.

Cannon, W. (1931). Again the James–Lange and the thalamic theories of emotion. *Psy. Rev., 38,* 281–295.

Lindsley, D. (1951). Emotion. In S. S. Stevens (Ed.), *Handbk. Exp. Psy.* New York: Wiley.

Schachter, S. & Singer, J. (1962). Cognitive, social, and physiological determinants of emotional state. *Psy. Rev., 69,* 379–399.

JOST'S LAWS. The German psychologist Adolf Jost (1874–?) formulated these laws based on his work, as well as the research by Ebbinghaus (1885), in the area of human learning and retention. Earlier studies (Ebbinghaus, 1885) reported that when lists of materials are learned on successive days ("distributed practice") using the same criterion each day, the number of trials to learn becomes progressively less. Jost (1897) expanded on this idea and proposed the following principles (*Jost's laws*): (1) given two associations of the same strength, but of different ages, the older one has greater value on a new repetition; (2) given two associations of the same strength, but of different ages, the older falls off less rapidly in a given length of time. Jost's data were rather meager for founding "laws" (Woodworth & Schlosberg, 1965), but more recent experiments have helped to corroborate his findings. For example, Youtz (1941) confirmed the fact that an older habit shows a larger learning increment after a single relearning trial and that when comparable parts of the materials are equated initially, as on the first recall, the amount of increment from new repetitions tends to increase in a logarithmic fashion. Thus, older associations (materials) require fewer trials to relearn than do younger associations. Inasmuch as younger habits show an excess of errors in the middle of a series of materials, the ratio of errors in the central position to those in the end position was used as one of the indicators of age (Hovland, 1951). Subsequently, Youtz (1941, p. 46) restated *Jost's first law* in the following terms "[O]f two series of associations which are overtly remembered to the same degree, the one exhibiting the most extensive dissipation of intralist inhibition will profit more on a new repetition." A principle in learning related to *Jost's law*, called the *law of diminishing returns* (Thorndike, 1907), states that in memorizing a series of items, each successive repetition increases the amount recalled less than does the one preceding it. As part of *Spearman's theory of intelligence* (Warren, 1934), this principle states that the more of an ability (e.g., intelligence) a person already has available, the less advantage accrues to his or her ability from further increments of it. All the studies conducted in psychology on the distribution of learning (and on the relations of retention, recall, and relearning) seem to fit together adequately and probably embody some fundamental law—which would supersede *Jost's laws*—even though that law has not yet been formulated (Woodworth & Schlosberg, 1965). *Jost's laws* are largely obsolete today, and the principles have been incorporated into the more modern area of human memory that employ newer concepts and terms such as *short-term memory* and *long-term memory* (Reber, 1995). See also FORGETTING/MEMORY, THEORIES OF; LEARNING THEORIES/LAWS.

REFERENCES

Ebbinghaus, H. von (1885). *Uber das Gedachtnis: Untersuchungen zur experimentellen Psychologie*. Leipzig: Duncker & Humbolt.

Jost, A. (1897). Die Assoziation festigkeit in ihrer Abhangigkeit von der Verteilung der Wiederholungen. *Z. Psy., 14,* 436–472.

Larguier des Bancels, J. (1901). Sur les methodes de memorisation. *Ann. Psy., 8,* 185–204.

Pentschew, C. (1903). Untersuchungen zur Okonomie und Technik des Lernens. *Ar. ges. Psy., 1,* 417–526.

Thorndike, E. (1907). *The elements of psychology*. New York: Seiler.

Warren, H. (Ed.) (1934). *Dictionary of psychology*. Cambridge, MA: Houghton Mifflin.

Youtz, A. (1941). An experimental evaluation of Jost's laws. *Psy. Mono.*, no. 238.

Hovland, C. (1951). Human learning and retention. In S. S. Stevens (Ed.), *Handbk. Exp. Psy.* New York: Wiley.

Woodworth, R., & Schlosberg, H. (1965). *Experimental psychology*. New York: Holt, Rinehart, & Winston.

Reber, A. (1995). *The Penguin dictionary of psychology*. New York: Penguin Books.

JUKE-BOX THEORY OF EMOTIONS. See SCHACHTER–SINGER'S THEORY OF EMOTIONS.

JULESZ'S OBJECT PERCEPTION THEORY. See PATTERN/OBJECT RECOGNITION THEORY.

JUNG'S THEORY OF PERSONALITY. The Swiss-born psychiatrist/psycho-analyst Carl Gustav Jung (1875–1961) first met Sigmund Freud in 1907 and was soon named Freud's successor (''my crown prince'') by Freud, but by 1914 Jung and Freud parted company—never to see one another again—essentially due to theoretical differences concerning the interpretation of psychoanalysis, the influence of *determinism* on personality (Freud thought personality was basically set or determined in the first few years of childhood; Jung believed it to be more malleable and changeable in later life by future goals), and the concepts of *libido* (Freud thought of it as ''sexual energy,'' while Jung regarded it as a generalized ''life energy'') and *unconscious* (Freud thought of it as the prime source of motivation with one-way master control over one's conscious thoughts and behavior; Jung partitioned it into the ''personal'' and ''collective'' unconscious where life's experiences are progressive and more flexibly selected and guided under their influence). Jung's (1913, 1936, 1940, 1953, 1960, 1964) approach toward personality and psychoanalytic theory and therapeutic practice became known as *analytical psychology*, wherein he formulated his unique notions about the myths and symbols that people have used throughout centuries of recorded history. The structure of ''total personality'' (i.e., the mind or *psyche*) in *Jung's theory* consists of a number of differentiated, but interacting, systems: the *ego* or conscious mind; the *personal unconscious* or repressed, suppressed, ignored, or forgotten experiences that may form ''complexes''; and the *collective, transpersonal unconscious* or storehouse of latent memory traces inherited from one's ancestral past. The notion of the *collective unconscious* is one of the most original and controversial features of *Jung's personality theory* (Hall & Lindzey, 1978). One of the components of the *collective unconscious* is called *archetypes* (other names for this component are *dominants, primordial images, imagoes, mythological images*, and *behavior patterns*; Jung, 1943; Coan, 1994), which are universal ideas that are emotion-laden and create images/visions that correspond to some aspect of the conscious situation in normal waking life. Other components of the *collective unconscious* are called the *per-*

sona—the masked or public face of personality; the *anima* and *animus*—a bisexual aspect where the feminine archetype in man is the *anima*, and the masculine archetype in woman is the *animus*; the *shadow*—the animal instincts that humans have inherited in their evolution from lower life forms and that may be manifested as recognition of original sin, the devil, or an enemy; and the *self*—comprising all aspects of the unconscious, it strives for equilibrium, integration, self-actualization, and unity and is expressed in the symbols of the mandala and the circle. According to Jung, the well-adjusted individual is one who seeks a compromise between the demands of the *collective unconscious* and the actualities of the external world. Jung also distinguished between the *extraversion* attitude—orientation of the individual toward the external/objective world—and the *introversion* attitude—orientation of the person toward the internal/subjective world. He described four fundamental *psychological types/functions*: thinking (ideational), feeling (evaluative), sensing (perceptual), and intuiting (unconscious or subliminal) aspects of processing information in the world (cf: Myers, 1962). Jung wrote broadly on such diverse topics as mythology, symbols, occult sciences, word associations, religion, dreams, telepathy, clairvoyance, spiritualism, and flying saucers. Jung borrowed concepts from the physical sciences (e.g., the principles of *equivalence, entropy*, and *synchronicity* in chemistry and physics) in describing the psychodynamics of personality. The *principle of entropy* as adapted by Jung (from the *second law of thermodynamics* in physics) states that the distribution of energy in the psyche seeks an equilibrium or balance. When Jung asserted that self-realization is the goal of psychic development, he meant that the dynamics of personality move toward a perfect balance of forces. The *principle of equivalence* states that if energy is expended in bringing about a certain condition, the amount expended will appear somewhere else in the system. This principle is similar to the *first law of thermodynamics* in physics and to Helmholtz's adaptation in psychology of the physical *principle of the conservation of energy*. The *principle of synchronicity* is a general statement concerning event interpretation that applies to events that occur together in time but that are not the cause of one another (see Progoff, 1973). Today, in spite of a few detractors (e.g., Glover, 1950) and a lack of contact with scientific psychology, Jung seems to have a number of devoted proponents and admirers throughout the world, and his influence has spread into many extrapsychology disciplines, including history, literature, literary criticism, anthropology, religion, and philosophy, among others. Perhaps Jung's *analytical psychology* has been dismissed by many psychologists because his theories are based on psychoanalytical and clinical findings (which include mythical and historical sources) rather than on experimental research. It has been suggested that what *Jungian theory* needs to make it more acceptable to scientific psychology is to test experimentally some of his hypotheses (Hall & Lindzey, 1978). See also DETERMINISM, DOCTRINE/THEORY OF; FREUD'S THEORY OF PERSONALITY; PERSONALITY THEORIES.

REFERENCES

Jung, C. (1912). *The psychology of the unconscious*. Leipzig: Deuticke.
Jung, C. (1913). The theory of psychoanalysis. In *Collected works*. Vol. 4. Princeton, NJ: Princeton University Press.
Jung, C. (1921). Psychological types. In *Collected works*. Vol. 6. Princeton, NJ: Princeton University Press.
Jung, C. (1936). The concept of the collective unconscious. In *Collected works*. Vol. 9. Part 1. Princeton, NJ: Princeton University Press.
Jung, C. (1940). *The integration of the personality*. London: Routledge & Kegan Paul.
Jung, C. (1943). The psychology of the unconscious. In *Collected works*. Vol. 7. Princeton, NJ: Princeton University Press.
Glover, E. (1950). *Freud or Jung*. New York: Norton.
Jung, C. (1953). *Modern man in search of a soul*. New York: Harcourt, Brace.
Read, H., Fordham, M., & Adler, G. (Eds.). (1953–1978). *C. G. Jung, Collected works*. 20 vols. Princeton, NJ: Princeton University Press.
Jung, C. (1957). *The undiscovered self*. Boston: Little, Brown.
Jung, C. (1960). A review of the complex theory. In *Collected works*. Vol. 8. Princeton, NJ: Princeton University Press.
Myers, I. (1962). *The Myers–Briggs Type Indicator*. Princeton, NJ: Educational Testing Service.
Jung, C. (Ed.) (1964). *Man and his symbols*. New York: Dell.
Progoff, I. (1973). *Jung, synchronicity, and human destiny*. New York: Julian.
McGuire, W. (Ed). (1974). *The Freud/Jung letters: The correspondence between Sigmund Freud and C. G. Jung*. Princeton, NJ: Princeton University Press.
Hall, C., & Lindzey, G. (1978). *Theories of personality*. New York: Wiley.
Coan, R. (1994). Archetypes. In R. J. Corsini (Ed.), *Ency. Psy.* New York: Wiley.
Haynie, N. (1994). Carl Jung. In R. J. Corsini (Ed.), *Ency. Psy.* New York: Wiley.

JUST-NOTICEABLE DIFFERENCES, PRINCIPLE OF. See WEBER'S LAW.

JUST-WORLD HYPOTHESIS. See ATTRIBUTION THEORY.

K

KAMIN EFFECT. See MOWRER'S THEORY; BLOCKING, PHENOME-NON/EFFECT OF.

KARDOS EFFECT. See PERCEPTION (I. GENERAL), THEORIES OF.

KELLEY'S ATTRIBUTION THEORY. See ATTRIBUTION THEORY.

KELLEY'S PRINCIPLE OF COVARIATION/CORRELATION. See AT-TRIBUTION THEORY.

KELLY'S PERSONAL CONSTRUCT THEORY. The American psychologist George A. Kelly (1905–1967) developed the *personal construct theory of personality*, which emphasizes the ways in which individuals interpret or construe events, and advances the viewpoint that each person unwittingly takes the role of "scientist" by observing events, formulating concepts to organize phenomena, and attempting to predict future events. According to Kelly (1955, 1963), people conduct mental "miniexperiments" in order to interpret and understand their own experiences. In this sense, people are actively engaged in the construction of their own subjective worlds, and one's perceptual processes are directed by the way one anticipates future events. The theory says that people are viewed as active and future-oriented, rather than passive or merely reactive, and they develop certain concepts, categories, and constructs with which to classify their experiences. With this approach, a concept such as *guilt* may be defined as the realization that the person has done something that he or she would not have predicted on the basis of the constructs that he or she used to describe himself or herself, and a concept such as *hostility* may be defined as a continuing and futile effort to find positive evidence for something that has already been recognized as a failure. *Kelly's theory* has two key features: it deals with both change and stability—including the aspects of process and structure in the individual; and it focuses on the uniqueness of the person (*idiographic*) as well as on the characteristics and processes that are common to all people (*nomothetic*). Kelly's major theoretical concept is the *construct*, which refers to a bipolar way of interpreting and perceiving events. For instance, the *construct/dimension* of "good–bad" is often used by individuals as they assess events and other people. Examples of other *constructs*—where the bipolar terms are not necessarily the logical opposite of each other—are "receive–give," "take–give," "unassertive–assertive," "unassertive–hostile," "hate–love," and "lust–love" (Pervin, 1996). When a *construct* becomes part of an individual's cognitive structure, it may be applied to anything or anyone. Kelly distinguishes among different types of *constructs*: *core constructs* (such as "weak–strong") versus *peripheral constructs* (such as "humorous–serious"); *verbal* versus *preverbal constructs*; and *superordinate* versus *subordinate constructs*. An individual's *personal constructs* are organized to form a *construct system* ranging from a simple system (containing only one or two levels of organization) to a complex system (containing multiple levels of organization). Complex construct systems allow greater differentiation and detailed predictions in one's perception of the world, while simple construct systems indicate that the person lumps all people and things into a few categories such as "good–bad" or "successful–unsuccessful" where the person's predictions are the same without regard to the situation or circumstances (Pervin, 1996). An individual's *personal construct* system may be assessed by Kelly's "Role Construct Repertory Test" ("Rep Test"). Interpreting Rep Test results is a subjective and laborious process because the test is as much a projective test as a rating scale. In the absence of an objective scoring system, the Rep Test has not been widely used for either clinical or research purposes, and its validity is largely unknown (Aiken, 1989). Although Kelly influenced later personality theorists (e.g., Mischel, 1968, 1990), the *theory of personal constructs* has advanced little since its initial development (cf: Epting, 1984). Originally, *Kelly's theory* was set down in a formal postulate fashion with 11 corollaries in his 1955 book, and it is difficult to classify or contrast it with other approaches (Peyser, 1994); Sechrest (1977) describes *Kelly's theory* as having many second cousins, but no siblings. Kelly's ideas arose from his clinical experience rather than from experimental research or systematic correlational studies, and there is relatively little current research based on *Kelly's theory* that is reported in the psychological literature (Pervin, 1996). See also FESTINGER'S COGNITIVE DISSONANCE THEORY; IDIOGRAPHIC/NOMOTHETIC LAWS; PERSONALITY THEORIES.

REFERENCES

Kelly, G. (1955). *The psychology of personal constructs*. New York: Norton.
Kelly, G. (1963). *A theory of personality*. New York: Norton.
Mischel, W. (1968). *Personality and assessment*. New York: Wiley.

Sechrest, L. (1977). Personal constructs theory. In R. J. Corsini (Ed.), *Current personality theories*. Itasca, IL: Peacock.

Epting, F. (1984). *Personal construct counseling and psychotherapy*. New York: Wiley.

Aiken, L. (1989). *Assessment of personality*. Boston: Allyn & Bacon.

Mischel, W. (1990). Personality dispositions revisited and revised: A view after three decades. In L. Pervin (Ed.), *Handbook of personality: Theory and research*. New York: Guilford.

Adams-Webber, J. (1994). Personal construct theory. In R. J. Corsini (Ed.), *Ency. Psy.* New York: Wiley.

Peyser, C. (1994). George A. Kelly. In R. J. Corsini (Ed.), *Ency. Psy.* New York: Wiley.

Pervin, L. (1996). *The science of personality*. New York: Wiley.

KENSHALO/NAFE QUANTITATIVE THEORY. See NAFE'S VASCULAR THEORY OF CUTANEOUS SENSITIVITY.

KINNEY'S LAW. See WHORF–SAPIR HYPOTHESIS/THEORY.

KIRSCHMANN'S LAW OF CONTRAST. See COLOR VISION, THEORIES/LAWS OF.

KJERSTAD–ROBINSON LAW. See SKAGGS–ROBINSON HYPOTHESIS.

KNOWLEDGE-ACROSS-SITUATIONS HYPOTHESIS. See ATTRIBUTION THEORY.

KOHLBERG'S THEORY OF MORALITY. The American psychologist Lawrence Kohlberg (1927–1987) proposed a *stage-dependent theory of moral development*, which is largely cognitive in nature and considers morality as a universal cognitive process that proceeds from one stage to the next in a definite and fixed manner at a pace that is determined by the individual's particular experiences and opportunities. According to Kohlberg (1969, 1978, 1981), a child progresses through three general levels of moral development: a *preconventional* level in which morality is essentially a matter of external rather than internal standards—this "premoral" level is indicated when the physical consequences of an action determine its "goodness" or "badness" regardless of the human meaning or value of the consequences and, also, where "right" action consists of things that instrumentally satisfy one's own needs (and mutuality, reciprocity, or concern for others is present only as they help the child fulfill his or her own needs); a *conventional* level in which morality derives from the child's performance of correct roles—this "conventional" level is exhibited when "good" behavior occurs in order to please or help others, and conformity-type behaviors occur where the child has the "intention" of doing "good" (also, at this level, fixed laws and authority figures are obeyed where "right" behavior consists of doing one's duty, respecting authority, and maintaining social conventions and rules for their own sake); and a *postconventional* level in which morality is basically one of shared standards, duties, and rights— this "self-accepted" morality level is shown when "right" action is defined by the standards agreed upon by the whole society and is designed to take account of an individual's rights, and where there is awareness that personal values differ where people must reach a consensus on certain social issues (also, this level is characterized by the orientation that "right" is defined by "conscience" in accord with universal principles of justice and respect for others). Kohlberg's three levels consist of two orientations each, and, thus, his *theory of morality* identifies six separate stages (three general levels times two orientations each): obedience–reward; instrumental exchange; conformist; law and order; social–contract; and universal–ethical principle. The central tenet of Kohlberg's original formulation (i.e., the presence of a universally fixed sequence of six moral stages) has not been supported by empirical investigations (cf: Kohlberg, 1978). On the other hand, research does indicate that an invariant level-to-level sequence may occur where *preconventional* morality is a prerequisite for *conventional* reasoning and where both must precede the appearance of *postconventional* morality. Critics of *Kohlberg's theory* have emphasized the role that social-cultural factors may play in the development of postconventional reasoning, especially experiences within the particular context of a jurisprudence system of justice. Thus, while Kohlberg's model may not provide "the" universal view of a moral person, it may be relevant to an individual living in the United States who has a constitutionally based legal system (Berzonsky, 1994). However, in the final analysis, the notion of *morality*—while it derives from a social codification of right and wrong—may be viewed as either *internal* (part of an individual's personal code) or *external* (imposed by society), and, although certain truths seem to be self-evident, it is probably not the case that a universal code of morality either exists or can be established (Reber, 1995). See also PIAGET'S THEORY OF DEVELOPMENTAL STAGES; SOCIAL LEARNING/COGNITION THEORIES.

REFERENCES

Kohlberg, L. (1958). The development of modes of moral thinking and choice in the years ten to sixteen. Unpublished doctoral dissertation. Chicago: University of Chicago Library.

Kohlberg, L. (1969). *Stages in development of moral thought and action*. New York: Holt.

Goldiamond, I. (1972). Moral behavior: A functional analysis. *Readings in psychology today*. Del Mar, CA: CRM.

Kurtines, W., & Greif, E. (1974). The development of moral thought: Review and evaluation of Kohlberg's approach. *Psy. Bull., 81*, 453–470.

Kohlberg, L. (1978). Revisions in the theory and practice of moral development. In W. Damon (Ed.), *New directions for child development: Moral development*. San Francisco: Jossey-Bass.

Colby, A. (1979). *Measurement of moral judgment: A manual and its results*. New York: Cambridge University Press.

Blasi, A. (1980). Bridging moral cognition and moral action: A critical review of the literature. *Psy. Bull., 88*, 1–45.

Kohlberg, L. (1981). *Essays on moral development*. Vol. 1. *The philosophy of moral development: Moral stages and the idea of justice*. San Francisco: Harper & Row.

Berzonsky, M. (1994). Moral development. In R. J. Corsini (Ed.), *Ency. Psy.* New York: Wiley.

Reber, A. (1995). *The Penguin dictionary of psychology*. New York: Penguin Books.

KONIG'S THEORY. See COLOR VISION, THEORIES/LAWS OF.

KORTE'S LAWS. The German psychologist A. Korte (1915) developed a series of general statements/laws that describe the optimal conditions for *apparent motion* when demonstrating the *phi phenomenon* (i.e., perceived motion produced when two stationary lights are flashed successively, where the sensation of "apparent" movement of the light from the first location to the second location occurs if the time interval between the flashing of the two lights is about 150 milliseconds; Wertheimer, 1912). Korte's *principles of apparent movement* (*phi*) are (1) when intensity of the lights is held constant, the time interval for optimal *phi* varies directly with the distance between the stimuli; (2) when time is held constant, the distance for optimal *phi* varies directly with intensity of the lights; and (3) when distance between the stimuli is held constant, the intensity for optimal *phi* varies inversely with the interval of time that is used. Thus, *Korte's laws* state that it is more difficult to perceive apparent motion or *phi* when the spatial separation between lights is too wide, when illumination is too low, and when the interstimulus interval is too short, even though decrements in one (or two) of the variables can be adjusted by increments in the other(s). The *phi phenomenon* may be observed in nonlaboratory settings such as in motion pictures ("movies"), television, animated displays, and various neon sign displays where the sensation of motion is overwhelming and, as Helmholtz (1866) might have said, "irresistible." *Korte's laws* have been revised and extended in recent experiments (see Kolers, 1964), and several other stimulus variables that determine optimal movement have been described (e.g., Bell & Lappin, 1973; Pantle & Picciano, 1976; Beck, Elsner, & Silverstein, 1977). See also APPARENT MOVEMENT, PRINCIPLES/THEORIES OF; UNCONSCIOUS INFERENCE, DOCTRINE OF.

REFERENCES

Helmholtz, H. von (1866). *Physiological optics*. Leipzig: Voss.

Linke, P. (1907). Die Stroboskopischen Tauschungen und das Problem des Sehens von Bewegungen. *Psy. Stud., 3*, 393–545.

Stratton, G. (1911). The psychology of change: How is the perception of movement related to that of succession? *Psy. Rev., 18*, 262–293.

Wertheimer, M. (1912). Experimentelle Studien uber das Sehen von Bewegung. *Z. Psy.,* *61,* 161–265.

Korte, A. (1915). Kinematoskopische Untersuchungen. *Z. Psy., 72,* 193–296.

Benussi, V. (1916). Versuche zur Analyse taktil erweckter Scheinbewenungen. *Ar. ges. Psy., 36,* 59–135.

Neuhaus, W. (1930). Experimentelle Untersuchung der Scheinbewegung. *Ar. ges. Psy., 75,* 315–458.

Fernberger, S. (1934). New phenomenon of apparent visual movement. *Amer. J. Psy., 46,* 309–314.

Neff, W. (1936). A critical investigation of the visual apprehension of movement. *Amer. J. Psy., 48,* 1–42.

Hall, K., Earle, A., & Crookes, T. (1952). A pendulum phenomenon in the visual perception of apparent movement. *Quar. J. Exp. Psy., 4,* 109–120.

Kolers, P. (1964). The illusion of movement. *Sci. Amer., 211,* 98–106.

Graham, C. (1965). Perception of movement. In C. Graham (Ed.), *Vision and visual perception.* New York: Wiley.

Bell, H., & Lappin, J. (1973). Sufficient conditions for the discrimination of motion. *Perc. & Psychophys., 14,* 45–50.

Pantle, A., & Picciano, L. (1976). A multistable movement display: Evidence for two separate motion systems in human vision. *Science, 193,* 500–502.

Beck, J., Elsner, A., & Silverstein, C. (1977). Position uncertainty and the perception of apparent movement. *Perc. & Psychophys., 21,* 33–38.

KRETSCHMER'S THEORY OF PERSONALITY. The German psychiatrist Ernst Kretschmer (1888–1964) devised a *theory of personality* based on the relationship of physical characteristics to personality attributes. Before *Kretschmer's theory* appeared (Kretschmer, 1921), various other viewpoints were advanced by investigators concerning the association between physical and personality traits (e.g., Lavater, 1804; Gall & Spurzheim, 1809; Rostan, 1824; Viola, 1909; Sigaud, 1914; and Naccarati, 1921). The early Greek physician Hippocrates (460–370 B.C.) suggested both a *typology of physique* and a *typology of temperament,* as well as indicated the relationships between the body's *humors* (liquid substances), temperament, and behavior that anticipated the modern importance of endocrine secretions as determinants of behavior. Hippocrates suggested a dichotomy concerning physiques that separated people into those who were thick and short versus those who were thin and long. He also indicated that these body types were accompanied by characteristic diseases and disorders. For example, the first type of person (thick and short) was prone to apoplexy, and the second type (thin and long) was prone to consumption. Kretschmer (1921) inaugurated *constitutional psychology* into the modern era (cf: Sheldon, 1944) based on observations he made in his psychiatric practice concerning the relationships between physique and manifest behavior, especially the behaviors displayed in manic-depressive psychosis and schizophrenia. As a result of his measurements of physique, Kretschmer described three fundamental types: *asthenic*—refers to a linear, frail physique (later called *leptosomic*; Coan, 1994);

athletic—a muscular, wide-shouldered physique; and *pyknic*—a plump, round-figured physique. A fourth, "mixed" type, *dysplastic*—a "rare or ugly" physique, was also described that applied to a small group of "deviant" cases. Kretschmer (1925) related the incidence of *physique types* to the two kinds of psychosis in his patients and concluded that there was a strong biological affinity between *manic-depression* and the *pyknic* body build and a similar association between *schizophrenia* and the *asthenic, athletic,* and *dysplastic* body builds. Criticisms of *Kretschmer's theory* focused on his failure to control adequately for differences in age between manic-depressives and schizophrenics. Thus, the common observation is suggested that with increasing age most people increase in weight and, thereby, are more likely to resemble Kretschmer's *pyknic* type. Also, because manic-depression typically occurs later in life than does schizophrenia, this may account for the particular relationships Kretschmer observed between physique and psychosis (Hall & Lindzey, 1978). See also GALEN'S DOCTRINE OF THE FOUR TEMPERAMENTS; PERSONALITY THEORIES; SHELDON'S TYPE THEORY.

REFERENCES

Lavater, J. (1804). *Essays on physiognomy: For the promotion of the knowledge and the love of mankind.* London: Whittingham.

Gall, F., & Spurzheim, J. (1809). *Recherches sur le Systeme nerveaux.* Paris: Schoell.

Rostan, L. (1824). *Cours elementaire d'hygiene.* Paris: Bechet.

Viola, G. (1909). *Le legge de correlazione morfologia dei tippi individuali.* Padova, Italy: Progperini.

Sigaud, C. (1914). *La forme humaine.* Paris: Maloine.

Kretschmer, E. (1921). *Korperbau und charakter.* Berlin: Springer.

Naccarati, S. (1921). The morphologic aspect of intelligence. *Ar. Psy.,* no. 45.

Kretschmer, E. (1925). *Physique and character.* New York: Harcourt.

Sheldon, W. (1944). Constitutional factors in personality. In J. McV. Hunt (Ed.), *Personality and the behavior disorders.* New York: Ronald Press.

Rees, L. (1973). Constitutional factors and abnormal behavior. In H. Eysenck (Ed.), *Handbook of abnormal psychology.* San Diego: Knapp.

Hall, C., & Lindzey, G. (1978). *Theories of personality.* New York: Wiley.

Coan, R. (1994). Personality types. In R. J. Corsini (Ed.), *Ency. Psy.* New York: Wiley.

L

LABELING/DEVIANCE THEORY. The *labeling theory* of deviant behavior postulates an interaction between individuals and their social environment where society both defines and produces *deviance*. That is, *labeling theory* focuses on society's reaction to personal behavior as a fundamental aspect of a deviance-producing process. While other models of deviance may place the source of deviance solely within the individual or solely within society, the *labeling theory* emphasizes the interactive processes between society and the individual (e.g., Becker, 1963; cf: Karle & Binder, 1994; Prentky, 1994). According to this view, deviance is created by other individuals' reactions to a given act or event where those with the ability and power to label are called the "influential audience." Certain behaviors are designated as illogical, deviant, or mentally ill when they have been codified appropriately and when a group has power to impose standards of codification. Thus, both the behavior and the person exhibiting the behavior become labeled as *deviant* (cf: Matza, 1964). In general, the study of deviance has been approached from two different theoretical aspects (Gibbons & Jones, 1975): deviance is an exceptional and consistent variation from statistical norms of the overall population, and deviance is defined by the occurrence of single "critical" events (e.g., violence, high-intensity behavior, emotions, or cognitions). In particular, theoretical positions on deviance include *internal factors* and *differences among individuals* with use of typologies and classification schemes such as insanity, criminality, mental illness, and learning disabilities (e.g., Scheff, 1974; Goldstein, Carr, Davidson, & Wehr, 1981); *social structural differences* where social alienation, enmity, and differential access to both legitimate and illegitimate opportunity are critical aspects of deviance (e.g., Merton, 1949); *interactionist* viewpoint—or *differential labeling theory*—where deviance arises from an interaction between individuals' performances and society's reaction to those performances (e.g., Becker, 1963); and *learning theory*, which argues that all behaviors, including both normal and deviant, are learned according to the laws of punishment, reinforcement, and modeling (e.g., Bandura, 1969, 1977). Various critics of *deviance theory* in general and *formal labeling theory* in particular suggest that the labeling of deviance (such as "criminal" and "mentally ill") is an unjust and irrational process and argue from research that shows that deviance is not absolute in character but may be attributed to an act, depending on the variance of the act from the experience of the audience, on the observability and location of the act, and on the implied motivation of the act (Davidson, 1994). See also BEHAVIOR THERAPY/COGNITIVE THERAPY, THEORIES OF; PYGMALION EFFECT.

REFERENCES

Merton, R. (1949). *Social theory and social structure*. New York: Free Press.

Becker, H. (1963). *Outsiders: Studies in the sociology of deviance*. New York: Free Press.

Matza, D. (1964). *Delinquency and drift*. New York: Wiley.

Bandura, A. (1969). *Principles of behavior modification*. New York: Holt, Rinehart, & Winston.

Scheff, T. (1974). The labeling theory of mental illness. *Amer. Soc. Rev., 39,* 444–452.

Gibbons, D., & Jones, J. (1975). *The study of deviance: Perspectives and problems*. Englewood Cliffs, NJ: Prentice-Hall.

Bandura, A. (1977). *Social learning theory*. Englewood Cliffs, NJ: Prentice-Hall.

Goldstein, A., Carr, E., Davidson, W., & Wehr, P. (1981). *In response to aggression*. New York: Pergamon Press.

Davidson, W. (1994). Labeling theory. In R. J. Corsini (Ed.), *Ency. Psy.* New York: Wiley.

Karle, W., & Binder, J. (1994). Mental illness: Attitudes toward. In R. J. Corsini (Ed.), *Ency. Psy.* New York: Wiley.

Prentky, R. (1994). Mental illness: Early history. In R. J. Corsini (Ed.), *Ency. Psy.* New York: Wiley.

LADD–FRANKLIN/FRANKLIN COLOR VISION THEORY. The American-German psychologist Christine Ladd-Franklin (née Christine Franklin) (1847–1930) proposed a *color vision theory* in 1892 that was a compromise between the *Young–Helmholtz* and the *Hering* (later, the *Hering–Hurvich–Jameson) theories*, and that has been called both a *genetic theory* (Judd, 1907; Warren, 1934) and an *evolutionary theory* (Osgood, 1953) of color vision. The *Ladd–Franklin theory* assumes that light energy liberates respective red-, green-, and blue-stimulating substances from a complex photosensitive molecule in the retinal nerve endings. When the red- and green-stimulating substances are present, they combine to form a yellow-stimulating substance, which, in turn, may combine with blue to form a white-stimulating substance. According to this theory, blue and red (or blue and green) cannot combine and, thereby, do not individually disappear in the mixtures of blue–red (or blue–green). Thus, the *Ladd–Franklin theory* postulates four primary colors (red, green, yellow, and blue) where separate cone mechanisms for each primary are assumed. This *four-receptor theory* was linked to various evolutionary facts (such as the evolutionary development of achromatic rod vision into chromatic cone vision and the relatively rapid evolution of the foveal area of the eye as compared to the periphery) and was able to give a convincing account of both color blindness and perimetry (stimulation of retinal perimeter areas) data (Osgood, 1953). The genetic and evolutionary aspects of the *Ladd–Franklin theory* may be stated in terms wherein various portions of the retina "recapitulate" the course of evolution and where all four types of color receptors are present near the fovea, but not at the periphery of the retina. According to Osgood (1953), the *Ladd–Franklin evolutionary theory of color vision* had much to recommend it, but it was never as popular as the *Young–Helmholtz theory*. See also COLOR VISION, THEORIES/LAWS OF; HERING–HURVICH–JAMESON COLOR VISION THEORY; RECAPITULATION, THEORY OF; YOUNG–HELMHOLTZ COLOR VISION THEORY.

REFERENCES

Ladd-Franklin, C. (1892). Eine neue Theorie der Lichtempfindungen. *Z. Psy. Physio. Sinn., 4,* 211.

Judd, C. (1907). *Psychology: General introduction.* New York: Scribners.

Ladd-Franklin, C. (1929). *Colour and colour theories.* New York: Harcourt, Brace.

Warren, H. (Ed.) (1934). *Dictionary of psychology.* Cambridge, MA: Houghton Mifflin.

Osgood, C. (1953). *Method and theory in experimental psychology.* New York: Oxford University Press.

LAG EFFECT. See TOTAL TIME HYPOTHESIS/LAW.

LAING'S THEORY OF SCHIZOPHRENIA. See SCHIZOPHRENIA, THEORIES OF.

LAMARCKIAN–LYSENKO DOCTRINE. See LAMARCK'S THEORY.

LAMARCK'S THEORY. = Lamarckian-Lysenko doctrine = Lamarckianism = Lamarckism. The French naturalist/evolutionist Jean-Baptiste Pierre Antoine de Monet Lamarck (1744–1829) presented his *theory of evolution* in 1800 in a public lecture in which he stated the first coherent theory of the process of evolution prior to *Darwin's theory of natural selection.* Lamarck formulated four "laws" in his theory: (1) there is a natural tendency toward increasing organic complexities; (2) new organs evolve by indirect environmental influences; (3) there is a *use–disuse principle* operative in changes to an organ where parts of the body used extensively to cope with the environment become larger and stronger, and where new habits are acquired, useless organs disappear; and (4) acquired characteristics are inheritable. Lamarck published his *theory of evolution* in 1809, the year Charles Darwin was born. Out of his interests in zoology and by comparing current species to fossil forms, Lamarck observed several lines of descent where each line was a chronological series of older to younger fossils leading to a modern species. To illustrate his *use–disuse principle*, Lamarck cited examples of the blacksmith who develops a bigger bicep in the arm that works the hammer and a giraffe stretching its neck to new lengths in pursuit of leaves to eat. The *principle of inheritable acquired characteristics* presumed that the modifications an organism acquires during its lifetime can be passed along to its offspring. However, there is no convincing evidence to support this principle, and most scientists today agree that acquired traits do not change genes transmitted by gametes to offspring—notwithstanding recent developments and techniques in biology called *genetic engineering, recombinant DNA,* and *gene cloning* where genetic manipulations can cause profound organismic changes and where the term *acquired characteristics* may require redefinition. Modern geneticists have affirmed that inheritance is determined solely by the reproductive cells and is unaffected by somatic (body) cells. Belief in the inheritance of acquired characteristics is, therefore, rejected (Harris & Levey, 1975). While the *Lamarckian theory of evolution* may be ridiculed by some people today because of its *inheritable acquired characteristics* assumption, that aspect of inheritance was generally accepted in Lamarck's time, and even Darwin himself could offer no acceptable alternative (Campbell, 1993). Also, the concept of *inheritable acquired characteristics* seems to have some survival value where it has been revived in certain contexts and in various guises by several early and modern biologists and psychologists, for example, Jean Piaget, Herbert Spencer, William McDougall, and Carl Jung (Lundin, 1994; Reber, 1995). In the 1930s, the Soviet geneticist/agronomist Trofim Denisovich Lysenko (1898–1976) formulated a *neo-Lamarckian theory of genetics*, which suggested that environment can alter the hereditary material. Lysenko rejected the popular *doctrine of neo-Mendelism*, and his theories were offered as Marxist orthodoxy, which won the official support of the Soviet government. However, during the 1950s, Soviet physicists and mathematicians had gained status and strength with the growth of the Soviet space program, and, as scientific support grew for Crick and Watson's 1953 *model of DNA* (see Watson & Crick, 1953; Watson, 1968; Crick, 1988; Newton, 1992), criticism mounted against Lysenko and his ideas. Lysenko was forced to resign his position as director of the Institute of Genetics and the Soviet Academy of Sciences in 1965 (Harris & Levey, 1975; Muir, 1994). In the final analysis, Lamarck probably deserves some credit for his unorthodox theory, which was visionary in many respects: it claimed that evolution was the best explanation for both the fossil record and the current diversity of life, it emphasized the great age of Earth, and it stressed adaptation to the environment as a primary product of evolution (Campbell, 1993). See also DARWIN'S EVOLUTION THEORY; MENDEL'S LAWS/ PRINCIPLES; WEISMANN'S THEORY.

REFERENCES

Lamarck, J. (1809). *Zoological philosophy: An exposition with regard to the natural history of animals.* London: Macmillan.

Watson, J., & Crick, F. (1953). Molecular structure of nucleic acids. A structure for deoxyribose nucleic acid. *Nature, 171*, 737–738.

Watson, J. (1968). *The double helix*. New York: Atheneum.

Harris, W., & Levey, J. (Eds.) (1975). *The new Columbia encyclopedia*. New York: Columbia University Press.

Crick, F. (1988). *What mad pursuit*. New York: Basic Books.

Newton, D. (1992). *James Watson & Francis Crick: Discovery of the double helix and beyond*. New York: Facts on File.

Campbell, N. (1993). *Biology*. Redwood City, CA: Benjamin/Cummings.

Lundin, R. (1994). Jean-Baptiste de Monet de Lamarck. In R. J. Corsini (Ed.), *Ency. Psy.* New York: Wiley.

Muir, H. (Ed.) (1994). *Larousse dictionary of scientists*. New York: Larousse.

Reber, A. (1995). *The Penguin dictionary of psychology*. New York: Penguin Books.

LAMBERT'S LAW/COSINE LAW. See ABNEY'S LAW.

LAND'S RETINEX THEORY. See COLOR VISION, THEORIES/LAWS OF.

LARGE NUMBERS, LAW OF. See PROBABILITY THEORY/LAWS.

LASHLEY'S THEORY. The American behaviorist/physiological psychologist Karl Spencer Lashley (1890–1958) developed two principles of brain functioning in his work on localization of functions: the *principle/theory of mass action* and the *principle/theory of equipotentiality* (Lashley, 1924, 1929). The concept of *mass action* refers to the operation of the cortex as a coordinated system where large masses of tissue are involved in all complex functioning. This principle contrasts with the competing theory that specific local areas of the brain mediate specific behaviors. Lashley's argument for *mass action* was based on the demonstration that the degree of disruption of a learned behavior is due not simply to the location of brain lesions but to the amount of tissue involved (Lashley was not suggesting that there was no localization of function but that such localization was only part of the explanation; Reber, 1995). As an example of *mass action*, Lashley taught cats to escape from a puzzle box, then removed various parts of the cortex of their brains. After the cats had recovered from the operation, they were placed in the box again. Lashley found that the cats could no longer perform the escape behavior, but with further training they were able to relearn the escape behavior even in cases where both frontal lobes had been removed entirely. Lashley concluded that the *principle of mass action* indicated that learning was not dependent on specific neural connections in the brain but on the brain as a whole and where the rate of relearning was a function of the total mass of brain tissue involved (Osgood, 1953). The *principle of equipotentiality* within neuropsychology/neurophysiology refers to the hypothesis that all the neurons that mediate a given sensory modality have a common competing function in addition to their specific functions (i.e., each has equal potential for participating in a sensory event within that modality). By extension, the principle applies also to the notion that within certain limits one portion of the cerebral cortex can take on the functions of another part (Krech, 1962). Thus, the *principle of equipotentiality* states that each part of the brain is just as important as any other, and if some parts of the brain are removed, other parts can carry on their functions. For instance, when Lashley removed the visual area of rats' brains—although they lost patterning—the rats could still discriminate differences in light intensity and could follow light (Lundin, 1994). The two theories of *equipotentiality* and *localization* (cf: Luria, 1973) form the basis for the major theoretical schools within neuropsychology. However, psychological research has not wholly supported either the *localization* or the *equipotentiality theory* (Golden, 1994). See also BEHAVIORIST THEORY.

REFERENCES

Lashley, K. (1924). Studies of cerebral function in learning. V. The retention of motor habits after destruction of the so-called motor areas in primates. *Ar. Neuro. Psychiat., 12*, 249–276.

Lashley, K., & McCarthy, D. (1926). The survival of the maze habit after cerebellar inquiries. *J. Comp. Psy., 6*, 423–432.

Lashley, K. (1929). *Brain mechanisms and intelligence*. Chicago: University of Chicago Press.

Lashley, K. (1942). An examination of the "continuity theory" as applied to discrimination learning. *J. Gen. Psy., 26*, 241–265.

Lashley, K. (1950). In search of the engram. *Symposium of the Society of Experimental Biology, 4*, 454–482.

Lashley, K., Chow, K., & Semmes, J. (1951). An examination of the electrical field theory of cerebral integration. *Psy. Rev., 58*, 123–136.

Osgood, C. (1953). *Method and theory in experimental psychology*. New York: Oxford University Press.

Krech, D. (1962). Cortical localization of function. In L. Postman (Ed.), *Psychology in the making*. New York: Knopf.

Luria, A. (1973). *The working brain*. New York: Basic Books.

Golden, C. (1994). Neuropsychology. In R. J. Corsini (Ed.), *Ency. Psy*. New York: Wiley.

Lundin, R. (1994). Karl Lashley. In R. J. Corsini (Ed.), *Ency. Psy*. New York: Wiley.

Reber, A. (1995). *The Penguin dictionary of psychology*. New York: Penguin Books.

LASHLEY–WADE HYPOTHESIS. See GENERALIZATION, PRINCIPLE OF.

LATENCY, LAW OF. See SKINNER'S DESCRIPTIVE BEHAVIOR/OPERANT CONDITIONING THEORY.

LATE SELECTION THEORIES. See ATTENTION, LAWS/PRINCIPLES/THEORIES OF.

LAZARUS' THEORY OF EMOTIONS. The American psychologist Richard S. Lazarus (1922–   ) proposed a *cognitive theory of emotions* that makes the concept of *appraisal* the keystone for analyzing and synthesizing the events that occur in an emotional episode (cf: *theory of induced emotion*—holds that the perception of emotional behavior or expression is sufficient to excite the same emotion in the person who perceives it; Warren, 1934). Lazarus (1982, 1984, 1991) argues that each emotion one experiences is based on a specific kind of *cognitive appraisal* that is accompanied by motor, behavioral, and physiological changes. Lazarus and his associates found that the *appraisal* of an event or situation and therefore a person's emotional reaction could be manipulated experimentally. *Appraisal*, according to Lazarus, falls into various categories: *primary*—initial evaluation leading to an incipient emotional response; *secondary*—an evaluation of one's relation to the environment leading to an altered emotional response; and *reappraisal*—evaluation of the significance of the secondary appraisal, or a psychological attempt to cope with stress in the situation. *Reappraisal* may not be based on the facts at hand but may be a ''defensive reappraisal'' where the person attempts to express a more compatible, friendly, or sympathetic point of view toward the situation or events. In Lazarus' (1966, 1980, 1993) approach, the notion of *coping* (in the reappraisal phase) functions as a mediator between events in the environment and one's emotional reaction. Thus, an individual may cope with a situation by reflecting on it, but it is the appraisal of one's conclusion (and not the reflection itself) that may alter the person's subsequent emotion. For example, you may feel uneasy over something that you have done or said long before you actually think about it, and subsequently you decide that you have behaved badly. See also ARNOLD'S THEORY OF EMOTIONS; COGNITIVE THEORIES OF EMOTIONS; EMOTIONS, THEORIES/LAWS OF; SCHACHTER–SINGER'S THEORY OF EMOTIONS.

REFERENCES

Warren, H. (Ed.) (1934). *Dictionary of psychology*. Cambridge, MA: Houghton Mifflin.

Lazarus, R. (1966). *Psychological stress and the coping process*. New York: McGraw-Hill.

Lazarus, R., Averill, J., & Opton, E. (1970). Towards a cognitive theory of emotion. In M. Arnold (Ed.), *Feelings and emotions*. New York: Academic Press.

Lazarus, R. (1980). The stress and coping paradigm. In L. Bond & J. Rosen (Eds.), *Competence and coping during adulthood*. Hanover, NH: University Press of New England.

Lazarus, R. (1982). Thoughts on the relations between emotion and cognition. *Amer. Psy., 37*, 1019–1024.

Lazarus, R. (1984). On the primacy of cognition. *Amer. Psy., 39*, 117–123.

Lazarus, R. (1991). Progress on a cognitive-motivational-relational theory of emotion. *Amer. Psy., 46*, 819–834.

Lazarus, R. (1993). From psychological stress to the emotions: A history of changing outlooks. *Ann. Rev. Psy., 44*, 1–21.

Arnold, M. (1994). Cognitive theories of emotion. In R. J. Corsini (Ed.), *Ency. Psy.* New
    York: Wiley.

LEADERSHIP, THEORIES OF. As defined in psychological research, the
term *leadership* involves the notion of persuading people to ignore their individual concerns and devote themselves instead to a common goal that is important for the welfare of the group (Hogan, Curphy, & Hogan, 1994). In another
definition (Fiedler & Chemers, 1994), *leadership* refers to the direction, supervision, or management of a group or an organization. Originally, *leadership* was
thought to be a fixed attribute of a person, a trait, or a series of traits (Baum,
Fisher, & Singer, 1985). Leaders may be "emergent" (i.e., informally acknowledged and elected by the group) or "appointed" (i.e., chosen by the organization
of which the group is a part). Empirical research on *leadership* has evolved from
the simplistic search for leadership traits (and the best way to relate to group
members) to the relatively complex view that emphasizes that different situations
require different types of leader personalities or behaviors. *Theories of leadership* may be classified as those stressing leader *traits/behaviors*, those emphasizing *contingencies/environmental influences*, those dealing with *transactional*
encounters, and those emphasizing *cognitive* processes. From the early 1900s to
about 1940, *leadership* research focused on the traits and personal characteristics
that distinguish leaders from followers. This general *trait theory* viewpoint has
also been called the *great man/great woman theory of leadership* (Baron &
Byrne, 1981). There have been studies in support of the *trait theory of leadership*, some of which have yielded positive results, but the differences found
between leader and followers were quite small and of little practical or theoretical value (cf: Stogdill, 1974). In one case, Lewin, Lippitt, and White (1939)
found that a democratic, participative leadership style produced better involvement and member satisfaction than either an autocratic or laissez-faire leadership
style. In another case, Stogdill and Coons (1957), using leader behavior rating
scales, identified the two behavior factors of *consideration*—concern for the
welfare of subordinates—and *structuring*—assigning roles, setting standards,
and evaluating performance—that helped to understand the leader's role in shaping the group's interaction. In a *humanistic* approach, McGregor (1960) described *Theory X*, which contained an assumption about the nature of the
worker—that human nature is basically lazy and externally motivated—and
Theory Y, which contained the assumption that human nature is basically responsible and self-directed. Another more recent orientation describes *Theory Z*
(Ouchi, 1981), which combines some of the positive features of the Japanese
workplace with some of the realities of the American workplace. *Theory Z*
suggests that American firms—like the Japanese "paternalistic" firms—offer
workers long-term (if not lifetime) employment when possible and restructuring
(when necessary) to avoid layoffs, both of which would enhance workers' loy-
alty. Many of the *leader behavior theories* have had a major impact on management thinking, but they have not been consistently supported by empirical

research. The *contingency leadership theories* (e.g., Fiedler, 1967) assert that the leader's environment is an important determinant of the leader's performance. The *contingency model* views the leadership situation as giving high, moderate, or low degree of power, influence, and control to the leader. In this approach, the effectiveness of the leader is contingent upon both the leader's personality and the characteristics of the situation. While the *contingency theories* have generated controversy, there appears to be substantial support for this approach (e.g., Strube & Garcia, 1981). The *path–goal theory* (House, 1971) is a contingency model involving the interaction of behavior and situation that states that the leader must motivate the subordinate individuals by stressing the relationship between the subordinates' needs and the organizational goals and by facilitating the ''path'' that subordinates must take to fulfill their own needs and the organization's goals. Research supports this approach concerning employee job satisfaction and motivation, but the theory's predictions concerning performance have not been well supported (Fiedler & Chemers, 1994). Another contingency model, called the *normative decision theory* (Vroom & Yetton, 1973), deals with the conditions under which leaders should take an autocratic role when making decisions. This theory assumes that individual decisions are more time-effective than group decisions, that subordinates who participate in the formulation of a decision are more committed to it, and that complex/ambiguous tasks require more information and consultation to achieve high-quality decisions. Further research is needed concerning the predictive validity of the *normative decision theory*, but the theory does indicate the best leadership style to use under various decision-making conditions. The *transactional theories of leadership* have replaced the older *situational theory* approach, which argued that leaders are best viewed in terms of the task faced by the group and the general situation within which it must operate. The *situational theory* tended to see leadership as a kind of ''one-way'' street; that is, it assumed that leaders influence and direct their groups but are not, in turn, affected by their followers. Many recent studies suggest, however, that leaders' behaviors are often strongly affected by the actions and demands of other group members (e.g., Fodor, 1978). With more current *transactional theories*, leadership is viewed as a reciprocal process of social influence in which leaders both direct followers and are, in turn, influenced by these individuals. *Transactional theory* also calls attention to the importance of the perceptions of both leaders and followers regarding the relationship between them (e.g., do the followers perceive the leader's position as legitimate or illegitimate?). The *transactional* viewpoint also argues that both characteristics of the leader and situational factors (such as the task faced by the group) must be taken into account. Thus, the *transactional* approach adopts a highly sophisticated account of the leadership process, and is much more complex than previous approaches. Leadership theorists have begun increasingly to study the *cognitive processes* inherent in leadership situations (e.g., Osborn & Hunt, 1975; Green & Mitchell, 1979). Leadership research is likely to continue in the study of both noncognitive and cognitive variables in the leader–

member relationship, as well as show increasing interest in the role of task characteristics in the determination of effective group and member performance (Fiedler & Chemers, 1994). See also OCCUPATION THEORIES; ORGANI-ZATIONAL/INDUSTRIAL/SYSTEMS THEORY; PERSONALITY THEO-RIES.

REFERENCES

Lewin, K., Lippitt, R., & White, R. (1939). Patterns of aggressive behavior in experi-mentally created social climates. *J. Soc. Psy., 10*, 271–299.

Coffin, T. (1944). A three-component theory of leadership. *J. Abn. Soc. Psy., 39*, 63–83.

Stogdill, R. (1948). Personal factors associated with leadership: A survey of the literature. *J. Psy., 25*, 35–71.

Stogdill, R., & Coons, A. (1957). *Leader behavior: Its description and measurement.* Columbus: Ohio State University, Bureau of Business Research.

McGregor, D. (1960). *The human side of enterprise.* New York: McGraw-Hill.

Blake, R., & Mouton, J. (1961). *Group dynamics: Key to decision making.* Houston, TX: Gulf.

Fiedler, F. (1967). *A theory of leadership effectiveness.* New York: McGraw-Hill.

House, R. (1971). A path-goal theory of leader-effectiveness. *Admin. Sci. Quar., 16*, 321–338.

Vroom, V., & Yetton, P. (1973). *Leadership and decision making.* Pittsburgh: University of Pittsburgh Press.

Stogdill, R. (1974). *Handbook of leadership.* New York: Free Press.

Osborn, R., & Hunt, J. (1975). An adaptive-reactive theory of leadership. *Org. & Admin. Sci., 6*, 27–44.

Blake, R., & Mouton, J. (1978). *The new managerial grid.* Houston, TX: Gulf.

Fodor, E. (1978). Simulated work climate as an influence on choice of leadership style. *Pers. Soc. Psy. Bull., 4*, 111–114.

Green, S., & Mitchell, T. (1979). Attributional processes of leaders in leader–member interactions. *Org. Beh. & Hum. Per., 23*, 429–458.

Baron, R., & Byrne, D. (1981). *Social psychology: Understanding human interaction.* Boston: Allyn & Bacon.

Ouchi, W. (1981). *Theory Z: How American business can meet the Japanese challenge.* Reading, MA: Addison-Wesley.

Strube, M., & Garcia, J. (1981). A metatheoretical analysis of Fiedler's contingency model of leadership effectiveness. *Psy. Bull., 90*, 307–321.

Baum, A., Fisher, J., & Singer, J. (1985). *Social psychology.* New York: Random House.

Eagly, A., Makhijani, M., & Klonsky, B. (1992). Gender and the evaluation of leaders: A meta-analysis. *Psy. Bull., 111*, 3–22.

Andrews, I. (1994a). Leadership styles. In R. J. Corsini (Ed.), *Ency. Psy.* New York: Wiley.

Andrews, I. (1994b). Leadership training. In R. J. Corsini (Ed.), *Ency. Psy.* New York: Wiley.

Bass, B. (1994). Leadership and supervision. In R. J. Corsini (Ed.), *Ency. Psy.* New York: Wiley.

Fiedler, F., & Chemers, M. (1994). Leadership effectiveness. In R. J. Corsini (Ed.), *Ency. Psy.* New York: Wiley.

Hogan, R., Curphy, G., & Hogan, J. (1994). What we know about leadership: Effectiveness and personality. *Amer. Psy., 49,* 493–504.

Eagly, A., Karan, S., & Makhijani, M. (1995). Gender and the effectiveness of leaders: A meta-analysis. *Psy. Bull., 117,* 125–145.

LEARNED HELPLESSNESS EFFECT/PHENOMENON/HYPOTHESIS/ THEORY. The American psychologist Martin E. P. Seligman (1942–   ) and his associates (Overmeier & Seligman, 1967; Seligman & Maier, 1967; Maier & Seligman, 1976; Seligman & Weiss, 1980) have demonstrated that when reinforcing outcomes are independent of an organism's responses, the individual learns that it will get the same outcomes whether it responds or not, and, thereby, responding is useless. In effect, the organism has learned to be inactive or to feel "helpless." Constant and unavoidable punishment eventually causes organisms to give up and quietly submit to the punishment. In the original experiments on *learned helplessness*, dogs were first restrained in a harness and given a series of severe, inescapable shocks. The next day, the dogs were placed in a simple, discriminated-avoidance situation. On each trial, when a conditioned stimulus (such as a tone) came on, shock followed after 10 seconds unless the dogs jumped over a low barrier. If they failed to jump, the conditioned stimulus remained on, and shocks continued for 50 seconds. Using this procedure, the dogs had an opportunity either to avoid or escape from the shock by jumping the barrier. Dogs that did not have "day-before" exposure to inescapable shock had no difficulty learning first to escape from shock and then to avoid it by jumping as soon as they heard the conditioned stimulus. On the other hand, the dogs that were pretrained with inescapable shock almost invariably failed to jump at all. Similar effects have been shown in experimental situations with a variety of species and different aversive stimuli. The effects often generalize from one highly aversive stimulus (such as water immersion) to another stimulus (such as shock). This pattern indicates that the aversiveness of the situation is the crucial aspect for most animals. The *learned helplessness* effects may be thought of as involving the long-known phenomenon of *Einstellung* (or *set*), which is defined as rigidity produced by earlier experience with testing/training conditions (Luchins, 1942). A certain amount of controversy raged for a number of years concerning whether *learned helplessness* is simply an effect of the suppression of punishment (of effective responses), or whether in some cognitive sense the organisms actually learn or really "know" that they have no control over what happens to them. The *cognitive* interpretation is called the *learned helplessness (LH) hypothesis* and is distinguished from the experimentally based *learned-helplessness effect*. There is no doubt about the "effect," but the status of the "hypothesis" is less certain (Staddon & Ettinger, 1989). Apparently, a great deal of interest in *learned helplessness* derives from Seligman's arguments that *learned helplessness* presents a model for understanding the ubiquitous malady of human depression (cf: Peterson & Seligman, 1984; Huesmann, 1978).

The *theory of learned helplessness* has been challenged, however, by other investigators who have explained the phenomenon in other ways. The issue is whether learning to be helpless in a particular situation generalizes only to similar situations or to a wide variety of them. For instance, McReynolds (1980) observed that when people experience a situation in which reinforcements are not contingent on their responding, their responding extinguishes. If the situation then changes to one where responding will be reinforced, the individuals will continue not to respond unless they perceive that the schedule of reinforcement has changed. The more similar the second situation is to the first, the more likely the person will act "helpless." Thus, the phenomenon of *learned helplessness* may be viewed as a failure to discriminate between the situation under which responding is reinforced and the situation under which it is not reinforced. Further research may determine whether *learned helplessness* is a stable personality trait, as Seligman argues, or whether it can be explained by instrumental/operant conditioning principles (Carlson, 1993). See also MIND/MENTAL SET, LAW OF; SKINNER'S DESCRIPTIVE BEHAVIOR/OPERANT CONDITIONING THEORY.

REFERENCES

Luchins, A. (1942). Mechanization in problem solving: The effect of Einstellung. *Psy. Mono., 54*, no. 248.

Overmeier, J., & Seligman, M. (1967). Effects of inescapable shock upon subsequent escape and avoidance learning. *J. Comp. Physio. Psy., 63*, 23–33.

Seligman, M., & Maier, S. (1967). Failure to escape traumatic shock. *J. Exp. Psy., 74*, 1–9.

Seligman, M. (1975). *Helplessness: On depression development and death.* San Francisco: Freeman.

Maier, S., & Seligman, M. (1976). Learned helplessness: Theory and evidence. *J. Exp. Psy.: Gen., 105*, 3–46.

Abramson, L., Seligman, M., & Teasdale, J. (1978). Learned helplessness in humans: Critique and reformulation. *J. Abn. Psy., 87*, 49–74.

Huesmann, L. (Ed.) (1978). Learned helplessness as a model of depression. (Special issue). *J. Abn. Psy., 87*, 1.

Wortman, C., & Dintzer, L. (1978). Is an attributional analysis of the learned helplessness phenomenon viable? A critique of the Abramson-Seligman-Teasdale reformulation. *J. Abn. Psy., 87*, 75–90.

McReynolds, W. (1980). Learned helplessness as a schedule-shift effect. *J. Res. Pers., 14*, 139–157.

Roth, S. (1980). Learned helplessness in humans: A review. *J. Pers., 48*, 103–133.

Seligman, M., & Weiss, J. (1980). Coping behavior: Learned helplessness, physiological activity, and learned inactivity. *Beh. Res. Theory, 18*, 459–512.

Peterson, C., & Seligman, M. (1984). Causal explanations as risk factors for depression. *Psy. Rev., 91*, 347–374.

Staddon, J., & Ettinger, R. (1989). *Learning: An introduction to the principles of adaptive behavior.* New York: Harcourt Brace Jovanovich.

Carlson, N. (1993). *Psychology: The science of behavior*. Boston: Allyn & Bacon.
Samuel, W. (1994). Learned helplessness. In R. J. Corsini (Ed.), *Ency. Psy*. New York: Wiley.

LEARNING THEORIES/LAWS. The term *learning* may be defined as "a relatively permanent change in behavior or in behavioral potentiality that results from experience and cannot be attributed to temporary body states such as those induced by illness, fatigue, or drugs" (Hergenhahn, 1982, p. 8). *Learning* is a general term to describe behavioral changes, while the term *conditioning* is a more specific term used to describe actual procedures that can modify behavior (e.g., *classical conditioning*, Pavlov, 1927; *instrumental/operant conditioning*, Thorndike, 1911; Skinner, 1938). In a chronological sequence of ideas in philosophy, the history of learning starts with the Greek philosopher Plato (427–347 B.C.) and his *rationalist* position (i.e., knowledge is available only through reasoning) concerning the conception of the universe in *dualistic* terms (abstract/ideation/nonsensory versus sensory experience); Plato maintained a *nativist* position in his *reminiscence theory of knowledge* (i.e., the belief that all knowledge is present in the human soul at birth, and, thus, "to know" was to remember the contents of the soul). Plato's famous student, Aristotle (384–322 B.C.), held that knowledge was gained both from sensory experience and from thinking/reasoning. However, for Aristotle (unlike Plato), the laws and forms in the universe did *not* have an existence independent of their *empirical* aspects but were simply observed relationships in nature. Thus, Aristotle's position was that of an *empiricist* (where knowledge is based on sensory experience), and he formulated his *laws of association* (such as the laws of *similarity*, *contrast*, and *contiguity*) within this empiricist context. According to Aristotle, sensory experience gives rise to ideas, and the ideas will stimulate other ideas in accordance with the principles of association. Later, in philosophy, the attempt to explain the relationship between ideas using the *laws of association* came to be known as *associationism*. Aristotle's ideas regarding associationism were so significant that they operate even today in all the major contemporary *learning theories*. Next, the French philosopher Rene Descartes (1596–1650) inferred from his famous edict, "I think, therefore I am," that sensory experience must be a reflection of a greater objective reality. Descartes also postulated a separation between the mind (which was free and capable of choice) and the body (which was similar to a predictable machine) where the pineal gland was the point of contact between the mind and body. The mind could move the gland from side to side to open or close the "pores" of the brain (allowing "animal spirits" to flow throughout the body and cause bodily movements in a *reflex action* fashion). Descartes relied heavily on *innate ideas* (such as the concepts of God, self, space, and time) that were not derivable from experience but were an integral part of the mind. Thomas Hobbes (1588–1679), however, opposed the notion that innate ideas were the source of knowledge. Instead, Hobbes held that sense impressions are the source of all knowledge and, with this belief, helped to pave the way for renewal of the concepts of *empiricism* and *associationism*. According to Hobbes, human behavior is controlled by "appetites" (events that are "good" and are approached by the individual) and "aversions" (events that are "evil" and avoided by the person); cf: Jeremy Bentham's (1748–1832) concept of the *pleasure principle*, which was hypothesized to control human behavior (Bentham, 1830) and which was later employed by Sigmund Freud as well as the *reinforcement* theorists. John Locke (1632–1704) also opposed the notion of innate ideas and suggested that the mind at birth is a blank tablet ("tabula rasa") upon which experience writes. Thus, according to Locke, there is nothing in the mind that is not first in the senses. Locke distinguished between *primary qualities* (characteristics of physical objects such as size, weight, solidity, mobility, and shape) and *secondary qualities* (things in the mind of the perceiver such as colors, odors, and tastes). Locke held that ideas are the elements that constitute the mind where the *laws of association* explain how the ideas come to be combined. George Berkeley (1685–1753) amended Locke's viewpoint by claiming that there are no primary qualities, only secondary qualities where the only reality is the mind. Because Berkeley asserted that the contents of the mind were derived from experience, he may still be considered an *empiricist*. Next, the philosopher David Hume (1711–1776) carried Berkeley's argument another step further and insisted that persons can know nothing for sure about ideas, and mind was no more than a stream of ideas, memories, feelings, and imaginings. Hume, also an *empiricist*, argued that the "laws of nature" are constructs of the imagination where the "lawfulness" observed in nature is in one's head and not in nature. Immanuel Kant (1724–1804) attempted to reconcile the viewpoints of *rationalism* (the manipulation of concepts) and *empiricism* (the examination of sensory experience). Kant suggested that *innate categories of thought* (such as unity, totality, reality, existence, and causality) existed where innate mental faculties are superimposed over one's sensory experiences, thereby giving them meaning and structure. Thus, according to Kant, the mind makes an active contribution to one's experience involving organization and meaning of sensory information; cf: *Gestalt theory* (Wertheimer, 1912) and *cognitive-developmental theory* (Piaget, 1970). In this sense, Kant kept the *doctrine of rationalism* vital by indicating the importance of mind as the source of knowledge. John Stuart Mill (1806–1873) accepted the earlier notion of Hobbes and Locke that complex ideas are combinations of simpler ideas but also added the innovative notion that a new totality—which bears little resemblance to its parts—may emerge in the process (cf: the later *Gestaltists'* assertion that "the whole is more than the sum of its parts"). Other historical influences on *modern learning theory* are Thomas Reid's (1717–1796) suggestion that there are 27 discrete areas of the brain where each corresponds to a specific innate *faculty*, that is, a power of the mind that influences how one perceives the world (Reid, 1849); Franz Joseph Gall's (1758–1828) assertion that a person's strong and weak faculties could be detected by analyzing the depressions and bumps on the individual's skull, a system of analysis/doctrine known as *phrenology* (Gall, 1835); Charles Darwin's (1809–1882) demonstration of the utility of behavior in adjusting to a changing environment and his evolutionary notion that human development is biologically continuous with that of lower animals (Darwin, 1859); and Hermann Ebbinghaus' (1850–1909) original experimental studies of learning and memory using "nonsense syllables," which demonstrated how the *law of frequency* operated in the formation of new verbal associations (Ebbinghaus, 1885). The so-called schools or isms in the history of psychology also influenced the shape of *modern learning theory*: *structuralism* (under Wilhelm Wundt and Edward B. Titchener), whose goal was to discover and examine the basic elements of thought ("sensations") through the method of *trained introspection* (self-analysis using predetermined modes of language or vocabulary); *functionalism* (under William James, John Dewey, and James R. Angell), whose goal was to discover how mental and behavioral processes are related to an organism's adaptation to its environment by analysis of the individual's acts and functions; and *behaviorism* (under John B. Watson), whose stated goal was to be totally objective and scientific in its study of external behavior, and where the study of inner consciousness was completely rejected. Of these schools of psychological thought, the approach of *behaviorism* probably had the most profound overall effect on American *learning theory* (Hergenhahn, 1982). Numerous theories dominated *modern learning theory* from about 1900 to 1960. Most of these may be called *intervening variable theories* because they attempted to explain hypothetical processes that intervene between observable environmental and behavioral events. One exception to the intervening variable approach is a metatheoretical/ atheoretical area of study in learning called the *experimental analysis of behavior* (e.g., Skinner, 1938; cf: Skinner, 1950), which refers to an emphasis upon examination, development, and application of the *principles of operant conditioning*. The *model of operant conditioning*, along with its many experimentally produced concepts (e.g., Honig, 1966), is considered to play an extremely important role in *learning theory* because it helps to explain how new and complex behaviors and phenomena are developed in individuals. Among the *intervening variable theories* (which attempted to deal with topics that the experimental analysis of behavior approach tends to avoid, such as memory, motivation, and cognition) are Tolman's (1932, 1949) *expectancy theory*—where "expectancies" were hypothesized to develop in the organism due solely to the temporal succession, or contiguity, of environmental events and not necessarily upon the consequences of responding; Pavlov's (1927) *physiological theory*—in which the relation between events and intervening variables used physiological referents to explain how learning occurs (cf: Hebb's, 1949), *neuropsychological theory* and also *irradiation theory*—a hypothesis that assumes that during learning, excitation spreads into neighboring structures such as nerves or muscles (Warren, 1934); Guthrie's (1935) *molecular/contiguity theory*—where temporally contiguous events, molecular stimulus events called "cues," molecular responses called "movements," and molar behaviors called "acts" were examined to understand an organism's behavior; and Hull's (1943, 1952) and Spence's (1956) *drive-reduction theory*—in which contiguity of stimulus with response, in addition to various drive-reduction concepts such as "habit," was hypothesized to account for learned behavior. Supplemental *modern learning theories* developed in the 1950s, 1960s, and 1970s have been called "miniature" theories (Hilgard, 1987; Lockwood, 1994), and they typically involve quantitative characteristics with a circumscribed range of content. Such miniature theories are illustrated by Estes' (1950) *mathematical learning/stimulus sampling theory*; Atkinson and Shiffrin's (1968) *information-processing/memory theory*; and Gregg and Simon's (1967) *stochastic/computer model theory*. Currently, there is reason to believe that the work by intervening variable theorists on *classical conditioning* and by experimental analysts on *operant conditioning* is converging on a common understanding of mutually employed concepts such as the key concept of *reinforcement* in *learning theory* (Lockwood, 1994). However, various important questions concerning learning processes and phenomena remain unanswered (Hergenhahn, 1982): How does learning vary as a function of *maturation*? Does learning depend on *reward*? How does learning vary as a function of *species*? How does learned behavior relate to *instinctive* behavior? Can some *associations* be learned more easily than others? How does learning vary as a function of *personality* characteristics? To what extent is learning a function of the total *environment*? and How do internal and external variables *interact* with type of learning? Most of what is now known about learning came out of the great debates among learning theorists that took place in the 1930s and 1940s. Such an atmosphere still exists in psychology, but the debate among learning theorists does not seem to be as intense today as it was during that earlier era. See also ASSOCIATION, LAWS/PRINCIPLES OF; BANDURA'S THEORY; BEHAVIORIST THEORY; DARWIN'S EVOLUTION THEORY; ESTES' STIMULUS SAMPLING THEORY; FORMAL DISCIPLINE THEORY; GESTALT THEORY/LAWS; GUTHRIE'S THEORY OF BEHAVIOR; HEBB'S THEORY OF PERCEPTUAL LEARNING; HULL'S LEARNING THEORY; MOWRER'S THEORY; PAVLOVIAN CONDITIONING PRINCIPLES/LAWS/THEORIES; PHRENOLOGY, DOCTRINE OF; PIAGET'S THEORY OF DEVELOPMENTAL STAGES; PUNISHMENT, THEORIES OF; REINFORCEMENT THEORY; REINFORCEMENT, THORNDIKE'S THEORY OF; SKINNER'S DESCRIPTIVE BEHAVIOR/OPERANT CONDITIONING THEORY; SPENCE'S THEORY; THORNDIKE'S LAW OF EFFECT; TOLMAN'S THEORY; WUNDT'S THEORIES/DOCTRINES.

REFERENCES

Bentham, J. (1830). *Works*. J. Bowruy (Ed.) Edinburgh: Hait.
Gall, F. (1835). *Works: On the functions of the brain and each of its parts*. Boston: Marsh, Capen, & Lyon.

Reid, T. (1849). *Essays on the intellectual powers of the mind.* Edinburgh: Macachian, Stewart.

Darwin, C. (1859). *On the origin of species by means of natural selection.* London: Murray.

Ebbinghaus, H. (1885). *Uber das Gedachtnis.* Leipzig: Duncker.

James, W. (1890). *Principles of psychology.* New York: Holt.

Wundt, W. (1897). *Outline of psychology.* Leipzig: Englemann.

Thorndike, E. (1911). *Animal intelligence: Experimental studies.* New York: Macmillan.

Wertheimer, M. (1912). Experimentelle studien uber das sehen von bewegung. *Z. Psy., 61,* 161–265.

Kuo, Z. (1921). Giving up instincts in psychology. *J. Philos., 18,* 645–664.

Pavlov, I. (1927). *Conditioned reflexes.* London: Oxford University Press.

Thurstone, L. L. (1930). The learning function. *J. Gen. Psy., 3,* 469–493.

Adams, D. (1931). A restatement of the problem of learning. *Brit. J. Psy., 22,* 150–178.

Tolman, E. (1932). *Purposive behavior in animals and men.* New York: Appleton-Century-Crofts.

Rexroad, C. (1933). An examination of conditioned reflex theory. *Psy. Rev., 40,* 457–466.

Warren, H. (Ed.) (1934). *Dictionary of psychology.* Cambridge, MA: Houghton Mifflin.

Dashiell, J. (1935). A survey and synthesis of learning theories. *Psy. Bull., 32,* 261–275.

Guthrie, E. R. (1935). *The psychology of learning.* New York: Harper.

Schlosberg, H. (1937). The relationship between success and the laws of conditioning. *Psy. Rev., 44,* 379–394.

Skinner, B. F. (1938). *The behavior of organisms: An experimental analysis.* New York: Appleton-Century-Crofts.

Hull, C. L. (1943). *Principles of behavior.* New York: Appleton-Century-Crofts.

Pitts, W. (1943). A general theory of learning and conditioning. *Psychometrika, 8,* 1–18.

Hilgard, E. (1948). *Theories of learning.* New York: Appleton-Century-Crofts.

Hebb, D. (1949). *The organization of behavior.* New York: Wiley.

Tolman, E. (1949). There is more than one kind of learning. *Psy. Rev., 56,* 144–155.

Estes, W. (1950). Toward a statistical theory of learning. *Psy. Rev., 57,* 94–107.

Skinner, B. F. (1950). Are theories of learning necessary? *Psy. Rev., 57,* 193–216.

Spence, K. (1951). Theoretical interpretations of learning. In S. S. Stevens (Ed.), *Handbk. Exp. Psy.* New York: Wiley.

Hull, C. L. (1952). *A behavior system: An introduction to behavior theory concerning the individual organism.* New Haven, CT: Yale University Press.

Spence, K. (1956). *Behavior theory and conditioning.* New Haven, CT: Yale University Press.

Honig, W. (Ed.) (1966). *Operant behavior: Areas of research and application.* New York: Appleton-Century-Crofts.

Gregg, L., & Simon, H. (1967). Process models and stochastic theories of simple concept formation. *J. Math. Psy., 4,* 246–276.

Atkinson, R., & Shiffrin, R. (1968). Human memory: A proposed system and its control processes. In K. Spence & J. Spence (Eds.), *The psychology of learning and motivation.* Vol. 2. New York: Academic Press.

Piaget, J. (1970). Piaget's theory. In P. Mussen (Ed.), *Carmichael's manual of child psychology.* Vol. 1. New York: Wiley.

Seligman, M. (1970). On the generality of the laws of learning. *Psy. Rev., 77,* 406–418.

Bower, G., & Hilgard, E. (1981). *Theories of learning*. Englewood Cliffs, NJ: Prentice-Hall.

Hergenhahn, B. (1982). *An introduction to theories of learning*. Englewood Cliffs, NJ: Prentice-Hall.

Hilgard, E. (1987). *Psychology in America: A historical survey*. San Diego: Harcourt Brace Jovanovich.

Lockwood, G. (1994). Learning theories. In R. J. Corsini (Ed.), *Ency. Psy.* New York: Wiley.

LEARNING THEORY, THORNDIKE'S. See REINFORCEMENT, THORN-DIKE'S THEORY OF.

LEAST ACTION, LAW/PRINCIPLE OF. See GESTALT THEORY/LAWS.

LEAST COMMITMENT, PRINCIPLE OF. See INFORMATION/INFORMATION-PROCESSING THEORY.

LEAST-EFFORT, GESTALT PRINCIPLE OF. See GESTALT THEORY/LAWS.

LEAST EFFORT, PRINCIPLE OF. This general principle states that when there are a number of possibilities for action, an individual will select the one that requires the *least amount of effort*. The principle has been invoked in a wide range of disciplines and in a diverse range of problems from rats learning to run mazes to the operation of economic systems. In the area of personality and social psychology, a principle called *least interest* found expression similar to that of *least effort*: in a personal relationship, whichever member of a couple is less interested in the relationship is the one who is able to set its terms. Zipf (1945, 1949) enumerated various functional relationships in the area of the law-fulness of language phenomena that exemplify the *principle of least effort*: the frequency of occurrence of words is inversely related to their length; that is, there is a universal tendency for people to use short words (e.g., "TV") more often than long ones (e.g., "television"); the lower the rank order in word frequency, the more different words are found at that rank (e.g., in a sample of 1,000 words there are many different words that occur once, and there are only a very few words that occur as frequently as 40 times per 1,000 words); the more "effortful" a sound is, the less frequent its occurrence tends to be; and the average number of different meanings per word is proportional to its fre-quency of occurrence. Zipf presented analyses and evidence indicating that there is a "grand harmony" or balance in the use of language. A related principle, called *economy of effort*, refers to the tendency of an organism in repeated performances to minimize the expenditure of energy by eliminating useless movements. This principle is also called *adaptive adaptation* by Borovski, who distinguished this law from that of *least effort* (Warren, 1934). See also ZIPF'S LAW.

REFERENCES

Warren, H. (Ed.) (1934). *Dictionary of psychology.* Cambridge, MA: Houghton Mifflin.
Zipf, G. (1945). The repetition of words, time-perspective, and semantic balance. *J. Gen. Psy., 32,* 127–148.
Zipf, G. (1949). *Human behavior and the principle of least effort.* Cambridge, MA: Addison-Wesley.

LEAST-ENERGY EXPENDITURE, PRINCIPLE OF. See GESTALT THE-ORY/LAWS.

LEE–HENDRICKS MODEL. See LOVE, THEORIES OF.

LEIBNITZ'S MONAD THEORY. See HERBART'S DOCTRINE OF AP-PERCEPTION.

LEPLEY HYPOTHESIS/LEPLEY–HULL HYPOTHESIS. See SERIAL POSITION EFFECT.

LEWIN'S FIELD THEORY. The German-born American psychologist Kurt Lewin (1890–1947) developed a *field theory of personality* that was influenced by Gestalt psychology and psychoanalysis. The concept of *field*, a major principle of the Gestaltists, refers to the determination of one's behavior by the psychophysical field, consisting of an organized system of stresses or forces, which is analogous in its dynamics to an electromagnetic/gravitational field in physics. In the *field theory* approach, an individual's perception of an object is determined by the total field in which the object is contained. According to Lewin, *field theory* provides a method of analyzing causal relations among mutually interdependent facts and of developing scientific constructs (Lewin, 1951). The principal features of *Lewin's field theory* are study of behavior as a function of the field that exists at the time the behavior occurs; analysis of behavior in the situation as a whole and from which the component parts may be distinguished; focus on the concrete person in a concrete situation that can be represented mathematically; and a preference for psychological, as opposed to physical or physiological, descriptions of the field in which underlying forces or needs determine behavior (Hall & Lindzey, 1978). Lewin's conceptualization of the structure of personality is cast in terms of spatial representations because such accounts can be treated in nonmetrical-mathematical ways, whereas ordinary verbal definitions do not lend themselves to such treatments. For example, the separation of the person from the rest of the universe is depicted by simply drawing an enclosed figure such as a circle, square, or triangle. The boundary of the figure defines the limits of the *person* where everything inside the boundary is "P" (the person) and everything outside the boundary is "non-P." Drawing another larger figure around the initial figure defines Lewin's concept of *psychological environment*, and the total area within both figures is called the *life space*. All the space outside the two figures represents the nonpsychological aspects of the universe. Thus, according to Lewin, *life space* (L) equals the *person* (P) plus the *psychological environment* (E). The L (also called *total psychological field*) is surrounded by a "foreign hull" that is part of the non-psychological or objective environment. Lewin's spatial representation separates the regions of P and the environment by "boundaries" that have degrees of "permeability" and various dimensions such as "nearness/remoteness." Regions of L are interconnected so that a "fact" in one region can affect a "fact" in another region (an influence between two facts is called an *event*). Connections between regions are said to exist when the individual can perform a "locomotion" between regions, and regions of P are considered connected when they can "communicate" with one another. The L also has the dimensions of "reality-unreality" and "past-future." All of Lewin's spatial concepts and relationships can be handled by the branch of mathematics called *topology*, and his structural concepts of personality are called *topological psychology* (Lewin, 1936). Lewin's invention of a new type of spatial representation was called *hodology* (the "science of paths"), wherein he was able to deal with the dynamic concepts such as force, distance, and direction (cf: Harary, Norman, & Cartwright, 1965). Lewin's account of the dynamics of his personality theory is called *vector psychology*, which includes development of the concepts of need, psychical energy, tension, force (vector), and valence. These dynamical constructs, in conjunction with his structural constructs, determine the particular locomotions of P and the way P structures her or his environment. Locomotions and restructurings are ways P reduces tension by satisfying needs. The ultimate goal of all psychological processes, according to Lewin, was to return P to a state of equilibrium. *Lewin's learning theory*, as part of his *personality development theory*, consisted of descriptions of the changes that occur in behavior and used concepts such as *cognitive restructuring, differentiation, motivation, changes in boundary conditions, integration*, and *organization*. Based on the amount of experimentation that Lewin's *personality theory* generated since its inception, it may be considered a "good" theory (see Cartwright, 1959; De-Rivera, 1976). In particular, *Lewin's field theory* instigated a great deal of experimental work in the areas of aspiration level/achievement motivation, interrupted/incompleted activities, regression, conflict, aggression, and cognitive dissonance/interpersonal relations. *Lewin's field theory* led to the development of an active area of investigation called *group dynamics* in social psychology (Lewin, 1948; Deutsch, 1968; Back, 1994) and provided the impetus for development of ecological/environmental psychology. Lewin's *theory of the person*, however, has made no important advances since the early 1940s, even though many of his concepts—such as life space, vector, valence, barrier, and tension system—have been assimilated into the mainstream of psychology. Formal criticisms of *Lewin's field theory* have occurred in four areas (Hall & Lindzey, 1978): Lewin's topological and vectorial systems do not provide anything new about the behavior they are supposed to explain (cf: Garrett, 1939); psychology should not ignore the objective environment (cf: Brunswik, 1943); Lewin does not account for the individual's past history (cf: Leeper, 1943); and Lewin misuses mathematical and physical concepts (cf: London, 1944). See also ACHIEVEMENT MOTIVATION, THEORY OF; FESTINGER'S COGNITIVE DISSONANCE THEORY; GESTALT THEORY/LAWS; HEIDER'S BALANCE THEORY; ZEIGARNIK EFFECT.

REFERENCES

Lewin, K. (1922). Das Problem der Willensmessung und das Grundgesetz der Assoziation. *Psy. Forsch., 1,* 191–302; *2,* 65–140.
Lewin, K. (1935). *A dynamic theory of personality.* New York: McGraw-Hill.
Lewin, K. (1936). *Principles of topological psychology.* New York: McGraw-Hill.
Garrett, H. (1939). Lewin's "topological" psychology: An evaluation. *Psy. Rev., 46,* 517–524.
Brunswik, E. (1943). Organismic achievement and environmental probability. *Psy. Rev., 50,* 255–272.
Leeper, R. (1943). *Lewin's topological and vectoral psychology: A digest and a critique.* Eugene: University of Oregon Press.
London, I. (1944). Psychologists' misuse of the auxiliary concepts of physics and mathematics. *Psy. Rev., 51,* 266–291.
Lewin, K. (1948). *Resolving social conflicts: Selected papers on group dynamics.* New York: Harper & Row.
Lewin, K. (1951). *Field theory in social science: Selected theoretical papers.* New York: Harper & Row.
Cartwright, D. (1959). Lewinian theory as a contemporary systematic framework. In S. Koch (Ed.), *Psychology: A study of a science.* Vol. 2. New York: McGraw-Hill.
Harary, F., Norman, R., & Cartwright, D. (1965). *Structural models: An introduction to the theory of directed graphs.* New York: Wiley.
Deutsch, M. (1968). Field theory in psychology. In G. Lindzey & E. Aronson (Eds.), *Handbook of social psychology.* Vol. 1. Cambridge, MA: Addison-Wesley.
DeRivera, J. (1976). *Field theory as human science: Contributions of Lewin's Berlin group.* New York: Halsted Press.
Hall, C., & Lindzey, G. (1978). *Theories of personality.* New York: Wiley.
Allred, G., Harper, J., & Wadham, R. (1994). Physics and the behavioral sciences. In R. J. Corsini (Ed.), *Ency. Psy.* New York: Wiley.
Back, K. (1994). Group dynamics. In R. J. Corsini (Ed.), *Ency. Psy.* New York: Wiley.
Lundin, R. (1994). Kurt Lewin. In R. J. Corsini (Ed.), *Ency. Psy.* New York: Wiley.
Reuder, M. (1994). Field theory. In R. J. Corsini (Ed.), *Ency. Psy.* New York: Wiley.

LEWINSOHN'S THEORY OF DEPRESSION. See DEPRESSION, THEORIES OF.

LIEBMANN EFFECT. See GESTALT THEORY/LAWS.

LIFE-SPAN DEVELOPMENT THEORIES. See AGING, THEORIES OF.

LIGHT, THEORIES OF. See VISION/SIGHT, THEORIES OF.

LIKELIHOOD PRINCIPLE. See UNCONSCIOUS INFERENCE, DOC-TRINE OF.

LIKING, THEORIES OF. See LOVE, THEORIES OF.

LINDSLEY'S ACTIVATION THEORY. Donald B. Lindsley's germinal work on activation in the general area of emotion showed the importance of the brain-stem portion of the brain called the *reticular substance*. Lindsley's (1951, 1982) *activation theory* was based, in particular, on research involving the electroencephalogram (EEG) and its relevance toward understanding the interaction of the cerebral cortex and the subcortical structures. The *activation theory* was not advanced as the only explanatory concept for emotional behavior, but it was related to the phenomenon of sleep–wakefulness, to EEG recordings of cortical activity, and to different types of abnormal behavior involving various psychiatric symptomatologies. The *activation theory* stated: (1) the EEG in emotion shows an *activation pattern* with reduction of alpha (synchronized) rhythms and induction of low-amplitude, fast activity; (2) the EEG *activation pattern* is reproducible by electrical stimulation of the brain-stem reticular formation (BSRF); (3) destruction of the rostral end of the BSRF abolishes EEG activation and allows restoration of rhythmic discharges in the thalamus/cortex; (4) the behavior associated with destruction of the rostral end of the BSRF is the opposite of emotional excitement, namely, apathy, somnolence, lethargy, and catalepsy; (5) the combined mechanism of the basal diencephalon and lower BSRF is identical with, or overlaps, the EEG activating mechanism, and this mechanism causes the objective features of emotional expressiveness to appear. Lindsley (1951) concluded that it was not legitimate on the basis of the existing experimental evidence to attempt to account for all the varieties of emotional expression, and further research was advised on the influences of learning, habituation, and memory on emotional expression. The *activation theory* was able to account for the extremes of emotional behavior but was not able to completely explain the intermediate and mixed states of emotional expressiveness. See also ACTIVATION/AROUSAL THEORY; EMOTIONS, THEORIES/LAWS OF; MOTIVATION, THEORIES OF; SLEEP, THEORIES OF.

REFERENCES

Berger, H. (1933). Uber das Elektrenkephalogramm des Menschen. VI. *Ar. Psychiat. Nervenkr., 99*, 555–574.

Darrow, C. (1935). Emotion as relative functional decortication: The role of conflict. *Psy. Rev., 42*, 566–578.

Jasper, H., & Andrews, H. (1938). Brain potentials and voluntary muscle activity in man. *J. Neurophysiol., 1,* 87–100.

Ranson, S., & Magoun, H. (1939). The hypothalamus. *Ergebn. Physiol., 41,* 56–163.

Williams, A. C., Jr. (1939). Some psychological correlates of the electroencephalogram. *Ar. Psy., N.Y.,* no. 240.

Lindsley, D. (1951). Emotion. In S. S. Stevens (Ed.), *Handbk. Exp. Psy.* New York: Wiley.

Lindsley, D. (1982). Neural mechanisms of arousal, attention, and information processing. In J. Orbach (Ed.), *Neuropsychology after Lashley.* Hillsdale, NJ: Erlbaum.

LINGUISTIC RELATIVITY HYPOTHESIS. See WHORF–SAPIR HYPOTHESIS/THEORY.

LIPOSTATIC THEORY. See HUNGER, THEORIES OF.

LIPPS' EMPATHY THEORY. The German philosopher/psychologist Theodor Lipps (1851–1914) formulated an *empathy theory* of aesthetic enjoyment (Lipps, 1897) in which aesthetic feeling was based in four different types of projection of the observer onto the perceived objects (cf: *conscious illusion theory*—holds that art-experience is a process of illusion or esthetic play resulting in a pleasurable free and conscious oscillation between semblance and reality; Warren, 1934): (1) a *general apperceptive empathy,* which involves the animation of the forms of common objects (e.g., perceiving a line as movement); (2) *empirical empathy,* which refers to the humanizing of natural objects (e.g., the phrase "babbling brook" may be used to describe a stream); (3) *mood empathy,* where one ascribes or incorporates feelings into colors or music (e.g., the painting was described as a "cheerful yellow," or the music had a "sad" and "melancholic" melody); and (4) *sensible appearance empathy,* where gestures and other bodily movements of individuals may be interpreted as indicators of their inner lives. Lipps maintained through these four types of empathy that *beauty* is a function of both the beholder/observer as well as the object itself (Peyser, 1994). See also ZEISING'S PRINCIPLE.

REFERENCES

James, W. (1890). *The principles of psychology.* New York: Holt.

Lipps, T. (1897). *Raumasthetik und geometrisch-optische Tauschungen.* Leipzig: Barth.

Lipps, T. (1898). *Komik und Humor. Eine psychologisch-asthetische Untersuchung.* Hamburg: Voss.

Lipps, T. (1905). *Psychological studies.* Baltimore: Williams & Wilkins.

Warren, H. (Ed.) (1934). *Dictionary of psychology.* Cambridge, MA: Houghton Mifflin.

Peyser, C. (1994). Theodor Lipps. In R. J. Corsini (Ed.), *Ency. Psy.* New York: Wiley.

LISTING'S LAW. See VISION/SIGHT, THEORIES OF.

LLOYD MORGAN'S/MORGAN'S CANON. See PARSIMONY, LAW OF.

LOCK-AND-KEY THEORY. See OLFACTORY/SMELL, THEORIES OF.

LOCUS OF CONTROL THEORY. See ROTTER'S SOCIAL LEARNING THEORY.

LOEB'S TROPISTIC THEORY. The German-born zoologist/physiologist Jacques Loeb (1859–1924) formulated a *theory of the tropism* as applied to animal behavior (Loeb, 1890, 1908). The term *tropism* refers to any unlearned movement or orientation of an organic unit as a whole toward a source of stimulation (cf: *phototropism*, which means "turning toward light"; *heliotropism* is "movement toward the sun," *geotropism* is "a simple orienting response, either negative or positive, to the lines of force of gravity," and *galvanotropism* is "a simple orienting response, either negative or positive, to electrical stimulation"). Modern convention reserves the term *tropism* for plants and the term *taxis* for such automatic movements when made by animate organisms (Warren, 1934; Reber, 1995). The *tropism*, according to Loeb, is a turning process—toward or away from specific objects in the environment—that is the key to instinct and to life in general. The *tropistic theory* states that an animal's response is a direct function of the stimulus, and the behavior is "forced" and does not require any explanation in terms of consciousness. Loeb's *continuous action theory of tropisms* holds that the orienting responses of animals depend on the continuous application of the stimulus and not on mere changes in intensity (cf: the *intensity theory of tropisms*, which holds that the tropic orientation of an organism to a stimulus is due to unequal intensity of stimulation of symmetrical points on the body; and the *direction theory of tropisms*, which asserts that the tropic orientation is determined by the direction or point in space from which the stimulus acts, rather than by its duration and intensity; Warren, 1934). Loeb, more than any other one person, formalized a mature and complete *mechanistic psychology* (i.e., the study of the problems of mind are reduced to the form of general physical problems; Leahey, 1994; cf: the *vitalism* approach of Bergson, 1911) in the closing years of the nineteenth century (Murphy & Kovach, 1972). As one of the early animal psychologists, Loeb influenced the thinking of John B. Watson, the founder of *behaviorism*. Loeb's basic impact on psychology was as a forerunner of an objective, scientific, and naturalistic psychology (Lundin, 1994). His work emphasized experimental methods and de-emphasized the role of consciousness in behavior (Schultz, 1969). See also BEHAVIORIST THEORY.

REFERENCES

Loeb, J. (1890). *Der Heliotropismus der Tiere*. Wurzburg: Hertz.

Loeb, J. (1908). *Forced movements, tropisms, and animal conduct*. Philadelphia: Lippincott.

Bergson, H. (1911). *Creative evolution*. New York: Holt.

Loeb, J. (1912). *The mechanistic conception of life: Biological essays.* Chicago: University of Chicago Press.

Warren, H. (Ed.) (1934). *Dictionary of psychology.* Cambridge, MA: Houghton Mifflin.

Schultz, D. (1969). *A history of modern psychology.* New York: Academic Press.

Murphy, G., & Kovach, J. (1972). *Historical introduction to modern psychology.* New York: Harcourt Brace Jovanovich.

Leahey, T. (1994). Mechanistic theory. In R. J. Corsini (Ed.), *Ency. Psy.* New York: Wiley.

Lundin, R. (1994). Jacques Loeb. In R. J. Corsini (Ed.), *Ency. Psy.* New York: Wiley.

Reber, A. (1995). *The Penguin dictionary of psychology.* New York: Penguin Books.

LOGAN'S MICROMOLAR THEORY. The American psychologist Frank A. Logan (1924–) formulated *micromolar theory*, which defines the quantitative aspects of various types of responses—such as speed, volume, and amplitude—where such aspects or dimensions become part of what the individual actually learns (Logan, 1956, 1960). In the classical view of response parameters, as exemplified in *Hull's* (1943) *macromolar theory*, response classes are defined in terms of their achievements (e.g., running a maze, pressing a lever), and variations in the response (e.g., speed amplitude) during training were taken to be indices of the strength of the "response tendency." Logan's *micromolar theory*, on the other hand, identifies a dimension (e.g., speed) as containing different responses that are selectively learned and influenced by differential reinforcement. *Logan's theory* is essentially a *utility* analysis where the *net utility* of a particular response—such as speed—is given by its *positive utility* minus its associated *negative utility*. The profile of *net utility* across a particular response (e.g., speed) continuum is then used to calculate the probability distribution of the various responses (e.g., speeds) (Bower & Hilgard, 1981). In experiments within the context of Hull–Spence's *stimulus–response incentive theory*, Logan found in one case that humans' performance speed (and "learning to learn") was dependent on practice speed. Logan also described the *hybrid theory of learning* that combines the features of various existing theories into a single system. Among the unique aspects of the *hybrid theory* is the hypothesization of two kinds of learning process: a cognitive-associative process for *classical conditioning* and a stimulus–response process for *operant conditioning* (Logan, 1977, 1979). The importance of Logan's *micromolar theory* has been primarily that of "conceptual housecleaning" within *learning theory* where several theoretical puzzles connected with the problem of how reinforcement shapes behavior have been unraveled and better understood (Bower & Hilgard, 1981). See also HULL'S LEARNING THEORY; PAVLOVIAN CONDITIONING PRINCIPLES/LAWS/THEORIES; SKINNER'S DESCRIPTIVE BEHAVIOR/ OPERANT CONDITIONING THEORY; SPENCE'S THEORY.

REFERENCES

Hull, C. (1943). *Principles of behavior.* New York: Appleton-Century-Crofts.

Logan, F. (1956). A micromolar approach to behavior theory. *Psy. Rev., 63,* 63–73.

Logan, F. (1960). *Incentive.* New Haven, CT: Yale University Press.

Logan, F., & Wagner, A. (1965). *Reward and punishment.* Boston: Allyn & Bacon.

Logan, F. (1970). *Fundamentals of learning and motivation.* Dubuque, IA: Brown.

Logan, F. (1977). Hybrid theory of classical conditioning. In G. Bower (Ed.), *The psychology of learning and motivation.* Vol. 2. New York: Academic Press.

Logan, F. (1979). Hybrid theory of operant conditioning. *Psy. Rev., 86,* 507–541.

Bower, G., & Hilgard, E. (1981). *Theories of learning.* Englewood Cliffs, NJ: Prentice-Hall.

LOMBROSIAN THEORY. Attempts to determine or predict who will be a *criminal* are not new. Various anthropological and psychological theories based on mental ability have provided explanations for criminal behavior (e.g., Dugdale, 1877; Goddard, 1910; cf: Danziger & Wheeler, 1975). The Italian anthropologist/criminologist Cesare Lombroso (1836–1909)—who wrote on the connection between genius and insanity—proposed his *theory of criminality* in the late nineteenth century (Lombroso, 1876/1911). According to Lombroso, criminals are throwbacks to prehuman evolution, and he considered the *physical characteristics* of criminals to resemble the characteristics of prehistoric humankind. Lombroso argued that people with a receding chin, flattened nose, low, flat forehead or other features of earlier forms of human life are more likely to be criminals. Lombroso showed that there was a relatively high incidence of these features among persons in jail. Criminals were deformed physically and could, therefore, be easily identified. A variation on *Lombroso's theory* in 1888 was called the *degeneracy theory of genius* and refers to the overdevelopment of certain capacities or traits that is accompanied by various defects and that indicates an instability of organization pointing toward degeneration (Warren, 1934). In this version, Lombroso suggested the innate disposition to criminal behavior as being associated with degeneration of hereditary cells, and he found most criminals have physical signs ("stigmata of degeneration") indicating the innate, constitutional disposition to crime (Wolman, 1973). Surprisingly, for a while, the *Lombrosian theory* was widely accepted, in spite of the fact that there was an equally high incidence of "criminal features" among noncriminal populations as there was among criminal populations. Eventually, however, *Lombroso's theory* was abandoned (Baum, Fisher, & Singer, 1985). See also KRETSCHMER'S THEORY OF PERSONALITY; SHELDON'S TYPE THEORY; TYPE THEORIES OF PERSONALITY.

REFERENCES

Lombroso, C. (1876/1911). *Criminal man.* New York: Putnam.

Dugdale, R. (1877). *The Jukes: A study in crime, pauperism, disease, and heredity.* New York: Putnam.

Goddard, H. (1910). *The criminal imbecile.* New York: Macmillan.

Warren, H. (Ed.) (1934). *Dictionary of psychology.* Cambridge, MA: Houghton Mifflin.

Wolman, B. (Ed.) (1973). *Dictionary of behavioral science.* New York: Van Nostrand Reinhold.

Danziger, S., & Wheeler, D. (1975). Economics of crime: Punishment or income redistribution. *Rev. Soc. Econ., 33*, 113–131.

Baum, A., Fisher, J., & Singer, J. (1985). *Social psychology*. New York: Random House.

LORENZ'S HYDRAULIC MODEL OF AGGRESSION. See HYDRAULIC THEORY.

LOTKA/LOTKA–PRICE LAW. This law was originally developed by Alfred J. Lotka, who was a demographer for the New York Metropolitan Life Insurance Company in the 1920s. *Lotka's law* states that the number of scientists publishing n papers is roughly proportional to n-squared where the constant of proportionality varies with the discipline. This law is somewhat similar to Vilfredo Pareto's (1848–1923) *law of income distribution* in economics. Derek de Solla Price (1976) subsequently refined *Lotka's law*, which now states that half of all scientific publications are made by the square root of the total number of scientific contributors. The *Lotka–Price law* of historiometry indicates the inequality of scientific productivity and is shown as highly skewed, hyperbolic-shaped distributions of creative output. See also PERSONALISTIC THEORY OF HISTORY.

REFERENCES

Lotka, A. (1926). The frequency distribution of scientific productivity. *J. Wash. Acad. Sci., 16*, 317–323.

Price, D. (1976). A general theory of bibliometric and other cumulative advantage processes. *Journal of the American Society of Information Sciences, 27*, 292–306.

Simonton, D. (1984). *Genius, creativity, and leadership*. Cambridge: Harvard University Press.

Zusne, L. (1985). Contributions to the history of psychology. xxxviii. The hyperbolic structure of eminence. *Psy. Rep., 57*, 1213–1214.

Furnham, A., & Bonnett, C. (1992). British research productivity in psychology 1980–1989. Does the Lotka–Price law apply to university departments as it does to individuals? *Pers. Indiv. Diff., 13*, 1333–1341.

Roeckelein, J. (1996). Contributions to the history of psychology: CIV. Eminence in psychology as measured by name counts and eponyms. *Psy. Rep., 78*, 243–253.

LOTZE'S THEORY OF LOCAL SIGNS. The German physiologist/psychologist Rudolph Hermann Lotze (1817–1881) developed a *theory/doctrine of local signs* that was typical of nineteenth-century thought in which philosophical concepts, rather than empirical data, dominated the area of the physiology of sense organs (Lotze, 1852). However, Lotze sought to unify physiological and psychological material in a coherent system in which both empirical findings and philosophical interpretations could be reconciled. Lotze argued that psychology must deal with the organism where the nervous system and the mind should be seen in relation to each other. On the other hand, Lotze maintained that it was foolish to suppose that the mere existence of physical and chemical process was an "explanation" of mind. He argued that exact science can give no clue as to the ultimate nature of mental processes where, in particular, the meanings of life, the reality of pleasures and pain, and the reality of one's ideals and dreams are not affected by the discovery of mechanical laws (Murphy & Kovach, 1972). A *local sign* is defined as an inherent qualitative factor by means of which one visual or tactual sensation can be distinguished from others in respect to position in space (Wolman, 1973). *Locality sign*, another term for *local sign*, is similarly defined as a specific character assumed to be inherent in the sensory experience aroused by a single receptor or by a single afferent neuron (and to differ for each receptor or for each afferent neuron). *Locality sign* or *local sign* is so called because it furnishes a cue to the position of the receptor-unit stimulated and hence to the location of the stimulus (Warren, 1934). The concept of *local signs* was applicable to most *nativistic* (i.e., inherent knowledge; cf: Helmholtz, 1856) *theories of space* (e.g., Hering, 1878) and *genetic theories* (e.g., Wundt, 1862, 1873). According to *Lotze's theory*, every tactual and visual sensation has its own specific *local sign* or "signature," which is an experiential intensity that is particular for the point stimulated—either on the retina for visual stimulation or on the skin for tactile stimulation. In the case of space perception, Lotze theorized that it was produced by the relationship between the *local signs* as the stimulation shifted across the receptor system. Lotze's *theory of local signs* was an attempt to find a compromise between the various views on space perception: the *theory of perceptual innateness* of I. Kant (1724–1804), the *experiential theory* of J. Herbart (1776–1841), and the theory of J. Muller (1801–1858), who taught that space perception is *innate*, but the elaboration of the world of space had to be *learned*. Lotze's view, both in visual and cutaneous space, was that psychological space is built up from sensations that in isolation would not be spatial but whose order of stimulation corresponds to transition of the stimulus from one point in physical space to another. *Lotze's theory of local signs* not only was highly important as an application of physiological findings and *associationist theory* to a complex problem but was one of the boldest, most fruitful attempts to make the muscular sensations play their part in mental life. Later, however, organismic and Gestalt approaches to psychology challenged Lotze's analytic, atomistic, and associationist conceptions such as his *local sign theory* (Murphy & Kovach, 1972). See also BERKELEY'S THEORY OF SPACE PERCEPTION; GESTALT THEORY/LAWS.

REFERENCES

Lotze, R. H. (1852). *Medicinische Psychologie oder, Physiologie der Seele*. Leipzig: Weidmann.

Helmholtz, H. von. (1856). *Handbuch der Physiologischen Optik*. Leipzig: Voss.

Wundt, W. (1862). *Beitrage zur Theorie der Sinneswahrnehmung*. Leipzig: Wunter'sck Verlaghandlung.

Lotze, R. H. (1864). *Microcosmus: An essay concerning man and his relation to the world*. Edinburgh: Clark.

Wundt, W. (1873). *Grundzuege der Physiologischen Psychologie*. Leipzig: Engelmann.

Hering, E. (1878). *Zur Lehre vom Lichtsinn*. Vienna: Gerolds.

Lotze, R. H. (1879). *Metaphysic, in three books, ontology, cosmology, and psychology*. Oxford: Clarendon Press.

Warren, H. (Ed.) (1934). *Dictionary of psychology*. Cambridge, MA: Houghton Mifflin.

Murphy, G., & Kovach, J. (1972). *Historical introduction to modern psychology*. New York: Harcourt Brace Jovanovich.

Wolman, B. (Ed.) (1973). *Dictionary of behavioral science*. New York: Van Nostrand Reinhold.

LOVE, THEORIES OF. In general, two contemporary definitions of *love* that may, or may not, carry sexual connotations, are "an internal feeling of strong liking/affection for some specific thing or person" and "an enduring sentiment toward a person providing a desire to be with that person and a concern for the happiness and satisfactions of that person" (Reber, 1995). An earlier definition of *love*, however, seemed to strongly imply a sexual component: "a feeling or sentiment of attachment toward some person, often growing out of sexual attraction, relations, or situations, and exhibiting a great diversity of psychological and physiological manifestations (Warren, 1934; cf: the *Coolidge effect*—the high continuous sexual performance shown by males of many species for extended periods of time with the introduction of new, receptive females; Zusne, 1987). Some dictionaries of psychological terms, interestingly, do not even attempt to give a definition of *love* (e.g., Wolman, 1973). Other approaches toward defining *love* are given in *psychoanalytic theory* where it is used variously as any affective state defined as the opposite of "hatred"; an emotion liable to sublimation or inhibition; and an equivalent to Eros and an instinctive force close either to the life instincts or to the sexual instincts, depending on early or late Freudian formulation. Only recently have social scientists systematically gathered information about *love* (e.g., Cook & Wilson, 1979; Pope, 1980; Hatfield & Walster, 1981). Using *love* as a scientific term leads to several types of conflicts or questions: Can love exist independent of sex/sexual expression? Is love innate, or is it an acquired emotional response? and Can the feeling of love be dissociated from the behavior, or does the emotion always contaminate the behavior? (Reber, 1995). The American social psychologist Zick Rubin (1944–) distinguishes between the conditions of *liking* and *loving* (Rubin, 1973). Romantic *love*, according to Rubin, generally includes such aspects as responsibility for the other person, tenderness, and self-disclosure. On the other hand, *liking* refers to an attraction for the other person that includes respect and the perception that the other person is similar to oneself. Rubin developed a *liking* and a *loving scale* to distinguish between the theoretical aspects of interpersonal attraction. Specifically, Rubin's *love scale* is constructed to evaluate three components: affiliative/dependent needs, predispositions to help, and exclusiveness. His *liking scale* is based on two primary components: a feeling that the liked person is similar to oneself, and an overall favorable evaluation of the liked person (Rubin, 1970, 1973). Another theoretical approach toward *love* is provided by Hatfield and Walster (1981) and Hatfield (1988), who distinguish between *passionate love*—a profound physiological arousal and an intensely emotional state with a confusion of feelings, tenderness and sexuality, elation and pain, anxiety and relief, and altruism and jealousy; and *companionate love*—a combination of friendly affection and deep attachment. In yet another approach, called the *Lee–Hendrick model*, Lee (1977) and Hendrick and Hendrick (1986) distinguish among six types/styles of *love*: *eros*—romantic and sexual love; *mania*—obsessive and demanding love; *ludis*—self-centered and playful love; *storge*—companionship and close-friends love; *agape*—saintly and "thou"-centered love; and *pragma*—logical and practical love. Winch's (1958) *theory of complementary needs* argues that people fall in love with those individuals who complement their own personalities and needs. However, other researchers do not agree completely with Winch's argument and suggest, instead, that people tend to select mates who possess similar (rather than complementary) personalities and needs (e.g., Schellenberg & Bee, 1960; Levinger, Senn, & Jorgensen, 1970). Stolller's (1978) *theory of love* asserts that hostility (i.e., the overt or hidden desire to harm another person) generates and enhances sexual excitement and passionate love. According to Stoller, the absence of hostility leads to sexual indifference and boredom. Tennov's (1979) theoretical approach is that *both* pleasure and pain are associated with love, and love may be stimulated by either condition. According to *Sternberg's triangular theory of love*, love may be conceived of as a three-dimensional triangular model where the three points of the figure are *intimacy* (the closeness two people feel toward one another, including reciprocal sharing and valuation), *commitment* (the decision to remain in the relationship), and *passion* (feelings of romance and physical/sexual attraction). In Sternberg's (1988) approach, relationships can involve different combinations of the models' three components where seven distinct love relationships (plus one of "nonlove") may be formed: liking, infatuated love, romantic love, empty love, companionate love, fatuous love, and consummate love. Generalizations from research on love indicate that there are subtle gender differences in how women and men experience love: men tend to be more "romantic" than women; men seem to fall *in* love faster and to fall *out* of love slower than women; women are more likely to experience the "agony" and the "ecstasy" of love than men; and women are more likely than men to disclose their feelings, both positive and negative, in casual relationships. Individuals in love exhibit, invariably, several behavioral cues such as paying attention to physical appearance and "preening," gazing deeply into each other's eyes, and touching and standing close to each other. The area of *love* and intimacy is relatively unexplored scientifically, and psychologists have just begun to investigate the conditions, feelings, emotions, and behaviors that occur when one individual loves another (Hatfield, 1994). See also INTERPERSONAL ATTRACTION THEORIES.

REFERENCES

Ellis, H. (1897/1936). *Studies in the psychology of sex.* 4 vols. New York: Random House.

Warren, H. (Ed.) (1934). *Dictionary of psychology.* Cambridge, MA: Houghton Mifflin.

Winch, R. (1958). *Mate selection: A study of complementary needs.* New York: Harper & Row.

Schellenberg, J., & Bee, L. (1960). A re-examination of the theory of complementary needs in mate selection. *Marr. & Fam. Liv., 22,* 227–232.

Levinger, G., Senn, D., & Jorgensen, B. (1970). Progress toward permanence in courtship: A test of the Kerckhoff–Davis hypothesis. *Sociometry, 33,* 427–443.

Rubin, Z. (1970). Measurement of romantic love. *J. Pers. Soc. Psy., 16,* 265–273.

Rubin, Z. (1973). *Liking and loving.* New York: Holt, Rinehart, & Winston.

Wolman, B. (Ed.) (1973). *Dictionary of behavioral science.* New York: Van Nostrand Reinhold.

Lee, J. (1977). *The colors of love.* New York: Bantam.

Stoller, R. (1978). *Sexual excitement.* New York: Pantheon.

Cook, M., & Wilson, G. (1979). *Love and attraction: An international conference.* Oxford: Pergamon Press.

Tennov, D. (1979). *Love and limerence.* New York: Stein & Day.

Pope, K. (1980). *On love and loving.* San Francisco: Jossey-Bass.

Hatfield, E., & Walster, G. (1981). *A new look at love.* Reading, MA: Addison-Wesley.

Hendrick, C., & Hendrick, S. (1986). A theory and method of love. *J. Pers. Soc. Psy., 50,* 392–402.

Sternberg, R. (1986). A triangular theory of love. *Psy. Rev., 93,* 119–135.

Zusne, L. (1987). *Eponyms in psychology.* Westport, CT: Greenwood Press.

Hatfield, E. (1988). Passionate and companionate love. In R. Sternberg & M. Barnes (Eds.), *The psychology of love.* New Haven, CT: Yale University Press.

Sternberg, R. (1988). *The triangle of love: Intimacy, passion, commitment.* New York: Basic Books.

Hatfield, E. (1994). Love. In R. J. Corsini (Ed.), *Ency. Psy.* New York: Wiley.

Reber, A. (1995). *The Penguin dictionary of psychology.* New York: Penguin Books.

LUNEBURG'S THEORY. See PERCEPTION (I. GENERAL), THEORIES OF.

LYSENKO'S THEORY. See LAMARCK'S THEORY.

M

MACH–BREUER–BROWN THEORY. See WITKIN'S PERCEPTION THEORY.

MACH–DVORAK PHENOMENON. See PERCEPTION (I. GENERAL), THEORIES OF.

MACHINE THEORY. See PERCEPTION (II. COMPARATIVE APPRAISAL), THEORIES OF.

MACH'S THEORY OF BODILY ROTATION. See WITKIN'S PERCEPTION THEORY.

MAIER'S LAW. This is a cynical "law" stated by the American psychologist Norman R. F. Maier (1900–) to the effect that "if the data do not fit the theory, the data must be disposed of." Apparently, Maier was chiding his colleagues for excessive concern with their own particular theoretical models (Reber, 1995).

REFERENCES

Maier, N.R.F. (1929). Reasoning in white rats. *Comp. Psy. Mono., 6*, no. 29.
Maier, N.R.F. (1930). Reasoning in humans: I. On direction. *J. Comp. Psy., 10*, 115–143.
Maier, N.R.F. (1932). The effect of cerebral destruction on reasoning and learning in rats. *J. Comp. Neurol., 54*, 45–75.
Maier, N.R.F., & Schneirla, T. (1942). Mechanisms in conditioning. *Psy. Rev., 49*, 117–133.

Maier, N.R.F. (1949). *Frustration: The study of behavior without a goal*. New York: McGraw-Hill.

Reber, A. (1995). *The Penguin dictionary of psychology*. New York: Penguin Books.

MANDLER'S THEORY OF EMOTION. See SCHACHTER–SINGER'S THEORY OF EMOTIONS.

MARBE'S LAW. See ASSOCIATION, LAWS/PRINCIPLES OF.

MASLOW'S THEORY OF PERSONALITY. The American psychologist Abraham H. Maslow (1908–1970) advanced a holistic, organismic, dynamic, and humanistic viewpoint of personality that has features similar to the theories of Kurt Goldstein and Andras Angyal. However, where Goldstein's and Angyal's theories were derived from the study of mentally unhealthy and brain-damaged individuals, Maslow's theory derives from the study of creative, healthy, and "self-actualized" persons. Consequently, Maslow's approach toward personality tends to be optimistic, health-oriented, and growth/potential-oriented. Maslow (1967) distinguished between the terms *basic needs* and *metaneeds* where needs were organized in a hierarchy or pyramid with the *basic needs* (such as food, air, water, sex, affection, and security) at the bottom and requiring satisfaction before moving up the pyramid to the *metaneeds* at the top. The list of *metaneeds* includes *wholeness and perfection*—the need for unity and completeness; *justice*—the need for fairness; *aliveness and richness*—the needs for spontaneity and complexity; *beauty*—the need for rightness and form; *goodness*—the need for benevolence; *uniqueness*—the need for individuality; *truth*—the need for reality; and *self-sufficiency*—the need for autonomy. According to Maslow's model, persons cannot be concerned with a lofty principle such as justice unless their "lower" need for food is met first. However, *metaneeds* are as important as *basic needs* in order to achieve a desirable state of *self-actualization*. When *metaneeds* are not fulfilled, the individual typically becomes cynical, alienated, and apathetic toward the world. Maslow (1959, 1962, 1970) identified certain *peak experiences* of living (such as maternal child-birth) that were characterized by profound feelings of spontaneity and harmony with the universe. Maslow cited various historical figures as illustrations of *self-actualized* persons: Beethoven, Einstein, Lincoln, Jefferson, Thoreau, Eleanor Roosevelt, and Walt Whitman. According to Maslow, such individuals possessed the requisite personality characteristics of *self-actualization*: realistic orientation of themselves within the world, complete acceptance of themselves and others, problem-oriented rather than self-oriented, highly private and detached, high levels of spontaneity and independence, and nonconformity to their culture. As a critic of science, Maslow (1956) asserted that the classical mechanistic approach of science (e.g., the *behavioristic* viewpoint in psychology) was inappropriate for characterizing the whole individual, and he advocated a *humanistic* approach, which he called the *third force* in American psychology, after the psychoanalytic and behavioristic approaches. Criticism of Maslow's *human-istic theory of personality* has been that it is more of a secular replacement for religion than it is a scientific psychology, that it accepts as true that which is yet only hypothetical, that it confuses theory with ideology, and that it substitutes rhetoric for research (Hall & Lindzey, 1978). See also ANGYAL'S PERSONALITY THEORY; GOLDSTEIN'S ORGANISMIC THEORY; PERSONALITY THEORIES.

REFERENCES

Maslow, A. (1943). A theory of human motivation. *Psy. Rev., 50,* 370–396.

Maslow, A. (1954). *Motivation and personality.* New York: Harper & Row.

Maslow, A. (1956). *The psychology of science.* New York: Harper & Row.

Maslow, A. (1959). Cognition of being in the peak experiences. *J. Genet. Psy., 94,* 43–66.

Maslow, A. (1962). *Toward a psychology of being.* Princeton, NJ: Van Nostrand.

Maslow, A. (1967). A theory of metamotivation: The biological rooting of the value–life. *J. Hum. Psy., 7,* 93–127.

Goble, F. (1970). *The third force: The psychology of Abraham Maslow.* New York: Grossman.

Maslow, A. (1970). *Religions, values, and peak experiences.* New York: Penguin Books.

Hall, C., & Lindzey, G. (1978). *Theories of personality.* New York: Wiley.

Smith, M. (1994). Humanistic psychology. In R. J. Corsini (Ed.), *Ency. Psy.* New York: Wiley.

MASS ACTION THEORY. See LASHLEY'S THEORY.

MATCHING LAW. See HERRNSTEIN'S MATCHING LAW.

McCOLLOUGH EFFECT. See EMMERT'S LAW.

McDOUGALL'S HORMIC/INSTINCT THEORY/DOCTRINE. The English-born social psychologist William McDougall (1871–1938) developed the system of psychology called *hormic* (meaning ''animal impulse'' or ''urge'') *psychology*, which was based on goal-oriented/purposeful behaviors that were assumed to be motivated by innate propensities or instincts. For McDougall (1908), goal-seeking behavior became the core of a psychology of all living organisms, and he defined purposive/goal seeking behavior as being spontaneous, persistent, variable, and repetitive. While McDougall emphasized the instinctive/innate nature of goal seeking, he did admit that some learning could occur (Lundin, 1994a). McDougall (1908) formulated a *theory of instincts* that became an important part of his *hormic psychology*, where instincts had three aspects: for any given instinct there was a perceptual predisposition to notice certain stimuli and not others (e.g., food odors were perceived by the organism when the hunger instinct was engaged); there was a predisposition for the organism to make movements toward the appropriate goal; and there was an ''emotional core,'' energy, or driving force in the organism between the perception of, and the movement toward, the goal. McDougall (1908) originally listed 12 major *instincts* in humans (i.e., hunger, rejection of particular substances, curiosity, escape, pugnacity, sex, maternal/paternal instinct, gregariousness, self-assertion, submission, construction, and acquisition), but by 1932 the list of *instincts* (or *propensities*) had increased to 17 (the 5 new instincts were crying out/appeal, laughter, comfort, rest/sleep, and migration). In addition to these *instincts*, there were other tendencies such as breathing, sneezing, and coughing. Complex forms of human behavior, according to McDougall, involved a combination (called *sentiments*) of two or more *instincts* (e.g., the sex and maternal/paternal instincts combined to account for a man's love for his wife). McDougall accepted the *doctrine of native capacities* where humans were endowed with certain potentials such as high intelligence and artistic, musical, and athletic talents, but an *instinct* had to operate as a push toward their fulfillment. McDougall's (1905) definition of psychology, that is, "the positive science of the conduct of living creatures"—which equated the term *conduct* with *behavior*—anticipated Watson's (1913) definition, that is, "the science of behavior" (Lundin, 1994a). However, ironically, McDougall was one of the more vigorous critics of Watsonian *behaviorism*, and, at one time, he attracted numerous adherents to his system of *hormic psychology*, particularly among social psychologists, sociologists, and anthropologists, many of whom considered Watson's position as too simplistic and sterile (Reber, 1995; cf: Watson & McDougall, 1929). McDougall's *hormic theory* contained several shortcomings, the primary one being the lack of precision in the definition and use of the concept of *instinct* (Lundin, 1994a, b). *Hormic psychology* and McDougall's *instinct theory* are mostly of historic interest, and, as far as human behavior is concerned, the *instinct doctrine* is not generally accepted today (except by Freudians). However, McDougall's ideas have led to a revival of interest in the concept of *instinct* among animal ethologists, and his notion of purposive/goal-directed behavior was advocated by some learning theorists (e.g., Tolman, 1932). See also ALLPORT'S THEORY OF PERSONALITY; BEHAVIORIST THEORY; LAMARCKIAN/LYSENKO DOCTRINE; SOUL THEORY; TOLMAN'S THEORY.

REFERENCES

McDougall, W. (1901). On the seat of psychological processes. *Brain, 24,* 577–630.
McDougall, W. (1905). *Physiological psychology.* London: Dent.
McDougall, W. (1908). *An introduction to social psychology.* Boston: Luce.
Watson, J. B. (1913). Psychology as the behaviorist views it. *Psy. Rev., 20,* 158–177.
McDougall, W. (1923). Purposive or mechanical psychology? *Psy. Rev., 30,* 273–288.
Watson, J. B., & McDougall, W. (1929). *The battle of behaviorism.* New York: Norton.
McDougall, W. (1932). *Energies of men: A study of the fundamental dynamics of psychology.* London: Methuen.
Tolman, E. (1932). *Purposive behavior in animals and men.* New York: Appleton-Century-Crofts.

McDougall, W. (1938). Further report on a Lamarckian experiment. *Brit. J. Psy.*, 28, 231–245.

Denny, M. (1994). Instinctive behavior. In R. J. Corsini (Ed.), *Ency. Psy.* New York: Wiley.

Lundin, R. (1994a). Hormic psychology. In R. J. Corsini (Ed.), *Ency. Psy.* New York: Wiley.

Lundin, R. (1994b). William McDougall. In R. J. Corsini (Ed.), *Ency. Psy.* New York: Wiley.

Riopelle, A. (1994). Instinct. In R. J. Corsini (Ed.), *Ency. Psy.* New York: Wiley.

Reber, A. (1995). *The Penguin dictionary of psychology.* New York: Penguin Books.

MEINONG'S THEORIES. The Austrian philosopher/psychologist Alexius Ritter von Handschuchsheim Meinong (1853–1920) studied under Franz Brentano (1838–1917), the founder of *act psychology* (i.e., a philosophical psychological system that was a precursor to *functionalism* and that focused on the *acts* or *processes* of mind as the fundamental source of empirical data; cf: the *structuralist's* approach, which argued that the basic subject matter of psychology was the *conscious* content of mind). Meinong's field was theoretical psychology and the theory of knowledge, and he formulated a *theory of assumptions,* a *theory of evidence,* a *theory of value,* and a *theory of objects;* cf: *Gegenstandstheorie* (''theory of objects'')—a branch of science originated by Meinong designed to study the properties and relations of objects as such, which the other sciences, particularly psychology, have neglected; Warren, 1934. In his *theory of objects,* Meinong accepted Plato's conceptions of ideal objects that subsist and other objects that exist, but he added a third aspect: objects that are nonexisting but have objective characteristics (cf: Meinong's *founding process*—an intellectual activity by which conscious contents are consolidated to form objects of higher order, termed *complexes;* Warren, 1934). Thus, it is possible to speak of impossible-to-exist entities such as ''round squares''; one can make true statements about many more things than the objects that exist. In his *theory of value,* Meinong (1894) appealed to the psychology of humans where people's emotional reactions, for example, are not balanced or consistent (e.g., one can show more sorrow in the nonexistence of the good than show pleasure in its existence or take displeasure in the existence of evil than joy in its nonexistence). Meinong's *value theory* anticipated contemporary thought with his various subdivisions of good and bad: good that is meritorious, good that is merely required, bad that is excusable, and bad that is inexcusable (Peyser, 1994). See also PERCEPTION (I. GENERAL), THEORIES OF.

REFERENCES

Meinong, A. (1891). Zur Psychologie der Komplexionen und Relationen. *Z. Psy.,* 2, 245–265.

Meinong, A. (1894). *Psychologisch-ethische untersuchungen zur werththeorie.* Graz, Austria: Leuschner & Lubensky.

Meinong, A. (1896). *Uber die bedeutung des Weber'schen gesetzes; Beitrage zur psychologie des vergleichens und messens.* Hamburg: Voss.

Meinong, A. (1899). Uber Gegenstande hoherer Ordnung und deren Verhaltnis zur inneren Wahrnehmung. *Z. Psy.*, *11*, 180–272.

Meinong, A. (1914). *Abhandlungen zur psychologie.* Leipzig: Barth.

Warren, H. (Ed.) (1934). *Dictionary of psychology.* Cambridge, MA: Houghton Mifflin.

Peyser, C. (1994). Alexius Meinong. In R. J. Corsini (Ed.), *Ency. Psy.* New York: Wiley.

MEMBRANE THEORY. See NEURON/NEURAL/NERVE THEORY.

MEMORY, THEORIES OF. See FORGETTING/MEMORY, THEORIES OF.

MENDELIAN RATIO. See MENDEL'S LAWS/PRINCIPLES.

MENDEL'S LAWS/PRINCIPLES. = Mendelian ratio = Mendel's theory of heredity = Mendelism. The Austrian botanist/experimental biologist Gregor Johann Mendel (1822–1884) was ordained as a priest in 1847, studied science in Vienna from 1851 to 1853, and returned later to the Brno monastery, becoming abbot in 1868. Mendel bred peas in the experimental garden of the monastery and grew almost 30,000 plants between 1856 and 1863. He artificially fertilized plants with specific characteristics; he crossed species that produced tall plants with those that produced short plants and counted the numbers of tall and short plants that appeared in the subsequent generations. All the plants of the first generation were tall, and the next generation consisted of some tall and some short in proportions of 3:1. Mendel suggested that each plant received one character from each of its parents, tallness being *dominant* and shortness being *recessive* or hidden and appearing only in later generations (Muir, 1994). The term *Mendelian ratio* refers to biparental offspring where the ratio is between those that possess a given unit character or combination of unit characters (dominants) and those that do not (recessives) possess the character. For a single *unit character* the ratio in the first filial generation is three dominants to one recessive. The term *Mendelism* refers to a *theory of inheritance* (based on *Mendel's law*) according to which the constitution of the offspring is determined by a certain number of independent factors, called *unit characters,* contributed by the parents. *Mendel's law* is a principle of hereditary transmission according to which the characters of the parents are transmitted to the offspring in units without change, some becoming perceptible in individuals of the first generation and others in those of later generations, with a definite ratio for each generation (Warren, 1934). Mendel's experiments led to the formulation of his *law of segregation* and *law of independent assortment.* Mendel's *first law/law of segregation* states that during meiosis (the process whereby a nucleus divides by two divisions into four nuclei), the two members of any pair of alleles (different sequences of genetic material occupying the same gene locus) possessed by an individual separate (segregate) into different gametes and subsequently into different offspring, neither having blended with or altered the other in any way while together in the same cell. Mendel's *second law/law of independent assortment* states that during meiosis all combinations of alleles are distributed to daughter nuclei with equal probability, the distribution of members of one pair having no influence on the distribution of members of any other pair. Mendel's *first law* is a consequence of the behavior of all chromosomes during meiosis; his *second law* is a consequence of the independent behavior of nonhomologous chromosomes during meiosis (Thain & Hickman, 1995). The English zoologist William Bateson (1861–1926) contributed to the establishment of the Mendelian concept of heredity and variations and gave the name *genetics* to the new science. Bateson experimented on hybridization in order to understand the transmission of inherited characteristics from parents to immediate offspring. In 1866, after Mendel's initial work in breeding peas was conducted, little further attention was given to *genetics* (cf: *Malthus' law*—a genetic-statistical principle proposed by T. R. Malthus, 1766–1834, that states that the population of any given region in respect to any given species tends to increase in geometrical progression, while the means of subsistence increases at a less rapid rate; Warren, 1934). However, Bateson "rediscovered" Mendel's findings and reinterpreted them in the light of more recent evidence. Bateson founded the *Journal of Genetics* in 1910 and served as a spokesman for the new science of *genetics*. Bateson also devised a *vibratory theory of inheritance* founded on the concepts of force and motion, but it never received much favor among his contemporary scientists (Lundin, 1994). During the 1920s, genetic research focused on mutations, and, as an alternative to *Darwin's theory of natural selection*, a widely accepted hypothesis held that evolution occurred in *rapid leaps*; cf: *punctuated equilibrium theory*—the notion that evolution occurred in bursts with long periods of little change between them as a result of radical changes in phenotype caused by mutations (Sutherland, 1996). This idea contrasted sharply with Darwin's view of *gradual* evolution due to environmental selection acting on continuous variations among individuals of a population. An important turning point for *evolution theory* was the birth of *population genetics*, especially in the 1930s, when *Mendelism* and *Darwinism* were reconciled, and the genetic basis of variation and natural selection was worked out. The results of Mendel's original experiments on garden peas have been extended to genetics and heritability in humans (cf: Humphreys, 1994; Jensen, 1994; Prentky, 1994), where it has been discovered that certain genetic disorders such as sickle-cell anemia, Tay-Sachs disease, and cystic fibrosis are inherited as simple recessive traits from phenotypically normal, heterozygous carriers. See also DARWIN'S EVOLUTION THEORY.

REFERENCES

Warren, H. (Ed.) (1934). *Dictionary of psychology*. Cambridge, MA: Houghton Mifflin.
Eysenck, H. (1994). Behavioral genetics. In R. J. Corsini (Ed.), *Ency. Psy.* New York: Wiley.

Humphreys, L. (1994). Heredity and intelligence. In R. J. Corsini (Ed.), *Ency. Psy.* New York: Wiley.

Jensen, A. (1994). Heritability. In R. J. Corsini (Ed.), *Ency. Psy.* New York: Wiley.

Lundin, R. (1994). William Bateson. In R. J. Corsini (Ed.), *Ency. Psy.* New York: Wiley.

Muir, H. (Ed.) (1994). *Larousse dictionary of scientists.* New York: Larousse.

Prentky, R. (1994). Heritability and personality. In R. J. Corsini (Ed.), *Ency. Psy.* New York: Wiley.

Thain, M., & Hickman, M. (1995). *The Penguin dictionary of biology.* New York: Penguin Books.

Sutherland, S. (1996). *The international dictionary of psychology.* New York: Crossroad.

MENDEL'S THEORY OF HEREDITY. See MENDEL'S LAWS/PRINCI-PLES.

MERKEL'S LAW. See HICK'S LAW.

MESMER'S THEORY. See HYPNOSIS/HYPNOTISM, THEORIES OF.

MEYER'S PSYCHOBIOLOGY THEORY. See MURPHY'S BIOSOCIAL THEORY.

MEYER'S THEORY OF HEARING. See AUDITION/HEARING, THEORIES OF.

MILL'S CANONS. See PARSIMONY, LAW/PRINCIPLE OF.

MIND–BODY THEORIES. Philosophers and scholars in all disciplines have struggled for centuries to define the nature of the human being. A prominent issue in this endeavor deals with the mind and body and the relationship between them, or what has been called the *mind–body problem* (Warren, 1934; Reuder, 1994a), leading to *mind–body theories* (Boring, 1957). Aristotle (384–322 B.C.) attempted to solve the problem as presented in Platonic *dualism* (i.e., reality consists of two different, relatively independent substances) by formulating a concrete, functional view of organic life. Later, Rene Descartes (1596–1650) proposed that matter (body) is "extended substance" and that the soul (mind) is "unextended substance" (cf: *soul theory*—which holds that mental phenomena are the manifestations of a specific substance, usually assumed to be distinct from material substance; *mind–dust theory*—the view that atoms or particles of mind exist extensively in the universe and are combined to form actual minds; and the *mind–stuff theory*—the view that mind is formed by the combination of atoms/particles that are held to be the same as those elements that appear to the observer as matter; Warren, 1934). Descartes held that these two kinds of substance interact with each other in the human organism, body affecting mind and mind affecting body, and his *dualistic* approach has come to be known as the *mind–body theory of interactionism.* Other early attempts to solving the *mind–body problem* were the *theory of occasionalism*—the view propounded by A. Geulincx (1624–1669) and N. Malebranche (1638–1715) that the concomitance between conscious and bodily processes is due to the intervention of the Deity, who determines that a specific conscious process shall occur on the occasion of a specific bodily process, and vice versa; and the *theory of preestablished harmony*—which refers to the relation between mental and physical events that assumes that they occur independently, that is, without either affecting the other causally, but that they harmonize and constitute parallel event series due to a fundamental or original characteristic of reality; this approach was one phase of a more general theory originated by Leibnitz (1646–1716); cf: Leibnitz's *law of sufficient reason*, which states that—given sufficient knowledge—one might discover why any specific occurrence is such as it is and not otherwise (Warren, 1934). More recent approaches to the *mind–body problem* are the *double-aspect theory*, which assumes that conscious experiences and brain processes are fundamentally identical, the two groups of phenomena being two manifestations or aspects of a single set of events (a synonym for this theory is the *identity hypothesis/theory*; Hoffding, 1908; Warren, 1934; Boring, 1957); the *theory of parallelism/psychophysicalism*, which is often confused with the *double-aspect theory* and states that for every variation in conscious processes or experiences, there is a concomitant variation in neural processes (this theory makes no assumption of a causal relation between the mind and body; the *theory of parallelism* was formulated by Spinoza, 1632–1677, and the *psychophysical* aspect was added by Fechner, 1803–1887); the *theory of epiphenomenalism*, which maintains that conscious processes are not in any sense causal agents, even with respect to one another, but are merely correlated with certain causally effective physiological processes; the *theory of phenomenalism*, which holds that human knowledge is limited to phenomena/experience and does not reach the real nature of things (proponents/precursors to this theory were Husserl's, 1859–1938, and Brentano's, 1838–1917, *psychological theory of intentionalism*, which defines the distinguishing feature of psychical phenomena—such as acts of perception or judgment—as their "intention" or reference to an object; this theory is synonymous with *act psychology*, in which the data are psychic activities, usually of a subject upon an object; cf: Brentano's *idiogenetic theory*, which holds that the function of judgment is an original or primordial mental fact; Warren, 1934); and the *theory of immaterialism*, which maintains that the existence of matter cannot be confidently affirmed inasmuch as all perceptual experiences are aspects of consciousness. There is general agreement by writers that *body* refers to the material, physical, or physiological characteristics of the organism and that such activities can be studied by the traditional empirical methods of science. However, the *mind, psyche,* or *soul* entity of the *mind–body problem* presents the most difficulty, where questions remain concerning whether such an entity even exists (cf: *synergy theory*, which holds that mental synthesis consists in a unitary response, whether perceptual or motor, aroused by the aggregate of sensory or other elements that are conceived as stimuli converging upon a single response mechanism; Warren, 1934; the *theory of mind/mind mechanism*, which is the use of one's existing concepts of people's mental states to explain their behavior; Premack & Woodruff, 1978; Leslie, 1987; and the *law of span*, which states that every mind tends to keep its total simultaneous cognitive output constant in quantity, however varying in quality; Warren, 1934). Questions remain, also, about how best to define the *mind* and how to apply the empirical methods of science to obtain descriptions and functional laws for such an inferred entity. See also FECHNER'S LAW; WEBER–FECHNER LAW.

REFERENCES

Hoffding, H. (1908). *Outlines of psychology*. London: Macmillan.

Warren, H. (Ed.) (1934). *Dictionary of psychology*. Cambridge, MA: Houghton Mifflin.

Boring, E. G. (1957). *A history of experimental psychology*. New York: Appleton-Century-Crofts.

Polten, E. (1973). *Critique of the psycho-physical identity theory*. The Hague: Mouton.

Cheng, D. (1975). *Philosophical aspects of the mind–body problem*. Honolulu: University of Hawaii Press.

Premack, D., & Woodruff, G. (1978). Does the chimpanzee have a "theory of mind"? *Beh. & Brain Sci.*, 515–526.

Levin, M. (1979). *Metaphysics and the mind–body problem*. Oxford: Clarendon Press.

Leslie, A. (1987). Pretence and representation: The origins of "theory of mind." *Psy. Rev., 94*, 412–426.

Reuder, M. (1994a). Mind/body problem. In R. J. Corsini (Ed.), *Ency. Psy*. New York: Wiley.

Reuder, M. (1994b). Monism/dualism. In R. J. Corsini (Ed.), *Ency. Psy*. New York: Wiley.

MIND/MENTAL SET, LAW OF. = set, law of. The term *set* is defined in the present context as a temporary condition of the organism that facilitates a certain specific type of activity (Warren, 1934); cf: the *set-theoretical model*, which refers to any model that treats the entities under consideration as elements arranged in a series or aggregate and formally represents the relations between the elements in terms of *set theory* that may be applied, among other things, to mathematical characterization, semantic features, word meaning, or human long-term memory (Reber, 1995). The related terms *mental/determining set* and *perceptual set* refer, respectively, to any condition, disposition, or tendency on the organism's part to respond in a particular manner, and to a kind of cognitive readiness for a particular stimulus or class of stimuli (called *Einstellung* in German). When *set* is associated with a problem-solving or task-oriented situation, the German word *Aufgabe* ("task") is used to capture the idea that each particular task or set of instructions for performing a particular task carries with it a cluster of constraints indicating the use of particular processes (cf: Ach's, 1905, *determining tendency*; Wheeler, 1929, refers to the *law of Aufgabe*). Thus, the *law of set/mental set* (cf: Woodworth & Sheehan, 1944, who refer to the *law of set*) in a psychological context refers to a temporary condition of responding that can arise from the task requirements (via overt or covert instructions), context, prior experiences, or expectations. At higher cognitive levels, *set* can alter the pattern of information pickup, the nature of what is perceived, and the probability that a particular problem may be solved (e.g., Luchins, 1942; cf: *fuzzy set theory*, which is the mathematical theory of sets that does not have sharp boundaries and, because most concepts are fuzzy in this sense—for example, ''bald,'' ''bad''—some believe the mathematical theory could throw light on cognition, but it has not so far done so; Sutherland, 1996). Other ways in which *set* interacts with cognitive processes are called *attentional set*, which refers to a condition whereby the observer is prepared to receive information of a particular type (or from a particular channel), and *functional fixedness* (or *functional fixity*), which is a *conceptual set* whereby objects that have been used for one function tend to be viewed as serving only that function, even though the situation may call for the use of the object in a different manner (Coren, 1994). See also ACH'S LAWS/PRINCIPLES/THEORY; WUNDT'S THEORIES/DOCTRINES.

REFERENCES

Ach, N. (1905). *Ueber die willenstatigkeit und das denken*. Gottingen: Vardenboek.

Wheeler, R. (1929). *The science of psychology: An introductory study*. New York: Crowell.

Warren, H. (Ed.) (1934). *Dictionary of psychology*. Cambridge, MA: Houghton Mifflin.

Gibson, J. (1941). A critical review of the concept of set in contemporary experimental psychology. *Psy. Bull., 38*, 781–817.

Luchins, A. (1942). Mechanization in problem solving—The effect of *Einstellung. Psy. Mono., 54*, no. 248.

Woodworth, R., & Sheehan, M. (1944). *First course in psychology*. New York: Holt.

Bruner, J. (1957). On perceptual readiness. *Psy. Rev., 64*, 123–152.

Coren, S. (1994). Set. In R. J. Corsini (Ed.), *Ency. Psy*. New York: Wiley.

Reber, A. (1995). *The Penguin dictionary of psychology*. New York: Penguin Books.

Sutherland, S. (1996). *The international dictionary of psychology*. New York: Crossroad.

MIND/MIND MECHANISM, THEORY OF. See MIND–BODY THEORIES.

MODERN SYNTHETIC THEORY. See DARWIN'S EVOLUTION THEORY/EVOLUTION, THEORY/LAWS OF.

MOON ILLUSION, THEORY OF. See EMMERT'S LAW.

MORAL DEVELOPMENT, PRINCIPLES/THEORY OF. See KOHLBERG'S THEORY OF MORALITY.

MORGAN'S CANON/LLOYD MORGAN'S CANON. See PARSIMONY, LAW/PRINCIPLE OF.

MOTIVATED FORGETTING, THEORY OF. See FORGETTING/MEMORY, THEORIES OF.

MOTIVATION, THEORIES OF. The term *motivation* comes from the same Latin stem "mot-" (meaning "move"), as does the term *emotion* (Leeper, 1948; Webb, 1948). The term *motive* applies to any internal force that activates and gives direction to behavior. Other related terms emphasize different aspects of motivation. For example, *need* stresses the aspect of lack or want; *drive* emphasizes the impelling and energizing aspect; and *incentive* focuses on the goal(s) of motivation (cf: *incentive theory*; Mook, 1987). In general, *motivation theories* deal with the reasons that behaviors occur and refer to the internal states of the organism as well as the external goals (rewards or reinforcers) in the environment. Typically, motivation involves the energization of behavior and goal direction where a distinction is made between the organism's *disposition* and its *arousal*. For example, a generalized state of hunger, anxiety, or fear may be called the individual's *disposition*, while the specific act of behaving toward, or away from, a particular goal is the result of its *arousal*. The concept of *motivation*, as a fundamental influence in many phenomena, cuts across the various areas in psychology of intelligence, learning, personality, and thinking. Research on motivation has studied both the type and intensity (formerly called *dynamogenesis*) of motives. Various *theories of motivation* have originated in the area of *dynamic psychology*, which is a traditional approach used to study behavior by examining its underlying forces. The *dynamic* approach is contrasted with the *descriptive* approach, which is concerned with naming, classifying, and diagnosing—while the *dynamic* approach is concerned with tracing behavior to its origins in prior experience. Woodworth (1918, 1958) developed the eclectic approach called *dynamic psychology*, which focused on the motivational forces of behavior where a variety of viewpoints (e.g., behaviorism, Gestalt psychology, functionalism, and structuralism) were brought together to study the common/central concepts of *drive* and *motive*. *Dynamic psychology* argued that humans are not motivated simply by a few universal drives or instincts but that each person has a unique spectrum of natural capacities, wishes, needs, purposes, and emotions that set the personality in motion. The Freudian *psychoanalytical* approach emphasized the interplay among drives as expressed in dynamic concepts such as *conflict*, *anxiety*, and *defense mechanisms*. The term *dynamic* attains its broadest meaning in the theoretical approach called *general systems theory* (e.g., Bertalanffy, 1968), even though *general systems theory* says little specifically about motivation and the motives that instigate and direct action. A great variety of *motivation theories* have been developed over the years and may be placed in three general categories (Pervin, 1994): (1) *hedonic/pleasure theories*—this forms the largest category of motivation theories and emphasizes the role of pleasure in organizing one's activities (cf: Young, 1966). The concept of *tension reduction* is important here, where pleasure is derived from reduction of tension through the discharge of energy, expression of an instinct, or reduction in drive level. Woodworth (1918) introduced the term *drive* into American psychology, and was used until the 1960s. Distinctions have been made between *needs* versus *drives/motives*, *innate* versus *acquired* drives, *primary* versus *secondary* drives, *viscerogenic* versus *psychogenic* drives, and *intrinsic* versus *extrinsic* motivation (see Koch, 1956; Hunt, 1965; Deci, 1994). Hull (1943, 1952) and Spence (1958) used the concept of *drive* extensively in their *stimulus–response learning theory*, where the organism was viewed as having primary/innate drives such as pain and hunger, as well as learned/secondary drives such as fears and the desire for money. Dollard and Miller (1950) extended Hull's work and emphasized the role of learned, secondary drives in behavior. They also integrated *Hullian learning theory* concepts with *Freudian theory* concepts. The concept of *need* was studied also within the tension-reduction, hedonistic/pleasure approach (Lewin, 1935). (2) *Cognitive/ need-to-know theories*—while some cognitive approaches to motivation remained tension-reduction models (e.g., Festinger's, 1957, *theory of cognitive dissonance*), other cognitive theories emphasized the motivation inherent in the *information-processing* activity of the organism (e.g., Kelly's, 1955, *cognitive theory of motivation*). (3) *Growth/actualization theories*—representative theorists in this category are Angyal (1941), Goldstein (1934), Maslow (1954), and Rogers (1961), who shared the common rejection of tension-reduction as the whole basis for human activity. Rather, these theorists emphasized the activities that lead to growth/self-fulfillment/self-actualization in the individual's personality. In general, most psychologists agree that the more active an organism is, the higher the level of motivation; they agree, also, that motivation energizes the human and nonhuman organism, but they often disagree as to just how motivation causes the energization. A fourth category of *motivation theory* concerns the role of *brain structures* and *neural mechanisms* in motivated behavior. Research in this area typically falls in the areas of *psychobiology*, *biopsychology*, or *neurobiology*. In one case, a part of the brain called the *reticular activating system* provides a physiological basis for the energizing effects of heightened motivation. Studies by Moruzzi and Magoun (1949) and Lindsley (1951) focused attention on the combined regions of the thalamus, reticular formation, and cortex in explaining both the specific and general arousal aspects of motivated organisms. On the other hand, the presumption of a single arousal system has been debated by researchers at both behavioral and physiological levels (cf: Routtenberg, 1968). The current impetus in research on motivation has shifted away from the study of generalized arousal/general motivation and toward the study of specific motivations (see Arnold & Levine, 1969; Bolles, 1975; Ferguson, 1994). See also ACHIEVEMENT MOTIVATION, THEORY OF; ACTIVATION/AROUSAL THEORY; ADLER'S THEORY OF PERSONALITY; AGGRESSION, THEORIES OF; CONTROL/SYSTEMS THEORY; DRIVE,

THEORIES OF; EMOTIONS, THEORIES/LAWS OF; FESTINGER'S COG-
NITIVE DISSONANCE THEORY; FREUD'S THEORY OF PERSONALITY;
GENERAL SYSTEM THEORY; HEDONISM, THEORY/LAW OF; HULL'S
LEARNING THEORY; HUNGER, THEORIES OF; JUNG'S THEORY OF
PERSONALITY; LEARNING THEORIES; McDOUGALL'S HORMIC/
INSTINCT THEORY/DOCTRINE; PERSONALITY THEORIES; REIN-
FORCEMENT THEORY; THIRST, THEORIES OF.

REFERENCES

Woodworth, R. (1918). *Dynamic psychology.* New York: Columbia University Press.

Goldstein, K. (1934). *The organism: A holistic approach to biology derived from pathological data in man.* New York: American Book.

Lewin, K. (1935). *A dynamic theory of personality.* New York: McGraw-Hill.

Angyal, A. (1941). *Foundations for a science of personality.* New York: Commonwealth
Foundation.

Hull, C. (1943). *Principles of behavior.* New York: Appleton-Century-Crofts.

Leeper, R. (1948). A motivational theory of emotion to replace "emotion as disorganized
response." *Psy. Rev., 55,* 5–21.

Webb, W. (1948). A motivational theory of emotions. *Psy. Rev., 55,* 329–335.

Moruzzi, G., & Magoun, H. (1949). Brain stem reticular formation and activation of the
EEG. *EEG Clin. Neurophysio., 1,* 455–473.

Dollard, J., & Miller, N. (1950). *Personality and psychotherapy: An analysis in terms
of learning, thinking, and culture.* New York: McGraw-Hill.

Lindsley, D. (1951). Emotion. In S. S. Stevens (Ed.), *Handbk. Exp. Psy.* New York:
Wiley.

Hull, C. (1952). *A behavior system: An introduction to behavior theory concerning the
individual organism.* New Haven, CT: Yale University Press.

Allport, G. (1953). The trend in motivational theory. *Amer. J. Orthopsy., 23,* 107–119.

Maslow, A. (1954). *Motivation and personality.* New York: Harper & Row.

Kelly, G. (1955). *The psychology of personal constructs.* New York: Norton.

Koch, S. (1956). Behavior as "intrinsically" regulated: Work notes towards a pretheory
of phenomena called "motivational." In M. Jones (Ed.), *Current theory and
research in motivation.* Vol. 4. Lincoln: University of Nebraska Press.

Festinger, L. (1957). *A theory of cognitive dissonance.* Stanford, CA: Stanford University
Press.

Spence, K. (1958). A theory of emotionally-based drive (D) and its relation to performance in simple learning situations. *Amer. Psy., 13,* 131–141.

Woodworth, R. (1958). *Dynamics of behavior.* New York: Holt.

Rogers, C. (1961). *On becoming a person.* Boston: Houghton Mifflin.

Hunt, J. (1965). Intrinsic motivation and its role in psychological development. In D.
Levine (Ed.), *Nebraska symposium on motivation.* Vol. 13. Lincoln: University
of Nebraska Press.

Young, P. (1966). Hedonic organization and regulation of behavior. *Psy. Rev., 73,* 59–
86.

Bertalanffy, L. von (1968). *General systems theory.* New York: Braziller.

Routtenberg, A. (1968). The two-arousal hypothesis: Reticular formation and limbic system. *Psy. Rev., 75,* 51–80.

Arnold, W., & Levine, D. (Eds.) (1969). *Nebraska symposium on motivation*. Lincoln: University of Nebraska Press.

Bolles, R. (1975). *Theory of motivation*. New York: Harper & Row.

Mook, D. (1987). *Motivation: The organization of action*. New York: Norton.

Deci, E. (1994). Intrinsic motivation. In R. J. Corsini (Ed.), *Ency. Psy.* New York: Wiley.

Ferguson, E. (1994). Motivation. In R. J. Corsini (Ed.), *Ency. Psy.* New York: Wiley.

Pervin, L. (1994). Dynamic psychology. In R. J. Corsini (Ed.), *Ency. Psy.* New York: Wiley.

MOWRER'S THEORY. The American psychologist Orval Hobart Mowrer (1907–1982) was a neo-Hullian who developed a *two-factor learning theory* that described the operation of two principles of reinforcement: instrumental responses involving the skeletal musculature that are mediated by the central nervous system and are reinforced and strengthened by drive reduction, and emotions such as fear and nausea involving the smooth musculature (e.g., glands, viscera, vascular tissue) that are mediated by the autonomic nervous system and are learned by sheer temporal contiguity of a conditioned stimulus to the elicitation of the emotional response (Mowrer, 1947). An example of *two-factor learning theory* in animal learning is the pairing of a buzzer with painful shocks in order to set up an association between the animal's state of fear and the buzzer and, at the same time, provide the opportunity for the animal to make some active avoidance response (such as jumping across a barrier separating two compartments in the cage) that, when performed, becomes reinforced through the hypothesized operation of *fear-reduction*. Mowrer also offered an analysis of *punishment* that involved a *passive* state in the organism where the animal reduces fear and avoids shock by doing nothing in the punishment situation. This is in contrast to the *active* avoidance situation where the animal reduces fear and avoids shock by doing something such as jumping out of the shock-compartment of the cage (cf: Bolles, 1972; see also the *Kamin effect*—animals trained on an avoidance task, when tested at different times after training, show a U-shaped curve of performance; they perform well at first and much worse after an hour or so; performance recovers after about two hours; Sutherland, 1996). In his later work, Mowrer (1956, 1960a) refined his analyses of instrumental behavior where positive habits were interpreted in the same way as punished habits, except the sign of the anticipated outcome was reversed. That is, the *proprioceptive feedback* from making a correct response is in ''favorable'' contiguity to the positive reinforcement (i.e., drive-reduction) so that it acquires secondary reinforcing capabilities by contiguity conditioning. Analogous to the way incipient punished responses are deterred, the incipient rewarded responses were pushed on through to completion because their proprioceptive response pattern was conditioned to the emotion of ''hope'' (that is, the anticipation of reward). In Mowrer's revision, there was not a direct associative connection between the external stimulus and the instrumental response, but, rather, feedback stimulation from the correct response becomes conditioned to a positive emotion (''hope'') that excites or gives energy to the completion of that response (cf: Sheffield, 1965). Today, it appears that even though Mowrer's (1960a, b) classification system for reinforcers/punishers is not discredited, it is very likely that his *drive-reduction hypothesis* is somewhat empirically inadequate (Hilgard & Bower, 1966; cf: Premack, 1959, 1962). See also HELSON'S ADAPTATION-LEVEL THEORY; HULL'S LEARNING THEORY; MOTIVATION, THEORIES OF; PREMACK'S PRINCIPLE/LAW; PUNISHMENT, THEORIES OF.

REFERENCES

Mowrer, O. H. (1947). On the dual nature of learning—A re-interpretation of ''conditioning'' and ''problem-solving.'' *Har. Ed. Rev., 17*, 102–148.

Mowrer, O. H. (1956). Two-factor learning theory reconsidered, with special reference to secondary reinforcement and the concept of habit. *Psy. Rev., 63*, 114–128.

Premack, D. (1959). Toward empirical behavior laws. I. Positive reinforcement. *Psy. Rev., 66*, 219–233.

Mowrer, O. H. (1960a). *Learning theory and behavior.* New York: Wiley.

Mowrer, O. H. (1960b). *Learning theory and the symbolic processes.* New York: Wiley.

Premack, D. (1962). Reversibility of the reinforcement relation. *Science, 136*, 255–257.

Sheffield, F. (1965). Relation between classical conditioning and instrumental learning. In W. Prokasy (Ed.), *Classical conditioning: A symposium.* New York: Appleton-Century-Crofts.

Hilgard, E., & Bower, G. (1966). *Theories of learning.* New York: Appleton-Century-Crofts.

Bolles, R. (1972). The avoidance learning problem. In G. Bower (Ed.), *The psychology of learning and motivation: Advances in research and theory.* Vol. 6. New York: Academic Press.

Bower, G., & Hilgard, E. (1981). *Theories of learning.* Englewood Cliffs, NJ: Prentice-Hall.

Rickert, E. (1994). Two-process learning theory. In R. J. Corsini (Ed.), *Ency. Psy.* New York: Wiley.

Sutherland, S. (1996). *The international dictionary of psychology.* New York: Crossroad.

MULLER EFFECT. See VISION/SIGHT, THEORIES OF.

MULLER–SCHUMANN LAW. See SKAGGS–ROBINSON HYPOTHESIS.

MULLER'S COLOR VISION THEORY. See COLOR VISION, THEORIES/ LAWS OF.

MULLER'S DOCTRINE OF SPECIFIC NERVE ENERGIES. = Specific nerve energies, law of. The German physiologist Johannes Peter Muller (1801– 1858) formulated the *doctrine/theory/law of specific energy of nerves* in 1826, which holds that each sensory nerve, however stimulated, gives rise to only one type of sensory process and a single quality of sensation. Stated another way, the *law of specific energies of nerve fibers* holds that the quality of sensation depends on the type of fiber excited, not on the form of physical energy that initiates the process (Osgood, 1953); cf: *Bowditch's law*—the principle that the nerves cannot be fatigued; they will keep transmitting impulses no matter how many consecutive times they are stimulated (Zusne, 1987). *Muller's law of specific nerve energies* is vividly expressed by the statement "If we could cross the auditory and optic nerves, we could see thunder and hear lightning" (Woodworth & Schlosberg, 1965). Earlier, in 1811, the Scottish anatomist Sir Charles Bell (1774–1842) suggested that each sensory nerve conveys one kind of quality or experience (e.g., visual nerves carry only visual impressions, auditory only auditory impressions, etc., Bell, 1811). Some writers have argued that Bell's name, rather than Muller's, should be attached to the law (Boring, 1957). Muller's contribution was that he gave the notion of *specific energies of nerves* explicit and precise formulation. Application of the law occupies almost 2% of an entire volume of Muller's *Handbuch* (Muller, 1833–1840). Muller actually formulated the *doctrine of specific nerve energies* under ten laws (Boring, 1957), but the essential generalization is that the various qualities of experience derive not from differences in the physical and environmental stimuli that impinge upon us but from the specific neural structures that each excites. Muller's particular form of the *doctrine of specific nerve energies* was eventually discredited by later physiological research. The plasticity of Muller's idea, however, gave it long life. The concept of *specific nerve energies*, at one time or another, has been referred to as a *doctrine*, a *hypothesis*, a *theory*, and a *law/principle* and has a rather consistent and even record of citation in textbooks across 112 years of psychology (Roeckelein, 1996). The *doctrine of specific nerve energies* made attempts at precision in the quest for neural foundations for sensory experience, and, consequently, it was highly useful as a guiding hypothesis in experimental psychology (Murphy & Kovach, 1972). See also ALL-OR-NONE LAW/PRINCIPLE.

REFERENCES

Bell, C. (1811). *Idea of a new anatomy of the brain.* London: Strahan & Preston.

Muller, J. (1833–1840). *Handbuch der physiologie des menschen.* 3 vols. Coblenz: Holscher.

Muller, J. (1842). *Elements of physiology.* London: Taylor & Walton.

Osgood, C. (1953). *Method and theory in experimental psychology.* New York: Oxford University Press.

Boring, E. G. (1957). *A history of experimental psychology.* New York: Appleton-Century-Crofts.

Woodworth, R., & Schlosberg, H. (1965). *Experimental psychology.* New York: Holt, Rinehart, & Winston.

Murphy, G., & Kovach, J. (1972). *Historical introduction to modern psychology.* New York: Harcourt Brace Jovanovich.

Zusne, L. (1987). *Eponyms in psychology*. Westport, CT: Greenwood Press.
Roeckelein, J. (1996). Citation of *laws* and *theories* in textbooks across 112 years of psychology. *Psy. Rep., 79*, 979–998.

MULTIFACTOR THEORY OF THIRST. See THIRST, THEORIES OF.

MULTIPLICATIVE LAW OF PROBABILITY. See PROBABILITY THEORY/LAWS.

MURPHY'S BIOSOCIAL THEORY. The American psychologist Gardner Murphy (1895–1979) formulated a *biosocial theory* (Murphy, 1947, 1951) that was popular in the 1950s and was eclectic in nature by combining holistic, evolutionary, functional, and biosocial concepts into a comprehensive psychological system (cf: Adolf Meyer's, 1957, integrative *theory of psychobiology*, which emphasized the importance of biological, social, and psychological influences on the person). While Murphy's approach overlapped with the theories of other psychologists, his systematization included some core ideas that were his own. For example, he emphasized sensory and activity needs in describing biological aspects of motivation, and he suggested that an organism's curiosity behavior emanated from a brain drive. Other concepts that were expanded by Murphy were *autism*—where cognitions move toward satisfaction of needs; *field theory*—in which personality is viewed as an organized field within a larger field involving a reciprocity of incoming and outgoing energies; *feedback*—where reality-testing based on outside information helps one escape from "autistic self-deception"; a *three-phase developmental theory*—in which all reality moves from an undifferentiated, homogeneous state, through a differentiated, heterogeneous reality, to an integrated and structured reality; and *canalization*—where needs tend to become more specific as a result of being satisfied in specific ways (Hartley, 1994a, b). Murphy's (1947) *canalization hypothesis* (cf: Holt's, 1931, *canalization hypothesis*) is one of his most important *learning theory* formulations and refers to the progressive differentiation ("narrowing") of the general and preferred ways in which one's drives may be satisfied. The idea of progressive "narrowing" of drives is invoked, also, in Freud's concept of *cathexis* (Murphy & Kovach, 1972). Murphy borrowed the term *canalization* from the French physician/psychiatrist Pierre Janet (1859–1947), and it has come today to have many meanings, depending on the context in which it is used. In the area of neurology, *canalization* refers to the formation and neural connections that facilitate the flow of the neural current (Warren, 1934; Wolman, 1973). In the area of evolutionary genetics, *canalization* is the idea that a particular epigenetic capability or behavior pattern continues to be observed in situations of less than optimal environments or, if disrupted by extreme conditions, to be relatively easy to restore when conditions are once more made appropriate (Reber, 1995). In the area of learning, comparative, and physiological psychology, the *canalization hypothesis* of Holt (1931) and Murphy (1947) were attempts to

break away from the associationistic model and the Pavlovian conditioning procedure as explanations for deeply ingrained and strongly motivated action patterns. Murphy's *canalization hypothesis* provided a conceptualization of drive
modification as a function of repeated satisfaction by stimuli within a limited
range and was distinguished from the phenomenon of *conditioning*, which involves what the English physiologist Charles Sherrington (1861–1952) called
preparatory responses—whereas Murphy's *canalization* involves *consummatory
responses*. Essentially, the *canalization hypothesis* attempts to account for the
process whereby an originally neutral stimulus acquires positive value as a satisfier and for narrowing the range from within which a drive may be satisfied.
It ·accounts for the acquisition of tastes and preferences, it illuminates conceptions of motivation and learning, it represents the biosocial process of development, and it gives important insights into numerous psychological phenomena
such as *conflict* and *ambivalence* (Hartley, 1994a). See also CONFLICT, THE-
ORIES OF; GOLDSTEIN'S ORGANISMIC THEORY.

REFERENCES

Holt, E. (1931). *Animal drive and learning process: An essay toward radical empiricism.*
    New York: Holt.
Warren, H. (Ed.) (1934). *Dictionary of psychology.* Cambridge, MA: Houghton Mifflin.
Murphy, G., Murphy, L., & Newcomb, T. (1937). *Experimental social psychology.* New
    York: Harper.
Murphy, G. (1947). *Personality: A biosocial approach to origins and structure.* New
    York: Harper.
Murphy, G. (1951). *Introduction to psychology.* New York: Harper.
Meyer, A. (1957). *Psychobiology: A science of man.* Springfield, IL: Thomas.
Hartley, E., & Perelman, M. (1963). Deprivation and the canalization of responses to
    food. *Psy. Rep., 13,* 647–650.
Murphy, G., & Kovach, J. (1972). *Historical introduction to modern psychology.* New
    York: Harcourt Brace Jovanovich.
Wolman, B. (Ed.) (1973). *Dictionary of behavioral science.* New York: Van Nostrand
    Reinhold.
Hartley, E. (1994a). Canalization. In R. J. Corsini (Ed.), *Ency. Psy.* New York: Wiley.
Hartley, E. (1994b). Gardner Murphy. In R. J. Corsini (Ed.), *Ency. Psy.* New York:
    Wiley.
Reber, A. (1995). *The Penguin dictionary of psychology.* New York: Penguin Books.

MURRAY'S THEORY OF PERSONALITY. The academically versatile
American psychologist Henry Alexander Murray (1893–1988) argued that the
fundamental goal of psychology should be to study *personality*, and this idiographic viewpoint, accordingly, has been called *personology* (Murray, 1938,
1968). Murray's wide-ranging, diverse, humanistic, and optimistic *personality
theory*, or *personological system*, is characterized by the following tenets
(Shneidman, 1994): (1) personality is shaped by numerous conscious and unconscious forces, by early childhood experiences, by individuals' habits, motivations, complexes, ambitions, wishes, needs, sentiments, dreams, and fantasies;

(2) a taxonomic approach where personality is precisely dissected and categorized (for instance, 20—later expanded to 30—human psychological needs were described, including the needs for aggression, achievement, affiliation, and abasement), where the person reacts to *press* (determinants of behavior) from the environment and other people, and where combinations of needs, *press*, and *press-need patterns* lead to *themas*, that is, characterizations of one's life; (3) a concern with time that involves longitudinal studies of personality and lives in progress (cf: White, 1963); (4) a multiform system of personality assessment including development of projective tests such as the Thematic Apperception Test (TAT) (Morgan & Murray, 1935; Murray, 1943) and a multifaceted orientation based on the works of Sigmund Freud, Carl Jung, Kurt Koffka, Kurt Lewin, Alfred North Whitehead, Talcott Parsons, Clyde Kluckhohn, and William McDougall; (5) a capacity for studying personages who were living, dead, fictional, historical, or archetypal (e.g., Murray, 1962a); and (6) a concern for diverse issues ranging from global problems such as prevention of nuclear war to reconciliation between religion and science (e.g., Murray, 1960). Murray's *theory of motivation* and *needs*, which is related closely to his accounts of the dynamics of personality, includes various novel concepts such as *press, press-need patterns* (cf: Baron, 1994), *thema, need integrate, unity thema, value-vector scheme*, and *regnancy* (Hall & Lindzey, 1978; Reber, 1995). Even though Murray's theories have undergone constant reexamination and modification (cf: Stern, 1970), his approach has always emphasized the importance on personality of unconscious sources of motivation and of the relationship between brain processes and psychological processes. Some critics of *Murray's personology theory* (e.g., Walsh, 1973) have argued that it loses power in being too broad in scope, that it gives a disproportionate amount of attention to the topic of motivation over that of learning, that it does not adequately explain the processes by which motives develop in one's personality, and that its concepts lack interface with empirical data. In general, Murray's writings and his research do not seem to be fashionable today within the psychological mainstream, and he is characterized as being too much of a poet and too little of a logical positivist (Hall & Lindzey, 1978). See also ACHIEVEMENT MOTIVATION, THEORY OF; IDIOGRAPHIC/NOMOTHETIC LAWS; PERSONALITY, THEORIES OF.

REFERENCES

Murray, H. (1933). The effect of fear upon estimates of the maliciousness of other personalities. *J. Soc. Psy., 4*, 310–329.

Morgan, C., & Murray, H. (1935). A method for investigating fantasies. *Ar. Neur. Psychiat., 34*, 289–306.

Murray, H. (1936). Basic concepts for a psychology of personality. *J. Gen. Psy., 15*, 241–268.

Murray, H. (1938). *Explorations in personality: A clinical and experimental study of fifty men of college age*. New York: Oxford University Press.

Murray, H. (1943). *Manual of Thematic Apperception Test.* Cambridge: Harvard University Press.

Murray, H. (1959). Preparations for the scaffold of a comprehensive system. In S. Koch (Ed.), *Psychology: A study of a science.* Vol. 3. New York: McGraw-Hill.

Murray, H. (1960). Two versions of man. In H. Shapley (Ed.), *Science ponders religion.* New York: Appleton-Century-Crofts.

Murray, H. (1962a). The personality and career of Satan. *J. Soc. Iss., 28,* 36–54.

Murray, H. (1962b). Prospect for psychology. *Science, 136,* 483–488.

White, R. (Ed.) (1963). *The study of lives.* New York: Atherton.

Murray, H. (1968). Components of an evolving personological system. In D. Sills (Ed.), *International encyclopedia of the social sciences.* New York: Macmillan & Free Press.

Stern, G. (1970). *People in context.* New York: Wiley.

Walsh, W. (1973). *Theories of person–environment interaction: Implications for the college student.* Iowa City, IA: American College Testing.

Hall, C., & Lindzey, G. (1978). *Theories of personality.* New York: Wiley.

Baron, A. (1994). Need-press theory. In R. J. Corsini (Ed.), *Ency. Psy.* New York: Wiley.

Shneidman, E. (1994). Henry A. Murray. In R. J. Corsini (Ed.), *Ency. Psy.* New York: Wiley.

Reber, A. (1995). *The Penguin dictionary of psychology.* New York: Penguin Books.

N

NAFE'S VASCULAR THEORY OF CUTANEOUS SENSITIVITY. The sense of touch consists of several partly independent senses: pressure on the skin, warmth, cold, pain, vibration, movement across the skin, and stretch of the skin. These sensations (*cutaneous senses*) depend on several kinds of receptors in the skin (Iggo & Andres, 1982); the cutaneous senses are sometimes known by the broader term *somatosensory system*. Two hypotheses have been proposed for the thermal receptors (cf: Osgood's, 1953, account and evaluation of *thermal sensitivity theories*: the *gradient theory*; Von Frey's *specific receptor theory*; Nafe's *vascular theory*; Jenkins' *concentration theory*), although there is little or no direct evidence in support of either (Kenshalo, 1971). The *specific terminal hypothesis* assumes a molecular configuration or other specific feature of the terminal membrane that governs differential responsiveness to thermal and mechanical stimuli. The *specific tissue hypothesis* assumes that afferent nerves are essentially alike, but they end in nonneural tissues whose characteristics are responsible for the stimulus specificities observed in the activity of the associated axon. An example of this latter type of hypothesis is the *vascular theory* proposed by Nafe (1934) and reviewed by Kenshalo (1970), in which the smooth muscles of the cutaneous vascular system contract when cooled and relax when warmed. According to this approach, the movement of the vessels initiates activity in the afferent nerves that terminate in the vessel walls. Another current theory, the *quantitative theory of cutaneous sensitivity* (Kenshalo & Nafe, 1962), is representative of several of the so-called *pattern theories of cutaneous sensory coding* (cf: Uttal, 1973). This theory holds that the qualities of cutaneous sensation are partly a function of the mechanical and thermal properties of the tissue in which the sensory nerves terminate and partly a function of variations in the temporal and spatial patterns of neural discharge of those nerves. According to Schwartz (1978), the *pattern theories of somatosensory coding* will require a great deal of experimental validation. However, on the basis of currently available information, it may be assumed that every different cutaneous sensation that can be discriminated is the result of a unique pattern of neural activity arriving at the points in the brain where it is interpreted (Kenshalo, 1971). See also ALRUTZ'S THEORY; CODING THEORIES/MODELS; GATE-CONTROL THEORY.

REFERENCES

Nafe, J. (1934). Pressure, pain, and temperature senses. In C. Murchison (Ed.), *A handbook of general experimental psychology*. Worcester, MA: Clark University Press.

Jenkins, W. (1939). Nafe's vascular theory and the preponderance of evidence. *Amer. J. Psy.*, *52*, 462–465.

Osgood, C. (1953). *Method and theory in experimental psychology*. New York: Oxford University Press.

Kenshalo, D., & Nafe, J. (1962). A quantitative theory of feeling—1960. *Psy. Rev.*, *69*, 17–33.

Kenshalo, D. (1970). Cutaneous temperature receptors: Some operating characteristics for a model. In J. Hardy (Ed.), *Physiological and behavioral temperature regulation*. Springfield, IL: Thomas.

Kenshalo, D. (1971). The cutaneous senses. In J. Kling & L. Riggs (Eds.), *Woodworth & Schlosberg's experimental psychology*. New York: Holt, Rinehart, & Winston.

Uttal, W. (1973). *The psychobiology of sensory coding*. New York: Harper & Row.

Schwartz, M. (1978). *Physiological psychology*. Englewood Cliffs, NJ: Prentice-Hall.

Iggo, A., & Andres, K. (1982). Morphology of cutaneous receptors. *Ann. Rev. Neurosci.*, *5*, 1–31.

NATIVISTIC/NATIVISM THEORIES/DOCTRINE. See LOTZE'S THEORY OF LOCAL SIGNS.

NATURALISTIC THEORY OF HISTORY. Two general approaches may be taken to explain how a science like psychology develops: the *naturalistic* (or *zeitgeist*—"spirit of the times") *theory* and the *personalistic* (or "great man/person") *theory* (Schultz, 1981; Reber, 1995). The *naturalistic theory* holds that "the *times* make the person" or at least make possible the acceptance of what she or he has to say. The *personalistic theory* suggests that scientific events would not have happened had it not been for the appearance of the great men and women; this theory maintains that "the *person* makes the times." Are the great men/great women the *causes* of progress, or are they merely its *symptoms*? Boring (1957) suggests that they are neither; they are the *agents* of progress. The *naturalistic theory* stresses the role of the social, cultural, and intellectual climate within which the investigator works and lives. However, the acceptance and use of a discovery may be limited by the dominant pattern of thought in a culture, region, or era. An idea that is too novel to gain acceptance in one period of civilization may be readily accepted a generation or a century later. Slow change seems to be the pattern for scientific progress. For example, Robert Whytt (1714–1766) first suggested the concept of *conditioning* of responses in

1763, but it was well over 100 years later—at a time when psychology was moving toward greater objectivity—that Ivan Pavlov (1849–1936) expanded and developed the concept in 1927 into a systematic body of knowledge. The great scholars, as Boring (1957) noted, have become *eponyms*; that is, their names have been given to systematic positions or laws (cf: Roeckelein, 1995); and this *personalistic* process has fostered the belief that a discovery was the result of one person's sudden insight (see Sutherland's, 1996, interesting definition of *law*: "In *science*, a generalization or theoretical postulate known to be true. In *psychology*, a generalization or theoretical postulate thought by at least *one person* to be true"; italics added). According to Boring (1963), eponymy may "distort" history by not taking proper account of the *zeitgeist* and of earlier neglected contributions. In the final analysis, however, the history of psychology should probably be considered in terms of both *personalistic* and *naturalistic* theories of history, with a major role being assigned to the influence of the *zeitgeist* (Schultz, 1981). See also PERSONALITY THEORIES.

REFERENCES

Fay, J. (1939). *American psychology before William James*. New Brunswick, NJ: Rutgers University Press.

Boring, E. G. (1957). *A history of experimental psychology*. New York: Appleton-Century-Crofts.

Boring, E. G. (1963). *History, psychology, and science: Selected papers*. New York: Wiley.

Curti, M. (1973). Psychological theories in American thought. Vol. 4. In P. Wiener (Ed.), *Dictionary of the history of ideas*. New York: Scribners.

Long, A. (1973). Psychological ideas in antiquity. Vol. 4. In P. Wiener (Ed.), *Dictionary of the history of ideas*. New York: Scribners.

Schultz, D. (1981). *A history of modern psychology*. New York: Academic Press.

Reber, A. (1995). *The Penguin dictionary of psychology*. New York: Penguin Books.

Roeckelein, J. (1995). Naming in psychology: Analyses of citation counts and eponyms. *Psy. Rep., 77*, 163–174.

Sutherland, S. (1996). *The international dictionary of psychology*. New York: Crossroad.

NATURAL SELECTION, LAW OF. See DARWIN'S EVOLUTION THEORY.

NEED ACHIEVEMENT THEORY. See ACHIEVEMENT MOTIVATION, THEORY OF.

NEED-REDUCTION THEORIES. See MOTIVATION, THEORIES OF.

NEED THEORIES. See MOTIVATION, THEORIES OF.

NEO-DISSOCIATION THEORY. See HYPNOSIS/HYPNOTISM, THEORIES OF.

NEO-FREUDIAN/NEO-ANALYTIC/PSYCHODYNAMIC/PSYCHOANA-LYTIC THEORIES. See PERSONALITY THEORIES.

NERNST–LILLIE THEORY. See NEURON/NEURAL/NERVE THEORY.

NEURAL QUANTUM THEORY. In psychology, the *classical theory* of sensory discrimination has been contrasted historically with the *neural quantum theory* in a controversy sometimes called the *sensory continuity–noncontinuity* issue (Corso, 1963) with origins in the area of psychophysics. Some early researchers in psychophysics (e.g., Lotze, 1852; Fechner, 1860) argued for the *noncontinuity* (or *discontinuity*) position that involved the concept of *threshold*, while other researchers (e.g., Muller, 1878; Jastrow, 1888) maintained that the sensory continuum consisted of a *continuous* series of intermediate degrees of sensation where there was no "true" threshold. The center of the controversy was whether the changes on the psychological continuum occur in a smooth/continuous manner as the value of the physical stimulus increases continuously along a specified dimension, or whether there is an abrupt, steplike change from "no sensation" to "sensation" or from "sensation" to a "difference in sensation" (Corso, 1967). The early *theory of threshold* (Fechner, 1860) held that the brain in its waking state was physiologically active, and, consequently, for an increasing stimulus to be detected, it had to generate neurological excitations that were larger than those already present as the result of the brain's spontaneous activity (cf: Herbart, 1824). The *sensory continuity–noncontinuity* issue dealt with the challenging question of how sensory mechanisms—which are composed of discrete neural elements that obey the *all-or-none law* of physiology—can convert continuous environmental energy into an apparently continuous change in sensory experience. Bekesy (1930, 1936) showed that *discrete* steps can be obtained in studies of sensory discrimination and, thereby, presented evidence for the *quantal* nature of sensory functions; cf: Corso (1961), who suggested that both the *quantal theory* and the *phi-gamma hypothesis* (which represents the *classical theory* of sensory discrimination and predicts the general form of the psychometric function to be the integral of the normal probability distribution or the "normal ogive" curve) are equally acceptable in predicting the same results and indicated that support of one theory to the exclusion of the other was not possible. The *neural quantum theory* was first introduced by Stevens, Morgan, and Volkmann (1941) within the context of *auditory* discrimination (cf: Corso, 1956, for *vision*; see Blackwell, 1953). Unlike the *classical theory*, which states that the proper form of the psychometric function for sensory discrimination is a normal ogive, the *neural quantum theory* asserts that the relationship between the proportion of judgments and corresponding stimulus values is best represented by a linear function, which implies that sensory discrimination is characterized by finite, discrete, or quantal steps. The *neural quantum theory* is intended to be consistent with the *all-or-none principle* since it is generally maintained that discriminatory judgments are mediated by the activities of underlying neural structures. In the psychological *theory of neural quantum*, the term *quantum* refers specifically to a "functionally" distinct unit in the neural mechanisms that are involved in sensory discrimination, and, in this context, the term *quantum* implies a perceptual unit, not a physical unit (such as used in contemporary physics to refer to energy units). Another version of this approach, the *quantal hypothesis* (Osgood, 1953), asserts that continuous increments in a physical variable produce discrete (quantal) increases in sensation (cf: the *law of quanta*—with a conscious responding system, the system makes a quantity of a certain kind of energy into a thing or object unlike the thing "out there"; Wheeler, 1940). It appears, on the basis of the existing data, that it cannot be determined whether the *theory of neural quantum* provides a better explanation of sensory discrimination than the *classical theory* (Corso, 1967). After making a critical review of the literature, Corso (1956) concluded that unequivocal support of the *neural quantum theory* is lacking, and the tenability of the *quantal hypothesis* as opposed to the *phi-gamma hypothesis* is extremely difficult to evaluate due to the severe restrictions in methodology and to the statistical limitations in the treatment of data. See also ALL-OR-NONE LAW/ PRINCIPLE; PSYCHOPHYSICAL LAWS/THEORY.

REFERENCES

Herbart, J. (1824). *Psychologie als wissenschaft, neu gegrundet auf erfahrung, metaphysik, und mathematik.* Konisberg, Germany: Unzer.

Lotze, R. (1852). *Medicinische psychologie, oder physiologie der seele.* Leipzig, Germany: Weidmann.

Fechner, G. (1860). *Elemente der psychophysik.* Leipzig, Germany: Breitkopf & Hartel.

Muller, G. (1878). *Zur grundlegung der psychophysik.* Berlin: Gruben.

Jastrow, J. (1888). A critique of psycho-physic methods. *Amer. J. Psy., 1,* 271–309.

Bekesy, G. von (1930). Uber das Fechner'sche gesetz und seine bedeutung fur die theorie der akustischen beobachtungsfehler und die theorie des horens. *Ann. Physik, 7,* 329–359.

Bekesy, G. von (1936). Uber die horschwelle und fuhlgrenze langsamer sinusformiger luftdruckschwankungen. *Ann. Physik, 26,* 554–566.

Wheeler, R. (1940). *The science of psychology.* New York: Crowell.

Stevens, S. S., Morgan, C., & Volkmann, J. (1941). Theory of the neural quantum in the discrimination of loudness and pitch. *Amer. J. Psy., 54,* 315–335.

Miller, G., & Garner, W. (1944). Effect of random presentation in the psychometric function: Implications for a quantal theory of discrimination. *Amer. J. Psy., 57,* 451–467.

Corso, J. (1951). The neural quantum in discrimination of pitch and loudness. *Amer. J. Psy., 64,* 350–368.

Blackwell, H. (1953). Evaluation of the neural quantum theory in vision. *Amer. J. Psy., 66,* 397–408.

Osgood, C. (1953). *Method and theory in experimental psychology.* New York: Oxford University Press.

Corso, J. (1956). The neural quantum theory of sensory discrimination. *Psy. Bull., 53,* 371–393.

Neisser, U. (1957). Response-sequences and the hypothesis of the neural quantum. *Amer. J. Psy., 70,* 512–527.

Corso, J. (1961). The quantal hypothesis and the threshold of audibility. *Amer. J. Psy., 74,* 191–204.

Corso, J. (1963). A theoretico-historical review of the threshold concept. *Psy. Bull., 60,* 356–370.

Norman, D. (1964). Sensory thresholds, response biases, and the neural quantum theory. *J. Math. Psy., 1,* 88–120.

Corso, J. (1967). *The experimental psychology of sensory behavior.* New York: Holt, Rinehart, & Winston.

Reber, A. (1995). *The Penguin dictionary of psychology.* New York: Penguin Books.

NEUROLINGUISTIC THEORY. See CHOMSKY'S PSYCHOLINGUISTIC THEORY.

NEURON/NEURAL/NERVE THEORY. The *neuron* (or *neurone, nerve cell*) is the basic structural and functional unit of the nervous system and consists of three main parts: a cell body ("soma") that contains the nucleus, an axon, and one or more dendrites (Carlson, 1994). A distinction is made between the terms *neuron* and *nerve* where a neuron is a single cell consisting of three parts (one of which is an axon), while a nerve is a bundle of many neural axons (see *Waller's law,* formulated in 1850, which states that if posterior roots of the spinal cord are cut on the central side of the ganglia, those portions of the cut nerves that lie within the spinal cord degenerate, while the peripheral portions of the same nerves—not being severed from the ganglia—do not degenerate; Warren, 1934). Neurons are cells that transmit information throughout the body, as well as within the brain (see *Dale's principle*—the proposal that only one kind of neurotransmitter substance is produced by a given neuron; there are now known to be exceptions to this principle; Zusne, 1987; Sutherland, 1996; see also the *drainage/diversion hypothesis,* which asserts that facilitation of neural conduction over certain neurons and its inhibition over others are due to a drainage of energy from paths of higher resistance into those of lower; and *du Bois Reymond's law,* which is the principle that the excitatory efficiency of an electric current that passes through neural tissue is dependent on the rate of current density *change* and not on current's absolute value; Warren, 1934). Many of the neurons in the human nervous system are extremely small (some axons are only about 0.1 millimeter long; other axons stretch up to a meter through the adult nervous system). It is estimated that the nervous system contains about 100 billion neurons (Williams & Herrup, 1988). The *neuron theory* holds that any sensorimotor neural pathway is not a continuous tissue but consists of separate nerve cells (the neurons) that are merely contiguous end-to-end. According to this view, the neuron is the histological/metabolic unit of the nervous system. The *neuron theory* (also called the *neuron doctrine*; Levinthal, 1983) was first named by von Waldeyer (1891) and was based on a viewpoint of the nervous system held by the Spanish physician/histologist Santiago Ramon y Cajal (1852–1934). Ramon y Cajal's (1899–1904) major work was on the microstructure of the nervous system and utilized the specialized histological staining techniques of the Italian histologist Camillo Golgi (1843–1926). The two men disagreed in their interpretations of neural structure (Ramon y Cajal maintained that nerve cells were discrete and that there was no physical continuity between one cell and another). The revolutionary Golgi stain technique (that impregnates neural tissue with silver) was crucial, historically, for the eventual confirmation of the *neuron theory*, which holds that neurons act as units and communicate via synapses rather than as a continuous network-like circuit (this latter notion, called the *reticularist theory*, is disregarded today; Sutherland, 1996). The dispute over this issue between Ramon y Cajal and Golgi became so heated that Golgi's 1906 Nobel Prize acceptance speech consisted of a fiery denunciation of the *neuron doctrine*. The controversy over the *neuron theory/doctrine* continued for more than 25 years afterward, despite the accumulation of evidence in its favor (Levinthal, 1983). Only with the advent of electron microscopic pictures in the 1950s were the opponents finally satisfied. The *neuron theory* was one of the most important neurological contributions for the history of psychology because it brought together numerous data concerning the nature of nervous physiology that psychologists could apply in their own disciplinary interests, notably in the areas of *learning theory* and the *theory of association* (Murphy & Kovach, 1972; cf: the *theory of psychoneural parallelism*, which holds that every fact of consciousness is concomitant with some neural change without implication of the reverse relation, namely, that all neural conditions are concomitant with conscious processes; Warren, 1934). Other notable issues and theories related to functioning of the neurons, nerves, and the nervous system were the *synaptic theory* of facilitation and inhibition and the *membrane theory* of nerve conduction. According to the *synaptic theory*, the actual pathway activated depends on the physiological properties of the synapse at the time, and the choice between alternatives that nerve impulses can take depends on slight and momentary factors such as *refractory phases* and *summation*. In 1895, the neurologist/psychoanalyst Sigmund Freud set out his assumptions about how the nervous system works (cf: *Jackson's law*, formulated in 1898, which states that when mental abilities are lost because of a neurological disorder, the abilities that appeared last in the course of evolution are lost first because it is the higher nervous centers—that is, those appearing last phylogenetically—that are first affected, and the lower/older centers are the last; Zusne, 1987); Freud hypothesized that neural elements are separated from one another by "contact barriers" (the idea of *synapses* was hotly contested when Freud proposed this), and one element can excite the next one only when the "contact barrier" (i.e., synapse) is crossed (Bloom, Lazerson, & Hofstadter, 1985). With Sherrington's (1906) contributions, as well as those made earlier by Exner (1882), the supposition that processes of *facilitation* and *inhibition* were *synaptic* functions was greatly strengthened. The nature of synaptic function, however, was not disclosed completely by Sherrington's methods. The work of Nernst (1908), Lillie (1923), and Lucas (1917) added theoretical and empirical understanding to the topics of depolarization, refractory phase, hyperexcitability, inhibition, and facilitation. The *membrane theory* of nerve conduction was developed along with the other discoveries of the nature of synapses and conduction. The German physical chemist Wilhelm Ostwald (1853–1932) first proposed the *membrane theory* in 1890; Julius Bernstein amplified and established it in 1902, and R. S. Lillie began a series of experiments that supported it in 1909 (Boring, 1942, 1957). The *membrane theory* of conduction is an explanation of the propagation of the nerve impulse (see Bishop, 1956) in terms of the electrochemical properties of surface films or membranes (cf: *Forbes–Gregg hypothesis*, which states that stimulus strength is translated by nerve fibers into frequency of discharge; this hypothesis was offered to explain how the nervous system handles varying stimulus intensities in spite of the *all-or-none law*, which precludes variability of the strength of discharge in a nerve fiber; Zusne, 1987). The eponymous *Nernst–Lillie theory of excitation and conduction* holds that excitation of a living cell results from a change in the electrical polarization of a protoplasmic membrane, following local change of ionic concentration at the membrane surface. The effect is automatically transmitted because of resulting secondary changes (such as permeability) in the properties of the membrane itself (Warren, 1934). The *membrane theory* accounted for the facts of *refractory phase* and *all-or-none transmission* and was well on its way toward acceptance among physiologists by 1920 (Boring, 1957). See also ALL-OR-NONE LAW/PRINCIPLE; ASSOCIATION, LAWS/PRINCIPLES OF; LEARNING THEORIES/LAWS; REFLEX ARC THEORY/CONCEPT; SPECIFIC NERVE ENERGIES, LAW OF.

REFERENCES

Exner, S. (1882). *Ar. ges. Physio., 28.*

Waldeyer, H. von (1891). Ueber einige neuere forschungen im gebiete der anatomie des centralnervensystems. *Deutsche Medizinische Wochenschrift, 17,* 1213–1218, 1244–1246, 1287–1289, 1331–1332, 1352–1356.

Ramon y Cajal, S. (1899–1904). *Textura del sistema nervioso del hombre y de los verte brados.* Madrid: Moya.

Sherrington, C. (1906). *The integrative action of the nervous system.* New Haven, CT: Yale University Press.

Nernst, W. (1908). Sur theorie des elektrischen reizes. *Ar. ges. Physio., 132,* 275–314.

Lucas, K. (1917). *The conduction of the nervous impulse.* London: Longmans, Green.

Lillie, R. S. (1923). *Protoplasmic action and nervous action.* Chicago: University of Chicago Press.

Warren, H. (Ed.) (1934). *Dictionary of psychology.* Cambridge, MA: Houghton Mifflin.

Boring, E. G. (1942). *Sensation and perception in the history of experimental psychology.* New York: Appleton-Century.

Bishop, G. (1956). Natural history of the nerve impulse. *Physio. Rev., 36,* 376–399.

Boring, E. G. (1957). *A history of experimental psychology*. New York: Appleton-Century-Crofts.

Murphy, G., & Kovach, J. (1972). *Historical introduction to modern psychology*. New York: Harcourt Brace Jovanovich.

Levinthal, C. (1983). *Introduction to physiological psychology*. Englewood Cliffs, NJ: Prentice-Hall.

Bloom, F., Lazerson, A., & Hofstadter, L. (1985). *Brain, mind, and behavior*. New York: Freeman.

Zusne, L. (1987). *Eponyms in psychology*. Westport, CT: Greenwood Press.

Williams, R., & Herrup, K. (1988). The control of neuron number. *Ann. Rev. Neurosci., 11*, 423–453.

Carlson, N. (1994). *Physiology of behavior*. Boston: Allyn & Bacon.

Sutherland, S. (1996). *The international dictionary of psychology*. New York: Crossroad.

NEUROTRANSMITTER/BIOGENIC AMINE THEORY OF DEPRESSION. See DEPRESSION, THEORIES OF.

NEWTON'S LAW/PRINCIPLES OF COLOR MIXTURE. The English physicist, mathematician, and philosopher Sir Isaac Newton (1642–1727) presented the first fruitful system for describing the data of *color mixture* in 1704. In an imaginative leap of speculation, Newton suggested that colors be arranged in a circle with white at the center and the spectral colors/hues (red, orange, yellow, green, blue, indigo, and violet) around the circumference, where the more "desaturated" a color, the closer it was to the center of the circle. Newton also had the idea of representing a given color's quantity by a small circle drawn about the position of the color on the large circle, and the area of the small circle was thought to be proportional to the quantity of the color. According to Newton, the position of a mixture of colors could be determined by calculating the center of gravity of the weighted individual components. Even though Newton had no way in 1704 of actually quantifying a color, his account contains generally all the principles of *color mixture* as developed by other scientists (e.g., Grassman, 1854) 150 years later. Newton's *color mixture law* states that if two color mixtures yield the same sensation of hue, their mixture will also yield that sensation. Newton's synonymous *law of equilibrium* in color mixing refers to the mixture of two hues to yield an intermediate hue. For example, if A and B are the hues that are mixed in proportions of *m* and *n*, then the resultant hue will be at a point on a line joining A and B so that AO/OB = *n/m* (Drever, 1952). Newton's famous *prismatic experiment* demonstrates how *color mixture* using light waves may be analyzed. If a white light is passed through a glass prism, it breaks up into all the "rainbow" colors of the spectrum, and if the entire spectrum of light wavelengths is recombined subsequently, the result is a white light again (Hochberg, 1965). See also COLOR MIXTURE, LAWS/THEORY OF; COLOR VISION, THEORIES/LAWS OF; GRASSMAN'S LAWS; VISION/SIGHT, THEORIES OF.

REFERENCES

Newton, I. (1704). *Opticks.* London: Innys.

Newton, I. (1730/1931). *Opticks.* London: Bell.

Grassman, H. (1853). Zur theorie der farbenmischung. *Pogg. Ann. Physik., 89*, 69.

Grassman, H. (1854). On the theory of compound colours. *Phil. Mag., 7*, 254–264.

Drever, J. (1952). *A dictionary of psychology.* Baltimore: Penguin Books.

Graham, C. (1965). Color mixture and color systems. In C. Graham (Ed.), *Vision and visual perception.* New York: Wiley.

Hochberg, J. (1965). *Perception.* Englewood Cliffs, NJ: Prentice-Hall.

NOMOTHETIC LAWS. See IDIOGRAPHIC/NOMOTHETIC LAWS.

NONCONTINUITY THEORY. See SPENCE'S THEORY.

NORMATIVE DECISION THEORY. See LEADERSHIP, THEORIES OF.

NOVELTY/DISRUPTION EFFECT. See EXPERIMENTER EFFECTS.

NULL HYPOTHESIS. The term *null hypothesis* refers to any statement, proposition, or assumption that serves as a tentative explanation of certain facts where the notion of *no difference* exists between the studied groups (e.g., the effects of a tested drug will be the *same* for both the *experimental* and *control* groups of subjects). When statistical analyses are used to test hypotheses, experimenters typically set up the *null hypothesis* prior to collecting data. This predetermined postulation allows for an evaluation of research results on the basis of sampling distribution and normal curve *probability theory.* A *null hypothesis* deals with the relationship between variables and is stated so that either it or its negation will result in information that can be used to advance a particular research hypothesis (Urbina, 1994). In the standard *hypothesis-testing* approach in science, one attempts to demonstrate the *falsity* of the *null hypothesis* (in a "straw-man" type of reasoning strategy called *falsification;* see Popper, 1935; e.g., a tested drug shows that there *is* a difference between the *experimental* and *control* groups of subjects), leaving one with the implication that the alternative (or mutually exclusive/opposite) hypothesis is the "correct" or acceptable one. After the data are collected, and the actual statistics are calculated, the researcher must decide whether or not to reject the *null hypothesis* (Lockwood, 1994). The concept of the *null hypothesis* was developed by the English geneticist/statistician Sir Ronald Aylmer Fisher (1890–1962) and approximates Sir Karl Popper's (1902–) philosophy of science approach that views science to be a process for the elimination of false theories (i.e., the major role of science is the *falsification* of incorrect theories). According to these viewpoints, science—particularly psychology—never "proves" hypotheses. Science shows only that certain hypotheses (e.g., the *null hypothesis*) have been disproved (Ray, 1996). Therefore, the *null hypothesis* itself cannot be proved without knowing the ''true'' state of affairs, but it can be disproved if the obtained results are too unlikely to be compatible with it. Decisions based on statistical *hypothesis testing* are usually cast in terms of levels of probability, or levels of confidence, as to the correctness of various outcomes vis-à-vis the *null hypothesis* (Urbina, 1994). See also PROBABILITY THEORY/LAWS.

REFERENCES

Fisher, R. (1925). *Statistical methods for research workers*. New York: Hafner.

Popper, K. (1935). *The logic of scientific discovery*. New York: Basic Books.

Lockwood, G. (1994). Hypothesis testing. In R. J. Corsini (Ed.), *Ency. Psy*. New York: Wiley.

Urbina, S. (1994). Errors (Type I and II). In R. J. Corsini (Ed.), *Ency. Psy*. New York: Wiley.

Ray, W. (1996). *Methods toward a science of behavior and experience*. Pacific Grove, CA: Brooks/Cole.

O

OBJECT PERCEPTION. See PATTERN/OBJECT RECOGNITION THEORY.

OCCAM'S RAZOR. See PARSIMONY, LAW/PRINCIPLE OF.

OCCASIONALISM, THEORY OF. See MIND–BODY THEORIES.

OCCUPATION THEORIES. See WORK/CAREER/OCCUPATION, THEORIES OF.

OHM'S ACOUSTIC/AUDITORY LAW. The German physicist Georg Simon Ohm (1787–1854) formulated this principle, which states that a complex tone is analyzed by the perceiver into its frequency components. In addition to the ability to objectively break down a complex sound into sine-wave components by means of a mathematical procedure (known as a *Fourier analysis*), the ear is able to carry out this analysis as well. The ear can carry out an analysis of complex tones into simpler components because of the way structures inside the ear vibrate in response to different frequencies and because individual neurons are tuned to respond to a narrow range of frequencies. Such an analysis takes place early in the auditory system, and, then at higher levels in the system, neural information about these frequency components is combined to create one's perception of sound (Goldstein, 1996). Although this analysis is not normally part of one's awareness, with training a hearer can learn to perceive individual *harmonics* (i.e., an overtone or partial, the frequency of which is a multiple of the fundamental tone or sine wave with the lowest frequency) in a complex sound. *Ohm's acoustic law* is a theoretical statement about the perceiver/hearer and is differentiated from a *Fourier analysis*, which is a theoretical statement about the physical stimulus. The word *acoustic* in *Ohm's acoustic law* (which was put in to distinguish it from *Ohm's electrical law* of I = E/R, where I is current in amperes, E is volts, and R is resistance) may be an unfortunate choice because it confuses the issue; it may have been better to call the law *Ohm's auditory law* (Reber, 1995). See also AUDITION/HEARING, THEORIES OF; FOURIER'S LAW/SERIES/ANALYSIS.

REFERENCES

Warren, H. (Ed.) (1934). *Dictionary of psychology*. Cambridge, MA: Houghton Mifflin.
Reber, A. (1995). *The Penguin dictionary of psychology*. New York: Penguin Books.
Goldstein, E. (1996). *Sensation and perception*. Pacific Grove, CA: Brooks/Cole.

OLFACTION/SMELL, THEORIES OF. The curious things about olfaction are that much of one's perceptual processing of odors is unconscious, that it is very difficult to recall smells, and that it is difficult to name them (Coren & Ward, 1989). However, the experience of a particular smell at a particular moment can stimulate numerous memories, often highly emotional, of episodes in which that smell was present (Engen, 1982, 1987). Smell seems to act according to two separate modes of action that may result in different perceptual and informational experiences: the "near" experience of the flavors of food and the "far" experience of air-borne smells (e.g., insects and some higher animals secrete volatile chemicals called *pheromones*, whose molecules travel through the air to other members of the species; cf: Gibbons, 1986; see also the *Lee–Boot effect*, which is the gradual slowing down of the estrus cycles of a group of female mice that are housed together; if they are then exposed to the odor of a male or to his urine, their cycles begin again; this latter effect, which is called the *Whitten effect*, is caused by a pheromone in the male's urine; cf: the *Vandenbergh effect*, which is the acceleration of the onset of puberty in female mice caused by a pheromone in the urine of a mature male mouse; Reber, 1995). Molecules that evoke the sensation of smell may be described as having a specific size, shape, weight, and "vibration frequency" (i.e., atoms in a given molecule move around in a characteristic pattern at predictable speeds that are different for different substances; Wright, 1982). Also, the particular atoms that make up a molecule (and the number of electrons available for chemical bonding with other molecules on the smell receptors) are likely to be important components of smell stimuli. However, as yet there is no consensus as to which of these factors is critical (Coren & Ward, 1989). As is the case with other senses, the mechanism by which the stimulus molecules cause an electrical response (the *transduction process*) in the receptors in the upper nasal passages (the "olfactory epithelium") is still something of a mystery. There are probably at least two classes of transduction mechanisms (Getchell & Getchell, 1987): highly selective processes where specific receptor-cell proteins ("specialists") form reversible chemical bonds with specific parts of odorant molecules; and less selective processes where chemicals directly affect the receptor cell membrane anywhere they contact it ("generalist" smell receptors). Several of the current *theories of olfaction* concerning the more selective ("specialist") mechanisms are the *lock-and-key theory* (also called the *stereochemical theory*)—which holds that variously shaped molecules fit into special sites on the receptor membrane like a key fitted into a lock; when a molecule fits into a receptor site, a change in the structure of the cell membrane occurs, allowing ions into or out of the cell and, consequently, generating an electrical current (Amoore, Johnson, & Rubin, 1964; cf: Seashore's, 1923, *law of complementary odors*); the *vibration theory*—which maintains that the stimulus molecule ruptures certain chemical bonds in the cell membrane, causing the release of stored-up energy, which, in turn, generates an electrical current and action potentials; which bonds are ruptured in which cells depends on the unique vibration frequency of each stimulus molecule (Wright, 1982); and the *gas chromatographic model*—which states that the rate of movement of an odorant molecule across the receptor surface determines the neural coding of its smell; that is, some molecules travel slowly across the receptor surface while others travel more rapidly, with the result that each molecule stimulates a different spatiotemporal pattern of receptors (Mozell, 1970; cf: the earlier *infrared theory* of Beck & Miles, 1947). The *gas chromatographic* approach is based on the observation that the same sort of "across-fiber patterns" that are found in the sense of *taste* seem to be present in the olfactory system, where it is likely that the "code" for smell qualities will be found in these patterns (e.g., Kauer, 1987). However, a *labeled-line theory*, such as applied to taste, may not be feasible for olfaction because it has many more types of labeled lines where there is no small list of primary smells for olfaction such as there is for taste. Thus, at present, there is no evidence of olfactory fibers falling into groups as the taste fibers seem to do (Kauer, 1987; Coren & Ward, 1989). The *stereochemical/lock-and-key* approach is based upon the identification of seven primary odors, each associated with a particular molecule shape (cf: Henning's, 1915, *smell theory/smell prism* which proposed six primary qualities: foul, fruity, burnt, resinous, spicy, and flowery; Seashore, 1923; Coren & Ward, 1989). The odors, proposed shapes, and typical stimuli are (Thorne, 1994): camphoraceous (spherically shaped; e.g., camphor or mothball), ethereal (small, flat, thin; e.g., dry-cleaning fluid); floral (key-shaped; e.g., rose); musky (disk-shaped; e.g., angelica root oil); minty (wedge-shaped; e.g., peppermint candy); pungent (shape unknown; e.g., vinegar); and putrid (shape unknown; e.g., rotten eggs). The phenomenon of *adaptation* is among the "laws" of olfaction (cf: other "laws" of smell such as *fusion, compensation, selectivity,* and *modulation*; Boring, Langfeld, & Weld, 1939). The perceived intensity of an odor is affected by *adaptation*, where only a brief period of exposure is sufficient to render an odor undetectable. In practical terms, *adaptation* may be beneficial to workers in an animal laboratory or zoo but nonbeneficial to coal miners who might need to detect an increase in intensity of a potentially lethal gas (Thorne, 1994). See also ADAPTATION, PRINCIPLES/LAWS OF; GUSTATION/TASTE, THEORIES OF.

REFERENCES

Henning, H. (1915). Der geruch. I. *Z. Psy.*, *73*, 161–257.

Seashore, C. (1923). *Introduction to psychology*. New York: Macmillan.

Beebe-Center, J. (1931). The variability of affective judgments upon odors. *J. Exp. Psy.* *14*, 91–93.

Dyson, G. (1938). The scientific basis of odour. *Chemistry and Industry, 57*, 647–651.

Boring, E. G., Langfeld, H., & Weld, H. (1939). *Introduction to psychology*. New York: Wiley.

Beck, L., & Miles, W. (1947). Some theoretical and experimental relationships between infrared absorption and olfaction. *Science, 106*, 511.

Pfaffman, C. (1951). Taste and smell. In S. S. Stevens (Ed.), *Handbk. Exp. Psy.* New York: Wiley.

Amoore, J., Johnson, J., & Rubin, M. (1964). The stereochemical theory of olfaction. *Sci. Amer., 210*, 42–49.

Pfaffman, C. (Ed.) (1969). *Olfaction and taste*. New York: Rockefeller University Press.

Mozell, M. (1970). Evidence for a chromatographic model of olfaction. *J. Gen. Physio., 56*, 46–63.

Porter, R., & Moore, J. (1981). Human kin recognition by olfactory cues. *Physio. & Beh., 27*, 493–495.

Amoore, J. (1982). Odor theory and odor classification. In E. Theimer (Ed.), *Fragrance chemistry—the science of the sense of smell*. New York: Academic Press.

Engen, T. (1982). *Perception of odors*. New York: Academic Press.

Wright, R. (1982). *The sense of smell*. Boca Raton, FL: CRC Press.

Gibbons, B. (1986). The intimate sense of smell. *National Geographic 170*, 324–361.

Engen, T. (1987). Remembering odors and their names. *Amer. Sci., 75*, 497–503.

Getchell, T., & Getchell, M. (1987). Peripheral mechanisms of olfaction: Biochemical and neurophysiology. In T. Finger & W. Silver (Eds.), *Neurobiology of taste and smell*. New York: Wiley.

Gilbert, A., & Wysocki, C. (1987). The smell survey: Results. *National Geographic, 172*, 514–525.

Kauer, J. (1987). Coding in the olfactory system. In T. Finger & W. Silver (Eds.), *Neurobiology of taste and smell*. New York: Wiley.

Coren, S., & Ward, L. (1989). *Sensation and perception*. New York: Harcourt Brace Jovanovich.

Ackerman, D. (1991). *A natural history of the senses*. New York: Vintage Books.

Thorne, B. (1994). Olfaction. In R. J. Corsini (Ed.), *Ency. Psy.* New York: Wiley.

Reber, A. (1995). *The Penguin dictionary of psychology*. New York: Penguin Books.

OPERANT CONDITIONING/BEHAVIOR, LAWS/THEORY OF. See SKINNER'S DESCRIPTIVE BEHAVIOR/OPERANT CONDITIONING THEORY.

OPERANT RESERVE, LAW OF. See SKINNER'S DESCRIPTIVE BEHAVIOR/OPERANT CONDITIONING THEORY.

OPPONENT-PROCESS COLOR VISION THEORY. See HERING–HURVICH–JAMESON COLOR VISION THEORY.

OPPONENT-PROCESS THEORY OF EMOTION. See SOLOMON'S OPPONENT-PROCESS THEORY OF EMOTIONS/FEELINGS/MOTIVA- TION.

ORGANISMIC THEORY. See GOLDSTEIN'S ORGANISMIC THEORY.

ORGANIZATIONAL/INDUSTRIAL/SYSTEMS THEORY. The branch of applied psychology called *organizational/industrial psychology* covers various areas such as industrial, military, economic, and personnel psychology and re- searches problems of tests and measurements, organizational behavior, personnel practices, human engineering/factors, the effects of work, fatigue, pay, satisfac- tion, and efficiency. In the present context, the term *organization* is defined as a complex social system made up of individuals, their facilities, and the products created. In this case, the following criteria may be applied: there must be co- ordination of personnel effort, personnel must have some set of common goals or purposes, there has to be some division of labor within the larger structure, and there has to be some degree of integrated functioning, including a hierarchy of authority (Reber, 1995; cf: *ego-alter theory*, which attempts to account for the origin or existence of *social* organizations in terms of innate egoism or altruism; Warren, 1934). The area of *systems theory* emphasizes the interaction and interrelated nature of behavior; according to this theory, an individual's behavior does not occur in a vacuum but rather is influenced by, and in turn influences, the environment in which it occurs (Kappenberg, 1994; cf: *chaos theory*—a viewpoint imported from the mathematics of nonlinear systems that has been applied to the behavior of complex systems such as humans, the weather, and wildlife populations; Gleick, 1987; see, also, *catastrophe theory*, which is a mathematical approach developed by Rene Thom that attempts to formalize the nature of abrupt discontinuities in functions; Reber, 1995; and Julian Simon's economics-based *grand theory*, 1996, that represents an "anti- entropy" position and emphasizes that evolving humans create more than they use or destroy). The general term *organizational dynamics* is used to refer col- lectively to the various dynamic patterns of shifting elements within an organ- izational unit where at least seven conceptual elements may be viewed in interrelationships: organizational processes, external environment, employees, formal structure, internal social system, technology, and coalitions within the organization (Kotter, 1978). Three topics of special interest to contemporary organizational psychologists concern managerial/leadership style, worker moti- vation/attitudes, and job satisfaction. Schein (1965) describes four different the- ories about the nature of individuals that are held by managers/leaders: the *rational-economic man theory*—argues that humans are primarily motivated by money; the leader's task is to manipulate the worker to perform his or her best within the limits of what one can be paid; workers' feelings, which are viewed as irrational, must be prevented from obstructing the expression of the workers' rational self-interest (Taylor, 1911; cf: McGregor's, 1960, *Theory X*); *social man* *theory*—holds that people are basically motivated by social needs that determine their sense of identity and meaning through relationships with others (Mayo, 1945); *self-actualizing man theory*—maintains that people are intrinsically motivated, as in the worker who has deeply personal, internalized reasons for doing a good job (Maslow, 1954; Argyris, 1964); and *complex man theory*—argues that different workers have different needs and capabilities, and managers/leaders must be sensitive to individual differences in the needs, fears, and abilities of workers (Vroom, 1960; Schein, 1965). The problem of worker motivation has been approached by three theories, among others: *goal-setting theory, equity theory*, and *expectancy theory*. Research on *goal-setting theory* (i.e., the proposal that specific and difficult goals lead to higher performance) suggests that goals provide both direction and mobilization of behaviors where the specificity of the goal acts as an internal stimulus (e.g., Locke, 1968). According to *equity theory* in a work setting, a worker is driven to perform by a need to maintain equilibrium or balance—that is, employees prefer jobs in which the "output" is equal to the "input"; if imbalances occur, workers adjust their input, output, or their psychological perceptions (cf: Wilpert, 1995). Currently, one of the most popular theories of worker motivation/attitudes is *expectancy theory*, which holds that workers' efforts are determined by expectancy of outcomes, their desirability, and the energy needed to achieve them (cf: *prospect theory*—an algebraic decision theory that attempts to explain departures from *expected utility theory*; it includes the *certainty effect, reflection effect*, and *isolation effect*; Sutherland, 1996; see, also, the *false-consensus effect*, which is the tendency to overestimate the degree to which one's opinions and beliefs are shared by others; and the *assimilation-contrast theory*, which is based on the assumption that attitudes are modified by changes in the relationship between one's originally held position, the opinion of the person effecting the change, and the source credibility; Reber, 1995). According to *expectancy theory*, workers ask themselves three questions: What can I reasonably expect from my efforts? Do I really want the rewards offered by management? If I give maximum effort, will it be reflected in my job evaluation? Another important issue in organizational psychology is the problem of job satisfaction (e.g., Kopelman, 1979; Ostroff, 1992). Among the theories of job satisfaction is the *personality-job fit theory* (cf: the *Peter principle*, which states that a person gets promoted up through the ranks of an organization until she or he reaches her or his level of incompetence; Reber, 1995), which asserts that a good fit, or match, between an individual's personality and an occupation results in maximal job satisfaction (Feldman & Arnold, 1985; Holland, 1985). See also CONTROL/SYSTEMS THEORY; EQUITY THEORY; EXCHANGE/SOCIAL EXCHANGE THEORY; HAWTHORNE EFFECT; LEADERSHIP, THEORIES OF; RISKY-SHIFT EFFECT; WORK/CAREER/OCCUPATION, THEORIES OF.

REFERENCES

Taylor, F. (1911). *The principles of scientific management*. New York: Harper.
Warren, H. (Ed.) (1934). *Dictionary of psychology*. Cambridge, MA: Houghton Mifflin.

Mayo, E. (1945). *The social problems of an industrial civilization*. Boston: Harvard Graduate School of Business.

Maslow, A. (1954). *Motivation and personality*. New York: Harper & Row.

McGregor, D. (1960). *The human side of enterprise*. New York: McGraw-Hill.

Vroom, V. (1960). *Some personality determinants of the effects of participation*. Englewood Cliffs, NJ: Prentice-Hall.

Argyris, C. (1964). *Integrating the individual and the organization*. New York: Wiley.

Schein, E. (1965). *Organizational psychology*. Englewood Cliffs, NJ: Prentice-Hall.

Locke, E. (1968). Toward a theory of task motivation and performance. *Org. Beh. & Hum. Per., 4*, 309–329.

Tausky, C., & Parke, E. (1976). Job enrichment, need theory, and reinforcement theory. In R. Dubin (Ed.), *Handbook of work, organization, and society*. Chicago: Rand-McNally.

Argyris, C., & Schon, D. (1978). *Organizational learning: A theory of action perspective*. Reading, MA: Addison-Wesley.

Kotter, J. (1978). *Organizational dynamics: Diagnosis and intervention*. Reading, MA: Addison-Wesley.

Kopelman, R. (1979). Directionally different expectancy theory predictions of work motivation and job satisfaction. *Mot. & Emo., 3*, 299–317.

Feldman, D., & Arnold, H. (1985). Personality types and career patterns: Some empirical evidence on Holland's model. *Can. J. Admin. Sci., 12*, 192–210.

Holland, J. (1985). *Making vocational choices: A theory of vocational personalities and work environments*. Englewood Cliffs, NJ: Prentice-Hall.

Gleick, J. (1987). *Chaos: Making a new science*. New York: Penguin Books.

Ostroff, C. (1992). The relationship between satisfaction, attitudes, and performance: An organizational level analysis. *J. App. Psy., 10*, 963–974.

Kappenberg, R. (1994). Conjoint therapy. In R. J. Corsini (Ed.), *Ency. Psy.* New York: Wiley.

Reber, A. (1995). *The Penguin dictionary of psychology*. New York: Penguin Books.

Wilpert, B. (1995). Organizational behavior. *Ann. Rev. Psy., 46*, 59–90.

Simon, J. (1996). *The ultimate resource 2*. Princeton, NJ: Princeton University Press.

Sutherland, S. (1996). *The international dictionary of psychology*. New York: Crossroad.

OSGOOD'S TRANSFER SURFACE/MODEL. See SKAGGS–ROBINSON HYPOTHESIS.

OVERATTRIBUTION EFFECT. See ATTRIBUTION THEORY.

OVERJUSTIFICATION EFFECT/HYPOTHESIS. See REINFORCEMENT THEORY.

P

PANDEMONIUM MODEL/THEORY. See PATTERN/OBJECT RECOGNITION THEORY.

PANUM PHENOMENON. See PERCEPTION (I. GENERAL), THEORIES OF.

PAPEZ-MacLEAN THEORIES. See EMOTIONS, THEORIES/LAWS OF.

PARALLELISM/PSYCHOPHYSICAL, THEORY/DOCTRINE OF. See MIND–BODY THEORIES.

PARALLEL LAW. See FECHNER'S LAW.

PARSIMONY, LAW/PRINCIPLE OF. = Lloyd Morgan's/Morgan's canon = Occam's razor = economy, principle of. The *law of parsimony* states that if two scientific propositions or two theories are equally tenable, the *simpler* one is to be preferred. Another name for this law is called *Lloyd Morgan's canon* in honor of the English zoologist/physiologist Conway Lloyd Morgan (1852–1936). Morgan articulated the principle in 1894 and cautioned against the explanatory excesses of the emerging field of comparative psychology by stating that in interpreting an animal's behavior, it is always preferable to adopt the psychologically *simplest* interpretation. Thus, *Morgan's canon* refers to the use of a lower, more ''primitive'' explanation of phenomena than to assume the activity of a higher, more ''mentalistic'' functioning (cf: Romanes', 1884, tendency to anthropomorphize animals' behavior). The canon was very influential in the development of the early behaviorists' programs and doctrines such as those proposed by Watson (1919) and Thorndike (1898). During Morgan's time, when the proof of *Darwin's evolutionary theory* was uppermost in the minds of psychologists and biologists, demonstration of *Morgan's canon* and the *law of parsimony* was an advancement in scientific thinking (Lundin, 1994; see, also, *J. S. Mill's* earlier *canons*, which are principles that govern inductive reasoning about cause–effect relationships and include the *laws* of *agreement, differences, joint agreement/disagreement, residues,* and *concomitant variation*; Copi, 1994; cf: *law of noncontradiction*—a canon of rational thinking that states that if a certain proposition is true, its exact opposite or contradictory is false; Warren, 1934). A third name for the *law of parsimony* is called the *principle of economy* and refers to a working rule for treatment of scientific data, according to which the *simplest* available explanation is to be preferred, that is, the explanation that involves the fewest or least complexly related concepts that are adequate. This was known also as the *law of simplicity* (and the *principle of ontological economy*), which was originally proposed by the English scholastic philosopher William of Occam (or Ockham) (c. 1285–c. 1349). Occam argued that reality exists only in individual things/events, and he further enjoined economy in explanation by stating, "What can be done with fewer assumptions is done in vain with more" (Harris & Levey, 1975). Today, *Occam's principle* is also called *Occam's razor*—the principle of scientific thinking that the *simplest* adequate explanation of a thing is to be preferred to any more complex explanations (Wolman, 1973). See also DARWIN'S EVOLUTION THEORY.

REFERENCES

Mill, J. S. (1874). *A system of logic.* New York: Harper.

Romanes, G. (1884). *Mental evolution in animals.* New York: Appleton.

Morgan, C. L. (1890/1891). *Animal life and intelligence.* London: Arnold.

Morgan, C. L. (1894). *An introduction to comparative psychology.* London: Scott.

Thorndike, E. (1898). *Animal intelligence.* New York: Macmillan.

Watson, J. B. (1919). *Psychology from the standpoint of a behaviorist.* Philadelphia: Lippincott.

Warren, H. (Ed.) (1934). *Dictionary of psychology.* Cambridge, MA: Houghton Mifflin.

Wolman, B. (Ed.). (1973). *Dictionary of behavioral science.* New York: Van Nostrand Reinhold.

Harris, W., & Levey, J. (Eds.) (1975). *The new Columbia encyclopedia.* New York: Columbia University Press.

Copi, I. (1994). Mill's canons. In R. J. Corsini (Ed.), *Ency. Psy.* New York: Wiley.

Lundin, R. (1994). Conway Lloyd Morgan. In R. J. Corsini (Ed.), *Ency. Psy.* New York: Wiley.

Reber, A. (1995). *The Penguin dictionary of psychology.* New York: Penguin Books.

PARTIAL REINFORCEMENT EXTINCTION EFFECT. See CAPALDI'S THEORY; REINFORCEMENT THEORY.

PASSING STRANGER/STRANGER ON A TRAIN EFFECT. See RECIPROCITY OF LIKING EFFECT.

PATH–GOAL THEORY. See LEADERSHIP, THEORIES OF.

PATTERN/OBJECT RECOGNITION THEORY. The perception of shape/form, including figural pattern and detail, is generally achieved by organisms through analysis of stimulus features from the sensory input (Uhr, 1966, 1973; cf: the *Hoffding step*—the Gestaltist's term for the mental step through which the perception of an image makes contact with a memory trace; Hoffding, 1887). Contour and edge perceptions are hypothesized to take place at the retinal level, and some vision experts propose that contour and edges are the basis of complex form perception. An *information-processing* analysis of vision requires an initial stage of figural synthesis, which is the way that stimulus information is transferred from the icon and synthesized into a form (e.g., Neisser, 1967). In order for pattern/shape recognition to occur, the synthesized information is subsequently transferred to memory to produce a unique response. One of the major problems for *pattern recognition* and perception theorists is to understand how the organism consistently recognizes forms/shapes when they are presented in different sizes and retinal locations, are degraded by poor or "noisy" environmental conditions, and are partially outlined in cartoon/picturelike formats (Anderson, 1994). The *pandemonium model/theory* was an early and influential computer model of *pattern perception* developed by Selfridge (1959). In its simplest form it was based on a number of perceiving elements (called "demons") that were tuned to detect specific features (e.g., a straight line, a half circle). Each low-level demon that was activated "shouted out," and the higher level demons decided what stimulus was presented by sifting through the "wild uproar" or *pandemonium* (Coren & Ward, 1989). One general approach in *pattern recognition theory* is the *feature extraction/feature theory*, which involves *template matching* processes—this assumes that various internal representations (i.e., "templates) of objects are stored in memory, and new stimuli are processed by comparing them with the templates until a match is found. However, as a *theory of human pattern recognition*, it is too simple, and it cannot, for example, account for the ability to recognize that a, A, *A*, and *a* are all examples of the same letter (Uttal, 1973; Reber, 1995). Most research in form/shape perception includes basic visual functions concerning luminance distribution, which produce lines or "Mach bands," discriminable differences in forms, figural aftereffects, visual illusion changes due to unspecified cues, and estimation of the vertical orientation (see Graham, 1965). Attneave and Arnoult (1956) studied the psychophysics of form and demonstrated that judgments of attributes of abstract forms could be related to stimulus *domain features* such as *complexity* and *area*. Gibson (1979) described three-dimensional perception and suggested that object perception can be based only on form perception; he argued that features are important where what counts is not the form per se but the *dimensions* of variation of form. Zusne (1970) made the terminological distinction that *form* is the more general term, and *shape* is more specific, even though the terms *form* and *shape* are frequently used interchangeably. Julesz (1981) hypothesized that the "primitives" for object perception are units called *textons*, which operate during the initial ("preattentive") stage of vision (cf: Enns, 1986; Northdurft, 1990). According to Julesz, texture formation in object perception is automatic and happens almost instantaneously. In her *feature integration theory* (*FIT*), Treisman (1993) suggests that the "primitives" of object perception operate in five stages (cf: Tarr, 1994). Treisman's *FIT* focuses on how different attributes such as shape, color, texture, and size are integrated into a simple object. However, Treisman does not spell out exactly how the process of feature combination works in her *FIT* (Goldstein, 1996). Another approach, *Biederman's* (1987) *recognition by components* (*RBC*) *theory*, is based on "primitives" also, but rather than being elementary properties such as color and shape, the "primitives" in *RBC theory* are volumetric primitives called *geons* (for *geometric ion*). The basic idea behind *RBC theory* is that objects are recognized by perceiving their *geons*. According to the *principle of componential recovery*, one can easily recognize an object if its *geons* can be identified. The basic message of *Biederman's theory* is that if enough information is available to enable one to identify an object's basic *geons*, the perceiver will be able to identify the object (Biederman, Cooper, Hummel, & Fiser, 1993). The theories by Julesz concerning *textons*, Treisman concerning *FIT*, and Biederman regarding *RBC* all have in common the idea that the perception of objects involves a number of stages, beginning with "primitives" and ending with the combination of primitives into the complete perception of an object (see Marr, 1982). See also GESTALT THEORY/LAWS; INFORMATION/INFORMATION-PROCESSING THEORY; PERCEPTION (I. GENERAL), THEORIES OF; PERCEPTION (II. COMPARATIVE APPRAISAL), THEORIES OF.

REFERENCES

Hoffding, H. (1887). *Psychologie in umrissen auf grundlage der erfahrung.* Leipzig: Reisland.

Attneave, F., & Arnoult, M. (1956). The quantitative study of shape and pattern perception. *Psy. Bull., 53,* 452–471.

Selfridge, O. (1959). Pandemonium: A paradigm for learning. In D. Blake & A. Uttley (Eds.), *Proceedings of the symposium on the mechanization of thought processes.* London: HM Stationery Office.

Graham, C. (Ed.) (1965). *Vision and visual perception.* New York: Wiley.

Uhr, L. (Ed.) (1966). *Pattern recognition: Theory, experiment, computer simulations, and dynamic models of form perception and discovery.* New York: Wiley.

Neisser, U. (1967). *Cognitive psychology.* New York: Appleton-Century-Crofts.

Zusne, L. (1970). *Visual perception of form.* New York: Academic Press.

Uhr, L. (1973). *Pattern recognition, learning, and thought.* Englewood Cliffs, NJ: Prentice-Hall.

Uttal, W. (1973). *The psychology of sensory coding.* New York: Harper & Row.

Gibson, J. (1979). *The ecological approach to visual perception.* Boston: Houghton Mifflin.

Julesz, B. (1981). Textons, the elements of texture perception, and their interactions. *Nature, 290,* 91–97.

Marr, D. (1982). *Vision.* San Francisco: Freeman.

Enns, J. (1986). Seeing textons in context. *Perc. & Psychophys., 39,* 143–147.

Biederman, I. (1987). Recognition-by-components: A theory of human image understanding. *Psy. Rev., 94*, 115–147.

Coren, S., & Ward, L. (1989). *Sensation and perception*. San Diego: Harcourt Brace Jovanovich.

Northdurft, H. (1990). Texton segregation by associated differences in global and local luminance distribution. *Proc. R. S. Lon., B239*, 295–320.

Biederman, I., Cooper, E., Hummel, J., & Fiser, J. (1993). Geon theory as an account of shape recognition in mind, brain, and machine. In J. Illingworth (Ed.), *Proceedings of the Fourth British Machine Vision Conference*. Guilford, Surrey, U.K.: BMVA Press.

Treisman, A. (1993). The perception of features and objects. In A. Baddeley & L. Weiskrantz (Eds.), *Attention: Selection, awareness, and control*. Oxford: Clarendon.

Anderson, N. (1994). Form/shape perception. In R. J. Corsini (Ed.), *Ency. Psy.* New York: Wiley.

Tarr, M. (1994). Visual representation. In V. Ramachandran (Ed.), *Encyclopedia of human behavior*. Vol. 4. New York: Academic Press.

Reber, A. (1995). *The Penguin dictionary of psychology*. New York: Penguin Books.

Goldstein, E. (1996). *Sensation and perception*. Pacific Grove, CA: Brooks/Cole.

PAVLOVIAN CONDITIONING PRINCIPLES/LAWS/THEORIES. The Russian physiologist Ivan Petrovich Pavlov (1849–1936) (note: Pavlov's name was spelled in various ways by some American writers in the 1920s and 1930s, such as "Pavloff," "Pawlow," Pavlow"; see Dunlap, 1922; Seashore, 1923; Hollingworth, 1928) was the first to explore extensively the characteristics of *classical conditioning* (Pavlov, 1927, 1928a), even though he was not the first to discover the *conditioned response* (also called the *conditional response*, the *conditioned reflex*, and the *conditional reflex*). Aristotle's *laws of association* anticipated the principle of conditioning; R. Whytt (1714–1766) and J. A. Unzer (1727–1799) laid down the foundations for the *doctrine of reflex action* (Peters, 1965); and Whytt (1763) recognized *psychic secretions* over a century before Pavlov (Hilgard & Bower, 1966). E. B. Twitmyer, in a doctoral dissertation in 1902 at the University of Pennsylvania, discovered the *conditioned response* (without actually using the term) in the course of an investigation of the knee jerk response (Woodworth, 1938; see Coon, 1982). Pavlov, along with another Russian scientist, Vladimir M. Bekhterev (1857–1927)—who is best known for his work on "associated reflexes" and the conditioning of motor withdrawal responses—both worked within the conditioning framework laid down by their Russian predecessor Ivan M. Sechenov (1829–1905). Sechenov (1863/1965) freely used the expression *psychic reflexes* and interpreted a person's voluntary behavior in reflex terms. Pavlov acknowledged the importance of having read Sechenov as he began to study psychic processes by physiological means (Hilgard & Bower, 1966). The procedure of *Pavlovian conditioning*, which is a particular form of learning, consists of the pairing of two stimuli, each of which initially produces a response that is different from the other one. Pavlov's *classical conditioning* experiment involved placing meat powder in a dog's mouth, whereupon salivation took place; the food was called the unconditioned stimulus (UCS), and the salivation was called the unconditioned reflex (UCR). Subsequently, some arbitrary stimulus, such as a light or bell, was combined with the presentation of the food. Eventually, after repetition and the optimal time relationships, the light or bell evoked salivation independently of the food: the light or bell became a conditioned stimulus (CS), and the response to it was called a conditioned reflex (CR) (Bower & Hilgard, 1981; cf: the *Rescorla–Wagner theory/model*, 1972, which states that the increment in the CS–CR association on any one trial is a decreasing function of the predictability of the CS). Many such conditioning studies indicate that the CR is seldom, if ever, an exact replica of the UCR and may differ markedly from it. This fact was recognized early by American researchers and led to the substitution of the term *response* for *reflex* inasmuch as the concept of *reflex* implies a fixed and stereotyped movement (Wickens, 1994). Pavlov developed a number of concepts and principles in his systematic study and theorizing about conditioning: reinforcement, extinction, spontaneous recovery, generalization (see the *law of coexistence* and the *law of contiguity*, which state that if two mental events occur at the same time, the recurrence of one tends to call forth the idea corresponding to the other; Warren, 1934; cf: Rescorla, 1976b), differentiation (cf: the *law of cohesion*—which states that acts that occur in close succession tend to become combined or unified and form an integrated act of more complex character; Warren, 1934), forward/backward/simultaneous/delayed and trace conditioning, inhibition (cf: Skinner, 1938; Rescorla, 1969, 1976a), association, irradiation, concentration, reciprocal induction (this phenomenon has been rediscovered in recent times and renamed *behavioral contrast*; see Reynolds, 1961), first and second signal systems, experimental neurosis, and higher-order conditioning. Pavlov's conditioning paradigm has come to be known as *classical conditioning* and is distinguished from other types of conditioning and learning (cf: Hilgard & Marquis, 1940, who coined the labels *classical* and *instrumental conditioning*. Other writers have used different labels for the two types of conditioning where the first term in the following pairs is the equivalent of *classical conditioning*, and the second term is the equivalent of *instrumental conditioning* (cf: Kimble, 1961): *associative shifting* versus *trial and error learning* (Thorndike, 1911); *Type I* versus *Type II* (Miller & Konorski, 1928; Konorski & Miller, 1937); *Type S, respondent* versus *Type R, operant* (Skinner, 1937); *conditioning* versus *success learning* (Schlosberg, 1937); and *conditioning* versus *problem-solving* (Mowrer, 1947). Pavlov has had a major impact on psychology, particularly *learning theory*, due to his systematic approach in experimentation, his *theories of association*, and his preferences for important topics of research. In Kimble's (1961) list of terms relevant to conditioning and learning, 31 terms are attributed to Pavlov, and only 21 other terms are attributed to all other psychologists combined. Razran (1965) estimated that by the year 1965 some 6,000 experiments had been conducted using Pavlov's exact *classical conditioning model* and were reported in at least 29 different languages. Even after the paradigm of *instrumental conditioning* was introduced and developed, it was found that most of the phenomena studied in the *classical conditioning* paradigm (e.g., reinforcement, generalization, extinction) still held up well (Razran, 1965). The first experiments on the phenomenon of *intermittent reinforcement* were conducted in Pavlov's laboratory, thereby anticipating modern and more extensive investigations of the topic of *schedules of reinforcement* (Ferster & Skinner, 1957; Skinner, 1969). As judged by evaluation studies and surveys, Pavlov ranks high—along with Freud and Wundt—as a major influence in American psychology today (Coan & Zagona, 1962; Roeckelein, 1995). See also ASSOCIATION, LAWS OF; INHIBITION, LAWS OF; LEARNING THEORIES.

REFERENCES

Whytt, R. (1763). *An essay on the vital and other involuntary motions of animals.* Edinburgh: Balfour.

Sechenov, I. (1863/1965). *Refleksy golovnogo mozga.* St. Petersburg. Translated as *Reflexes of the brain.* Cambridge: MIT Press.

Pavlov, I. (1902). *The work of the digestive glands.* London: Griffin.

Thorndike, E. (1911). *Animal intelligence.* New York: Macmillan.

Dunlap, K. (1922). *The elements of scientific psychology.* St. Louis: Mosby.

Seashore, C. (1923). *Introduction to psychology.* New York: Macmillan.

Pavlov, I. (1927). *Conditioned reflexes.* New York: Dover.

Bekhterev, V. (1928). *General principles of human reflexology, an introduction to the objective study of personality.* New York: International.

Hollingworth, H. (1928). *Psychology: Its facts and principles.* New York: Appleton.

Miller, S., & Konorski, J. (1928). Sur une forme particuliero des reflexes conditionnels. *C. R. Soc. Bio. Paris, 99,* 1155–1157.

Pavlov, I. (1928a). *Lectures on conditioned reflexes.* New York: International.

Pavlov, I. (1928b). *Twenty-five years of objective study of the higher nervous activity (behavior) of animals.* Dover, NH: Pinter.

Pavlov, I. (1932). The reply of a physiologist to psychologists. *Psy. Rev., 39,* 91–127.

Loucks, R. (1933). An appraisal of Pavlov's systematization of behavior from the experimental standpoint. *J. Com. Psy., 15,* 1–47.

Warren, H. (Ed.) (1934). *Dictionary of psychology.* Cambridge, MA: Houghton Mifflin.

Konorski, J., & Miller, S. (1937). On two types of conditioned reflex. *J. Gen. Psy., 16,* 264–272.

Schlosberg, H. (1937). The relationship between success and the laws of conditioning. *Psy. Rev., 44,* 379–394.

Skinner, B. F. (1937). Two types of conditioned reflex: A reply to Konorski and Miller. *J. Gen. Psy., 16,* 272–279.

Skinner, B. F. (1938). *The behavior of organisms: An experimental analysis.* Englewood Cliffs, NJ: Prentice-Hall.

Woodworth, R. (1938). *Experimental psychology.* New York: Holt.

Hilgard, E., & Marquis, D. (1940). *Conditioning and learning.* New York: Appleton-Century-Crofts.

Mowrer, O. H. (1947). On the dual nature of learning—a reinterpretation of "conditioning" and "problem-solving." *Harv. Ed. Rev., 17,* 102–148.

Ferster, C., & Skinner, B. F. (1957). *Schedules of reinforcement*. New York: Appleton-Century-Crofts.

Kimble, G. (1961). *Hilgard and Marquis' conditioning and learning*. New York: Appleton-Century-Crofts.

Reynolds, G. (1961). Behavioral contrast. *J. Exp. Anal. Beh., 4*, 57–71.

Coan, R., & Zagona, S. (1962). Contemporary ratings of psychological theorists. *Psy. Rec., 12*, 315–322.

Peters, R. (Ed.) (1965). *Brett's history of psychology*. Cambridge: MIT Press.

Razran, G. (1965). Russian physiologists' psychology and American experimental psychology. *Psy. Bull., 63*, 42–64.

Hilgard, E., & Bower, G. (1966). *Theories of learning*. New York: Appleton-Century-Crofts.

Rescorla, R. (1969). Pavlovian conditioned inhibition. *Psy. Bull., 72*, 77–94.

Skinner, B. F. (1969). *Contingencies of reinforcement: A theoretical analysis*. New York: Appleton-Century-Crofts.

Rescorla, R., & Wagner, A. (1972). A theory of Pavlovian conditioning: Variations in the effectiveness of reinforcement and nonreinforcement. In A. Black & W. Prokasy (Eds.), *Classical conditioning: II. Current research and theory*. New York: Appleton-Century-Crofts.

Rescorla, R. (1976a) Pavlovian excitatory and inhibitory conditioning. In W. Estes (Ed.), *Handbook of learning and cognitive processes*. Vol. 2. Hillsdale, NJ: Erlbaum.

Rescorla, R. (1976b). Stimulus generalization: Some predictions from a model of Pavlovian conditioning. *J. Exp. Psy.: Anim. Beh. Proc., 2*, 88–96.

Bower, G., & Hilgard, E. (1981). *Theories of learning*. Englewood Cliffs, NJ: Prentice-Hall.

Coon, D. (1982). Eponymy, obscurity, Twitmyer, and Pavlov. *J. Hist. Beh. Sci., 18*, 255–262.

Wickens, D. (1994). Classical conditioning. In R. J. Corsini (Ed.), *Ency. Psy.* New York: Wiley.

Roeckelein, J. (1995). Naming in psychology: Analyses of citation counts and eponyms. *Psy. Rep., 77*, 163–174.

PERCEPTION (I. GENERAL), THEORIES OF. The area in psychology called *perception* refers to the study of the *central* processes that give coherence and unity to sensory (*peripheral* processes) input. Involved in these processes are physical, physiological, neurological, sensory, cognitive, and affective components of behavior. *Theories of perception*, much like *theories of learning*, are very far-reaching and encompass nearly every area of psychology. Most *theories of perception* start with the recognition that what is perceived is not uniquely determined by physical stimulation but is a complex process dependent on a number of other factors, such as *attention*—focusing on selectively chosen stimuli (e.g., the *Broadbent filtering effect*—the phenomenon, in a dichotic listening task, of not hearing the message in the unattended ear when the hearer complies with instructions to listen only to the message presented to the other ear; Zusne, 1987); *constancy*—stabilizing of the perceptual world despite changes in sensory input; *motivation*—physical and psychological drive level of the individual; *or-*

ganization—sensory elements are grouped and ordered into coherent wholes (see Wheeler's, 1930, *organismic laws*—where parts of behavior are accounted for in terms of the whole; and his *law of individuation*—the principle that parts come into existence from wholes through a process of individuation; cf: *distributive law*—the principle that an operation performed on a complex whole affects each part of this complex in the same way as if performed on that part separately; Warren, 1934); *set*—cognitive and emotional predispositions toward a stimulus array; *learning*—the degree to which perceptions are acquired from experience versus innate origins and the degree that learning adapts to, and changes, perception; *distortion/hallucination*—misperceptions due to emotional feelings, drugs, lack of sleep, sensory deprivation, stress, and mental disorders that may be classified as *top-down processes*; and *illusion*—normal perceptions concerning unpredictability and information often due to conflicting sensory cues (e.g., the *shrinkage* illusion of the *Ansbacher effect*, also called the *Ansbacher shrinkage effect/H. C. Brown shrinkage effect*—a lighted arc placed at the edge of a disc and rotated in a dark room will appear to be shorter the greater is the velocity of the rotation; see also the *texture* illusion of the *Spillman–Redies effect*, the *geometric* illusion of the *Bourdon effect/illusion*; Zusne, 1987; the *subliminal* illusion of the *Poetzl effect*, and the *movement* illusion of the *Ternus phenomenon*; Sutherland, 1996). One major theoretical approach, the *classical theory*, has dominated perceptual inquiry for many years (Hochberg, 1994). The *classical theory* began with the physiological studies of the German physiologist Johannes Muller (1801–1858) concerning the division of sensory experience into the modalities of vision, touch, and smell. Muller argued that the organized perceived world is actually composed of separate channels of experience, each of which depends on the action of some specific and identifiable part of the sensory nervous system (Muller, 1842). Later, the German physicist Hermann von Helmholtz (1821–1894) subdivided the sensory modalities themselves into elementary sensations, each of which reflected the normal activity from the stimulation of specific receptor nerve cells by particular physical energies (Helmholtz, 1856). The German physicist and psychologist Gustav Fechner (1801–1887) developed the classical psychophysical methods to measure the effects on experience of small stimulation differences, which provided the tools for perceptual analysis in sensory research (Fechner, 1860/1966). The analytic approach of these early researchers accounted for many major features of sensory experience. For example, Helmholtz's *visual perceptual theory* (which receives little support today) related the three fundamental visual sensations of red, green, and violet to the physical aspect of long-, middle-, and short-wavelengths of light, respectively. Helmholtz (1863) also proposed a *perceptual theory of audition* (which also receives little support today), in which the fundamental sensations for differences in pitch were due to differing receptor cell activity and responses made to the frequency components of sound waves entering the ear. The early studies in the physiology of sensation and perception continue today as a vital area devoted to sensory research, principally in the domains of visual and auditory science. The *classical perceptual theory* of the 1800s set the stage for subsequent investigations of perceptual experience involving the properties of things and events such as shape, brightness, distance, movement, and space (cf: *Luneburg's theory of visual space*—a geometric theory that binocular visual space, in contrast to physical space, is best described as a Riemannian space of constant Gaussian curvature; Zusne, 1987). In one case, the perception of *three-dimensional space* posed a problem to early researchers because three dimensions are not directly specified by the two-dimensional array of light that enters the eye (cf: the *Hess effect* and the *Pulfrich phenomenon/effect*—a visual stereoscopic effect in which a regularly swinging pendulum will be perceived to follow an elliptical path when viewed monocularly through a medium-density filter; and the *Mach–Dvorak phenomenon*— stereoscopic depth perceived as a result of delaying the presentation of a moving object to one eye as compared to the other; see, also, the *panum phenomenon*— an effect observed in the stereoscopic image produced by three equal, parallel lines, two of them close together and presented to one eye, the third line presented to the other eye; if the single line is made to overlap one of the other two lines, the combined line will appear to be closer to the viewer than the other line in the pair; Warren, 1934; Zusne, 1987; Reber, 1995; Sutherland, 1996). A traditional *theory of depth perception* is that clues about the third dimension of space are provided by an *unconscious inference* process concerning nearness and farness of objects in the world. This viewpoint emphasizes that, because the use of such cues involves no conscious process, depth clues are available in a direct manner rather than being mediated by conscious deduction. Cues for depth, such as linear/size perspective, interposition, aerial perspective, and atmospheric conditions of haze, were known and used by painters for generations before research in perception took place. In the early *classical perceptual theory*, it was assumed that depth perception was achieved through the learned association of such visual cues with memories of previous muscle-stretch and touch sensations (cf: Thorndike, 1899; Gibson & Walk, 1960, also found that some organisms respond to visual depth cues without previous visual experience). Thus, concerning space perception at least, there appears to be a need to identify some innate visual mechanisms for depth response where a fundamental revision of the *classical theory* is required (Hochberg, 1994). Three other major sets of phenomena present problems for the *classical perceptual theory*: constancies, illusions, and perceptual organization. The most systematic opposition to the *classical theory of perception* was *Gestalt theory*, which argued that the configuration (''gestalt'') of the stimulating energies, not the energies themselves, is the essential stimulus attribute to which the nervous system responds (cf: *reorganization theory*, which states that the primary process involved in *learning* is the altering of existing mental structures and is commonly found in opposition to *associationistic theory*, which holds that structural reorganization is not necessary in learning new responses; Reber, 1995; cf: also the *Gelb phenomenon/effect*—where a spinning black wheel illuminated by a circle of light in a dark room looks white, but looks blacker if a white piece of paper is put into the light just in front of it; the effect suggests that brightness constancy is, in part, determined by the gradients of luminance between neighboring surfaces; and the *Kardos effect*—the phenomenon concerning brightness constancy where a white rotating disc exactly covered by a shadow looks dark gray or black; Sutherland, 1996; see also the *Fuchs phenomenon* for other perceptual effects; Zusne, 1987). The Gestalt *laws of perceptual organization*—such as figure-ground, proximity, similarity (also called the *law of equality*; Reber, 1995), and so on—presented relevant demonstrations of perceptual experience, even though they were not quantitatively or objectively studied (cf: *law of precision*, which states that organization occurs in such a way that its products, namely, the whole field—perceptual, ideational, and behavioral—become as well articulated as possible; Warren, 1934). Attempts to formulate a theory from the Gestaltist demonstrations focused on radically different notions of the nervous system and attempts to objectively formulate the *laws of perceptual organization* (largely based on the *principle of simplicity*) have not flourished. Current versions of the *classical theory* can better explain the Gestaltist demonstrations than can *Gestalt theory* or its successors (Hochberg, 1994). An early view from *classical theory* concerning the illusions and constancies is that they both are aspects of one process, and *Helmholtz's theory of unconscious inference*, based on "unnoticed sensations," has been revitalized (e.g., Rock, 1977), even though the theory is difficult to test. Theories of *direct perception* and the *constancy hypothesis* (Reber, 1995)—the notion that perceptions are direct responses to physical properties of the environment (e.g., Gibson, 1950; cf: *Gibson effect*—vertical lines appear curved when viewed through a wedge prism; the apparent curvature diminishes with prolonged viewing, but when the prism is removed, vertical lines appear again but curved in the opposite direction; Zusne, 1987)—make Helmholtz's inference-like mental processes and the concept of *unconscious inference* unnecessary (cf: the *constructivist theory of perception*, which holds that perceptual experience is more than a direct response to stimulation; Reber, 1995). However, while a few mathematical analyses of the direct theoretical approach have been offered (e.g., explanation of the phenomenon of *motion parallax*; Hay, 1966), there is no good evidence to completely support the *direct perception theory*, and the *classical theory* concerning explanations of various constancy/illusion phenomena remains strong among contemporary perceptual psychologists. Three avenues of research have been preeminent in providing opportunities to test and amend the *classical theory*: infant perception/perceptual development (e.g., Walk, 1981); perceptual adaptation/rearranged sensory input (e.g., Kornheiser, 1976); and complex sensory channels (e.g., Sekuler & Ganz, 1963). Hochberg (1994) reviewed evidence concerning mental structure and inference in perception and concluded that what we perceive is not fully determined by direct sensory response to object properties alone but requires the addition of cognitive factors as well—as the *classical theory* proposed—to understand completely the perceptual process. See also APPARENT MOVEMENT, PRINCIPLES/THEORIES OF; ATTENTION, LAWS/PRINCI-

PLES/THEORIES OF; FECHNER'S LAW; GESTALT THEORY/LAWS; LEARNING THEORIES/LAWS; MIND/MENTAL SET, LAW OF; PERCEPTION (II. COMPARATIVE APPRAISAL), THEORIES OF; TOP-DOWN PROCESSING/THEORIES; UNCONSCIOUS INFERENCE, DOCTRINE OF; YOUNG–HELMHOLTZ COLOR VISION THEORY.

REFERENCES

Muller, J. (1842). *Elements of physiology*. London: Taylor & Walton.

Helmholtz, H. von (1856). *Handbuch der physiologischen optik*. Leipzig: Voss.

Fechner, G. (1860/1966). *Elements of psychophysics*. D. Howes & E. G. Boring (Eds.) New York: Holt, Rinehart, & Winston.

Helmholtz, H. von (1863). *Lehre von dem tonempfindungen als grundlage fur die theorie der musik*. Leipzig: Voss.

Hering, E. (1878/1964). *Outlines of a theory of the light sense*. Cambridge: Harvard University Press.

Thorndike, E. (1899). The instinctive reactions of young chicks. *Psy. Rev., 6*, 282–291.

Wheeler, R. (1930). The individual and the group: An application of eight organismic laws. In R. Wheeler, *Readings in psychology*. New York: Crowell.

Warren, H. (Ed.) (1934). *Dictionary of psychology*. Cambridge, MA: Houghton Mifflin.

Gibson, J. (1950). *The perception of the visual world*. Boston: Houghton Mifflin.

O'Neill, W. (1958). Basic issues in perceptual theory. *Psy. Rev., 65*, 348–361.

Gibson, E., & Walk, R. (1960). The "visual cliff." *Sci. Amer., 202*, 64–71.

Sekuler, R., & Ganz, L. (1963). Aftereffects of seen motion with a stabilized retinal image. *Science, 139*, 419–420.

Hay, J. (1966). Optical motions and space perception: An extension of Gibson's analysis. *Psy. Rev., 73*, 550–565.

Avant, L., & Helson, H. (1973). Theories of perception. In B. Wolman (Ed.), *Handbook of general psychology*. Englewood Cliffs, NJ: Prentice-Hall.

Carterette, E., & Friedman, M. (Eds.) (1974). *Handbook of perception*. New York: Academic Press.

Kornheiser, A. (1976). Adaptation to laterally displaced vision: A review. *Psy. Bull., 83*, 783–816.

Gibson, J. (1977). The theory of affordances. In R. Shaw & J. Bransford (Eds.), *Perceiving, acting, and knowing: Toward an ecological psychology*. Hillsdale, NJ: Erlbaum.

Rock, I. (1977). In defense of unconscious inference. In W. Epstein (Ed.), *Stability and constancy in visual perception*. New York: Wiley.

Walk, R. (1981). *Perceptual development*. Monterey, CA: Brooks/Cole.

Zusne, L. (1987). *Eponyms in psychology*. Westport, CT: Greenwood Press.

Hochberg, J. (1994). Perception. In R. J. Corsini (Ed.), *Ency. Psy.* New York: Wiley.

Walk, R. (1994a). Illusions. In R. J. Corsini (Ed.), *Ency. Psy.* New York: Wiley.

Walk, R. (1994b). Perceptual organization. In R. J. Corsini (Ed.), *Ency. Psy.* New York: Wiley.

Reber, A. (1995). *The Penguin dictionary of psychology*. New York: Penguin Books.

Sutherland, S. (1996). *The international dictionary of psychology*. New York: Crossroad.

PERCEPTION (II. COMPARATIVE APPRAISAL), THEORIES OF. The American social psychologist Floyd Henry Allport (1890–1978) reviewed and critiqued the major *theories of perception* and, subsequently, proposed his own *perceptual theory of structure (event-structure* or *enestruence*), which held that social structure had no anatomical or physical basis but consisted of cycles of events that return upon themselves to complete and maintain the cycle (Allport, 1955). Allport appraised the following 13 *theories of perception*: core-context, Gestalt, topological field, cell-assembly, sensory-tonic field, set and motor adjustments, adaptation-level, probabilistic functionalism, transactional functionalism, directive state, hypotheses, behavior, and cybernetic theories. The *core-context theory* of perception (Titchener, 1909; Boring, 1946) states that a perception consists in its earlier stage of three items: a number of sensations consolidated into a group under the laws of attention and the special properties of sensory connection; images from past experiences that supplement the sensations; and meaning (i.e., "context;" cf: *atmosphere/context effects* and *context theory*, which maintain that all behavior must be analyzed within the context in which it occurs; Reber, 1995). Allport (1955) considered the *core-context theory* to be parsimonious and in agreement with the limited range of facts used to support it; though the theory centered on "object meaning," it had a potentiality for generalization. The theory was found weak, however, in logical consistency and explanatory value. Its chief merit was that it recognized the part played in perception by "object" and "situational" meaning. The *Gestalt theory of perception* (Wertheimer, 1912; Kohler, 1929; Koffka, 1935) employs basic principles such as form-concept/isomorphism; field/forces; flexibility/transformation/transposition; symmetry/goodness of form; and organization. Kohler (1929) proposed the *dynamic theory* ("psychic dynamism"), according to which physiological processes are determined by dynamic conditions (e.g., by forces involved in the central nervous system field as a whole) rather than by structural conditions (e.g., neural structures and connections). The *dynamic theory* has been contrasted with the *machine theory*, which states that physiological processes are machinelike and determined by constant conditions (e.g., by neural topography) rather than by dynamic conditions (Warren, 1934). Wertheimer (1912) proposed the *short-circuit theory*, which states that phenomenal movement—such as the *phi phenomenon*—is due to a short-circuit between the regions of the brain excited by each stimulus, thereby giving rise to a new structured unity (Warren, 1934). Six major principles cover most of the *Gestalt laws*, demonstrations, and experimental exhibits; however, no fewer than 114 *laws of gestalten* have been formulated by various writers (cf: Helson, 1933), but they have been edited down to a list of 14 (Boring, 1942). The *Gestalt theory* is essentially consistent, parsimonious, and based on a large number of experiments that support its phenomenological generalizations. However, concerning *brain-field theory*, the Gestalt approach has difficulties with the facts of brain physiology and also has problems with some genetic and clinical observations (Allport, 1955). The *topological field theory* of perception (e.g., Lewin, 1936) is an offshoot of the Gestalt movement in psychology, and, while it makes use of *fields* and related Gestalt principles, it has no direct concern about physiological bases or *isomorphism* (i.e., the hypothesis that there is a point-by-point relationship between the two systems of excitatory fields in the cortex and conscious experience or between the perception of the stimulus and the brain). *Lewin's field theory* is short on logical consistency because it does not discriminate well between phenomenological and physicalistic data (Allport, 1955). The *cell-assembly theory* of perception, also called *Hebb's theory of perceptual learning* (Hebb, 1949), holds that perception is not an innate process but has to be learned. The theory maintains that a particular perception depends on the excitation of particular brain cells (*cell assemblies*) at some point in the central nervous system. The *cell assembly* is Hebb's basic unit of perception and represents the physiological basis of the simplest percept. Complex perceptions (*phase sequences*) are formed out of the basic assemblies by the principles of mutual facilitation in conduction and consolidation in timing. The *cell-assembly theory* is fairly logical, parsimonious, and built on facts of neurophysiology, genetic development, and brain pathology. However, the theory has trouble with the concept of *equipotentiality* (Lashley, 1929) and does not handle well the aspects of dimension, constancy, and frame of reference (Allport, 1955). The *sensory-tonic field theory* of perception (Werner & Wapner, 1949, 1952) deals with the relationship between *tonic* events (e.g., changes in postural/muscular tension) and *sensory* events (e.g., a conscious experience such as a sensory quality). The attempt of *sensory-tonic theory* was to show that tonic factors interact with sensory factors in perception and that a "field" is present in which the body and the perceived object interact. The *sensory-tonic theory* is well supported by experimental findings, but it fails to explain the interrelation of sensory and tonic factors in a clear and logical manner (Allport, 1955). The *set and motor adjustments theory* of perception holds that *set* (i.e., a disposition to respond in a particular way; includes perceptual set, or *Einstellung*, and task-oriented set, or *Aufgabe*) and the actual behaviors that prepare the organism provide a basis for understanding the motor aspects of perception (Freeman, 1939). The *set and motor adjustments theory* is logical, unified, and based on experimental findings and is in general agreement with motor physiology; however, the theory fails to unite exteroceptive sensory and motor elements in the perceptual process (Allport, 1955; cf: an early, curious, and nonperceptual principle concerning the relationship between sensory and motor events is the *law of dynamogenesis*, which states that any change in sensory stimulation has a corresponding effect in altering muscular activity or tension; Baldwin, 1894; Triplett, 1898). The *adaptation-level theory* of perception (Helson, 1948) is a formulation of sensory-context effects that maintains that the neutral, adapted background provides a standard against which new stimuli are perceived (cf: the *law of relativity*, which states that an experience is understood only in its relation to other experiences, as when the visual localization of an object depends on the perception of the relation of the object to the frame of reference; Warren, 1934). The theory has been extended from explanations in the area of sensory processes to those of attitudes and attitude change. The theory states that the concept of *adaptation-level* represents a weighted geometric mean of all the stimuli that have been judged on a particular dimension. The *adaptation-level theory* is logical, supported by experimental facts, and has good generalizability and parsimony. However, the theory does not seem applicable to the phenomena of configuration, and it falls short in interpreting the non-quantitative aspects of perceptual aggregates, including object and situational meaning (Allport, 1955). The *probabilistic functionalism theory* of perception (e.g., Brunswik, 1956) argues that the veridical distal relationship with objects in the environment is dependent on the statistical validity of the cue-to-object relationships where the attainment of distal objects is never better than an approximate or "probable" achievement. The theory stresses that perception is a process of discovering which aspects of the stimulus provide the most useful/functional cues. The *transactional theory* of perception (e.g., Ittelson, 1952; Kilpatrick, 1952; Ames, 1953) is based on the notion that perception results from acquired, but unconscious, assumptions about the environment, represented as probabilities of transactions occurring within it. Thus, the relationship between *probabilistic theory* and *transactional theory* is very close: both deal with the "dimensional" aspect of perception, both are "molar," both rely on past experience, both give a strategic position to cues and their probabilistic weighting, both involve unconscious inferences or judgments of the perceiver, and both hold an intermediate ground between the stimulus object and some activity of the organism. The main difference, on the other hand, between the theories is that whereas *probabilistic theory* is concerned with phenomenological "attainment" of perceptual objects, *transactional functionalism* contains a more specific statement of the perceptual significance of action and purpose (Allport, 1955). The *directive-state theory* of perception (e.g., Bruner & Postman, 1947) divides the determinants of perception into two contrasting categories: the *autochthonous* (structural) aspects, including the stimulus and effects of stimulation on the receptors, afferent neurons, and sensory cortical areas, and the *behavioral* (motivational) "New Look" aspects, including the needs, tensions, values, defenses, and emotions of the person (cf: the *fashioning effect* of *role theory* whereby the role adopted by a person influences both that person's behavior and his or her self-perceptions; Reber, 1995). Corresponding to these are two contrasting programs of experiment and theory: the *formal* and the *functional*. Taken together, the behavioral determinants form a *central directive state* where they may be viewed as independent variables in an experimental setting. Experimental evidence (which has not gone unchallenged) for the *directive-state theory* derives from six areas: the effect of bodily needs on what is perceived; the effect of reward and punishment on perceptual content; the influence of values on speed of object-recognition; effects of needs and values on the dimensionality of the percept; personality as a perceptual determinant; and the effect on perception of the emotionally disturbing nature of the stimulus-object. The *directive-state theory*, while it opened a new field of dynamic possibilities, does not offer enough agreement with the available facts; however, the theory does show the importance of taking individual cases into account (Allport, 1955). The *hypothesis-theory* of perception (e.g., Tolman & Brunswik, 1935) is a reformulation of the *directive-state theory* and states that all cognitive processes, whether they take the form of perceiving, thinking, or recalling, represent *hypotheses* that are usually unconscious and that the organism sets up in a given situation. Such hypotheses require "answers" in the form of further experience that will either confirm or disprove them (for the same notion in a *learning* context, see Restle, 1962). Adjustment of the organism to the environment proceeds by such a process of hypothesis confirmation or rejection. The *hypothesis theory* is in accord with experimental findings and draws together many of the discordant results of the *directive-state* experiments and moves generally in the direction of a unified theory. However, it is deficient in explanatory principles for hypothesis checking, stimulus-transformation, monopoly, and similar concepts/processes (Allport, 1955). The *behavior theory* of perception (e.g., Hull, 1943; Spence, 1951) is based on the *association* or *S-R* notion of the linkage of a stimulus or stimulus-pattern to a reaction and the gradual strengthening of such a connection. Learning involves the increasing of *habit strength* where the strengthening takes place through repeated trials accompanied by reinforcement (need-state or drive-reduction). Another notion of learning (e.g., Tolman, 1932) has the organism learn *meanings* and *relationships* rather than the specific movements to be made in a situation (the *field* or *S-S* type of theory). The *S-S* type of learning is related to perception by the similarity in acquisition of elements: in learning, cognitions are expected suddenly, and in perception, a percept is a very brief, all-or-none event as well. Thus, the cognitive and other aspects of *S-S learning theory*, particularly, seem to fit a phenomenological/perceptual frame of reference better than a physicalistic/S-R framework; however, *S-S, field*, or *cognition-like theories* have not succeeded in becoming general for all the phenomena of perception. Some of the *S-S theories* have almost completely discounted the evidence that past experience is an important determinant of perceptual behavior. The *S-S learning models* of perception have been lacking in explicit reference, explanatory value, parsimony, and generalizability (Allport, 1955). The *cybernetic-theory* of perception (see Wiener, 1948; Von Foerster, 1950–1952) is based on the modern development of technological communication and control systems (the term *cybernetic* means "helmsman," or "one who steers"). The specific contributions of *cybernetics* to the study of perception are relatively few, but the following *cybernetic* concepts/principles may prove fruitful to perceptual theory ultimately: *open systems* (involving irreversibility, steady state, negative entropy), *information, coding, feedback loops, negative feedback, oscillation, scanning, teleological mechanisms*, and *repeating circuits*. The correspondence between some *cybernetic* concepts and perceptual/imagery phenomena is good, but other notions such as digitalization of information in the nervous system, time limitations of the reverberating circuit, and scanning device seem more dubious. On the whole, however, the *cybernetics theory* has contributed valuable structural ideas and suggestions for the *theory of open systems* and neurophysiology (Allport, 1955). After appraising the major theories of perception, Allport (1955) concluded that most of the theories contain certain common generalizations such as internal relatedness, self-closedness/circularity, and space/time building, and he asserted that such generalizations represent the most substantial insights into the nature of the perceptual act and the best explanations of why things appear as they do to the perceiver. See also ALLPORT'S THEORY OF ENESTRUENCE; CONTROL SYSTEMS/THEORY; GESTALT THEORY/LAWS; HELSON'S ADAPTATION-LEVEL THEORY; HULL'S LEARNING THEORY; INFORMATION/INFORMATION-PROCESSING THEORY; LEWIN'S FIELD THEORY; PARSIMONY, LAW/PRINCIPLE OF; PERCEPTION (I. GENERAL), THEORIES OF; SPENCE'S THEORY; TOLMAN'S THEORY.

REFERENCES

Baldwin, J. (1894). *Handbook of psychology*. New York: Holt.

Triplett, N. (1898). The dynamogenic factors in peacemaking and competition. *Amer. J. Psy., 9*, 507–533.

Titchener, E. (1909). *Experimental psychology and the thought processes*. New York: Macmillan.

Wertheimer, M. (1912). Experimentelle studien uber das sehen von bewegung. *Z. Psy., 61*, 161–265.

Kohler, W. (1929). *Gestalt psychology*. New York: Liveright.

Lashley, K. (1929). *Brain mechanisms and intelligence*. Chicago: University of Chicago Press.

Tolman, E. (1932). *Purposive behavior in animals and men*. New York: Century.

Helson, H. (1933). The fundamental propositions of gestalt psychology. *Psy. Rev., 40*, 13–32.

Warren, H. (Ed.) (1934). *Dictionary of psychology*. Cambridge, MA: Houghton Mifflin.

Koffka, K. (1935). *Principles of gestalt psychology*. New York: Harcourt.

Tolman, E., & Brunswik, E. (1935). The organism and the causal texture of the environment. *Psy. Rev., 42*, 43–77.

Lewin, K. (1936). *Principles of topological psychology*. New York: McGraw-Hill.

Freeman, G. (1939). The problem of set. *Amer. J. Psy., 52*, 16–30.

Boring, E. G. (1942). *Sensation and perception in the history of experimental psychology*. New York: Appleton-Century-Crofts.

Hull, C. (1943). *Principles of behavior: An introduction to behavior theory*. New York: Appleton-Century-Crofts.

Boring, E. G. (1946). The perception of objects. *Amer. J. Physics, 14*, 99–107.

Bruner, J., & Postman, L. (1947). Tension and tension-release as organizing factors in perception. *J. Pers., 15*, 300–308.

Helson, H. (1948). Adaptation-level as a basis for a quantitative theory of frames of reference. *Psy. Rev., 55*, 297–313.

Wiener, N. (1948). *Cybernetics*. New York: Wiley.

Hebb, D. (1949). *The organization of behavior*. New York: Wiley.

Werner, H., & Wapner, S. (1949). Sensory-tonic field theory of perception. *J. Pers., 18*, 88–107.

Von Foerster, H. (Ed.) (1950–1952). *Cybernetics.* New York: Josiah Macy, Jr. Foundation.

Spence, K. (1951). Theoretical interpretations of learning. In C. Stone (Ed.), *Comparative psychology.* New York: Prentice-Hall.

Ittelson, W. (1952). *The Ames demonstrations in perception.* Princeton, NJ: Princeton University Press.

Kilpatrick, F. (Ed.) (1952). *Human behavior from the transactional point of view.* Princeton, NJ: Institute for Associated Research.

Werner, H., & Wapner, S. (1952). Toward a general theory of perception. *Psy. Rev., 59,* 324–338.

Ames, A. (1953). Reconsideration of the origin and nature of perception. In S. Ratner (Ed.), *Vision and action.* New Brunswick, NJ: Rutgers University Press.

Allport, F. (1955). *Theories of perception and the concept of structure.* New York: Wiley.

Brunswik, E. (1956). *Perception and the representative design of psychological experiments.* Berkeley: University of California Press.

Restle, F. (1962). The selection of strategies in cue learning. *Psy. Rev., 69,* 329–343.

Reber, A. (1995). *The Penguin dictionary of psychology.* New York: Penguin Books.

PERCEPTUAL ORGANIZATION, LAWS OF. See GESTALT THEORY/LAWS.

PERIPHERAL THEORIES OF HUNGER. See HUNGER, THEORIES OF.

PERKY EFFECT. See IMAGERY/MENTAL IMAGERY, THEORIES OF.

PERMISSIVE AMINE THEORY OF DEPRESSION. See DEPRESSION, THEORIES OF.

PERSEVERATION THEORY. See INTERFERENCE THEORIES OF FORGETTING.

PERSONALISTIC THEORY OF HISTORY. See NATURALISTIC THEORY OF HISTORY.

PERSONALITY-JOB FIT THEORY. See ORGANIZATIONAL/INDUSTRIAL/SYSTEMS THEORY.

PERSONALITY THEORIES. A *theory of personality* is a set of unproven speculations about various aspects of human behavior that often invites argument from research-oriented psychologists who decry the lack of quantification and the proliferation of untestable hypotheses found in most personality theories, while personality theorists, in turn, criticize the laboratory approach toward understanding behavior as being too artificial and trivial (Ewen, 1994). Hall and Lindzey (1978) discuss in detail what personality is, and what a theory is, what a theory of personality is and assess over 15 major personality theories (see especially, Table 17.1, p. 692). The personality theorist typically devises a variety of interrelated concepts, constructs, and terms that provide convenient descriptions of behavior and establish a framework for organizing substantial amounts of data. However, the definition of the term *personality* itself seems to be so resistant to a simple consensual statement and so broad in usage that most psychology textbooks (other than textbooks on personality theories) use it strategically as the title of a chapter and then write freely about it without incurring any of the definitional or positivistic responsibilities attached to it (cf: *implicit theory of personality*, which refers to the unconsciously held ideas that most laypeople have about the personalities of others, where they establish a complex web of assumptions about the traits and behaviors of others and assume that they will act in accordance with those assumptions; Reber, 1995). One approach toward understanding the term *personality* is to examine it according to the role it has played in psychological theory, rather than to list the numerous definitions. Thus, the following roles, or theory-categories, of personality may be cited: (1) *type theories*—individuals are described and classified based on a pattern of traits or other dispositional characteristics (e.g., the ancient Greek physician Hippocrates hypothesized the four basic temperament types of sanguine, choleric, melancholic, and phlegmatic; W. Sheldon proposed personality characteristics as related to the three body types or "somatotypes" of endomorph, mesomorph, and ectomorph; C. Jung classified individuals as to introvert versus extravert types; cf: Coan, 1994); (2) *trait theories* assume that personality may be described as a compendium of particular ways ("traits") and dispositions of behaving, thinking, feeling, and reacting (e.g., G. Allport's *cardinal, central,* and *secondary* traits; the factor analytic approach of R. B. Cattell, who identified 16 basic dimensions as the "core" of personality; and H. Eysenck's approach of two fundamental dimensions—introversion versus extraversion and stability versus unstability—as the core personality; cf: the current *big five model* of personality traits that identifies the basic five factors in personality as extroversion, agreeableness, conscientiousness, neuroticism, and openness to experience; Digman, 1990); (3) *psychodynamic/psychoanalytic theories*, which characterize personality by the "integration" of systems (such as the manner in which unconscious mental forces interplay with thoughts, feelings, and behavior), the motivation of the individual, and the concern with the development of personality over time (e.g., the personality theories of S. Freud, C. Jung, A. Adler, R. Laing, F. Perls, and the "neo-Freudians" such as E. Fromm, H. S. Sullivan, and K. Horney); (4) *behavioristic theories*, which extend *learning theory* to the study of personality and assess personality from an outside (rather than an internal) perspective by measuring observable behaviors and reinforcement contingencies (e.g., the approaches of J. B. Watson and B. F. Skinner); (5) *social learning/social cognitive theories* (including *situationism* and *interactionism*; Reber, 1995), which examine factors, in addition to external observable behaviors, such as complex social roles, memory, retention processes, modeling, observational learning, and self-regulatory processes as they contribute to the functioning of personality (e.g., the approaches of J. Dollard and N. Miller, A. Bandura, J. Rotter, W. Mischel, A. Staats, H. Eysenck, and J. Wolpe); (6) *humanistic theories* (also called the *phenomenological perspective,* and the *third force* in psychology—so-called because it developed as a reaction to both *psychoanalytic* and *learning* theories) emphasize internal experiences, feelings, thoughts, and the basic self-perceived worth of the individual human being where self-actualization/self-realization are overall goals (e.g., the theories of C. Rogers and A. Maslow). Maddi (1972), Corsini (1977), Hall and Lindzey (1978), Ewen (1980), Schultz (1981), and Pervin (1993, 1996) show the range that personality theorists cover concerning the *core* and *structure* of personality, the *development* and *dynamics* of personality, and the *criteria* of the *healthy personality* (cf: Vinacke, 1994). The contributions that personality theories have made to psychology include insights into dream interpretation, the causes and dynamics of psychopathology, new and creative developments in psychotherapy, facilitation of learning in work and educational settings, expanded methods of literary analysis, and fuller understanding of the nature of religious beliefs and prejudices. Some of the constructs that originated in *personality theory* and have enjoyed widespread acceptance in psychology include the phenomena of the unconscious, parapraxes ("Freudian slips"), anxiety-reducing defense mechanisms, narcissism, transference of emotions, resistance in therapy, anxiety, introversion and extraversion, inferiority and superiority complexes, lifestyle, body language, compensation, identity crisis, intrapsychic conflict, traits, and needs for self-esteem, self-hate, self-actualization, and achievement (Ewen, 1994). General criticisms and evaluations of *personality theory* include Hall and Lindzey's (1978) suggestion that the field of personality would benefit enormously from an increased sophistication in methodology, from more sensitive discrimination between effective literary style and powerful theorizing, from more freedom concerning an obligation to justify theoretical formulations that depart from normative or customary views of behavior, and from avoidance of theoretical "imperialism." Also, Ewen (1994) suggests that too few of the useless constructs in the psychology of personality have been discarded by the theorists who created them, that personality theorists have been far too free with neologisms—that is, coining new words or terms or using existing terms in novel ways (Reber, 1995, observes that using neologisms is often considered to be a creative act of an innovative individual; however, he then suggests that it may also be regarded as a symptom characteristic of certain pathological conditions such as schizophrenia and some forms of aphasia—where excessive use of neologisms incur a waste of time and effort through the unnecessary duplication of ideas—and that the inability of personality theorists to resolve the most fundamental issues (such as the nature of human motivation) may lead people to question the merits of the entire field of personality psychology. On balance, however, despite such assessments, the area of *personality theory* seems to represent a potentially useful contrast and adjunct to the often narrow scope of modern empirical research in psychology. See also ADLER'S THEORY OF PERSONALITY; ALLPORT'S THEORY OF PERSONALITY; ANGYAL'S PERSONALITY THEORY; CATTELL'S THEORY OF PERSONALITY; ERIKSON'S THEORY OF PERSONALITY; EYSENCK'S THEORY OF PERSONALITY; FREUD'S THEORY OF PERSONALITY; FROMM'S THEORY OF PERSONALITY; GALEN'S DOCTRINE OF THE FOUR TEMPERAMENTS; GOLDSTEIN'S ORGANISMIC THEORY; HORNEY'S THEORY OF PERSONALITY; JUNG'S THEORY OF PERSONALITY; KELLY'S PERSONAL CONSTRUCT THEORY; KRETSCHMER'S THEORY OF PERSONALITY; MASLOW'S THEORY OF PERSONALITY; MURPHY'S BIOSOCIAL THEORY; MURRAY'S THEORY OF PERSONALITY; RANK'S THEORY OF PERSONALITY; REICH'S ORGONE/ORGONOMY THEORY; ROGERS' THEORY OF PERSONALITY; SHELDON'S TYPE THEORY; SULLIVAN'S THEORY OF PERSONALITY.

REFERENCES

Maddi, S. (1972). *Personality theories: A comparative analysis.* Homewood, IL: Dorsey.

Corsini, R. J. (Ed.) (1977). *Current personality theories.* Itasca, IL: Peacock.

Hall, C., & Lindzey, G. (1978). *Theories of personality.* New York: Wiley.

Ewen, R. (1980). *An introduction to theories of personality.* New York: Academic Press.

Schultz, D. (1981). *Theories of personality.* Monterey, CA: Brooks/Cole.

Corsini, R. J., & Marsella, A. (Eds.) (1983). *Personality theory, research, and assessment.* Itasca, IL: Peacock.

Pervin, L. (1985). Personality: Current controversies, issues, and directions. *Ann. Rev. Psy., 36,* 83–114.

Digman, J. (1990). Personality structure: Emergence of the five-factor model. *Ann. Rev. Psy., 41,* 417–440.

Pervin, L. (1993). *Personality: Theory and research.* New York: Wiley.

Coan, R. (1994). Personality types. In R. J. Corsini (Ed.), *Ency. Psy.* New York: Wiley.

Ewen, R. (1994). Personality theories. In R. J. Corsini (Ed.), *Ency. Psy.* New York: Wiley.

Vinacke, W. (1994). Healthy personality. In R. J. Corsini (Ed.), *Ency. Psy.* New York: Wiley.

Reber, A. (1995). *The Penguin dictionary of psychology.* New York: Penguin Books.

Pervin, L. (1996). *The science of personality.* New York: Wiley.

PERSON-CENTERED THEORY. See ROGERS' THEORY OF PERSONALITY.

PERSON PERCEPTION. See IMPRESSION FORMATION, THEORIES OF.

PETER PRINCIPLE. See ORGANIZATIONAL/INDUSTRIAL/SYSTEMS THEORY.

PHENOMENALISM, THEORY OF. See MIND-BODY THEORIES.

PHENOMENOLOGICAL (HUMANISTIC) THEORIES OF PERSONAL-ITY. See PERSONALITY THEORIES.

PHI-GAMMA HYPOTHESIS. See NEURAL QUANTUM THEORY.

PHI PHENOMENON. See APPARENT MOVEMENT, PRINCIPLES/THE-ORIES OF; GESTALT THEORY/LAWS; KORTE'S LAWS.

PHONEMIC RESTORATION EFFECT. See WHORF–SAPIR HYPOTHE-SIS/THEORY.

PHOTOCHEMICAL THEORY. See VISION/SIGHT, THEORIES OF.

PHYSICAL CORRELATE THEORY. See STEVENS' POWER LAW.

PHYSIOLOGICAL THEORY OF GENERALIZATION. See GENERALI-ZATION, PRINCIPLE OF.

PIAGET'S PRINCIPLE OF CONSERVATION. See PIAGET'S THEORY OF DEVELOPMENTAL STAGES.

PIAGET'S THEORY OF DEVELOPMENTAL STAGES. The Swiss biol-ogist, psychologist, and genetic epistemologist Jean Piaget (1896–1980) for-mulated a *theory of cognitive development* where development was considered to be a continuous and creative interaction between the child and the environ-ment, and where both the child's body and sensory activities contribute to the development of intelligence and thinking skills (Piaget, 1926, 1929, 1936, 1954, 1970, 1975). According to Piaget, four major and distinct stages occur sequen-tially in development where each child must pass through all four stages. How-ever, the stages are not rigidly fixed in a time sequence, but they can overlap, and the ages are only approximate concerning the appearance of a given stage. Piaget's stages are (1) the *sensorimotor* stage—from birth to approximately two years of age; the infant at this stage is learning to use its body, and all experience is gained immediately through the senses where adequate sensory stimulation is important in developing the child's abilities; the term *practical intelligence* is used to describe behavior at this stage, where the infant learns to act in the world without thinking about what is happening; (2) the *preoperational* stage— occurs from about two to seven years of age during the child's preschool years when she or he can begin to use words—from one/two-word sentences at age two to about eight/ten-word sentences at age five—and can understand that objects can be moved from place to place and maintain an existence even when she or he does not perceive the movements of the object; a more complete understanding of *object permanence* occurs during this period where the child's image-based thinking improves and develops with a capacity called *represen-*

tation; with *representation*, the child can think about some actions when they are not being performed, can think about events when they are not actually happening, and can think of objects when they are not present; (3) the *concrete operations* stage—appears from about 7 to 11 years of age during the child's school age where the child continues to use "intuitive" thought that characterized the preoperational period; during this stage the child also begins to develop an understanding of "concrete operations" such as *conservation* of liquid and addition and multiplication of classes of objects where she or he is able to carry out transformations mentally without carrying them out physically; (4) the *formal operations* stage—occurs from about 11 to 15 years of age during the beginning of adolescence and continues to develop throughout adulthood; the individual at this stage is able to think in a hypothetical way and to carry out systematic tests of the various possible explanations of a phenomenon or a specific event; rational patterns of thinking now develop where symbolic meanings are understood, and abstract mental strategies are possible. While adults may behave at the *sensorimotor* level (e.g., ice-skating or bicycle riding where deep understanding of what is happening is not necessary), the difference between the infant and the adult is that the infant does not yet recognize a distinction between her or his own knowledge or actions and the objects in the world that are acted upon. One of the limitations of the *concrete-operations* stage is that while the child may be able to deal with concrete objects and events in an "actual" situation, she or he cannot deal with such things in a "hypothetical" situation. The development of "higher-order" systems of thought takes time, and all capacities do not develop simultaneously. This fact was viewed by Piaget particularly in the sequential (not simultaneous) development of the different types of *conservation* (i.e., the understanding that quantitative aspects of a set of materials or other stimulus display are not changed or affected by transformations of the display itself): *conservation of number* develops first, followed by *conservation of amount*, followed by *conservation of weight*, and so on. Inasmuch as the *concrete-operations* child cannot yet tie together and coordinate her or his various operational systems, each type of *conservation problem* seems like a new and separate problem to her or him. During the *formal-operations* stage, the child is able to coordinate and integrate two separate dimensions together (such as "weight" and "distance"), as well as to understand and appreciate abstract principles and hypothetical cases, both of which are prerequisite to study in fields such as mathematics, science, ethics, and languages (cf: Piaget & Inhelder, 1956, 1969). According to Piaget, a child's intelligence and understanding of events seem to be *constructed* as a result of encounters between the child and her or his environment where she or he experiences a discrepancy between what is already understood and what the environment is presenting to her or him. Piaget employs the concepts of *schemes, assimilation, accommodation,* and *equilibration* in his discussions of the "construction of an understanding." A *scheme* is an organized action or mental structure that the child holds at a particular time. The terms *assimilation* and *accommodation* refer to the interaction and adjustment that the individual makes between her or his scheme and the objects and events in the world. *Assimilation* is the person's active attempt to apply particular schemes to events, and *accommodation* is the person's adjustment of her or his schemes to the events to be known. The term *equilibriation* was used by Piaget to summarize the joint effects of *assimilation* and *accommodation*. The mind constantly seeks a psychological equilibrium between these two processes, much like the internal physiological processes of the body that naturally seek equilibrium, balance, or homeostasis. The fundamental problem for Piaget's theory, say some developmentalists, and one for which no convincing answer has yet been found is the issue of spontaneity and novelty in the child's development: How does "new" knowledge arise out of a cognitive structure that did not, in any distinctive or discernible way, contain the "new" knowledge, and, once "new" knowledge does emerge, how does it come to be regarded as necessarily connected to other knowledge? (Murray, 1994). A current alternative to *Piaget's theory of cognitive development* is the *information-processing model* (McShane, 1991), which describes the process of taking in, remembering or forgetting, and using information. This approach draws an analogy between the mind and the computer to explain cognitive development. See also ACCOMMODATION, LAW/PRINCIPLE OF; CONSTRUCTIVIST THEORY OF PERCEPTION; PLAY, THEORIES OF.

REFERENCES

Piaget, J. (1926). *The language and thought of the child*. New York: World.

Piaget, J. (1929). *The child's conception of the world*. New York: Littlefield, Adams.

Piaget, J. (1936). *Origins of intelligence*. New York: International Universities Press.

Piaget, J. (1954). *The construction of reality in the child*. New York: Basic Books.

Piaget, J., & Inhelder, B. (1956). *The child's conception of space*. London: Routledge & Kegan Paul.

Piaget, J., & Inhelder, B. (1969). *The psychology of the child*. New York: Basic Books.

Piaget, J. (1970). Piaget's theory. In P. Mussen (Ed.), *Carmichael's manual of child psychology*. New York: Wiley.

Piaget, J. (1975). *L'equilibration des structures cognitives*. Paris: Presses Universitaires de France.

Wadsworth, B. (1978). *Piaget for the classroom teacher*. New York: Longman.

Vuyk, R. (1981). Overview and critique of *Piaget's genetic epistemology 1965–1980*. New York: Academic Press.

McShane, J. (1991). *Cognitive development: An information processing approach*. Oxford: Blackwell.

Murray, F. (1994). Piaget's theory. In R. J. Corsini (Ed.), *Ency. Psy.* New York: Wiley.

PIANO THEORY OF HEARING. See AUDITION/HEARING, THEORIES OF.

PIECEMEAL ACTIVITY, LAW OF. See REDINTEGRATION, PRINCIPLE/LAW OF.

PIPER'S LAW. See RICCO'S/PIPER'S LAW.

PLACEBO EFFECT. See EXPERIMENTER EFFECTS.

PLACE/PLACE-VOLLEY/PLACE-FREQUENCY THEORY. See AUDI-TION/HEARING, THEORIES OF.

PLAY, THEORIES OF. The term *play* has many different meanings. Reber (1995) notes there are at least 55 distinguishable meanings for *play*. At the core of most meanings is the notion that *play* involves diversion or recreation and is an activity not necessarily to be taken seriously. *Play* is activity for its own sake and can be viewed, at least for children, as what they do when allowed to freely choose activity. An early *theory of play*, the *instinctive theory* (Groos, 1898; cf: Bruner, Jolly, & Sylva, 1976), held that play allowed animals to perfect their instinctive skills and asserted that the very existence of youth was largely for the sake of play (cf: *surplus energy theory*, which holds that play activities of human and subhuman young are due to the superabundance of energy in grow-ing organisms; Warren, 1934). A more recent, similar theory, *competence theory* (White, 1959), argues the developmental need for competence or effectiveness in one's environment where play is one form of activity that helps in such development. Another earlier theory, the *recapitulation theory* (Hall, 1904), maintains that play is an evolutionary link between the child and all biological and cultural stages that have preceded human beings on the phylogenetic scale. The *autotelic theory* or *motivational model* (e.g., Berlyne, 1969; cf: Ellis, 1973; Day, 1979) stresses that play is an activity that is done for its own sake with the reward residing in the process itself. Although this approach recognizes ultimate useful outcomes of playful activity, it is concerned mainly with im-mediate satisfactions such as pleasure, fun, spontaneity, and reduction of un-certainty. An opposing viewpoint is that play is a useful activity that enhances the growth and development of an individual toward maturity and adulthood. Consistent with this approach is Piaget's (1963) *stage theory of cognitive de-velopment*, which posits that at each stage of development certain types of play become predominant (cf: *Froebelism* and the use of *instructive play* in kinder-garten; Zusne, 1987). Day (1979) developed a typology that distinguished five forms of play: *exploratory*, *creative*, *diversive*, *mimetic*, and *cathartic play* (see, also, *practice theory of play*, which states that the function of play is to give the organism practice on tasks that it will have to perform in earnest in later life; Sutherland, 1996). Day has also proposed a principle by which all activities can be measured along a *playfulness–workfulness* continuum where the concept of *playfulness* may be a method of comparing all forms of behavior including those observed on jobs and in games with the goal of identifying the motivation to participate in such activities. See also PIAGET'S THEORY OF DEVEL-OPMENTAL STAGES; RECAPITULATION, THEORY/LAW OF.

REFERENCES

Groos, K. (1898). *The play of animals*. New York: Appleton.

Hall, G. S. (1904). *Adolescence: Its psychology and its relations to physiology, anthropology, sociology, sex, crime, religion, and education*. Englewood Cliffs, NJ: Prentice-Hall.

Warren, H. (Ed.) (1934). *Dictionary of psychology*. Cambridge, MA: Houghton Mifflin.

White, R. (1959). Motivation reconsidered: The concept of competence. *Psy. Rev., 66*, 297–333.

Piaget, J. (1963). *The origins of intelligence in children*. New York: Norton.

Berlyne, D. (1969). Laughter, humor, and play. In G. Lindzey & E. Aronson (Eds.), *Handbook of social psychology*. Vol. 3. Reading, MA: Addison-Wesley.

Ellis, M. (1973). *Why people play*. Englewood Cliffs, NJ: Prentice-Hall.

Bruner, J., Jolly, A., & Sylva, K. (Eds.) (1976). *Play—Its role in development and evolution*. New York: Basic Books.

Day, H. (1979). Why people play. *Loisir et Societe, 2*, 129–147.

Sutton-Smith, B. (1980). Children's play: Some sources of play theorizing. In K. Rubin (Ed.), *New directions for child development—children's play*. San Francisco: Jossey-Bass.

Hutt, C. (1981). Toward a taxonomy and conceptual model of play. In H. Day (Ed.), *Advances in intrinsic motivation and aesthetics*. New York: Plenum.

Zusne, L. (1987). *Eponyms in psychology*. Westport, CT: Greenwood Press.

Reber, A. (1995). *The Penguin dictionary of psychology*. New York: Penguin Books.

Sutherland, S. (1996). *The international dictionary of psychology*. New York: Crossroad.

PLEASURE-PAIN, DOCTRINE/THEORY/LAW OF. See HEDONISM, THEORY/LAW OF.

PLEASURE PRINCIPLE. See HEDONISM, THEORY/LAW OF; FREUD'S THEORY OF PERSONALITY.

PLUTCHIK'S MODEL OF EMOTIONS. Robert Plutchik (1962, 1980), like Izard (1984) and Tomkins (1980), independently developed an approach toward the understanding of emotions that is based largely on the *evolutionary theory* of Charles Darwin (1872). Plutchik's model shows how "primary" emotions such as surprise and fear may blend into "secondary" emotions such as awe, as well as indicates how various emotions such as fear, terror, and apprehension may involve one "primary" emotion experienced at several different levels of intensity. Plutchik's model is shown both as a two-dimensional circle and a three-dimensional ellipse so that, when viewed as a two-dimensional circle (analogous to a color *wheel*), it indicates how the eight primary emotions (joy, acceptance, fear, surprise, sadness, disgust, anger, anticipation) may be mixed/ blended to give various secondary emotions (awe, disappointment, remorse, contempt, aggressiveness, optimism, love, submission). When the model is viewed as a three-dimensional ellipse (analogous to a color *spindle*), emotional intensity may be assessed for the primary and secondary emotions. According to Plutchik, diversity in human emotion is a product of variations in emotional intensity, as well as a blending of primary emotions. Each vertical slice in his model is a primary emotion that can be subdivided into emotional expressions of varied intensity ranging from most intense at the top of the model to least intense at the bottom of the model. Plutchik joins the ranks of those *evolutionary theorists of emotion* who assume that evolution equips us with a small number of primary emotions that have proven adaptive and survival value. *Plutchik's model*, when viewed as two- and three-dimensional figures, appears to be a combination of the earlier models of emotion by Schlosberg (1954) and of activation/arousal by Lindsley (1951). See also ACTIVATION/AROUSAL THEORY; EKMAN–FRIESEN'S THEORY OF EMOTIONS; EMOTIONS, THEORIES/LAWS OF; FACIAL-FEEDBACK HYPOTHESIS; IZARD'S THEORY OF EMOTIONS.

REFERENCES

Darwin, C. (1872). *Expression of the emotions in man and animals*. London: Murray.
Lindsley, D. (1951). Emotion. In S. S. Stevens (Ed.), *Handbk. Exp. Psy.* New York: Wiley.
Schlosberg, H. (1954). Three dimensions of emotion. *Psy. Rev., 61,* 81–88.
Plutchik, R. (1962). *The emotions: Facts, theories, and a new model*. New York: Random House.
Plutchik, R. (1980). *Emotion: A psychoevolutionary synthesis*. New York: Harper & Row.
Tomkins, S. (1980). Affect as amplification: Some modifications in theory. In R. Plutchik & H. Kellerman (Eds.), *Emotion, theory, research, and experience*. New York: Academic Press.
Izard, C. (1984). Emotion-cognition relationships and human development. In C. Izard, J. Kagan, & R. Zajonc (Eds.), *Emotions, cognition, and behavior*. Cambridge, England: Cambridge University Press.

POETZL EFFECT. See PERCEPTION (I. GENERAL), THEORIES OF.

PORTER'S LAW. See FERRY–PORTER LAW.

POSTREMITY PRINCIPLE. See GUTHRIE'S THEORY OF BEHAVIOR.

POWER LAW OF PRACTICE. See TOTAL TIME HYPOTHESIS/LAW.

PREESTABLISHED HARMONY, THEORY/DOCTRINE OF. See MIND–BODY THEORIES.

PREFERENCE, THEORY OF. See DEMBER–EARL THEORY OF CHOICE/PREFERENCE.

PREJUDICE, THEORIES OF. The term *prejudice* refers to an act of ''pre-judging'' or ''preconception'' and is the formation of an attitude prior to having sufficient information. A *prejudice* can be either negative or positive in evaluative terms concerning any particular thing, person, event, or idea. A *prejudice* has also been defined as an attitude, either for or against a certain unproved hypothesis, that prevents one from evaluating new evidence correctly; *prejudice* carries an emotional implication, whereas the synonym *bias* lacks an emotional component (Warren, 1934). More commonly, in social psychology, *prejudice* refers to a negative attitude toward a particular group of persons based on negative traits assumed to be uniformly displayed by all members of that group. A related term, *discrimination*, refers to external, observable behaviors, while *prejudice* is applied more to internal, inferred attitudes (Dovidio & Gaertner, 1986). Another related term, *stereotype*, refers to a set of relatively fixed, simplistic overgeneralizations about a group or class of people. Stereotypes and prejudices differ in two ways: the former are more cognitive and concerned with thinking, whereas the latter are more affective and concerned with feelings. Consequently, stereotypes can be relatively neutral, while prejudices are essentially positive or negative, usually negative (Hilton & von Hippel, 1996). One of the oldest theories of prejudice, the *realistic conflict theory*, maintains that prejudice stems from competition between social groups over valued commodities or opportunities where the greater the competition, the greater the members of the groups come to assess each other in more and more negative ways (Baron, 1992). Another theoretical approach, the *us-versus-them effect* or the *self-categorization theory* (Turner, Hogg, Oakes, Reicher, & Wetherell, 1987), assumes that people have a tendency to divide the social world into two distinct categories—*us* or *them*. That is, individuals view other persons as belonging either to their own social group (usually termed the *ingroup*) or to another group (called the *outgroup*). Such distinctions are based on many dimensions such as religion, race, age, sex, ethnicity, geographical location, and occupation. The *dual-processes theory* of prejudice (Devine, 1989) is based on the distinction between uncontrolled/automatic versus controlled/conscious mental processes. This theory states that stereotypes pervade the culture and exert an automatic/unconscious influence on one's perceptions of members of stereotyped groups. One implication of the *dual-processes theory* is that overcoming prejudice is like attempting to resist any well-learned habit. The *contact hypothesis* (Stephan, 1987) suggests that patterns of prejudice and stereotypes can be broken by direct intergroup contact: there are potential benefits for resisting prejudice when there is close acquaintance with members of other groups. Cook (1985) argues that intergroup contact reduces prejudice only under certain conditions: when the groups that interact are roughly equal in social, economic, or task-related status, when the contact situation involves cooperation and interdependence where the groups work toward shared goals, when contact between the groups is informal and on a one-to-one basis, when contact occurs in a setting where existing norms favor group equality, and when the persons involved view each other as typical members of their respective groups. See also ATTITUDE/ATTITUDE CHANGE, THEORIES OF; FESTINGER'S COGNITIVE DISSONANCE THEORY.

REFERENCES

Warren, H. (Ed.) (1934). *Dictionary of psychology.* Cambridge, MA: Houghton Mifflin.

Allport, G. (1954). *The nature of prejudice.* Cambridge, MA: Addison-Wesley.

Cook, S. (1985). Experimenting on social issues: The case of school desegregation. *Amer. Psy., 40,* 452–460.

Dovidio, J., & Gaertner, S. (Eds.) (1986). *Prejudice, discrimination, and racism.* Orlando, FL: Academic Press.

Stephan, W. (1987). The contact hypothesis in intergroup relations. *Rev. Pers. & Soc. Psy., 9,* 41–67.

Turner, J., Hogg, M., Oakes, P., Reicher, S., & Wetherell, M. (1987). *Rediscovering the social group: A self-categorization theory.* Oxford, England: Blackwell.

Devine, P. (1989). Stereotypes and prejudice: Their automatic and controlled components. *J. Pers. Soc. Psy., 57,* 165–188.

Baron, R. (1992). *Psychology.* Boston: Allyn & Bacon.

Hilton, J., & von Hippel, W. (1996). Stereotypes. *Ann. Rev. Psy., 47,* 237–271.

PREMACK'S PRINCIPLE/LAW. The American psychologist David Premack (1925–   ) offered a reappraisal of the concepts of *reinforcement* and Thorndike's *law of effect* that served to increase the generality of these terms (Premack, 1959, 1965). *Premack's principle/law* states that any response that occurs with a fairly high frequency can be used to reinforce a response that occurs with a relatively lower frequency. *Premack's principle* is based on the implicit assumption that the organism's responses/activities that are to be reinforced are neutral and have no intrinsic value. With the counterassumption that an organism engages in a variety of activities that vary in their intrinsic value, Premack ties the reinforcement relation to a preference ranking of the activities where a given activity can be used to reinforce those of lesser value but not those of higher value. Premack (1959) proposed that a generally valid index of value for both humans and nonhumans would be *response rate* in a free-operant situation in which the activity is freely available to the subject. Premack presented data from children, monkeys, and rats that suggest that his predictions concerning the reinforcing effects of certain behaviors over others is generally accurate. He also demonstrated that it is possible to reverse the reinforcement relation between two activities by altering level of deprivation or motivation (Premack, 1962). *Premack's principle* has the merit of being operational, of generating novel experiments, and of describing many social behaviors and activities that may be used as human reinforcers. However, there have been some criticisms and difficulties with *Premack's principle* (also called the *probability-differential theory of reinforcement* and the *prepotent response theory*). For example, Timberlake and Allison's (1974) *response-deprivation theory of reinforcement* and Timberlake's (1980) *equilibrium theory of learned performance* provide a more *general* theory to handle all results consistent with *Premack's theory* as well as consider other results/studies that disconfirm his theory. See also REINFORCEMENT THEORY; REINFORCEMENT, THORNDIKE'S THEORY OF; THORNDIKE'S LAW OF EFFECT.

REFERENCES

Premack, D. (1959). Toward empirical behavior laws. I. Positive reinforcement. *Psy. Rev., 66,* 219–233.

Premack, D. (1962). Reversibility of the reinforcement relation. *Science, 136,* 255–257.

Premack, D. (1965). Reinforcement theory. In M. Jones (Ed.), *Nebraska symposium on motivation.* Lincoln: University of Nebraska Press.

Timberlake, W., & Allison, J. (1974). Response deprivation: An empirical approach to instrumental performance. *Psy. Rev., 81,* 146–164.

Timberlake, W. (1980). A molar equilibrium theory of learned performance. In G. Bower (Ed.), *The psychology of learning and motivation.* Vol. 14. New York: Academic Press.

PREPOTENCY, LAW OF. See SKINNER'S DESCRIPTIVE BEHAVIOR/ OPERANT CONDITIONING THEORY.

PREPOTENT RESPONSE THEORY. See PREMACK'S PRINCIPLE/LAW; REINFORCEMENT THEORY.

PRETESTING EFFECT. See EXPERIMENTER EFFECTS.

PRIOR ENTRY, LAW OF. See VIGILANCE, THEORIES OF.

PROACTIVE INHIBITION, LAW OF. See INTERFERENCE THEORIES.

PROBABILISTIC FUNCTIONALISM, THEORY OF. See PERCEPTION (II. COMPARATIVE APPRAISAL), THEORIES OF.

PROBABILITY THEORY/LAWS. The mathematical foundation of *probability theory* forms the basis for all the statistical techniques of psychology. *Probability theory* originated in games of gambling where, on the basis of a relatively small number of trials (e.g., roulette-wheel spins, dice throws, poker hands), some decisions needed to be made about the likelihood of particular events occurring in the long run, given the basic assumption of the uniformity of nature and the mutual cancellation of complementary errors (Reber, 1995). The earliest contributions to *probability* and the *laws of chance* (Gates, 1926, and Mowrer, 1960, refer to the probability principles as *laws of chance*; cf: *aleatory theory*—the belief that changes in society over time are largely due to chance; Sutherland, 1996) were made by the French mathematician/astronomer Pierre Simon de Laplace (1749–1827), who is credited with founding the modern form of *probability theory* (Muir, 1994). In the early 1800s, Laplace postulated seven general principles of the calculus of probabilities. Laplace was also the pioneer of the *theory of errors* (i.e., the assumption that ''error'' behaves in a random way as an additive component of any score and where random error is distributed in a ''normal'' way), but the contributions of the German mathematician Carl Friedrich Gauss (1777–1855) were so striking that the normal *law of error* is sometimes (incorrectly, it would seem, because of Laplace's priority) called the *Gaussian law* (Boring, 1957). As the *theory of probability* developed, in addition to serving as a model of games of chance, it served also as a model for many other kinds of things having little obvious connection with games—such as results in the sciences. One feature is common to most applications of *probability theory*: the observer is uncertain about what the outcome of some observation will be and eventually must infer or guess what will happen (see the *gambler's fallacy*—the mistaken belief that, in a series of *independent* chance events, future events can be predicted from past ones; e.g., the fallacious belief that if a coin has come down heads many times in succession, it has an increased probability of coming down tails on the next throw; cf: the *base-rate fallacy*, which is the tendency to ignore the base-rate at which events occur when making decisions; Reber, 1995; and the *principle of equal distribution of ignorance*, formulated by G. Bode in 1854, which states that when the relative probabilities of two or more events are unknown, the chances of their occurrences are equal; Warren, 1934). In particular, the observer needs to know what will happen "in the long run" if observations could be made indefinitely (cf: the *law of averages*, which states that the arithmetic mean of a group of observations has a probability of occurrence that is greater than that of any single observation; Warren, 1934). The logical machinery of "in the long run" is formalized in the *theory of probability*. The theory alone does not tell anyone how to decide on events (cf: the mathematical *law of least squares*, which refers to deciding on the most acceptable values from among a series of unknown quantities by taking the minimum sum of the squared residual errors of the observations; Warren, 1934), but it does give ways of evaluating the degree of risk one takes for some decisions (Hays, 1994). There are diverse views of the nature of probability and the topic is not without controversy (Ferguson & Takane, 1989). Three approaches to probability have been employed: the *subjective/personalistic* approach (e.g.,"It will probably rain today"), the *formal mathematical* approach (e.g., "The probability of an event is the ratio of the number of favorable cases to the total number of equally likely cases"), and the *empirical relative-frequency* approach (e.g., "A population of events is defined where probability is the relative frequency in the population and is a population parameter"). In recent years, interest in *subjective probability* and *Bayesian statistics* (see *Bayes' theorem*, which states the relation among the various conditional probabilities of various events; Hays, 1994) has increased (de Finetti, 1978). The basic *laws/theorems of probability* (cf: *law of large numbers*—the larger the sample taken from a population, the more likely is the sample's mean to approximate that of the whole population; and the *central-limit theorem*—as the size of any sample of scores becomes large, the sampling distribution of the mean approaches the normal distribution; Hays, 1994) that are central to *probability theory* are the *additive law of probability*, which states that in a given set of mutually exclusive events the probability of occurrence of one event *or* another event is equal to the *sum* of their separate probabilities, and the *multiplicative law of probability*, which states that the probability of the *joint* occurrence of two or more independent events is the *product* of their individual probabilities (Howell, 1989). See also DECISION-MAKING THEORIES; ESTES' STIMULUS SAMPLING THEORY; HYPOTHESIS-TESTING THEORY.

REFERENCES

Gates, A. (1926). *Elementary psychology*. New York: Macmillan.

Warren, H. (Ed.) (1934). *Dictionary of psychology*. Cambridge, MA: Houghton Mifflin.

Boring, E. G. (1957). *A history of experimental psychology*. New York: Appleton-Century-Crofts.

Mowrer, O. H. (1960). *Learning theory and the symbolic processes*. New York: Wiley.

de Finetti, B. (1978). Probability: Interpretations. In W. Kruskal & J. Turner (Eds.), *International encyclopedia of statistics*. New York: Free Press.

Ferguson, G., & Takane, Y. (1989). *Statistical analysis in psychology and education*. New York: McGraw-Hill.

Howell, D. (1989). *Fundamental statistics for the behavioral sciences*. Boston: PWS-Kent.

Hays, W. (1994). *Statistics*. New York: Harcourt, Brace.

Muir, H. (Ed.) (1994). *Larousse dictionary of scientists*. New York: Larousse.

Reber, A. (1995). *The Penguin dictionary of psychology*. New York: Penguin Books.

Sutherland, S. (1996). *The international dictionary of psychology*. New York: Crossroad.

PROCESS INTERACTION SYSTEM/THEORY. See COMMUNICATION THEORY.

PROGRESSION, LAW OF. See WEBER'S LAW.

PROGRESSIVE TELEOLOGICAL-REGRESSION HYPOTHESIS. See SCHIZOPHRENIA, THEORIES OF.

PROPORTION, PRINCIPLE OF. See ZEISING'S PRINCIPLE.

PROPOSITIONAL THEORY OF MEMORY. See FORGETTING/MEMORY, THEORIES OF.

PROSPECT THEORY. See ORGANIZATIONAL/INDUSTRIAL/SYSTEMS THEORY.

PSYCHIC RESULTANTS, LAW OF. See WUNDT'S THEORIES.

PSYCHOANALYTIC/LIBIDINAL THEORY OF DEPRESSION. See DEPRESSION, THEORIES OF.

PSYCHOANALYTIC THEORIES OF PERSONALITY. See PERSONAL-
ITY THEORIES.

PSYCHODYNAMIC THEORIES OF PERSONALITY. See PERSONAL-
ITY THEORIES.

PSYCHOGENIC THEORIES OF ABNORMALITY. See PSYCHOPA-
THOLOGY, THEORIES OF.

PSYCHOLOGICAL LAW OF RELATIVITY. See WUNDT'S THEORIES.

PSYCHOPATHOLOGY, THEORIES OF. The general term *psychopathology*
refers to the scientific study of mental disorders that includes findings from the
fields of psychology, psychiatry, pharmacology, neurology, and endocrinology,
among others, and is distinguished from the actual practice of clinical psychologists and psychiatrists in the treatment of individuals with mental disorders.
The specific terms *psychopathy, sociopathy, sociopathic personality,* and *psychopathic personality* refer to a personality disorder characterized by amorality,
a lack of affect, and a diminished sense of anxiety/guilt associated with antisocial
behaviors. These terms, once popular, are now little used since the term *antisocial personality disorder* is more preferred in mainstream psychology today
but with the absence of the clinical features of anxiety/guilt under the newer
term (Reber, 1995). The process of *diagnosis of psychopathology* refers to classifying information relevant to an individual's behavioral and emotional state
and the subsequent assignment of a name/label to that state taken from a commonly accepted classification system. This psychodiagnostic process has often
been criticized because of the labeling practice where, once identified as a patient, the individual may then feel the "victim" of an illness and may fail to
take responsibility for resolution of problems (Matarazzo & Pankratz, 1994).
Different historical perspectives and *theories of psychopathology* have been provided (e.g., Zilboorg & Henry, 1941; Neugebauer, 1979) ranging from beliefs
in demons, witches, and supernatural powers inhabiting the afflicted person, to
use of mental status examinations by judges to distinguish mental retardation
from mental illness. The comprehensive diagnostic system of psychopathology
used today began with the German-born psychiatrist Emil Kraepelin (1855–
1926), who made careful observations of patients and statistical tabulations of
symptoms. Kraepelin (1883) concluded that there were two major mental disorders largely caused by physiological/biological factors: *dementia praecox*
(which was subdivided into simple, hebephrenia, catatonia, and paranoia) and
manic-depressive psychosis (which had many subdivisions depending on the
regularity/irregularity of the cycles of mania and depression). Kraepelin's
nosological term *dementia praecox* was criticized severely for almost 50 years
on the basis that the alleged irreversible behavioral deterioration in this condition
was actually reversible. Later, the Swiss psychiatrist Eugen Bleuler (1857–1939)

advanced Kraepelin's basic subtypes of disorder but substituted the term *schizophrenia* for *dementia praecox* (Bleuler, 1916). In 1945, the U.S. Army Medical Department developed a revised classification system where *schizophrenic* patients were no longer forced into the Kraepelin-type system. Today, the *Diagnostic and Statistical Manual of Mental Disorders* (American Psychiatric Association, 1994) is used by most psychologists and psychiatrists treating the *psychopathologies* in the United States (cf: *International Classification of Diseases* as the international classificatory system; Reber, 1995). The personality theorist Theodore Millon (1967) described a number of *theories of psychopathology* under the rubrics *biophysical theories* (e.g., viewpoints of E. Bleuler and W. Sheldon), *intrapsychic theories* (e.g., approaches of S. Freud, E. Erikson, K. Horney, H. S. Sullivan, E. Fromm, and C. Jung), *behavioral theories* (e.g., viewpoints of B. F. Skinner, H. Eysenck, J. Dollard, N. Miller, and A. Bandura), and *phenomenological theories* (e.g., theoretical positions of C. Rogers, R. May, R. D. Laing, and A. Maslow). Millon (1967) states that the term *psychopathology* is defined in the context of the theory one employs. For instance, an *idiographically oriented* humanist theorist who emphasizes the importance of phenomenological experience will include uniqueness and self-discomfort in the definition, while a *nomothetically oriented* biochemical theorist will formulate a definition in terms of biochemical dysfunctions. According to Millon, once a particular theory has been selected, the definition of *psychopathology* follows logically and inevitably. No single definition conveys the wide range of observations and orientations with which psychopathology may be examined (cf: Reber, 1995). Current *models/theories in psychopathology* and therapy include physiological/biochemical, psychoanalytic, learning, cognitive, humanistic, and predispositional/diathesis-stress paradigms where the definition of *abnormal/abnormality* yields several criteria (e.g., statistical rarity, subjective distress, disability, and norm violations), but none of which, by itself, is completely satisfactory. At this stage, too little is known about *psychopathology* and its treatment to settle conclusively on any one paradigm (Davison & Neale, 1990). See also IDIOGRAPHIC/NOMOTHETIC LAWS; LABELING/DEVIANCE THEORY; PERSONALITY THEORIES.

REFERENCES

Kraepelin, E. (1883). *Clinical psychiatry.* New York: Macmillan.

Bleuler, E. (1916). *Textbook of psychiatry.* New York: Macmillan.

Zilboorg, G., & Henry, G. (1941). *A history of medical psychology.* New York: Norton.

Millon, T. (Ed.) (1967). *Theories of psychopathology.* Philadelphia: Saunders.

Zubin, J. (1967). Classification of behavior disorders. *Ann. Rev. Psy., 18*, 373–406.

Sokal, R. (1974). Classification: Purposes, principles, progress, prospects. *Science, 185*, 1115–1123.

Hare, R., & Schalling, D. (Eds.) (1978). *Psychopathic behavior: Approaches to research.* New York: Wiley.

Neugebauer, R. (1979). Medieval and early modern theories of mental illness. *Ar. Gen. Psychiat., 36*, 477–483.

Spitzer, R., & Williams, J. (1980). Classification in psychiatry. In A. Kaplan, A. Freed-
    man, & B. Sadok (Eds.), *Comprehensive textbook of psychiatry. III.* Baltimore:
    Williams & Wilkins.
Garfield, S. (1981). Psychotherapy: A 40-year appraisal. *Amer. Psy., 36,* 174–183.
Davison, G., & Neale, J. (1990). *Abnormal psychology.* New York: Wiley.
American Psychiatric Association (1994). *Diagnostic and statistical manual of mental
    disorders.* Washington, DC: American Psychiatric Association.
Matarazzo, J., & Pankratz, L. (1994). Diagnoses. In R. J. Corsini (Ed.), *Ency. Psy.* New
    York: Wiley.
Reber, A. (1995). *The Penguin dictionary of psychology.* New York: Penguin Books.

PSYCHOPHYSICAL LAWS/THEORY. See FECHNER'S LAW; STEVENS'
POWER LAW; WEBER'S LAW.

PSYCHOPHYSICAL PARALLELISM, DOCTRINE OF. See MIND–
BODY THEORIES.

PSYCHOSOCIAL/PSYCHOLOGICAL THEORIES OF PERSONALITY.
See ERIKSON'S THEORY OF PERSONALITY.

PULFRICH PHENOMENON/EFFECT. See PERCEPTION (I. GENERAL),
THEORIES OF.

PUNISHMENT, THEORIES OF. In the context of *operant conditioning* (i.e.,
learning from consequences; Skinner, 1938, 1953), while the term *reinforcement*
refers to an increase in the frequency of a behavior, the term *punishment* denotes
a decrease in the frequency of a behavior (see Solomon, 1964; Azrin & Holz,
1966). One way in which *punishment* may be administered is through the application of some aversive stimulus (e.g., give a spanking, an electric shock,
etc.) contingent upon a particular behavior—this is called *positive punishment.*
Another method for punishing a particular behavior is the elimination or removal
of a desired stimulus (e.g., take away television/movie privileges, etc.) contingent upon that behavior—this procedure is called *negative punishment.* It is
useful to distinguish between the terms *punishment* (i.e., the procedure or process) and *punisher* (i.e., the thing or stimulus used in decreasing a given behavior). The punishing stimulus itself may be short in duration, simple to
administer, and well defined (as in most laboratory studies where electric shock
is used), but it may also be an extended, complex event (as in cases where
society incarcerates a legal offender). Punishers may be given, also, for the
performance of some response (e.g., a rat pressing the ''wrong'' bar) or for the
nonperformance of a response (e.g., a rat's failure to press the bar). The term
punishment is often confused by the layperson with the term *negative reinforcement*: correct usage has the former term referring to a *decrease* in behavior,
while the latter term refers to an *increase* in behavior due to the removal of an

aversive stimulus. A number and variety of theories have been proposed to account for the fact that punishment and aversive stimuli change an organism's behavior. An early theory by Thorndike (1932) held that a punishing stimulus that was contingent upon a response simply decreased the strength of that stimulus–response connection. However, contemporary theories have stressed both the contribution of an emotional state (e.g., fear) elicited by the noxious stimulus and the learning of avoidance responses that interfere with a previously learned response (cf: Estes, 1944). Another theoretical position, the *two-stage process theory* of Mowrer (1960), assumes that the response followed by punishment produces certain internal and external stimuli that, by virtue of their contiguity with the aversive stimulus, acquire the capacity to arouse fear (cf: the *single-factor theory*, Estes, 1969). According to Mowrer's theory, two learning processes are involved: fear conditioning via classical conditioning, and the subsequent learning of an instrumental response that eliminates/controls the fear. Another *theory of punishment* is Dinsmoor's (1954, 1955) *avoidance hypothesis*, which explains the reduction in the frequency of the punished behavior in terms of simple stimulus–response principles of *avoidance learning*. This theory holds that there is an interference between behaviors where punished behaviors decrease and are suppressed because of an increase in *other* behaviors that *compete* with the punished response (cf: Dunham, 1971). Current thinking on how effective a given punishment situation is depends on various factors, such as the characteristics of the punishing stimulus, desire to merely suppress an undesirable behavior temporarily or to eliminate it permanently, the specific behavior being punished, and the particular individual being punished (Engel, 1994). See also ESTES' STIMULUS SAMPLING THEORY; LEARNING, THEORIES OF; MOWRER'S THEORY; REINFORCEMENT THEORY; SKINNER'S DESCRIPTIVE BEHAVIOR/OPERANT CONDITIONING THEORY.

REFERENCES

Thorndike, E. (1932). Reward and punishment in animal learning. *Comp. Psy. Mono., 8*, no. 39.

Skinner, B. F. (1938). *The behavior of organisms: An experimental analysis.* New York: Appleton-Century-Crofts.

Estes, W. (1944). An experimental study of punishment. *Psy. Mono.*, no. 263.

Skinner, B. F. (1953). *Science and human behavior.* New York: Macmillan.

Dinsmoor, J. (1954). Punishment. I. The avoidance hypothesis. *Psy. Rev., 61*, 34–46.

Dinsmoor, J. (1955). Punishment. II. An interpretation of empirical findings. *Psy. Rev., 62*, 96–105.

Mowrer, O. H. (1960). *Learning theory and behavior.* New York: Wiley.

Solomon, R. (1964). Punishment. *Amer. Psy., 19*, 239–253.

Azrin, N., & Holz, W. (1966). Punishment. In W. Honig (Ed.), *Operant behavior: Areas of research and application.* New York: Appleton-Century-Crofts.

Estes, W. (1969). Outline of a theory of punishment. In B. Campbell & R. Church (Eds.), *Punishment and aversive behavior.* New York: Appleton-Century-Crofts.

Dunham, P. (1971). Punishment: Method and theory. *Psy. Rev., 78*, 58–70.

Walters, G., & Grusec, J. (1977). *Punishment*. San Francisco: Freeman.

Engel, J. (1994). Punishment. In R. J. Corsini (Ed.), *Ency. Psy.* New York: Wiley.

Reber, A. (1995). *The Penguin dictionary of psychology*. New York: Penguin Books.

PURKINJE EFFECT/PHENOMENON/SHIFT. The Czech physiologist Jan Evangelista Purkinje (1787–1869) (also spelled "Purkyne") described the change in color sensitivity as a visual stimulus moved from the center of the visual field, to the periphery—where colors become gray at the periphery of the field, and different colors change at different visual field locations. Purkinje (1825) also reported that visual *accommodation* was caused by changes in the shape of the eye's lens. The *Purkinje effect/phenomenon/shift* refers to the manner in which colors emerge from darkness at dawn: initially there is only black and gray with red as the darkest, next the blues appear, and finally the reds appear. The *Purkinje effect* occurs when the illumination of objects is reduced, and the red and orange hues (at the long-wavelength end of the electromagnetic spectrum) lose their perceived brightness faster than the green and blue hues (at the short-wavelength end of the spectrum). Consequently, the reds are relatively bright in strong light, and the greens and blues are bright in dim light. The greens and blues in dim light are not only relatively bright but also "whitish" because of the colorless contribution of the rods under such conditions. The shift is caused by the differential activity of the rods, which have a greater overall sensitivity than the cones: at sunset we shift from cone to rod vision, and at sunrise we shift from rod to cone vision. The *Purkinje effect* fails to occur under conditions where the stimulus light is confined strictly to the rod-free region of the retina and when considering cases of *night blindness* or *nyctalopia*—which is due often to a deficiency of vitamin A or to a congenital retinal defect. In addition to the *Purkinje effect*, Purkinje's name is honored in the terms *Purkinje figures*—the network of interwoven blood vessels of the retina that may be perceived under conditions of low ambient illumination and when a small bright light is positioned just under the eye as the person stares at a blank screen or wall; *Purkinje–Sanson images*—the perception by one person—by looking at a second person's eye—of three separate images of an object that the second person looks at, where one image is from the surface of the cornea, one is from the back of the lens, and one is from the front of the lens; and *Purkinje after-image*—the second positive afterimage that follows stimulation by a bright light that is a hue complement to the original stimulus. Purkinje's other research in sensory psychology included work on *afterimages* (or *Bidwell's ghost*, which is another term for the *Purkinje afterimage*), *dark adaptation*, the location and nature of the *blind spot* in the retina, a comparison of *monocular* and *binocular* vision, the "flight of colors" (i.e., the succession of colors that occurs in a visual afterimage), and the physiology of *optics*. The *Purkinje shift* led the German scientist Johannes von Kries (1895) to postulate the existence of two separate visual systems (rods and cones), and the *Purkinje effect* also helped the Austrian-American scientist Selig Hecht (1937) to establish firmly the *duplicity* *theory* of rod and cone visual systems for modern theories of vision (Peyser, 1994). See also HECHT'S COLOR VISION THEORY; VISION/SIGHT, THEORIES OF; von KRIES' COLOR VISION THEORY.

REFERENCES

Purkinje, J. (1819). *Beitrage zur kenntniss des sehens in subjectiver hinsicht.* Prague: Calve.

Purkinje, J. (1825). *Neue beitrage zur kenntniss des sehens in subjectiver hinsicht.* Berlin: Reimer.

von Kries, J. (1895). Uber die natur gewisser mit den psychischen vorgangen verknupfter gehirnzustande. *Z. Psy., 8,* 1–33.

Hecht, S. (1937). Rods, cones, and the chemical basis of vision. *Physio. Rev., 17,* 239–290.

Peyser, C. (1994). Jan Evangelista Purkinje. In R. J. Corsini (Ed.), *Ency. Psy.* New York: Wiley.

PURPOSIVE/COGNITIVE THEORY. See REINFORCEMENT THEORY; TOLMAN'S THEORY.

PYGMALION EFFECT. This phenomenon is derived from a play (called *Pygmalion*) by the Ireland-born British dramatist/critic George Bernard Shaw (1856–1950). Originally, the name *Pygmalion* came from a Greek legend in which *Pygmalion*, a king of Cyprus and a sculptor, made a statue of a maiden (named *Galatea*). Aphrodite—the goddess of love and beauty—gave the statue life after she discovered that *Pygmalion* fell in love with the statue. The term *pygmalionism* refers to a pathological condition in which one falls in love with one's own creation (Reber, 1995). The *Pygmalion effect*, on the other hand, is the observed effect in which people come to behave in ways that correspond to others' expectations concerning them. The effect is similar to the concept of *self-fulfilling prophesy*; that is, things turn out just as one expected or prophesied that they would, not necessarily because of one's prescience but because one behaved in a manner that optimized these very outcomes (Merton, 1948). The *Pygmalion effect* is particularly relevant to the social and psychological dynamics between teacher and students in the classroom. Rosenthal and Jacobson (1968) were the first to use the concept *Pygmalion effect*—in their book "Pygmalion in the Classroom" which describes the effects of teachers' expectations on students' behavior (cf: Dusek, 1975; Braun, 1976; Nash, 1976). See also EXPERIMENTER EFFECTS; HALO EFFECT; LABELING/DEVIANCE THEORY.

REFERENCES

Merton, R. (1948). The self-fulfilling prophesy. *Antioch Review, 8,* 193–210.

Rosenthal, R., & Jacobson, L. (1968). *Pygmalion in the classroom: Teacher expectation and pupils' intellectual development.* New York: Holt, Rinehart, & Winston.

Elashoff, D., & Snow, R. (Eds.) (1971). *Pygmalion reconsidered.* Worthington, OH: Jones.

Dusek, J. (1975). Do teachers bias children's learning? *Rev. Ed. Res., 45,* 661–684.

Braun, C. (1976). Teacher expectation: Sociopsychological dynamics. *Rev. Ed. Res., 46,* 185–213.

Nash, R. (1976). *Teacher expectations and pupil learning.* London: Routledge & Kegan Paul.

Cooper, H. (1979). Pygmalion grows up: A model for teacher expectation, communication, and performance influence. *Rev. Ed. Res., 49,* 389–410.

Bar-Tal, D. (1994). Pygmalion effect. In R. J. Corsini (Ed.), *Ency. Psy.* New York: Wiley.

Shaw, R. (1994). Self-fulfilling prophecies. In R. J. Corsini (Ed.), *Ency. Psy.* New York: Wiley.

Reber, A. (1995). *The Penguin dictionary of psychology.* New York: Penguin Books.

Q

QUANTAL HYPOTHESIS. See NEURAL QUANTUM THEORY.

QUANTUM THEORY. See VISION/SIGHT, THEORIES OF.

R

RANK'S THEORY OF PERSONALITY. The Austrian psychoanalyst Otto Rank (1884–1939) formulated a *theory of personality* that may be characterized as an *intrapsychic conflict model* (Maddi, 1972) where all functioning of the individual is expressive of the dual tendency to minimize both the fear of life and the fear of death. According to Rank (1929, 1945), life is equivalent to the processes of separation and individualization, whereas death is the opposite processes of union and fusion. The two opposing fears of life and death are experienced as uncomfortable tension states, much as the concept of *anxiety* has been stressed by other conflict theorists. However, Rank prefers the more definite term *fear* over the diffuse term *anxiety*. While the individual does possess biological instincts, they do not provide the intrinsic basis for conflict. More important for conflict is the tendency for living things to individuate and separate. Rank (1929) asserted that the mere act of being born is a deeply traumatic experience because the newborn must relinquish the warm and relatively constant environment of the womb where one's needs were met automatically. Rank initially considered the birth trauma to be the most significant event in one's life. However, later in his career, he came to consider birth only the first in a long series of separation experiences that are caused by biological, psychological, and social factors that are indistinguishable from life. Another important core characteristic in *Rank's theory* is the concept of *will*, which is analogous to Freud's concept of *ego*, and to Sullivan's concept of *self*. Rank's concept of *will* refers to an organized sense of self-identity and functions consciously to aid in the development of a basis for minimizing both the life and death fears. Rank argued that the highest form of living involved a mature expression of will—over that of counterwill and guilt—where it provided the basis for successful expression of the core tendency of minimizing both fear of life and fear of death. In general, *Rank's personality theory* has never been very popular in mainstream psychology. However, in at least two research cases, Rank's theorizing has proven useful for explanation of empirical results "after the fact" (Mackinnon, 1965; Crutchfield, 1955), even though such research was not planned a priori or explicitly to measure or validate Rank's concepts. The overall fruitfulness of Rank's theoretical position, however, has not yet been empirically demonstrated (Maddi, 1972). See also CONFLICT, THEORIES OF; PERSONALITY THEORIES.

REFERENCES

Rank, O. (1929). *The trauma of birth.* New York: Harcourt, Brace.

Rank, O. (1945). *Will therapy and truth and reality.* New York: Knopf.

Karpf, F. (1953). *The psychology and psychotherapy of Otto Rank.* New York: Philosophical Library.

Crutchfield, R. (1955). Conformity and character. *Amer. Psy., 10,* 191–198.

Taft, J. (1958). *Otto Rank: A biographical study based on notebooks, letters, collected writings, therapeutic achievements and personal associations.* New York: Julian Press.

Mackinnon, D. (1965). Personality and the realization of creative potential. *Amer. Psy., 20,* 273–281.

Maddi, S. (1972). *Personality theories: A comparative analysis.* Homewood, IL: Dorsey Press.

Menaker, E. (1982). *Otto Rank: A rediscovered legacy.* New York: Columbia University Press.

RANSCHBURG INHIBITION/EFFECT. See INHIBITION, LAWS OF.

RATIONAL-ECONOMIC MAN THEORY. See ORGANIZATIONAL/INDUSTRIAL/SYSTEMS THEORY.

RATIONAL-EMOTIVE THERAPY THEORY. See ABC THEORY.

RAVEN'S PROGRESSIVE MATRICES THEORY. See INTELLIGENCE, THEORIES/LAWS OF.

REACTANCE THEORY. A common tendency in human behavior is to react against any attempted restrictions imposed on the individual. The term *psychological reactance* is defined as the motivational state aroused when a person perceives that a specific behavioral freedom is threatened with elimination or is actually eliminated (Brehm, 1994). *Reactance theory* (Brehm, 1966) holds that under such conditions of threats to personal freedom, oppositional behaviors may be understood as manifestations of a single motivational state and includes the assumption that when reactance motivation is aroused, the person makes attempts to restore the threatened or eliminated freedom. *Reactance theory* makes two predictions: because the desirability of an object or event is assumed to be related to the opportunity to choose it, the more the individual perceives that others are attempting to limit one's opportunities, the more attractive the object or event becomes; and when a person perceives that strong pressure is being exerted to force a particular decision, the person will tend to become contrary and resist the pressure by selecting an opposing perspective (Reber, 1995). *Reactance theory* maintains that individuals possess a finite number of specific behavioral freedoms (i.e., behaviors—including emotions, attitudes, beliefs, and overt acts—are free if the person is currently engaging in them, or expects to engage in them in the future). The theory does not assume any need or desire for freedom per se but allows for a wide variation in individual differences concerning ''free'' behaviors. In general, the more important the freedom is to the person, the greater the magnitude of the threat; and the greater the number of freedoms threatened, the greater will be the reactance aroused. An example of a reactance situation is the desire of a girl to marry a boyfriend in spite of parental opposition. According to *reactance theory*, the girl will attempt to restore the threatened freedom (of marrying the person whom she chooses). In such cases, two ''counterforces'' serve to influence restorative action: as the magnitude of pressure to comply increases, both reactance arousal and the motive to comply (by relinquishing the freedom) will increase, and if the costs of direct restorative action are sufficiently high, direct opposition may be prevented. Thus, *compliance* motives counteract/influence *reactance* arousal to determine the resulting behavioral tendency. How much one desires to restore freedom, as well as how strongly the individual actually attempts to do so, will reflect the interplay between *compliance* forces and *reactance*. Costs of direct opposition, on the other hand, should act mainly as a suppressor of overt action and, given a chance to restore freedom without incurring unreasonably high costs, the individual is predicted to do so (Brehm, 1994). Research on *reactance theory* (e.g., Brehm & Brehm, 1981) has shown considerable empirical support for the theory, which has been applied to a wide variety of psychological issues and problems. See also ATTITUDE/ATTITUDE CHANGE, THEORIES OF; ATTRIBUTION THEORY.

REFERENCES

Brehm, J. (1966). *A theory of psychological reactance*. New York: Academic Press.

Clee, M., & Wicklund, R. (1980). Consumer behavior and psychological reactance. *J. Consumer Res., 6*, 389–405.

Brehm, S., & Brehm, J. (1981). *Psychological reactance: A theory of freedom and control*. New York: Academic Press.

Brehm, S. (1994). Reactance theory. In R. J. Corsini (Ed.), *Ency. Psy*. New York: Wiley.

Reber, A. (1995). *The Penguin dictionary of psychology*. New York: Penguin Books.

READINESS, LAW OF. This is one of the accessory principles to *Thorndike's law of effect*. The *law of readiness* states that when a stimulus–response unit is ready to conduct, it yields a satisfying effect as long as nothing interferes with its conducting action. When Thorndike proposed his *law of readiness* in 1913, it was little more than a guess that was stated in terms of ''conduction units'' as to the physiological conditions underlying its operation in the acquisition of behavior. Today, the *law of readiness* and its correlate the *law of unreadiness*—where satisfaction is not forthcoming if the conducting unit is not ready—are important only as historical curiosities in the area of learning and conditioning (Murphy & Kovach, 1972; Bower & Hilgard, 1981). See also EFFECT, LAW OF; EXERCISE, LAW OF; REINFORCEMENT, THORNDIKE'S THEORY OF.

REFERENCES

Thorndike, E. (1913). *Educational psychology*. Vol. 2. *The psychology of learning*. New York: Teachers College, Columbia University.

Keller, F., & Schoenfeld, W. (1950). *Principles of psychology*. New York: Appleton-Century-Crofts.

Cruze, W. (1951). *General psychology for college students*. New York: Prentice-Hall.

Chaplin, J., & Krawiec, T. (1968). *Systems and theories of psychology*. New York: Holt, Rinehart, & Winston.

Murphy, G., & Kovach, J. (1972). *Historical introduction to modern psychology*. New York: Harcourt Brace Jovanovich.

Bower, G., & Hilgard, E. (1981). *Theories of learning*. Englewood Cliffs, NJ: Prentice-Hall.

REAFFERENCE THEORY/PRINCIPLE. The term *reafference*, coined by the German physiologists E. von Holst and H. Mittelstaedt (1950), refers to a distinction between "active" sensory input, which is the result of some movement of the animal, and "passive" input, which occurs independently of the organism. The *principle of reafference* has come to be a cover term for those sensory events that are produced by voluntary movements of a sense organ (e.g., events resulting from the movement of an image across the retina that accompany voluntary movements of the eye). This is contrasted with *exafference*, which are those sensory events produced by changes in the stimulus itself (e.g., events resulting from movement of an image across the retina that accompany real displacements of the physical object) (Reber, 1995). The seminal studies by von Holst and Mittelstaedt (1950) examined the *optokinetic reflex* in the fly—which is a movement of the fly in response to movement of the visual world and compensates for external movement. As a result of the *optokinetic reflex*, the fly's eye is able to look at the same part of the environment successively—this is similar to nystagmus in the human eye where rapid movement of the eyes in one direction is followed by a slow drift in the opposite direction. During operation of this reflex system, an *efference/effector copy* is left at some place in the nervous system, and the effector that is activated by the efferent message has some influence on new stimulation that enters the receptor. The *afferent/sensory* message is compared to the *efference/effector copy*, and, if they match, the copy is nullified. If the *afference* matches the *efference* copy, it is called *reafference*. However, afferent stimulation that does not match an efference copy is called *exafference*. *Reafference theory* is an example of the application of control/feedback systems to behavior analysis. In control systems, the mismatch between the *afference* and the motor copy results in an error signal that, in the normal fly, is corrected by *negative feedback*. When the fly's head is rotated, the error signal becomes *positive feedback*. An example of *reafference/feedback* in human behavior is shown in the classical perception studies by Stratton (1896, 1897), who reported that any movement made while wearing inverting lenses caused the individuals' world to swing and whirl about them (cf: Kohler, 1962); the left-right reversal of the customary relation of image displacement to body movement caused the field to appear to move in the direction of the person's movements, only faster. As with the fly, there is a *positive* rather than a *negative feedback* loop involving the *efference copy*. Humans have the capability to cope and adapt with such inverted-image-lens situations so that the world eventually appears stationary during head movements. The fly, however, does not have such an adaptive capability and, as a consequence, circles to exhaustion (McBurney & Collings, 1977). See also CONTROL/SYSTEMS THEORY.

REFERENCES

Stratton, G. (1896). Some preliminary experiments on vision without inversion of the retinal image. *Psy. Rev., 3*, 611–617.

Stratton, G. (1897). Vision without inversion of the retinal image. *Psy. Rev., 4*, 341–360, 463–481.

von Holst, E., & Mittelstaedt, H. (1950). Das reafferenz-prinzip. *Die Naturwissen schaften, 20*, 464–467.

Kohler, I. (1962). Experiments with goggles. *Sci. Amer., 206*, 62–72.

McBurney, D., & Collings, V. (1977). *Introduction to sensation/perception.* Englewood Cliffs, NJ: Prentice-Hall.

Reber, A. (1995). *The Penguin dictionary of psychology.* New York: Penguin Books.

REALISTIC CONFLICT THEORY. See CONFLICT, THEORIES OF; PREJUDICE, THEORIES OF.

REBER'S LAW. This is a self-styled/self-proclaimed principle by the American psychologist/lexicographer Arthur Samuel Reber (1940–   ), which states that the closer anything is examined, the more complex it is seen to be (for other semihumorous "laws," note *Murphy's laws*: anything that can possibly go wrong will go wrong; anything that goes wrong will do so at the worst possible time; and anything you plan will cost more and take longer; Reber, 1995). *Reber's law* is a self-conscious or self-reflective outcome of his work on his dictionary and stands at the extreme "personalistic" end of the *personalistic* versus *naturalistic* continuum concerning the development of *lawful* concepts in science (Schultz, 1969). Enunciation of this "law" indicates, perhaps, that *laws* in psychology may be created suddenly in the immediate present by individuals and not necessarily developed through painstaking assessment, distillation, and refinement processes involving the "checks and balances" of other investigators' inputs over a relatively long period of time. See also NATURALISTIC THEORY OF HISTORY.

REFERENCES

Schultz, D. (1969). *A history of modern psychology*. New York: Academic Press.

Reber, A. (1995). *The Penguin dictionary of psychology*. New York: Penguin Books.

Roeckelein, J. (1996). Citation of *laws* and *theories* in textbooks across 112 years of psychology. *Psy. Rep., 79*, 979–998.

RECAPITULATION THEORY/LAW OF. = biogenetic recapitulation theory. This theory, developed and taught by the American psychologist Granville Stanley Hall (1844–1924) and often referred to as both a *principle* and a *doctrine*, states that the development of an individual organism is a microcosmic reenactment of the evolution of its species and emphasizes the predetermined progression in development (Hall, 1904a). Hall's *recapitulation theory* was the direct outcome of the impact of *Darwin's evolutionary theory* on Hall's attempts to understand mental development (Diehl, 1986). Hall (1923) argued that evolution, rather than physics, should form the basis for science, and he saw in evolution a noteworthy organizing principle that unites the phylogenetic emergence of the species with the ontogenetic development of a single individual. Hence, the well-known phrase ''Ontogeny recapitulates phylogeny'' (originally called the *biogenetic law* by E. Haeckel; see Eysenck & Arnold, 1972) captures the essence of the *theory of recapitulation*. Hall's *evolutionary recapitulation theory* was extended as *development theory* into educational contexts and assumed that every child from the moment of conception to maturity re-creates every stage of development through which the human race from its lowest animal beginnings has passed (Hall, 1904b, 1923). Thus, the *theory of recapitulation* has had heuristic manifestations in two areas: evolutionary biology/embryology and developmental psychology/perception-cognition. In the area of embryology, *Baer's/von Baer's law* is often confused with the *theory of recapitulation/biogenetic law*. *Baer's law* is the doctrine that the embryos of different kinds of organisms are at first similar and develop for a time along similar lines, those organisms least closely related diverging first, the others diverging at later periods in proportion to the closeness of relationship (Warren, 1934). The *recapitulation theory* has been applied also, unsuccessfully, to anthropological contexts (and renamed the *culture-epoch theory*) where all cultures were assumed to evolve through a series of *epochs* or stages (such as hunting, pastoral, agricultural, industrial), and where each person in a culture passed through the same steps as demonstrated in the cultural sequence. The *culture-epoch theory* is also known as the *monotypic evolution theory* and the *unilineal/unilinear theory* of cultural evolution (Warren, 1934). Hall's notion that the ontogenetic history of individuals represents a *recapitulation*, or repeating, of the species' phylogenetic history is largely discounted today (McKinney, 1994). See also DEVELOPMENTAL THEORY; PLAY, THEORIES OF.

REFERENCES

Hall, G. S. (1904a). *Adolescence: Its psychology and its relations to physiology, anthropology, sociology, sex, crime, religion, and education.* Vol. 1. Englewood Cliffs, NJ: Prentice-Hall.

Hall, G. S. (1904b). Coeducation. *Add. & Proc. Nat. Ed. Assoc.*, June 27–July 1, 538–542.

Hall, G. S. (1923). *Life and confessions of a psychologist.* New York: Appleton.

Warren, H. (Ed.) (1934). *Dictionary of psychology.* Cambridge, MA: Houghton Mifflin.

Eysenck, H., & Arnold, W. (Eds.) (1972). *Encyclopedia of psychology.* New York: Herder and Herder.

Ross, D. (1972). *G. Stanley Hall: The psychologist as prophet.* Chicago: University of Chicago Press.

Diehl, L. (1986). The paradox of G. Stanley Hall. *Amer. Psy., 4,* 868–878.

McKinney, J. (1994). Child psychology. In R. J. Corsini (Ed.), *Ency. Psy.* New York: Wiley.

RECENCY, LAW OF. See ASSOCIATION, LAWS/PRINCIPLES OF.

RECIPROCITY LAW. See BUNSEN–ROSCOE LAW; LOVE, THEORIES OF.

RECIPROCITY OF LIKING EFFECT. The *principle of reciprocity* is a basic, common-sense generalization concerning relationships and interpersonal encounters that suggests that we often treat other people as they have treated us; (however, cf: the curious phenomena of the *passing stranger/stranger on a train effect*, where a person will divulge the most private information about himself or herself to a perfect stranger, and the *hard-to-get effect*, where one is selective in his or her social choices in order to appear as more desirable than those who are more readily available; Reber, 1995). In the context of Fritz Heider's (1946, 1958) *balance theory*, *reciprocity* is the principle that social attraction is mutual: if I know you like me, it increases the likelihood that I will like you. In the context of *interpersonal attraction theory*, an important determinant of attraction is *reciprocity* and the nature of others' feelings toward us. Many studies indicate that the more others like us, the greater our liking toward them (e.g., Condon & Crano, 1988). The *reciprocity of liking effect* seems to be so strong that it occurs even when it is suspected that the positive sentiments one hears are merely attempts at flattery (Drachman, deCarufel, & Insko, 1978). In the area of *helping/prosocial behavior*, the *principle of reciprocity* becomes the *norm of reciprocity* (Sears, Peplau, Freedman, & Taylor, 1988), which posits that we should help those who help us, that a larger favor is reciprocated more often than a smaller one, and that returning a favor is more likely when the original help is perceived to be given intentionally and voluntarily (cf: Latane & Nida, 1981). In the context of aggressive motivation, the *principle of reciprocity* may be experienced when dealing with others, especially difficult people. When others engage in direct provocation toward us, we tend to treat them much as they have treated us. Thus, according to the *reciprocity principle*, when verbally or physically provoked by others, we tend to respond in kind, often with the unfortunate result that aggression spirals upward, as sarcastic comments give way to direct insults, which, in turn, often lead to physical violence (Baron, 1992). See also AGGRESSION, THEORIES OF; BYSTANDER INTERVENTION EFFECT; HEIDER'S BALANCE THEORY; INTERPERSONAL ATTRACTION THEORIES; LOVE, THEORIES OF.

REFERENCES

Heider, F. (1946). Attitudes and cognitive organization. *J. Psy., 21*, 107–112.

Heider, F. (1958). *The psychology of interpersonal relations.* New York: Wiley.

Drachman, D., deCarufel, A., & Insko, C. (1978). The extra credit effect in interpersonal attraction. *J. Exp. Soc. Psy., 14*, 458–465.

Latane, B., & Nida, S. (1981). Ten years of research on group size and helping. *Psy. Bull., 89*, 308–324.

Condon, J., & Crano, W. (1988). Inferred evaluation and the relation between attitude similarity and interpersonal attraction. *J. Pers. Soc. Psy., 54*, 789–797.

Sears, D., Peplau, L., Freedman, J., & Taylor, S. (1988). *Social psychology.* Englewood Cliffs, NJ: Prentice-Hall.

Baron, R. (1992). *Psychology.* Boston: Allyn & Bacon.

Reber, A. (1995). *The Penguin dictionary of psychology.* New York: Penguin Books.

RECONPOSRE THEORY OF DEPRESSION. See DEPRESSION, THEORIES OF.

RECONSTRUCTION THEORY. See FORGETTING, THEORIES OF.

REDINTEGRATION, PRINCIPLE/LAWS OF. The Scottish philosopher Sir William Hamilton (1788–1856) first proposed the *principle of redintegration*, which refers to an impression one has that tends to bring back into consciousness the whole situation of which it was a part at one time (cf: *law of piecemeal activity*—Thorndike's principle that a learned response may still be given when only part of the original stimulus situation is presented; Sutherland, 1996). *Hamilton's theory* concerning the nature of memory and association was able to identify a continuing weakness in the *associationistic doctrine*: it presupposed the existence of individual parts of the mind, each of which sets off another part of the mind without any unifying principle to make the parts hold together. Hamilton critiqued the associationists, who considered a sequence of mental events as a "remembering mind" that contained only one single idea at a time. He taught, on the other hand, that the process of perception is such that any one of the elements simultaneously experienced was capable, when presented later, of bringing back the total experience. The person *redintegrates* in memory the original situation where one recalls not only a series of elements but a pattern of elements as well. Thus, *Hamilton's principle of redintegration* suggests that any given mental event is only a part of a much larger whole. Hamilton may have expected too much of his *redintegration hypothesis* concerning memory, and he failed to explain the process of forgetting (Peters, 1965). Hamilton also seemed to neglect the facts of serial association and the occasional explanatory ineffectiveness of the *redintegration principle* (Murphy & Kovach, 1972). Hollingworth (1926) used the term *redintegration* to describe the "functional" process, rather than the "recall" process, in which the part acts for the whole context. Hollingworth (1928, 1930) also described the *law of redintegration* as the capability of one aspect of a situation to bring it back in its entirety or the reestablishment of a whole situation or experience by bringing together its several parts ("reintegration") (cf: Griffith's, 1929, *principle of redintegration*). While the terms *redintegration* and *reintegration* essentially are synonymous, and even though the shorter form (reintegration) is more euphonic, historic usage from William Hamilton (1859/1860) on down favors the spelling "redintegration" (Warren, 1934). The *law/principle of redintegration* was adopted and used by the Scottish psychologist Alexander Bain (1818–1903) as well as by the American philosopher/psychologist William James (1842–1910). The concept of *redintegration* has undergone various logical, contextual, and terminological changes (cf: Bradley, 1883; Semon, 1904), and it has served as the starting point for much modern discussion of learning (Murphy & Kovach, 1972). See also ASSOCIATION, LAWS/PRINCIPLES OF; FORGETTING/MEMORY, THEORIES OF; GESTALT THEORY/LAWS; LEARNING THEORIES/LAWS.

REFERENCES

Hamilton, W. (1859/1860). *Lectures on metaphysics and logic*. London, England: Blackwood.
Bradley, F. (1883). *Principles of logic*. London: Kegan Paul, Trench.
Semon, R. (1904). *Die mneme*. Leipzig: Engelmann.
Hollingworth, H. (1926). *The psychology of thought*. New York: Appleton.
Hollingworth, H. (1928). *Psychology: Its facts and principles*. New York: Appleton.
Griffith, C. (1929). *General introduction to psychology*. New York: Macmillan.
Hollingworth, H. (1930). *Abnormal psychology*. New York: Ronald Press.
Warren, H. (Ed.) (1934). *Dictionary of psychology*. Cambridge, MA: Houghton Mifflin.
Peters, R. (Ed.) (1965). *Brett's history of psychology*. Cambridge: MIT Press.
Murphy, G., & Kovach, J. (1972). *Historical introduction to modern psychology*. New York: Harcourt Brace Jovanovich.
Sutherland, S. (1996). *The international dictionary of psychology*. New York: Crossroad.

REFLEX ARC THEORY/CONCEPT. The American philosopher/educator John Dewey (1859–1952) adapted the physiologist's *model of the reflex arc* to the study of psychological action. The *reflex arc* was the hypothesized neural unit that represented the functioning of a reflex where the abstract arc is schematically indicated by a sensory (afferent) neuron stimulated by physical energy and a motor (efferent) neuron to which the impulse is transmitted via an intermediary neuron. The *reflex arc* is also called the *reflex circuit* (Reber, 1995). In his theoretical approach, Dewey attacked the psychological molecularism, elementism, and reductionism of the *reflex arc* with its distinction between stimulus and response (Dewey, 1896). Dewey argued that the behavior involved in a reflex response cannot be meaningfully reduced to its basic sensory-motor elements anymore than consciousness can be meaningfully analyzed into its elementary components. He maintained that behavior should be treated not as an artificial scientific construct, but rather in terms of its functional significance to the organism in adapting to the environment (Schultz, 1981; cf: Hull, 1929). Dewey was concerned also about the contemporaneous cleavage of the organism into a body and a mind. In his paper on the *reflex arc*, Dewey (1896) struggled to rid psychology of the ancient mind–body dualism and suggested that behavior should be viewed as so integrated that it is impossible to split it up into disparate things. Dewey's *reflec arc theory* was an attempt to show how behavior and psychological events need to be viewed as whole entities, and his approach was a significant protest against the artificial fragmentation of behavior imbedded in the *reflex arc paradigm* of his day (Pronko, 1994). See also MIND–BODY THEORIES; NEURON/NEURAL/NERVE THEORY.

REFERENCES

Dewey, J. (1886). *Psychology*. New York: Harper.
Dewey, J. (1896). The reflec arc concept in psychology. *Psy. Rev., 3*, 357–370.
Hull, C. (1929). A functional interpretation of the conditioned reflex. *Psy. Rev., 36*, 498–511.
Schultz, D. (1981). *A history of modern psychology*. New York: Academic Press.
Pronko, N. (1994). Reflex arc concept. In R. J. Corsini (Ed.), *Ency. Psy.* New York: Wiley.
Reber, A. (1995). *The Penguin dictionary of psychology*. New York: Penguin Books.

REFLEX FATIGUE, LAW OF. See SKINNER'S DESCRIPTIVE BEHAVIOR/OPERANT CONDITIONING THEORY.

REFLEX RESERVE, PRINCIPLE OF. See SKINNER'S DESCRIPTIVE BEHAVIOR/OPERANT CONDITIONING THEORY.

REFRACTORY PHASE, LAW OF. See SKINNER'S DESCRIPTIVE BEHAVIOR/OPERANT CONDITIONING THEORY.

REICHENBACH PHENOMENON. See REICH'S ORGONE/ORGONOMY THEORY.

REICHER–WHEELER EFFECT. See TOP-DOWN PROCESSING/THEORIES.

REICH'S ORGONE/ORGONOMY THEORY. The Austrian-born American psychoanalyst Wilhelm Reich (1897–1957) formulated a ''dissident'' *psycho-*

analytic theory called the *orgone theory* (Wolman, 1973), which was based on the assumption that a specific form of energy called *orgone energy* filled all space and accounted for all life (Reich, 1933, 1942, 1945; cf: *Reichenbach phenomenon*, which is a force or emanation, called the "od," "odic," or "odylic" force, that a "sensitive" person could allegedly see issuing from all matter; this and "N-rays" and "auras" proved to be cases of self-deception; Zusne, 1987). Reich suggested that not only were patients' symptoms evidence of neurosis but that their character structure itself may be neurotic. Reich called his therapeutic approach *character analysis* wherein he often elicited intense emotions from patients with the result that changes occurred in their bodily attitudes, tonus, and posture. Reich attacked the problems of neurosis by attacking the somatic muscular "armor" of his patients. An individual's emotions, according to Reich, came to mean the manifestations of a tangible biological energy called *orgone* (from the terms *organism* and *orgasm*), and the function of the physiological act of the orgasm was to regulate the organism's energy (Nelson, 1994). One of the problems with such a concept as *orgone* and a theory of "being" as *orgone theory* is the identification of the *orgone*. In order to demonstrate the existence of something (like *orgone*), one must be able to determine where it is not, so as to know where it is. That is, if something exists uniformly everywhere, it might as well be nowhere (Reber, 1995). The issue of *orgone* identity led Reich to construct a device he called the *orgone accumulator*—a box composed of layers of different metals that collected "orgones" and concentrated them on the person sitting inside, much to the benefit of their sex lives ("if it worked, it would be in great demand"—Sutherland, 1996)— and that led to some serious legal problems with the U.S. Food and Drug Administration. The term *orgonomy* refers to Reich's personality theory and associated therapeutic practices, which involved elaborate programs and massage, manipulations, prodding, probing, and encouraging the patient/client to experience the ultimate *orgastic release* that Reich believed to be the evidence of therapeutic breakthrough. The current consensus of opinion is that *Reich's orgone theory* was basically a psychoanalytic system that was transformed into something that became ludicrous and totally dismissible (Reber, 1995). See also PERSONALITY THEORIES.

REFERENCES

Reich, W. (1933). *Charakter analyse*. Leipzig: Sexpol Verlag.

Reich, W. (1942). *The function of the orgasm*. New York: Farrar, Straus.

Reich, W. (1945). The masochistic character. In W. Reich (Ed.), *Character analysis*. New York: Orgone Institute Press.

Wolman, B. (Ed.) (1973). *Dictionary of behavioral science*. New York: Van Nostrand Reinhold.

Zusne, L. (1987). *Eponyms in psychology*. Westport, CT: Greenwood Press.

Nelson, A. (1994). Wilhelm Reich. In R. J. Corsini (Ed.), *Ency. Psy.* New York: Wiley.

Reber, A. (1995). *The Penguin dictionary of psychology*. New York: Penguin Books.

Sutherland, S. (1996). *The international dictionary of psychology*. New York: Crossroad.

REINFORCEMENT, THORNDIKE'S THEORY OF. = learning theory, Thorndike's. E. L. Thorndike (1874–1949) anticipated the *modern theory of reinforcement* in his *law of effect* (Thorndike, 1898), where he considered the consequences of a response to be essential to the strengthening of the associative bond between stimulus and response. Thus, according to *Thorndike's theory of reinforcement*, the "satisfying consequences" (e.g., rewards or escape from punishment) strengthen a stimulus–response connection, while "annoying consequences" (e.g., punishment) weaken the connection. Thorndike argued that psychology's main goal should be to study behavior (i.e., stimulus–response units) and not conscious experience or mental elements. His *instrumental conditioning* approach was to develop the notion of "connectionism" and the *laws of connection* (see Thorndike, 1907; Titchener, 1928), that is, the connections between situations and responses, rather than the associations between *ideas* that were formulated by earlier psychologists and philosophers. *Thorndike's* (1898) *theory of reinforcement* resembled Pavlov's *law of reinforcement*, which was reported four years after Thorndike's *law of effect* first appeared. Many consider Thorndike to be the "father" of American learning psychology (Bugelski, 1994), and his classical experiments involving animals in "puzzle-boxes" (where the animal learned to get out of a cagelike box, and its behavior was instrumental in receiving food as a consequence) emphasized the "trial-and-error" aspects of learning (also called the *irradiation theory*; Reber, 1995) as well as the stimulus–response "connections" that occurred by chance and served to strengthen certain functional behaviors. The term "satisfier" that Thorndike used in his theory (i.e., "a stimulus–response bond or connection is strengthened when the response is followed by a satisfier") had been synonymous with the term *reward* until later psychologists (e.g., Hull, 1943; Skinner, 1938) advanced arguments for using the term *reinforcement* over the terms *satisfier* or *reward*. Terminology was, and continues to be, important in the area of *learning theory* development. Thus, while Thorndike's terms *satisfier* and *annoyer* may be outdated by the terminology in more current learning theories, it was an empirical advance over the much earlier rational philosophical approach, such as the Aristotelian terms *pleasure* and *pain*. Thorndike's two-part *reinforcement theory*—that is, that one learns (retains) whatever responses are followed by *satisfiers* and does not learn (eliminates) responses that are followed by *annoyers*—and his *laws of learning* (i.e., exercise, readiness, effect, belongingness, associative shifting) served for many years at the beginning of the twentieth century in this country as the basis for educational programs and systems (see Thorndike, 1910, 1913, 1931, 1932). See also ASSOCIATIVE SHIFTING, LAW OF; BELONGINGNESS, PRINCIPLE OF; EFFECT, LAW OF; EXERCISE, LAW OF; READINESS, LAW OF.

REFERENCES

Thorndike, E. L. (1898). Animal intelligence: An experimental study of the associative processes in animals. *Psy. Rev. Mono. Supp. 2*, 1–109.

Thorndike, E. L. (1907). *The elements of psychology.* New York: Seiler.

Thorndike, E. L. (1910). The contribution of psychology to education. *J. Ed. Psy., 1*, 5–12.

Thorndike, E. L. (1913). *The psychology of learning.* New York: Teachers College Press.

Titchener, E. B. (1928). *A textbook of psychology.* New York: Macmillan.

Thorndike, E. L. (1931). *Human learning.* New York: Appleton-Century-Crofts.

Thorndike, E. L. (1932). *The fundamentals of learning.* New York: Teachers College Press.

Thorndike, E. L. (1933a). An experimental study of rewards. *Teach. Coll. Contr. Ed.,* no. 580.

Thorndike, E. L. (1933b). A theory of the action of the after-effects of a connection upon it. *Psy. Rev., 40*, 434–439.

Skinner, B. F. (1938). *The behavior of organisms: An experimental analysis.* New York: Appleton-Century-Crofts.

Hull, C. (1943). *Principles of behavior.* New York: Appleton-Century-Crofts.

Thorndike, E. L. (1949). *Selected writings from a connectionist's psychology.* New York: Appleton-Century-Crofts.

Bugelski, B. R. (1994). Thorndike's laws of learning. In R. J. Corsini (Ed.), *Ency. Psy.* New York: Wiley.

Reber, A. (1995). *The Penguin dictionary of psychology.* New York: Penguin Books.

REINFORCEMENT THEORY. The term *reinforcement* contains a considerable amount of diversity of usage in psychology where most of the definitional variations stem from theoretical issues in *learning theory* concerning what reinforcement is and how it functions (Reber, 1995; cf: Warren, 1919, who describes the *law of reinforcement*). Common to most approaches, however, is the tautological reference to an operation of strengthening, supporting, or solidifying something (e.g., a learned response or a stimulus–response connection) or the event that so strengthens or supports it. In the empirical context of *Pavlovian classical conditioning*, *reinforcement* is defined as the unconditioned stimulus as it is related to, or paired with, the neutral or conditioned stimulus. In the context of *instrumental* or *operant conditioning*, *reinforcement* is defined as the events (usually stimuli; cf: Premack, 1962) that are consequences of a voluntary response or behavior where such behavior subsequently increases in frequency of occurrence. A related term, *reward*, is used by some psychologists as synonymous with *reinforcement*. When writers do not equate these two terms, however, the distinction usually centers around the ascribed subjective "satisfying" or "pleasurable" aspects of events ("rewards") versus the objectively measured influences that events have on behaviors ("reinforcers"). Psychologists also distinguish between *intrinsic* versus *extrinsic rewards*. *Intrinsic rewards* are activities that are interesting and fun to do in themselves, even though they produce no external benefits (e.g., painting, writing poetry), and *extrinsic rewards* are response outcomes that are satisfying independent of the events that produce them (e.g., money, food, public recognition). Kassin and Lepper (1984) and others have suggested that external reward for behavior produces an *overjustification effect* where providing an external reward for a behavior when there previously was none causes a person to question the justification for responding in the first place. *Intrinsic* and *extrinsic rewards* may be thought of as part of the *incentive theory of motivation* (Mook, 1987), which maintains that external stimuli motivate responding by "pulling" the behavior from the individual and is contrasted with the biological, drive-reduction, and arousal theories of motivation, which assert that behavior is "pushed" by events inside the organism. In other distinctions, the term *reinforcement* refers to the *procedure* of presenting/removing a stimulus event, and the term *reinforcer* refers to the actual consequent stimulus *event* itself. Historically, Thorndike (1898) preferred the terms *reward* and *punishment* to the older, more philosophically based terms *pleasure* and *pain*, but he also substituted the terms *satisfiers* and *annoyers* for *rewards* and *punishments* because this gave more range to possible kinds of behavioral aftereffects. By the late 1930s, both Hull (1943) and Skinner (1938) followed up on Thorndike's theory, but they changed his terminology where *satisfiers* now became *reinforcements*. In Hull's (1943) *drive-reduction theory*, *reinforcement* was defined in terms of decreasing degrees of drive stimulation where *rewards* or *satisfiers* now became *drive-reducers*, and learning could take place only when drives were diminished. In Skinner's (1938) *descriptive-behavioral* approach, however, the term *drive* was too vague and subjective so the term *deprivation* was used in its place. Thus, for Skinner, as for Thorndike, a *reinforcer* was anything that would result in a stronger/faster rate of performance of some activity that previously would occur only by chance (cf: the *trans-situationality principle*—the false generalization that a reinforcer that is effective in one situation will be as effective in all; Sutherland, 1996). In the period when Hull and Skinner were arguing for the importance of rewards/reinforcers for learning, other theoretical positions were formulated also. Guthrie (1935) asserted that one learns what one happens to do just before the stimulus that leads to the response is removed. According to Guthrie's *associative/contiguity theory*, one learns what one did *last*, and rewards are just a convenient way of making the stimuli disappear, and what one learns is to make both adaptive and non-adaptive responses where rewards are irrelevant. Tolman's (1932) *purposive/cognitive theory* held that learning was a matter of frequency of association between stimuli and responses where rewards were related only to the level of motivation. Another *theory of reinforcement*, Premack's (1959, 1962) *prepotent response theory*, is stated entirely in terms of responses and their probabilities: of any two responses the more probable response will reinforce the less probable one where the "prepotent" response is designated as the reinforcer. A critical test for *Premack's theory* was in its verification of the *indifference principle* (i.e., the contentions that the reinforcing power of a response depends solely on its probability, and it makes no difference how response probability was determined). In spite of various potential problems with *Premack's theory*, some writers (e.g., Adams, 1980) score it high in inventiveness: being able to reverse reinforcement relations is a particularly important finding that cannot be generated by competing reinforcement theories. A refinement to Premack's approach is called the *disequilibrium principle* (e.g., Timberlake & Farmer-Dougan, 1991), which proposes that the key to reinforcement is not just how much time one spends on a given activity, but whether a person spends as much time on it as she or he would like. Other *theories of reinforcement* include Harlow's (1950), Butler's (1953), and Montgomery's (1954) notions about sensory reinforcement and stimulus-centered drives as determinants of behavior. Brown (1953) recognized that the *stimulus-centered theorists'* work in exploratory and curiosity behavior were offering a drive *increase* theory of reinforcement in opposition to the drive *reduction* theory of reinforcement (such as Hull's approach). The *theory of stimulus-centered drive* by Harlow, Butler, and Montgomery also related well to the physiological *arousal theory* of drive and the discovery of the functioning of the "ascending reticular activating system" of the brain. In defense of the *arousal theorists'* approach to defining reinforcement (as against the *drive-reduction theorists'* criticisms), the *inverted-U hypothesis* was offered to show how a theory can explain the reinforcing effects of *both* drive decrease and drive increase (cf: Hebb, 1955; Malmo, 1959): when the organism is below the optimum point of arousal, an increase in drive is rewarding, but when one is above the optimum point, the drive level is aversive, and a decrease in drive is rewarding. Thus, *arousal theory* has been useful as an attempt to integrate externally based drives and internally based drives and as a link with contemporary findings in brain physiology, but it is not as yet a fully functioning *theory of reinforcement* (Adams, 1980). Accessory concepts to *reinforcement theory* are the terms *primary reinforcers, secondary reinforcers, positive reinforcement, negative reinforcement, partial reinforcement paradox/ effect* (see Capaldi, 1966), and *schedules of reinforcement*—including *continuous, fixed ratio, variable ratio, fixed interval*, and *variable interval* schedules (see Ferster & Skinner, 1957; Schoenfeld, 1970). The concept of *reinforcement* provides overlapping and even contradictory definitions to psychologists who find themselves often trapped lexicographically into the use of the term where part of the difficulty results from attempts to treat the concept (perhaps "wrong-headedly") as if it represented a single fundamental principle that operated in all circumstances (Reber, 1995). The ambiguities in the definitions of *reinforcer* and *reinforcement* are likely to remain unresolved for some time, but the worth of the concepts has already been demonstrated in countless studies and applications (Shaw, 1994). See also GUTHRIE'S THEORY OF BEHAVIOR; HULL'S LEARNING THEORY; INVERTED-U HYPOTHESIS; LEARNING THEORIES/LAWS; MOTIVATION, THEORIES OF; PAVLOVIAN CONDITIONING PRINCIPLES/LAWS/THEORIES; PREMACK'S PRINCIPLE/ LAW; PUNISHMENT, THEORIES OF; REINFORCEMENT, THORNDIKE'S THEORY OF; SKINNER'S DESCRIPTIVE BEHAVIOR/OPERANT CONDITIONING THEORY; TOLMAN'S THEORY.

REFERENCES

Thorndike, E. (1898). Animal intelligence: An experimental study of the associative processes in animals. *Psy. Rev. Mono. Supp., 2*, 1–109.

Warren, H. (1919). *Human psychology*. Boston: Houghton Mifflin.

Tolman, E. (1932). *Purposive behavior in animals and men*. New York: Appleton-Century-Crofts.

Guthrie, E. (1935). *The psychology of learning*. New York: Harper & Row.

Skinner, B. F. (1938). *The behavior of organisms: An experimental analysis*. New York: Appleton-Century-Crofts.

Hull, C. (1943). *The principles of behavior*. New York: Appleton-Century-Crofts.

Harlow, H. (1950). Learning and satiation of response in intrinsically motivated complex puzzle performance by monkeys. *J. Comp. Physio. Psy., 43*, 289–294.

Brown, J. (1953). Comments on Professor Harlow's paper. In *Current theory and research in motivation: A symposium*. Lincoln: University of Nebraska Press.

Butler, R. (1953). Discrimination learning by Rhesus monkeys to visual-exploration motivation. *J. Comp. Physio. Psy., 46*, 95–98.

Montgomery, K. (1954). The role of the exploratory drive in learning. *J. Comp. Physio. Psy., 47*, 60–64.

Hebb, D. (1955). Drives and C.N.S. (conceptual nervous system). *Psy. Rev., 62*, 243–255.

Ferster, C., & Skinner, B. F. (1957). *Schedules of reinforcement*. New York: Appleton-Century-Crofts.

Malmo, R. (1959). Activation: A neuropsychological dimension. *Psy. Rev., 66*, 367–386.

Premack, D. (1959). Toward empirical behavioral laws: I. Positive reinforcement. *Psy. Rev., 66*, 219–233.

Premack, D. (1962). Reversibility of the reinforcement relation. *Science, 136*, 255–257.

Capaldi, E. (1966). Partial reinforcement: An hypothesis of sequential effects. *Psy. Rev., 73*, 459–477.

Schoenfeld, W. (Ed.) (1970). *The theory of reinforcement schedules*. New York: Appleton-Century-Crofts.

Adams, J. (1980). *Learning and memory: An introduction*. Homewood, IL: Dorsey Press.

Kassin, S., & Lepper, M. (1984). Oversufficient and insufficient justification effects: Cognitive and behavioral development. *Advances in Motivation & Achievement, 3*, 73–106.

Mook, D. (1987). *Motivation: The organization of action*. New York: Norton.

Timberlake, W., & Farmer-Dougan, V. (1991). Reinforcement in applied settings: Figuring out ahead of time what will work. *Psy. Bull., 110*, 379–391.

Bugelski, B. R. (1994). Rewards. In R. J. Corsini (Ed.), *Ency. Psy.* New York: Wiley.

Kimble, G. (1994). Reinforcement. In R. J. Corsini (Ed.), *Ency. Psy.* New York: Wiley.

Shaw, R. (1994). Reinforcers. In R. J. Corsini (Ed.), *Ency. Psy.* New York: Wiley.

Reber, A. (1995). *The Penguin dictionary of psychology*. New York: Penguin Books.

Sutherland, S. (1996). *The international dictionary of psychology*. New York: Crossroad.

RELATIVITY/RELATIVE EFFECT, LAW OF. See HERRNSTEIN'S MATCHING LAW.

REM SLEEP, THEORY OF. See SLEEP, THEORIES OF.

REORGANIZATION THEORY. See PERCEPTION (I. GENERAL), THEORIES OF.

REPAIR/RESTORATION THEORY. See SLEEP, THEORIES OF.

REPETITION EFFECT. See SERIAL-POSITION EFFECT.

RESCORLA–WAGNER THEORY/MODEL. See BLOCKING, PHENOM-ENON/EFFECT OF; PAVLOVIAN CONDITIONING PRINCIPLES/LAWS/THEORIES.

RESONANCE, RESONANCE/PLACE, RESONANCE/VOLLEY THEO-RIES. See AUDITION/HEARING, THEORIES OF.

RESPONSE MAGNITUDE, LAW OF. See SKINNER'S DESCRIPTIVE BE-HAVIOR/OPERANT CONDITIONING THEORY.

RETICULARIST THEORY. See NEURON/NEURAL/NERVE THEORY.

RETROACTIVE INHIBITION, LAW OF. See INTERFERENCE THEO-RIES.

REVERSION, LAW OF. See GALTON'S LAWS.

REWARD THEORY OF INTERPERSONAL ATTRACTION. See INTER-PERSONAL ATTRACTION THEORIES.

RIBOT'S LAW. The French psychologist Theodule Armand Ribot (1839–1916) formulated this principle concerning amnesia, which states that retrograde memory loss affects events that occurred closer in time to the onset of amnesia, and these events are remembered less well than those events that occurred further back in time (Zusne, 1987). Thus, according to *Ribot's law*, in a traumatic retrograde amnesia situation, memories for events occurring immediately before the accident are most likely to be lost. This principle does not always hold, but it was an important first step in going from clinical description to scientific theory (Kihlstrom & Glisky, 1994). See also FORGETTING/MEMORY, THE-ORIES OF; JACKSON'S LAW.

REFERENCES

Ribot, T. (1881). *Les maladies de la memoire*. Paris: Alcan.
Ribot, T. (1885). *Les maladies de la personalite*. Paris: Alcan.
Zusne, L. (1987). *Eponyms in psychology*. Westport, CT: Greenwood Press.
Kihlstrom, J., & Glisky, E. (1994). Amnesia. In V. Ramachandran (Ed.), *Encyclopedia of human behavior*. San Diego: Academic Press.
Reber, A. (1995). *The Penguin dictionary of psychology*. New York: Penguin Books.

RICCO'S/PIPER'S LAWS. The first generalized principle in the area of visual thresholds and cutaneous-thermal thresholds, developed by the Italian astronomer Annibele Ricco (1844–1919), states that in considering very small areas of the retina, such as less than 10-degrees of arc, the absolute threshold is inversely proportional to the area that is stimulated (Ricco, 1877). *Ricco's law* holds well for both fovea and periphery areas of the retina where it states that the product of area stimulated times the luminance is a constant for threshold, but for larger areas the law does not apply well (Bartlett, 1965). A principle related to *Ricco's law*, called *Piper's law*, was named in honor of the German physiologist Hans Edmund Piper (1877–1915) and states that for uniform and moderately sized areas of the retina the absolute threshold is inversely proportional to the square root of the area that is stimulated. Thus, the two related laws of visual threshold and retinal area effects may be compared where *Ricco's law* states that $L \times A = C$, and *Piper's law* states that $L \times$ square root $A = C$ (L = luminance or extant "brightness," A = amount of retinal area stimulated, and C = a constant for absolute threshold). Neither of these two laws, however, holds over the full range of stimulus areas (Brown & Mueller, 1965). *Ricco's law* deals with "spatial summation" in the visual system, while another related law, the *Bunsen–Roscoe law*, deals with "temporal summation" and states that $IT = C$ (I = threshold intensity or "brightness," T = light flash duration up to .1 second, and C = a constant). See also BUNSEN–ROSCOE LAW; VISION/SIGHT, THEORIES OF.

REFERENCES

Ricco, A. (1877). Relazione fra il minimo angolo visuale e l'intensita luminosa. *Mem. Reg. Acc. Sci. Let. Art. Mod., 17,* 47–160.

Piper, H. (1911). Uber die netzhautstrome. *Ar. Anat. Physio., Leipzig,* 85–132.

Riopelle, A., & Chow, A. (1953). Scotopic area-intensity relations at various retinal locations. *J. Exp. Psy., 46,* 314–318.

Bartlett, N. (1965). Thresholds as dependent on some energy relations and characteristics of the subject. In C. Graham (Ed.), *Vision and visual perception.* New York: Wiley.

Brown, J., & Mueller, C. (1965). Brightness discrimination and brightness contrast. In C. Graham (Ed.), *Vision and visual perception.* New York: Wiley.

Zusne, L. (1987). *Eponyms in psychology.* Westport, CT: Greenwood Press.

RISKY-SHIFT/CHOICE SHIFT EFFECT. See DECISION-MAKING THEORIES.

ROGERS' THEORY OF PERSONALITY. The American psychologist Carl Rogers (1902–1987) developed a theory of personality that is essentially humanistic and phenomenological in nature and falls between the *psychoanalytic* approach (e.g., Freud, 1953–1974) and the *behavioristic* orientation (e.g., Skinner, 1938, 1953; cf: Rogers & Skinner, 1956). The humanistic outlook (called the *third force*) toward personality is one of optimism where it is argued that individuals contain within themselves the potentialities for healthy and creative growth if they accept the responsibility for their own lives. This orientation differs from the "pessimism" of the *psychoanalytic* approach and the "mechanization" of the *behavioristic* approach. The phenomenological aspect of *Rogers' theory* refers to an emphasis on the person's "inner life" where experiences, values, beliefs, perceptions, and feelings are examined. Rogers' notions of personality and personality change grew out of his clinical experience and therapeutic relationships, which also led to his development of a method of psychotherapy called *nondirective*, or *client-centered*, therapy. In *client-centered* therapy, the client comes to perceive the therapist as providing "unconditional positive regard" as well as gaining an understanding of one's internal frame of reference. The goal in this approach is to help a person's *self-concept* become more congruent with his or her total experience and to become a fully functioning individual (Rogers, 1951, 1980). Rogers (1942) offered a relatively simple theory of how people can change their attitudes and behavior within a permissive climate with an empathic therapist. He also presented a more sophisticated 19-proposition *theory of self* (Rogers, 1951) highlighted by postulates such as reality for the individual is the field as perceived, perceptions may be ignored when they are inconsistent with the concept of *self*, and when the *self-concept* is safe from threat, it can examine contradictory perceptions and incorporate them into a revised concept of *self*. Rogers' *theory of self* was later expanded and published as a more formal theory (Rogers, 1959; cf: Krause, 1964; Raimy, 1975). The dynamics of *Rogers' personality theory* focuses on the selective tendencies of the organism to grow, actualize, enhance, and maintain its experiences, where the major motivating force is the *self-actualizing* drive, and the main goal of life is to become a "whole" (i.e., "self-actualized") person. Rogers' *motivational theory of personality* emphasizes the two learned needs of "positive regard" and "self-regard" (Rogers, 1959). Rogers' *client-centered therapy* is an established and widely used method of treatment, and his *person-centered theory* has become a significant stimulus for research in personality (Hall & Lindzey, 1978). On the other hand, criticisms of his theory include the observation (e.g., Smith, 1950) that his approach is based on a naive type of phenomenology where data from unreliable self-reports are used, and the assertion by psychoanalytically oriented psychologists that Rogers ignores the influence of the unconscious in determining behavior (Hall & Lindzey, 1977; cf: Rogers, 1977). See also FREUD'S THEORY OF PERSONALITY; MASLOW'S THEORY OF PERSONALITY; PERSONALITY THEORIES; SKINNER'S DESCRIPTIVE BEHAVIOR/OPERANT CONDITIONING THEORY.

REFERENCES

Skinner, B. F. (1938). *The behavior of organisms: An experimental analysis.* New York: Appleton-Century-Crofts.

Rogers, C. (1942). *Counseling and psychotherapy: Newer concepts in practice.* Boston: Houghton Mifflin.

Rogers, C. (1947). Some observations on the organization of personality. *Amer. Psy., 2,* 358–368.

Smith, M. (1950). The phenomenological approach in personality theory: Some critical remarks. *J. Abn. Soc. Psy., 45,* 516–522.

Rogers, C. (1951). *Client-centered therapy: Its current practice, implications, and theory.* Boston: Houghton Mifflin.

Freud, S. (1953–1974). *The standard edition of the complete psychological works of Sigmund Freud.* J. Strachey (Ed.). London: Hogarth Press.

Skinner, B. F. (1953). *Science and human behavior.* New York: Macmillan.

Rogers, C., & Skinner, B. F. (1956). Some issues concerning the control of human behavior: A symposium. *Science, 124,* 1057–1066.

Rogers, C. (1959). A theory of therapy, personality, and interpersonal relationships, as developed in the client-centered framework. In S. Koch (Ed.), *Psychology: A study of a science.* Vol. 3. New York: McGraw-Hill.

Rogers, C. (1961). *On becoming a person.* Boston: Houghton Mifflin.

Krause, M. (1964). An analysis of Carl R. Rogers' theory of personality. *Genet. Psy. Mono., 69,* 49–99.

Epstein, S. (1973). The self-concept revisited or a theory of a theory. *Amer. Psy., 28,* 404–416.

Rogers, C. (1974). In retrospect: Forty-six years. *Amer. Psy., 29,* 115–123.

Raimy, V. (1975). *Misunderstandings of the self: Cognitive psychotherapy and the misconception hypothesis.* San Francisco: Jossey-Bass.

Rogers, C. (1977). *Carl Rogers on personal power.* New York: Delacorte.

Hall, C., & Lindzey, G. (1978). *Theories of personality.* New York: Wiley.

Rogers, C. (1980). *A way of being.* Boston: Houghton Mifflin.

Wylie, R. (1994). Self-concept. In R. J. Corsini (Ed.), *Ency. Psy.* New York: Wiley.

ROTTER'S SOCIAL LEARNING THEORY. The American psychologist Julian Bernard Rotter (1916–) formulated a *social learning theory* that combined the Hullian concept of *reinforcement* with the Tolmanian concept of *cognition* to describe situations where the individual has a number of behavioral options (Rotter, 1954, 1982). In Rotter's approach, each potential behavior of the person is related to an outcome that has a particular reinforcement *value* associated with it, as well as an *expectancy* concerning the likelihood of the reinforcers following each behavior. Thus, *Rotter's theory* may be characterized as an *expectancy-value model* where the likelihood of a behavior's occurring is a function of both the value of the reinforcer associated with it and the probability of the reinforcer occurring (Feather, 1982). In Rotter's model, the value and probability of various reinforcers are unique to the person, and it is the person's internal value and expectancy calculations that are important rather than some objective measure of value and probability. Rotter proposed that situations may be assessed also in terms of the outcomes (i.e., expectancy and value of reinforcers) associated with specific behaviors (Rotter, 1981), as well as suggested that individuals develop expectations that hold across many situations (called *generalized expectancies*; Rotter, 1966, 1971, 1990). Among Rotter's *generalized expectancies* concepts are *interpersonal trust* (the degree to which one can rely on the word of others; Rotter, 1971), which has received little research interest, and *internal* versus *external locus of control of reinforcement* (also called simply *locus of control*), which has received a great deal of research attention (Lefcourt, 1984; Rotter, 1990). Persons who score high on *internal locus of control* expect that outcomes or reinforcers will depend mostly on their own efforts, whereas persons scoring high on *external locus of control* have an expectancy that outcomes will depend largely on luck, chance, fate, or other external forces; external locus of control individuals feel relatively helpless in relation to events (Pervin, 1996). Rotter developed the "Internal-External (I-E) Scale" to measure individual differences in generalized expectancies concerning the extent to which punishments and rewards are under external or internal control (Rotter, 1966). Variations of the I-E Scale have appeared also in research in the areas of health and children's behavior (e.g., Strickland, 1989). While Rotter's approach has had a large impact on research in personality and social learning psychology for about a decade (his 1966 monograph on *generalized expectancies* was the most frequently cited single article in the social sciences since 1969), his influence has declined recently—perhaps because the *locus of control* scale has been found to be more complex than was originally expected (Pervin, 1996). See also BANDURA'S THEORY; REINFORCEMENT THE-ORY.

REFERENCES

Rotter, J. (1954). *Social learning and clinical psychology.* Englewood Cliffs, NJ: Prentice-Hall.

Phares, E. (1957). Expectancy changes in skill and chance situations. *J. Abn. Soc. Psy., 54,* 339–342.

Lefcourt, H. (1966). Internal versus external control of reinforcement: A review. *Psy. Bull., 65,* 206–220.

Rotter, J. (1966). Generalized expectancies for internal versus external control of reinforcement. *Psy. Mono., 80,* no. 609.

Rotter, J. (1971). Generalized expectancies for interpersonal trust. *Amer. Psy., 26,* 443–452.

Rotter, J., Chance, J., & Phares, E. (Eds.) (1972). *Applications of a social learning theory of personality.* New York: Holt, Rinehart, & Winston.

Collins, B. (1974). Four components of the Rotter internal-external scale: Belief in a difficult world, a just world, a predictable world, and a politically responsive world. *J. Pers. Soc. Psy., 29,* 381–391.

Levenson, H. (1974). Activism and powerful others: Distinctions within the concept of internal-external control. *J. Pers. Assess., 38,* 377–383.

Rotter, J. (1975). Some problems and misconceptions related to the construct of internal versus external control of reinforcement. *J. Cons. & Clin. Psy., 43,* 56–67.

Rotter, J. (1981). The psychological situation in social learning theory. In D. Magnusson (Ed.), *Toward a psychology of situations.* Hillsdale, NJ: Erlbaum.

Feather, N. (Ed.) (1982). *Expectancies and actions: Expectancy-value models in psychology*. Hillsdale, NJ: Erlbaum.

Rotter, J. (1982). *The development and applications of social learning theory: Selected papers*. New York: Praeger.

Lefcourt, H. (Ed.) (1984). *Research with the locus of control construct*. Orlando, FL: Academic Press.

Strickland, B. (1989). Internal-external control expectancies: From contingency to creativity. *Amer. Psy., 44*, 1–12.

Rotter, J. (1990). Internal versus external controls of reinforcement. *Amer. Psy., 45*, 489–493.

Phares, E. (1994a). Locus of control. In R. J. Corsini (Ed.), *Ency. Psy.* New York: Wiley.

Phares, E. (1994b). Social learning theories. In R. J. Corsini (Ed.), *Ency. Psy.* New York: Wiley.

Vinacke, W. (1994). Inner/outer-directed behavior. In R. J. Corsini (Ed.), *Ency. Psy.* New York: Wiley.

Pervin, L. (1996). *The science of personality*. New York: Wiley.

RUTHERFORD'S FREQUENCY THEORY. See AUDITION/HEARING, THEORIES OF.

S

SCHACHTER–SINGER'S THEORY OF EMOTIONS. The American psychologists Stanley Schachter and Jerome Singer (1962) proposed a *theory of emotions* that challenged certain aspects of both the *cognitive theory of emotions* and the earlier *James–Lange theory* (James, 1890). Where these other theories assumed that each emotion is associated with a specific physiological state or condition (cf: Funkenstein, 1955), Schachter and Singer argued that individuals who are in a state of physiological arousal for which they have no explanation will *label* that state as an emotion that is appropriate to the situation in which they find themselves (e.g., the arousal will be labeled as "happy" if the person is at a party, but the *same* arousal state will be labeled as "angry" if the person is confronting another person in an argument). The experiments of Schachter and his associates point out the fact that emotions seem to depend on two components (*Schachter–Singer's theory* is sometimes called a *two-factor theory*; Baron, 1992): (1) some kind of objective physiological arousal and (2) a subjective cognitive or mental process and appraisal whereby persons interpret and label their bodily changes. People who have no reasonable or objective explanation for their internal, emotional, or aroused state may interpret their mood in subjective terms according to their perception of the present environment. The *Schachter–Singer theory* has also been called the *jukebox theory of emotions* (e.g., Kagan & Havemann, 1968) because one's physiology is aroused by some stimulus, where the arousing stimulus is compared to the coin placed in a jukebox. The stimulus sets off patterns of brain activity, especially in the hypothalamus, which, in turn, activates the autonomic nervous system and the endocrine glands, causing a state of general physiological arousal. The body's sensory receptors report these physiological changes to the brain. However, the sensations are vague and can be labeled in many different ways, just as a jukebox activated by the coin can be made to play any one of a number of different songs depending on which button is pushed. While the experiments of Schachter and his associates seem to support a *cognitive theory of emotions*, they may actually come closer to the *James–Lange theory* because the *Schachter–Singer theory* implies that the physiological arousal state comes about first, and the cognitive label that defines the emotion comes afterward. Some theorists (e.g., Arnold, 1994) argue that Schachter's experiments are interesting but not relevant for a theory of emotion inasmuch as people do not normally look for a label to identify their emotions. The alternative view is that emotions are felt without attending to the physiological changes that accompany them, and people react to the object or event and not to a physiological state. On the other hand, while some recent studies of emotion have not always agreed with Schachter and Singer's (1962) viewpoint, many investigators do offer support for the contention that people often interpret their emotions in terms of external cues (e.g., Dutton & Aron, 1974). The *Schachter–Singer theory* has also been fruitful in suggesting the important research question of the origin or source of one's physiological arousal. For example, one source of arousal that has been explored in recent years is the discrepancy between *actual* and *expected* events (Baron, 1992). According to the *discrepancy-evaluation/constructivity theory* (Mandler, 1990), the greater the gap between what a person *expects* and what *actually* does happen in a given situation, the greater the resulting arousal. Such arousal is then interpreted cognitively to yield subjective experiences of emotion. The *discrepancy-evaluation/constructivity theory* further suggests that arousal level determines the intensity of the emotional experience, while cognitive evaluation determines its specific identity or quality. Thus, the *discrepancy-evaluation/constructivity theory* extends the *Schachter–Singer theory* by identifying a key cause of the arousal that people interpret—in terms of external cues—as one emotion or another. See also ATTRIBUTION THEORY; COGNITIVE THEORIES OF EMOTIONS; EMOTIONS, THEORIES/LAWS OF.

REFERENCES

James, W. (1890). *The principles of psychology*. New York: Holt.

Funkenstein, D. (1955). The physiology of fear and anger. *Sci. Amer., 192*, 74–80.

Schachter, S., & Singer, J. (1962). Cognitive, social, and physiological determinants of emotional state. *Psy. Rev., 69*, 379–399.

Kagan, J., & Havemann, E. (1968). *Psychology: An introduction*. New York: Harcourt, Brace, & World.

Dutton, D., & Aron, A. (1974). Some evidence for heightened sexual attraction under conditions of high anxiety. *J. Pers. Soc. Psy., 30*, 510–517.

Mandler, G. (1990). A constructivity theory of emotion. In N. Stein, B. Leventhal, & T. Tragbasso (Eds.), *Psychological and biological approaches to emotion*. Hillsdale, NJ: Erlbaum.

Baron, R. (1992). *Psychology*. Boston: Allyn & Bacon.

Arnold, M. (1994). Cognitive theories of emotion. In R. J. Corsini (Ed.), *Ency. Psy.* New York: Wiley.

Sinclair, R., Hoffman, C., Mark, M., Martin, L., & Pickering, T. (1994). Construct accessibility and the misattribution of arousal: Schachter and Singer revisited. *Psy. Sci., 5*, 15–19.

SCHAFER–MURPHY EFFECT. See GESTALT THEORY/LAWS.

SCHIZOPHRENIA, THEORIES OF. The term *schizophrenia* is a general label for a number of psychotic disorders with various behavioral, emotional, and cognitive features. The term was originated by the Swiss psychiatrist Eugen Bleuler (1857–1939) in 1911, who offered it as a replacement for the term *dementia praecox* (Bleuler, 1911). In its literal meaning, *schizophrenia* is a "splitting in the mind," a connotation reflecting a dissociation or separation between the functions of feeling/emotion, on one hand, and those of cognition/ thinking, on the other hand. The "split" is taken to mean a horizontal direction, rather than a vertical direction, which indicates the disorder called *multiple personality* (which is often confused by laypeople with *schizophrenia*). In the simplest terms, *multiple personality* is a "split *within* self," while *schizophrenia* is a "split *between* self and others." Various categories, descriptions, and subtypes of schizophrenia have been developed (e.g., acute, borderline, catatonic, childhood/infantile autism, chronic, disorganized, hebephrenic, latent, paranoid/ paraphrenic, process, reactive, residual, schizoaffective, simple, and undifferentiated), but there are certain common aspects to all types (Reber, 1995): (1) deterioration from previous levels of social, cognitive, and vocational functioning; (2) onset before midlife (i.e., about 45–50 years of age); (3) a duration of at least six months; and (4) a pattern of psychotic features including thought disturbances, bizarre delusions, hallucinations, disturbed sense of self, and a loss of reality testing. The *progressive teleological-regression hypothesis* (Arieti, 1974) is a theory of schizophrenia that maintains that the disorder results from a process of active concretization, that is, a purposeful returning to lower levels of psychodynamic and behavioral adaptation that, while momentarily effective in reducing anxiety, tends ultimately toward repetitive behaviors and results in a failure to maintain integration. In general, current *theories of schizophrenia* focus on biochemical abnormalities, with some cases of schizophrenia appearing to be of genetic origin perhaps triggered by environmental stresses (cf: *brain-spot hypothesis*—a term applied by E. Southard to theories that emphasize organic factors in the etiology of mental disease; the *mind-twist hypothesis*, which emphasizes a functional, rather than a structural, basis of mental disorders; Warren, 1934; and *Sutton's law*, named after the notorious Willie Sutton who robbed banks "because that's where the money was," and is the principle when applied to clinical diagnosis that one should look for a disorder where or in whom it is most likely to be found and emphasizes the predisposing factors in all diseases and disorders; Reber, 1995). The major theoretical models of the etiology of schizophrenia are the *specific gene theory*—which assumes that the disorder is caused by one or more faulty genes that produce metabolic disturbances (e.g.,

Rosenthal, 1971; Gottesman & Shields, 1972; Kety, 1976; Dworkin, Lenzen-wenger, & Moldin, 1987; cf: Meehl, 1962; see, also, the *founder effect* con-cerning population genetics and the high rate of schizophrenia in residents of Sweden above the Arctic Circle; Reber, 1995); *psychoanalytic theory*—which today gives primacy to aggressive impulses and suggests that the threats of the intense *id* impulses may provoke schizophrenia depending on the strength of the *ego*; however, few data are available on the psychoanalytic position, and there is no evidence that *ego* impairments cause schizophrenia (Davison & Neale, 1990); *labeling theory*—which assumes that the crucial factor in schizophrenia is the act of assigning a diagnostic label to the individual where the label then influences the way in which the person continues to behave and also determines the reactions of other people to the individual's behavior; that is, the social role *is* the disorder, and it is determined by the labeling process (e.g., Scheff, 1966; cf: Rosenhan, 1973, 1975; Murphy, 1976); *experiential theory*—which assumes that one's family is a key factor is producing schizophrenic behavior in the person where, in a process called "mystification," the parent systematically strips the child's feelings and perceptions about him- or herself and the world of all validity so that the child comes to doubt his or her hold on reality (e.g., Laing's, 1969, *theory of schizophrenia* as a "double-bind, no-win situation"; cf: Davison & Neale, 1990, who state that there seems to be little substantiating evidence for this position); *biochemical/neurological theories*—in this category, at this time, no single biochemical or neurological theory has unequivocal sup-port; however, there are promising, but incomplete, findings concerning areas both of brain pathology and of excess activity of the neurotransmitter *dopamine* regarding the incidence of schizophrenia (e.g., Taubes, 1994); *social class the-ory*—which emphasizes the consistent correlations found between lowest so-cioeconomic class and the diagnosis of schizophrenia (e.g., Hollingshead & Redlich, 1958; Kohn, 1968); in this category, the *sociogenic hypothesis* states that simply being in a low social class may in itself cause schizophrenia, and the *social drift theory* suggests that during the course of their developing psy-chosis, schizophrenics may "drift" into the poverty-ridden areas of the city (e.g., Turner & Wagonfeld, 1967); the *environmental stress/family theories*—which view schizophrenia as a reaction to a stressful environment, or family, that presents overwhelming and anxiety-producing conditions; the *diathesis-stress hypothesis* refers to a predisposition to develop a particular disorder—in this case, schizophrenia—as a result of interaction between stressful demands and personal traits; the term *schizophrenogenic parent/mother* has been coined for the allegedly cold, rejecting, distant, aloof, dominant, and conflict-inducing parent who is said to produce schizophrenia in one's offspring (e.g., Fromm-Reichmann, 1948); early researchers studying schizophrenia looked for, and found, pathology in one or both parents of psychotic children (e.g., Mahler, 1965); however, more current research (e.g., Werry, 1979) suggests that there is no valid scientific evidence confirming that parental disorders precede and precipitate their children's disturbances. Another prominent early viewpoint, the *double-bind theory*, emphasized the situation faced by a person who receives contradictory or "mixed" messages from a powerful person (usually the parent) who has difficulty with close affectionate relationships but cannot admit to such feelings. In the *double-bind* scenario, the parent communicates withdrawal and coldness when the child approaches but then reaches out toward the child with simulated love when he or she pulls back from the coldness; in this way, the child is caught in a *double bind*: no course of action can possibly prove satisfactory, and all assumptions about what she or he is supposed to do will be disconfirmed (cf: Fowles, 1992; Enfield, 1994). The *constitutional-predisposition theory* combines the *genetic* and the *environmental theories* and argues that a variety of disparate dispositions are inherited but that the emergence of a diagnosable schizophrenic disorder is dependent on the degree of these dispositions and the extent to which they are encouraged by particular types of enviromental conditions; this point of view has the largest number of adherents among specialists (Reber, 1995); and the *two-syndrome hypothesis/theory* suggests that schizophrenia is composed of two separate syndromes: Type 1, which is related to *dopamine sensitivity* and produces positive symptoms such as delusions and hallucinations, and Type 2, which is related to *genetics* and *brain abnormalities* and produces negative symptoms such as flat effect and social withdrawal (e.g., Crow, 1985; Gottesman, 1991). See also LABELING/DEVIANCE THEORY; PSYCHOPATHOLOGY, THEORIES OF.

REFERENCES

Bleuler, E. (1911). *Dementia praecox: Or the group of schizophrenias*. New York: International Universities Press.

Warren, H. (Ed.) (1934). *Dictionary of psychology*. Cambridge, MA: Houghton Mifflin.

Fromm-Reichmann, F. (1948). Notes on the development of treatment of schizophrenics by psychoanalytic psychotherapy. *Psychiatry, 11*, 263–273.

Hollingshead, A., & Redlich, F. (1958). *Social class and mental illness: A community study*. New York: Wiley.

Meehl, P. (1962). Schizotaxia, schizotypy, schizophrenia. *Amer. Psy., 17*, 827–838.

Mahler, M. (1965). On early infantile psychosis. The symbiotic and autistic syndromes. *J. Amer. Acad. Psychiat., 4*, 554–568.

Scheff, T. (1966). *Being mentally ill: A sociological theory*. Chicago: Aldine.

Turner, R., & Wagonfeld, M. (1967). Occupational mobility and schizophrenia. *Amer. Socio. Rev., 32*, 104–113.

Kohn, M. (1968). Social class and schizophrenia: A critical review. In D. Rosenthal & S. Kety (Eds.), *The transmission of schizophrenia*. Elmsford, NY: Pergamon.

Laing, R. (1969). *The divided self: A study of sanity and madness*. New York: Pantheon.

Rosenthal, D. (1971). *Genetics of psychopathology*. New York: McGraw-Hill.

Gottesman, I., & Shields, J. (1972). *Schizophrenia and genetics: A twin study vantage point*. New York: Academic Press.

Rosenhan, D. (1973). On being sane in insane places. *Science, 197*, 250–258.

Arieti, S. (1974). *Interpretations of schizophrenia*. New York: Basic Books.

Rosenhan, D. (1975). The contextual nature of psychiatric diagnoses. *J. Abn. Psy., 84*, 462–474.

Kety, S. (1976). Genetic aspects of schizophrenia. *Psychiat. Ann., 6*, 11–32.

Murphy, J. (1976). Psychiatric labeling in cross-cultural perspective. *Science, 191*, 1019–1028.

Werry, J. (1979). The childhood psychoses. In H. Quay & J. Werry (Eds.), *Psychopathological disorders of childhood*. New York: Wiley.

Crow, T. (1985). The two syndrome concept: Origins and current status. *Schizo. Bull., 11*, 471–486.

Dworkin, R., Lenzenwenger, M., & Moldin, S. (1987). Genetics and the phenomenology of schizophrenia. In P. Harvey & E. Walker (Eds.), *Positive and negative symptoms of psychosis*. Hillsdale, NJ: Erlbaum.

Davison, G., & Neale, J. (1990). *Abnormal psychology*. New York: Wiley.

Gottesman, I. (1991). *Schizophrenia genesis: The origins of madness*. New York: Freeman.

Fowles, D. (1992). Schizophrenia: Diathesis-stress revisited. *Ann. Rev. Psy., 43*, 303–336.

Enfield, R. (1994). Double bind. In R. J. Corsini (Ed.), *Ency. Psy.* New York: Wiley.

Lovass, O. (1994). Autism. In R. J. Corsini (Ed.), *Ency. Psy.* New York: Wiley.

Mendel, W. (1994). Schizophrenia. In R. J. Corsini (Ed.), *Ency. Psy.* New York: Wiley.

Taubes, G. (1994). Will new dopamine receptors offer a key to schizophrenia? *Science, 265*, 1034–1035.

Reber, A. (1995). *The Penguin dictionary of psychology*. New York: Penguin Books.

SECONDARY REINFORCEMENT, PRINCIPLE OF. See REINFORCEMENT THEORY; SKINNER'S DESCRIPTIVE BEHAVIOR/OPERANT CONDITIONING THEORY.

SEGREGATION, LAW OF. See MENDEL'S LAWS/PRINCIPLES.

SELF-ACTUALIZING MAN THEORY. See ORGANIZATIONAL/INDUSTRIAL/SYSTEMS THEORY.

SELF-CATEGORIZATION THEORY. See PREJUDICE, THEORIES OF.

SELF-CONCEPT THEORY. See ROGERS' THEORY OF PERSONALITY.

SELF-PERCEPTION THEORY. See ATTRIBUTION THEORY.

SELYE'S THEORY/MODEL OF STRESS. The Austrian-born Canadian endocrinologist/psychologist Hans Selye (1907–1982) was one of the first modern psychologists to systematically examine *stress* and its effects on the organism, although medical interest in *stress* goes back to the Greek physician Hippocrates (460–377 B.C.). In the 1920s, the American physiologist Walter B. Cannon (1871–1945) verified that the "stress response" is part of a unified mind–body system (Cannon, 1929), where a variety of stressors (such as lack of oxygen, extreme cold, emotional states) trigger the flow of adrenaline and noradrenaline, which, in turn, enter the bloodstream from sympathetic nerve endings in the inner portion of the adrenal glands. Such physiological events help to prepare and adapt the body for what Cannon called the "flight or fight" syndrome, or what is known today as *Cannon's emergency syndrome* (Cannon, 1932). Hans Selye (1936, 1976) spent 40 years of research on *stress* and expanded Cannon's findings to the extent that today *stress* is a major concept in both medicine and psychology. Based on his study of hormone-action in rats and after many disappointments with his experiments, Selye discovered that many stressors such as surgical trauma, heat, cold, electric shock, and immobilizing restraint all had similar physiological effects on the organism. The body's adaptive response to stress seemed so general to Selye that he called it the *general adaptation syndrome (GAS)*, which is defined as the pattern of nonspecific bodily mechanisms activated in response to a continuing threat by almost any severe stressor. According to *Selye's theory*, the *GAS* is divided into three stages: (1) alarm reaction—initially, the stressor results in a state of alarm ("shock" and "countershock" phases) and mobilization where the body's resistance drops below its normal level; (2) resistance—this stage develops where the adrenal cortex secretes protective corticosteroids, and where the body becomes highly susceptible to additional and unrelated stresses; and (3) exhaustion—this stage occurs if the danger from stress is prolonged, and the individual may become seriously ill and die. The *GAS* has been observed in cases of prolonged exposure to psychological (e.g., maternal separation), environmental (e.g., cold), and physiological (e.g., poison) types of stressors. However, newer research indicates that there are subtle differences in the body's reactions to different stressors, and one weakness of *Selye's model* is that it fails to account for cognitive processes in determining how individuals interpret a specific event to be stressful or not (Baron, 1992). Nevertheless, most medical experts agree with Selye's basic point that prolonged stress can produce physical deterioration (cf: the field of *behavioral medicine* and its perspectives on stress; Pomerleau & Brady, 1979). Extending from Selye's work on stress is the development of a new field of study in psychology called *psychoneuroimmunology* (and *health psychology*), which seeks to examine how stress, emotions, and upsetting thoughts affect the body's immune system to make the person more susceptible to disease (e.g., Geiser, 1989; Ader, Felten, & Cohen, 1990; O'Leary, 1990; Taylor, 1990). See also ACCOMMODATION, LAW/PRINCIPLE OF; CONFLICT, THEORIES OF; HABITUATION, PRINCIPLE/LAW OF; LAZARUS' THEORY OF EMOTIONS.

REFERENCES

Cannon, W. (1929). *Bodily changes in pain, hunger, fear, and rage*. New York: Branford.
Cannon, W. (1932). *The wisdom of the body*. New York: Norton.
Selye, H. (1936). A syndrome produced by diverse nocuous agents. *Nature, 138*, 32.
Selye, H. (1950). *Stress*. Montreal: Acta.
Selye, H. (1956). *The stress of life*. New York: McGraw-Hill.

Selye, H. (1976). *Stress in health and disease*. Toronto: Butterworth.

Pomerleau, O., & Brady, J. (Eds.) (1979). *Behavioral medicine: Theory and practice*. Baltimore: Williams & Wilkins.

Selye, H. (1980). *Selye's guide to stress research*. New York: Van Nostrand Reinhold.

Breznitz, S., & Goldberger, L. (1983). *Handbook of stress*. New York: Free Press.

Geiser, D. (1989). Psychosocial influences on human immunity. *Clin. Psy. Rev., 9*, 689–715.

Ader, R., Felten, D., & Cohen, N. (1990). Interactions between the brain and the immune system. *Ann. Rev. Pharm. & Tox., 30*, 561–602.

O'Leary, A. (1990). Stress, emotion, and human immune function. *Psy. Bull., 108*, 363–382.

Taylor, S. (1990). Health psychology. *Amer. Psy., 45*, 40–50.

Baron, R. (1992). *Psychology*. Boston, MA: Allyn & Bacon.

Anisman, H. (1994). Stress consequences. In R. J. Corsini (Ed.), *Ency. Psy*. New York: Wiley.

Stotland, E. (1994). Stress. In R. J. Corsini (Ed.), *Ency. Psy*. New York: Wiley.

SEMIOTIC THEORY. See CHOMSKY'S PSYCHOLINGUISTIC THEORY.

SENSORY-TONIC FIELD THEORY. See PERCEPTION (II. COMPARA-TIVE APPRAISAL), THEORIES OF.

SEQUENTIAL PATTERNING THEORY. See CAPALDI'S THEORY.

SERIAL-POSITION EFFECT. = serial position curve. The *serial-position effect* is the generalization that in a free-recall experiment the chance of an individual item from a list being recalled is a function of the location of that item in the serial presentation of the list during learning. The items that were toward the beginning of the list and those toward the end are more likely to be correctly recalled than those in the middle. When the results of a serial-position learning task are graphed, with correct recall of items plotted against the serial position of the item during presentation, the curve is characteristically bow-shaped with high probabilities of recall for the first few (called the *primacy effect*) and for the last few (called the *recency effect*) items. The *serial-position curve* is the same in form for meaningful material as for nonsense syllables (cf: *Hunter–McCrary law*; McCrary & Hunter, 1953; Smith & Smith, 1958). An early theory of the *serial-position effect/curve* was given by Lepley (1934) and Hull (1935) and made great use of the *doctrine of remote associations* (Ebbinghaus, 1885) and the acquisition of inhibitory connections to suppress the observed remote errors: such inhibitory factors were assumed to pile up most in suppressing responses in the middle of the list, and, as a result, most errors should occur at the middle positions. The major premises of this *Lepley–Hull hypothesis* concerning remote associations, however, have been discredited along with the theory that was constructed on that basis (Bower & Hilgard, 1981). Another *theory of the serial-position effect/curve* was proposed independently by Jensen (1962a, b) and Feigenbaum and Simon (1962). In Jensen's view, the items on a list that are learned first, or best, are the ones to which the learner first attends (i.e., the first item or two in the list), and these first-learned items then serve as an "anchor point" for learning the rest of the list. Jensen's theory, however, has been criticized because of its vagueness concerning the basic learning mechanism and the implausibility of the argument concerning the attachment of items to "expanding" anchor points (Bower & Hilgard, 1981). Feigenbaum and Simon (1962) pointed out that there are ways of distorting the characteristic shape of the serial-position curve. For instance, if one item is made clearly distinct from other items (cf: Kohler & von Restorff, 1935), it will be learned much faster, or, if half the list is colored red and the other half black, the curve shows a large decrease in errors on the last item of the red half of the list and the first item of the black half (Wishner, Shipley, & Hurvich, 1957). Feigenbaum and Simon developed an *information-processing theory of serial learning* where "anchor points" and a "macroprocessing system" describe the serial-position results (Feigenbaum & Simon, 1961). Feigenbaum and Simon's theory—in addition to other response-learning and guessing factors (e.g., Slamecka, 1964)—gives a good account of most facts known about the serial-learning curve (Kling & Riggs, 1971). See also FORGETTING/MEMORY, THEORIES OF; INFORMATION/INFORMATION-PROCESSING THEORY; von RESTORFF EFFECT.

REFERENCES

Ebbinghaus, H. von (1885). *Uber der gedachtnis*. Leipzig: Duncker.

Lepley, W. (1934). Serial reactions considered as conditioned reactions. *Psy. Mono., 46*, no. 205.

Hull, C. (1935). The conflicting psychologies of learning—a way out. *Psy. Rev., 42*, 491–516.

Kohler, W., & von Restorff, H. (1935). Analyse von vorgangen im spurenfeld. II. Zur theorie der reproduktion. *Psy. Forsch., 21*, 56–112.

McCrary, J., & Hunter, W. (1953). Serial position curves in verbal learning. *Science, 117*, 131–134.

Wishner, J., Shipley, T., & Hurvich, M. (1957). The serial-position curve as a function of organization. *Amer. J. Psy., 70*, 258–262.

Smith, K., & Smith, W. (1958). *The behavior of man: An introduction to psychology*. New York: Holt.

Feigenbaum, E., & Simon, H. (1961). Comment: The distinctiveness of stimuli. *Psy. Rev., 68*, 285–288.

Feigenbaum, E., & Simon, H. (1962). A theory of the serial position effect. *Brit. J. Psy., 53*, 307–320.

Jensen, A. (1962a). An empirical theory of the serial-position effect. *J. Psy., 53*, 127–142.

Jensen, A. (1962b). Temporal and spatial effects of serial position. *Amer. J. Psy., 75*, 390–400.

Slamecka, N. (1964). An inquiry into the doctrine of remote associations. *Psy. Rev., 71*, 61–76.

Jensen, A., & Rohwer, W. (1965). What is learned in serial learning? *J. Verb. Learn. Verb. Beh., 4*, 62–72.

Kling, J., & Riggs, L. (1971). *Woodworth and Schlosberg's experimental psychology.* New York: Holt, Rinehart, & Winston.

Bower, G., & Hilgard, E. (1981). *Theories of learning.* Englewood Cliffs, NJ: Prentice-Hall.

SET, LAW OF. See MIND/MENTAL SET, LAW OF.

SET/MOTOR ADJUSTMENTS THEORY. See PERCEPTION (II. COMPARATIVE APPRAISAL), THEORIES OF.

SET-POINT THEORY. See HUNGER, THEORIES OF.

SET THEORY. See MIND/MENTAL SET, LAW OF.

SHELDON'S TYPE THEORY. The American psychologist/physician William Herbert Sheldon (1899–1977) formulated a *constitutional theory of personality* that emphasized the importance of the physical structure of the body and biological-hereditary factors (''constitutional'' variables) as major determinants of behavior. The term *constitution* refers to those aspects of the person that are relatively fixed and unchanging (such as morphology, physiology, genes, endocrine functioning) and is contrasted with those aspects that are relatively more labile and susceptible to modification by environmental pressures such as education, habits, and attitudes (Sheldon, 1940; cf: Kretschmer, 1921). The *constitutional psychologist* looks to the biological substratum of the person for factors that are important to the explanation of human behavior. *Constitutional psychology* assumes the role of a facilitator or bridge connecting the biological with the behavioral domains (Hall & Lindzey, 1978). In Sheldon's view, a hypothetical biological structure (*morphogenotype*) underlies the external, observable physique (*phenotype*) that determines physical development and shapes behavior. In order to measure physique, Sheldon devised a photographic technique using pictures of persons' front, side, and rear in standard poses. This procedure was called the *somatotype performance test* (Sheldon, 1954). After examining and judging about 4,000 of these photographs, Sheldon and his associates concluded that there were three primary dimensions or components concerning the measurement and assessment of the physical structure of the human body: *endomorphy*—a body that appears soft and spherical; *mesomorphy*—a body that appears to be hard, rectangular, and muscular; and *ectomorphy*—a body that appears to be linear, thin, and fragile. All subjects in Sheldon's photographs could be assigned a score of from one to seven for each of the components and, with further anthropometric measurements, a complete description of the *somatotyping* process of individuals could be made (Sheldon, 1954, 1971). According to Sheldon, the notion of *somatotype* was an abstraction from the complexity of any specific physique, and he developed various *secondary components* by way of accounting for the great variation across individuals. *Secondary components* included *dysplasia*—an inconsistent/uneven mixture of the three primary components in different parts of the body; *gynandromorphy*—called the "g index" and referring to the degree that one's physique possesses characteristics ordinarily associated with the opposite sex; and *textural aspect*—a highly subjective physical aspect reflecting "aesthetic pleasingness" (Sheldon, 1940, 1949). Sheldon also developed three *primary components of temperament* along with their associative *traits*: *viscerotonia* (this was paired with *endomorphy*)—characterized by enjoyment of food, people, and affection; *somatotonia* (this was paired with *mesomorphy*)—love of physical adventure and risk taking; and *cerebrotonia* (this was paired with *ectomorphy*)—desire for isolation, solitude, and concealment. The three temperament dimensions, in conjunction with a list of 20 defining traits for each dimension, constituted Sheldon's *scale for temperament* (Sheldon, 1942). Sheldon's research led to the strong confirmation of the *constitutional psychologist's* expectation that there is a noteworthy continuity between the structural/physical aspects of the person and his or her functional/behavioral qualities. Although Sheldon was successful in isolating and measuring dimensions for describing physique and temperament, he cautioned that the dimensions should not be examined in isolation one by one, but, rather, the *pattern* of relations between the variables should be studied. Perhaps the most frequent criticism of *Sheldon's constitutional theory* is that it is no theory at all but simply consists of one general assumption—the continuity between structure and behavior—and a set of descriptive concepts for scaling physique and behavior (Hall & Lindzey, 1978). Other criticisms have focused on procedural flaws in Sheldon's research (e.g., Humphreys, 1957) and on the fact that his notion of *somatotype* is not invariant in the presence of nutrition, age, and other environmental changes. See also KRETSCHMER'S THEORY OF PERSONALITY; PERSONALITY THEORIES.

REFERENCES

Kretschmer, E. (1921). *Korper und charakter.* Berlin: Springer.

Viola, G. (1933). *La costituzione individuale.* Bologna, Italy: Cappeli.

Sheldon, W. (1940). *The varieties of human physique: An introduction to constitutional psychology.* New York: Harper.

Sheldon, W. (1942). *The varieties of temperament: A psychology of constitutional differences.* New York: Harper.

Sheldon, W. (1949). *Varieties of delinquent youth: An introduction to constitutional psychiatry.* New York: Harper.

Sheldon, W. (1954). *Atlas of men: A guide for somatotyping the adult male at all ages.* New York: Harper.

Humphreys, L. (1957). Characteristics of type concepts with special reference to Sheldon's typology. *Psy. Bull., 54,* 218–228.

Parnell, R. (1958). *Behavior and physique: An introduction to practical and applied somatometry.* London: Arnold.

Sheldon, W. (1971). The New York study of physical constitution and psychotic pattern. *J. Hist. Beh. Sci., 7*, 115–126.

Hall, C., & Lindzey, G. (1978). *Theories of personality.* New York: Wiley.

Coan, R. (1994). Personality types. In R. J. Corsini (Ed.), *Ency. Psy.* New York: Wiley.

Corey, G. (1994). Constitutional types. In R. J. Corsini (Ed.), *Ency. Psy.* New York: Wiley.

SIGNAL DETECTION, THEORY OF. The *theory of signal detection* (*TSD*) is a mathematical theory of the detection of physical signals that measures not only an observer's ability to detect a stimulus when it is present but also one's guessing behavior as reflected in a "yes" response when, in fact, no signal is present (Green & Swets, 1966; Egan, 1975). *TSD* is based on the assumption that sensitivity to a signal is not merely a result of its intensity (as *classical psychophysical theory* asserts; cf: Swets, 1961) but is dependent also on the amount of "noise" present, the motivation of the participant, and the criterion that the individual sets for responding. *TSD* represents an innovation in thinking about the way in which information is processed in psychophysical experiments and constitutes *the* major theoretical development in psychophysics since Gustav Fechner's pioneering work of over a century ago (Dember & Warm, 1979). Other models of psychophysical discrimination, such as the *phi-gamma* and *neural quantum* positions, can be viewed as *two-state theories* of perceptual processing (Massaro, 1975). *Two-state theories* imply that in any detection experiment, the perceptual system can signify only two possible states on a given trial: a detection state in which a stimulus is present and a nondetection state in which a stimulus is not present. *TSD*, on the other hand, is a *multistate theory* that assumes that every trial contains some degree of interference or "noise" that emanates from several possible sources, such as spontaneous firing in the nervous system, changes inherent in the environment or in the equipment used for generating stimuli, and factors deliberately introduced by the experimenter. Such noise always results in a greater-than-zero level of sensation, and the stimulus to be detected always occurs against a background of noise. A major assumption of *TSD* is that the amount of neural stimulation is normally distributed, and the individual's decision to respond "yes" (i.e., "I detected a signal") is given by whether the total stimulation contributed either by noise alone or by noise plus signal exceeds the set-response criterion. The proportion of *hits* (i.e., cases in which the person responded "yes" where a signal was actually present) to *false alarms* (i.e., cases in which the person responded "yes," but where there was no physical signal present) can be varied by manipulating the participant's criterion. A method of representing the data from a *TSD* experiment is called the *receiver-operating characteristic* (*ROC*) curve, which plots the number of *hits* and *false alarms* depending on the number of *catch trials* (i.e., the trials where there was no signal present). The result of *ROC* curve plotting is a sensitive measure of the participant's true sensory sensitivity. Performance indices of *TSD* are the response criterion—called *beta*, which is a nonperceptual measure that reflects bias in responding—and a perceptual index—called *d-prime*, which specifies the sensitivity of a given observer and, as such, reflects the observer's ability to discriminate signal from noise. The value of *d-prime* is defined as the separation between the means of the noise and the signal-plus-noise distributions expressed in terms of their standard deviation. The larger the value of *d-prime*, the more detectable the signal and/or the greater the sensory capability of the observer (Coren & Ward, 1989). While all aspects of *TSD* have not received unanimous and unqualified support (cf: Hohle, 1965; Parducci & Sandusky, 1970), enough favorable evidence has accumulated so that it has gained general acceptance among researchers concerned with perceptual processes. The principal advantage of *TSD* is that it permits the inherent detectability of the signal to be separated from attitudinal and motivational variables that influence the observer's criteria for judgment, and *TSD* becomes useful (e.g., Clark & Yang, 1974) when it is of interest to learn whether an experimental outcome is attributable to a change in the perceptual system, to variations in response bias, or to both. Wright (1974) developed a theoretical framework that attempts to bring together *TSD*, the *phi-gamma hypothesis*, and the *neural quantum theory* and indicates that the two major variants of classical threshold theory and the contemporary *TSD* may not be as far apart as they might seem. Eventually, it may be possible to integrate these approaches under a single theoretical model (Dember & Warm, 1979). See also ELICITED OBSERVING RATE HYPOTHESIS; NEURAL QUANTUM THEORY; PHI-GAMMA HYPOTHESIS.

REFERENCES

Tanner, W., & Swets, J. (1954). A decision-making theory of visual detection. *Psy. Rev.,* *61*, 401–409.

Swets, J. (1961). Is there a sensory threshold? *Science, 134*, 168–177.

Swets, J., Tanner, W., & Birdsall, T. (1961). Decision processes in perception. *Psy. Rev.,* *68*, 301–340.

Atkinson, R. (1963). A variable sensitivity theory of signal detection. *Psy. Rev., 70*, 91–106.

Hohle, R. (1965). Detection of a visual signal with low background noise: An experimental comparison of two theories. *J. Exp. Psy., 70*, 459–463.

Green, D., & Swets, J. (1966). *Signal detection and psychophysics*. New York: Wiley.

Krantz, D. (1969). Threshold theories of signal detection. *Psy. Rev., 76*, 308–324.

Parducci, A., & Sandusky, A. (1970). Limits on the applicability of signal detection theory. *Perc. & Psychophys., 7*, 63–64.

Swets, J. (1973). The relative operating characteristic in psychology. *Science, 182*, 990–1000.

Clark, W., & Yang, J. (1974). Acupunctural analgesia: Evaluation by signal detection theory. *Science, 184*, 1096–1098.

Wright, A. (1974). Psychometric and psychophysical theory within a framework of response bias. *Psy. Rev., 81*, 322–347.

Egan, J. (1975). *Signal detection theory and ROC-analysis*. New York: Academic Press.

Massaro, D. (1975). *Experimental psychology and information processing.* Chicago: Rand McNally.

Dember, W., & Warm, J. (1979). *Psychology of perception.* New York: Holt, Rinehart, & Winston.

Coren, S., & Ward, L. (1989). *Sensation and perception.* San Diego: Harcourt Brace Jovanovich.

SIMILARITY, LAW OF. See ASSOCIATION, LAWS/PRINCIPLES OF; GESTALT THEORY/LAWS.

SIMILARITY PARADOX. See SKAGGS–ROBINSON HYPOTHESIS.

SITUATIONAL THEORY OF LEADERSHIP. See LEADERSHIP, THEORIES OF.

SIZE-DISTANCE INVARIANCE HYPOTHESIS. See EMMERT'S LAW.

SKAGGS–ROBINSON HYPOTHESIS. This hypothesis, credited to the American psychologists Ernest Burton Skaggs (1893–?) and Edward Stevens Robinson (1893–1937), derived from the *similarity paradox* in the area of serial and transfer phenomena in human verbal learning. The classical statement, formulated in 1925–1927, of the relationship between similarity of learned material and interference in human learning was that "the greater the similarity, the greater the interference" (Osgood, 1953; cf: *Kjerstad–Robinson law*, formulated in 1919, which states that in verbal learning the amount of material learned during equal portions of the learning time is the same for different lengths of the material to be learned; and the *Muller–Schumann law*, formulated in 1893, which states that once an association has been formed between two items, it becomes more difficult to establish an association between either one of these items and a third one; Zusne, 1987). This lawful statement was connected to the work of McGeoch and others (e.g., McGeoch & McGeoch, 1937), but when it is carried to its logical conclusion, it leads to an impossible state of affairs. That is, a stimulus situation can never be precisely identical from case to case, nor can the response, but they may be maximally similar, which is when the greatest facilitation, or ordinary learning, takes place. As Osgood (1953, p. 530) states the *similarity paradox*, "ordinary learning is at once the *theoretical* condition for maximal *interference*, but obviously the *practical* condition for maximal *facilitation*." A distinction was made by Wylie (1919) between stimulus and response activities where the transfer effect in a learning task is positive when an "old" response is associated with a new stimulus but negative when an "old" stimulus must be associated with a new response. This principle has been shown to be valid only within broad limits of materials, but it fails to account for degrees of either stimulus or response similarity. Robinson (1927) was one of the first psychologists to clearly conceive/address the *similarity paradox*, and he proposed (via J. McGeoch's "christening") what is known as the *Skaggs–Robinson hypothesis* as a resolution. The experimental aspects of this hypothesis show a "high peak–low valley–medium peak" curve when the relationship is graphed between the variables of "degree of stimulus similarity on a descending scale" on the abscissa and "efficiency of recall of material" on the ordinate. Thus, the hypothesis states that facilitation of learning is greatest when successively practiced materials are identical ("high peak") and least (with greatest interference) when similarity of materials is moderate ("low valley"). Facilitation of learning increases again as materials become least similar ("medium peak") but never attains the level of the "high peak" condition. Several experiments give limited validation to the poorly defined *Skaggs–Robinson hypothesis* (e.g., Cheng, 1929; Harden, 1929; Kennelly, 1941). Later, in the 1940s, many other studies on serial and transfer learning were conducted to examine the *Skaggs–Robinson hypothesis* and attempt to explain the fundamental *similarity paradox* (i.e., that responses can never be truly identical, yet ordinary learning takes place). Osgood (1949) attempted a resolution of the paradox by proposing a model called the *transfer and retroaction surface*. Osgood's *transfer surface* represented an important systematic attempt to integrate a large range of transfer and retroaction phenomena, but it proved to be inadequate for a number of reasons (e.g., although the verbal learning data give evidence of differences in transfer between identical, similar, and unrelated stimuli, or responses, they have not shown a "continuous gradient" of effects as similarity is varied over the intermediate range; Bower & Hilgard, 1981). The demise of the *Skaggs–Robinson hypothesis* was facilitated by its nonanalytic formulation, which did not specify the locus of intertask similarity. The hypothesis lapsed into disuse as the analysis of similarity relations in retroaction, as in transfer, shifted to the investigation of stimulus and response functions (Postman, 1971). See also ASSIMILATION, LAW OF; TRANSFER OF TRAINING, THORNDIKE'S THEORY OF.

REFERENCES

Wylie, H. (1919). An experimental study of transfer of response in the white rat. *Beh. Mono., 3*, no. 16.

Robinson, E. (1920). Some factors determining the degree of retroactive inhibition. *Psy. Mono., 28*, no. 128.

Skaggs, E. (1925). Further studies in retroactive inhibition. *Psy. Mono., 34*, no. 161.

Robinson, E. (1927). The similarity factor in retroaction. *Amer. J. Psy., 39*, 297–312.

Cheng, N. (1929). Retroactive effect and degree of similarity. *J. Exp. Psy., 12*, 444–449.

Harden, L. (1929). A quantitative study of the similarity factor in retroactive inhibition. *J. Gen. Psy., 2*, 421–432.

McGeoch, J., & McGeoch, G. (1937). Studies in retroactive inhibition: X. The influence of similarity of meaning between lists of paired associates. *J. Exp. Psy., 21*, 320–329.

Kennelly, T. (1941). The role of similarity in retroactive inhibition. *Ar. Psy., N.Y., 37*, no. 260.

Osgood, C. (1949). The similarity paradox in human learning: A resolution. *Psy. Rev., 56*, 132–143.

Osgood, C. (1953). *Method and theory in experimental psychology.* New York: Oxford University Press.

Postman, L. (1971). Transfer, interference, and forgetting. In J. Kling & L. Riggs (Eds.), *Woodworth and Schlosberg's experimental psychology.* New York: Holt, Rinehart, & Winston.

Bower, G., & Hilgard, E. (1981). *Theories of learning.* Englewood Cliffs, NJ: Prentice-Hall.

Zusne, L. (1987). *Eponyms in psychology.* Westport, CT: Greenwood Press.

SKINNER'S DESCRIPTIVE BEHAVIOR/OPERANT CONDITIONING THEORY. The American psychologist Burrhus Frederic Skinner (1904–1990) developed a distinctive approach to understanding human and animal learning and behavior called *operant reinforcement/conditioning.* In examining Skinner's approach, it is noteworthy that he rejected the use of formal theory in learning and psychology (e.g., Skinner, 1950, 1956), especially the postulate-theorem, hypothetico-deductive type of approach to theorizing (see Hull, 1943, 1952). Skinner's position is characterized by a heavy emphasis on the study of "emitted" responses (operants) that are strongly influenced by the consequences (reinforcement) of the responses rather than on "stimulus-elicited" (respondent) responses. Skinner also focused on individual subjects where behavioral laws and equations are expected to apply, rather than on groups of individuals yielding generalized/statistical results. According to Skinner, the employment of a *functional analysis of behavior* (i.e., behavior described in terms of cause-and-effect relationships) allows one to achieve maximum control of behavior. In such an analysis, there would be no need to make inferences or to discuss the mechanisms operating *within* the organism (such as "self," "feelings," or "personality"). Essentially, Skinner developed a program for a descriptive science where understanding of behavior and its environmental consequences—with no concern for intervening events—leads to laws and universal principles of behavior. Skinner assumed that behavior was orderly and modifiable, and the behavioral scientists' goal should be to understand, predict, and control behavior. A key concept in Skinner's program (*operant reinforcement* theory) of behavioral change is the principle of *positive reinforcement,* which refers to a stimulus or environmental event following a behavior and causing an *increase* in the frequency of that behavior (cf: Wolman, 1973, who cites 10 variants on this same principle). Other important concepts in Skinner's approach are positive and negative punishment, negative reinforcement, extinction, shaping, differential reinforcement, schedules of reinforcement (including fixed interval, fixed ratio, variable interval, and variable ratio schedules), superstitious behavior, conditioned/secondary reinforcer, generalized reinforcer, stimulus generalization, stimulus discrimination, and chaining (cf: *associative-chain theory* of the early behaviorists concerning complex behavior; Reber, 1995). In his early work, Skinner (1938) described various *static laws of the reflex*: *law of the threshold*— the intensity of the stimulus must reach or exceed a certain critical value, called the threshold, in order to elicit a response (cf: *Vierordt's law*, which states that the more mobile a part of the body is, the lower the two-point threshold of the skin over it; Warren, 1934; Reber, 1995; *Vierordt's law* is also defined in the area of time perception as the principle that short intervals are overestimated, and long ones are underestimated; Woodrow, 1951; Sutherland, 1996); the *law of latency*; *law of response magnitude*; *law of afterdischarge*; and the *law of temporal summation*. Skinner also described the *dynamic laws of reflex strength*: *law of the refractory phase*; *law of reflex fatigue*; *law of facilitation*; *law of inhibition* (cf: *law of conflicting associations*—principle of mental association where a thought similar to the desired association tends to inhibit that association; Warren, 1934); *law of conditioning of Type S*; *law of extinction of Type S*; *law of conditioning of Type R* (cf: the *law of resolution*, formulated by H. S. Jennings, which states that the resolution of one physiological state into another becomes easier and more rapid after it has taken place a number of times; Warren, 1934); and the *law of extinction of Type R*. Skinner's (1938) concept of *reflex reserve* employed two measures of responses within extinction: rate of responding and total number of responses before responding returns to its normal rate prior to conditioning. The total number of responses during extinction, often described as ''resistance to extinction,'' was formerly called the *reflex reserve* by Skinner (using a figure of speech to describe a kind of reservoir of responses ready to be emitted during extinction), but he later apparently rejected the concept because of his subsequent interpretation of appropriate scientific concepts rather than because of any change in the factual relationships described (Hilgard & Bower, 1966; cf: Skinner, 1950). Skinner (1938) also states a number of *laws of the interaction of reflexes*: *law of compatibility*; *law of prepotency*; *law of algebraic summation*; *law of blending*; *law of spatial summation*; *law of chaining*; and the *law of induction*. Other laws in Skinner's (1938) early work are *law of the extinction of chained reflexes*; *law of stimulus discrimination in Type S*; *law of stimulus discrimination in Type R*; and the *law of the operant reserve*. In general, except for slight differences in terminology, Skinner's views of learning are quite similar to those of Thorndike after 1930. Except for the way each researcher measured the dependent variables, Thorndike's *instrumental conditioning* and Skinner's *operant conditioning* may be considered to be the same set of procedures (Hergenhahn, 1982). Skinner's principles have been successfully applied to teaching and learning settings, to understanding various social problems, to behavior modification and therapy in the clinical setting, to psychopharmacology, to threshold and laboratory studies, and to warfare contexts. The experimental results reported by Skinner, his associates, and his students employing the *idiographic*, or single-subject, design present a degree of lawfulness and precise regularity in behavior analysis and control that is virtually unparalleled among psychologists (Hall & Lindzey, 1978). Perhaps the criticism most widely leveled at Skinner is that his theory is no theory at all where he has little appreciation for the role of theory and mediating processes in building the science of psychology (see Skinner, 1969; cf: the term *hyphen psychologist*, which is a half-humorous sobriquet applied by "pure" behaviorists to theorists who invoke mediational processes, mental constructs, and hypothesized entities occurring between presentation of a simulus and the organism's response; Reber, 1995). Other criticisms against Skinner's approach include the argument that it is too simplistic and elemental to represent the full complexity of human behavior, especially language behavior. This assessment typically issues from the humanistic, holistic, and cognitive psychologists and theorists. Skinner's proponents/followers are viewed, also, as being insular and demonstrating no responsibility for the task of coordinating their work closely with that of others who study learning. However, Skinner's position has served acutely to highlight the fundamental opposition between scientists who believe that progress is to be made only by rigorous examination of actual behavior resulting in the discovery of a few generalizations versus those who believe that behavioral observations are interesting only to the degree that they reveal underlying laws of the mind that are only partially revealed in the behavior (Bower & Hilgard, 1981). See also INHIBITION, LAWS OF; LEARNING, THEORIES/LAWS; THORNDIKE'S LAW OF EFFECT.

REFERENCES

Warren, H. (Ed.) (1934). *Dictionary of psychology*. Cambridge, MA: Houghton Mifflin.

Skinner, B. F. (1935). The generic nature of the concepts of stimulus and response. *J. Genet. Psy., 12*, 40–65.

Skinner, B. F. (1938). *The behavior of organisms: An experimental analysis*. New York: Appleton-Century-Crofts.

Hull, C. (1943). *Principles of behavior*. New York: Appleton-Century-Crofts.

Skinner, B. F. (1948). *Walden two*. New York: Macmillan.

Skinner, B. F. (1950). Are theories of learning necessary? *Psy. Rev., 57*, 193–216.

Woodrow, H. (1951). Time perception. In S. S. Stevens (Ed.), *Handbk. Exp. Psy*. New York: Wiley.

Hull, C. (1952). *A behavior system*. New Haven, CT: Yale University Press.

Skinner, B. F. (1953). *Science and human behavior*. New York: Macmillan.

Rogers, C. (1956). Some issues concerning the control of human behavior. *Science, 124*, 1057–1066.

Skinner, B. F. (1956). A case history in scientific method. *Amer. Psy., 11*, 221–233.

Ferster, C., & Skinner, B. F. (1957). *Schedules of reinforcement*. New York: Appleton-Century-Crofts.

Skinner, B. F. (1957). *Verbal behavior*. New York: Appleton-Century-Crofts.

Skinner, B. F. (1958). Teaching machines. *Science, 128*, 969–977.

Skinner, B. F. (1960). Pigeons in a Pelican. *Amer. Psy., 15*, 28–37.

Skinner, B. F. (1961). *Cumulative record*. New York: Appleton-Century-Crofts.

Skinner, B. F. (1963). Behaviorism at fifty. *Science, 140*, 951–958.

Hilgard, E., & Bower, G. (1966). *Theories of learning.* New York: Appleton-Century-Crofts.

Skinner, B. F. (1968). *The technology of teaching.* New York: Appleton-Century-Crofts.

Skinner, B. F. (1969). *Contingencies of reinforcement: A theoretical analysis.* New York: Appleton-Century-Crofts.

Chomsky, N. (1971). The case against B. F. Skinner. *N.Y. Review of Books,* December 30, 18–24.

Skinner, B. F. (1971). *Beyond freedom and dignity.* New York: Knopf.

Wolman, B. (Ed.) (1973). *Handbook of general psychology.* Englewood Cliffs, NJ: Prentice-Hall.

Skinner, B. F. (1974). *About behaviorism.* New York: Knopf.

Skinner, B. F. (1976). *Particulars of my life.* New York: Knopf.

Honig, W., & Staddon, J. (Eds.) (1977). *Handbook of operant behavior.* Englewood Cliffs, NJ: Prentice-Hall.

Hall, C., & Lindzey, G. (1978). *Theories of personality.* New York: Wiley.

Bower, G., & Hilgard, E. (1981). *Theories of learning.* Englewood Cliffs, NJ: Prentice-Hall.

Hergenhahn, B. (1982). *An introduction to theories of learning.* Englewood Cliffs, NJ: Prentice-Hall.

Skinner, B. F. (1984a). *A matter of consequences.* Washington Square, NY: New York University Press.

Skinner, B. F. (1984b). *The shaping of a behaviorist.* Washington Square, NY: New York University Press.

Reber, A. (1995). *The Penguin dictionary of psychology.* New York: Penguin Books.

Sutherland, S. (1996). *The international dictionary of psychology.* New York: Crossroad.

SLEEP, THEORIES OF. The experience of *sleep* is characterized by a particular loss of consciousness accompanied by a variety of behavioral and neurophysiological effects. In modern psychology, sleep and the various stages of sleep are defined and characterized typically by particular physiological events, specifically by distinctive brain-wave patterns as recorded by an electroencephalograph, metabolic processes, muscle tone (cf: *Isakower phenomenon*—strange hallucinations usually felt in the mouth, hands, or skin; they include the feelings of an object pulsating or approaching/receding, and they occur mainly when falling asleep; Sutherland, 1996), heart and respiration rates, and the presence/absence of rapid eye movements (REMs). Periods of *REM sleep* (see *REM sleep theories*; Atkinson, Atkinson, Smith, & Hilgard, 1987) are evident by its primary defining feature, the rapid eye movements, and several less detectable factors, including a lack of *delta waves* (slow, large-amplitude brain waves), flaccid musculature, fluctuating heartbeat, erratic respiration, genital changes, and dreaming (80–85% reliability of dreaming during REM sleep). Non-REM sleep (NREM), on the other hand, is usually divided into four separate stages based on the proportion of *delta waves* observed: stage 1 is 0% of total brain activity, *delta*; stage 2 is up to 20% *delta waves*; stage 3 is between 20–50% *delta* waves;

and stage 4 is over 50% *delta waves*. Stages 3 and 4 are often referred to collectively as *slow-wave sleep*; in all the stages there is a progressively deeper and deeper sleep and all are characterized by a lack of REM, a regular heartbeat, rhythmic respiration, low levels of metabolic activity, and moderate-to-high muscle tone (Reber, 1995; cf: Wolman, 1973). In terms of *arousal theory*, the current conception of sleep is that it must be considered as a condition that is qualitatively different, as well as quantitatively different, from the state of wakefulness. There are active mechanisms controlling sleep just as there are active mechanisms controlling arousal during wakefulness. Sleep should be considered not as one condition but as two separate ones where *quiet sleep* (or NREM sleep) and *active sleep* (or REM sleep) constitute the *duality of sleep* (Levinthal, 1983). Estimates suggest that people spend nearly a third of their lives sleeping. Laboratory studies indicate that most individuals find it difficult to stay awake for more than 60 hours, even though some "marathoners" have remained awake for close to 19 days. With sleep deprivation, most people get cranky and have difficulty concentrating, especially on boring tasks (Horne, 1985). Among the major theories that have been formulated to explain the function/purpose of sleep is the *repair/restorative theory* (e.g., Webb, 1981; cf: Cohen, 1979; Shapiro, 1982), which suggests that sleep serves an important recuperative function, allowing one to recover not only from physical fatigue but also from emotional and intellectual demands (cf: *extensions of waking life theory*; Plotnik, 1993). Another theory, called the *adaptive nonresponding theory* or the *evolutionary/ circadian theory* (e.g., Kleitman, 1963; Campbell & Tobler, 1984), argues that sleep is a part of circadian rhythms and evolved as a means of conserving energy (see *energy conservation theory*; McGee & Wilson, 1984) and protecting individuals from predators (Allison & Cicchetti, 1976; Hobson, 1989). The *evolutionary/circadian theory* helps explain differences in sleep patterns across species where animals that sleep the longest (e.g., opposums and cats) are least threatened by the environment and can easily find food and shelter, while animals that sleep very little (e.g., horses and sheep) have diets that require constant foraging for food, and their only defense against predators is vigilance and running away. A *common/popular theory* is that people sleep in order to dream (Dement, 1960; Roffwarg, Munzio, & Dement, 1966) and assumes that dreaming is an important activity for good health (cf: Vogel, 1975). Recently, Webb (1988) has proposed a theory of sleep that combines some of the best explanatory features of the *restorative* and *adaptive nonresponding theories*. This new theory explains sleep as a function of *sleep demand* (based on the time of wakefulness preceding sleep), *circadian tendencies* (i.e., bodily rhythms whose cycle corresponds to approximately 24 hours and that include endocrine activity, metabolic function, and body temperature), *behaviors* that facilitate or inhibit sleep (such as body position, noise, or worrying), and several other variables such as species differences and developmental stages. See also DREAMS, THEORIES OF.

REFERENCES

Dement, W. (1960). The effect of dream deprivation. *Science, 131,* 1705–1707.

Kleitman, N. (1963). *Sleep and wakefulness.* Chicago: University of Chicago Press.

Roffwarg, H., Munzio, J., & Dement, W. (1966). Ontogenic development of the human sleep-dream cycle. *Science, 152,* 604–619.

Chase, M., Kripke, D., & Walter, P. (Eds.) (1972–1981). *Sleep research.* Vols. 1–10. Los Angeles: BIS/BRI.

Wolman, B. (Ed.) (1973). *Dictionary of behavioral science.* New York: Van Nostrand Reinhold.

Vogel, G. (1975). A review of REM sleep deprivation. *Ar. Gen. Psychiat., 32,* 749–761.

Allison, T., & Cicchetti, D. (1976). Sleep in mammals: Ecological and constitutional correlates. *Science, 194,* 732–734.

Cohen, D. (1979). *Sleep and dreaming: Origin, nature, and functions.* New York: Pergamon.

Webb, W. (1981). Some theories about sleep and their clinical implications. *Psychiatric Annals, 11,* 415–422.

Shapiro, C. (1982). Energy expenditure and restorative sleep. *Bio. Psy., 15,* 229–239.

Levinthal, C. (1983). *Introduction to physiological psychology.* Englewood Cliffs, NJ: Prentice-Hall.

Campbell, S., & Tobler, I. (1984). Animal sleep: A review of sleep duration across phylogeny. *Neuroscience & Biobehavioral Reviews, 8,* 269–300.

McGee, M., & Wilson, D. (1984). *Psychology: Science and application.* New York: West.

Horne, J. (1985). Sleep function, with particular reference to sleep deprivation. *Ann. Clin. Res., 17,* 199–208.

Atkinson, R. L., Atkinson, R. C., Smith, E., & Hilgard, E. (1987). *Introduction to psychology.* New York: Harcourt Brace Jovanovich.

Webb, W. (1988). An objective behavioral model of sleep. *Sleep, 11,* 488–496.

Hobson, J. (1989). *Sleep.* New York: Freeman.

Plotnik, R. (1993). *Introduction to psychology.* Pacific Grove, CA: Brooks/Cole.

Webb, W. (1994). Sleep. In R. J. Corsini (Ed.), *Ency. Psy.* New York: Wiley.

Reber, A. (1995). *The Penguin dictionary of psychology.* New York: Penguin Books.

Sutherland, S. (1996). *The international dictionary of psychology.* New York: Crossroad.

SMELL, LAWS/THEORIES OF. See OLFACTION/SMELL, THEORIES OF.

SOCIAL COMPARISON/EVALUATION THEORY. See FESTINGER'S COGNITIVE DISSONANCE THEORY.

SOCIAL EXCHANGE THEORY. See EXCHANGE/SOCIAL EXCHANGE THEORY.

SOCIAL FACILITATION THEORY. See ZAJONC'S AROUSAL AND CONFLUENCE THEORIES.

SOCIAL IMPACT THEORY. See INFECTION THEORY/EFFECT.

SOCIAL LEARNING/COGNITION THEORIES. See BANDURA'S THE-ORY; ROTTER'S SOCIAL LEARNING THEORY.

SOCIAL MAN THEORY. See ORGANIZATIONAL/INDUSTRIAL/SYS-TEMS THEORY.

SOCIAL PENETRATION THEORY. See EXCHANGE/SOCIAL EX-CHANGE THEORY.

SOLOMON'S OPPONENT-PROCESS THEORY OF EMOTIONS/FEEL-INGS/MOTIVATION. The American psychologist Richard Lester Solomon (1918–1995) formulated a theory that applies a homeostatic (i.e., a state of physiological equilibrium, balance, or stability) model to the experience of emotion where it is assumed that emotions have *hedonic* value; that is, they vary in their ability to be unpleasant or pleasant. Solomon's (1980, 1982) *opponent-process theory* states that an emotional response will be followed in a short time by its *hedonic opposite*. For instance, if one currently feels anger, it will give way to a feeling of calm shortly; if one feels fear, it will give way to relief; and if one feels depression, it will give way to euphoria. It is a major tenet of Solomon's *opponent-process theory* that the brain automatically activates opposing, or opponent, processes in order to protect itself from emotional extremes and, further, to restore a state of equilibrium to the individual. In most cases, the states of emotional opposites are of roughly the same intensity so that they balance out each other. *Solomon's theory* proposes, however, that when the same stimulus or event repeatedly elicits the same emotion, the first reaction will gradually weaken in intensity, with the overall result of the opponent reaction's gaining in strength. The *opponent-process theory* suggests that the eventual dominance achieved by the opponent emotional states can explain why some individuals may engage in risky and thrill-seeking behaviors such as high-stakes gambling, running dangerous river rapids, and skydiving. See also EMOTIONS, THEORIES/LAWS OF; OPPONENT-PROCESS COLOR VISION THEORY.

REFERENCES

Solomon, R., & Corbit, J. (1974). An opponent-process theory of motivation. I. Temporal dynamics of affect. *Psy. Rev., 81*, 119–145.

Solomon, R. (1980). The opponent-process theory of acquired motivation: The costs of pleasure and benefits of pain. *Amer. Psy., 35*, 691–712.

Solomon, R. (1982). The opponent-process in acquired motivation. In D. Pfaff (Ed.), *The physiological mechanisms of motivation*. New York: Springer-Verlag.

SOUL THEORY. See MIND–BODY THEORIES.

SOUND-PATTERN/WAVE-PATTERN THEORY. See AUDITION/HEAR-ING, THEORIES OF.

SPACE PERCEPTION THEORY. See BERKELEY'S THEORY OF VI-SUAL SPACE PERCEPTION.

SPATIAL SUMMATION, LAW OF. See SKINNER'S DESCRIPTIVE BE-HAVIOR/OPERANT CONDITIONING THEORY.

SPEARMAN'S TWO-FACTOR THEORY. See INTELLIGENCE, THEO-RIES/LAWS OF.

SPECIFIC NERVE ENERGIES, LAW OF. See MULLER'S DOCTRINE OF SPECIFIC NERVE ENERGIES.

SPECIFIC TERMINAL/SPECIFIC TISSUE HYPOTHESES. See NAFE'S THEORY OF CUTANEOUS SENSITIVITY.

SPENCE'S THEORY. The American psychologist and neo-Hullian Kenneth W. Spence (1907–1967) formulated a *theory of discrimination learning* known as *continuity theory*, which was developed against an elaborate theoretical foun-dation established by Clark Hull (1943, 1952). The interconnection of *Spence's theory* with Hull's framework has led some writers to label *Spence's theory* the *Hull–Spence theory of discrimination* (Schwartz, 1978). In the typical discrim-ination paradigm, the subject is positively reinforced for responding in the pres-ence of one stimulus ("positive" stimulus) and not reinforced in the presence of another stimulus ("negative" stimulus). With differential training, the subject comes to respond promptly to the positive stimulus, but not to the negative stimulus. Spence (1936) provided the classical/traditional *continuity* approach to discrimination learning where the only concepts needed to explain discrimina-tion were simple conditioning, extinction, and stimulus generalization. Spence assumed that the cumulative effects from reinforced responding to the positive stimulus build up a strong "excitatory tendency," whereas "conditioned inhi-bition" accumulates with the negative stimulus due to the frustration that is consequent on nonreinforced responses made in the presence of the negative stimulus. It was also assumed that the excitatory and inhibitory tendencies gen-eralize to similar stimuli with amount of generalization decreasing with decreas-ing similarity. The overall tendency to respond to any stimulus was given by the generalized excitation minus generalized inhibition to that particular stimu-lus. Spence's relatively simple theory has shown itself to be very serviceable in giving good accounts concerning discrimination learning (Kimble, 1961); how-ever, over the years, some of the theory's incompleteness and inadequacies have been noted. For example, the phenomenon of *behavioral contrast* (Reynolds,

1961) indicates a process of "negative induction" rather than Spence's classical theory prediction of "positive induction," and the phenomenon of *errorless discrimination learning* (Terrace, 1963) runs counter to the classical theory explanation of discrimination. Another issue that faced Spence's theorizing was to specify what it is exactly that a subject learns in discrimination training. Against Spence's *absolute stimulus theory* (where a subject learns specific stimulus–response connections) were the opposing viewpoints provided by the *relational theory* (e.g., Kohler, 1925), which held that the subject learns "relations" between stimuli (such as instructions to a subject to "choose the *larger* one of the two stimuli"). Thus, the *relational theory* suggested that the relation between stimuli that a subject learns is one that transcends the specific ("absolute") stimulus pair used to exemplify the relation, and indicates that subjects "transpose" the relation along a particular dimension (cf: Spence, 1937, 1942; Honig, 1962). Such *relational theory* studies are called *transposition* experiments (see Hebert & Krantz, 1965). Despite the parsimony of *Spence's theory* and the supporting evidence for it, other results have suggested that the "absolute" stimulus aspect was either inadequate or incomplete in some ways (see Riley, 1958). Subsequently, a more comprehensive *theory of transposition* was proposed by Zeiler (1963), which assumed that the subject perceives each stimulus in relation to an internal norm or *adaptation level* (cf: Helson, 1964). Spence's *theory of discrimination learning* places great emphasis upon the gradual accumulation of "habit strength" and upon the algebraic summation of gradients of generalization based on reinforcement and extinction. In general, this *continuity theory* (Spence, 1940, 1945) has been contrasted with one that emphasizes the problem-solving behavior of organisms in discrimination learning. The opposing theory, called *noncontinuity theory*, implies that learning a discrimination is not a continuous accumulation of positive and negative habit strength or some similar process, but, rather, an organism "tries out" hypotheses about the discrimination problem he or she is faced with by testing one hypothesis and then another (*hypothesis-testing theory*) until the correct solution is found (cf: Krechevsky, 1932, 1938; Lashley, 1942). Apparently, both the *continuity* and *noncontinuity theories* have something worthwhile to say, and it is a credit to Spence's theorizing that his classic formulation and experimental argumentation was prominent for so many years in the analysis of discrimination learning. Few miniature theories in psychology have proven so viable and robust against subsequent research (Bower & Hilgard, 1981). See also HELSON'S ADAPTATION-LEVEL THEORY; HULL'S LEARNING THEORY.

REFERENCES

Kohler, W. (1925). *The mentality of apes.* New York: Harcourt Brace Jovanovich.
Krechevsky, I. (1932). "Hypotheses" in rats. *Psy. Rev., 38,* 516–532.
Spence, K. (1936). The nature of discrimination learning in animals. *Psy. Rev., 43,* 427–449.

Spence, K. (1937). The differential response in animals to stimuli varying within a single dimension. *Psy. Rev., 44*, 430–444.

Krechevsky, I. (1938). A study of the continuity of the problem-solving process. *Psy. Rev., 45*, 107–133.

Spence, K. (1940). Continuous versus non-continuous interpretations of discrimination learning. *Psy. Rev., 47*, 271–288.

Lashley, K. (1942). An examination of the "continuity theory" as applied to discrimination learning. *J. Gen. Psy., 26*, 241–265.

Spence, K. (1942). The basis of solution by chimpanzees of the intermediate size problem. *J. Exp. Psy., 31*, 257–271.

Hull, C. (1943). *Principles of behavior*. New York: Appleton-Century-Crofts.

Spence, K. (1945). An experimental test of the continuity and non-continuity theories of discrimination learning. *J. Exp. Psy., 35*, 253–266.

Hull, C. (1952). *A behavior system: An introduction to behavior theory concerning the individual organism*. New Haven, CT: Yale University Press.

Spence, K. (1956). *Behavior theory and conditioning*. New Haven, CT: Yale University Press.

Riley, D. (1958). The nature of the effective stimulus in animal discrimination learning: Transposition reconsidered. *Psy. Rev., 65*, 1–7.

Kimble, G. (1961). *Hilgard and Marquis' conditioning and learning*. New York: Appleton-Century-Crofts.

Reynolds, G. (1961). Behavioral contrast. *J. Exp. Anal. Beh., 4*, 57–71.

Honig, W. (1962). Prediction of preference, transposition, and transposition-reversal from the generalization gradient. *J. Exp. Psy., 64*, 239–248.

Terrace, H. (1963). Discrimination learning with and without errors. *J. Exp. Anal. Beh., 6*, 1–27.

Zeiler, M. (1963). The ratio theory of intermediate size discrimination. *Psy. Rev., 70*, 516–533.

Helson, H. (1964). *Adaptation-level theory*. New York: Harper & Row.

Hebert, J., & Krantz, D. (1965). Transposition: A reevaluation. *Psy. Bull., 63*, 244–257.

Schwartz, B. (1978). *Psychology of learning and behavior*. New York: Norton.

Bower, G., & Hilgard, E. (1981). *Theories of learning*. Englewood Cliffs, NJ: Prentice-Hall.

SPILLMAN–REDIES EFFECT. See PERCEPTION (I. GENERAL), THEORIES OF.

SPREADING-ACTIVATION MODEL OF MEMORY. See FORGETTING/MEMORY, THEORIES OF.

STATIC LAWS OF THE REFLEX. See SKINNER'S DESCRIPTIVE BEHAVIOR/OPERANT CONDITIONING THEORY.

STEREOCHEMICAL THEORY. See OLFACTION/SMELL, THEORIES OF.

STERNBERG–LUBART'S INVESTMENT THEORY OF CREATIVITY. See INTELLIGENCE, THEORIES OF.

STERNBERG'S TRIANGULAR THEORY OF LOVE. See LOVE, THEORIES OF.

STERNBERG'S TRIARCHIC THEORY OF INTELLIGENCE. See INTELLIGENCE, THEORIES/LAWS OF.

STEVENS' POWER LAW. The American psychologist/psychophysicist Stanley Smith Stevens (1906–1973) proposed this generalization, which states that the psychophysical relationship between a physical stimulus and the psychological experience or perceived magnitude of that stimulus is given by the equation: $P = k S^n$, where perceived magnitude (P) equals a constant (k) times the stimulus intensity (S) raised to a power, n. On the basis of the stability of his data, Stevens (1957, 1958, 1960, 1961) proposed that the psychophysical law is best represented as a power relation rather than a logarithmic relation as described by *Fechner's law*. Stevens (1957) and Stevens and Galanter (1957) distinguish between two kinds of perceptual continua, *prothetic* and *metathetic*. *Prothetic* continua are concerned with "how much" and represent dimensions on which discriminations involve an additive process on the physiological level (examples of this continua are loudness, brightness, heaviness, and duration), and *metathetic* continua are concerned with "what kind" or "where" and represent dimensions on which discriminations involve a substitutive process at the physiological level (such as pitch and apparent inclination). Stevens pointed out that while Fechner's assumption (*Fechner's law*; Fechner, 1860) of the equality of "just noticeable differences" (JNDs) may hold for *metathetic* dimensions, it definitely does not hold for *prothetic* dimensions. Using the "magnitude methods" (magnitude estimation and magnitude production), Stevens found that psychophysical magnitude did not increase as a logarithmic function of stimulus magnitude, as Fechner had believed, but rather as a power function in accord with Plateau's (1872) prediction. That is, perceived magnitude is proportional to physical magnitude raised to some power (*Stevens' power law*). The consistency of Stevens' power function obtained in magnitude estimation experiments has led some writers to comment that it is one of the most firmly established quantitative statements in psychology (Engen, 1971; Marks, 1974; cf: Warren's, 1969, *physical correlate theory*). The magnitude-judgment techniques of Stevens have led to the development of what has been called the "new psychophysics" in which perceived magnitude is measured directly rather than indirectly as in the classical approach developed by Fechner. Dember and Warm (1979) review a number of challenges to *Stevens' power law* and conclude that until the many factors that contribute to the complexities of the judgmental process can be isolated and fully explained, it may be premature to speak of *the* psychophysical law; the newer investigations hold the promise of generating a broader approach to psychophysical measurement and, perhaps, of generating more general psychological laws, of which the psychophysical law may only be a special case. See also FECHNER'S LAW; WEBER'S LAW.

REFERENCES

Fechner, G. (1860). *Elemente der psychophysik.* Leipzig: Breitkopf & Hartel.

Plateau, J. (1872). Sur la mesure des sensations physiques, et sur la loi quilie l'intensite de ces sensations a l'intensite de la cause excitante. *Bull. l'Acad. R. S. Let. Beaux-Arts Bel., 33* 376–388.

Stevens, S. S. (1957). On the psychophysical law. *Psy. Rev., 64,* 153–181.

Stevens, S. S., & Galanter, E. (1957). Ratio scales and category scales for a dozen perceptual continua. *J. Exp. Psy., 54,* 377–409.

Stevens, S. S. (1958). Problems and methods of psychophysics. *Psy. Bull., 55,* 177–196.

Stevens, S. S. (1960). The psychophysics of sensory function. *Amer. Sci., 48,* 226–254.

Stevens, S. S. (1961). To honor Fechner and repeal his law. *Science, 133,* 80–86.

Stevens, S. S. (1962). The surprising simplicity of sensory metrics. *Amer. Psy., 17,* 29–39.

Stevens, S. S. (1968). Mathematics, statistics, and the schemapiric view. *Science, 161,* 849–856.

Warren, R. (1969). Visual intensity judgments: An empirical rule and a theory. *Psy. Rev., 76,* 16–30.

Engen, T. (1971). Psychophysics II. Scaling methods. In J. Kling & L. Riggs (Eds.), *Woodworth and Schlosberg's experimental psychology.* New York: Holt, Rinehart, & Winston.

Stevens, S. S. (1971). Issues in psychophysical measurement. *Psy. Rev., 78,* 428–450.

Marks, L. (1974). *Sensory processes: The new psychophysics.* New York: Academic Press.

Stevens, S. S. (1975). *Psychophysics: Introduction to its perceptual, neural, and social prospects.* New York: Wiley.

Dember, W., & Warm, J. (1979). *Psychology of perception.* New York: Holt, Rinehart, & Winston.

STILES' COLOR VISION THEORY. In 1946, Walter Stanley Stiles (1901–?) formulated his version of a *line-element theory* of trichromatic visual processes, which he later revised and elaborated (Stiles, 1953, 1959). The *line-element* type of theory is concerned with an isomorphic relation between visual data and a mathematical space, without necessarily making inferences regarding intervening processes such as specific physiological factors or events. *Stiles' theory* has been regarded as an improvement over Helmholtz's earlier *line-element theory* (Graham, 1965) and consisted of quantitative extensions of Helmholtz's (1856–1866) data, such as substitution of a two-color technique for Helmholtz's double-peaked fundamental curves and changes in Fechnerian relationships of two-color thresholds. According to other formulations by Stiles, luminances of differently colored (but equally bright) lights are not additive and, thereby, do not concur with *Abney's law* concerning the mixture of heterochromatic lumi-

nances. Stiles' updated theory (1953, 1959) indicated the usefulness of a five-
or seven-*receptor theory* where the attempt was to reconcile his *line-element
theory* with the older Fechner fractions for visual hue (especially "blue") mechanisms. See also ABNEY'S LAW; COLOR MIXTURE, LAWS/THEORY OF;
COLOR VISION, THEORIES/LAWS OF; GRASSMAN'S LAWS; STILES–
CRAWFORD EFFECT; YOUNG–HELMHOLTZ COLOR VISION THEORY.

REFERENCES

Helmholtz, H. von (1856–1866). *Handbuch der physiologischen optik.* Leipzig: Voss.
Stiles, W. (1939). The directional sensitivity of the retina and the spectral sensitivities
    of the rods and cones. *Proc. R. S. Lon., 127B,* 64–105.
Stiles, W. (1946). A modified Helmholtz line-element in brightness-colour space. *Proc.
    Phy. Soc., Lon., 58,* 41–65.
Stiles, W. (1953). Further studies of visual mechanisms by the two colour threshold
    method. *Coloquio sobre problemas opticos de la vision. I. Conferencias gener-
    ales.* Madrid: Union International de Physique Pure et Appliquee.
Stiles, W. (1955). The basic data of colour-matching. *Phys. Soc. Yearbk.* London: Phys-
    ical Society.
Stiles, W. (1959). Color vision: The approach through increment-threshold sensitivity.
    Proc. Nat. Acad. Sci., 45, 100–114.
Stiles, W., & Burch, J. (1959). National Physical Laboratory Colour-Matching Investi-
    gation: Final Report (1958). *Optica Acta, 6,* 1–26.
Graham, C. (1965). Color: Data and theories. In C. Graham (Ed.), *Vision and visual
    perception.* New York: Wiley.

STILES–CRAWFORD EFFECT. In 1933, the English physicist Walter Stanley Stiles (1901–?) and the English physiologist Brian Hewson Crawford
showed that light falling on different parts of the pupil of the eye is not equally
effective in producing a sensory result, even though the light may reach the
same point on the retina. In particular, the *Stiles–Crawford effect* is a demonstration that light rays passing through the edge of the pupil stimulate the retina
less than those rays passing through the center of the pupil because edge rays
and center rays do not meet the same conditions along their paths going to a
given point on the retina. The majority of the *Stiles–Crawford effect* is due to
the properties of the retina itself and is related to foveal cone vision in the light-
adapted eye. The effect is found also in any part of the retina when deep red
illumination is used as the light source, indicating again that the phenomenon
is obtained predominantly as a response of the cones in the retina. The exact
origin of the *Stiles–Crawford effect* is not certain (Bartley, 1951), but best
guesses ascribe it either to the shape of the cones or to the direction in which
they point, and where the total internal reflection within the conical part of the
cones may be responsible for a concentration of the light in the peripheral areas
(O'Brien, 1946). The fact that the *Stiles–Crawford effect* is absent in pure rod
vision may indicate that the phenomenon is due to differences between rods and
cones in shape, in refractive index, and in the distribution of the photoreceptive

pigments. The quantitative characteristics of the *Stiles–Crawford effect* have been calculated in detail by Moon and Spencer (1944). See also ABNEY'S LAW; STILES' COLOR VISION THEORY.

REFERENCES

Stiles, W., & Crawford, B. (1933). The luminous efficiency of rays entering the eye pupil at different points. *Proc. R. S. Lon., 112B*, 428–450.

Stiles, W., & Crawford, B. (1934). The liminal brightness increment for white light for different conditions of the foveal and parafoveal retina. *Proc. R. S. Lon., 116B*, 55–102.

Moon, P., & Spencer, D. (1944). On the Stiles–Crawford effect. *J. Opt. Soc. Amer., 34*, 319–329.

O'Brien, B. (1946). Theory of the Stiles–Crawford effect. *J. Opt. Soc. Amer., 36*, 506–509.

Bartley, S. (1951). The psychophysiology of vision. In S. S. Stevens (Ed.), *Handbk. Exp. Psy.* New York: Wiley.

STIMULUS-CENTERED THEORY. See REINFORCEMENT THEORY.

STIMULUS DISCRIMINATION IN TYPE R, LAW OF. See SKINNER'S DESCRIPTIVE BEHAVIOR/OPERANT CONDITIONING THEORY.

STIMULUS DISCRIMINATION IN TYPE S, LAW OF. See SKINNER'S DESCRIPTIVE BEHAVIOR/OPERANT CONDITIONING THEORY.

STIMULUS–RESPONSE/OPERANT CONDITIONING THEORY OF WORK. See WORK/CAREER/OCCUPATION, THEORIES OF.

STOMACH-CONTRACTION THEORY. See HUNGER, THEORIES OF.

STROOP EFFECT/INTERFERENCE EFFECT/STROOP TEST. This phenomenon is named in honor of the American psychologist John Ridley Stroop (1897–?), who designed a test in 1935 that measures an individual's degree of cognitive control. The original test consisted of a series of colored cards on which names of colors other than the color of the cards was printed. The person was asked to name the *color* of the *card* rather than to read the name written. The degree to which individuals are subject to the interference of the printed words is the measure of cognitive control (Wolman, 1973). In another version of testing materials, the *Stroop effect* is the process by which a printed color word (such as the word *red*) interferes with a person's ability to name the color of ink in which the word is printed if the ink color is not the color named by the word. Psychologists studying attention processes are interested in highly practiced cognitive and motor tasks such as reading, typing, or riding a bicycle. Learning such tasks initially requires a great deal of concentrated effort, but with practice, performance of the tasks becomes automatic (cf: *Humphrey's law*—which states that once performance of a task has become automatized, conscious thought about the task, while performing it, impairs performance; Sutherland, 1996). The term *automaticity* refers to one or more of the following conditions: performance becomes increasingly effortless; performance can be carried out without any conscious attention; and other tasks can be performed at the same time without interference (e.g., Shiffrin & Schneider, 1977; Logan, 1980). The *Stroop test* is a good illustration of *automaticity* in reading where the person must name the ink color of a word without reading the word itself. This task satisfies two out of three criteria for *automaticity*—it is carried out without attention, and it appears to be effortless. However, the third criterion is violated: it does interfere with naming the ink color. The *Stroop test* is a reminder not to take *automaticity* for granted: tasks may seem automatic in many ways, yet they still make considerable demands on the person's attention. In the *Stroop test*, most people cannot completely ignore the words and simply name the colors. The tendency to think of the words and pronounce them is difficult to resist. The *Stroop effect* indicates that even when one tries to suppress a well-practiced memory, it tends to be retrieved automatically when the appropriate stimulus occurs. Egeth, Blecker, and Kamlet (1969) conducted a "converging operations" experiment (see Garner, Hake, & Eriksen, 1956) to decide which is more important in the *Stroop effect*, the *perceptual* system or the *response* system. They were able to eliminate the perceptual system explanation as a cause of the effect and concluded that a response process system accounts for the *Stroop effect*. Other studies on the *Stroop phenomenon* lead also to the conclusion that response competition is an important contributing factor to *Stroop interference* (see Elmes, Kantowitz, & Roediger, 1992). See also ATTENTION, LAWS/PRINCIPLES/THEORIES OF.

REFERENCES

Stroop, J. (1935). Studies of interference in serial verbal reactions. *J. Exp. Psy., 18*, 643–662.

Garner, W., Hake, H., & Eriksen, C. (1956). Operationism and the concept of perception. *Psy. Rev., 63*, 149–159.

Egeth, H., Blecker, D., & Kamlet, A. (1969). Verbal interference in a perceptual comparison task. *Perc. & Psychophys., 6*, 355–356.

Dyer, F. (1973). The Stroop phenomenon and its use in the study of perceptual, cognitive, and response processes. *Mem. & Cog., 1*, 106–120.

Wolman, B. (Ed.) (1973). *Dictionary of behavioral science*. New York: Van Nostrand Reinhold.

Shiffrin, R., & Schneider, W. (1977). Controlled and automatic human information processing. II. Perceptual learning, automatic attending, and a general theory. *Psy. Rev., 84*, 127–190.

Logan, G. (1980). Attention and automaticity in Stroop and priming tasks: Theory and data. *Cog. Psy., 12*, 523–553.

Elmes, D., Kantowitz, B., & Roediger, H. (1992). *Research methods in psychology*. St. Paul, MN: West.
Sutherland, S. (1996). *The international dictionary of psychology*. New York: Crossroad.

STUMPF'S THEORY OF MUSICAL CONSONANCE AND DISSO-NANCE. The German philosopher/psychologist/musician Karl Stumpf (1848–1946) proposed a *theory of consonance and dissonance* in music that stated that tonal combinations judged most consonant are those that tend to fuse together. The greater the degree of fusion (as in an octave), the greater is the consonance. Likewise, in dissonance, when tones are played together, the degree to which they separate out and can be heard as single tones, the greater is the dissonance (Stumpf, 1883–1890). The phenomenon of *combination tones* (also called *resultant tones*) is the occurrence of an additional tone that is perceived when two separate tones are sounded simultaneously. According to the *combinational tone theory*, there are two types of combination tones: the *difference tone* (sometimes called the *grave harmonic*; Warren, 1934), whose frequency is the difference in the frequencies of the generating tones, and the *summation tone*, whose frequency is the sum of the frequencies of the generating tones. *Stumpf's theory* emphasized the fact that tones an octave apart seem to "fuse" into one psychical unity, and such fusion involves musical consonance. But when one tone is sounded together with another tone a semitone higher, the hearer is keenly aware of the distinctness of the two tones and at the same time finds the combination highly discordant. The degree of fusion between tones was regarded by Stumpf as the basis for musical consonance. The fact that the increasing complexity of vibration ratios is, in general, accompanied by decreasing consonance fits well with *Stumpf's theory*. Stumpf's emphasis on "fusion" makes it distinctly not a physical but a psychological theory (Murphy & Kovach, 1972). In the course of his work in audition/learning, a controversy arose between Stumpf and Wilhelm Wundt (the founder of structuralism) around the question of whether a trained introspectionist of the Wundtian variety or a trained musician (i.e., Stumpf) was more qualified to make tonal judgments. The problem was never resolved (Lundin, 1994). See also AUDITION/HEARING, THEORIES OF; FESTINGER'S COGNITIVE DISSONANCE THEORY; WUNDT'S THEORIES/DOCTRINES.

REFERENCES

Stumpf, K. (1883–1890). *Tonpsychologie*. Leipzig: Hirzel.
Stumpf, K. (1898–1924). *Beitrage zur akustik und musik wissenschaft*. Leipzig: Barth.
Warren, H. (Ed.) (1934). *Dictionary of psychology*. Cambridge, MA: Houghton Mifflin.
Murphy, G., & Kovach, J. (1972). *Historical introduction to modern psychology*. New York: Harcourt Brace Jovanovich.
Lundin, R. (1994). Carl Stumpf. In R. J. Corsini (Ed.), *Ency. Psy.* New York: Wiley.

SUBJECT EFFECTS. See EXPERIMENTER EFFECTS.

SUBTRACTIVE COLOR MIXTURE, PRINCIPLE OF. See COLOR MIX-
TURE, LAWS/THEORY OF.

SULLIVAN'S THEORY OF PERSONALITY. The American psychiatrist
Harry Stack Sullivan (1892–1949) developed the *interpersonal theory of psychiatry*, which defines the hypothetical entity of *personality* as the "relatively
enduring pattern of recurrent interpersonal situations which characterize a human
life" (Sullivan, 1953, p. 111) and views the individual's basic existence in terms
of one's relationships with other people. *Sullivan's theory of personality* favors
concepts and variables from the fields of social psychology and *field theory*
(Lewin, 1951; Sullivan, 1964). According to Sullivan's approach, the essential
unit in personality study is the interpersonal situation, not the individual, where
the structure and organization of personality consist of intersocial events rather
than intrapsychic events. Primary concepts in *Sullivan's theory* are *dynamisms*—
habits or enduring patterns of energy transformations such as overt talking or
covert thinking that are directed toward one or more persons and serve to satisfy
one's basic needs; *personifications*—an image one has of oneself or others consisting of feelings, attitudes, and experiences concerning need-satisfaction and
anxiety; personifications that are shared by a number of other people are called
stereotypes; and *cognitive processes*—include *prototaxic* experience (or the discrete series of sensations, images, feelings, and states of the organism), *parataxic*
experience (or perceiving causal relationships between events that may include
superstitious thinking), and *syntaxic* experience (or consensually validated symbol activity such as using words and numbers that give logical order to human
communication). Sullivan's account of the dynamics of personality emphasizes
the concept of *tension-reduction*—tension may arise from anxiety or from the
needs of the individual where unsatisfied needs may lead to apathy behavior or
to other dynamisms (such as "somnolent detachment," or falling asleep, in
infants as a result of inescapable anxiety). Sullivan rejected the notion of *instincts* as a primary source of human motivation, and dismissed Freud's concept
of *libido*. According to Sullivan, personality development occurs in six distinctive stages (cf: *stage theories* of S. Freud and E. Erikson): infancy, childhood,
juvenile era, preadolescence, early adolescence, and late adolescence. Sullivan
asserted that personality is not set at an early age, but, rather, it may change
with variations in interpersonal situations and new learning experiences. If re-
gressions in personality due to failure, anxiety, or pain occur in a person's life,
the help of a therapist acting as a *participant observer* in the *psychiatric interview* setting was advised (Sullivan, 1954). While *Sullivan's interpersonal theory*
is a "down-to-earth" formulation that invites and encourages empirical testing,
critics of his theory argue that he (and other social-psychological personality
theorists) has cut the personality off from its vital biological heritage and fails
to specify the precise learning mechanisms by which a society molds its citizens
(Hall & Lindzey, 1978). See also LEWIN'S FIELD THEORY; PERSONALITY
THEORIES.

REFERENCES

Sullivan, H. S. (1940). *Conceptions of modern psychiatry.* New York: Norton.

Lewin, K. (1951). *Field theory in social science: Selected theoretical papers.* D. Cartwright (Ed.) New York: Harper & Row.

Sullivan, H. S. (1953). *The interpersonal theory of psychiatry.* New York: Norton.

Sullivan, H. S. (1954). *The psychiatric interview.* New York: Norton.

Sullivan, H. S. (1962). *Schizophrenia as a human process.* New York: Norton.

Sullivan, H. S. (1964). *The fusion of psychiatry and social science.* New York: Norton.

Mullahy, P. (1973). *The beginnings of modern American psychiatry: The ideas of Harry Stack Sullivan.* Boston: Houghton Mifflin.

Hall, C., & Lindzey, G. (1978). *Theories of personality.* New York: Wiley.

SURROUNDEDNESS, LAW OF. See GESTALT THEORY/LAWS.

SUSTAINED ATTENTION THEORIES. See VIGILANCE, THEORIES OF.

SUTTON'S LAW. See SCHIZOPHRENIA, THEORIES OF.

SYMBOLIC DISTANCE EFFECT. See HICK'S LAW.

SYNAPTIC/SYNAPSE THEORY. See NEURON/NEURAL/NERVE THEORY.

SYNCHRONICITY PRINCIPLE. See JUNG'S THEORY OF PERSONALITY.

SYSTEMATIC DESENSITIZATION TECHNIQUE. See WOLPE'S THEORY/TECHNIQUE OF RECIPROCAL INHIBITION.

SYSTEMS THEORY. See CONTROL/SYSTEMS THEORY; ORGANIZATIONAL/INDUSTRIAL/SYSTEMS THEORY.

T

TALBOT–PLATEAU LAW. = Talbot's law. Named in honor of the English physicist William H. F. Talbot (1800–1877) and the Belgian physicist Joseph A. Plateau (1801–1883), this generalized principle states that when a periodic visual stimulus is repeated at a rate that is adequately high so that to an observer it appears to be fused, it will match in brightness a steady light that has the same time-average luminance. For instance, if the flickering light consists of equally long "on" and "off" periods, the steady state will have one-half the brightness (called *Talbot brightness*) of the "on" phase. The *Talbot–Plateau law* is demonstrated by use of the *Talbot–Plateau disc*, which is a white disc with concentric bands, each band showing black and white alternately, but with the same quantity of black and white, divided differently in each band (1/1, 2/2, 4/4, etc.). When rotated, this disc extinguishes the flicker sensations and shows a uniform gray color. Thus, an intermittent stimulus may be seen as continuous. The effect may also be demonstrated by interrupting a beam of light with a rotating disc (Postman & Egan, 1949). The disc, in this case, has segments cut out of it so that part of the time the light may pass through. Under conditions where the light passes only 50% of the time, and the disc is rotated slowly so the light is interrupted only two or three times a second, the observer sees the light as interrupted (i.e., as alternations of light and dark). However, as the rotation speed of the disc slowly increases, a point is reached at which the light appears as continuous, and the brilliance of the continuous light will be the same as if the total amount of light had been distributed uniformly over a whole revolution of the disc. The *Talbot–Plateau law* was challenged by Fick (1863) and Grunbaum (1898), who noted that it may not hold under special circumstances such as high intensity and conditions where fusion of a peripheral field occurs when the eye is fixated. However, the law's validity is now generally accepted under most conditions (see Hyde, 1906; Hecht & Wolf, 1932; Wolf & Zerrahn-Wolf, 1935; cf: Arnold, 1934). The validity of the *Talbot–Plateau law* has an interesting implication for the functional nature of the visual system: it suggests that the response of this system is proportional to stimulus luminance in those regions that precede the location where fusion occurs (Brown, 1965). See also FERRY–PORTER LAW; VISION/SIGHT, THEORIES OF.

REFERENCES

Talbot, W. (1834). Experiments on light. *Phil. Trans. Roy. Soc. Lon., 3*, 298.

Plateau, J. (1835). Sur un principe de photometrie. *Bull. l'Aca. Roy. Sci., Brux., 2*, 52–59.

Fick, A. (1863). Uber den zeitlichen verlauf der erregung in der netzhaut. *Ar. Anat. Physio.,* 739–764.

Plateau, J. (1872). Sur la mesure des sensations physiques, et sur la loi qui lie l'intensite de ces sensations a l'intensite de la cause excitante. *Bull. l'Acad. R. S. Let. Beaux-Arts Bel., 33*, 376–388.

Grunbaum, O. (1898). On the intermittent stimulation of the retina. *J. Physio., 22*, 433–450.

Hyde, E. (1906). Talbot's law as applied to the rotating sectored disc. *Bull. Bur. Stan., 2*, 1–32.

Hecht, S., & Wolf, E. (1932). Intermittent stimulation by light. I. The validity of Talbot's law for Mya. *J. Gen. Physio., 15*, 369–389.

Arnold, W. (1934). On the theoretical significance of Talbot's law. *J. Gen. Physio., 17*, 97–101.

Wolf, E., & Zerrahn-Wolf, G. (1935). The validity of Talbot's law for the eye of the honey bee. *J. Gen. Physio., 18*, 865–868.

Postman, L., & Egan, J. (1949). *Experimental psychology: An introduction.* New York: Harper & Brothers.

Brown, J. (1965). Flicker and intermittent stimulation. In C. Graham (Ed.), *Vision and visual perception.* New York: Wiley.

TARCHANOFF PHENOMENON. See ELECTRODERMAL ACTIVITY/PHENOMENA.

TASTE, THEORIES OF. See GUSTATION/TASTE, THEORIES OF.

TELEPHONE THEORY OF HEARING. See AUDITION/HEARING, THEORIES OF.

TEMPORAL SUMMATION, LAW OF. See SKINNER'S DESCRIPTIVE BEHAVIOR/OPERANT CONDITIONING THEORY.

TENSION, LAW OF. See WEBER'S LAW.

TENSION-REDUCTION THEORIES. See MOTIVATION, THEORIES OF.

TERNUS PHENOMENON. See PERCEPTION (I. GENERAL), THEORIES OF.

TETRACHROMATIC THEORY. See HERING–HURVICH–JAMESON COLOR VISION THEORY.

THERMOSTATIC THEORY. See HUNGER, THEORIES OF.

THIRST, THEORIES OF. The term *thirst* may be defined operationally as the internal, physiological state that results from water deprivation for a given period of time and is usually characterized by a dryness in the mouth, throat, and mucous membranes of the pharynx; in terms of motivation, *thirst* is a need/ drive state resulting from liquid deprivation that produces a desire for fluids, specifically water, and motivates water-seeking behavior (Reber, 1995). An early *peripheral theory of thirst*, the *dry-mouth theory* (Cannon, 1934), emphasized the relationship of salivary-gland function and moisture receptors in the mouth. The common notion that drinking results simply when the mouth is dry has a long history going back to Hippocrates (c. 460–377 B.C.). The *dry-mouth theory of thirst* was later revived in the eighteenth century by Albrecht von Haller and has continued to enjoy great popularity because of its intuitive appeal (Grossman, 1973). *Cannon's theory*, however, has not survived the test of time and experimentation. For example, removal of the salivary glands in dogs does not disrupt the regulation of water intake in terms of the amount of liquid consumed, nor does the administration of drugs that induce excessive salivation. Severing the nerves associated with the mouth and throat also appears to be ineffective in amount of liquid consumed (Levinthal, 1983). The organism's need for water is metered by brain mechanisms that give rise to the sensation of thirst when the body's water stores become depleted. The brain seems to be sensitive to at least two different signals: (1) short periods of water deprivation result primarily in a loss of water from the general circulation system producing a state of low volume (called *hypovolemia*) and low blood pressure; and (2) with long periods of deprivation, water is drawn out of the cells to compensate for the critically low volume in the circulatory system, where prolonged deprivation of cellular dehydration accounts for 65–70% of the body's water loss with vascular hypovolemia accounting for the remaining 30–35% of the loss (Grossman, 1994). A *multifactor theory of thirst* (Adolph, Barker, & Hoy, 1954) takes such cellular dehydration effects into account (cf: Gilman, 1937; Fitzsimons, 1961). Based on the distinction between intracellular and extracellular fluids, two kinds of thirst may be considered: *cellular dehydration thirst* and *hypovolemic thirst*. A current view of water regulation, called the *double-depletion hypothesis of thirst* (Epstein, 1973), is that while *cellular dehydration thirst* and *hypovolemic thirst* are often present together, they are independent regulatory activities with independent neural systems in control. However, the neural systems for *cellular dehydration* and *hypovolemic thirst* are both disrupted after extensive lesions of the lateral hypothalamus. Also, the relative contributions of peripheral factors, cellular dehydration factors, and hypovolemic factors appear to vary according to the species being studied (Levinthal, 1983). See also HUNGER, THEORIES OF.

REFERENCES

Cannon, W. (1934). Hunger and thirst. In C. Murchison (Ed.), *Handbook of general experimental psychology*. Worcester, MA: Clark University Press.

Gilman, A. (1937). The relation between blood osmotic pressure, fluid distribution, and voluntary water intake. *Amer. J. Physio., 120*, 323–328.

Adolph, E., Barker, J., & Hoy, P. (1954). Multiple factors in thirst. *Amer. J. Physio., 178*, 538–562.

Fitzsimons, J. (1961). Drinking by rats depleted of body fluid without increase in osmotic pressure. *J. Physio., 159*, 297–309.

Adolph, E. (1964). Regulation of body water content through water injection. In M. Wayner (Ed.), *Thirst*. New York: Macmillan.

Epstein, A. (1973). Epilogue: Retrospect and prognosis. In A. Epstein, H. Kissileff, & E. Stellar (Eds.), *The neuropsychology of thirst: New findings and advances in concepts*. Washington, DC: Hemisphere.

Grossman, S. (1973). *Essentials of physiological psychology*. New York: Wiley.

Grossman, S. (1975). Role of the hypothalamus in the regulation of food and water intake. *Psy. Rev., 82*, 200–224.

Grossman, S. (1979). The biology of motivation. *Ann. Rev. Psy., 30*, 209–242.

Levinthal, C. (1983). *Introduction to physiological psychology*. Englewood Cliffs, NJ: Prentice-Hall.

Stricker, E. (1990). *Handbook of behavioral neurobiology*. Vol. 10. *Neurobiology of food and fluid intake*. New York: Plenum Press.

Grossman, S. (1994). Physiological needs. In R. J. Corsini (Ed.), *Ency. Psy.* New York: Wiley.

Reber, A. (1995). *The Penguin dictionary of psychology*. New York: Penguin Books.

THORNDIKE'S LAW OF EFFECT. See EFFECT, LAW OF.

THREE-ELEMENT/TRI-RECEPTOR/TRICHROMATIC COLOR VISION THEORY. See YOUNG–HELMHOLTZ COLOR VISION THEORY.

THREE-STAGE/PROCESS THEORY OF MEMORY. See FORGETTING/MEMORY, THEORIES OF.

THRESHOLD, LAW OF. See SKINNER'S DESCRIPTIVE BEHAVIOR/OPERANT CONDITIONING THEORY.

THURSTONE'S LAW OF COMPARATIVE JUDGMENT. The American psychologist/psychometrician Louis Leon Thurstone (1887–1955) formulated a mathematical model, called the *law of comparative judgment*, based on the scaling principle used by Gustav Fechner (1803–1887), that stated that regardless of the physical values involved, stimulus differences that are detected equally often are subjectively equal. The *law of comparative judgment* refers to a subject's perception of how two or more stimuli compare on a particular dimension and applies to the scaling of attributes (such as "beauty") for which there are no specifiable physical correlates or physically specifiable attributes (Thurstone, 1927). The law employs the psychophysical method of "paired-comparisons" that was first introduced by Cohn (1894) in his study of color preferences and then developed further by Thurstone. The paired-comparisons method is regarded as the most appropriate way of obtaining subjective/value judgments (Engen, 1971). In the traditional method of paired-comparisons, every object in a set is presented for judgment in a pairwise fashion with every other object in the set (e.g., comparing tones according to "loudness," paintings according to "beauty," odors according to "pleasantness," and faces according to "similarity"; cf: Folgemann, 1933). The power in the approach derives from the application of multidimensional and factor-analytic techniques to the data to reveal the underlying dimensions along which the judgments were made (Reber, 1995). *Thurstone's law of comparative judgment* made it possible to obtain perceptual scale values associated with a single stimulus by starting quantitatively with individual difference measures. His law of the psychological distance between stimuli was cast in an equation involving a standard (z) score, variances, standard deviations, and a correlation coefficient (Engen, 1971, p. 52). However, because experimental data on the values in the equation are usually not available, *Thurstone's law of comparative judgment* equation cannot be tested directly (cf: Guilford, 1954; Thurstone, 1959). Torgerson (1958) showed how the theoretical principles of *Thurstone's law of comparative judgment* were applicable to the special case of psychometric rating scales and data (cf: Galton, 1879–1880), and he proposed a *law of categorical judgment*, which holds that an individual's psychological continuum can be divided into a specified number of ordered categories or steps. *Torgerson's law of categorical judgment* ideally should provide a scale with equal intervals for psychological measurement. Unfortunately, it is very difficult to obtain stable, useful, and valid ratings at even an ordinal scale level due to various biases in the observers and variability in the objects or persons rated (see Guilford, 1954). It is almost always necessary to provide the raters with a common anchor or reference point in order to obtain reliable data in such rating situations (Engen, 1971). See also DECISION-MAKING THEORIES; PSYCHOPHYSICAL LAWS/THEORY.

REFERENCES

Galton, F. (1879–1880). Psychometric experiments. *Brain, 2,* 149–162.

Cohn, J. (1894). Experimentelle untersuchungen uber die gefuhlsbetonung der farben, helligkeiten, und ihrer combinationen. *Phil. Stud., 10,* 562–603.

Thurstone, L. L. (1927). A law of comparative judgment. *Psy. Rev., 34,* 273–286.

Folgemann, E. (1933). An experimental study of composer-preferences of four outstand-
    ing orchestras. *J. Exp. Psy., 16*, 709–724.
Guilford, J. P. (1954). *Psychometric methods*. New York: McGraw-Hill.
Torgerson, W. (1958). *Theory and methods of scaling*. New York: Wiley.
Thurstone, L. L. (1959). *The measurement of values*. Chicago: University of Chicago
    Press.
Engen, T. (1971). Psychophysics. II. Scaling methods. In J. Kling & L. Riggs (Eds.),
    Woodworth and Schlosberg's experimental psychology. New York: Holt, Rine-
    hart, & Winston.
Gulliksen, H. (1994). Scaling. In R. J. Corsini (Ed.), *Ency. Psy.* New York: Wiley.
Reber, A. (1995). *The Penguin dictionary of psychology*. New York: Penguin Books.

THURSTONE'S PRIMARY MENTAL ABILITIES MODEL/THEORY.
See INTELLIGENCE, THEORIES/LAWS OF.

TIME PERCEPTION, LAW/THEORY OF. See SKINNER'S DESCRIP-
TIVE BEHAVIOR/OPERANT CONDITIONING THEORY.

TIP-OF-THE-TONGUE PHENOMENON. See FORGETTING/MEMORY,
THEORIES OF.

TOLMAN'S THEORY. The American psychologist Edward Chace Tolman
(1886–1959) formulated a "purposive" *behavioristic learning theory* that is also
called the *sign-gestalt theory* and *expectancy theory* to emphasize the cognitive
nature of his approach (cf: the *stimulus–response learning theories* of Thorndike,
1932; Guthrie, 1935; Skinner, 1938; and Hull, 1943). In his theory, Tolman
(1932) was concerned with concepts such as *knowledge, thinking, planning,
intention, inference,* and *purpose.* He described animals' behavior in terms of
their motives, cognitions ("bits of knowledge"), expectations, and purposes
much as if animals possessed human characteristics of thought (it has been said
that while Hull attempted to "make men into rats" with his *stimulus–response*
approach to learning, Tolman attempted to "make rats into men" with his
cognitive-purposive approach to learning). The main tenets of *Tolman's theory*
are that behavior should be analyzed in terms of actions (large-scale basis or
"molar") rather than of movements (small-scale basis or "molecular"; cf:
Royce, 1994), that behavior is goal-directed ("purposive"), and that behavior
in seeking a particular goal varies according to environmental circumstances.
Among Tolman's learning constructs is *expectancy*—a three-term associative
unit involving a stimulus, a response to it, and another stimulus that follows the
response—and a *cognitive map*—a mental map of the environment that indicates
routes, paths, and environmental relationships that determine what responses the
organism will make. One of the basic assumptions of *Tolman's theory* is that
knowledge is acquired as a simple result of exposure and attention to environmental events; no reward is necessary, just contiguity of experienced events

where expectancies are strengthened every time objective events occur in sequence. Tolman viewed the concept of *extinction* as a weakening/loss of a specific expectancy and the concept of *inference* as the process by which new positive events at a goal-location could work their way back to affect any subsequent response selection. Tolman asserted that organisms have internal representations that allow them to demonstrate "goal learning" and discriminations. Evidence for this position comes from experiments on *reward expectancy* (e.g., Cowles & Nissen, 1937; Trapold, 1970), *place learning* (e.g., Tolman, Ritchie, & Kalish, 1946; cf: Restle, 1957), *latent learning/latent extinction* (e.g., Menzel, 1978), *partial reinforcement extinction effect/discrimination hypothesis* (e.g., Capaldi, 1966), *provisional expectancies/hypotheses theory* (e.g., Krechevsky, 1932, 1933), and *vicarious trial-and-error* (e.g., Muenzinger, 1938; Mowrer, 1960). *Tolman's theory* anticipated many of the later significant developments in learning theory. For example, the current topics of "decision processes," "subjective probability," and "subjective utility" involve concepts that are similar to Tolman's *expectancy value* and *object valence*; Rotter's (1954) *behavioral potential theory* and *expectancy-reinforcement theory* are close to Tolman's *means-ends readiness* and *valence*; Deutsch's (1960) *structural model* contains aspects similar to Tolman's *insightful behavior of rats*; and Logan's (1979) *hybrid theory* of classical conditioning and incentive learning centers on Tolman's *sensory-sensory contiguity principle of association*. However, Tolman's approach has been criticized as containing too many superfluous and surplus meanings, as being too anthropomorphic, unparsimonious, teleological, and vitalistic. Tolman's system was not tight enough to endure, and there is no "Tolman's law" to give him immortality. The *latent learning* experiment is probably as uniquely Tolman's as the *nonsense syllable* is uniquely Ebbinghaus's. Perhaps, in the final analysis, Tolman's contribution to learning may lie in his emphasis upon the cognitive aspects of behavior, which gave a new challenge to rigid behaviorism (Bower & Hilgard, 1981). See also AMSEL'S HYPOTHESIS/THEORY; CAPALDI'S THEORY; GUTHRIE'S THEORY OF BEHAVIOR; HULL'S LEARNING THEORY; LOGAN'S MICROMOLAR THEORY; SKINNER'S DESCRIPTIVE BEHAVIOR/OPERANT CONDITIONING THEORY.

REFERENCES

Krechevsky, I. (1932). "Hypotheses" in rats. *Psy. Rev., 39*, 516–532.

Thorndike, E. (1932). *The fundamentals of learning*. New York: Teachers College, Columbia University.

Tolman, E. C. (1932). *Purposive behavior in animals and men*. New York: Appleton-Century-Crofts.

Krechevsky, I. (1933). The docile nature of "hypotheses." *J. Comp. Psy., 16*, 99–116.

Guthrie, E. (1935). *The psychology of learning*. New York: Harper & Row.

Cowles, J., & Nissen, H. (1937). Reward expectancy in delayed responses of chimpanzees. *J. Comp. Psy., 24*, 345–358.

Muenzinger, K. (1938). Vicarious trial and error at a point of choice: I. A general survey of its relation to learning efficiency. *J. Genet. Psy., 53*, 75–86.

Skinner, B. F. (1938). *The behavior of organisms: An experimental analysis.* New York: Appleton-Century-Crofts.

Hull, C. (1943). *Principles of behavior.* New York: Appleton-Century-Crofts.

Tolman, E. C., Ritchie, B., & Kalish, D. (1946). Studies in spatial learning: II. Place learning versus response learning. *J. Exp. Psy., 36*, 221–229.

Rotter, J. (1954). *Social learning and clinical psychology.* Englewood Cliffs, NJ: Prentice-Hall.

Restle, F. (1957). Discrimination of cues in mazes: A resolution of the "place-vs. response" question. *Psy. Rev., 64*, 217–228.

Tolman, E. C. (1959). Principles of purposive behavior. In S. Koch (Ed.), *Psychology: A study of a science.* Vol. 2. New York: McGraw-Hill.

Deutsch, J. (1960). *The structural basis of behavior.* Chicago: University of Chicago Press.

Mowrer, O. H. (1960). *Learning theory and behavior.* New York: Wiley.

Capaldi, E. (1966). Partial reinforcement: An hypothesis of sequential effects. *Psy. Rev., 73*, 459–477.

Trapold, M. (1970). Are expectancies based upon different positive reinforcing events discriminably different? *Learn. & Mot., 1*, 129–140.

Menzel, E. (1978). Cognitive mapping in chimpanzees. In S. Hulse, H. Fowler, & W. Honig (Eds.), *Cognitive processes in animal behavior.* Hillsdale, NJ: Erlbaum.

Logan, F. (1979). Hybrid theory of operant conditioning. *Psy. Rev., 86*, 507–541.

Bower, G., & Hilgard, E. (1981). *Theories of learning.* Englewood Cliffs, NJ: Prentice-Hall.

Royce, J. (1994). Molar/molecular constructs. In R. J. Corsini (Ed.), *Ency. Psy.* New York: Wiley.

TONES/COMBINATIONAL, THEORY OF. See STUMPF'S THEORY OF MUSICAL CONSONANCE AND DISSONANCE.

TOP-DOWN PROCESSING/THEORIES. *Top-down processing* is a generic term referring to the flow of information/data in any given aspect of *cognitive* or *perceptual theory.* For example, when one takes "meaning" or "familiarity" of stimuli into account when perceiving the world, it is called *top-down processing* because processing is based on "higher-level" information such as the meaningful context in which a stimulus is observed (cf: *bottom-up processing*), as well as other information that causes the observer to expect that another stimulus will be presented (Goldstein, 1996). The *word-superiority effect* (*WSE*) (i.e., the finding, first reported by J. McK. Cattell in 1885, that a letter can be identified at a lower threshold and responded to more rapidly when it is part of a familiar word than if it is presented in isolation) is a good example of *top-down processing.* The *WSE* is also called the *Reicher–Wheeler effect*; Zusne (1987). Thus, processes that originate in the brain and influence the selection, organization, or interpretation of sensory data are called "conceptually driven," "hypothesis-driven," or *top-down processing.* Abstract thoughts, prior knowledge, beliefs, values, past experience, expectations, memory, motivations, cultural background, and language all influence and direct *top-down processing*. Usually, both *top-down* and *bottom-up processing* interact as one attempts to perceive the environment in some comprehensive, organized, and cohesive fashion (Zimbardo & Weber, 1994). See also BOTTOM-UP PROCESSING/ THEORIES; INFORMATION/INFORMATION-PROCESSING THEORY; PATTERN/OBJECT RECOGNITION THEORY; PERCEPTION (I. GENERAL), THEORIES OF; PERCEPTION (II. COMPARATIVE APPRAISAL) THEORIES OF.

REFERENCES

Cattell, J. McK. (1885). Uber die zeit der erkennung und benennung von schriftzeichen, bildern, und farben. *Phil. Stud., 2,* 635–650.

Zusne, L. (1987). *Eponyms in psychology.* Westport, CT: Greenwood Press.

Zimbardo, P., & Weber, A. (1994). *Psychology.* New York: HarperCollins.

Reber, A. (1995). *The Penguin dictionary of psychology.* New York: Penguin Books.

Goldstein, E. B. (1996). *Sensation and perception.* Pacific Grove, CA: Brooks/Cole.

TORGERSON'S LAW OF CATEGORICAL JUDGMENT. See THURSTONE'S LAW OF COMPARATIVE JUDGMENT.

TOTAL TIME HYPOTHESIS/LAW. The American psychologist B. R. Bugelski (1913–1995) explored the *total time hypothesis* in a learning context (Bugelski, 1962, 1964), suggesting that total time (number of trials multiplied by trial time) to learn material in paired-associate learning tasks equals a constant. Houston (1981) elevated this hypothesis to the status of a *law*. The *total time law* refers to the notion that the amount of learning that will occur in a given time interval is relatively constant no matter how that time is spent in rehearsing the material to be learned (cf: *deJong's law*—the principle that the time taken to perform a task is an exponential function of the time spent practicing it; the *power law of practice*—the time taken to perform a mental task decreases as a fractional power of the number of trials; and the *law of fixation*—the principle that with repeated practice learned material becomes more or less permanently fixed in the mind; Sutherland, 1996). Bugelski's (1962) study supported the *total time law* where he found that the total time required to learn a list of nonsense syllables (presented in pairs as "paired associates" in which subjects were asked to anticipate and say aloud the second syllable of each pair when shown the first syllable) was unaffected by the rate at which items were presented within that total time. Subsequent to Bugelski's work, many other researchers have elaborated upon, and supported, the *total time hypothesis/law* (e.g., Cooper & Pantle, 1967; cf: the *lag effect* as an exception to the *total time hypothesis*; Baddeley, 1976). The *total time law* has potential value for educators and teachers because it suggests that the patterns of rehearsal that a person uses when learning materials is relatively unimportant and that an essential aspect in learning is that the individual keeps on working; Bugelski (1964, p. 26) stated: "It takes a certain amount of time to learn something, regardless of the length of the practice period." See also LEARNING THEORIES/LAWS.

REFERENCES

Bugelski, B. R. (1962). Presentation time, total time, and mediation in paired-associate learning. *J. Exp. Psy.*, *63*, 409–412.

Bugelski, B. R. (1964). *The psychology of learning applied to teaching*. New York: Bobbs-Merrill.

Cooper, E., & Pantle, A. (1967). The total-time hypothesis in verbal learning. *Psy. Bull.*, *68*, 221–234.

Bugelski, B. R. (1970a). Presentation time and the total-time hypothesis: A methodological amendment. *J. Exp. Psy.*, *84*, 529–530.

Bugelski, B. R. (1970b). Words and things and images. *Amer. Psy.*, *25*, 1002–1012.

Baddeley, A. (1976). *The psychology of memory*. New York: Basic Books.

Bugelski, B. R. (1979). *The principles of learning and memory*. New York: Praeger.

Houston, J. (1981). *Fundamentals of learning and memory*. New York: Academic Press.

Sutherland, S. (1996). *The international dictionary of psychology*. New York: Crossroad.

TRACE THEORY. See FORGETTING/MEMORY, THEORIES OF; GESTALT THEORY/LAWS.

TRAIT THEORIES OF PERSONALITY. See PERSONALITY THEORIES.

TRAIT THEORY OF LEADERSHIP. See LEADERSHIP, THEORIES OF.

TRANSACTIONAL ANALYSIS TECHNIQUE. See BERNE'S SCRIPT THEORY.

TRANSACTIONAL THEORIES OF LEADERSHIP. See LEADERSHIP, THEORIES OF.

TRANSACTIONAL THEORY. See PERCEPTION (II. COMPARATIVE APPRAISAL), THEORIES OF.

TRANSFER OF TRAINING, THORNDIKE'S THEORY OF. = identical elements theory. In general, the topic of transfer of training refers to the situation where something learned in one task (e.g., learning to fly a helicopter) may be carried over ("transferred") to another task (e.g., learning to fly a jet aircraft) and where the transfer may either facilitate or inhibit the learning of the second task. Transfer of training is often attributed to the existence of "identical elements" in the two functions or to the process of generalization (cf: *instance/episode/exemplar theory*, which holds that memory and knowledge systems are built up directly on the basis of specific instances or episodes in one's experience; this theory is contrasted, generally, with *abstraction/prototype theory*, which argues that memory/knowledge is built up by processes of abstract information that is extracted from specific episodes that one experiences; Reber, 1995). Early accounts of the operation of transfer of training emphasized the *faculty* (i.e., a power or agency of the mind such as feeling, will, intellect) that was involved in the learning situation. The historic school and system of psychology called *faculty psychology* (see Leahey, 1994) approached the study of the human mind by attempting to account for mental processes in terms of a fixed number of such "faculties." A *faculty* was defined in such a broad manner as to cover all the operations of memory and observation and was supposed to be strengthened by exercise on any sort of material. In an educational context, the *theory of faculty training* held that training to learn one set of materials (e.g., learning Latin) would prepare one to excel on another set of materials (e.g., learning English). Although largely discredited today, *faculty psychology* has recently been revived under the *modularity hypothesis/theory* where cognitive and perceptual modules (e.g., a language module; a numerical module) are hypothesized (Reber, 1995). Thorndike's (1903) pioneer experimental work was in opposition to the postulates of the traditional *faculty theory*. Thorndike proposed that transfer of material was possible only so far as *identical elements* of behavior could be carried over from one learning task to another one. Thorndike and Woodworth (1901) conducted transfer experiments that attacked a correlate of the *faculty theory* called the *doctrine of formal discipline* (i.e., the educational approach that suggests that some courses should be studied—independently of the content that they might have—because they serve generally to "train the mind"). The transfer effects that Thorndike and Woodworth found were due to specific methods, habits, and ideas that were carried over from the practice tasks that were given previously. Their conclusions were that improvements in performance were due to definite factors (rather than general tendencies), and these definite factors comprised "common" or "identical" elements. Thorndike (1903, 1913) consistently held that a change in one function alters any other only insofar as the two functions have identical elements as factors. In more recent times, psychologists seem to prefer the term *common factors* over the term *identical elements*, but Thorndike's *identical elements* approach to transfer of training situations still serves as a useful prescription that points toward features and factors that are definite and concrete vis-à-vis the cause of any observed transfer effect. See also EFFECT, LAW OF; FORMAL DISCIPLINE/ TRAINING, THEORY/DOCTRINE OF; GENERALIZATION, PRINCIPLE OF; REINFORCEMENT, THORNDIKE'S THEORY OF.

REFERENCES

Thorndike, E., & Woodworth, R. (1901). The influence of improvement in one mental function upon the efficiency of other functions. *Psy. Rev., 8*, 247–261, 384–395, 553–564.

Thorndike, E. (1903). *Educational psychology*. New York: Lemcke & Buechner.
Thorndike, E. (1913). *Educational psychology*. Vol. 2. *The psychology of learning*. New York: Teachers College, Columbia University.
Gibson, E. (1953). Improvement in perceptual judgments as a function of controlled practice or training. *Psy. Bull., 50*, 401–431.
Osgood, C. (1953). *Method and theory in experimental psychology*. New York: Oxford University Press.
Leahey, T. (1994). Faculty psychology. In R. J. Corsini (Ed.), *Ency. Psy.* New York: Wiley.
Reber, A. (1995). *The Penguin dictionary of psychology*. New York: Penguin Books.

TRANSFORMATIONAL THEORY OF LANGUAGE. See CHOMSKY'S PSYCHOLINGUISTIC THEORY.

TRANSSITUATIONALITY PRINCIPLE. See REINFORCEMENT THEORY.

TRAVELING WAVE THEORY. See AUDITION/HEARING, THEORIES OF.

TREISMAN'S FEATURE INTEGRATION THEORY. See PATTERN/OBJECT RECOGNITION THEORY.

TROXLER EFFECT. See VISION/SIGHT, THEORIES OF.

TWO-FACTOR LEARNING THEORY. See MOWRER'S THEORY.

TWO-FACTOR THEORY OF WORK. See WORK/CAREER/OCCUPATION, THEORIES OF.

TWO-STAGE PROCESS THEORY. See PUNISHMENT, THEORIES OF.

TWO-SYNDROME HYPOTHESIS. See SCHIZOPHRENIA, THEORIES OF.

TYPE THEORIES OF PERSONALITY. See PERSONALITY THEORIES.

U

UNCONSCIOUS INFERENCE, DOCTRINE OF. The German physiologist/
psychologist Hermann Ludwig Ferdinand Helmholtz (1821–1894) developed the
doctrine of unconscious inference (in German, "unbewusster Schluss"), which
refers to a judgment one makes on the basis of a limited amount of data or
evidence and is made without conscious awareness (Helmholtz, 1856–1866; cf:
Wundt, 1862; Chalmers, 1996). The notion of *unconscious inference* was offered
by Helmholtz as an explanation for many perceptual phenomena (see Allport,
1955; cf: the *likelihood principle*—Helmholtz's idea that people interpret sensations in such a way as to perceive what is most likely to have given rise to
those sensations; Sutherland, 1996). For example, concerning the perceptual
principle of interposition: when two objects (A and B) are arranged before an
observer such that A is partially blocking B, the observer makes an *unconscious
inference* and concludes that object A must be closer to him or her than object
B. Historically, the *doctrine of unconscious inference* was a very important part
of Helmholtz's *theory of perception* and was a corollary of the *empiricist* position—the viewpoint that knowledge results from experience, induction, and
learning, and where in its once extreme form it asserted that mind at birth was
a "blank slate" or *tabula rasa* upon which experience writes its messages. The
empiricist position competed with the viewpoints of *nativism*—the doctrine that
the capacity to perceive time and space is inborn, genetic, or inherited; *rationalism*—the perspective that truth is received through the use of rational thought
and deductive reasoning; and *a priorism*—the doctrine that the mind comes
equipped with innate ideas where genuine knowledge is possible independent
of experience. *Unconscious inference* may be viewed also in connection with
Helmholtz's *theory of color contrast* (which never gained general acceptance):
red and verdigris are color complementaries and contrast with each other; a gray-
colored stimulus figure appears on a red ground; it contrasts with the red, and,
by *unconscious inference*, the observer sees it as the opposite ("greenish")

color. Helmholtz argued that perception may contain many experiential data that are not immediately represented in the stimulus and are, in a sense, additions that accrue to the perception in accordance with its development in past experience. Helmholtz decided to call these unconsciously determined phenomena *inferences*, and, in an attempt both to affirm and to deny their inferential nature, he used the paradoxical phrase *unconscious inference*. Helmholtz made three positive statements concerning *unconscious inferences*: they are normally "irresistible" (i.e., they are immediate, unconscious, and not correctible by conscious reasoning); they are formed by experience (i.e., they develop by "association" and "repetition" into unconscious inferences); and they are, in their results, like conscious inferences from analogy and are thus inductive (i.e., the brain makes generalizations quickly and automatically in perception) (Boring, 1957). See also CONSTRUCTIVIST THEORY OF PERCEPTION; PERCEPTION (I. GENERAL), THEORIES OF; PERCEPTION (II. COMPARATIVE APPRAISAL), THEORIES OF.

REFERENCES

Helmholtz, H. von (1856–1866). *Physiological optics*. Leipzig: Voss.

Wundt, W. (1862). *Beitrage zur theorie der sinneswahrnehmung*. Leipzig: Wunter'sck Verlaghandlung.

Allport, F. (1955). *Theories of perception and the concept of structure*. New York: Wiley.

Boring, E. G. (1957). *A history of experimental psychology*. New York: Appleton-Century-Crofts.

Hochberg, J. (1994). Unconscious inference. In R. J. Corsini (Ed.), *Ency. Psy*. New York: Wiley.

Chalmers, D. (1996). *The conscious mind: In search of a fundamental theory*. New York: Oxford University Press.

Sutherland, S. (1996). *The international dictionary of psychology*. New York: Crossroad.

UNIT HYPOTHESIS. See GENERALIZATION, PRINCIPLE OF.

UNIVERSALISTIC THEORIES. See WORK/CAREER/OCCUPATION, THEORIES OF.

UNLEARNING HYPOTHESIS. See INTERFERENCE THEORIES.

USE, LAW OF. This is one of the corollaries of Thorndike's (1898) *law of exercise*, which states that behaviors, stimulus–response connections, and functions that are exercised, rehearsed, or practiced are strengthened as compared to those behaviors, bonds, or functions that are not used. Some early writers (e.g., Gates, 1926) held that the repeated use of a stimulus–response connection unit (neurones) brought about certain synaptic changes that made the passage of the nerve impulse more rapid in the future. Gates called this native capacity of nervous structure modifiability the *law of modification by exercise* or, more simply, the *law of use* (cf: the *use/disuse, use-inheritance theory* advanced by

J. B. Lamarck, which holds that the structural or functional changes in organs brought about by their use or their disuse are passed onto the progeny; Warren, 1934). The idea of a physiological change in nervous structure during the practice (use) of stimulus–response connections anticipated Hebb's (1947, 1972) later concepts in perception/learning of *cell assembly* and *phase sequence*, where groups of neurons are functionally interrelated and organized into a complex "closed circuit" by repeated stimulation. See also DISUSE, LAW/THEORY OF; EFFECT, LAW OF; EXERCISE, LAW OF; FREQUENCY, LAW OF; HEBB'S THEORY OF PERCEPTUAL LEARNING; LAMARCK'S THEORY.

REFERENCES

Thorndike, E. (1898). *Animal intelligence.* New York: Macmillan.

Gates, A. (1926). *Elementary psychology.* New York: Macmillan.

Thorndike, E., Bregman, E., Tilton, J., & Woodyard, E. (1928). *Adult learning.* New York: Macmillan.

Trowbridge, M., & Cason, H. (1932). An experimental study of Thorndike's theory of learning. *J. Gen. Psy., 7,* 245–258.

Warren, H. (Ed.) (1934). *Dictionary of psychology.* Cambridge, MA: Houghton Mifflin.

Hebb, D. (1947). *Organization of behavior.* New York: Wiley.

Hebb, D. (1972). *Textbook of psychology.* Philadelphia: Saunders.

US-VERSUS-THEM EFFECT. See PREJUDICE, THEORIES OF.

UTILITY THEORY. See DECISION-MAKING THEORIES.

V

VANDENBERGH EFFECT. See OLFACTION/SMELL, THEORIES OF.

VASCULAR THEORY. See NAFE'S THEORY OF CUTANEOUS SENSITIVITY.

VIBRATION THEORY. See OLFACTION/SMELL, THEORIES OF.

VIBRATORY THEORY OF INHERITANCE. See MENDEL'S LAWS/ PRINCIPLES.

VIERORDT'S LAW. See SKINNER'S DESCRIPTIVE BEHAVIOR/OPERANT CONDITIONING THEORY.

VIGILANCE, THEORIES OF. = sustained attention theories. In general, *theories of vigilance* refer to the systematic accounts of how observers maintain their focus of *attention* (i.e., the selective aspects of perception that function to help an organism focus on certain features of the environment to the exclusion of other features) and remain alert to stimuli over prolonged periods of time (i.e., *sustained attention*; cf: the *law of prior entry*—the principle that if a subject is attending to one of two possible stimuli, and if they occur simultaneously, the one to which he or she is attending tends to be perceived as having occurred before the other; in social psychology, this is called the *prior entry effect* where the first impressions of a person tend to dominate and are not easily changed by further acquaintance; Sutherland, 1996; see also Woodworth's, 1921, *laws of attention*: *selection*—of two or more inconsistent responses to the same situation, only one is made at the same time; *advantage*—one of the alternative responses has an initial advantage over the others due to such factors as intensity and change in the stimulus; *shifting*—the response that has the initial advantage loses its advantage shortly, and an alternative response is made, provided the situation remains the same; *tendency*—a tendency when aroused to activity facilitates responses that are in its line and inhibits others; and *combination*—a single response may be made to two or more stimuli, and two or more stimuli may arouse a single joint response). The various specific *theories/models of vigilance* attempt to deal with certain common questions in an observer's behavior during a vigilance task: How is background information stored? How are decisions made during observation? and How do neural attention units function? A sampling of the *vigilance theories* and some of their major tenets are *expectancy theory*—observers act as "temporal averaging instruments" who form expectancies as to the approximate time course of critical signal appearances on the basis of samples of signal input; readiness to detect a signal is assumed to be positively related to level of expectancy; *elicited observing rate hypothesis*—the observer constantly makes sequential decisions about whether or not to emit observing responses toward the display that is monitored; detection failures occur when the subject does not emit the observing responses due to fatigue or low motivation or does so in an imperfect fashion; *signal detection theory*—the decrement function typically found in a vigilance task reflects a shift to a more conservative response criterion and decision process, rather than a decline in alertness or perceptual sensitivity to signals; *activation/arousal theory*—instead of a "cognitive" appraisal of vigilance, this approach emphasizes a neurophysiological explanation whereby sensory input has two general functions: to convey information about the environment and to "tone up" the brain with a background of diffuse activity that helps cortical transmission via increased alertness; the orientation suggests that the monotonous aspects of vigilance tasks reduce the level of nonspecific activity that is necessary to maintain continued alertness and, consequently, lead to a decline in the efficiency of signal detection; and *habituation theory*—habituation is a lessening of neural responsiveness due to repeated stimulation and is an "active process of inhibition"; this approach argues that the degree of neural habituation in a given task is directly related to the frequency of stimulus presentation so that with the development of habituation the observer's ability to discriminate critical signals is degraded, attention to the task becomes increasingly more difficult, and performance declines over a period of time; this theory holds that habituation accumulates more rapidly at fast, than at slow, rates and results in a decline in performance at fast stimulus/event rates. The current status of *vigilance theories* is that each model focuses on a somewhat different aspect of the sustained attention situation, even though many theories can account for similar data. To date, the task remains of synthesizing the various theoretical positions of vigilance into a unified framework where stronger "lawful" cause–effect statements may be provided (Dember & Warm, 1979). See also ACTIVATION/AROUSAL THEORY; ATTENTION, LAWS/PRINCIPLES/THEORIES OF; ELICITED OBSERVING RATE HYPOTHESIS; HABITUATION, PRINCIPLE/LAW OF; IMPRESSION FORMATION, THEORIES OF; SIGNAL DETECTION THEORY.

REFERENCES

Woodworth, R. (1921). *Psychology: A study of mental life*. New York: Holt.

Mackworth, N. (1948). The breakdown of vigilance during prolonged visual search. *Quar. J. Exp. Psy., 1*, 6–21.

Deese, J. (1955). Some problems in the theory of vigilance. *Psy. Rev., 62*, 359–368.

Malmo, R. (1959). Activation: A neuropsychological dimension. *Psy. Rev., 66*, 367–386.

Baker, C. (1963). Further toward a theory of vigilance. In D. Buckner & J. McGrath (Eds.), *Vigilance: A symposium*. New York: McGraw-Hill.

Davies, D., & Tune, G. (1969). *Human vigilance performance*. New York: American Elsevier.

Mackworth, J. (1969). *Vigilance and habituation*. Baltimore: Penguin Books.

Loeb, M., & Alluisi, E. (1970). Influence on display, task, and organismic variables on indices of monitoring behavior. *Acta Psy., 33*, 343–366.

Broadbent, D. (1971). *Decision and stress*. New York: Academic Press.

Stroh, C. (1971). *Vigilance: The problem of sustained attention*. New York: Pergamon.

Mackie, R. (Ed.) (1977). *Vigilance: Theory, operational performance and physiological correlates*. New York: Plenum.

Dember, W., & Warm, J. (1979). *Psychology of perception*. New York: Holt, Rinehart, & Winston.

Parasuraman, R., & Davies, D. (1989). *Varieties of attention*. Orlando, FL: Academic Press.

Sutherland, S. (1996). *The international dictionary of psychology*. New York: Crossroad.

VISION/SIGHT, THEORIES OF. One of the earliest theories that attempted to describe a mechanism for human vision was proposed by the Greek mathematician/mystic Pythagoras (c. 582–507 B.C.). He asserted that rays of light sprang from the eyes themselves, much like twin spotlights; somehow, the light striking objects in front of the observer triggered a reaction in the eye, and vision was the result (Levinthal, 1983). However, by the fifteenth century *Pythagoras' theory* was reversed, where the eyes were considered the receivers, not senders, of light. By that time, some of the greatest scientists of the day began to investigate the question of light's effect on the eye. For example, Leonardo da Vinci (1452–1519) made detailed drawings of the eye's anatomy; Johannes Kepler (1571–1630) formulated the basic *laws of light refraction*, which explained how light rays can be bent as they travel from one medium to another; and Rene Descartes (1596–1650) conducted studies concerning the application of these *refraction laws* to the structural features of the eye, which led to a basic understanding of how the eye focused incoming light. By 1666, Sir Isaac Newton's (1642–1727) experiments on the composition of light itself was the formal beginning of inquiries into the physical nature of light as well as inquiries into the way the eye interprets color phenomena (cf: the *inverse square law*—the principle that the intensity of a stimulus that reaches the receptor from a distant source varies inversely as the square of the distance of the source from the receptor; the *law of illumination*—the principle that the illumination upon a surface varies directly as the luminous intensity of the light source, inversely as the square of its distance, and directly as the cosine of the angle made by the light rays with the perpendicular to the surface; Warren, 1934; and the *Arago phenomenon*—the relative insensitivity to light of the very center of the visual field at very low levels of illumination; Reber, 1995). According to modern *vision theory* (e.g., Geldard, 1972), the stimulus for the sensory modality of vision/sight is electromagnetic radiation (light) between approximately 380 and 740 nanometers (*nm*, where 1 *nm* = 1 billionth of a meter), and where the initial processing of visual information is the receptor system consisting of photosensitive cells (*rods* and *cones*) in the retina of the eye. Vision is the process of transforming ("transducing") physical light energy into biological neural impulses that can then be interpreted by the brain. The electromagnetic radiation can vary in intensity (which is perceived as a difference in brightness level) and wavelength (which is perceived as a difference in color). The *quantum theory of vision* (e.g., Harris & Levey, 1975) maintains that light energy travels to the eye in the form of discrete or discontinuous changes in energy where wavelength frequencies correspond to definite energies of the light quanta called *photons*. The Dutch physicist Christiaan Huygens (1629–1693) first proposed the *undulatory theory*, which forms a part of the *wave theory of light* that supplanted the earlier *corpuscular/particle theory*. The *wave theory* offers a ready explanation of interference, diffraction, and polarization of light but fails to explain the interaction of light with matter, the emission and absorption of light, photoelectricity, and other phenomena. These can be explained only by a quasi-*corpuscular theory* involving packets of energy—light quanta or photons. The *quantum theory* was introduced by the German physicist Max Planck (1858–1947) in 1900. Ultimately, it appears that two models are required to explain the phenomenon of light. According to the *complementarity principle* of the Danish physicist Niels Bohr (1885–1962), a system such as an electron can be described *either* in terms of *particles* or in terms of *wave motion* (Illingworth, 1991). *Theories of vision* are systematic attempts to account for the various phenomena of visual perception in relation to the known structure and functions of the visual organs. Included by extension is the study of photoreceptors, the action of nerves and nerve endings (cf: *Hering's law of equal innervation*—the muscles of each eye always operate in synchrony because they receive the same innervation; Sutherland, 1996), responses to light in lower organisms, the higher psychological implications of light, color, form, and their temporal and spatial relations (cf: *Harvey's principle*—when a grating is viewed, the number of vertical stripes per unit of total breadth is overestimated and the number of horizontal stripes is underestimated; Sutherland, 1996; and the *law of identical visual direction*—in binocular vision, any pair of corresponding lines of direction in objective space are represented by a single line of direction in visual space; Warren, 1934). The anatomical and physiological basis for vision may be hypothesized much as is the case for the *theories of color vision,* for example, the three-component *Young–Helmholtz theory*; the *antagonistic/opponent-process theory of Hering*; the *Ladd–Franklin genetic theory*; and the *von Kries duplicity theory* (Warren, 1934). The cone cells ("daylight vision") in the retina are responsible for chromatic/color vision and visual acuity (see *Charpentier's law*—in the retinal fovea, the product of the area of a stimulus and its intensity is constant for stimuli at threshold intensities; and the *blue-arc phenomenon*—an effect produced by a stimulus at the center of the visual field against a dark background; it consists of a pair of bluish, luminous arcs seen as connecting the stimulus with the locus of the blind spot; Warren, 1934; see also the *Troxler effect*—the fading of visual objects in the periphery of the visual field when a point in its center is steadily fixated; this is due to the organization of the peripheral retina, which requires larger eye movements than are needed in the fovea, to break the adaptation brought about by steady fixation; Zusne, 1987; and the *Ditchburn–Riggs effect*—phenomenon of the rapid cessation of vision of contours when the image of the contours undergoes prolonged stabilization with respect to the retina; Pritchard, 1961). The rod cells ("night-time vision") are sensitive to minute amounts of light but are not sensitive to colors (cf: Kaneko's, 1979, *photochemical theory of vision*). Because of the anatomical features of the visual system, the *left* visual field is represented in the *right* occipital lobe of the brain, and the *right* visual field is represented in the *left* occipital lobe (see Sperry, 1974). It is much easier to trace anatomically the visual pathway from the retina to the occipital lobes than it is to explain and understand how the eyes and the brain interact to produce the perception of vision (Bowen, 1994; cf: the *Cheshire cat effect*, which relies on the phenomenon of binocular rivalry—where each eye has a different input from the same part of the visual field—and motion in the field of one eye can cause either the entire image to disappear or parts of the image to be erased; the movement captures the brain's attention momentarily; Crick & Koch, 1997). More is known about how photochemical processes/mechanisms operate in the rod cells than about the cone cells. In addition to responding directly to light, the receptor cells are affected also by the surrounding receptor cells. Studies have shown that there are both inhibitory and excitatory effects when neighboring receptor cells fire simultaneously (Hartline & Ratliff, 1957). Other studies indicate that various cells in the visual cortex are maximally activated by objects in the visual field with specific shapes, of particular orientations, and moving in particular directions. For instance, Hubel and Wiesel (1965) hypothesized the existence of four general types of hierarchically organized cells (simple, complex, lower-order hypercomplex, and upper-order hypercomplex), and this notion has found anatomical support from other research, but the theory that those cells are arranged hierarchically is not yet supported (see Kelly & VanEssen, 1974). Over 100 years ago, the German physician/psychologist Hermann Aubert (1826–1892) provided a number of theoretical and lawful propositions concerning visual *acuity* and *perception* (cf: *Listing's law* concerning visual *accommodation*—if the eye moves from a primary position to any other position, the torsional rotation of the eyeball in the new position is the same as it would be if the eye had turned about a fixed axis, and lies at right angles to the initial and final directions of the line of regard; Warren, 1934; and *Alexander's law*, which refers to nystagmus, produced either by rotation or thermally, which can be accentuated voluntarily by moving the eyes in the direction of the jerky component of the nystagmus; Zusne, 1987). Among Aubert's eponymous referents are the following: the *Aubert–Fleischl paradox/phenomenon*—a perceptual effect whereby a moving stimulus seems to move more slowly when the observer fixates on the stimulus than when she or he fixates on the background (Aubert, 1886); the *Aubert–Forster phenomenon*—when two objects of different physical sizes are placed at different distances from the observer such that both subtend the same number of degrees of visual arc, the physically closer one can be recognized over a greater area of the retina than the physically more distant one (Aubert, 1865); the *Aubert phenomenon*—when a single vertical straight-line stimulus is presented to an observer, the line will be perceptually displaced as the observer tilts his or her head (Aubert, 1886; cf: the *Muller effect*—when an observer views a luminous vertical rod in the dark, it appears to be tilted out of vertical in the same direction as the head; this effect occurs only with small tilts of the head; Sutherland, 1996); and the *Aubert–Forster law*—a generalization regarding visual acuity based on the *Aubert–Forster phenomenon* that states that objectively small objects can be distinguished as two at greater distances from the fovea than objectively larger objects subtending the same visual angle (Aubert, 1865). See also ADAPTATION, PRINCIPLES/LAWS OF; COLOR VISION, THEORIES/LAWS OF; PURKINJE EFFECT/PHENOMENON/SHIFT.

REFERENCES

Aubert, H. (1865). *Physiologie der netzhant.* Breslau: Morgenstern.

Aubert, H. (1886) Die bewegungsempfindung. *Ar. ges. Physio., 39,* 347–370.

Warren H. (Ed.) (1934). *Dictionary of psychology.* Cambridge, MA: Houghton Mifflin.

Hartline, H., & Ratliff, F. (1957). Inhibitory interaction of receptor units in the eye of limulus. *J. Gen. Physio., 40,* 357–376.

Pritchard, R. (1961). Stabilized images on the retina. *Sci. Amer., 204,* 72–78.

Hubel, D., & Wiesel, T. (1965). Receptive fields and functional architecture in two nonstriate visual areas (18 and 19) of the cat. *J. Neurophysio., 28,* 229–289.

Geldard, F. (1972). *The human senses.* New York: Wiley.

Kelly, J., & VanEssen, D. (1974). Cell structure and function in the visual cortex of the cat. *J. Physio., 238,* 515–547.

Sperry, R. (1974). Lateral specialization in the surgically separated hemispheres. In F. Schmitt & F. Worden, (Eds.), *The neurosciences: Third study program.* Cambridge: MIT Press.

Harris, W., & Levey, J. (Eds.) (1975). *The new Columbia encyclopedia.* New York: Columbia University Press.

Gregory, R. (1978). *Eye and brain: The psychology of seeing.* New York: McGraw-Hill.

Kaneko, A. (1979). Physiology of the retina. *Ann. Rev. Neuroscience, 2,* 169–191.

Levinthal, C. (1983). *Introduction to physiological psychology.* Englewood Cliffs, NJ: Prentice-Hall.

Zusne, L. (1987). *Eponyms in psychology*. Westport, CT: Greenwood Press.

Illingworth, V. (Ed.) (1991). *The Penguin dictionary of physics*. New York: Penguin Books.

Bowen, D. (1994). Vision (theories of). In R. J. Corsini (Ed.) *Ency. Psy.* New York: Wiley.

Harris, M., & Humphreys, G. (1994). *Computational theories of vision*. In A. Colman (Ed.), *Companion encyclopedia of psychology*. London: Routledge.

Reber, A. (1995). *The Penguin dictionary of psychology*. New York: Penguin Books.

Sutherland, S. (1996). *The international dictionary of psychology*. New York: Crossroad.

Crick, F., & Koch, C. (1997). The problem of consciousness. In *Sci. Amer.* (Special Issue), *Mysteries of the mind*, vol. 7, no. 1.

VISUAL-ORIENTATION HYPOTHESIS. See ATTRIBUTION THEORY.

VIVIDNESS/CLEARNESS, LAW OF. See ASSOCIATION, LAWS/PRINCIPLES OF.

VOLLEY/PERIODICITY THEORY. See AUDITION/HEARING, THEORIES OF.

von KRIES' COLOR VISION THEORY. = duplicity/duplexity theory. The *duplicity/duplexity theory of vision* was first proposed by Max Schultze (1866), and later by H. Parinaud (1898) and Johannes von Kries (1895). The theory states that vision is mediated by two (''duplex'') classes of retinal receptors, the cones, which are ''chromatic'' and sensitive to color wavelengths and used in high illumination (''photopic vision''), and the rods, which are ''achromatic'' and used in low illumination (''scotopic vision''). Since the two classes of receptors manifest different wavelength relationships, the shape of a specific function that relates brightness to color may be used to indicate whether rod or cone vision is predominant in a given situation. There are anatomical differences between the rods and cones, even though these two types of receptors are very similar (Woodworth & Schlosberg, 1965): (1) the rods are smaller and seem to be less highly developed than the cones; (2) there are no rods (only closely packed cones) in the foveal area of the retina; (3) the cones have a better (''one-to-one'') supply of nerves; (4) the substance rhodopsin (''visual purple'') is present in the rods but not in the cones; and (5) nocturnal animals possess mostly rods and very few cones. Today, the *von Kries duplicity theory of vision* is so well established that it counts as a strong statement of fact (von Kries, 1929; Woodworth & Schlosberg, 1965). See also COLOR VISION, THEORIES OF.

REFERENCES

Schultze, M. (1866). Zur anatomie und physiologie der retina. *Ar. Mikr. Anat., 2,* 175–286.

Kries, J. von (1895). Uber die natur gewisser mit den psychischen vorgangen verknupfter gehirnzustande. *Z. Psy., 8,* 1–33.

Parinaud, H (1898). *La vision*. Paris: Octave Doin.

Kries, J. von (1929). Zur theorie des tages–und dammerungssehens. In A. Bethe, G. Bergmann, G. Embden, & A. Ellinger (Eds.), *Handbuch der normalen und pathologischen physiologie*. Berlin: Springer.

Woodworth, R., & Schlosberg, H. (1965). *Experimental psychology*. New York: Holt, Rinehart, & Winston.

von RESTORFF EFFECT. The German psychologist/physician Hedwig von Restorff (1903–?) developed the generalization that if in a given series of stimuli to be learned (such as a list of words), one of them is made physically distinctive in some way (e.g., printed in large type or in a different color from the others), it will be easier to learn and recall. This phenomenon, called the *von Restorff effect*, is also known as the *isolation effect* (Jensen, 1962; Reber, 1995) and the *Kohler–Restorff phenomenon* (Zusne, 1987) and refers to the tendency to remember unusual items better than the more common items (von Restorff, 1933). The experiments by von Restorff (1933) and Kohler and von Restorff (1935) provided a *trace theory* basis for the Gestalt psychologists to explain the forgetting of material. A trace regarding learned materials could become distorted through its interactions with a mass of related traces similar to it. Thus, associative interference in forgetting experiments was related to the material to be remembered. Von Restorff (1933) showed that part of the difficulty of learning a list of nonsense syllables stems from their homogeneity: they are all undistinguishable and equally confusable with one another. However, if one item is perceptually distinguishable, then that unique item will be remembered better than the other items. Kohler and von Restorff (1935) thought of the unique item as standing out like a figure against a ground of all the homogeneous items. Being thus distinguished, the trace laid down for the unique item would be isolated from the traces of the rest of the items and therefore not be distorted by interactions with those traces. Accounts of the *von Restorff effect* by stimulus–response associationists have proceeded along similar lines, using principles of *stimulus generalization* and *associative interference* (Bower & Hilgard, 1981). See also INTERFERENCE THEORIES OF FORGETTING; TOP-DOWN PROCESSING/THEORIES; TRACE THEORY.

REFERENCES

Restorff, H. von (1933). Analyse von vorgangen im spurenfeld. I. Uber die wirkung von bereichsbildungen im spurenfeld. *Psy. Forsch., 18*, 299–342.

Kohler, W., & Restorff, H. von (1935). Analyse von vorgangen im spurenfeld. II. Zur theorie der reproduktion. *Psy. Forsch., 21*, 56–112.

Jensen, A. (1962). The von Restorff isolation effect with minimal response learning. *J. Exp. Psy., 64*, 123–125.

Bower, G., & Hilgard, E. (1981). *Theories of learning*. Englewood Cliffs, NJ: Prentice-Hall.

Zusne, L. (1987). *Eponyms in psychology*. Westport, CT: Greenwood Press.

Reber, A. (1995). *The Penguin dictionary of psychology*. New York: Penguin Books.

W

WEBER-FECHNER LAW. See FECHNER'S LAW.

WEBER'S LAW. = Weber's fraction = Weber's function = Weber's ratio. The German physiologist/psychophysicist Ernst Heinrich Weber (1795–1878) formulated this psychophysical generalization, which states that the *just-noticeable differences* (or *JNDs*), that is, the differences between two stimuli that are detected as often as they are undetected, in stimuli are proportional to the magnitude of the original stimulus (Weber, 1834). Weber described the relationship between existing stimulation and changes in that stimulation in what historians of psychology have called the *first quantitative law of psychology* (Schultz & Schultz, 1987; cf: the *quotient hypothesis*, which is an interpretation of *Weber's law* according to which the quotients/ratios of any two successive *JNDs* in a given sensory series are always equal; and *Breton's law*, which is a formula proposed by P. Breton as a substitute for *Weber's law* that states a parabolic relation between stimulus and *JND*; Warren, 1934). In formal terms, *Weber's law* states that delta I/I = k, where I is the intensity of the comparison stimulus, delta I is the increment in intensity just detectable, and k is a constant. The law holds reasonably well for the midrange of most stimulus dimensions but tends to break down when very low- or very high-intensity stimuli are used. For instance, for very low-intensity tones the *Weber fraction* is somewhat larger than it is for moderately loud tones (Reber, 1995). Representative values of the *Weber ratio* for the intermediate range of some sensory dimensions are brightness, .02 to .05; visual wavelength, .002 to .006; loudness, .1 to .2; auditory frequency, .002 to .035; taste (salt), .15 to .25; smell, .2 to .4; cutaneous pressure, .14 to .16; and deep pressure, .01 to .03. The *law of progression* (Warren, 1934) refers to a formulation devised by the Belgian psychophysicist J.L.R. Delboeuf (1831–1896) as a partial substitute for *Weber's law* and states that successive sensation increments increase by arithmetical progression when the corresponding stimulus-increments increase by geometric progression. Delboeuf's *law of degradation*, another partial substitute for *Weber's law*, states that a sensation is always strongest as it enters consciousness and from then on becomes less intense; and Delboeuf's *law of tension* states that any change in external stimuli produces a condition of disequilibrium/tension in the organism that constitutes the excitation whose conscious accompaniment is the "sensation" (Boring, 1957). An indication of the enduring significance of *Weber's law* is given by Roeckelein (1996): in a random sample of 136 introductory psychology textbooks published from 1885 through 1996, *Weber's law* was cited and described in over 60% of the books (an extremely high percentage for all the laws found in this study), suggesting that it is one of the most popular and frequently cited laws in the psychological literature. Titchener (1907) mentioned *Weber's law* in more than 18 different contexts (e.g., *Weber's law* for affection, for auditory sensations, for cutaneous sensations, for organic sensations, etc.). *Weber's law* has even been applied successfully to plants' response systems (Fuller, 1934). Smith and Guthrie (1924) mention only one law in their book: *Weber's law* (Roeckelein, 1996). See also FECHNER'S LAW; FULLERTON-CATTELL LAW.

REFERENCES

Weber, E. (1834). *De pulsu, resorptione, auditu et tactu*. Leipzig: Koehler.

Gamble, E. (1898). The applicability of Weber's law to smell. *Amer. J. Psy., 10*, 82–142.

Titchener, E. (1907). *An outline of psychology*. New York: Macmillan.

Smith, S., & Guthrie, E. (1924). *General psychology in terms of behavior*. New York: Appleton.

Yoshioka, J. (1929). Weber's law in the discrimination of maze distance by the white rat. *Univ. Cal. Pub. Psy., 4*, 155–184.

Fuller, H. (1934). Plant behavior. *J. Gen. Psy., 11*, 379–394.

Warren, H. (Ed.) (1934). *Dictionary of psychology*. Cambridge, MA: Houghton Mifflin.

Boring, E. G. (1957). *A history of experimental psychology*. New York: Appleton-Century-Crofts.

Schultz, D., & Schultz, S. (1987). *A history of modern psychology*. San Diego: Harcourt Brace Jovanovich.

Reber, A. (1995). *The Penguin dictionary of psychology*. New York: Penguin Books.

Roeckelein, J. (1996). Citation of *laws* and *theories* in textbooks across 112 years of psychology. *Psy. Rep., 79*, 979–998.

WEDENSKY INHIBITION/EFFECT. See SKINNER'S DESCRIPTIVE BEHAVIOR/OPERANT CONDITIONING THEORY.

WEISMANN'S THEORY. = Weismannism. The German biologist August Friedrich Leopold Weismann (1834–1914) formulated a *theory of genetics* that negated the principle that acquired characteristics are inherited and postulated a *continuity* of germ plasm through generations (Wolman, 1973). Weismann was a strong supporter of Charles Darwin's (1859, 1871) *theory of evolution*. In an attempt to disprove the idea of acquired characteristics proposed by Jean-Baptiste Lamarck (1744–1829), Weismann amputated the tails from mice during five successive generations and found that there was no reduction in the propensity to grow tails. Weissmann's early work on the sex cells and development of the Hydrozoa (invertebrate sea animals such as jellyfish, sea anemones, hydroids) led him to develop his *germ plasm/continuity theory*, which postulated that the information required for the development and final form of an organism must be contained within the germ cells, the egg and sperm (he located the germ plasm in what are called today the chromosomes), and be transmitted unchanged from generation to generation. In Weismann's view, germ plasms gave the *continuity* from parent to offspring; all other cells are merely a vehicle to convey the germ plasm, and it alone is—in a sense—immortal; other cells are destined to die. Weismann also noted that some form of reduction division, which is now known to occur during meiosis, must occur if the genetic material were *not* to double on each generation. Weismann's ideas are only broadly correct, but it is surprising that he was able in the 1880s to get so near the modern view. He was wrong in his belief that the germ plasm is unalterable and immune to environmental effects, as others were later to demonstrate (Millar, Millar, Millar, & Millar, 1996). Weismann's theories appeared in a series of essays, translated as "Essays upon Heredity and Kindred Biological Problems" (1889–1892), and his "Vortrage uber Descendenztheorie" (1902) was an important contribution to *evolutionary theory* (Muir, 1994). See also DARWIN'S EVOLUTION THEORY; LAMARCK'S THEORY; MENDEL'S LAWS/PRINCIPLES.

REFERENCES

Darwin, C. (1859). *The origin of species*. London: Murray.
Darwin, C. (1871). *The descent of man*. London: Murray.
Wolman, B. (Ed.) (1973). *Dictionary of behavioral science*. New York: Van Nostrand Reinhold.
Muir, H. (Ed.) (1994). *Larousse dictionary of scientists*. New York: Larousse.
Millar, D., Millar, I., Millar, J., & Millar, M. (1996). *The Cambridge dictionary of scientists*. New York: Cambridge University Press.

WERTHEIMER'S PERCEPTUAL THEORY. See GESTALT THEORY/ LAWS.

WEVER–BRAY EFFECT. See AUDITION/HEARING, THEORIES OF.

WHORF–SAPIR HYPOTHESIS/THEORY. = Whorfian hypothesis = Whorf's hypothesis = linguistic relativity hypothesis = Sapir–Whorf hypothesis. The American linguists Benjamin Lee Whorf (1897–1941) and Edward Sapir (1884–1939) formulated the *Whorf–Sapir linguistic hypothesis*, which states that one's language influences the nature of one's perceptions and thoughts (Whorf, 1956). There are two forms of the *linguistic relativity hypothesis*: a "weak" form (which argues that only perceptions are so influenced; e.g., an Eskimo's perception of snow is distinguishable from a non-Eskimo's because the former has many different words in his or her language for different variations in types of snow), and a "strong" form (which asserts that abstract conceptual processes are so affected; e.g., the Hopi Indian language handles time in a relativistic manner as compared with the English language breakdown of time into past, present, and future). Unfortunately, very little convincing evidence supports completely the *Whorf–Sapir hypothesis* (Reber, 1995; cf: Rosch, 1973; Kay & Kempton, 1984). An early view of the relationship between language and thought was J. B. Watson's (1878–1958) *behaviorist* approach, which asserted that one learns to talk in much the same way that other muscular skills (such as riding a bicycle) are learned, and when one subsequently makes the same muscular movements in a more hidden form (i.e., to oneself rather than aloud), it is called *thought*. According to Watson (1924), what psychologists have called *thought* is nothing but talking to oneself (see also the *motor theory of speech perception* propounded by A. M. Liberman, which holds that speech is assumed to be perceived by an implicit, covert system that "maps" the acoustic properties of the input against a set of deep motor representations of idealized articulation; Reber, 1995). However, Watson's extreme *behaviorist* view that thought depends only on the implicit muscle movements of speech has proven to be inadequate (see Smith, Brown, Toman, & Goodman, 1947; note also *Kinney's law* concerning temporal factors and behavioral/quantitative aspects of speech deficiency in postnatally developing *deafness* where the length of time over which changes in speech develop is directly proportional to the length of time during which normal speech has been present; Zusne, 1987; and the *phonemic restoration effect*, which is the generalization that a dramatically altered acoustic element in speech is extremely difficult to detect and where replacing various speech sounds with others still sounds like proper speech; Reber, 1995). Other competing theories concerning the relationship between language and thought are Piaget's (1954) *cognitive stage development theory*, which emphasizes the idea that language is a result or by-product of a child's advances in cognitive abilities, particularly the ability to symbolize (which develops at the end of infancy); and Vygotsky's and Luria's *linguistic theory*, which portrays language and thought as developing together and aiding each other in the process (Vygotsky, 1934/1962). The notion of *linguistic relativity* (like most "large" theories in psychology) is not the kind of theory that will ever be proven completely right or wrong, and, most likely, language differences affect people's thinking and perception in some ways, as well as cognitive abilities and perceptions influencing one's language in other ways (Gray, 1994). See also CHOMSKY'S PSYCHOLINGUISTIC THEORY; PIAGET'S THEORY OF DEVELOPMENTAL STAGES.

REFERENCES

Watson, J. B. (1924). *Behaviorism*. Chicago: University of Chicago Press.

Vygotsky, L. (1934/1962). *Thought and language*. Cambridge: MIT Press.

Smith, S., Brown, H., Toman, J., & Goodman, L. (1947). The lack of cerebral effects of d-tubercurarine. *Anesthesiology, 8*, 1–14.

Piaget, J. (1954). *The construction of reality in the child*. New York: Basic Books.

Whorf, B. (1956). *Language, thought, and reality*. New York: Wiley.

Rosch, E. (1973). On the internal structure of perceptual and semantic categories. In T. Moore (Ed.), *Cognitive development and the acquisition of language*. New York: Academic Press.

Kay, P., & Kempton, W. (1984). What is the Sapir–Whorf hypothesis? *Amer. Anthro., 86*, 65–79.

Zusne, L. (1987). *Eponyms in psychology*. Westport, CT: Greenwood Press.

Gray, P. (1994). *Psychology*. New York: Worth.

Reber, A. (1995). *The Penguin dictionary of psychology*. New York: Penguin Books.

WITKIN'S PERCEPTION/PERSONALITY/COGNITIVE STYLE THEORY. The American psychologist Herman A. Witkin (1916–1979) conducted research on *cognitive styles* in the 1940s, in particular on individual differences in the perception of the upright in space. An earlier approach toward understanding visual space perception, especially one related to the perception of rotation/movement in space, was provided by the Austrian physicist/philosopher Ernst Mach (1838–1916) in his *theory of bodily rotation* (also called the *Mach–Breuer–Brown theory of labyrinthine functioning*; Zusne, 1987), where he suggested that the sense organs for this experience were to be found in the semicircular canals of the inner ear. *Mach's theory* (1886/1959, 1902), with some modification, is still prevalent today (Boring, 1957). In Witkin's theoretical approach, when stationary visual and bodily cues are placed in opposition, and one has to judge whether an object is upright, some persons are more influenced by the *visual* cues (*field-dependent* individuals), while others depend more on *bodily* cues (*field-independent* individuals) (Witkin & Goodenough, 1977, 1981). The factors of *field dependence* and *field independence* represent a dimension along which one's perceptions may be placed concerning dependence on (or independence from) cues in the environment (called the *field*). In the first and simplest test (called the *rod and frame test* or RFT) used to study this dimension, a subject had to align a stimulus (such as a rod) so that it was "truly" vertical when a second stimulus (such as a frame around the rod) was varied with respect to the true vertical. Persons who can set the rod relatively accurately—independently of the orientation of the frame—are called *field-independent* because they rely on bodily sensation cues rather than on cues in the field. The more the tilt in the field controls the person's setting of the rod, the more *field-dependent* the person (Reuder, 1994). Later, Witkin and others conducted more elaborate studies using chairs and whole rooms that could be tilted. The study of the trait *field dependence* began in the area of perception, but the large individual differences that were found in tests such as RFT (cf: Andrulis, 1994) encouraged research in other areas such as personality, emotions, cognitive style, neuropsychological processes, and psychopathology. Witkin argued that people move, in general, from *field dependence* toward *field independence* as they mature. However, those who become most *field-independent* are those raised in ways that foster personal autonomy and a secure sense of self. Witkin's research led to a variety of studies including dreaming, cultural differences in socialization, intellectual processes, interpersonal relations (e.g., between teachers and students, therapists and patients, and parents and children), brain laterality, and chromosomal aberrations (Korchin, 1994). See also BERKELEY'S THEORY OF VISUAL SPACE PERCEPTION; COGNITIVE STYLE MODELS; GESTALT THEORY/LAWS; PERCEPTION (II. COMPARATIVE APPRAISAL), THEORIES OF; PERSONALITY, THEORIES OF.

REFERENCES

Mach, E. (1886/1959). *The analysis of sensations and the relation of the physical to the psychical.* New York: Dover.

Mach, E. (1902). *The analysis of experience.* Jena, East Germany: Fisher.

Witkin, H. (1950). Individual differences in ease of perception of embedded figures. *J. Pers., 19,* 1–15.

Boring, E. G. (1957). *A history of experimental psychology.* New York: Appleton-Century-Crofts.

Witkin, H., & Goodenough, D. (1977). Field dependence and interpersonal behavior. *Psy. Bull., 84,* 661–689.

Witkin, H., Goodenough, D., & Oltman, P. (1979). Psychological differentiation: Current status. *J. Pers. Soc. Psy., 37,* 1127–1145.

Witkin, H., & Goodenough, D. (1981). *Cognitive styles: Essence and origins—Field dependence and field independence.* New York: International Universities Press.

Zusne, L. (1987). *Eponyms in psychology.* Westport, CT: Greenwood Press.

Andrulis, R. (1994). Hidden figures test. In R. J. Corsini (Ed.), *Ency. Psy.* New York: Wiley.

Korchin, S. (1994). Herman A. Witkin. In R. J. Corsini (Ed.), *Ency. Psy.* New York: Wiley.

Reuder, M. (1994). Field dependency. In R. J. Corsini (Ed.), *Ency. Psy.* New York: Wiley.

Walk, R. (1994). Perceptual style. In R. J. Corsini (Ed.), *Ency. Psy.* New York: Wiley.

WOLPE'S THEORY/TECHNIQUE OF RECIPROCAL INHIBITION. The South African-born American psychiatrist Joseph Wolpe (1915–   ) conducted experimental studies early in his career on the production and cure of neuroses in animals that demonstrated that the neuroses could be produced by learning and also could be reversible by learning. Later, Wolpe derived psychotherapeutic techniques from his research for treating neuroses in humans (Wolpe, 1954, 1958). *Wolpe's theory* and technique constituted one of the many varieties of *behavior modification* (or *behavior therapy*, which is a procedure of direct intervention to alter a person's behaviors to situations that are deemed by oneself or by others to be changeworthy; Krasner, 1971; cf: Franks, 1994). Wolpe's approach, called *reciprocal inhibition*, is a form of behavior therapy that is based on the neurological concept of *reciprocal innervation*, that is, the inhibition of the action of one neural pathway by the activity of another. As a *general theory of behavior modification*, Wolpe's *reciprocal inhibition* refers to the inhibition of one response (e.g., yelling) by the occurrence of another mutually incompatible response (e.g., talking softly). The specific method used in *reciprocal inhibition* is called *desensitization* or *systematic desensitization*. In a clinical context, especially in the treatment of phobias (''irrational fears''), the procedure of *systematic desensitization* is designed to produce a decrease in anxiety (i.e., ''de-sensitize'') toward some feared situation or object (e.g., snakes). This is accomplished by exposing the client to a series of approximations to the anxiety-producing stimulus under relaxed conditions until, eventually, the anxiety reaction becomes extinguished. The procedure of *systematic desensitization* has come under heavy criticism from psychoanalytically oriented therapists and theorists over the issue of the *symptom substitution hypothesis* (i.e., the idea that if only the surface or superficial behavioral manifestations of a neurosis are treated in psychotherapy, the presumed unresolved underlying conflict will ''erupt'' elsewhere, and new symptoms will emerge). The notion of *symptom substitution* derives from the assumption (not accepted by all psychologists) that psychological disturbances are analogous to medical disturbances (as in the *medical/disease model* of illness) in that they can be treated only by removal of the root cause of the disorder (Reber, 1995). Wolpe has suggested that variables such as food, expression of aggression, and sexual feeling might work also to reciprocally inhibit avoidance behavior or anxiety feelings. Wolpe's work on the direct reeducation of sexual behavior foreshadowed Masters and Johnson's (1966) widely publicized studies, and his emphasis on expression of feeling foreshadowed the procedure of assertiveness training (Fischer, 1994; Ullman, 1994). See also BEHAVIOR THERAPY/COGNITIVE THERAPY, THEORIES OF.

REFERENCES

Wolpe, J. (1952). Experimental neurosis as learned behavior. *Brit. J. Psy., 43*, 243–268.

Wolpe, J. (1954). Reciprocal inhibition as the main basis of psychotherapeutic effects. *Ar. Neuro. Psychiat., 72*, 205–226.

Wolpe, J. (1958). *Psychotherapy by reciprocal inhibition*. Stanford, CA: Stanford University Press.

Masters, W., & Johnson, V. (1966). *Human sexual response*. Boston: Little, Brown.

Krasner, L. (1971). Behavior therapy. *Ann. Rev. Psy., 22*, 483–532.

Fischer, C. (1994). Assertiveness training. In R. J. Corsini (Ed.), *Ency. Psy.* New York: Wiley.

Franks, C. (1994). Behavior therapy: Problems and issues. In R. J. Corsini (Ed.), *Ency. Psy.* New York: Wiley.

Ullman, L. (1994). Behavior modification. In R. J. Corsini (Ed.), *Ency. Psy.* New York: Wiley.

Reber, A. (1995). *The Penguin dictionary of psychology.* New York: Penguin Books.

WORD-SUPERIORITY EFFECT. See TOP-DOWN PROCESSING/THEORIES.

WORK ADJUSTMENT, THEORY OF. See WORK/CAREER/OCCUPATION, THEORIES OF.

WORK/CAREER/OCCUPATION, THEORIES OF. The psychological study of work, career, and occupational factors ranges from *theories of decision making* in career development (e.g., Osipow, 1968) to ergonomic/ergopsychometry/anthropometry (e.g., Roebuck, Kroemer, & Thomson, 1975; Chapanis, 1976), human engineering/human factors (e.g., McCormick & Sanders, 1981), work fatigue/efficiency (e.g., Gilbreth, 1911), applications research, and work *motivation theories* (e.g., Gray & Starke, 1979). *Theories of career development* fall into one of several kinds: trait-oriented, systems-oriented, personality-oriented, or developmental; while no single approach seems to be predominant, each has its own particular utility for career/work/occupation counselors. Once a person makes a career decision, potential problems exist in terms of worker productivity, adjustment to the stress and strain of the workplace, and level of job satisfaction (Osipow, 1994). *Theories in vocational psychology* may be divided into four main categories (Super, 1994): matching approaches (involves theories and methods based on studies in the area of *differential psychology* and on *situational theories*), phenomenological approaches (involves *self-concept theory* and *congruence theory*), developmental approaches (includes *role theory* and *life-stage theory*), and decision-making approaches. *Theories of work/job efficiency* attempt to account for effective work performance and how stress, strain, boredom, fatigue, and other negative consequences of work affect one's health and well-being (Spokane, 1994). The *theories of work motivation* may be categorized into two broad areas (Gray & Starke, 1979): *universalistic theories*—which posit widespread applicability to the work environment, and *contingency theories*—which focus on individual differences that influence motivation levels. Among the *universalistic theories* are Maslow's (1943) *hierarchy of needs theory*—which proposes that human behavior is a result of attempts to satisfy currently unsatisfied needs where the needs are arranged in a hierarchical order such that the satisfaction of a prior level of need leads to a need for satisfaction at a succeeding level; Herzberg's *two-factor theory*—which asserts that job satisfaction and dissatisfaction are caused by different work-related factors such as achievement, recognition, advancement, growth, and responsibility as satisfiers and lack of company policy, administration, technical supervision, salary, job security, fringe benefits, and status as dissatisfiers (Herzberg, Mausner, & Snyderman, 1959); and McClelland's *achievement motivation theory*—which focuses on the needs of power, affiliation, and achievement as prominent work-related factors (McClelland, Atkinson, Clark, & Lowell, 1953). Among the *contingency theories* are Skinner's (1971) *stimulus–response/operant conditioning theory*—which argues that human behavior is not motivated by needs within an individual but by the external environment and the rewards and punishments that it provides; Adams' (1963) *equity theory*—which assumes that individuals are motivated by a desire to be treated equitably on their jobs; and Vroom's (1964) *expectancy theory*—which asserts that a person's motivation to perform is a function of both perceived desirability and attainability of outcomes. Closely related to work motivation is the issue of occupational adjustment, which also is a major source of personal identity and role definition. One well-formulated *theory of work adjustment* (Lofquist & Dawis, 1969) maintains that occupational environments provide different patterns of reinforcement, which interact with a person's needs and abilities where harmony between an individual and the work environment results in satisfaction and, as a consequence, greater level of work stability. The *theories of motivation and adjustment* have practical implications for work-related activities in organizations and contribute to the maximization of job satisfaction and worker morale (Baron, 1994). See also LEADERSHIP, THEORIES OF; MOTIVATION, THEORIES OF; OR-GANIZATIONAL/INDUSTRIAL/SYSTEMS THEORY; SELF-CONCEPT/SELF THEORY.

REFERENCES

Taylor, F. (1903). *Shop management*. New York: Harper.
Gilbreth, F. (1911). *Motion study, a method for increasing efficiency*. New York: Van Nostrand.
Maslow, A. (1943). A theory of human motivation. *Psy. Rev., 50*, 370–396.
McClelland, D., Atkinson, J., Clark, R., & Lowell, E. (1953). *The achievement motive*. New York: Appleton-Century-Crofts.
Herzberg, F., Mausner, B., & Snyderman, B. (1959). *The motivation to work*. New York: Wiley.
Adams, J. (1963). Toward an understanding of inequity. *J. Abn. Soc. Psy., 67*, 422–436.
Vroom V. (1964). *Work and motivation*. New York: Wiley.
Osipow, S. (1968). *Theories of career development*. Englewood Cliffs, NJ: Prentice-Hall.
Lofquist, L., & Dawis, R. (1969). *Adjustment to work*. New York: Appleton-Century-Crofts.
Skinner, B. F. (1971). *Beyond freedom and dignity*. New York: Bantam Books.
Roebuck, J., Kroemer, K., & Thomson, W. (1975). *Engineering anthropometry methods*. New York: Wiley.
Chapanis, A. (1976). Ergonomics in a world of new values. *Ergonomics, 19*, 252–268.
Gray, J., & Starke, F. (1979). *Organizational behavior: Concepts and applications*. Columbus, OH: Merrill.
McCormick, E., & Sanders, M. (1981). *Human factors in engineering and design*. New York: Wiley.

Baron, A. (1994). Morale in organizations. In R. J. Corsini (Ed.), *Ency. Psy.* New York: Wiley.

Osipow, S. (1994). Career counseling. In R. J. Corsini (Ed.), *Ency. Psy.* New York: Wiley.

Spokane, A. (1994). Work efficiency. In R. J. Corsini (Ed.), *Ency. Psy.* New York: Wiley.

Super, D. (1994). Career development. In R. J. Corsini (Ed.), *Ency. Psy.* New York: Wiley.

WUNDT'S THEORIES/DOCTRINES/PRINCIPLES. The German physiologist, psychologist, philosopher, and founder of experimental psychology Wilhelm Max Wundt (1832–1920) created and developed the first school of psychological thought, called *structuralism*, whose basic tenet was that sensations were the proper subject matter of psychology. Using the method of *introspection* (i.e., looking within one's own experience and reporting on it), Wundt and his students investigated subjects' immediate experience through exacting attention to sensations and feelings. The goals of *structuralism* were to analyze conscious processes into basic elements, to determine how these elements are connected, and to establish the laws of these connections. Wundt proposed a *tridimensional theory of feeling* where an equilibrium between pleasure–displeasure, tension–relaxation, and excitement–calm/depression occupied three independent and distinct dimensions of feeling. Wundt held that emotions were complex compounds of the elementary feelings and that each of the feelings could be effectively described by defining its position on each of the three dimensions (cf: Wundt's three *principles of emotional expression* formulated in 1900 as a reformulation of *Darwin's principles*: the *principles of innervation, association of analogous sensations,* and *relation of movements to images*; Warren, 1934). *Wundt's theory of feelings* stimulated a great deal of research in his own and rival laboratories but did not withstand the test of time (Schultz, 1969). Wundt postulated his *doctrine of apperception* to explain how the various elements of conscious experience are combined to form unified conscious experiences. He used the term *apperception* in a fashion similar to that of the German philosopher/psychologist Johann Herbart (1776–1841) to refer to the active mental process of selecting and structuring internal experience. The term *apperception* is rarely used today in experimental psychology, but the concepts underlying it are important, especially to many cognitively oriented psychologists (Reber, 1995). Wundt designated the active process of combining the various elements into a unity as his *law of psychic resultants* (also called the *principle of creative synthesis*), which states that the combination of elements creates new properties where every psychic compound has characteristics that are more than the sum of the characteristics of the elements (Wundt, 1896; cf: Mill, 1874). In a sense, Wundt's *principle of creative synthesis* (via J. S. Mill) and *law of psychic resultants* anticipated the Gestalt theorists' viewpoint that the "whole is more than the sum of its parts," where something new is created out of the synthesis of the elemental parts of experience (Schultz, 1969). At the turn of the century, Wundt was involved in an academic controversy called *imageless thought*. The controversy about the nature of thinking was between Wundt and E. B. Titchener, on one hand, and the members of the "Wurzburg school," on the other hand. Wundt postulated that consciousness was made up of only three elements: sensations, images, and feelings; Titchener placed major emphasis on images as the vehicles of thought. The Wurzburg psychologists hypothesized that subjects' responses were due to *determining tendencies* or *sets* without the use of imagery (i.e., they argued for "imageless thought"). The topic of images/imagery waned with the advent of *behaviorism* in the early 1900s, but then in the 1960s and 1970s, it was revived with the development of the *cognitive* approach in psychology, and imagery began to play a significant role in the areas of learning, perception, thinking, and meaning. Wundt's wide-ranging laboratory investigations of psychological phenomena included the psychology and physiology of seeing, hearing, the "lower" senses, optics, reaction-time experiments, word associations, folk psychology, and psychophysics (e.g., Wundt adopted a purely psychological interpretation of *Weber's law* that he considered to be an example of the *psychological law of relativity*; cf: Muller, 1878). While there were signs reflecting the narrowness of Wundt's new experimental psychology, it was through Wundt's vision largely that the conception of an independent inductive psychology became a reality (Murphy & Kovach, 1972). See also ACH'S LAWS/PRINCIPLES/THEORY; BEHAVIORIST THEORY; DONDERS' LAW; GESTALT THEORY/LAWS; HERBART'S DOCTRINE OF APPERCEPTION.

REFERENCES

Wundt, W. (1862). *Beitrage zur theorie der sinneswahrnehmung*. Leipzig: Wunter'sck Verlaghandlung.

Wundt, W. (1873). *Grundzuege der physiologischen psychologie*. Leipzig: Engelmann.

Mill, J. S. (1874). *A system of logic*. New York: Harper.

Muller, G. (1878). *Zur grundlegung der psychophysik*. Berlin: Gruben.

Wundt, W. (1896). *Grundriss der psychologie*. Leipzig: Engelmann.

Wundt, W. (1897). *Principles of psychology*. Leipzig: Engelmann.

Warren, H. (Ed.) (1934). *Dictionary of psychology*. Cambridge, MA: Houghton Mifflin.

Schultz, D. (1969). *A history of modern psychology*. New York: Academic Press.

Murphy, G., & Kovach, J. (1972). *Historical introduction to modern psychology*. New York: Harcourt Brace Jovanovich.

Reber, A. (1995). *The Penguin dictionary of psychology*. New York: Penguin Books.

X

X, THEORY. See LEADERSHIP, THEORIES OF.

Y

Y, THEORY. See LEADERSHIP, THEORIES OF.

YERKES–DODSON LAW. This is a statement of the relationship between arousal level and quality of performance formulated by R. M. Yerkes and J. D. Dodson in 1908. The law, also called the *inverted-U hypothesis*, suggests that there is an optimal level of arousal (e.g., motivation, anxiety) for tasks where moderate levels of arousal facilitate problem solving, but if stress or anxiety is too high (or too low), the person does not process the important and relevant cues (or ignores them), and optimal learning and performance fail to occur. Thus, the *Yerkes–Dodson law* states that increased drive will improve performance up to a point, beyond which there is deterioration of performance. However, the law may need to be qualified by various factors, one of which is task "complexity." That is, the complexity of the task to be performed may need to be examined and controlled wherein the optimal level of motivation should be higher for a simple task than it is for a complex task. For example, solving difficult mathematical problems within a time limit (a complex task) may be best accomplished by only a slight level of arousal instead of being highly aroused or excited. On the other hand, sorting and reshelving library books all day (a simple task) may best be done by creating a high level of motivation in the person. On the whole, the *Yerkes–Dodson law* seems reasonable and useful, but it has received only mixed support (see Neiss, 1988; Teigen, 1994). See also AROUSAL THEORY; INVERTED-U HYPOTHESIS.

REFERENCES

Yerkes, R., & Dodson, J. (1908). The relation of strength of stimulus to rapidity of habit formation. *J. Comp. Neurol. & Psy., 18*, 459–482.

Neiss, R. (1988). Re-conceptualizing arousal: Psychobiological states and motor performance. *Psy. Rev., 103*, 345–366.

Anderson, K., Revelle, W., & Lynch, M. (1989). Caffeine, impulsivity, and memory scanning: A comparison of two explanations for the Yerkes–Dodson effect. *Mot. & Emo., 13*, 1–20.

Anderson, K. (1994). Impulsivity, caffeine, and task difficulty: A within-subjects test of the Yerkes–Dodson law. *Pers. Indiv. Diff., 16*, 813–819.

Teigen, K. (1994). Yerkes–Dodson: A law for all seasons. *Theory & Psy., 4*, 525–547.

YOUNG–HELMHOLTZ COLOR VISION THEORY. = Helmholtz's color vision theory = Young's color vision theory = three-element/trireceptor/triple receptor/trichromatic color vision theory. In 1801, the English physician/physicist Thomas Young (1773–1829) proposed that color vision was due to three different kinds of visual fibers. Young's original theory was based on Isaac Newton's (1642–1727) earlier demonstration in physics of the existence of three primary colors (red, green, and blue). Because Young found it difficult to conceive of each sensitive point in the retina containing an infinite number of particles to be capable of vibrating in perfect unison with every possible undulation of light energy, he suggested that there are only three kinds of fibers corresponding to three primary colors (red, green, and blue). Young expanded his theory somewhat in 1807, but it remained essentially unrecognized as it sat in the Philosophical Transactions of the Royal Society of London until 1852, when Hermann von Helmholtz rediscovered and popularized it (the Scottish physicist James Clerk Maxwell, 1831–1879, is reputed, also, to have "rediscovered" Young's early work at about the same time as did Helmholz). Hermann von Helmholtz (1821–1894) wrote his quantitative *line-element* treatment of color vision and color discrimination shortly before his death. As he developed his quantitative theory, Helmholtz (1891, 1892) studied whether or not hue could be discriminated on the basis of gradations in the intensity of three fundamental processes (red, green, blue) that are evoked whenever the retinal cones are stimulated by light energy. Today, the theory is known as the *Young–Helmholtz theory*, and it postulates three types of cones (red, green, blue), each containing a different chemical substance where each is sensitive maximally to a different region of the electromagnetic spectrum. Consistent with the *law of specific energies*, the red cones (if stimulated in isolation) would give a "red" sensation, green cones would give a "green" sensation, and blue cones would give a "blue" sensation. Also, according to the theory, the rate of firing ("excitability") of each cone type depends on the wavelength of the stimulating light. Thus, the phenomenal or subjective experience of *hue* depends on the relative frequencies of impulses set up in the three types of fibers, *brightness* depends on the total frequency of impulses in all three fibers, and *saturation* depends on the amount of white produced in any quantifiable fusion of the fibers. All the other *hues* (including yellow, purple, and white or gray) are due to various combinations of the three component activities. The *Young–Helmholtz color vision theory* contains widely accepted ideas by psychologists today and has the advantages of accounting for the *laws of color mixing* and of *parsimony* over other theories that advance the involvement of more than three receptor processes in the visual experience. However, the *Young–Helmholtz theory* does have a number of difficulties: accounting fully for the experiences of the color-blind (cf: *Daltonism*, which is red-green color blindness and is named for John Dalton, 1766–1894, an English chemist who had it and first described it; Reber, 1995); accounting for the *brightness* functions of both normal and color-blind observers; and accounting for contrary evidence that shows that the blue component in color vision has different properties than either the red or green components (Osgood, 1953). See also COLOR MIXTURE, LAWS/THEORY OF; COLOR VISION, THEORIES/LAWS OF; SPECIFIC NERVE ENERGIES, LAW OF.

REFERENCES

Young, T. (1801). On the mechanism of the eye. *Phil. Trans. Roy. Soc. Lon., 91*, 23–88.

Young, T. (1807). On the theory of light and colours. In W. Savage (Ed.), *Lectures in natural philosophy*. Vol. 2. London: Joseph Johnson, St. Paul's Church Yard.

Helmholtz, H. von (1852). On the theory of compound colours. *Phil. Mag., 4*, 519–534.

Helmholtz, H. von (1891). Versuch einer erweiterten anwendung des Fechnerschen gesetzes im farbensystem. *Z. Psy. Physio. Sinn., 2*, 1–30.

Helmholtz, H. von (1892). Versuch das psychophysische gesetz auf die farben unterschiede trichromatischer augen anzuwenden. *Z. Psy. Physio. Sinn. 3*, 1–20.

Osgood, C. (1953). *Method and theory in experimental psychology*. New York: Oxford University Press.

Reber, A. (1995). *The Penguin dictionary of psychology*. New York: Penguin Books.

YOUNG'S COLOR VISION THEORY. See YOUNG–HELMHOLTZ COLOR VISION THEORY.

Z

Z, THEORY. See LEADERSHIP, THEORIES OF.

ZAJONC'S AROUSAL AND CONFLUENCE THEORIES. The Polish-born social psychologist Robert B. Zajonc (1923–   ) proposed the following generalization concerning *social facilitation* (i.e., the tendency to perform a task better in the presence of others than when alone) and *social interference* (i.e., a decline in performance when observers are present): the presence of others facilitates performance of *dominant* (i.e., simple, habitual, or instinctive) responses and interferes with performance of *nondominant* (i.e., complex, nonhabitual, or unnatural) responses (Zajonc, 1965). Zajonc explained both *facilitation* and *interference effects* by linking them to the more general phenomenon of the effect of high *arousal* (drive) on performance. That is, high *arousal* typically improves performance of simple or well-learned tasks and worsens performance of complex or poorly learned tasks (cf: Yerkes & Dodson, 1908). According to *Zajonc's theory*, the main effect of the presence of others is to increase *arousal* after which easy responses are easier, and difficult responses become more difficult. Studies of the influence of others' presence and the effects of being observed on one's performance go back to the late 1800s (e.g., Triplett, 1898) and the early 1900s (e.g., Allport, 1920) and reported *social facilitation* in some experiments but *social interference* in other studies. *Zajonc's theory* was able to explain both types of outcome, suggesting that the mere presence of others who are members of one's own species may enhance *arousal* innately (Zajonc, 1965). Reber (1995) cites *social facilitation* in athletes, children, chickens, and even cockroaches (which "learn a maze faster if watched by other roaches"). Other theorists, however, explain such *arousal* in somewhat different terms; for instance, terms such as *evaluation anxiety* (e.g., Geen, 1991), *self-perception* of one's skill at the task (e.g., Sanna, 1992), and *self-consciousness* (e.g., Baumeister & Showers, 1986). Zajonc has theorized also concerning the influence of environmental factors on human intelligence, in particular the relationship between birth order and intelligence (Zajonc & Marcus, 1975). In attempting to answer the finding of several studies that first-borns tend to have higher IQs than second-borns, who tend to have higher IQs than third-borns, and so on, Zajonc's *confluence theory* suggests that each individual's intellectual growth depends to an important degree on the intellectual environment in which the child develops (Zajonc, 1976). Zajonc's *confluence theory* and his interpretation of the correlation between birth order and intelligence, however, are not universally accepted and have been the source of heated debate (Baron, 1992). See also ACTIVATION/AROUSAL THEORY; COGNITIVE THEORIES OF EMOTIONS; YERKES–DODSON LAW.

REFERENCES

Triplett, N. (1898). The dynamogenic factors in peacemaking and competition. *Amer. J. Psy.*, 9, 507–533.

Yerkes, R., & Dodson, J. (1908). The relation of strength of stimulus to rapidity of habit formation. *J. Comp. Neurol. & Psy.*, 18, 459–482.

Allport, F. (1920). The influence of the group upon association and thought. *J. Exp. Psy.*, 3, 159–182.

Rasmussen, E. (1939). Social facilitation. *Acta Psy.*, 4, 275–294.

Zajonc, R. (1965). Social facilitation. *Science, 149*, 269–274.

Quarter, J., & Marcus, A. (1971). Drive level and the audience effect: A test of Zajonc's theory. *J. Soc. Psy.*, 83, 99–105.

Zajonc, R., & Marcus, G. (1975). Birth order and intellectual development. *Psy. Rev.*, 82, 74–88.

Zajonc, R. (1976). Family configuration and intelligence: Variations in scholastic aptitude scores parallel trends in family size and the spacing of children. *Science, 192*, 226–236.

Zajonc, R. (1980). Feeling and thinking: Preferences need no inferences. *Amer. Psy.*, 35, 151–175.

Zajonc, R. (1985). Emotion and facial efference: A theory reclaimed. *Science, 228*, 15–21.

Baumeister, R., & Showers, C. (1986). A review of paradoxical performance effects: Choking under pressure in sports and mental tests. *Euro. J. Soc. Psy.*, 16, 361–383.

Geen, R. (1991). Social motivation. *Ann. Rev. Psy.*, 42, 377–399.

Baron, R. (1992). *Psychology.* Boston: Allyn & Bacon.

Sanna, L. (1992). Self-efficacy theory: Implications for social facilitation and social loafing. *J. Pers. Soc. Psy.*, 62, 774–786.

Reber, A. (1995). *The Penguin dictionary of psychology.* New York: Penguin Books.

ZEIGARNIK EFFECT/PHENOMENON. This is the seemingly paradoxical assertion by the Russian psychologist Bliuma Zeigarnik (1900–?) that the recall of unfinished tasks is superior to the recall of completed tasks. Zeigarnik (1927) is noted for her doctoral dissertation, which was the first formal test of Lewin's *Gestalt theory* concerning the idea that attainment of a goal relieves tension. In a typical experimental activity of the *Zeigarnik effect*, subjects are asked to perform 15–22 different tasks; some tasks are manual (e.g., stringing beads), and some are mental (e.g., solving puzzles). On half of the activities, subjects are allowed to continue until completion, but on the other half of the tasks the subjects are asked to stop and move on to a new activity. Following this phase, the task materials are removed, and the subjects are asked to recall some of the activities that they had just experienced. Results of this simple procedure typically show that the number of incompleted or unfinished tasks (called "I") that are recalled is higher than the number of completed tasks (called "C"). A calculated ratio, using "I/C," was always greater than 1.0 in Zeigarnik's experiments. In some cases, the I/C ratio was subsequently related to a person's "ambition" level. Among the possible alternative explanations that may account for the *Zeigarnik effect* are that subjects may implicitly assume that the interrupted tasks will be completed at a later time; task interruption may set up a new motive involving resentment toward the interrupter, which causes better memory; the interruption of a task emphasizes that task; the subject may attempt to achieve "closure" concerning the incompleted tasks; subjects' personal histories in being rewarded for attending to unsolved problems may lead to better memory; and fulfillment and completion may be defined differently by different persons in terms of their own sense of satisfaction. Studies have shown that the *Zeigarnik effect* is less likely to occur if the subject is ego-involved in the task and is most likely to occur if the subject has a genuine level of aspiration in the interrupted task (i.e., the task is possible of being achieved ultimately). Other studies have shown that the differential effect between I and C tasks seems to be quite temporary and is typically lost over a period of 24 hours (Hilgard, 1966). Prentice (1944) provides a comprehensive review of the *Zeigarnik effect*. See also GESTALT THEORY/LAWS; LEWIN'S FIELD THEORY.

REFERENCES

Zeigarnik, B. (1927). Untersuchungen zur handlungsund affektpsychologie. Herausgegeben von K. Lewin, 3. Das behalten erledigter und unerlediger handlungen. *Psy. Forsch., 9*, 1–85.

Ovsiankina, M. (1928). Die wiederaufnahme unterbrochener handlungen. *Psy. Forsch., 11*, 302–379.

Freeman, G. (1930). Changes in tonus during completed and interrupted mental work. *J. Gen. Psy., 4*, 309–333.

Pachauri, A. (1936). A study of Gestalt problems in completed and interrupted tasks. *Brit. J. Psy., 27*, 170–180.

Prentice, W. (1944). The interruption of tasks. *Psy. Rev., 51*, 329–340.

Glixman, A. (1949). Recall of completed and incompleted activities under varying degrees of stress. *J. Exp. Psy., 39*, 281–295.

Atkinson, J. (1953). The achievement motive and recall of interrupted and completed tasks. *J. Exp. Psy., 46*, 381–390.

Hilgard, E. (1966). Methods and procedures in the study of learning. In S. S. Stevens (Ed.), *Handbk. Exp. Psy.* New York: Wiley.

Reeve, J., Cole, S., & Olson, B. (1986). The Zeigarnik effect and intrinsic motivation: Are they the same? *Mot. & Emo., 10*, 233–245.

Denmark, F. (1994). Zeigarnik effect. In R. J. Corsini (Ed.), *Ency. Psy.* New York: Wiley.

ZEILER'S THEORY. See SPENCE'S THEORY.

ZEISING'S PRINCIPLE. This generalization refers to a term—*golden section*—that was used by Adolph Zeising and called attention to the aesthetic value of the geometric relationships inherent in a rectangle (Warren, 1934). That is, the *golden section* is the division of a line or area into two parts, or the relations of the sides of a rectangle, in such a manner that the ratio of the smaller to the larger equals the ratio of the larger to the whole (Harris & Levey, 1975). This *principle of proportion* was investigated experimentally by Gustav Fechner (1897) in the area called *experimental aesthetics* (Lindauer, 1994). Fechner's seminal research on preferences for shapes gave *experimental aesthetics* its "reductionistic" quality (i.e., examining aesthetics from "below" from a structural point of view). Investigations have been made by researchers for an *aesthetic formula* (cf: Birkhoff, 1933). In one case, the aesthetic measure (M) of balance or unity (represented by the number 1) was defined as the ratio of order (O) to complexity (C); in the resulting formula, $M = O/C$, the various components of an artwork can be physically specified, measured, and evaluated where the closer it is to 1, the more "harmonious" the object (Lindauer, 1994). *Zeising's principle* attempts to answer the persistent question in aesthetics concerning the dimensions of preferred shapes such as encompassed in the concept of the *golden section* (Zusne, 1970). See also FECHNER'S LAW; WEBER'S LAW.

REFERENCES

Fechner, G. (1897). *Vorschule der aesthetik.* Leipzig: Breithopf & Haertel.

Birkhoff, G. (1933). *Aesthetic measure.* Cambridge: Harvard University Press.

Warren, H. (Ed.) (1934). *Dictionary of psychology.* Cambridge, MA: Houghton Mifflin.

Valentine, C. (1962). *The experimental psychology of beauty.* London: Methuen.

Zusne, L. (1970). *Visual perception of form.* New York: Academic Press.

Harris, W., & Levey, J. (Eds.) (1975). *The new Columbia encyclopedia.* New York: Columbia University Press.

Child, I. (1978). Aesthetic theories. In E. Carterette & M. Friedman (Eds.), *Handbook of perception.* Vol. 10. New York: Academic Press.

Lindauer, M. (1994). Experimental aesthetics. In R. J. Corsini (Ed.), *Ency. Psy.* New York: Wiley.

ZIPF'S LAW. This generalization was developed by George Kingsley Zipf (1903–1950) and states that an equilibrium exists between *uniformity* and *diversity* in examining various psychological phenomena. In general, *Zipf's law* describes the relationship between the frequency with which a certain event occurs (e.g., the frequency of usage of a word in a language) and the number of events that occur with that frequency. In particular, *Zipf's law* states that when examining certain aspects of language, it is predicted that there are a very large number of very short words (e.g., "auto") that occur with high frequency and progressively fewer longer words (e.g., "automobile") that occur with lower frequency. Zipf hypothesized that such *uniformities* or "tendencies" in language usage were the result of a biological *principle of least effort*. While this latter notion has not been validated by other researchers (these uniformities are now known to be merely the necessary result of particular stochastic processes; Reber, 1995), Zipf's *linguistic hypothesis* that frequency of word usage and word length are inversely related seems to be a pervasive and apparent phenomenon of language usage, especially in the present age of computers and the perceived need for rapid communication. See also LEAST EFFORT, PRINCIPLE OF.

REFERENCES

Condon, E. (1928). Statistics of vocabulary. *Science, 67,* 300.

Zipf, G. (1935). *The psycho-biology of language.* Boston: Houghton Mifflin.

Skinner, B. F. (1936). The verbal summator and a method for the study of latent speech. *J. Psy., 2,* 71–107.

Zipf, G. (1945a). The meaning-frequency relationship of words. *J. Gen. Psy., 33,* 251–256.

Zipf, G. (1945b). The repetition of words, time-perspective, and semantic balance. *J. Gen. Psy., 32,* 127–148.

Reber, A. (1995). *The Penguin dictionary of psychology.* New York: Penguin Books.

APPENDIX A

Frequency of Usage of Concepts as Sampled in Psychology Textbooks, 1885–1996

A random sample was taken of over 136 introductory textbooks (see *Appendix B*) published between 1885 and 1996, in order to record the names of, and frequency of occurrence of, the terms *law* and *theory* in these books. This appendix gives information from that survey and is offered as an empirical set of raw data, or data bank, for possible use by historians and researchers concerned with historiographic analyses of psychology; cf: J. E. Roeckelein (1996c), "Citation of *Laws* and *Theories* in Textbooks across 112 Years of Psychology, *Psychological Reports*, 79, 979–998.

Entries on the following *laws* and *theories* tables refer to percent of reference made by writers collectively within a given time period. For example, a "0" entry means that none (zero percent) of the writers in that time period made reference in their books to that given term; a "57" entry means that 57% of the writers in that time period made reference in their books to that given term; and so on.

There are over 800 laws and theories listed in this appendix; the total time period is broken down into five separate subperiods (columns).

Entries are based on the precise term that was used in a given textbook. Sometimes, there were synonymous terms for a single concept, and these were given only a single entry if both terms happened to be used in the same book. For example, "tetrachromatic theory" is synonymous with "opponent-process theory," which is synonymous with "Hering's color theory." An attempt was made to record only single ("presence versus absence") entries for any given term for any given textbook. Moreover, a name (such as Jung, Adler, etc.) may be mentioned in a book, but it's entered here only if the term *theory* or *law* has been *explicitly* attached to it by the writer.

In addition to synonymous terms appearing on these lists, the designation "general" occurs in parenthesis after some of the terms. This refers to the use of the word *theory* in a general context or meaning (such as "learning *theories*") and is distinguished from specific usage (such as "Hull–Spence learning *theory*"). Again, redundancy of usage was avoided in recording data from any given textbook, and the term *law* or *theory* had to be explicitly connected to the concept in order for it to serve as an acceptable datum entry.

Finally, it will be noticed that some terms are included under both the *laws* and the *theories* rubrics; this is because they appeared that way in the textbooks surveyed.

	1885-1919	1920-39	1940-59	1960-79	1980-96
Laws in 112 Years of Psychology					
abstraction, laws of	4	0	0	0	0
accommodation, law of	4	0	0	0	0
Ach's laws	0	3	0	0	0
action, law of	4	0	0	3	0
adaptation, law of	0	7	0	0	0
adjustment, laws of	4	0	0	0	0
Adrian's rate law	0	0	0	0	3
advantage, laws of	0	3	0	0	0
affinity, laws of	0	0	3	0	0
after-image, law of	0	3	0	0	0
all-or-none law	8	30	48	34	53
analysis, law of	4	0	0	0	0
Archimedes' law	0	0	0	0	3
assimilation, law of	0	7	0	0	0
association, law(s) of	83	50	31	11	3
attention, law(s) of	17	13	7	0	0
Bell-Magendie law	0	0	3	0	0
belongingness, law of	0	0	7	0	0
Bloch's law	0	0	0	3	0
Bunsen-Roscoe law	0	0	3	0	0
cadence, law of	0	3	0	0	0
Cermak's parallel laws	0	3	0	0	0
chance, laws of	0	3	0	0	0
classical conditioning, laws of	0	0	7	0	16
coincidences, law of	4	0	0	0	0
color vision, laws of	0	3	0	0	0
combination, law of	0	3	0	0	0
comparative judgment, law of	0	0	3	0	0
complementary odors, law of	0	3	0	0	0
Comte's law	0	0	0	0	3
configuration, law of	0	3	0	0	0
connection, laws of	0	3	0	0	0
conservation of energy, law of	0	3	3	0	0
constancy, laws of	0	0	3	0	0
contiguity, law of	29	43	17	9	0

	1885-1919	1920-39	1940-59	1960-79	1980-96
Laws in 112 Years of Psychology					
continuity, law of	0	3	0	0	0
contradictory representation, law of	4	0	0	0	0
contrast, law of	8	23	10	0	0
degeneration, law of	4	0	0	0	0
difference, law of	4	0	0	0	0
diffusion, law of	8	0	0	0	0
diminishing returns, law of	4	3	3	0	0
disaggregation, law of	4	0	0	0	0
dissociation, law of	8	0	0	0	0
disuse, law of	0	3	3	0	3
docility, laws of	4	0	0	0	0
dynamogenesis, laws of	8	3	0	0	0
effect, law of	0	40	66	46	78
Emmert's law	0	7	7	6	9
error, law of	4	3	0	0	0
evolution, laws of	13	7	3	0	0
excess discharge, law of	4	0	0	0	0
exclusion, law of	4	0	0	0	0
exercise, law of	0	23	28	3	6
Fechner's law	21	3	3	14	19
Fourier's law	0	10	3	0	0
frequency, law of	0	27	31	0	0
Galton's reversion law	4	0	0	0	0
Gauss' law	0	3	0	0	0
genetics, laws of	0	3	7	0	9
gravitation/gravity, law of	17	0	0	0	0
growth, law of	8	0	7	0	0
habit, law of	21	13	10	0	0
hedonic law	4	0	0	0	0
Heyman's law	0	3	0	0	0
Hick's law	0	0	0	3	0
Hogan's law	0	0	0	0	3
Hunter-McCrary law	0	0	3	0	0
idiographic laws	0	0	3	0	0
individual variation, law of	4	3	0	3	0

	1885-1919	1920-39	1940-59	1960-79	1980-96
Laws in 112 Years of Psychology					
inertia, law of	13	0	0	0	0
inheritance, law of	4	3	0	0	0
insight, law of	0	3	0	0	0
intelligence, laws of	8	0	0	0	0
intensity, law of	13	20	24	0	0
Jost's law	0	10	10	0	0
Korte's laws	0	3	0	0	0
learning, laws of	0	27	28	14	6
least effort, law of	0	7	14	3	3
least resistance, law of	4	0	0	0	0
Marbe's law	0	0	0	6	0
matching law	0	0	0	6	0
Mendel's law	4	10	21	6	0
mental growth & decay, law of	4	3	0	0	0
mind's set, law of	8	3	0	0	0
moral law	4	0	0	0	0
mosaic law	4	0	0	0	0
motives, laws of	4	0	0	0	0
natural selection, law of	0	0	3	3	3
nervous action, laws of	8	3	10	0	0
neural processes, laws of	4	0	0	0	0
new insight, law of	0	3	0	0	0
Newton's color laws	8	17	21	9	0
nomothetic laws	0	0	3	0	3
Ohm's law	0	7	0	6	0
olfaction, laws of	0	3	0	0	0
operant conditioning, laws of	0	0	0	0	13
overlearning, law of	0	0	0	3	0
parsimony, law of	0	23	24	14	9
partial activity, law of	4	0	0	0	0
perceptual organization/Gestalt laws*	0	7	28	46	72
power law, Stevens'	0	0	3	14	13
practice, law of	4	0	7	0	0
Premack ("grandma's") law	0	0	0	14	22
preparedness laws	0	0	0	0	3

	1885-1919	1920-39	1940-59	1960-79	1980-96

Laws in 112 Years of Psychology

	1885-1919	1920-39	1940-59	1960-79	1980-96
primacy, law of	0	0	21	3	0
probability, laws of	0	0	7	9	0
psychophysical law	17	3	0	3	0
qualitative discrimination, laws of	4	0	0	0	0
Raoult's law	0	0	0	3	0
reaction to stimuli, law of	4	3	0	0	0
readiness, law of	4	7	10	0	0
recency, law of	0	13	28	3	0
reciprocal innervation, law of	0	0	0	3	0
redintegration, law of	0	7	0	0	0
referred pain, law of	0	3	0	0	0
reflex pain, law of	0	3	0	0	0
regression, law of	0	3	0	0	0
reinforcement, law of	0	0	21	14	13
reinstatement, law of	4	0	0	0	0
relative effect, law of	21	0	0	3	0
repetition, law of	0	3	0	0	0
resemblance, law of	4	0	0	0	0
retention/recall, laws of	0	0	7	0	0
retroaction, laws of	0	0	0	3	0
S-R/R-R laws	0	0	3	0	0
segregation law	0	0	0	3	0
selection, laws of	4	7	0	0	0
self-conservation, law of	4	0	0	0	0
sensation, laws of	4	0	0	0	0
sentiment formation, laws of	0	0	3	0	0
set, law of	0	0	7	0	0
shifting, law of	0	3	0	0	0
similarity, law of	17	33	17	0	0
smell, laws of	0	7	0	0	0
smell-mixture, laws of	0	3	0	0	0
specific nerve energy, law of	8	3	7	6	6
succession/perceptual, laws of	4	3	0	0	0
suggestion, laws of	8	0	0	0	0
survival, law of	0	0	0	3	0

Laws in 112 Years of Psychology	1885-1919	1920-39	1940-59	1960-79	1980-96
Talbot-Plateau law	0	10	0	0	0
taste, laws of	0	3	0	0	0
tendency, law of	0	3	0	0	0
thought, laws of	13	0	0	0	0
threshold(s), law of	8	0	0	0	0
tonal sequences, laws of	0	3	0	0	0
totality, law of	4	0	0	0	0
transfer of training laws	0	3	7	6	0
universal natural laws	4	0	0	0	0
use, law of	0	10	7	0	0
value, law of	0	0	3	0	0
varying concomitants, law of	4	0	0	0	0
Vierordt's law	0	3	0	0	0
voluntary interest, law of	4	0	0	0	0
Weber's law	67	53	48	54	81
Weber-Fechner law	4	7	21	11	3
Yerkes-Dodson law	0	0	0	20	53

(Includes laws/principles of: contiguity, proximity, continuation, similarity, simplicity, grouping, closure, common fate, symmetry, continuity, contrast, constancy, aerial/linear perspective, interposition, clearness, figure-ground, texture gradients, light & shadow, relative size, and pragnanz: good figure/shape).

	1885-1919	1920-39	1940-59	1960-79	1980-96
Theories in 112 Years of Psychology					
ability, theories of	0	0	3	0	0
abnormality, theories of	0	3	0	0	0
abstraction, theories of	4	0	0	0	0
accumulating damages theory	0	0	0	0	3
achievement motivation, theory of	0	0	0	3	6
activation synthesis theory of dreaming	0	0	0	0	13
activation/arousal theory	0	0	0	23	44
active theory of sleep	0	0	0	3	3
activity/action theory	4	7	0	0	22
adaptation, theory of	0	7	0	0	0
adaptation-level (Helson) theory	0	0	3	3	6
adaptive nonresponding theory	0	0	0	0	3
Adler's theory	0	7	7	14	16
adolescence, theories of	0	0	0	0	3
adulthood, theories of	0	0	0	0	3
affections, theories of	13	17	0	0	0
affective-arousal theory	4	0	0	3	3
after-image, theory of	0	3	0	0	0
aggression, theories of	0	0	0	6	28
aging, theories of	0	0	0	0	16
Allport's trait theory	0	0	0	6	13
aminostatic theory	0	0	0	0	3
amnesia, theories of	0	0	0	0	3
ampullar sense, theory of	0	3	0	0	0
analysis-by-synthesis theory	0	0	0	3	0
anxiety disorder, theories of	0	0	0	0	9
anxiety, theories of	0	0	7	0	0
apparent distance theory	0	0	0	0	3
applied psychology, theory of	0	3	0	0	0
Aquinas' theories	0	0	10	0	0
Aristotle's theory of feeling	4	0	0	0	0
Aristotle's theory of heart & nerves	4	0	0	0	0
Aristotle's theory of pleasure-pain	8	0	0	0	0
Arnold's theory of emotion	0	0	0	0	3
Asch's theory	0	3	0	6	0

	1885-1919	1920-39	1940-59	1960-79	1980-96
Theories in 112 Years of Psychology					
assimilation-contrast theory	0	0	0	3	0
association theory	17	7	14	11	3
assortive mating theory	0	0	0	3	0
atomistic theory of mind	4	3	3	0	0
attention theory of schizophrenia	0	0	0	3	0
attention, theory of	25	3	3	0	0
attenuation theory	0	0	0	0	6
attitude/attitude change, theories of	0	3	0	11	0
attribution theory	0	0	0	14	66
audition/hearing, theories of	17	40	24	15	22
auditory beats, theory of	0	3	0	0	0
automation theory	4	0	0	0	0
babble-luck theory	0	0	0	0	3
balance theory	0	0	3	17	34
Bandura's theory	0	0	0	3	3
Beck's cognitive theory	0	0	0	0	6
behavior therapy, theories of	0	0	7	9	0
behavioral adaptive theory of sleep	0	0	0	0	3
behaviorist theory	0	3	3	20	31
Bem's self-perception theory	0	0	0	9	19
Berkeley's theory of vision	13	0	0	0	0
big five theory of personality	0	0	0	0	3
Binet's theory	0	0	3	0	0
biochemical theories of abnormality	0	0	0	0	6
biogenetic recapitulation theory	0	0	0	3	0
biogenic theory of abnormality	0	0	0	0	3
biological limit theory of aging	0	0	0	0	3
biological rhythm theory of sleep	0	0	0	0	6
biological/biosocial theory	0	3	0	3	19
Boring's theory of hearing	0	3	0	0	0
bottom-up theories	0	0	0	0	3
Brehm's theory	0	0	0	3	0
Bridges' theory of emotions	0	0	0	0	3
brightness discrimination, theory of	0	0	0	3	0
brood-excitation theory	0	0	0	3	0

	1885-1919	1920-39	1940-59	1960-79	1980-96
Theories in 112 Years of Psychology					
Bruner's theory	0	0	0	3	0
Cannon/Cannon-Bard theory	0	16	28	57	78
cardinal value, theory of	4	0	0	0	0
Cattell's personality theory	0	0	0	11	13
cell theory	0	3	0	0	0
central/centralist theory of thinking	0	0	31	9	0
chain-reflex theory	0	0	3	0	0
chemical theory of inhibition	0	3	0	0	0
choice, theory of	0	0	0	3	0
Chomsky's theory	0	0	0	9	6
chromaxie theory	0	3	0	0	0
circumstances theory	0	0	3	0	0
classic organization theories	0	0	0	0	3
cochlea action theory	4	0	0	0	0
coding theories	0	0	0	3	0
coefficient of belief, theories of	4	0	0	0	0
cognitive dissonance theory	0	0	0	60	56
cognitive economy, theory of	0	0	0	3	0
cognitive/cognitive appraisal theory	0	0	10	40	94
cold adaptation, theory of	0	3	0	0	0
collective unconscious theory	0	0	0	3	0
color blindness, theory of	0	7	0	0	0
color constancy, theories of	0	0	0	3	0
color mixture, theory of	0	3	3	0	0
color vision, theories of	29	43	31	17	25
common sense theory of emotions	0	0	3	0	0
communication theory	0	0	0	3	0
comparator/comparison theories	0	0	0	3	3
compensatory theory of dreaming	0	0	0	3	0
competence/control theories	0	0	0	0	6
component theories of intelligence	0	0	0	0	3
composite theory of color vision	0	0	0	0	3
Condillac's theory of attention	4	0	0	0	0
conditioning, theories of	0	0	3	3	9
conflict, theory of	0	0	0	6	3

	1885-1919	1920-39	1940-59	1960-79	1980-96
Theories in 112 Years of Psychology					
confluence theory	0	0	0	0	3
confusion theory	0	3	0	0	0
congruity theory	0	0	0	6	0
connectionism, theory of	0	0	3	0	0
conscience, theories of	8	0	0	0	0
consciousness, theories of	13	7	0	0	3
consistency/consonance theories	0	3	0	3	16
consolidation theory	0	0	0	6	3
constitutional theory of personality	0	0	0	3	3
consummatory-response theory	0	0	0	3	0
contact theory of prejudice	0	0	0	0	3
contextual theories of intelligence	0	0	0	0	3
contiguity theory	0	0	7	3	0
contingency theory of leadership	0	0	0	0	16
continuity theory	0	0	0	3	3
contrast, theory of	0	3	0	0	0
copy theory	0	0	7	0	6
correlation theory of personality	0	0	0	3	0
correspondence, theories of	0	0	3	0	0
correspondent interference theory	0	0	0	0	6
Cottrell's theory	0	0	0	0	3
crest-of-the-wave theory	0	0	0	3	0
crisis theory	0	0	0	3	0
cross-cultural theories of intelligence	0	0	0	0	3
cultural theories of personality	0	0	0	3	0
cybernetic theory	0	0	0	3	0
Darwin's evolution theory	17	7	28	37	34
data perception, theories of	0	0	0	0	3
death theory	0	0	0	0	3
decay theory	0	0	3	17	34
decision theory	0	0	0	3	0
definitional theory	0	0	0	0	3
degeneracy, theories of	0	7	0	0	0
depression, theories of	0	0	0	0	25
deprivation theories	0	0	0	0	3

	1885-1919	1920-39	1940-59	1960-79	1980-96
Theories in 112 Years of Psychology					
depth-of-processing theory	0	0	0	0	3
destiny, theories of	0	0	3	0	0
determinism, theory of	4	0	7	0	0
developmental theory	0	3	7	11	9
dialectical humanism, theory of	0	0	0	3	0
diathesis-stress theory	0	0	0	6	6
differential theories of intelligence	0	0	0	0	3
differentiation theory	0	0	3	0	0
diffusion of responsibility theory	0	0	0	0	3
dimensional theories of emotions	0	0	0	0	6
disengagement theory	0	0	0	0	16
disguise theory of symbolism	0	0	0	3	0
displacement theory	0	0	3	0	3
dispositional theories of personality	0	0	0	0	3
distraction-conflict theory	0	0	0	0	3
disuse, theory of	0	0	0	6	0
divided consciousness theory	0	0	0	0	3
Dollard/Dollard-Miller's theory of personality	0	0	0	17	6
dominant-recessive genes theory	0	0	0	0	3
dopamine theory of schizophrenia	0	0	0	0	6
double-aspect theory	13	10	3	0	0
double-blind theory	0	0	0	3	3
dream theory	0	3	10	11	19
drive, theories of	0	0	0	29	28
drive-reduction theory	0	0	7	9	47
dry mouth theory	0	0	0	0	3
dual code/coding theory	0	0	0	0	9
dual hypothalamic control theory	0	0	0	0	3
dual-trace theory	0	0	0	3	6
duplicity/duplexity theory	0	13	14	9	19
dynamic theory	0	3	0	0	0
early selection theory	0	0	0	0	6
eating, theories of	0	0	0	3	0
Ebbinghaus' theory of color	4	0	0	0	0
ecological theory	0	0	0	0	16

	1885-1919	1920-39	1940-59	1960-79	1980-96

Theories in 112 Years of Psychology

	1885-1919	1920-39	1940-59	1960-79	1980-96
effect theory of attention reflex	4	0	0	0	0
elasticity theory of light	4	0	0	0	0
emboitement, theory of	4	0	0	0	0
emergency theory	0	0	3	3	0
emotion, theories of (general)	13	13	31	46	69
emotivist theory of morality	0	0	0	3	0
empiricist theory of perception	0	0	0	3	0
encoding specificity theory	0	0	0	0	3
energizing theory of emotions	0	0	10	3	0
energy conservation theory of sleep	0	0	0	0	3
energy regulation, theories of	0	0	3	3	0
entelechean theory	0	0	3	0	0
environmental theory	0	0	0	0	3
Epicurian theory	0	0	0	3	0
equilibrium theory of personal space	0	0	0	0	3
equipotentiality theory	0	0	3	0	3
equity theory	0	0	0	6	16
Erikson's psychosocial theory	0	0	0	23	41
errors, theory of	4	0	0	0	0
Estes' stimulus sampling theory	0	0	3	0	0
ethical ideal, theories of	4	0	0	0	0
evaluation theories	0	0	0	3	0
event-structure theory (F. Allport)	0	0	3	0	0
Ewald's theory of hearing	0	3	0	0	0
exchange/social exchange theory	0	0	0	3	22
exemplar theory	0	0	0	0	3
existential theory of abnormality	0	0	0	6	9
expectancy/value expectancy theory	0	0	0	9	16
experience theory of learning	0	3	0	0	0
extensions-of-waking-life theory	0	0	0	0	3
extensity theory of pitch	0	3	0	0	0
extrinsic theory	0	0	0	0	3
eye movement theory	0	0	3	0	0
Eysenck's theory of personality	0	0	0	6	6
facial-feedback theory (Tomkins)	0	3	0	0	9

	1885-1919	1920-39	1940-59	1960-79	1980-96
Theories in 112 Years of Psychology					
facilitation theory of attention	0	0	3	0	0
factor theories of intelligence	0	0	0	0	16
faculty theory	0	7	3	0	0
family configuration theory	0	0	0	0	3
fat-cell theory	0	0	0	0	3
fear, theories of	0	0	3	0	0
feature analysis theory	0	0	0	3	3
Fechner's theory	4	0	3	0	0
feedback theory	0	0	0	6	9
feeling(s), theories of	13	20	7	0	0
field theory (K. Lewin)	0	0	14	23	3
filter theory (D. Broadbent)	0	0	0	9	19
Fodor's theory of intelligence	0	0	0	0	3
Forbes' theory of color vision	0	3	0	0	0
forced-movement theory	0	0	3	0	0
forgetting, theories of	0	3	10	23	13
formal discipline, theory of	0	0	7	6	0
formal theories of intelligence	0	0	0	0	3
frames of intelligence theory	0	0	0	0	3
frequency theories of hearing	0	3	10	14	66
frequency theory of learning	0	3	7	0	0
Freud's theory of forgetting	0	3	0	0	0
Freud's theory of the unconscious	0	3	0	0	0
Freudian theory	0	33	48	71	88
Fromm's theory of personality	0	0	0	6	3
frustration-drive/frustration-aggression theory	0	0	0	0	6
functional autonomy theory (G. Allport)	0	0	0	0	6
functional theories of emotion	0	0	0	3	6
gain-loss theory	0	0	0	9	6
gate-control theory of pain	0	0	0	11	66
gender identification theories	0	0	0	3	38
general factor theory of intelligence	0	0	3	3	0
generative theory of language	0	0	0	3	3
genetic/genetic clock theory	17	7	3	6	9
Gestalt theory	0	20	14	9	3

	1885-1919	1920-39	1940-59	1960-79	1980-96
Theories in 112 Years of Psychology					
Gilligan's theory of moral development	0	0	0	0	3
glucostatic theory	0	0	0	14	19
Granit's theory of color vision	0	0	0	6	0
gravitation theory	0	0	0	3	0
great man/person theory	0	0	3	3	13
Groos' theory of play	0	3	0	0	0
group factor theory of intelligence	0	3	3	3	0
Guilford's theory of intelligence	0	0	0	0	6
gustation/taste, theories of	4	7	3	0	3
Guthrie's theory of behavior	0	0	0	3	0
habit, behaviorist theory of	0	3	3	0	0
handedness, theory of	0	3	0	0	0
Harlow's error factor theory	0	0	3	0	0
hedonic/hedonistic theory	0	0	3	6	3
Heider's balance theory	0	0	0	3	0
Helmholtz's color theory	17	13	3	0	0
Helmholtz's theory of hearing	25	23	14	6	3
Henning's theory of smell	0	3	0	0	0
Herbart's theory of feeling	4	0	0	0	0
Hering-Hurvich-Jameson theory	0	0	0	14	0
hierarchical theory of motivation	0	0	0	3	6
higher-units theory (Bryan & Harter)	0	0	3	0	0
historic theories of abnormality	0	0	0	0	3
Holzinger & Harman's intelligence theory	0	0	3	0	0
homeostatic theory	0	0	0	6	0
homosexuality, theories of	0	0	0	0	6
hopelessness theory of depression	0	0	0	0	3
hormic theory of action	0	3	3	0	0
Hull/Hull-Spence theory	0	0	0	15	3
human-relations theories	0	0	0	0	3
humanistic/self-integrative theory	0	0	0	9	47
humor, theories of	0	3	0	0	0
humoral/humors, theory of	0	0	7	3	13
hunger, theories of	0	0	3	11	0
hylomorphic theory	0	0	3	0	0

	1885-1919	1920-39	1940-59	1960-79	1980-96
Theories in 112 Years of Psychology					
hypnosis/hypnotism, theories of	13	0	0	0	22
hypothesis-testing theory	0	0	0	0	3
hysteria, theories of	0	0	3	3	0
idealistic/idealism theory	8	0	0	0	0
ideas, theory of innate	13	0	0	0	0
identical components theory	0	0	3	0	0
identical points, theory of	4	0	0	0	0
identity theory	0	7	0	3	0
ideomotor theory	0	3	3	0	0
idiographic theories of personality	0	0	0	3	0
illusions, theories of	0	3	0	0	0
imagination, theory of	0	3	0	0	0
imitation, theories of	4	0	0	3	0
implicit theories of personality	0	0	0	20	28
impression management theory	0	0	0	0	6
incentive theory of motivation	0	0	0	0	25
indeterminism, theory of	4	0	0	0	0
individual meta theory	0	0	0	0	3
individuation theory	0	0	3	0	0
infant attachment theories	0	0	0	9	19
information/information-processing theory	0	0	0	17	34
inhibition theory of attention	0	0	3	0	0
innate capacity theory	0	0	0	3	0
innervation, theory of	4	0	0	0	0
inoculation theory	0	0	0	0	3
instincts, theory of	0	13	10	11	44
integration theory	0	0	3	0	0
intellectualist theory	4	0	0	0	0
intelligence, theories of (general)	0	7	21	3	41
intensity theory of learning	0	3	0	0	0
interactive/interactionist theories	4	0	0	3	6
interference theory of forgetting	0	0	3	37	38
interference theory of inhibition	0	3	0	0	0
interjectional theory of speech	0	10	0	0	0
intermittency theory	0	0	0	3	0

	1885-1919	1920-39	1940-59	1960-79	1980-96
Theories in 112 Years of Psychology					
interpersonal attraction theories	0	0	0	11	9
intrapsychic theories	0	0	0	3	0
intrinsic theory of motivation	0	0	0	0	3
intuition, theories of	4	0	0	0	0
intuitive theory of morality	0	0	0	3	0
Izard's theory of emotion	0	0	0	3	9
James' theory of emotion	0	7	0	3	0
James' theory of habit	0	3	0	0	0
James' theory of retention/recollection	4	0	0	0	0
James' theory of sensation	4	0	0	0	0
James-Lange/Lange-James theory	29	73	55	71	100
judgmental theory of affection	0	3	0	0	0
juke-box theory of emotions	0	0	0	9	0
Jung's theory of personality	0	3	10	31	34
Kantian theory	13	0	0	0	0
Keith's theory of audition	0	3	0	0	0
Kelley's attribution theory	0	0	0	0	6
Kelly's personal construct theory	0	0	0	15	13
Kempf's theory of neurosis	0	7	0	0	0
Klein's theory of psychosexual development	0	0	0	3	0
knowledge, theory of	13	0	0	0	0
known and knowing, theory of the	4	0	0	0	0
Kohlberg's theory	0	0	0	11	22
Kohler's theory of traces	0	3	0	0	0
Konig's color theory	4	0	0	0	0
Kretschmer's theory of personality	0	0	7	0	0
Kruger's theory of audition	4	0	0	0	0
labeling theory	0	0	0	0	6
Ladd-Franklin/Franklin theory	21	40	28	9	0
Laing's theory of schizophrenia	0	0	0	3	0
Lamarck's theory	0	3	7	3	0
language/language development theories of	13	10	3	17	38
lapsed intelligence, theory of	4	0	0	0	0
late selection theories of attention	0	0	0	0	6
leadership theories (general)	0	0	0	14	0

	1885-1919	1920-39	1940-59	1960-79	1980-96

Theories in 112 Years of Psychology

	1885-1919	1920-39	1940-59	1960-79	1980-96
learned helplessness theory	0	0	0	0	6
learned inattention theory of schizophrenia	0	0	0	0	3
learning theories (general)	0	17	52	57	59
levels of processing theory	0	0	0	0	16
Lewinsohn's theory of depression	0	0	0	3	0
libidinal theory of depression	0	0	0	0	3
liking, theories of	0	0	0	0	3
Lindsley's activation theory	0	0	0	3	0
linguistic competence, theories of	0	0	0	0	3
lipostatic theory	0	0	0	0	9
Lipps' theory of ideas	4	0	0	0	0
local indices theory	4	0	0	0	0
local sign, theory of	0	7	0	0	0
local stimulus theory of drive	0	0	3	0	0
localization theory	4	7	0	0	3
lock-and-key theory	0	0	0	0	3
loop theory	0	3	0	0	0
love, theories of	0	0	0	3	6
magic, theories of	0	3	0	0	0
Maslow's theory	0	0	3	17	31
mass action theory	0	7	3	0	0
materialist identity theory	0	0	0	0	3
maturation, theories of	0	0	0	6	0
McClelland's theory	0	0	0	3	0
McDougall's theory of instincts	0	0	0	3	0
McDougall's theory of play	0	3	0	0	0
McDougall's theory of temperament	0	3	3	0	0
McGuire's attitude theory	0	0	0	3	0
meaning, theories of	0	10	3	0	0
mechanistic/mechanical theories	0	3	10	3	0
mediation theory	0	0	0	9	3
membrane theory of nerve excitation	0	7	14	0	0
memory, theories of (general)	4	3	3	11	0
Mendelian theory of heredity	0	0	7	0	0
mental unity, organic theory of	4	0	0	0	0

	1885-1919	1920-39	1940-59	1960-79	1980-96
Theories in 112 Years of Psychology					
meta theories of personality	0	0	0	0	3
Meyer's hydraulic theory of hearing	0	3	0	0	0
Mill's logical theory	4	0	0	0	0
mind-body theories	0	3	3	0	0
mind-stuff theory	4	0	0	0	0
mind/mental functions, theory of	0	3	0	0	3
misapplied constancy, theory of	0	0	0	0	6
modeling theory	0	0	0	0	3
molar theories	0	0	0	3	0
molecular theories	0	0	0	3	0
monoamine theory of depression	0	0	0	0	3
monogenic biochemical theories of schizophrenia	0	0	0	3	0
mood disorders, theories of	0	0	0	0	6
moon illusion, theory of	0	0	3	0	0
moral development/reasoning, theories of	8	0	0	6	3
motivation, theories of (general)	0	3	0	34	41
motivator-hygiene theory	0	0	0	0	3
motor/motion/movement theory	0	17	10	14	0
Mowrer's theory	0	0	0	9	0
Muller theory of color vision	4	0	3	0	0
multiple-factor/intelligences theory	0	0	7	3	34
multiple-stage/S-R theory	0	0	0	3	0
Murray's theory of needs	0	0	0	6	3
music, theory of	0	3	0	0	0
Nafe's theory of cutaneous sensitivity	0	3	3	0	0
nativist theories	13	10	0	0	3
need theory	0	0	0	0	9
need-reduction theory	0	0	3	0	3
negative practice theory	0	3	0	0	0
neo-Freudian theories	0	0	0	6	13
neoanalytic theories	0	0	0	3	0
neodissociation theory	0	0	0	0	22
network theories of memory	0	0	0	0	6
neural/nerve theory	0	13	0	6	3
neurocultural theory	0	0	0	0	3

	1885-1919	1920-39	1940-59	1960-79	1980-96
Theories in 112 Years of Psychology					
neurological theories of emotion	0	0	0	3	0
neurophysiological theory of intelligence	0	0	0	0	3
neurosis, theories of	0	3	0	6	0
neurovascular theory	0	0	0	0	3
noise, theory of	0	3	0	0	0
nomothetic theories	0	0	0	3	0
non-process theory of trace	0	3	0	0	0
noncontinuity theory	0	0	0	3	3
nonstate theories of hypnosis	0	0	0	0	9
norepinephrine theory	0	0	0	0	3
now-print theory of memory	0	0	0	0	6
object-relations theory of depression	0	0	0	0	6
observational learning theory	0	0	0	3	0
olfactory qualities, theory of	4	0	0	0	0
one-stage theories	0	0	0	3	0
onomatopoeic theory of speech	0	10	0	0	0
opponent-process theory (Hering)	21	37	21	40	87
opponent-process theory of addiction	0	0	0	0	3
opponent-process theory of emotion (Solomon)	0	0	0	3	13
optimization theory	0	0	0	3	9
organic selection, theory of	4	0	0	0	0
organismic theory	0	0	7	6	0
organizational theory	0	0	0	0	9
paired associated sentences theory	0	0	0	0	3
pandemonium theory	0	0	0	3	6
Papez-Maclean theory	0	0	0	3	0
parallelism theory	8	0	0	0	0
passive theory of sleep	0	0	0	3	0
pathognomic (ding-dong) theory	0	3	0	0	0
pattern/pattern recognition theory	0	3	7	6	6
Pavlovian conditioning theory	0	3	3	0	0
perception, theories of (general)	8	7	14	11	6
periodicity theory	0	0	0	6	0
peripheral theory of emotion	0	3	7	9	3
peripheral theory of thinking	0	3	28	0	0

	1885-1919	1920-39	1940-59	1960-79	1980-96
Theories in 112 Years of Psychology					
permissive amine theory	0	0	0	0	3
person-centered approach theory	0	0	0	0	3
personality theories (general)	0	3	28	60	41
perspective theory of perception	0	0	0	3	0
phenomenological theories of personality	0	0	0	6	9
photochemical theory of seeing	4	3	3	0	0
photographic theory of consciousness	0	0	0	0	3
phylogenetic theory of affection	0	3	0	0	0
physiological theory of emotions	0	0	7	9	3
Piaget's theory	0	0	3	37	66
piano theory of hearing	0	0	3	0	0
place/place-volley/place-frequency theory	0	0	17	38	75
plastic medium theory	4	0	0	0	0
Plato's theory of pain	4	0	0	0	0
play, theories of	0	3	3	0	0
pleasure and pain theories	8	13	3	0	0
positive incentive theory of addiction	0	0	0	0	3
practice, theory of	0	0	3	0	0
preconscious processing theory	0	0	0	0	3
predictive contingency theory	0	0	0	0	6
prejudice, theories of	0	0	0	6	6
preparedness theory	0	0	0	0	3
prescriptivist theory of morality	0	0	0	3	0
pressure sensation, theory of	4	0	0	0	0
pressure sense, theory of	0	7	0	0	0
primitive theory of mind	0	3	0	0	0
private theories of personality	0	0	0	3	0
probability theory	0	0	3	0	3
problem-solving theory	0	0	0	6	0
programming/programmed theory of aging	0	0	0	0	6
projection, theory of	4	0	0	0	0
propositional code theory	0	0	0	0	3
prospect theory of reasoning	0	0	0	0	3
prototypic feature/matching theory	0	0	0	0	13
psychic trauma theory	0	0	0	3	0

	1885-1919	1920-39	1940-59	1960-79	1980-96
Theories in 112 Years of Psychology					
psychoanalytic theories of personality	0	7	45	71	78
psychodynamic theories of personality	0	0	7	11	31
psychogenic theories of abnormality	0	0	0	0	3
psycholinguistic theory	0	0	0	0	6
psychological/psychosocial theories of personality	0	0	3	3	9
psychopathology, theories of	0	0	0	6	22
psychophysical theory	0	3	0	0	0
quantum theory of vision	0	7	0	0	0
racial theories of intelligence	0	0	0	3	0
Rank's theory	0	0	3	0	0
Raven's theory of intelligence	0	0	0	0	3
reactance theory	0	0	0	0	3
reading, theory of	0	0	0	0	3
realism/reality, theories of	4	3	0	0	0
reasoning/reason, theory of	4	3	0	0	0
recapitulation theory	4	7	7	0	0
recency theory of learning	0	3	0	0	0
recitation theory	0	0	0	3	0
recognition, theories of	0	0	3	0	3
reconstruction theory of memory	0	0	0	3	0
reflex attention, theory of	4	0	0	0	0
reflex theory	8	7	0	3	0
Reich's theory of personality	0	0	0	3	0
reincarnation, theory of	0	3	0	0	0
reinforcement theory	0	0	10	20	9
reinforcement/behavior-regulation theory	0	0	0	0	6
relativity, theory of	0	3	0	0	0
religious theories of healing	0	0	3	0	0
REM sleep, theories of	0	0	0	0	3
repair/restoration theory of sleep	0	0	0	0	9
repression, theory of	0	0	3	3	0
residue theory of pitch	0	0	0	3	0
resonance theory of hearing	0	20	14	9	3
response bias theory	0	0	0	6	0
response inhibition theory of obesity	0	0	0	3	0

	1885-1919	1920-39	1940-59	1960-79	1980-96

Theories in 112 Years of Psychology

	1885-1919	1920-39	1940-59	1960-79	1980-96
retention, theories of	0	0	3	0	0
reticular theory	0	0	0	0	3
retinex theory	0	0	0	0	3
retrieval failure theory	0	0	0	0	6
retroactive inhibition theory	0	0	3	0	0
reward-cost theory	0	0	0	3	6
Rogers' theory	0	0	0	20	25
role/social role theory	0	0	0	6	13
Rotter's locus of control theory	0	0	0	0	3
roundness of spots, theory of	0	3	0	0	0
Rutherford's frequency theory	0	0	0	3	0
sampling theory	0	0	3	6	0
satiation theory of cortical conduction	0	0	0	3	0
scapegoat theory of prejudice	0	0	0	3	6
Schachter-Singer's theory	0	0	0	17	69
Schanz' color theory	0	3	0	0	0
schema theory of memory	0	0	0	0	9
Schiller-Spencer theory of play	0	3	0	0	0
scholastic theory (general)	0	0	3	0	0
scholastic theory of abstraction	4	0	0	0	0
script/reconstructive script theory	0	0	0	0	6
search theory of memory	0	0	0	3	0
seasons of a man's life theory	0	0	0	0	3
selection, theory of	0	3	3	0	0
selective filter theory	0	0	0	0	3
self-concept/self theories	4	7	0	34	75
self-control/commitment, theory of	0	0	0	3	0
self-discrepancy theory	0	0	0	0	3
self-fulfilling prophecy theory	0	0	0	0	3
self-justification theory	0	0	0	0	3
self-presentation theory	0	0	0	0	3
Selye's theory of stress	0	0	0	3	3
Selz's theory of thought	0	3	0	0	0
sensation, theory of (general)	4	0	3	3	0
sensory theory of pleasant/unpleasantness	0	3	0	0	0

	1885-1919	1920-39	1940-59	1960-79	1980-96
Theories in 112 Years of Psychology					
sensory-tonic theory of perception	0	0	0	6	0
serial learning, theory of	0	0	0	3	0
set-point theory	0	0	0	0	16
sex role, theories of	0	0	0	3	3
sex/sex typing theories	0	0	0	6	3
Sheldon's type theory	0	0	3	3	0
shock, theory of	0	0	3	0	0
signal-detection theory	0	0	0	26	56
similarity-attraction theory	0	0	0	0	3
sin theory of psychopathology	0	0	0	3	0
situational theory of leadership	0	0	0	3	6
skilled memory theory	0	0	0	0	3
Skinner's descriptive behavior theory	0	0	0	14	9
sleep, theories of	0	7	0	6	13
slot theory of short-term memory	0	0	0	0	3
small-group phenomena, theory of	0	0	0	3	0
smell, theories of (general)	0	13	0	0	0
Snygg & Combs' theory of personality	0	0	0	3	0
social comparison/evaluation theory	0	0	0	17	25
social impact theory	0	0	0	0	13
social interest theory	0	0	0	0	3
social learning/cognition theories	0	0	0	37	100
social psychology/interaction theories	0	0	0	3	9
soul, theory of the	4	0	0	0	0
sound pattern theory	0	0	3	0	0
Soviet theory of emotion	0	0	0	3	0
space perception theory	21	13	0	0	0
special process theory of hypnosis	0	0	0	0	9
specific nerve energies theory	4	17	3	0	3
specificity theory	0	0	0	3	6
Spencer's theory of integration of feelings	8	0	0	0	0
spirit theory of behavior	0	0	0	3	0
spiritual theory of reflex attention	4	0	0	0	0
spreading activation theory	0	0	0	0	3
Sroufe's theory of emotion	0	0	0	0	3

	1885-1919	1920-39	1940-59	1960-79	1980-96
Theories in 112 Years of Psychology					
stage theories of development (general)	0	0	0	9	28
state theories of hypnosis	0	0	0	0	6
statistical configuration theory	0	0	0	0	3
stereochemical theory of smell	0	0	3	3	9
stimulus theory of hunger	0	0	0	3	0
stimulus-response (S-R) theories	0	0	10	20	16
stimulus-substitution, theory of	0	3	7	3	0
stress, theories of	0	0	0	0	9
structural theory of language/intelligence	0	0	0	6	6
structuralist theory of development	0	0	3	3	0
subconscious, theories of	0	7	0	0	0
subjectivity, theory of	4	0	0	0	0
substance abuse, theories of	0	0	0	0	3
Sullivan's theory of personality	0	0	0	6	6
suppression, theory of	4	0	0	0	0
synaesthesia, theory of	0	3	0	0	0
synaptic/synapse theory	0	13	3	3	0
tubula rasa theory	0	0	0	3	0
tactile perception, theories of	8	10	0	0	0
taking-into-account theory	0	0	0	0	3
teleological theory	4	0	0	0	0
telephone theory of hearing	0	10	7	9	3
temperament, theories of	0	3	3	0	0
temperature sense, theory of	4	3	0	0	0
template-matching theory	0	0	0	6	13
temporal theories of pitch perception	0	0	0	0	3
tendencies, positive & negative theory of	4	0	0	0	0
tension-reduction theories	0	0	3	3	0
testing, theory of	0	0	3	0	0
texture gradient theory	0	0	0	3	0
thalamic theory	0	7	14	3	6
thermostatic theory of hunger	0	0	0	9	0
Thibaut & Kelley's theory	0	0	0	0	3
thinking, theories of	0	3	21	3	0
thirst, theories of	0	0	3	6	0

	1885-1919	1920-39	1940-59	1960-79	1980-96
Theories in 112 Years of Psychology					
Thorndike's synthetic theory	0	0	7	0	0
three-element/trichromatic vision theory	0	0	0	14	81
three-process theory of memory	0	0	0	3	0
threshold theory	0	0	0	0	6
Thurstone's primary mental abilities theory	0	0	10	0	3
tickle, theory of	0	3	0	0	0
time perception theories	0	3	0	0	0
Tolman's sign-Gestalt theory	0	0	0	3	0
Tolman's theory of motivation	0	0	0	3	0
tones/combinational theory of tones	13	7	0	0	0
top-down theories	0	0	0	0	3
toxin theories of schizophrenia	0	0	0	3	0
trace theory of memory	0	0	3	9	3
trait theories of personality (general)	0	0	17	31	66
transactional theory	0	0	0	0	3
transcendentalist theory of the self	4	0	0	0	0
transfer of training theories	0	0	7	0	0
transformational theory of language	0	0	0	3	3
trauma, theory of	0	0	0	3	0
traveling wave theory	0	0	0	3	0
trial and error theory	0	0	3	0	0
triangular theory of love	0	0	0	0	19
triarchic theory of intelligence (Sternberg)	0	0	0	0	47
triple aspect theory	0	3	0	0	0
triple receptor theory	0	0	0	3	0
Troland's theory of retroflex action	0	3	0	0	0
turmoil theory of adolescence	0	0	0	0	3
two-cue theory	0	0	0	0	3
two-factor theory of intelligence (Spearman)	0	10	21	3	25
two-point threshold, theory of	0	3	0	0	0
two-process theory of forgetting	0	0	0	6	0
two-stage/factor/process theories	0	0	7	17	13
type/body types theories (general)	0	0	31	14	25
unconscious inference theory	0	0	0	0	3
unimodal theory of intelligence	0	3	3	0	0

	1885-1919	1920-39	1940-59	1960-79	1980-96
Theories in 112 Years of Psychology					
utilitarian theory	4	0	0	0	0
vascular/visceral theory	0	0	7	0	0
Venable's theory of color vision	0	3	0	0	0
verbal behavior, general theory of	0	0	3	0	0
vestibular sense, theories of	0	3	0	0	0
vision/sight, theories of (general)	33	17	3	6	0
visual extensity, theories of	8	0	0	0	0
vitalism, theory of	4	0	3	0	0
volition/voluntarism, theory of	8	0	0	0	0
Volkmann's theory of feeling	4	0	0	0	0
volley theory of hearing	0	0	24	20	19
volley theory of neural excitation	0	3	0	0	0
von Kries' color theory	4	3	0	0	0
Vygotsky's theory of cognitive development	0	0	0	0	3
wave pattern theories of hearing	0	3	0	0	0
wear-and-tear theories of aging	0	0	0	0	13
Weber's law, theory of	0	3	0	0	0
Wechsler's theory of intelligence	0	0	0	0	3
Weismann's theory	0	3	0	0	0
Wertheimer's perceptual theory	0	0	0	3	0
white, theory of	0	3	0	0	0
Whorf's theory	0	0	3	0	0
will, theories of	0	0	3	0	0
Wrightson's theory of audition	0	3	0	0	0
Wundt's theory of association of mental elements	4	0	0	0	0
Wundt's theory of color	4	0	0	0	0
Wundt's tridimensional theory of feeling	0	10	7	0	0
Wurzburg theory of thought	0	3	0	0	0
X, theory	0	0	0	0	3
Y, theory	0	0	0	0	3
Young's theory of color sensations	8	3	0	0	0
Young-Helmholtz color theory	4	20	45	49	53
Z, theory	0	0	0	0	3
Zajonc's arousal theory	0	0	0	0	6

APPENDIX B

References—Textbooks Surveyed for Collection of Laws and Theories in 112 Years of Psychology

The following textbooks in psychology were surveyed for collection of Laws and Theories in 112 Years of Psychology. The following five time periods (covering 112 years) are included in this listing of references:

1. Textbooks published from 1885 through 1919.
2. Textbooks published from 1920 through 1939.
3. Textbooks published from 1940 through 1959.
4. Textbooks published from 1960 through 1979.
5. Textbooks published from 1980 through 1996.

Angell, J. R. (1908) *Psychology*. New York: Henry Holt.

Asher, E., Tiffin, J. & Knight, F. (1953) *Introduction to general psychology*. Boston: D. C. Heath.

Atkinson, R., Atkinson, R., Smith, E., & Hilgard, E. (1987) *Introduction to Psychology*. New York: Harcourt Brace Jovanovich.

Averill, L. A. (1943) *Introductory psychology*. New York: Macmillan.

Baldwin, J. M. (1894) *Handbook of psychology*. New York: Henry Holt.

Baldwin, J. M. (1906) *Handbook of psychology*. New York: Henry Holt.

Baron, R. (1989) *Psychology: The essential science*. Boston: Allyn & Bacon.

Baron, R., Byrne, D., & Kantowitz, B. (1977) *Psychology: Understanding behavior*. Philadelphia: W. Saunders.

Benjamin, L., Hopkins, J., & Nation, J. (1994) *Psychology*. New York: Macmillan.

Bentley, M. (1934) *The new field of psychology*. New York: D. Appleton-Century.

Bootzin, R., Loftus, E., & Zajonc, R. (1983) *Psychology today*. New York: Random House.

Boring, E. G., Langfeld, H. S., & Weld, H. P. (1935) *Psychology: A factual textbook*. New York: John Wiley.

Boring, E. G., Langfeld, H. S., & Weld, H. P. (1939) *Introduction to psychology*. New York: John Wiley.

Brennan, R. E. (1952) *General psychology.* New York: Macmillan.

Brown, W., & Gilhousen, H. C. (1950) *College psychology.* New York: Prentice-Hall.

Brown, R., & Herrnstein, R. J. (1975) *Psychology.* Boston: Little, Brown.

Buell, C. S. (1900) *Essentials of psychology.* Boston: Ginn.

Bugelski, B. R. (1960) *An introduction to the principles of psychology.* New York: Holt, Rinehart, & Winston.

Buss, A. (1973) *Psychology: Man in perspective.* New York: John Wiley.

Calkins, M. W. (1905) *An introduction to psychology.* New York: Macmillan.

Calkins, M. W. (1916) *An introduction to psychology.* New York: Macmillan.

Carlson, N. R. (1993) *Psychology: The science of behavior.* Boston: Allyn & Bacon.

Carmichael, L. (1957) *Basic psychology.* New York: Random House.

Carr, H. A. (1925) *Psychology: A study of mental activity.* New York: Longmans, Green.

Cattell, R. B. (1941) *General psychology.* Cambridge, MA: Sci-Art.

Cole, L. E. (1939) *General psychology.* New York: McGraw-Hill.

Crider, A., Goethals, G., Kavanaugh, R., & Solomon, P. (1986) *Psychology.* Glenview, IL: Scott, Foresman.

Crooks, R., & Stein, J. (1991) *Psychology: Science, behavior, and life.* Chicago: Holt, Rinehart, & Winston.

Cruze, W. W. (1951) *General psychology for college students.* New York: Prentice-Hall.

Davidoff, L. L. (1976) *Introduction to psychology.* New York: McGraw-Hill.

Deese, J. (1967) *General psychology.* Boston: Allyn and Bacon.

Dewey, J. (1898) *Psychology.* New York: Harper and Brothers.

Dockeray, F. C. (1936) *General psychology.* New York: Prentice-Hall.

Dresser, H. W. (1924) *Psychology in theory and application.* New York: T. Y. Crowell.

Dunlap, K. (1922) *The elements of scientific psychology.* St. Louis, MO: C. V. Mosby.

Dunlap, K. (1936) *Elements of psychology.* St. Louis, MO: C. V. Mosby.

Ebbinghaus, H. (1908) *Psychology: An elementary text-book.* Boston: D. C. Heath.

Edwards, D. C. (1968) *General psychology.* New York: Macmillan.

Engle, T. L. (1950) *Psychology: Its principles and applications.* New York: World Book.

Fantino, E., & Reynolds, G. (1975) *Introduction to contemporary psychology.* San Francisco: W. H. Freeman.

Feldman, R. S. (1987) *Understanding psychology.* New York: McGraw-Hill.

Fernberger, S. W. (1936) *Elementary general psychology.* New York: F. S. Crofts.

Franz, S., & Gordon, K. (1933) *Psychology.* New York: McGraw-Hill.

Freeman, E. (1939) *Principles of general psychology.* New York: Henry Holt.

Gannon, T. J. (1954) *Psychology: The unity of human behavior.* New York: Ginn.

Garrett, H. E. (1955) *General psychology.* New York: American Book.

Gates, A. I. (1926) *Elementary psychology.* New York: Macmillan.

Gault, R. H., & Howard, D. T. (1926) *Outline of general psychology.* New York: Longmans, Green.

Geiwitz, J. (1976) *Looking at ourselves: An invitation to psychology.* Boston: Little, Brown.

Goleman, D., Engen, T., & Davids, A. (1982) *Introductory psychology.* New York: Random House.

Griffith, C. R. (1924) *General introduction to psychology.* New York: Macmillan.

Griffith, C. R. (1929) *General introduction to psychology.* New York: Macmillan.

Guthrie, E. R., & Edwards, A. L. (1949) *Psychology: A first course in human behavior.* New York: Harper.

Haber, A., & Runyon, R. P. (1974) *Fundamentals of psychology*. Reading, MA: Addison-Wesley.

Haber, R. N., & Fried, A. H. (1975) *An introduction to psychology*. New York: Holt, Rinehart, & Winston.

Halleck, R. P. (1895) *Psychology and psychic culture*. New York: American Book.

Halonen, J., & Santrock, J. (1996) *Psychology: Contexts of behavior*. Chicago: Brown & Benchmark.

Harlow, H., McGaugh, J., & Thompson, R. (1971) *Psychology*. San Francisco: Albion.

Harmon, F. L. (1951) *Principles of psychology*. Milwaukee, WI: Bruce.

Hilgard, E. R. (1953) *Introduction to psychology*. New York: Harcourt, Brace.

Hilgard, E. R. (1957) *Introduction to psychology*. New York: Harcourt, Brace.

Hill, W. F. (1970) *Psychology: Principles and problems*. Philadelphia: J. B. Lippincott.

Hoffding, H. (1908) *Outlines of psychology*. London: Macmillan.

Hollingworth, H. L. (1928) *Psychology: Its facts and principles*. New York: D. Appleton.

Holtzman, W. H. (1978) *Introduction to psychology*. New York: Harper and Row.

Hothersall, D. (1985) *Psychology*. Columbus, OH.: Charles E. Merrill.

Hunter, W. S. (1919) *General psychology*. Chicago: University of Chicago Press.

James, W. (1890) *The principles of psychology*. New York: Henry Holt (Dover ed.: 1950, New York: Dover).

Johnson, D. M. (1948) *Essentials of psychology*. New York: McGraw-Hill.

Judd, C. H. (1907) *Psychology: General introduction*. New York: Charles Scribner's Sons.

Kagan, J., & Havemann, E. (1968) *Psychology: An introduction*. New York: Harcourt, Brace, and World.

Kagan, J., & Havemann, E. (1980) *Psychology: An introduction*. New York: Harcourt Brace Jovanovich.

Kalat, J. (1986) *Introduction to psychology*. Belmont, CA: Wadsworth.

Keller, F. S., & Schoenfeld, W. N. (1950) *Principles of psychology*. New York: Appleton-Century-Crofts.

Kendler, H. H. (1963) *Basic psychology*. New York: Appleton-Century-Crofts.

Kimble, G. A., & Garmezy, N. (1956) *Principles of general psychology*. New York: Ronald Press.

Krech, D., Crutchfield, R. S., & Livson, N. (1974) *Elements of psychology*. New York: Alfred A. Knopf.

Kulpe, O. (1909) *Outlines of psychology*. New York: Macmillan.

Ladd, G. T. (1898) *Outlines of descriptive psychology*. New York: Charles Scribner's Sons.

Lamberth, J., McCullers, J., & Mellgren, R. (1976) *Foundations of psychology*. New York: Harper & Row.

Lazerson, A. (1975) *Psychology today: An introduction*. New York: CRM/Random House.

Lefton, L. A. (1994) *Psychology*. Needham Heights, MA: Allyn & Bacon.

Leuba, C. U. (1961) *Man: A general psychology*. New York: Holt, Rinehart, & Winston.

Lindgren, H. C., & Byrne, D. (1965) *Psychology: Introd. to the study of human behavior*. New York: Wiley.

Lindzey, G., Hall, C. S., & Thompson, R. F. (1978) *Psychology*. New York: Worth.

London, P. (1978) *Beginning psychology*. Homewood, IL: Dorsey Press.

Lotze, H. (1885) *Outlines of psychology*. Minneapolis, MN: S. M. Williams.

Lund, F. H. (1933) *Psychology: An empirical study of behavior*. New York: Ronald Press.

Maher, M. (1900) *Psychology*. New York: Longmans, Green.

McDougall, W. (1924) *Outline of psychology*. New York: Charles Scribner's Sons.

McGee, M. G., & Wilson, D. W. (1984) *Psychology: Science and application*. New York: West.

McMahon, F. B. (1972) *Psychology the hybrid science*. Englewood Cliffs, NJ: Prentice-Hall.

Mednick, S., Higgins, J., & Kirschenbaum, J. (1975) *Psychology: Explorations in behavior and experience*. New York: Wiley.

Mischel, W., & Mischel, H. N. (1977) *Essentials of psychology*. New York: Random House.

Morgan, C. T. (1956) *Introduction to psychology*. New York: McGraw-Hill.

Morris, C. G. (1990) *Psychology: An introduction*. Englewood Cliffs, NJ: Prentice-Hall.

Morris, C. G. (1996) *Psychology*. Upper Saddle River, NJ: Prentice-Hall.

Munn, N. L. (1946) *Psychology*. New York: Houghton Mifflin.

Murphy, G. (1951) *An introduction to psychology*. New York: Harper and Brothers.

Myers, D. G. (1996) *Exploring psychology*. New York: Worth.

Newman, P. R., & Newman, B. M. (1983) *Principles of psychology*. Homewood, IL: Dorsey Press.

Papalia, D., & Olds, S. W. (1988) *Psychology*. New York: McGraw-Hill.

Perrin, F.A.C. (1932) *Psychology: Its methods and principles*. New York: Henry Holt.

Pettijohn, T. F. (1987) *Psychology: A concise introduction*. Guilford, CT: Dushkin.

Phillips, D. E. (1927) *An elementary psychology*. New York: Ginn.

Pillsbury, W. B. (1926) *The essentials of psychology*. New York: Macmillan.

Plotnik, R. (1993) *Introduction to psychology*. Pacific Grove CA: Brooks/Cole.

Price, R., Glickstein, M., Horton, D., Sherman, S., & Fazio, R. (1987) *Principles of psychology*. Glenview, IL: Scott, Foresman.

Prothro, E. T., & Teska, P. T. (1950) *Psychology*. New York: Ginn.

Rathus, S. A. (1993) *Psychology*. New York: Harcourt Brace Jovanovich.

Reid, A. C. (1938) *Elements of psychology*. New York: Prentice-Hall.

Robertson, G. C. (1896) *Elements of psychology*. New York: Charles Scribner's Sons.

Roediger, H., Capaldi, E., Paris, S., & Polivy, J. (1991) *Psychology*. New York: HarperCollins.

Royce, J. (1903) *Outlines of psychology*. New York: Macmillan.

Rubin, Z., Peplau, L., & Salovey, P. (1993) *Psychology*. Boston: Houghton Mifflin.

Ruch, F. L. (1958) *Psychology and life*. Fairlawn, NJ: Scott, Foresman.

Ruch, F. L. (1963) *Psychology and life*. Chicago: Scott, Foresman.

Ruja, H. (1955) *Psychology for life*. New York: McGraw-Hill.

Sanford, F. H. (1965) *Psychology: A scientific study of man*. Belmont, CA: Wadsworth.

Scarr, S., & VanderZanden, J. (1984) *Understanding psychology*. New York: Random House.

Seamon, J., & Kenrick, D. (1992) *Psychology*. Englewood Cliffs, NJ: Prentice-Hall.

Seashore, C. E. (1923) *Introduction to psychology*. New York: Macmillan.

Shaver, K., & Tarpy, R. (1993) *Psychology*. New York: Macmillan.

Shepard, D. L. (1977) *Psychology: The science of human behavior*. Chicago: Science Research Associates.

Sidis, B. (1914) *The foundations of normal and abnormal psychology*. Boston: Gorham Press.

Smith, K. U., & Smith, M. F. (1973) *Psychology: An introduction to behavior science.* Boston: Little, Brown.

Smith, K. U., & Smith, W. M. (1958) *The behavior of man: An introduction to psychology.* New York: Henry Holt.

Smith, R., Sarason, I., & Sarason, B. (1978) *Psychology: The frontier of behavior.* New York: Harper & Row.

Smith, S., & Guthrie, E. R. (1924) *General psychology in terms of behavior.* New York: D. Appleton.

Spencer, H. (1892) *The principles of psychology.* New York: D. Appleton.

Stagner, R., & Karwoski, T. F. (1952) *Psychology.* New York: McGraw-Hill.

Starch, D., Stanton, H. M., & Koerth, W. (1937) *Controlling human behavior.* New York: Macmillan.

Stroud, J. B. (1938) *Introduction to general psychology.* New York: Prentice-Hall.

Thompson, W., & DeBold, R. C. (1971) *Psychology: A systematic introduction.* New York: McGraw-Hill.

Thorndike, E. L. (1907) *The elements of psychology.* New York: A. G. Seiler.

Thorndike, E. L. (1920) *The elements of psychology.* New York: A. G. Seiler.

Titchener, E. B. (1898) *An outline of psychology.* New York: Macmillan.

Titchener, E. B. (1907) *An outline of psychology.* New York: Macmillan.

Titchener, E. B. (1915) *A beginner's psychology.* New York: Macmillan.

Titchener, E. B. (1928) *A textbook of psychology.* New York: Macmillan.

Vinacke, W. E. (1968) *Foundations of psychology.* New York: American Book.

Wade, C., & Tavris, C. (1996) *Psychology.* New York: HarperCollins.

Warren, H. C. (1919) *Human psychology.* Boston: Houghton Mifflin.

Watson, J. B. (1919) *Psychology: From the standpoint of a behaviorist.* Phila.: J. B. Lippincott.

Weiten, W. (1989) *Psychology: Themes and variations.* Pacific Grove, CA: Brooks/Cole.

Weld, H. P. (1928) *Psychology as science.* New York: Henry Holt.

Wheeler, L., Goodale, R., & Deese, J. (1975) *General psychology.* Boston: Allyn & Bacon.

Wheeler, R. H. (1929) *The science of psychology: An introductory study.* New York: Thomas Y. Crowell.

Wickens, D. D. (1955) *Psychology.* New York: Dryden Press.

Williams, G. W. (1960) *Psychology: A first course.* New York: Harcourt, Brace, and World.

Wolff, W. (1956) *Essentials of psychology.* New York: Grune and Stratton.

Wood, E., and Wood, S. (1993) *The world of psychology.* Boston: Allyn & Bacon.

Woodworth, R. S. (1921) *Psychology: A study of mental life.* New York: Henry Holt.

Woodworth, R. S. (1940) *Psychology.* New York: Henry Holt.

Woodworth, R. S., & Marquis, D. G. (1947) *Psychology.* New York: Henry Holt.

Woodworth, R. S., & Sheehan, M. R. (1944) *First course in psychology.* New York: Henry Holt.

SELECTED BIBLIOGRAPHY

Buss, A. (1973). *Psychology: Man in perspective*. New York: Wiley.

Einstein, A. (1959). Space-time. *Encyclopaedia Britannica*. Chicago: Encyclopaedia Britannica.

English, H., & English, A. (1976). *A comprehensive dictionary of psychological and psychoanalytical terms*. New York: McKay.

Gergen, K. (1994). Diachronic versus synchronic models. In R. J. Corsini (Ed.), *Encyclopedia of psychology*. New York: Wiley.

Harriman, P. (1966). *Handbook of psychological terms*. Totowa, NJ: Littlefield, Adams.

Hill, W. (1970). *Psychology: Principles and problems*. Philadelphia: J. B. Lippincott.

Hume, D. (1739–1740). *A treatise of human nature*. London: Noon.

Marx, M. (1976). *Introduction to psychology*. New York: Macmillan.

Marx, M., & Goodson, F. (Eds.) (1976). *Theories in contemporary psychology*. New York: Macmillan.

Marx, M., & Hillix, W. (1979). *Systems and theories in psychology*. New York: McGraw-Hill.

Roe, K., & Frederick, R. (1981). *Dictionary of theoretical concepts in biology*. Metuchen, NJ: Scarecrow Press.

Roeckelein, J. (1995). Naming in psychology: Analyses of citation counts and eponyms. *Psychological Reports, 77*, 163–174.

Roeckelein, J. (1996a). Citation of *laws* and *theories* in textbooks across 112 years of psychology. *Psychological Reports, 79*, 979–998.

Roeckelein, J. (1996b). Contributions to the history of psychology: CIV. Eminence in psychology as measured by name counts and eponyms. *Psychological Reports, 78*, 243–253.

Roeckelein, J. (1996c). Gender differences in naming and eponymy in psychology. *Psychological Reports, 79*, 435–442.

Roeckelein, J. (1997a). Hierarchy of the sciences and terminological sharing of laws among the sciences. *Psychological Reports, 81*, 739–746.

Roeckelein, J. (1997b). Psychology among the sciences: Comparisons of numbers of theories and laws cited in textbooks. *Psychological Reports, 80*, 131–141.

Royce, J. (1994). Theoretical psychology. In R. J. Corsini (Ed.), *Encyclopedia of psychology*. New York: Wiley.

Turner, M. (1967). *Philosophy and the science of behavior*. New York: Appleton-Century-Crofts.

Viney, W. (1993). *A history of psychology: Ideas and context*. Boston: Allyn & Bacon.

Webster's third new international dictionary of the English language. (1986). Unabridged. Springfield, MA: Merriam-Webster.

Wolman, B. (1973). *Dictionary of behavioral science*. New York: Van Nostrand Reinhold.

SUBJECT INDEX

Page numbers for main entries in the Dictionary are set in **boldfaced** type.

A priorism, doctrine of, 463
ABC theory, **1,** 70, 101, 397
Abney's effect, 2
Abney's law, **2,** 103, 290, 444–446
Abnormality, theories of, 3
Absolute stimulus theory, 441
Abstraction, laws/principles of, 3, 98, 114, 263
Abstraction/prototype theory, 112, 461
Accommodation, law/principle of, **3–5,** 75, 225, 230, 379, 392, 424, 470
Achievement motivation, theory of, **5–6,** 59, 306, 329, 336, 340
Achievement motivation theory of work, 7, 482
Achievement need, theory of, 5–6
Ach's laws/principles/theory, **7–8,** 327, 484
Across-fiber pattern theory, 220
Activation/arousal theory, **8–10,** 41, 164, 307, 329, 382, 467, 490
Activation model of memory organization, 10, 189
Activation-synthesis theory, 10, 151
Activity theory of aging, 20
Actor-observer discrepancy effect, 58
Adams zone theory, 105

Adaptation, principles/laws of, **10–12,** 78, 104, 121, 129, 208, 225–226, 231, 351, 392, 471
Adaptation-level theory, 12, 124, 231, 369, 370, 441
Adaptive adaptation, principle of, 303
Adaptive nonresponding theory, 12, 437
Additive color mixture, principle of, 13, 102–103
Additive law of probability, 13, 386
Adler's theory of personality, 11, **13–15,** 77, 79–80, 100–101, 117, 150, 193, 197, 200, 233, 240, 329, 376
Advantage, law of, 466
Aesthetics, principle of, 15, 492
Afterdischarge, law of, 15, 434
Aftereffects hypothesis, 37, 89
Afterimage law, 15, 78, 160
Afterimages, positive/negative, theory of, 78, 104, 392
Aggression, theories of, **15–18,** 66, 117, 192, 197, 246, 329, 403
Aging, theories of, **18–22,** 143, 307
Agreement, law of, 357
Aleatory theory, 385
Alexander's law, 22, 471
Algebraic summation, law of, 22, 434

Algorithmic-heuristic theory, **22–24,** 84, 190, 260, 263

Alienation theories, 24

Allegiance effect, 145

All-or-none law/principle, **24–25,** 112, 333, 341–342, 345

Allport's conformity hypothesis, **25–26,** 86, 135

Allport's functional autonomy principle, **26–28,** 29–30

Allport's theory of enestruence, **28,** 165, 368, 372

Allport's theory of personality, 14, 27, **29–31,** 91, 251, 320, 376

Alpha movement effect, 37

Alrutz's theory, **31–32** 339

Amsel's hypothesis/theory, **32–33** 90, 242, 457

Analogue theory of memory, 33, 189

Ancestral inheritance, law of, 33, 201

Angyal's personality theory, **33–35,** 215, 318–319, 329, 376

Animal magnetism, theory of, 35, 246, 247

Ansbacher effect/shrinkage effect, 35, 364

Anxiety, theories of, **35–37**

Anxiety-stress theory, 36

Apparent movement, principles/theories of, **37–39,** 63, 83, 177, 212, 259, 283, 366, 377

Apperception, doctrine of, 39, 232, 483

Appraisal theories of emotions, 39, 40, 100–101, 292

Arago phenomenon, 469

Aristotle's doctrines/theories, **39–40,** 212, 224, 230

Arnold's theory of emotions, **40–41,** 101, 164, 292

Arousal theory, 9, 41, 271, 328–329, 410, 419, 437, 486, 489

Asch conformity effect, **41–43,** 135

Ashby's law of requisite variety, 43

Assimilation, law of, 4, **43–44** 225, 432

Assimilation-contrast theory, 354

Association, doctrine of, 44, 313, 425

Association, laws/principles of, 8, 40, 43, **44–48,** 76, 82, 114, 121, 144, 189, 191, 212, 222, 225, 267, 268, 298–299, 301, 318, 345, 360, 362, 365, 402–404, 431

Association of ideas, doctrine of, 44, 47

Associative-chain theory, 434

Associative/contiguity theory, 48, 222, 344, 409

Associative facilitation effect, 43

Associative interference effect, 43, 473

Associative learning, principle of, 45

Associative shifting, law of, **48,** 75, 207, 222–223, 361, 407

Atmosphere/context effects, 368

Attachment, principle of, 48. *See also* Infant attachment theories

Attention, laws/principles/theories of, **48–52,** 65, 82–83, 97, 113–114, 120, 154, 175, 186, 226, 291, 327, 363, 366, 447, 466–467, 472

Attenuation theory of attention, 50

Attitude/attitude change, theories of, 26, **52–56,** 59, 108, 237, 255, 260, 383, 398

Attribution/attitude boomerang effect, 56, 60

Attribution theory, 56, **57–60,** 63–64, 75, 123, 125, 144, 185, 198, 230, 254–255, 278, 279, 281, 355, 398, 419, 423, 472

Aubert phenomenon, 61, 471

Aubert-Fleischl paradox/phenomenon, 61, 471

Aubert-Forster phenomenon/law, 61, 471

Audition/hearing, theories of, **61–63,** 73, 172, 191–192, 230, 246, 324, 350, 379–380, 412, 417, 440, 448, 452, 462, 472, 476

Aufgabe, law of the, 63, 326, 369

Augmentation principle, 59, 63, 255

Autokinetic effect, 37, 63

Automaticity hypothesis, 57, 63, 447

Autotelic theory, 63, 380

Averages, law of, 386

Avoidance hypothesis, 63, 391

Baer/von Baer's law, 64, 401

Bait-shyness effect, 202–203

Balance, principles/theory of, 4, 19, 57, 64, 255, 379, 402, 439

Baldwin effect, **64–65**

Bandura's theory, 17, **65–67,** 70, 192, 301, 416, 439

Barnum effect/phenomenon, **67–68**

Bartlett's schemata theory, **68**

Base-rate fallacy, 386

Bateson's vibratory theory, 68

Bayes's theorem, 386

Beauty/physical appearance principle, 269, 308

Beck's cognitive therapy theory, 68, 70

Behavior theory of perception, 69, 371

Behavior therapy/cognitive therapy, theories of, 66, 68, **69–71,** 102, 287, 479–80

Behavioral contrast effect/phenomenon, 71, 206, 361, 440

Behavioral potential theory, 457

Behaviorist/behavioristic/behaviorism theory, **71–73,** 110–111, 164, 222, 259, 291, 300–301, 309, 318, 320, 374, 389, 413–414, 456, 477, 484

Bekesy's theory, 61, 73

Bell-Magendie law, **73–74**

Belongingness, law/principle of, 48, **74–75,** 210, 212, 407

Bem's self-perception theory, 75, 185–186

Beneke's doctrine of traces, 75

Berkeley's theory of visual space perception, **75–76,** 228, 241, 313, 440, 479

Berne's script theory, **76–77,** 460

Beta movement effect, 37–38

Bezold-Brucke effect/phenomenon/hue shift, **77–78,** 234–235

Bichat, law of, **78–79**

Biederman's theory, 79, 359

Big five model/theory of personality, 79, 374

Biochemical theories of depression, 138

Biochemical theories of personality/abnormality, 79, 200

Biochemical/neurological theories of schizophrenia, 79, 421

Biofeedback, principles of, 79, 121

Biogenetic recapitulation theory, 79, 142, 401

Biogenic amine theories, 138

Biological evolution, doctrine of, 79, 128

Biological theories of depression, 138

Birth order theory, 14, **79–81**

Blau's exchange theory, 172

Blending, law of, 81, 434

Bloch's law, 81, 84–85

Blocking, phenomenon/effect of, **81–83,** 279, 412

Blood-glucose theory, 244

Blue-arc phenomenon, 470

Bodily humors, doctrine of, 199

Bodily rotation, theory of, 478

Bohr's complementarity principle, 83

Bottom-up processing theories, **83,** 458–459

Bourdon effect/illusion, 364

Bowditch's law, 24, 83, 333

Brain-field theory, 38, 83, 368

Brain-spot hypothesis, 420

Breton's law, 474

Brewster effect, 85

Broadbent's filter theory/model/effect, 50, 83, 259, 363

Broca-Sulzer effect, 85

Brown shrinkage effect, 364

Bruce effect, **83–84**

Brucke effect, 85

Bruner's theory of instruction, 23, 84

Brunswik's probabilistic functionalism theory, 84

Bunsen-Roscoe law, 81, **84–85,** 402, 413

Bystander intervention effect, 26, 42, **85–86,** 135, 403

Canalization hypothesis, 87, 334–335

Cannon/Cannon-Bard theory, 9, **87–89,** 160, 164, 186, 274, 424

Capaldi's theory, 32, **89–90,** 357, 425, 457

Career development theories, 90, 481

Catastrophe theory, 353

Catecholamine hypothesis/theory of depression, 90, 138

Categorical judgment, law of, 455

Cattell's theory of personality, **90–93,** 178, 376

Celestial illusion effect, 161

Cell assembly theory, 93, 369, 465

Central-limit theorem, 386

Certainty effect, 354

Chaining, law of, 93, 434

Chance, laws of, 93, 385

Change, law of, 230

Chaos theory, 353

Character analysis theory, 406

Charpentier's law, 93, 470

Chemical profile theory, 93, 244

Cheshire cat effect, 470

Choice, theory of, 93, 132, 136

Chomsky's psycholinguistic theory, **93–95,** 219, 259, 343, 425, 462, 477

Classical conditioning, laws of, 95, 298, 301, 310, 360–61

Classical strength theory, 95, 132

Classical theory of sensory discrimination, 95, 341

Clever Hans effect/phenomenon, **95–96,** 175–76

Closure, principle of, 96, 211

Cluster hypothesis, 217

Cocktail party phenomenon, 50, 97, 210, 212

Coding theories **97–98** 107–108, 165, 212, 220, 252, 338–39, 351

Coercion to the biosocial mean, law of, 92

Coexistence, law of, 361

Cognitive algebra theory, 98, 254

Cognitive appraisal theory, 41, 98, 164, 419

Cognitive consistency theories of attitude change, 53

Cognitive developmental theories, 142, 167, 299, 377–80, 477

Cognitive dissonance, theory of, 4, 55, 59, 64, 117, 133, 166, 329. *See also* Festinger's cognitive dissance theory

Cognitive style models, 3, 23, **98–100,** 478–79

Cognitive theories of emotions, 39, 41, 98, **100–102,** 292, 418–19, 490

Cognitive theory, 5, 46, 83, 94, 97, 100–101, 111–12, 120, 132, 138–139, 170, 185, 206, 251–52, 257, 281, 293–94, 329, 371, 456, 458, 484

Cognitive therapy, theories of, 1, 70, 102, 204

Cohesion, law of, 361

Cohort effects, 19

Color-contingent aftereffect, 160

Color contrast phenomenon, 234

Color mixing, principles of, 102, 488

Color mixture, laws/theory of, 2, 13, **102–4,** 104–105, 217–18, 234, 346, 445, 449, 487

Color vision, theories/laws of, 11, 78, 103, **104–6,** 217–18, 228, 233–35, 239, 281, 283, 287–88, 290, 332, 346, 445, 471–72, 488

Combination, law of, 467

Combination/resultant tones, phenomenon/theory of, 448

Common direction/common fate/good continuation, law of, 210–211

Commonsense theory of emotions, 273

Communication theory, 84, **106–9,** 259–60, 387

Comparative judgment, law of, 109, 133, 459. *See also* Thurstone's law of comparative judgement

Compatibility, law of, 109, 434

Compensatory theory of dreaming, 109

Competence theory, 109, 380

Complementarity, law/principle of, 103, 469

Complementary needs, theory of, 109, 315

Complementary odors, law of, 110, 351

Complex man theory, 354

Componential recovery, principle of, 110, 359

Comte's law, **110–11**

Concentration theory of cutaneous cold, 31, 338

Concept learning/concept formation, theories of, **111–13**

Concomitant variation, law of, 357

Condillac's theory of attention, 49–50, **113–14**

Conditioning of Type R, law of, 114, 434

Conditioning of Type S, law of, 114, 434

Conflict, theories of, 26, 55, **115–19,** 123, 132–33, 166, 185–86, 239, 335, 396–97, 400, 424
Conflicting associations, law of, 434
Confluence theory, 119. *See also* Zajonc's arousal and confluence theories
Conformity hypothesis/theory, 42. *See also* Allport's conformity hypothesis
Connection, laws of, 45, 119, 407
Conscious illusion theory, 308
Conservation of energy, law/principle of, 19, 119, 211, 277
Consolidation hypothesis/theory, 119, 187
Constancy hypothesis, 161, 363, 366
Constitutional theories of personality, 119, 284–85, 427
Constitutional-predisposition theory of schizophrenia, 422
Constructivist theory of perception, **119–20,** 177, 230, 249, 366, 379, 464
Contact hypothesis of prejudice, 120, 383
Contemporary model of emotions, 164
Context, law of, 120, 267
Context theory, 76, 212, 368
Context theory of distance, 76
Contiguity, law of, 44–46, 121, 189, 212–222, 225, 298, 361
Contiguity learning theory, 48, 81, 154, 222, 331, 409, 456–57
Contingency theories of work motivation, 121, 481
Contingency theory of leadership, 121, 294
Continuity, law/principle of, 121, 151, 210
Continuity theory, 25, 121, 142, 341, 428, 440–41, 475
Continuous action theory of tropisms, 309
Contrast, law of, 44–46, 104, 121, 191, 212, 298
Contrast effect, 89, 104, 124, 210, 234
Control/systems theory, 79, **121–23,** 127, 208, 257, 260, 329, 354, 372, 400, 450
Coolidge effect, 123, 314
Cooperation/competition, theories of, 115, 123, 270
Core-context theory, 123, 368

Corpuscular/particle theory, 469
Correspondent inference theory, 58, 123, 255
Counterintuitive theory of emotions, 273
Covariation/correlation principle, 59, 123
Creative synthesis, principle of, 123, 483
Crespi effect, **123–25,** 231
Criminality, theory of, 311
Critical period hypothesis/phenomenon, 257
Cue-selection models, 112
Cultural bias hypothesis, 125, 265
Cultural-norm hypothesis, 57, 125
Culture-epoch theory, 125, 401
Cumulative deficits phenomenon/theory, **125–26,** 246
Cupboard theory, 48, **126–27,** 257
Cybernetic theory, 121–22, 127
Cybernetic theory of perception, 127, 371

Dale's principle, 343
Daltonism, 488
Darwin's evolution theory/evolution, theory/laws of, 12, 65, 79, **128–31,** 156, 171, 192, 219, 271–72, 288–89, 300–301, 323, 327, 340, 356–57, 381, 401, 476
Darwin's theory of emotions, **131,** 156, 164, 483
Decay theory of memory, 131, 187
Decision-making theories, 42, 86, 95, 117, **132–34,** 175, 186, 202, 219, 260, 387, 413, 455, 465, 481
Degeneracy theory of genius, 134, 311
Degradation, law of, 134, 475
Degrees of consciousness theory, 232
Deindividuation theory, 42, 86, **134–35**
DeJong's law, 135, 459
Delta movement effect, 37–38
Dember-Earl theory of choice/preference, 93, **136–37,** 382
Demoralization hypothesis, 137, 145
Denervation, law of, **137,** 226
Depression, theories of, 90, **137–40,** 158, 231, 285, 296, 306, 346, 373, 387, 403
Depression/negative contrast effect, 124
Descartes' theory of innate ideas, 113, 298

Determining tendency, principle of, 7, 326, 484

Determinism, doctrine/theory of, **140–42,** 230, 256, 276–77

Deutsch's structural model, 457

Developmental theory, 20, 121, 130, **142–43,** 167, 334, 401, 477

Devil effect, 227

Diagnosis of psychopathology, 143

Diathesis-stress theory of abnormality, 143, 421

Differences, law of, 357

Differential emotions theory, 271

Differential forgetting, theory of, 143, 268

Differentiation hypothesis, 143, 268

Diminishing returns, law of, 144, 275

Direct perception theory, 120, 144, 366

Direction theory of tropisms, 309

Directive-state theory, 144, 370

Discounting principle, 59, 144, 255

Discrepancy-evaluation/constructivity theory, 144, 419

Discrimination learning theory, 144, 170, 440–41

Discrimination/generalization hypothesis, 89

Disease/medical model, 69

Disengagement theory, 20

Disequilibrium principle, 144, 410

Disinhibition, principle of, 262

Dispositional attribution effect, 57

Dispositional (type/trait) theories of personality, 144

Dissociation, law of, 144

Dissociation by varying concomitants, law of, 46

Dissonance theory. *See* Festinget's cognitive dissonance theory

Distributive law, 364

Disuse, law/theory of, **144–45,** 174, 464–65

Ditchburn-Riggs effect, 145, 470

Dodo hypothesis, 137, **145–46,** 195, 258

Dominator-modulator theory, 104

Donders' law; Donders' reaction time techniques, **146–47,** 238, 484

Dopamine theory of schizophrenia, 147, 421–22

Doppler effect/principle/shift, **148**

Double-aspect theory, 149, 325

Double-bind hypothesis/theory, 149, 422

Double-depletion hypothesis, 149, 453

Drainage/diversion hypothesis, 343

Dream theory, 10, 109, **149–52,** 437

Drive, theories of, 9, 16, 152, 224, 328–30

Drive-reduction theory/hypothesis, 16, 152, 301, 329, 331–32, 371, 409–10

Dry-mouth theory, 152, 453

Dual coding hypothesis/model/system/theory, 97, 152, 252

Dual-processes theory of prejudice, 152, 383

Du Bois Reymond, law of, 343

Duplicity/duplexity theory, 152, 392–93, 469–70, 472

Duration, law of, 45, 191

Dynamic laws of reflex strength, 152, 434

Dynamic theory, 153, 328, 368

Dynamogenesis, law of, 64–65, 153, 328, 369

Early selection theories, 50, 154

Ebbinghaus' doctrine of remote associations, 154, 425

Economy, principle of, 154, 356–57

Economy of effort, principle of, 303

Effect, law of, 16, 48, 74–75, 89, 144, **154–56,** 165, 174, 222, 229–30, 236, 241, 384, 399, 407, 454, 461, 465

Egan effect, 62

Ego development, theories of, 29, 142

Ego-alter theory, 353

Ego-state theory, 117, 156, 248

Einstellung effect, 156, 296, 326, 369

Ekman-Friesen theory of emotions, 131, **156–57,** 164, 180, 272, 382

Elaboration likelihood model, 54

Elation/positive contrast effect, 124

Electrodermal activity/phenomena, **157–58,** 183, 452

Electrolyte metabolism theory of depression, 138, 158

Elicited observing rate hypothesis, **159,** 430, 467

Emboitement, theory of, **159–60**

Emergency theory, 87, 160

Emmert's law, 15, 76, **160–62,** 319, 327, 431

Emotional contagion/primitive emotional contagion, theory of, 162

Emotions, theories/laws of, 9, 41, 88, 101, 131, 156, 158, **162–65,** 180, 200, 272, 274, 292, 307, 330, 356, 382, 418–19, 439, 483

Empirical law of effect, 154, 165, 169

Empiricist theory, 75, 113, 298–99, 463

Encoding, theory of taste quality, 220

Encoding specificity hypothesis/principle, 97, 165

Energy conservation theory, 165, 437

Energy metabolism theory, 165, 244

Enestruence, theory of, 165, 368. *See also* Allport's theory of enestruence

Entropy principle, 165, 208, 277

Environmental/stress/family theories, 421–22

Enzyme theory of taste, 220

Epiphenomenalism, theory of, 165, 325

Epsilon movement effect, 37–38

Equal distribution of ignorance, principle of, 386

Equality, law of, 366

Equalization, principle of, 214

Equilibrium, law of, 346

Equilibrium theory of learned performance, 172, 384

Equipotentiality, principle/theory of, 165, 290–91, 369

Equity theory, 117, **165–67,** 173, 270, 354

Equity theory of work, 167, 482

Equivalence principle, 167, 277

Erikson's theory of personality, 142–43, **167–69,** 376, 390

Error, law of, 386

Errorless discrimination learning, phenomenon of, 441

Errors, theory of, 169, 385

Essential identity law, 25

Estes's stimulus sampling theory, **169–71,** 301, 387, 391

Ethological theory, 15, 224, 246, 256–57, 320

Euclid's law, 160

Event-structure theory, 165, 368. *See also* Allport's theory of enestruence

Evolution, laws of, 128, 171, 288, 381

Evolutionary theory of color vision, 287

Evolutionary/circadian theory of sleep, 171, 437

Ewald's sound pattern theory, 172

Exafference, principle of, 399

Exchange/social exchange theory, 166, **172–74,** 270, 354, 438–39

Exercise, law of, 144, **174,** 191, 399, 407, 464–65

Existential/phenomenological theories of abnormality, 174

Expectancy effect, 174–75

Expectancy theory, 456–57, 467

Expectancy theory of work, 175, 354, 482

Expectancy-reinforcement theory, 300, 457

Expectancy-value theory, 132, 175, 415, 457

Expected utility theory, 354

Experiential theory, 421, 464

Experimenter effects, 6, 96, 174, **175–77,** 227–28, 248, 347, 380, 385, 393, 448

Extinction, laws of, 206

Extensions of waking life theory, 177, 434

Extinction of chained reflexes, law of, 177, 434

Extinction theory, 32, 89, 222

Extinction of Type R, law of, 177, 434

Extinction of Type S, law of, 177, 434

Eye movement theory, 38, 120, 177

Eysenck's theory of personality, **177–79,** 200, 376

Facial feedback hypothesis, 131, 156, 162–64, **180–81,** 272, 382

Facilitation, law of, 181, 344, 434

Faculty theory, 113, 181, 299, 461

False-consensus effect, 354

Fashioning effect/role theory, 370, 481

Feature analysis/extraction theory, 181, 358

Feature theory of memory, 181, 188

Feature integration theory, 359

Fechner-Helmholtz law, 181–82

Fechner's law, **181–83,** 198, 326, 367, 390, 443–44, 474–75, 492

Fere phenomenon, 158, 183

Ferry-Porter law, **183–84,** 382, 452

Festinger's cognitive dissonance theory, 4, 55, 59, 64, 117, 133, 144, 166, **184–86,** 187, 263, 280, 306, 329–30, 383, 438, 448

Field dependence/independence, theory of, 99, 186, 478–79

Field theory, 184, 186, 208, 304–306, 334, 371, 449

Fight or flight theory, 87, 186

Figure-ground relationships, principle of, 210, 214, 231

Filial regression, law of, 186, 201

Filter theory/model, 50, 186

First quantitative law of psychology, 474

Fiske and Maddi's personality theory, 187

Fitts' law, 187, 259

Fixation, law of, 187, 459

Fluctuation theory, 170

Forbes' color vision theory, 104

Forbes-Gregg hypothesis, 187, 345

Forgetting, law of, 187

Forgetting/memory, theories of, 10, 33, 119, 131, 144, 181, **187–90,** 222, 253, 268, 275, 322, 328, 387, 403–404, 412, 426, 442, 454, 456, 460

Forgetting/transfer, laws of, 267

Formal behaviorist theory, 72

Formal discipline/training, theory/doctrine of, 23, 190, 301, 461

Founder effect, 321, 421

Fourier's law/series/analysis, **190–91,** 349–50

Frequency, law of, 45–46, 174, **191,** 300, 465

Frequency theories of hearing, 61, 192

Frequency/repetition, principle of, 46, 191

Frequency/telephone theory, 61, 191

Freud's doctrine of catharsis, 192

Freud's instinct theory, 29, **192–93,** 194–95, 197

Freud's theory of personality, 14, 35–36, 77, 91, 100–101, 117, 142–43, 145, 149, 167, 168, 188, 192, **193–95,** 196–

97, 230, 232–33, 239–40, 246, 248, 256–57, 262, 276–77, 314, 328–30, 334, 376, 381, 396, 414

Froebelism theory, 380

Fromm's theory of personality, 11, **196–97,** 376

Frustration hypothesis/theory, 32

Frustration-aggression hypothesis/theory, 15–16, 192, 197

Frustration-fixation hypothesis, 16

Frustration-regression hypothesis, 16

Fuchs phenomenon, 197, 366

Fullerton-Cattell law, **197–98,** 475

Functional autonomy principle. *See* All-port's funchional autonomy principle

Functional theories of attitude change, 53–54

Fundamental attribution error, 57, 198, 255

Fuzzy set theory, 198, 327

Gain-loss theory, 19, 173, 199, 269

Galen's doctrine of the four tempera-ments, **199–200,** 243, 273, 285, 376

Galton's laws, 33, 186, **200–202,** 412

Gambler's fallacy, 202, 386

Game theory, 132, 172, 202

Gamma movement effect, 37–38

Garcia effect, **202–3**

Gardner's multiple intelligences theory, 203, 265

Gas chromatographic model, 203, 351

Gate-control theory, **203–5,** 339

Gaussian law, 386

Gegenstandstheorie, 321

Gelb phenomenon/effect, 205, 365

Generalization, principles of, 38, 43, 48, 71, 170, **205–7,** 291, 377, 440, 460–61, 464

Generalization-differentiation theory, 207, 268

General feedback theory, 121

General systems theory, 78, **207–9,** 328, 330

Genetic continuity, principle of, 209, 475

Genetic programming theories, 20, 257, 313

Genetic theories of depression, 138

Genetic theory of color vision, 287
Genetics, laws of, 201, 209
Geons hypothesis, 359
Germ-plasm/continuity theory, 209, 476
Gestalt theory/laws, 74–75, 96, 119, 121,
     207, **209–13,** 214, 216, 228, 254, 271,
     299, 301, 303–304, 306, 313, 359,
     365, 367–68, 372–73, 377, 404, 420,
     431, 450, 460, 476, 479, 484, 490–91
Gestalten, laws of, 368
Gibson effect, 213, 366
Gibson's direct perception theory, 213
Glucostatic theory, 213, 244
Goal-setting theory, 213, 354
Golden section, principle of, 492
Goldstein's organismic theory, 34, **213–
     16,** 318–19, 329, 335, 353, 376
Good continuation, principle of, 210–12,
     216
Graceful degradation, principle of, 216,
     259
Gradient theory, 205–206, 338
Grand theory, 353
Granit-Harper law, 216–17
Granit's color vision theory, **216–17**
Grassmann's laws, 2, 103, **217–18,** 346,
     445
Great man/great person theory, 218, 339
Great man/great woman theory of leader-
     ship, 218, 293
Greatest economy, law of, 211
Greenspoon effect, **218–19**
Groos' theory of play, 219, 380
Groupthink phenomenon, 26, 42, 132,
     219
Growth/actualization theories, 318–19,
     329
Guilford's structure-of-intellect model/the-
     ory, 219, 265
Gustation/taste, theories of, **219–21,** 232,
     351, 452
Guthrie's theory of behavior, 25, 47–48,
     154–55, 170, **221–23,** 241, 300–301,
     382, 409–410, 457

Habit/habit formation, laws/principles of,
     12, 206, **224–25,** 241, 301

Habituation, principle/law/theory of, 11–
     12, 137, **225–27,** 424, 467
Halo effect, 176, **227,** 393
Hamilton's hypothesis of space, 76, 228
Hamilton's principle of least action/law
     of least resistance, 211, 228
Hard-to-get effect, 402
Harp theory, 61
Harvey's principle, 228, 469
Hawthorne effect, 175–76, 228, 354
Hebb's theory of perceptual learning,
     228, 300–301, 369, 465
Hecht's color vision theory, 105, **228–29,**
     392–93
Hedonic relativity, principle of, 236
Hedonism, theory/law, 40, 134, **229–30,**
     328, 330, 381, 439
Heider's balance theory, 230, 306, 402–
     403
Heisenberg's principle of uncertainty/in-
     determinacy, 141, 230
Helmholtz's color vision theory, 75, 228,
     230, 364, 444, 463, 487–88
Helmholtz's likelihood principle, 119,
     230, 463
Helmholtz's theory of hearing, 61, 230,
     364
Helplessness/hopelessness theory of de-
     pression, 231
Helson's adaptation-level theory, 12, 124,
     231–32, 332, 369–70, 372, 441
Henning's theory/pyramid of taste, 220,
     232
Henning's theory of smell, 232, 351
Herbart's doctrine of apperception, 39,
     116, **232–33,** 304, 484
Hering-Hurvich-Jameson color vision the-
     ory, 105, 216–17, **233–35,** 245, 287–
     88, 352, 453
Hering's color theory, 105, 233–35, 287,
     469
Hering's law of equal innervation, 235,
     469
Herrnstein's matching law, 155, **235–37,**
     319, 411
Hess effect, 237, 365
Heuristic theory of persuasion, 54, 237
Heyman's law of inhibition, 237, 262

Hick-Hyman law, 238
Hick's law, 147, **237–39,** 260, 324, 450
Hierarchical associations theory of memory, 170
Hierarchy of needs theory of work motivation, 239, 481
Hierarchy theory of motivation, 239
Hilgard's hidden observer hypothesis, 239, 247–48
Historic theories of abnormality, 239
Hoffding step/phenomenon, 239, 358
Holistic theory, 34, 207, 214–15, 318, 334
Homans' exchange theory, 172
Homeostasis, principle of, 121, 208, 239, 243, 439
Honi effect/phenomenon, 116, 239
Hormonal theory of hunger, 239, 244
Horner's law, 104, 239
Horney's theory of personality, 24, 117, 197, **239–41**
Horopter theory, 75, 241
Horwicz's theory of attention, 49
Hull's learning theory, 32, 47, 72, 111–12, 152, 170, 205–206, 224–25, **241–43,** 247, 301, 310, 329–30, 332, 372, 409–410, 440–41, 456–57
Hull-Spence theory of discrimination, 440
Humoral/humors theory, 199–200, 243, 284
Humphrey's law, 243, 447
Hunger, theories of, 93, 165, 213, 239, **243–45,** 249, 308, 330, 373, 427, 446, 453–54
Hunger-pang theory, 243, 245
Hunter-McCrary law, 245, 425
Hurvich-Jameson color vision theory, 233–35, 245
Hutt's microdiagnosis theory, 125, 246
Huygen's wave theory of light, 246
Hybrid theory, 246, 310, 457
Hydraulic theory, 16–17, 61–62, **246,** 312
Hyphen psychologist, 435
Hypnosis/hypnotism, theories of, 5, 35, 156, 239, **246–49,** 324, 340
Hypnotherapy, theories of, 248–49
Hypothalamic theory, 243–44, 249
Hypothesis-testing theory, 119, 249, 347–48, 387, 441

Hypothesis theory, 249, 347, 371
Hypothetico-deductive learning theory, 72

Identical elements theory, 170, 250, 460–61
Identical visual direction, law of, 469
Identity hypothesis/theory, 250, 325
Idiogenetic theory, 325
Idiographic/nomothetic laws, 29–30, 80, 141, **250–51,** 280, 336, 347, 389, 434
Illumination, law of, 468
Image theories, 116, 252, 484
Imagery/mental imagery, theories of, 152, 189, **251–53,** 373
Immaterialism, theory of, 253, 325
Implicit theory of personality, 374
Impression formation, theories of, 98, **253–56,** 270, 376, 467
Impression management theory, 255
Incentive theory, 256, 310, 328, 409
Income distribution, law of, 312
Independence hypothesis, 256, 268, 478
Independent assortment, law of, 256, 322–23
Indeterminism, doctrine/theory of, 141, 256
Indifference principle, 256, 409
Individuality theory, 256, 265
Individuation, law of, 364
Induced emotion, theory of, 292
Induced movement effect, 37–38
Induction, law of, 104, 256, 434
Infant attachment theories, 48, 126–27, **256–58**
Infection theory/effect, **258–59** 439
Inference theory, 38, 259
Informal behaviorist theory, 72
Information/information-processing theory, 43, 53, 82–83, 97, 108, 112, 187, 189, 212, 216, 237–38, 255, **259–61,** 303, 329, 358–59, 372, 379, 426, 459
Information-processing/levels of processing models, 259, 261, 301
Infrared theory, 261, 351
Inheritable acquired characteristics, principle of, 289
Inheritance, laws of, 201, 261, 322–23
Inheritance, polygenic theory of, 200

Inhibition, laws of, **261–63,** 344, 362, 397, 434–35
Inhibitory potential, principle of, 241, 262, 361, 434, 440
Instance/episode/exemplar theory, 460
Instinct theory, 16, 246, 257, 263, 277, 314, 319–20, 380, 449
Instructional theory, 23, 263
Instrumental conditioning, principles of, 263, 297–98, 361–62, 407–408, 434
Insufficient-justification effect, 185, 263
Integration theory, 121, 254
Intelligence, theories/laws of, 125–26, 202–203, 219, 256, **263–67,** 397, 440, 443, 456, 490
Intensity theory of tropisms, 309
Intensity/vividness, law of, 46, 267
Intentionalism, psychological theory of, 267, 325
Interaction/interactionism, theory/doctrine of, 267, 286, 325, 374
Interaction of reflexes, law of, 267, 434
Interference theories of forgetting, 120, 143, 187, 189, 207, 256, 262, **267–69,** 373, 385, 412, 464, 473
Interpersonal attraction theories, 173, 199, **269–70,** 315, 402–403, 412
Interpersonal perception, 254–55, 270
Interpersonal stage development theory, 167
Intervening variable theories, 241, 300
Intrapsychic theories, 389, 396
Intuitive theory of emotions, 273
Inverse square law, 468
Inverted-U hypothesis, **271,** 410, 486
Irradiation theory, 300, 407
Isakower phenomenon, 271, 436
Isolation effect, 354, 473
Isomorphism, phenomenon/hypothesis of, 212, 271, 369
Izard's theory of emotions, 131, 156, 164, 180, **271–72,** 382

Jackson's law, 273, 344, 412
James-Lange/Lange-James theory of emotions, 87–88, 101, 156, 164, **273–74,** 418–19
Joint agreement/disagreement, law of, 357

Jost's laws, 144, **274–76**
Juke-box theory of emotions, 276, 418
Julesz's object perception theory, 276
Jung's theory of personality, 100–101, 149, 165, 167, 193, 233, 240, **276–78,** 330, 376, 450
Just-noticeable differences, principle/law of, 182, 197, 278, 443, 474
Just-world hypothesis, 58, 278

Kamin effect, 279, 331
Kardos effect, 279, 366
Kelley's attribution theory, 279
Kelley's principle of covariation/correlation, 279
Kelly's personal construct theory, 99, 101, 186, **279–81,** 376
Kenshalo/Nafe quantitative theory, 281
Kinney's law, 281, 477
Kirschmann's law of contrast, 104, 281
Kjerstad-Robinson law, 281, 431
Knowledge-across-situations hypothesis, 58, 281
Kohlberg's theory of morality, **281–83,** 327
Kohler-Restorff phenomenon, 473
Konig's theory, 104, 283
Korte's laws, 38, **283–84,** 377
Kretschmer's theory of personality, 119, 200, **284–85,** 311, 376, 428

Labeled-line theory, 220, 351
Labeling/deviance theory, **286–87,** 389, 393, 421–22
Ladd-Franklin/Franklin color vision theory, 104–105, **287–88,** 469
Lag effect, 288, 459
Laing's theory of schizophrenia, 288, 421
Lamarckian-Lysenko doctrine, 288–89, 320
Lamarck's theory, 130, **288–90,** 316, 465, 476
Lambert's law/cosine law, 2, 290
Land's retinex theory, 105, 290
Large numbers, law of, 290, 386
Lashley's theory, 165, **290–91,** 319
Lashley-Wade hypothesis, 206, 291
Late selection theories, 50, 291

Latency, law of, 291, 434

Latent inhibition, principle of, 262

Lateral hypothalamus/feeding center theory, 243–44

Lazarus' theory of emotions, 41, 101, **292–93** 424

Leadership, theories of, 121, 218, **293–96,** 347, 354, 358, 431, 460, 482, 485–86, 489

Learned helplessness effect/phenomenon/hypothesis/theory, 138–39, **296–98**

Learning theories/laws, 15, 36, 44, 46–47, 70, 82, 112, 124, 142–43, 154, 208, 210, 223–25, 242, 256–57, 260, 275, **298–303,** 310, 329–30, 334, 344–45, 361–62, 367, 371, 391, 404, 407–408, 410, 435, 460

Learning theory, Thorndike's, 303, 407

Least action, law of, 211, 303

Least commitment, principle of, 259, 303

Least constraint, law of, 211

Least interest principle, 303

Least squares, law of, 386

Least-effort, Gestalt principle of, 211, 303

Least effort, principle of, 211, **303–4,** 493

Least-energy expenditure, principle of, 211, 304

Lee-Boot effect, 350

Lee-Hendricks model, 304, 315

Leibnitz's monad theory, 113, 232, 304

Lepley hypothesis/Lepley-Hull hypothesis, 304, 425

Lewin's field theory, 184, 186, 208, 212, **304–6,** 369, 372, 490–91

Lewinsohn's theory of depression, 306

Liberalized stimulus-response theory, 72

Libido theory, 35, 194, 239, 256, 276, 449

Liebmann effect, 210, 306

Life-span development theories, 19, 307

Light, theories of, 307, 468

Likelihood principle, 119, 307, 463

Liking, theories of, 307

Lindsley's activation theory, 9, **307–8**

Line-element theory, 228, 444, 487

Linguistic relativity hypothesis, 308, 476–77

Lipostatic theory, 244, 308

Lipps' empathy theory, **308**

Listing's law, 308, 470

Liveliness, law of, 45, 191

Lloyd Morgan's/Morgan's canon, 308, 356–57

Lock-and-key theory, 309, 351

Locus of control theory, 309, 416

Loeb's tropistic theory, **309–10**

Logan's micromolar theory, 242, 246, **310–11,** 457

Lombrosian theory, 134, **311–12**

Lorenz's hydraulic model of aggression, 16, 246, **312**

Lotka/Lotka-Price law, **312**

Lotze's theory of local signs, **312–14,** 339

Love, theories of, 109, 123, 173, 270, 304, 307, **314–16,** 402–403, 443

Luneburg's theory of visual space, 316, 365

Lysenko's theory, 288–89, 316

Mach-Breuer-Brown theory of labyrinthine functioning, 317, 478

Mach-Dvorak phenomenon, 317, 365

Machine theory, 317, 368

Mach's theory of bodily rotation, 317, 478

Macromolar theory, 310

Maier's law, **317–18**

Malthus' law, 323

Mandler's theory of emotion, 318

Marbe's law, 46, 318

Maslow's theory of personality, 14, 197, 239, **318–19,** 329, 376, 414, 481

Mass action, principle/theory of, 290, 319

Matching law, 235–36, 319

Match-mismatch model, 226

Mathematical learning theory, 112, 169, 242, 301

McCollough effect, 160, 319

McDougall's hormic/instinct theory/doctrine, 29–30, 263, **319–21,** 330

Meaning shift effects, 254

Mediational theories, 112
Medical/disease model, 480
Meinong's theories, **321–22**
Membrane theory of nerve conduction, 322, 344–45
Memory, theories of, 68, 97, 151, 170, 212, 322
Mendelian ratio, 322
Mendel's laws/principles, 68, 130, 209, 256, 261, 289, **322–24,** 324, 423, 466, 476
Mendel's theory of heredity, 322, 324
Mental laws of association, 45
Mental self-government theory, 265
Merkel's law, 237, 324
Mesmer's theory, 324
Meyer's psychobiology theory, 324, 334
Meyer's theory of hearing, 246, 324
Micromolar theory, 310
Mill's canons, 324, 357
Mind-body theories, 149, 165, 250, 253, 267, **324–26,** 349, 356, 382, 390, 439
Mind-dust theory, 324
Mind/mental set, law of, 8, 63, 156, 198, 226–27, 296–97, **326–27,** 364, 367, 369, 427, 484
Mind/mind mechanism, theory of, 327
Mind-stuff theory, 324
Mind-twist hypothesis, 420
Minitheories of emotion, 163
Modern synthetic theory of evolution, 130, 327
Modification by exercise, law of, 464
Modularity hypothesis/theory, 461
Molecular/contiguity theory, 300
Moon illusion, theory of, 161, 327
Moral development, principles/theory of, 281–82, 327
Morgan's canon/Lloyd Morgan's canon, 328
Motivated forgetting, theory of, 187–88, 194, 328
Motivation, theories of, 7, 9, 27, 152–53, 164, 256, 307, **328–31,** 332, 336, 340, 380, 410, 452, 481–82
Motivational hedonic theory, 229
Motor theory of speech perception, 477

Mowrer's theory, 152, 242, 279, 301, **331–32,** 391, 462
Muller effect, 332, 471
Muller's color vision theory, 332
Muller's doctrine of specific nerve energies, 83, **332–34,** 440
Muller-Schumann law, 332, 431
Muller's zone theory, 105
Multifactor theory of thirst, 334, 453
Multiple intelligences theory, 265
Multiplicative law of probability, 334, 387
Murphy's biosocial theory, 34, 87, 215, 324, **334–35,** 376
Murphy's laws, 400
Murray's theory of personality, 29, **335–37,** 376

Nafe's vascular theory of cutaneous sensitivity, 31, 281, **338–39,** 440, 466
Native capacities, doctrine of, 201, 320
Nativistic/nativism theories/doctrine, 75, 298, 313, 339, 463
Natural selection, law of, 129, 340
Naturalistic theory of history, 218, 251, **339–40,** 373, 400–401
Need achievement theory, 6, 340
Need-reduction theories, 16, 152, 301, 329, 331–32, 340
Need theories, 318, 328–29, 336, 340
Negative adaptation, principle of, 10, 225
Negative afterimages phenomenon, 78, 160, 234
Negative law of effect, 154–55
Negative transfer of training effect, 43, 267
Neobehaviorist theory, 72
Neo-dissociation theory, 247, 340
Neo-Freudian/neo-analytic/psychodynamic/ psychoanalytic theories, 341, 374
Neo-Lamarckian theory of genetics, 289
Neo-Mendelism doctrine, 289
Nernst-Lillie theory of excitation and conduction, 341, 345
Neural quantum theory, 95, **341–43,** 377, 395, 429–30
Neurocognitive theory of dreams, 151

Neurolinguistic theory, 94, 343
Neuromuscular inhibition, theory of, 262
Neuron/neural/nerve theory, 4, 74, 97, 187, 273, 322, 341, **343–46,** 412, 450
Neuropsychological theory, 300
Neurotransmitter/biogenic amine theory of depression, 346
Newton's laws/principles of color mixture, 2, 103, 217–18, **346–47**
Nomothetic laws, 29–30, 80, 141, 280, 347, 389
Noncontinuity theory, 341, 347, 441
Noncontradiction, law of, 357
Normative decision theory, 294, 347
Norm of reciprocity, principle of, 402
Novelty/disruption effect, 175, 347
Null hypothesis, 249, **347–48**

Object perception theory, 83, 349
Obliteration theory, 187
Observational learning theory, 66
Observer effect, 175–76
Occam's razor/principle, 349, 356–57
Occasionalism, theory of, 325, 349
Occupation theories, 295, 349
Ohm's acoustic/auditory law, 191, **349–50**
Olfaction/smell, theories of, 11, 84, 110, 203, 232, 261, 309, **350–52,** 438, 442, 466
Operant conditioning/behavior, laws/theory of, 297–98, 300–301, 310, 352, 390, 408, 433–34
Operant reserve, law of the, 352, 434
Opponent-process color vision theory, 105, 216, 233–35, 352, 439, 469
Opponent-process theory of emotion, 353, 439
Organic evolution, theory of, 128
Organizational/industrial/systems theory, 122, 133, 208, 213, 295, **353–55,** 373, 376, 387, 397, 423, 439, 450, 482
Organismic laws, 364
Organismic theory, 34, 213–14, 313, 318, 353
Osgood's transfer/retroaction surface model, 267, 355, 432

Overattribution effect, 57, 355
Overjustification effect/hypothesis, 355, 408

Pandemonium model/theory, 356, 358
Panum phenomenon, 356, 365
Papez-MacLean theories, 163, 356
Paradoxical cold phenomenon, 31
Parallelism/psychophysicalism, theory/doctrine of, 325, 356
Parallel law, 182, 356
Parsimony, law/principle of, 130, 154, 308, 324, 328, 349, **356–57,** 372, 487
Partial reinforcement extinction effect, 89, 357, 410, 457
Passing stranger/stranger on a train effect, 357, 402
Path-goal theory, 294, 358
Pattern/object recognition theory, 79, 83, 110, 181, 239, 260, 276, 349, 356, **358–60,** 459, 462
Pattern theories of cutaneous sensory coding, 338
Pavlovian conditioning principles/laws/theories, 95, 205–206, 222, 241, 262, 298, 300–301, 310, 340, **360–63,** 407–408, 410, 412
Perception (I. General), theories of, 8, 28, 35, 76, 83, 120, 136, 144, 161, 197, 205, 212–13, 237, 255, 279, 317, 321, 356, **363–67,** 372, 382, 390, 411, 442, 453, 459, 464
Perception (II. Comparative appraisal), theories of, 28, 69, 76, 83–84, 93, 120, 123, 127, 144, 153, 161, 228, 231, 249, 317, 359, **367–73,** 385, 425, 427, 459–60, 464, 479
Perceptual organization, laws of, 74–75, 209–212, 366, 373
Perceptual theories of attitude change, 53–54
Periodicity theory, 61–62
Peripheral theories of hunger/thirst, 243–44, 373, 453
Perky effect, 252, 373
Permissive amine theory of depression, 138, 373

Perseveration theory, 267, 373
Personalistic theory of history, 251, 312, 339–40, 373, 400
Personality-job fit theory, 354, 373
Personality theories, 17, 34, 67, 79, 92, 168, 177–78, 185, 195–97, 199–200, 214–15, 224, 233, 251, 255, 258, 277, 280, 284–85, 295, 305, 319, 330, 335–36, 340–41, **373–76,** 388–89, 397, 406, 414, 428, 449, 460, 462, 479
Person-centered theory, 305, 335, 376, 414
Person perception theory, 254–55, 270, 376
Peter principle, 354, 376
Phenomenalism, theory of, 325, 376
Phenomenological (humanistic) theories of personality, 375, 377, 389, 413
Phi-gamma hypothesis, 341–42, 377, 429–30
Phi phenomenon, 37, 212, 283, 368, 377
Phonemic restoration effect, 377, 477
Photochemical theory, 377, 470
Photographic law, 85
Phrenology, doctrine of, 300–301
Physical correlate theory, 377, 443
Physiological laws of association, 45
Physiological theory of generalization, 205, 377
Piaget's principle of conservation, 377
Piaget's theory of developmental stages, 3, 4, 43, 99, 142, 167–68, 261, 263, 266, 282, 301, **377–79,** 477
Piano theory of hearing, 61, 379
Piecemeal activity, law of, 379, 403
Piper's law, 380, 413
Pituitary adrenal axis theories, 138
Placebo effect, 176, 380
Place/place-volley/place-frequency theory, 61–62, 380
Planned behavior theory, 54
Play, theories of, 63, 109, 219, 379, **380–81,** 401
Pleasure-pain, doctrine/theory/law of, 40, 230, 381, 407
Pleasure/reality principles, 35, 193, 229–30, 299, 328–29, 381

Plutchik's model of emotions, 156, 164, 272, **381–82**
Polychromatic hypothesis, 217
Porter's law, 183–84, 382
Positive transfer of training effect, 43
Postremity principle, 222, 382
Potzl/Poetzl phenomenon/effect, 151, 364, 382
Power law, 183, 377, 390, 443–44
Power law of practice, 382, 459
Practice theory of play, 380
Pragnanz, law of, 211
Precision, law of, 366
Preestablished harmony, theory/doctrine of, 325, 382
Preference, theory of, 136, 382
Prejudice, theories of, 55, 116–17, 120, 152, **382–84,** 400, 423, 465
Premack's principle/law, 90, 332, **384–85,** 410
Prepotency, law of, 385, 434
Prepotent response theory, 384–85, 409
Pretesting effect, 175, 385
Primary laws of association, 45
Primary-recency effects, 254, 425
Primitive emotional contagion, theory of, 180
Prior entry, effect/law of, 385, 466
Proactive inhibition, law of, 187, 262, 267, 385
Probabilistic functionalism, theory of, 370, 385
Probability-differential theory of reinforcement, 384
Probability theory/laws, 13, 93, 132–33, 140, 169–70, 202, 290, 334, 347–48, **385–87**
Process interaction system/theory, 107, 387
Process theory of decision making, 170
Progression, law of, 387, 474
Progressive matrices theory, 264
Progressive teleological-regression hypothesis, 387, 420
Proportion, principle of, 387, 492
Propositional theory of memory, 188, 387
Prospect theory, 354, 387

Prototype theory of memory, 112, 189
Provisional expectancies/hypotheses theory, 457
Proximity, law/principle of, 191, 210, 212, 269–70
Psychic resultants, law of, 387, 483
Psychoanalytic/libidinal theory of depression, 139, 387
Psychoanalytic theories of personality, 15, 167, 193–95, 239, 250, 256–57, 314, 328, 388, 406, 413–14, 421
Psychoanalytic theory of dreams, 151
Psychobiology, theory of, 329, 334
Psychodynamic theories of personality, 29, 193–95, 374, 388
Psychogenic theories of abnormality, 388
Psycholinguistics theory, 93
Psychological law of relativity, 388, 484
Psychoneural parallelism, theory of, 344
Psychopathology, theories of, 3, 24, 79, 139, 143, 174, 239, **388–90,** 422
Psychophysical laws/theory, 182, 197–98, 341–42, 364, 390, 429, 443, 455
Psychophysical parallelism, doctrine of, 390
Psychosexual development, theory of, 142, 167, 194
Psychosocial development, theory of, 142, 167–68
Psychosocial/psychological theories of personality, 390
Pulfrich phenomenon/effect, 365, 390
Punctuated equilibrium theory, 323
Punishment, theories of, 36, 63, 222, 301, 331–32, **390–92,** 410, 462
Purkinje effect/phenomenon/shift, 12, 216–17, **392–93,** 471
Purposive/cognitive theory, 72, 320, 393, 409, 456
Pygmalion effect/Pygmalionism, 176, 227, 287, **393–94**

Quanta, the law of, 342
Quantal hypothesis, 341–42, 395
Quantitative theory of cutaneous sensitivity, 338
Quantum theory, 140, 341–42, 395, 469
Quotient hypothesis, 474

Radical behaviorist theory, 72
Rank's theory of personality, 376, **396–97**
Ranschburg inhibition/effect, 262, 397
Rational-economic man theory, 353, 397
Rational-emotive therapy theory, 1, 69, 397
Rationalism/rationalist, doctrine of, 209, 298–99, 463
Raven's progressive matrices theory, 397
Reactance theory, 122, **397–98**
Reactive inhibition, principle of, 262
Readiness, law of, 155, 191, **398–99,** 407
Reafference theory/principle, **399–400**
Realistic conflict theory, 116, 383, 400
Reber's law, **400–401**
Recapitulation, theory/law of, 64, 79, 125, 160, 288, 380, **401–2**
Recency, law of, 45–46, 402
Reciprocal inhibition technique/theory, 69, 262
Reciprocity law, 84–85, 402
Reciprocity of liking effect, 357, **402–3**
Recognition by components theory, 359
Reconposre theory of depression, 138, 403
Reconstruction theory, 187–88, 403
Redintegration, principle/laws of, 379, **403–4**
Redshift effect, 148
Reflection effect, 354
Reflex action, doctrine of, 298, 360
Reflex arc theory/concept, 215, 345, **404–5**
Reflex fatigue, law of, 405, 434
Reflex reserve, principle of, 405, 434
Refractory phase, law of, 25, 405, 434
Reichenbach phenomenon, 405–6
Reicher-Wheeler effect, 405, 458
Reich's orgone/orgonomy theory, 376, **405–6**
Reinforcement, Thorndike's theory of, 75, 119, 155, 263, 301, 303, 384, 399, **407–8,** 410, 461
Reinforcement/theory, 36, 48, 55, 89, 144, 185, 222, 230, 236, 256, 263, 271, 299, 301, 310, 330–31, 355, 357,

384, 390–91, 393, 407, **408–11,** 415–16, 423, 433, 446, 462
Relational theory, 441
Relativity/relative effect, law of, 236, 369, 411
REM sleep, theory of, 150–51, 411, 436
Reminiscence theory of knowledge, 298
Reorganization theory, 365, 411
Repair/restoration theory, 412, 437
Repetition, law/effect of, 191, 230, 412
Requisite variety, law of, 260
Rescorla-Wagner model, 82, 361, 412
Residues, law of, 357
Resistance, law of, 350
Resolution, law of, 434
Resonance, resonance/place, resonance/volley theories, 61, 412
Response-deprivation theory of reinforcement, 384
Response generalization, principle of, 205
Response magnitude, law of, 412, 434
Reticularist theory, 344, 412
Retinex theory, 105
Retrieval failure theory, 187
Retroactive inhibition, law of, 187, 262, 267, 412
Reverse halo effect, 227
Reversion, law of, 201, 412
Reward theory of interpersonal attraction, 269, 412
Ribot's law, 49, **412**
Ricco's/Piper's laws, 85, 380, **413**
Risky-shift/choice shift effect, 132, 354, 413
Rogers' theory of personality, 14, 197, 215, 329, 376, **413–15,** 423
Rosenthal effect, 96, 175–76
Rotter's social learning/theory, 66, 309, **415–17,** 439, 457
Rutherford's frequency theory, 61, 417

Schachter-Singer's theory of emotions, 41, 101, 144, 164, 276, 292, 318, **418–20**
Schafer-Murphy effect, 210, 420
Schanz's color vision theory, 104
Schemata theory of memory, 4, 68

Schizophrenia, theories of, 79, 143, 147, 149, 288, 387, **420–23,** 450, 462
Schizophrenogenic parent/mother hypothesis, 421
Script theory, 76–77
Secondary laws of association, 45
Secondary reinforcement, principle of, 423
Segregation, law of, 322, 423
Selection, law of, 154–55, 466
Selective attention theories, 81, 170
Selective social interaction theory, 20
Self-actualizing man theory, 214, 277, 318, 354, 375, 414, 423
Self-categorization theory, 383, 423
Self-concept/self theory, 29, 208, 277, 375, 414, 423, 481–82
Self-perception theory, 58, 423, 489
Self-serving bias effect, 59
Selye's theory/model of stress, 12, 208, **423–25**
Semiotic theory, 94, 425
Sensitization, principle of, 226
Sensory discrimination, classical theory of, 341
Sensory-tonic field theory, 369, 425
Sequential patterning theory, 89, 425
Serial-position/serial learning effect, 154, 189, 245, 304, 412, **425–27**
Set, law of, 326–27, 427
Set/motor adjustments theory, 369, 427
Set-point theory, 244, 427
Set size effects, 254
Set-theoretical model, 326
Set theory, 6, 326, 427
Sheldon's type theory, 119, 200, 285, 311, 376, **427–29**
Shifting, law of, 466
Short-circuit theory, 368
Signal detection, theory of, 107–108, 159, **429–31,** 467
Sign gestalt theory, 456
Similarity, law of, 44–46, 189, 191, 210, 212, 298, 431
Similarity-attraction theory, 269
Similarity paradox, 431–32
Simplicity, law of, 210–211, 357, 366
Situational attribution effect, 57

Situational theory of leadership, 294, 431
Size-distance invariance hypothesis, 160–61, 431
Skaggs-Robinson hypothesis, 267–68, 281, 332, 355, **431–33**
Skinner's descriptive behavior/operant conditioning theory, 15, 22, 25, 70, 72, 81, 93, 94, 109, 114, 152, 177, 181, 191, 219, 237, 256, 262–63, 267, 291, 297, 301, 310, 352, 385, 391, 405, 409–410, 412, 414, 423, **433–36**, 440, 442, 446, 452, 454, 456–57, 466, 475, 482
Sleep, theories of, 9, 12, 151, 165, 171, 271, 307, 411–12, **436–38**
Smell, laws/theories of, 438
Snowball effect, 258
Social class theories of schizophrenia, 421
Social comparison/evaluation theory, 185, 438
Social drift theory, 421
Social exchange theory, 269–70, 438
Social facilitation theory, 438, 489
Social impact theory, 258, 439
Social learning/cognition theories, 16–17, 65, 143, 192, 282, 374, 415, 439
Social learning model, 69, 415
Social man theory, 353–54, 439
Social penetration theory, 173, 439
Societal progress theory, 108
Sociogenic hypothesis, 421
Sociological theory of communication, 108
Solomon's opponent-process theory of emotions/feelings/motivation, 164, 353, **439**
Soul theory, 320, 324, 439
Sound-pattern/wave-pattern theory, 61–62, 440
Space perception theory, 75, 313, 440
Span, law of, 326
Spatial summation, law of, 434, 440
Spearman's two-factor theory, 264, 275, 440
Specific gene theory, 420
Specific nerve energies, law of, 345, 440, 487–88. *See also* Muller's doctrine of specific nerve engines

Specific receptor theory, 338
Specific terminal/specific tissue hypotheses, 338, 440
Spence's theory, 121, 144, 205, 224–25, 242, 259, 301, 310, 329, 347, 372, **440–42**, 492
Spillman-Redies effect, 364, 442
Spiritual theories of reflex attention, 49
Spot theory of temperature senses, 31
Spreading-activation model of memory, 9, 189, 442
Square root law, 197
Stage theories of development/personality, 142, 257, 281–82, 377–79, 449, 481
Static laws of the reflex, 262, 434, 442
Statistical learning theory, 89, 169
Stereochemical theory of smell, 351, 442
Sternberg-Lubart's investment theory of creativity, 265, 443
Sternberg's triangular theory of love, 315, 443
Sternberg's triarchic theory of intelligence, 265, 443
Stevens' power law, 183, 377, 390, **443–44**
Stiles' color vision theory, 228, **444–45**
Stiles-Crawford effect, **445–46**
Stimulus aftereffects hypothesis, 89
Stimulus association, principle of, 48
Stimulus-centered theory, 446
Stimulus discrimination in Type R, law of, 434, 446
Stimulus discrimination in Type S, law of, 434, 446
Stimulus generalization, principle of, 38, 170, 205, 473
Stimulus preexposure effect, 262
Stimulus-response theory, 111, 310, 329, 456
Stimulus-response/operant conditioning theory of work, 446, 482
Stimulus sampling theory, 169
Stochastic/computer model theory, 301
Stomach-contraction theory, 243, 446
Stroboscopic movement effect, 37–38
Strong law of effect, 154

Stroop effect/interference effect/Stroop test, 243, **446–48**
Structure-of-intellect model/theory, 265
Stumpf's theory of musical consonance and dissonance, **448,** 458
Subject effects, 176, 448
Subjective expected utility, 132, 457
Subtractive color mixture, principles of, 102–103, 449
Sufficient reason, law of, 325
Sullivan's theory of personality, 150, 167–68, 270, 376, 396, **449–50**
Surplus energy theory, 380
Surroundedness, law of, 210, 450
Sustained attention theories, 450, 466–67
Sutton's law, 420, 450
Symbolic distance effect, 238, 450
Symptom substitution hypothesis, 480
Synaptic depression model, 226
Synaptic/synapse theory, 344, 450
Synchronicity principle, 277, 450
Synergy theory, 325
Synthetic heat phenomenon, 31
Systematic desensitization technique, 222, 450, 480
Systems theory, 121, 353, 372, 450

Talbot-Plateau law, 184, **451–52**
Tarchanoff phenomenon, 158, 452
Taste, theories/laws of, 452. *See* Gustation/taste, theories of
Taste aversion effect, 202–203
Telephone theory of hearing, 61, 452
Template matching theory, 358
Temporal summation, law of, 434, 452
Tendency, law of, 467
Tension, law of, 452, 475
Tension-reduction theories, 185, 329, 449, 452
Ternus phenomenon, 364, 453
Tetrachromatic theory, 453. *See also* Hering–Hurvich–Jameson Color Vision Theory
Texton hypothesis, 358
Thalamic theory, 87
Thermal sensitivity theories, 338
Thermostatic theory, 244, 453
Thibaut & Kelley's exchange theory, 172

Thirst, theories of, 149, 152, 245, 330, 334, **453–54**
Thorndike's law of effect, 47–48, 169–70, 174, 223, 229, 241, 301, 384, 398, 435, 454. *See also* Effect, law of
Thought, motor theory of, 200, 477
Three-element/tri-receptor/trichromatic color vision theory, 454. *See also* Young-Helmholtz color vision theory
Three-phase developmental theory, 334
Three-primaries law, 103
Three-stage/process theory of memory, 187, 454
Threshold, law/theory of, 341, 434, 454
Thurstone's law of comparative judgment, 109, 133, **454–56,** 459
Thurstone's primary mental abilities model/theory, 265, 456
Time perception, law/theory of, 456
Tip-of-the-tongue phenomenon, 188, 456
Tolman's theory, 32, 47, 72, 90, 300–301, 320, 372, 393, 409–410, 415, **456–58**
Tones/combinational, theory of, 458
Top-down processing/theories, 83, 212, 364, 367, 405, **458–59,** 473, 481
Topological field theory, 305, 368
Torgerson's law of categorical judgment, 455, 459
Total time hypothesis/law, 135, 187, 288, 382, **459–60**
Toxicosis effect, 202–203
Traces, doctrine of, 212
Trace theory, 68, 89, 187, 212, 460, 473
Trait theories of personality, 29, 91, 224, 374, 460
Trait theory of leadership, 293, 460
Transactional analysis technique, 77, 460
Transactional functionalism theory, 370
Transactional theories of leadership, 293–94, 460
Transactional theory, 77, 370, 460
Transfer of training, Thorndike's theory of, 43, 48, 181, 250, 268, 432, **460–62**
Transformational theory of language, 462
Transposition, phenomenon of, 441
Transsituationality principle, 409, 462
Traveling wave theory, 61, 462
Treisman's feature integration theory, 462

Trichromatic theory, 105, 216
Tricomponent model of attitude, 52
Tridimensional theory of feeling, 483
Tripartite personality theory, 77, 193–94, 200, 233
Tropism, theory of the. *See* Loeb's tropistic theory
Troxler effect, 462, 470
Two-factor theory, 418
Two-factor learning theory, 331, 462
Two-factor theory of work, 462, 481
Two-stage process theory, 391, 462
Two-step theory of communication, 108
Two-syndrome hypothesis, 422, 462
Type theories of personality, 200, 277, 284–85, 311, 374, 462

Unconscious inference, doctrine of, 7, 120, 259, 283, 307, 365–67, **463–64**
Undulatory theory, 469
Unit hypothesis, 205, 464
Universalistic theories, 464, 481
Unlearning hypothesis, 268, 464
Unreadiness, law of, 399
Use, law of, 144, 174, 191, **464–65**
Use/disuse, use-inheritance theory, 288–89, 464
Us-versus-them effect, 383, 465
Utility theory, 132, 159, 229, 310, 465

Vandenbergh effect, 350, 466
Vascular theory, 466. *See also* Nafe's vascular theory of cutaneous sensitivity
Venable's color vision theory, 104
Vibration theory, 350–51, 466
Vibratory theory of inheritance, 323, 466
Vierordt's law, 434, 466
Vigilance, theories of, 50, 159, 227, 238, 385, 450, **466–68**
Vision/sight, theories of, 22, 61, 83, 93, 103, 161, 184, 191, 228, 235, 246, 307, 308, 332, 346, 377, 393, 395, 413, 452, 462, **468–72**
Visual-orientation hypothesis, 58, 472
Vividness/clearness, law of, 46, 472
Volley/periodicity theory, 61, 472
Von Kries' color vision theory, 152, 392–93, 469, **472–73**

Von Kries-Schrodinger zone theory, 105
Von Restorff effect, 212, 426, **473**

Waller's law, 343
Wave theory of light, 469
Weak law of effect, 154
Weber-Fechner law, 182, 198, 231, 326, 474
Weber's law, 134, 182–83, 197–98, 278, 387, 390, 444, 452, **474–75,** 484, 492
Wedensky inhibition/effect, 262, 475
Weismann's theory, 130, 209, 289, **475–76**
Wertheimer's perceptual theory, 476
Wever-Bray effect, 61, 476
Whitten effect, 350
Whorf-Sapir hypothesis/theory, 94, 281, 308, 377, **476–78**
Witkin's perception/personality/cognitive style theory, 76, 186, 317, **478–79**
Wolpe's theory/technique of reciprocal inhibition, 70, 450, **479–81**
Word-superiority effect, 458, 481
Work adjustment, theory of, 481–82
Work/career/occupation, theories of, 6, 90, 121, 167, 175, 239, 349, 354, 446, 462, 464, **481–83**
Wundt's theories/doctrines/principles, 39, 49, 123, 233, 301, 327, 387–88, 448, **483–84**

X, Theory, 293, 353, 485

Y, Theory, 293, 486
Yerkes-Dodson law, 271, **486–87,** 490
Young-Helmholtz color vision theory, 104–105, 216–17, 230, 234–35, 287–88, 367, 445, 454, 469, **487–88**
Young's color vision theory, **488**

Z, Theory, 293, 489
Zajonc's arousal and confluence theories, 101, 119, 438, **489–90**
Zeigarnik effect/phenomenon, 8, 306, **490–92**
Zeiler's theory, 492
Zeising's principle, 15, 308, 387, **492**
Zipf's law, 304, **492–93**

About the Author

JON E. ROECKELEIN is Professor of Psychology in the Department of Psychology at Mesa Community College, Mesa Arizona.

ISBN 0-313-30460-2

90000>

EAN

9 780313 304606

HARDCOVER BAR CODE